D1360694

PHILANTHROPIC FOUNDATIONS

New Scholarship, New Possibilities

Edited by
Ellen Condliffe Lagemann

Indiana University Press

Bloomington and Indianapolis

This book is a publication of

Indiana University Press
601 North Morton Street
Bloomington, Indiana 47404-3797 USA

www.indiana.edu/~iupress

Telephone orders 800-842-6796
Fax orders 812-855-7931
Orders by e-mail iuporder@indiana.edu

The paper used in this publication meets the minimum requirements
of American National Standard for Information Sciences—
Permanence of Paper for Printed Library Materials,
ANSI Z39.48-1984.

Manufactured in the United States of America

Library of Congress Cataloging-in-Publication Data
Philanthropic foundations : new scholarship, new possibilities /
    edited by Ellen Condliffe Lagemann.
        p.   cm. — (Philanthropic studies)
    Includes bibliographical references and index.
    ISBN 0-253-33500-0 (cl : alk. paper)
    1. Charitable organization—United States—History.
    2. Endowments—United States—History.   I. Lagemann, Ellen
    Condliffe, date.   II. Series.
    HV40.8.U6P55   1999
    361.7'6'0973—dc21   98-55922
1 2 3 4 5   04 03 02 01 99

Contents

ACKNOWLEDGMENTS

AN EDITED VOLUME is always the work of many people, and I should like to thank some of the people who helped make this collection possible.

The papers gathered here emerged from a series of seminars organized by the Center for the Study of American Culture and Education at the New York University School of Education. Their purpose was to encourage good, critical writing about the history of foundations by inviting doctoral students from across the country to present their dissertations-in-progress to working seminars of other scholars and foundation personnel. After several years of seminars, we organized two larger conferences, one held at New York University in the fall of 1996 and another held in Indianapolis at the Center on Philanthropy at Indiana University in the fall of 1997. These various meetings were made possible by the Lilly Endowment, which not only supported the gatherings but made available the wisdom and keen interest of Susan Wisely, director of evaluation for the Endowment. Susan knows how to be a program officer who is first and foremost a colleague and friend. Before his retirement from the Endowment, Robert Lynn also played an invaluable role in dreaming up this project.

Throughout most of the life of this project, Susan Kastan has served as its coordinator, ably handling a myriad of logistical details. In addition, Dwight Burlingame and Warren Ilchman of the IU Center on Philanthropy offered generous help with local arrangements for the fall 1997 meeting.

Over the years, we have had a few "regulars" at our meetings who have always asked incisive questions, challenged vague hypotheses, and added valuable data and experience to our conversations. Chief among these, in addition to some of the authors, have been Miriam Chamberlain, Sarah Englehardt, Paul Mattingly, Fritz Mosher, Jim Smith, and Frank Sutton.

All the papers benefited from the unusually savvy comments of panel moderators. Roger Geiger, Peter Dobkin Hall, Michael Katz, Stanley Katz, Robert Lynn, Steven Schlossman, and Judith Sealander not only improved the papers with their insights, but also contributed invaluably to the liveliness of the two conferences.

Last but hardly least important, I should like to thank the authors whose work is presented here. They have made the supposedly thankless task of editing a collection of essays an education and a pleasure. Beyond that, they have stolen time from amazingly busy lives to write, revise, and revise again. Their labors are testimony to our collective commitment to studying philanthropic foundations.

E.C.L.

INTRODUCTION

Foundations in History

New Possibilities for Scholarship and Practice

Ellen Condliffe Lagemann

THROUGHOUT THE TWENTIETH CENTURY, philanthropic foundations have played a variety of crucial roles in U.S. society. They have facilitated the development of ideas, provided important support to the arts, funded experimental programs in medicine, and helped spread American culture around the world. Despite that, until relatively recently, their history was known only in superficial, general outline.

The reasons for this are several. First, until recently there were few, if any, social theories that helped direct scholarly attention to foundations. This was because the great social theorists whose ideas have provided the baseline for most social research in our era lived at a time when "the foundation" had not yet been invented as a means for channeling funds and directing social energies. The writings of the great theorists constantly recalled one to the significance of social classes, bureaucracy, ideology, and charisma, but they did not direct equal attention to the ways in which patronage was organized. Because theories help raise questions for research, a lack until recently of theories that turned the spotlight on foundations has been a barrier to research.

At least as important, foundations themselves have discouraged scholarly writing. Having been the subject of hostile Congressional investigations on at least four occasions, they have been extremely skittish about opening their files to outside scholars. Many have preferred to chronicle their own achievements, the result being chronologies of grants that foundations officers believed successful, with little or no sense of external context or of the full array of internal considerations involved in deciding to fund one project and not some others.

Boring to read and insignificant in the insight offered into the crucial interface between foundations and surrounding institutions, foundation histories of this sort provided a false façade behind which trustees and foundation officers and staff could feel securely proud of their apparently altruistic, apolitical contributions to knowledge, culture, or humankind. If such "house histories" were useful as tokens to be ceremonially presented to arriving or retiring personnel, their chief, though unannounced and perhaps unintended, function seems to have been to help deflect scholars from undertaking research about foundations. The genre of foundation history was too stilted and the literature too uninteresting to those who did not have direct knowledge of a particular foundation to attract scholars seriously engaged in the social or political history of the United States.

Despite those long-standing barriers to the development of critical scholarship about foundations and their histories, things are now changing. As the essays collected here attest, the history of foundations is attracting scholars from across the social disciplines and now stands in fruitful relation to some of the most interesting and productive lines of research in history and the social sciences.

One of these, taken up primarily by intellectual, cultural, and educational historians, pertains to "the organization of knowledge" in the United States and other societies around the world.[1] Studies of this problem originated from widespread disenchantment with approaches to intellectual history that presumed knowledge was a fabric of free-standing ideas that was largely self-generating and detached from the surrounding social context. Research into the organization of knowledge has been characterized by relating the history of ideas to the people, social processes, and social structures that have been involved in their formulation, transformation, and dissemination. Not surprisingly, this has yielded important new insights into intellectual disciplines and professions and the schools, colleges, universities, libraries, professional associations, and research organizations to which those have been related.[2]

Because foundations have been such important actors in the social history of ideas, research into the organization of knowledge has inevitably drawn scholars to consider their activities. Initial interest in the motivations behind foundation grant making has prompted investigators to scrutinize foundation interactions with other agencies of governance, not only the federal, state, and local governments, but also voluntary associations engaged in all sorts of knowledge-generating and knowledge-regulating activities.[3] Work of this kind has added significantly to what we know about policy making in the United States.

If new substantive questions have encouraged the study of foundation history, so have new theoretical perspectives. One important example is work associated with "the new institutionalism" developed in the late 1970s by sociologists, economists, and organizational theorists studying organizational behavior. This perspective grew out of new awareness that the formal and even the informal rules that different institutions have followed as they sought to fulfill their missions were neither the only nor necessarily the most important variables to consider in analyzing organizational strategies and actions.[4] Because this recognition broadened the relevant context for organizational studies, the new institutionalism threw the spotlight on foundations. This has yielded research and writing about foundation involvement in institutions as different as art museums and community colleges.[5] At the same time, by fostering awareness that foundations operate within a field or sector composed of like institutions, which tends to make the operations of already like institutions more and more similar, the new institutionalism has generated many new questions about foundations as organizations.[6]

Significant, therefore, not only for the empirical data already garnered, but also for the analytic insights now available to guide continuing research, studies built around a neo-institutionalist perspective are kindred to another line of research that is, yet again, providing fruitful stimulus for the study of foundation histories. This is research intended to "bring the state back in" or, more precisely, to counter the trend evident in political science since the 1950s to consider politics as primarily an interaction between and among discrete interest groups and government agencies. Proponents of "bringing the state back in" are concerned instead with focusing attention on the full range of administrative, legal, bureaucratic, and coercive systems that different political regimes or states together comprise.[7] Because foundations sit in a gray zone between the public and private sectors and have been vitally involved in helping to transfer rights, responsibilities, and powers between the two, interest in states and changing state functions has, once again, stirred new interest in foundation histories.[8]

If writing about foundations has been stimulated by relatively recent developments in history and the social sciences, it has been made possible at an even more basic level by changing attitudes among philanthropists. Obviously, possibilities for studying foundations depend on the willingness of foundation trustees and officers to open their files and to help finance research. Advances in scholarship therefore reflect the fact that, in recent years, more and more foundation personnel have come to realize that outside scrutiny may be beneficial internally and is, in any case, a responsibility for trusts set up to manage, use, and distribute tax-free, essentially public money.

This new openness to scholarly investigation is not universal, though it is increasingly widespread, and it has supported the emergence of a new infrastructure for scholarship. Many foundations now make their files accessible to outside scholars and some have donated their records to archive centers such as the Rockefeller Archive Center in Pocantico, New York, and the Joseph and Matthew Payton Philanthropic Studies Library at Indiana

University, in Indianapolis. Some foundations have also made grants to support research. This has helped finance new academic centers such as the Center on Philanthropy at Indiana University as well as fellowship programs such as the Aspen Institute's Nonprofit Sector Research Fund. Finally, as foundation work has itself been professionalized, professional organizations such as the Independent Sector, the Council on Foundations, and Association for Research on Nonprofit Organization and Voluntary Action (ARNOVA) have begun to develop forums for scholarly research. Some organizations publish journals and scholarly indices, and many invite scholars to present their ideas at annual meetings.

Supported by this infrastructure and increasingly attractive to scholars, the history of foundations is at an interesting and critical point as a field of study. In the development of scholarly specialties, there are always tensions between increasing specialization and the possibilities for enriching more general conversations. In fields of study directly related to fields of professional practice, there is an additional tension between scholarly and practice-oriented interests and concerns. Now that there are a significant number of scholars of high competence engaged in writing about foundations and their histories, and significant (though not sufficient) resources are available to encourage continuing investigation, the history of foundations is at a point where those tensions are likely to intensify. This will pose difficult but important intellectual and organizational problems not only for scholars writing about foundation histories, but also for the foundation officials who must decide whether and how to support them.

The pros and cons of specialization are well known. In the case at hand, specialization would mean approaching the history of foundations as a discrete field of study or as part of what some describe as the new field of "philanthropic studies." This approach is likely to foster a sense of intellectual and social community among scholars, which can facilitate all the processes that make for good scholarship. Within a community of peers formed around a specialized field of study, it is relatively easy to exchange and criticize work in progress and to build research programs that are deliberately designed to have a cumulative effect. Within a community of peers, standards and generative themes and questions are likely to emerge.

Despite that, the obvious ease of communication that can result when everyone has read the same books and learned the same language is offset by the limitations of isolation. Scholars who practice within specialized fields are less likely to have to articulate for a general audience the significance of their research than scholars who work in more general areas. Having read the same literature, their peers are likely instantly and on their own to appreciate the importance of one research topic or another. This can be comfortable. And yet, being somewhat removed from challenges concerning the value of one's investigations—challenges built around the famous "so what" questions historians dread, but ignore at their peril—can increasingly lead scholars to address technical and abstruse topics rather than ones integral to enduring human dilemmas or current social problems.

Happily, the problem of specialization is not a zero-sum matter. Specialization need not obviate participation in general scholarly and public debates. However, as a subject such as the history of foundations attracts sufficient personnel and resources to become a distinct field, it is natural for scholars to drift in that direction. It is always easier to preach to the converted, presenting work at specialized conferences such as those organized by ARNOVA or the Independent Sector, than to preach to the unconverted, trying to secure a place on the conference programs of the Organization of American Historians or the American Historical Association, neither of which has been especially friendly to research on new topics, such as foundations and their histories. Clearly, however, scholars writing about foundations need to communicate with both specialists and generalists. Hence, scholars and the foundation personnel who support their work will need to support specialization directed toward more scholarship of critical interest, while trying also to ensure that such work remain in its fundamental concerns oriented toward questions of moment to those who are not foundation history aficionados. The quest must be for ever more incisive histories, addressed to ever larger, more diverse audiences.

If the history of foundations is at a developmental moment when possibilities for specialization need to be approached with caution, a careful balance must still be achieved between the interests of scholars and those of practitioners. Too often in scholarly fields that have direct relevance to one or more fields of practice, education being a prime example, relations between scholars and practitioners are non-existent, hostile, or, at best, tainted with suspicion.[9] To date, however, this problem seems not to have loomed large in conversations between scholars writing about foundations and their histories and professionals working inside foundations. Perhaps that is because scholars of philanthropy, unlike scholars of education, have not stood in authority relationships to practitioners. Whereas teachers usually have to study at least some education research to secure a license to practice, which introduces an expert/practitioner hierarchy into that field, foundation officers and staff are not required to engage in similar license-related professional preparation. Whatever accounts for the difference, foundation personnel often seem genuinely interested in what scholars can offer as they ponder questions of strategy, accountability, and success and failure in grant making.

Given the opportunities for relatively open exchange between scholars and practitioners currently available in this field, the challenge for scholars will be to serve two masters: responding to the demands of their disciplinary peers while speaking in ways useful to the more practical interests of their colleagues in foundations. This might mean that historians writing institutional histories of foundations should locate the particular foundation they are studying in relation to both the histories of the fields in which that foundation has been active *and* current foundation staff concerns about programmatic direction and effectiveness. The goal would not be to address those programmatic concerns directly, direct lessons drawn from past to present usually being more facile than true. The goal would rather be to use current concerns to help one understand through contrast the concerns that were important in the past.

Serving two masters could also mean that historians undertaking wide-angle studies of foundation history would define their topics in reference both to disciplinary developments of the kind I pointed to as spurs to recent research *and* to questions of current high interest to a wide range of foundation personnel. Today, for example, many foundation professionals are worried about the possibility of a new round of Congressional investigations, which could result in more extreme restrictions on activity than was the case in 1968 when the Tax Reform Act imposed some relatively mild new regulations on foundations. This worry invites close historical scrutiny of earlier investigations, which could also be worth studying from the perspective of issues having to do with the continuous negotiations involved in defining publicly acceptable aggregations of private resources and power.

Beyond the matter of possible Congressional investigations, there is keen interest today in differences between, and appropriate roles for, "conservative" and "liberal" foundations. Interest in this topic has been stimulated by a report written by Sally Covington for the National Committee for Responsible Philanthropy; this report demonstrated the extraordinary purposiveness and effectiveness of a small group of "conservative" foundations with expressly right-wing ideological commitments.[10] Greeted with both praise and skepticism, the report begs for greater historical depth on the issues raised. How valid are distinctions between "conservative" and "liberal" foundations when examined over a longer time frame? Have foundations always sought influence of the kind the "conservative" foundations appear to have achieved today, or are we witnessing a new phenomenon? And what changes in the social and political context pertain to what seems to be the increasing political polarization of foundations?

The matter of "conservative" and "liberal" foundations also raises a host of philosophical questions of concern to practitioners in the foundation field. What, if any, are the differences between foundations and political associations of various kinds? Are there special ethical concerns that distinguish the two types of organizations? Given the political context of the late 1990s, is it any longer possible to identify, let alone pursue "*the* public interest" or even "*a* public interest"? Last, but hardly least important, when do liberal commitments to "objectivity" and "disinterest" stand in the ways of defending other liberal values, including those derived from the visions of equality and social justice that nurtured liberalism in the first place? Questions of that order could and should inform historical studies of foundation philanthropy. As more and more well-contextualized, critical histories of foundation appear, they can and should become topics for lively and important conversation among foundation personnel.

One topic that is already much in discussion among foundation personnel is evaluation—a problem that could benefit from historical consideration. As currently conceived, evaluation tends to be approached narrowly, primarily as a matter of assessing how well a grantee has accomplished what he or she proposed to do. Too rarely does talk about evaluation further imply examining how effectively a foundation has operated and whether, with the benefit of hindsight, its investments were at once prudent and daring, imaginative and wise. Of course, foundation personnel operate under heavy responsibilities not only to use the funds at their disposal in thoughtful and creative ways, but also constantly to reappraise the purposes they have identified as intermediaries to typically lofty goals such as "improving mankind." Still, fully rounded evaluations that take into account all sides of the philanthropic transaction are rare. They are rare because foundation personnel are no more eager to be evaluated by their peers than physicians, teachers, or other professional workers are. That notwithstanding, fully rounded evaluations are vital to the health of individual foundations as well as to the long-term viability of the very institution, "the foundation." Free from the heat of the moment and therefore encouraging dispassionate thinking, foundation histories can help practitioners realize the full benefit of self-scrutiny.

Obviously, one could endlessly multiply examples of the hypothetical uses to which foundation history could be put, and one could compile a very long list of topics that might be approached in ways that would simultaneously generate new and deeper knowledge about the historic significance of foundations, achieve a balance between scholarly and practitioner perspectives, and address audiences generally interested in politics, policy making, and public affairs. But delineating hypotheticals is not the purpose of this book. The purpose of this book is rather to present examples of cutting-edge work about foundations and their histories and, in doing so, to offer scholars and foundation personnel the opportunity to ponder the problems and possibilities of foundation history.

Some of the essays collected here speak directly to questions about "the foundation" as an organization and its place in American society. This is especially true of the three essays that compose Part I of the book. Peter Dobkin Hall analyzes the long history of trusteeship, in the process tracing the ways in which political ideals of equality have stood in tension with the reality of human and material inequalities throughout U.S. history. David Hammack sets the history of foundations within the wide sweep of American history since the Civil War. His concern is to call attention to the ways in which foundations have intervened in markets for nonprofit services. Moving toward the present, Peter Frumkin focuses on developments following the Tax Reform Act of 1968, his argument being that professionalization was one of the unintended consequences of that Act.

Part II shifts the focus from foundations as organizations to foundations as actors in specific developments in American culture. Meg Jacobs traces the ways in which the Twentieth Century Fund, unlike some of its peer institutions, purposefully helped nurture the culture of consumerism that emerged in this country in the 1930s. Focusing on several foundations, Elizabeth Toon describes the strategies used to educate the public about health early in the twentieth century. Julia Grant's subject is the creation of the profession and science of child development, which was largely the result of interests pursued by the Rockefeller philanthropies, especially the Laura Spelman Rockefeller Memorial, during the 1920s and 1930s. Finally, Guy Alchon focuses on Mary Van Kleeck, an important early researcher at the Russell Sage Foundation, in order to reconsider her effort to reconcile Christian and social-science ideals.

Part III extends the focus of Part II. That is, it offers essays that move outward from foundations to reconstruct some of the ways in which foundations have contributed to social movements. Alice O'Connor and Greg Raynor both study the Ford Foundation and what was called "the gray areas project." O'Connor concentrates on the 1960s and considers the Ford program nationally, her interest being what Ford's turn to activism tells us about an expanding liberal state. Raynor, by contrast, concentrates on New York City as a case study in the intersection of local and national policy change over twenty years. J. Craig Jenkins and Abigail Halci survey foundations generally to reconstruct their influence on social movements generally, especially the civil-rights and women's movements. Writing about foundations controlled by grant recipients or grantees, Susan Ostrander analyzes the ways in which an unusual organizational form opened new possibilities for financing social change. Rosa Proietto returns to the Ford Foundation in order to trace how it contributed to the development of women's studies in the United States.

Like Part I, Part IV of this book consists of essays about foundations as organizations, only this time the subject is foundation history. The purpose here is to consider some of the problems and possibilities of this kind of research and writing. Barry Karl details the difficulty of the enterprise by telling the story of his own long engagement in the field. By contrast, using the Ford Foundation as a case study, Richard Magat writes about the constraints that historians sometimes face when foundations are reluctant to allow full scrutiny of their activities. Ruth Crocker introduces biography into the mix through a portrait of Margaret Olivia Sage and the various motivations that led her to create the Russell Sage Foundation. Rightly critical of the existing literature for its focus on large, national foundations, Bill McKersie argues for more attention to foundations engaged in local grant making, while Lucy Bernholz suggests more regional work and more attention to the practitioner. Finally, Susan Kasten categorizes and comments on some of the recent historical writings about foundations.

Although the essays differ in style and subject, all should convey, along with the substantive material at hand, a sense of the importance of foundation history. However much progress there may have been in recent years in recapturing what foundations have done over the last century and how they have interacted with a host of different institutions, the history of foundations is still largely uncharted. If this collection of essays can stimulate further work and, much more important, thoughtful conversations between scholars and foundation personnel about the kinds of histories that could at once advance scholarship and practice, its purposes will have been amply met. If this comes about, the historical literature will be enriched and possibilities for reflective philanthropy enhanced.

Notes

1. Alexandra Oleson and John Voss, *The Organization of Knowledge in Modern America, 1860–1920* (Baltimore: Johns Hopkins University Press, 1979), and Joanne Brown and David K. Van Keuren, eds., *The Estate of Social Knowledge* (Baltimore: Johns Hopkins University Press, 1991), discuss and exemplify this line of research.

2. There is a vast literature one could cite. The following are exemplary: Martin Bulmer, *The Chicago School of Sociology: Institutionalization, Diversity, and the Rise of Sociological Research* (Chicago: University of Chicago Press, 1984); Roger L. Geiger, *To Advance Knowledge: The Growth of American Research Universities, 1900–1940* (New York: Oxford University Press, 1986) and *Research and Relevant Knowledge: American Research Universities since World War II* (New York: Oxford University Press, 1993); and Kenneth M. Ludmerer, *Learning to Heal: The Development of American Medical Education* (New York: Basic Books, 1983).

3. An emphasis on motivations for grantmaking was particularly evident in early works such as Robert F. Arnove, ed., *Philanthropy and Cultural Imperialism: The Foundation at Home and Abroad* (Bloomington: Indiana University Press, 1980), and Edward

H. Berman, *The Influence of the Carnegie, Ford, and Rockefeller Foundation on American Foreign Policy: The Ideology of Philanthropy* (Albany: SUNY Press, 1983). Among the more recent works that illustrate this broader approach are Hamilton Cravens, *Before Headstart: The Iowa Station and America's Children* (Chapel Hill: University of North Carolina Press, 1993); John Ettling, *The Germ of Laziness: Rockefeller Philanthropy and Public Health in the New South* (Cambridge, Mass.: Harvard University Press, 1981); Margot Horn, *Before It's Too Late: The Child Guidance Movement in the United States, 1922–1945* (Philadelphia: Temple University Press, 1989); Ellen Condliffe Lagemann, *Private Power for the Public Good: A History of the Carnegie Foundation for the Advancement of Teaching* (Middletown, Conn.: Wesleyan University Press, 1983) and *The Politics of Knowledge: The Carnegie Corporation, Philanthropy, and Public Policy* (Chicago: University of Chicago Press, 1992); and Steven C. Wheatley, *The Politics of Philanthropy: Abraham Flexner and Medical Education* (Madison: University of Wisconsin Press, 1988).

4. John W. Meyer and Brian Rowan, "Institutionalized Organizations: Formal Structure as Myth and Ceremony," in *The New Institutionalism in Organizational Analysis*, ed. Walter W. Powell and Paul J. DiMaggio (Chicago: University of Chicago Press, 1991), 41–62.

5. Paul J. DiMaggio, ed., *Nonprofit Enterprise in the Arts: Studies in Mission and Constraint* (New York: Oxford University Press, 1986), and Steven Brint and Jerome Karabel, *The Diverted Dream: Community Colleges and the Promise of Educational Opportunity in America, 1900–1985* (New York: Oxford University Press, 1989).

6. Peter Frumkin, "Philanthropy: Strangled Freedom," *American Scholar* 64 (Summer 1995): 590–597.

7. Theda Skocpol, "Bringing the State Back In: Strategies of Analysis in Current Research," in *Bringing the State Back In*, ed. Peter B. Evans, Dietrich Rueschemeyer, and Theda Skocpol (Cambridge: Cambridge University Press, 1985); and Ira Katznelson, "The State to the Rescue? Political Science and History Reconnect," *Social Research* 59 (Winter 1992): 719–37.

8. As one example, see Guy Alcon, *The Invisible Hand of Planning: Capitalism, Social Science, and the State in the 1920s* (Princeton: Princeton University Press, 1985).

9. I have detailed this in "Contested Terrain: A History of Education Research, 1890–1990," *Educational Researcher* 26 (December 1997): 5–17.

10. Sally Covington, *Moving a Public Policy Agenda: The Strategic Philanthropy of Conservative Foundations*. A Report to the National Committee for Responsive Philanthropy (Washington, D.C., July 1997).

PART I

Foundations as Organizations

1 | Resolving the Dilemmas of Democratic Governance

The Historical Development of Trusteeship in America, 1636–1996

Peter Dobkin Hall

T HE CENTRAL PARADOX OF American life is the coexistent ideals of political equality enshrined in our institutions of law and government and the realities of unequally distributed wealth, influence, and talent. While the Constitution ensures to each citizen no more than one vote and equal standing before the law, in the marketplaces of commerce and ideas, those with the time, money, skills, and motivation to devote to capturing the attention of the public and of government officials have always been favored.[1]

Classic democratic theory as it stood at the end of the eighteenth century posited institutions of government which were *de jure* subservient to the popular will as expressed through the ballot—but were, as Tocqueville suggested, *de facto* masters, since, without intermediary bodies which permitted the people to assemble themselves, citizens had no way of making their wishes known to elected officials.[2] But popular intermediary bodies presented a dilemma of which eighteenth-century political theorists were well aware. Formed around special interests—geographical, commercial, religious—they not only diminished the sovereignty of the state by representing themselves rather than government as legitimate forums for the expression of the popular will, they also favored propertied minorities with the resources to devote to their establishment and perpetuation.[3]

The Founding Fathers, having overthrown the greatest military power on earth using voluntary associations such as the Sons of Liberty, knew all too well the dangers posed by nongovernmental popular assemblies and, regardless of their other differences, united in denouncing them. In 1783, the establishment of the Society of the Cincinnati, a national veterans' organization of Continental officers, sparked an intense national outcry against "self-created societies" as engines of monarchical and aristocratic scheming.[4] In the 1790s, the formation of "democratic societies" by Jefferson's followers provoked a similar outcry from conservatives—who linked them to the excesses of the French Revolution and the disorders connected with Fries and the Whiskey rebellions.[5] In his "Farewell Address to Congress" in 1796, Washington warned against "all combinations and Associations" representing "a small but artful and enterprising minority of the Community" through which "cunning, ambitious and unprincipled men will be enabled to subvert the Power of the People, and to usurp for themselves the reins of Government."[6]

But while democratic theory presented compelling arguments against allowing the people to assemble themselves, practical experience with republican institutions—once they were in place—offered dilemmas that could not be ignored. When the religious dissenters allied with Jefferson agitated for the disestablishment of religion, the conservatives responded by offering statutes that permitted the citizenry to vote for *which* sect should receive tax support.[7] Such machinations underscored the shortcomings of defining democracy in purely representative terms (since a popular sovereignty approach to freedom of worship so obviously abridged the rights of religious minorities, who were forced to contribute to the support of majority sects) and pointed to the need to consider the methods of expanding the range of ways in which the people could make their voices heard.

Constitutional guarantees of rights of speech, worship, press, and assembly embodied in the First Amendment only partially addressed the problem, since they protected the rights only of individuals, not of collectivities. Extending these rights to associations was problematic because, under English law, all collectivities had a governmental or quasi-governmental character as delegations of authority from the sovereign to individuals empowering them to act as groups. There was no legal or constitutional precedent for nongovernmental associations' acting in the public interest; nor was the egalitarian logic underlying the assertion of inalienable individual rights compatible with extending such rights to collectivities, which, by their very nature, diminished the abilities of other individuals to exercise their rights.

Jefferson himself was surprisingly unimaginative in addressing these issues. He was willing to countenance voluntary associations as an extension of the right to assemble freely—as long as these bodies could not hold property or endure beyond the lives of the citizens who organized them. Without "personality" in the legal sense, such short-term propertyless alliances seemed harmless. And as far as more ambitious enterprises were concerned, he held to established British precedent: regarding propertied corporations as contingent delegations of government authority that government could alter or abolish without regard to private rights. As Jefferson would write to New Hampshire governor William Plumer on the eve of the state's efforts to take control of Dartmouth College, the idea that institutions, established for the use of the nation, cannot be touched or modified, even to make them answer their end, because of rights gratuitously supposed to be in those employed to manage them in trust for the public, may, perhaps, be a salutary provision against the abuses of a monarch, but it is most absurd against the nation itself. Yet our lawyers and priests generally inculcate this doctrine; and suppose that preceding generations held the earth more freely than we do; had a right to impose laws on us, unalterable by ourselves; and that we, in a like manner, can make laws, and impose burdens on future generations, which they will have no right to alter; in fine, that the earth belongs to the dead, but not to the living.[8]

If Jefferson dodged the issue, Jeffersonians in states such as Massachusetts, where the associational impulse ran more strongly than in Virginia, could not. In an 1802 memorandum, which perfectly expresses the uncertainty and ambivalence of Americans of the earlier nineteenth century in regard to associations, James Sullivan, a Jeffersonian leader serving as Massachusetts attorney general, wrote,

There is no legal decision, no precedent established in the government, on which to predicate an opinion, or to form decisive answers. This subject may eventually engage the attention, and employ the learning of all the men in the commonwealth. The feelings of interest, the dictates of prudence, the calculations of policy, and even the prevalency of parties, may give the whole contest a complexion which is at this time inconceivable to any one. The giving a decided opinion, therefore, without a precedent, or established rule to guide my mind would be of little avail; and might hereafter be considered as presumptuous and imprudent.

The great end of government, is to unite and consolidate the interests of all the subjects. A sense of security, and an assurance of protection, concentrates the public favourable opinion in support of the social compact. The creation of a great variety of corporate interests, in themselves powerful and important, must have a direct tendency to weaken the powers of government. When those are multiplied, and all the ability of the state is engaged in one or the other; and when the interests may militate with each other essentially, it is in vain to reason upon naked principles unfortified by established rules. No one can foresee what the event will be, no body can predict the consequences, while every one will lament the calamity.[9]

Sullivan, like all Americans across the political spectrum in the first decades of the nineteenth century, found himself reluctantly accepting the necessity of intermediary associations. In the process, the focus of debate shifted from the question of whether these entities should be allowed to exist to the more clearly defined question of how to ensure that they served—

or at least were not destructive to—the public interest. Attention to this question eventually settled on the issue of organizational governance, particularly board composition and lines of accountability, internal and external. Although the debate by no means confined itself to matters involving eleemosynary enterprises—the governance of commercial associations (business corporations), religious bodies, and public agencies was also a hotly contested subject—this essay will focus primarily on nonproprietary entities providing educational, health, human, and religious services.

Because the dilemma to which this essay addresses itself is so central to democratic polities, it is unresolvable. The perpetual tension between constitutional, legal, and electoral ideals of equality and human and material realities of inequality reposits itself periodically with the emergence of new productive technologies, demographic shifts, political or economic empowerments of groups (propertyless men, minorities, women), and other restructurings of the institutional landscape. The repositing of this tension— and the recurrent efforts of Americans to resolve it—is the theme running through this exploration of the evolution of organizational governance.

Over the past century and a half, the effort to temper the potential subversiveness of voluntary enterprise has centered on mechanisms of accountability. This essay will explore the dimensions of success and failure in creating and implementing these mechanisms.

"All that can be required of a trustee to invest, is, that he shall conduct himself faithfully and exercise a sound discretion": Fiduciary Accountability

Massachusetts led the nation both in the chartering of corporations and in the establishment of testamentary and charitable trusts. By the second decade of the nineteenth century, wealthy Bostonians were leaving increasing proportions of their estates in trust, and charities such as the Massachusetts General Hospital and Harvard were accumulating formidable endowments. The boundaries between private and eleemosynary interests were not always clear: many trust estates contained provisions in behalf of charitable institutions; certain charitable institutions managed private trusts on behalf of individuals; and more frequently than not, the same group of businessmen and lawyers both sat on the tightly interlocked boards of for-profit and nonprofit corporations and served as trustees for families and individuals.

This proliferation of corporations and trusts was tied to a massive shift of Boston capital from holdings in family-owned shipping firms and land to diversified portfolios of government bonds, mortgages, and the stocks of publicly held banking, insurance, and manufacturing corporations.[10] Because the value of these assets was subject to fluctuation in the rapidly growing economy, trustees became increasingly worried about liability issues: Could beneficiaries hold them accountable for the performance of investments? Were some investments more risky than others? What degrees of risk would be tolerated by the courts?

Much depended on the resolution of these questions. Economic growth created an insatiable demand for capital. But legal uncertainties constrained the willingness of fiduciaries to invest imaginatively, particularly in the securities of firms based on new manufacturing and transportation technologies. In the 1820s, a group of Boston trustees, hoping to discover the legal limits of fiduciary prudence, brought a test case before the state's Supreme Judicial Court. The suit involved the estate of merchant John McLean, who had died in 1823, leaving a $50,000 trust to support his widow, and on her death to be divided between Harvard College and the Massachusetts General Hospital.

Jonathan and Francis Amory, the trustees of the McLean estate, invested extensively in manufacturing stocks, which yielded generous dividends, despite their fluctuating value. In 1828, on Mrs. McLean's death, they turned over to the college and hospital stocks whose book value had sunk to $30,000. The residual legatees brought suit, charging that the bequest had been squandered by risky investments and demanding that the deficiency be made good by the trustees.

In setting forth his opinion, Justice Samuel Putnam (himself a well-connected Bostonian with extensive interests in manufacturing) carefully reviewed both the legal and the practical issues defining the duties of trustees as fiduciaries. Depending almost entirely on English precedents, he quoted an eighteenth-century Lord Chancellor's opinion which stated that to hold trustees accountable for diminutions of principal (in the absence of obvious mismanagement) would impose such a burden on trustees that no sensible person "would undertake such a hazardous responsibility." Putnam devoted most of his attention to the question of risk in investing. Again citing British precedents, he pointed out that neither government securities nor the "safe and productive stock" of banks was any less prone to fluctuations in value than stocks in trading and manufacturing companies. "It may well be doubted," Putnam declared, "if more confidence should be reposed in the engagements of the public, than in the promises and conduct of private corporations which are managed by substantial and prudent directors." Indeed, he suggested, investors might be better off placing their faith in private firms: "They are amenable to the law. The holder may pursue his legal remedy and compel them or their officers to do justice. But the government can only be supplicated." Putnam was similarly dismissive of arguments that investments in banks and insurance companies were less risky than manufacturing stocks because their value was no less dependent on the solvency of their debtors and the competency of their managers.[11]

"Do what you will," Putnam intoned, "the capital is at hazard":

> Investments on mortgages of real estate, after the most careful investigation, may be involved, and ultimately fail, and so the capital, which was originally supposed to be as firm as the earth itself, will be dissolved.

> All that can be required of a trustee to invest, is, that he shall conduct himself faithfully and exercise a sound discretion. He is to observe how men of prudence, discretion and intelligence manage their own affairs, not in regard to speculation, but in regard to the permanent disposition of their funds, considering the probable income, as well as the probable safety of the capital to be invested.

This formulation, known as the Prudent Man (Person) Rule, has been the fiduciary standard to which trustees have been held ever since. Trustees are not held accountable for financial losses incident to the normal fluctuation of markets. Nor have states presumed to restrict investment vehicles.

Recent years have brought changes in the interpretation of fiduciary prudence. Until the 1970s, many trustees used the breadth of discretion granted by the rule to make long-term investments in closely held businesses, for the purpose of maintaining family control of businesses and preventing hostile takeovers. The excess holdings provisions of the 1969 Tax Reform Act—and a number of state statutes that embodied its regulatory thrust— prohibited the charitable institutions from holding controlling interests in business firms and required them to diversify their portfolios (though a number of major foundations obtained special acts of Congress to enable them to avoid these restrictions). Subsequently, a number of influential legal scholars asserted that fiduciary prudence required "maximum return" on investments through diversified portfolios.[12] Other recent refinements in the rule concern the power of trustees to delegate asset management to investment professionals. Though traditionally prohibited, such delegation was approved in the Third Restatement of Trusts and, in effect, became licit in states that adopted the American Bar Association's Model Nonstock Corporation Statute, which, in shifting fiduciary accountability from the stricter trust to the more flexible corporate director standard, expanded the range of financial mechanisms available to boards.[13] In addition, federal statutes passed in the 1970s—ERISA (Employees Retirement Insurance Security Act) and UMIFA (Uniform Management of Institutional Funds Act)—posit guidelines and oversight mechanisms for managers of endowments and pension funds which favor maximum return investment policies and effectively diminish trustees' discretion.

"Who are the society?—where is the control? Shall the officers in the executive department govern the whole movement, responsible only to God?": Voluntary Associations and the Problem of Accountability

Although both the common law and statutory perspectives treated eleemosynary corporations as public bodies, the question of who the public was and how it could express its will within such entities remained unclear. The situation of Dartmouth College, as a corporation established to enforce the intentions of its donors—as represented by its self-perpetuating board of trustees—was fairly clear-cut. But it shed little light on the lines of accountability in organizations whose governing boards were elected by their members.

The problem of accountability in membership organizations troubled many early-nineteenth-century commentators. In 1828, Rev. William Ellery Channing, the leader of Boston Unitarianism, used a review-essay of the annual reports of several of the city's charitable institutions to raise broad concerns about the hazards posed to democracy by voluntary associations. "They accumulate power in a few hands," Channing wrote,

> and this takes place just in proportion to the surface over which they spread. In a large institution, a few men rule, a few do everything; and if the institution happens to be directed to objects about which conflict and controversy exist, a few are able to excite in the mass strong and bitter passions, and by these to obtain an immense ascendancy. Through such an Association, widely spread, yet closely connected by party feeling, a few leaders can send their voices and spirit far and wide, and, where great funds are accumulated, can league a host of instruments, and by menace and appeals to interest, can silence opposition. Accordingly, we fear that in this country, an influence is growing up through widely spread Societies, altogether at war with the spirit of our institutions, and which, unless jealously watched, will gradually but surely encroach on freedom of thought, of speech, and of the press.

"We are persuaded," he continued,

> that by an artful multiplication of societies, devoted apparently to different objects, but all swayed by the same leaders, and all intended to bear against a hated party, as cruel a persecution may be carried on in a free country as in a despotism. Public opinion may be so combined, and inflamed, and brought to bear on odious individuals or opinions, that it will be as perilous to think and speak with manly freedom, as if an Inquisition were open before us. . . . They are perilous instruments. They ought to be suspected. They are a kind of irregular government created within our Constitutional government. Let them be watched closely. As soon as

we find them resolved or even disposed to bear down on a respectable man or set of men, or to force on the community measures about which wise and good men differ, let us feel that a dangerous engine is at work among us, and oppose to it our steady and stern disapprobation.[14]

Channing's concerns were echoed and amplified a decade later by Rev. Francis Wayland, president of Brown University and America's leading political economist, in a book on the limits of moral responsibility.[15] Wayland was concerned not only with the tendency of associations to concentrate power in the hands of a few, but with the specific mechanisms through which they represented or, in his opinion, failed to represent the views of their members and, hence, the public. Most voluntary associations, Wayland charged, were

> principally, organizations, for the sake of convenience in the collection and transmission of funds, in support of objects of unquestionable utility. They have a constitution, and various officers; but these, for the most part, are merely matters of form. . . . The members bind themselves to no particular belief. The only requisite for membership is the payment of a certain sum of money. When this payment ceases, membership ceases, and no question is asked. The seceding member neither forfeits any social privilege, nor is exposed to any odium; he has changed his opinions respecting the object, or his means are less ample; or he does not choose any longer to appropriate them in this manner: and his decision in this case is always held to be ultimate and without offense. There is no principle brought to bear upon him but his individual sense of duty; and he acts, in respect to the matter of this society, as in respect to every other, from the sole dictates of his understanding and conscience.[16]

Although acknowledging that associations could be forces for good, he questioned the extent to which, by allowing individuals to delegate charitable responsibilities to others, they created a troubling kind of limited moral liability:

> when men are thus associated, it is well known that their feeling of moral responsibility is vastly less acute than when they act as individuals. Associations will perpetrate acts, at which every member of the association would individually revolt. Hence, the common proverb that "corporate bodies have no consciences." The leaders throw the responsibility upon the members, and the members throw it back again upon the leaders, and between the two, we find that although the thing has been done, yet who is to be blamed for it, it is by no means easy to ascertain.[17]

Wayland's ideas about how to remedy the lack of mechanisms of accountability within membership organizations were peculiarly Jeffersonian in character. His first concern had to do with organizations "whose object it is to produce a change either in the opinions or the practices of the community"—which he felt peculiarly prone to abuse. "When men are thus associated in masses," he wrote, "the impulsive forces" are strengthened and "the restraints of moral responsibility weakened," with invariably evil consequences. All too frequently, associations seeking to promote their ideas forged coalitions with political groups and, in doing so, became corrupted: in such situations, "the primary object of the association is lost sight of, and the thing itself becomes a mere system of machinery, working for no other purpose than for the advancement of turbulent and selfish agitators." Conjuring up apocalyptic visions of social catastrophe, Wayland asked, "what were the French Jacobin clubs but voluntary associations?"

> At first, they were mere societies for the harmless purpose of discussing theoretical questions of civil politics. Soon they were changed into associations, for the purpose of carrying into practice those truths which they supposed themselves to have demonstrated. They were next multiplied, by the establishment of affiliated branches in every town of France, (each one, however, governed and directed by the central association in Paris,) until they were able to control the public sentiment of the nation. They then boldly assumed the government of the empire. The throne and the legislative assemblies were prostrate at their feet. The right of franchise, that palladium of liberty, was valueless; for elect whom you would to be a legislator, he dared not disobey the mandate of the club. Legislative proceedings were regularly decided upon, in the meetings of these voluntary associations before they were brought forward in the assembly; and the representatives of the people did nothing but record the mandates of a sanguinary mob. Thus was a tyranny enacted, to which the history of the world affords no parallel; and all this was done by men, who, at first, were associated to discuss abstract principles of right, and who were merely pledged to carry into effect some truly salutary measures of reform.[18]

Guarding voluntary associations from "the evils to which they are manifestly exposed" required both statutory constraints on the scope of corporate activity and internal mechanisms to limit the discretion of trustees. As to the first, Wayland believed that:

> 1. The object for which men associate should be capable of so exact and palpable definition, that it may be always clearly distinguished from every other that might from time to time be amalgamated with it. It should not only be capable of such definition, but it should, moreover, be actually and palpably defined. When this is done, every one will have it in his power, at once, to know whether or not such object has at any-time been departed from or transcended.
> 2. The manner in which it is proposed to carry such object into effect, should be clearly and accurately set forth. Unless this be done, no one will know when he unites in such an association, what course of conduct he may or may not be held responsible for. If I agree to unite in promoting

an object by all suitable means, I leave the question of suitableness to be decided upon by a committee, or by a majority, and hence may make myself responsible for acts of the most unquestionable wrong.

3. The object itself, and the manner in which it is to be promoted, should be perfectly and entirely innocent; that is, they must be such as are incapable of violating the rights of any human being. As individuals, we are under moral obligation to adopt this rule. How much more, when we act in masses, proverbially liable to err, either from excitement, from party spirit, or from confidence in their own power. Unless these principles be adopted, voluntary associations will manifestly tend to retard rather, than advance the progress of truth; and they will be among the most fruitful sources of mischief to a free community.[19]

But even these external constraints were insufficient to prevent powerful factions from taking control of associations and putting them to evil purposes. In addition, internal rules were needed to regulate "the members of voluntary associations, in their relations with each other." Wayland urged his readers to regard joining associations as a serious commitment, based on wholehearted agreement "both of the object itself, and also of the manner in which it is to be accomplished." Members should be wary of the all too likely possibility that associations would act in their names without securing their approval—and unless they fully agreed with such actions, they should be prepared to withdraw from membership. Voluntary associations, Wayland wrote, must abide by the "precise terms" of their contract with their members:

> They have no power to do any thing in a manner different from that which was specified in the original compact. The moment any departure is made from the original agreement, the association is, in fact, dissolved. The individual members agreed to unite for one specific purpose; if the purpose be changed, another association is formed, with which the previous members have nothing to do, unless they form a new and different compact. Thus, suppose I join a temperance society, by signing a pledge to abstain from spirituous liquors, and by my example and precept, in such manner as I think proper, to promote temperance among my fellowmen. This is a distinct and definite matter. It binds me to a particular and specified course of conduct. But this is all. I delegate nothing to any one. I put myself in no one's power. I surrender neither, my understanding, nor my conscience, nor my liberty, to any man, nor to any set of men. I am in all these things as I was before.[20]

Wayland's radically individualistic and anti-institutional conception of voluntary associations minimized the role of the board and placed primary responsibility for governance in the hands of their membership. This put him in conflict with colleagues such as Yale professor and abolitionist Leonard Bacon, whose response to Wayland's views constitutes the first fully articulated rationale for board governance.

Bacon and Wayland's debate was sparked by a struggle between pro- and anti-slavery forces in the major national interdenominational bodies, the American Tract Society (ATS) and the American Board of Commissioners for Foreign Missions (ABCFM). At the time their debate began, the possibilities of voluntary associations, for good or for ill, were still largely unknown. In the abstract, they seemed infinitely malleable; as real entities, however, which aggregate property and interests, they took on—as both Wayland and Bacon discovered—an intractable personhood (what sociologists call the "Iron Law of Oligarchy"). More than this, because these associations were national institutions, their offices were necessarily distant from their contributors—which made it difficult for donors to monitor how their contributions were being used (a classic example of what today's economists call contract failure).

By the 1840s, the initially fragile associational efforts of the evangelicals had taken on a life of their own. The largest of their organizations took in hundreds of thousands of dollars a year in contributions and had built up large staffs to coordinate the activities of hundreds of missionaries and to print and distribute tens of thousands of publications around the world.[21] The American Board of Commissioners for Foreign Missions, which had began in 1811 with three clergymen who volunteered as secretaries, by 1846 had a full-time salaried staff that supervised the activities of more than 300 missionaries and assistants in 93 missions. It boasted annual revenues of more than a quarter of a million dollars—making it one of the largest corporations in the United States (by comparison, Harvard's endowment at this point was less than half a million dollars, and its annual revenues were less than $50,000). The American Tract Society—which boasted annual revenues of nearly $154,000 in 1846—had a salaried staff of 12 corresponding secretaries and clerks who supervised the activities of 175 field agents who sold its publications throughout the United States.

As these organizations matured, their governance structures also became more elaborate, and their power accordingly altered. Because they were national organizations, their trustees were in no position to oversee their day-to-day operations—a problem they solved by delegating authority to "prudential committees" (what we would call executive committees). Additional committees were spawned, as the need arose, to take on other special responsibilities. As the organizations and their financial needs grew, they sought to broaden their constituencies by enlarging their boards, by creating dual boards, or by seeking direct affiliation with the governing bodies of particular denominations. While in theory these increased numbers should have made organizations more accountable to relevant stakeholders, since larger boards represented more of the public and included a greater range of stakeholders, in Bacon's view this growth actually had the opposite effect. Larger boards increased the power of salaried executives and board insiders.

Writing as one of the most experienced trustees in the country, Bacon in 1847 set forth his concerns about governance in an article published in the *New Englander*, entitled "Responsibility in the Management of Societies."[22] It was a remarkable piece, not only because of the detailed description and analysis that Bacon provided of two of the largest societies, but also because, rather than using his essay as an opportunity to attack his enemies or denounce specific abuses, he took it as an occasion to reflect in very concrete and organizational terms on the process of governance, the mechanics of associational accountability, and the broader issues of moral agency.[23]

Bacon began his essay by describing and praising the "new order of things" in which "associated enterprises for the propagation of Christianity, at home and abroad, have become almost the greatest of the material and visible interests of the Christian commonwealth," which had come to "act irresistibly on all the relations of churches to each other, on the development and culture of piety, on the administration of the gospel in the pulpit, and even on theological dogmas."[24] While taking pains to emphasize that he in no way sighed "for the good old days . . . when the spirit of aggression against the empire of darkness, slumbered in the church," he made clear his concern that "in an age of activity and of religious enterprises" there was danger "that important truths may be forgotten or undervalued in the zeal and hurry of the movement." He pointed in particular to the impact of their enormous growth both on their understanding of their own purposes and, more importantly, on their relation to the churches, the clergy, and the public. He expressed particular "uneasiness" that the power "accumulating in the hands of the secretaries and executive committees" had made these societies dangerously self-serving.

Bacon proceeded to examine the role of management and the uncritical faith that seemed to be placed in it. Though he noted that in most cases "the executive department of a great benevolent society" was "chiefly in the hands of ministers of the gospel," this fact did not render them immune from corruption. After pointing out the enormous importance of these executive positions—which, because of their power to influence public opinion and the actions of believers, had become, in a very real sense, offices of "the highest moment in the religious world," self-serving—he went on to point out that what made them true to their trust and effective as managers was not their clerical status, but their personal qualities. This, Bacon argued, was an insufficient safeguard and, in consequence, raised fundamental questions about associations, their managers, and the nature of the trust imposed on them: "Ought the executive department of a great voluntary society, for missions or for any similar enterprise, to be really and formally responsible to anybody?—if so, to whom, and how?" Bacon asked. "Who are the society?—where is the control? Shall the officers in the executive department govern the whole movement, responsible only to God? Or shall they be under the government of some constituency?"[25]

After a detailed description and analysis of the scope and scale of the operations of the American Board of Commissioners of Foreign Missions and the American Tract Society, Bacon posed his fundamental concerns more concretely. First, he argued, "a true responsibility of the executive to some superior or constituent power, is a security against mismanagement and the gradual perversion of the trust," not because of "fraudulent mismanagement," but "in consequence of devoting their minds too engrossingly to the one particular interest which they have in hand."[26] "Great perversions of trusts" (what we today would call mission displacement), Bacon noted, tended to occur inadvertently, as a by-product of routine, taking place "for the most part unconsciously, gradually, and with the best intentions."[27] Bacon believed that the solution to this problem was not to eliminate managers and board committees, but to require them to report fully and regularly on their activities.

A second reason for "making the executive administration of these societies, truly and formally responsible to some definite constituency" was the tendency of power to accumulate dangerously in the hands of a few. "Power, and especially executive power, if placed in irresponsible hands, grows and accumulates till nothing but the violence of revolution can resist it. For the same reason the power which is necessarily involved in the administration of these great societies, and of others like them, and which must necessarily be entrusted to a few hands, should be carefully guarded and bounded by corresponding responsibility. . . . "[28]

Bacon's third argument in favor of increasing the accountability of executives was that failure to do so might invite public hostility toward the societies—as had recently happened to the Masonic fraternal order. "An irresponsible executive at the head of one of these great movements," Bacon warned, "is constantly liable to suspicion and assault. . . . There are men, and in this country of ours they are not insignificant in numbers or in the faculty of making themselves felt, whose instinctive jealousies are kindled at the sight of power, and who can not rest till they have ascertained that there is some adequate security against the possible abuse of it." More dangerous still, Bacon argued, was the tendency of such organizations to insulate themselves from legitimate criticism and, in so doing, act to destroy "the influence and reputation, of the refractory individuals who . . . have dared to embarrass the great and blessed cause."[29]

Bacon's argument, as it emerged, suggested a conception of accountability that was neither to the public (in a political sense) nor to market forces. While he conceded that "great associations" were necessarily dependent on the public of donors "to commend their objects and . . . methods to the largest possible number of individuals, in order to enlist the largest possible number of supporters and friends," this kind of accountability did not fully address the fundamental questions of accountability, since, as presently constituted, donors had no means of influencing—or even monitoring—the ways in which their funds were used. Political accountability, on the other hand, meant that organizations would have to submit to the judgment of a public hostile or indifferent to their causes, while giving entrenched managers undue advantage because of the enormous power of the societies they controlled to influence public opinion. Having dismissed political or market accountability as unworkable, Bacon considered the alternative of accountability to churches and denominations. This he found equally unsatisfactory, because merging the activities of the churches with the operations of the missionary and tract societies merely shifted the problem of unaccountable bureaucracy to the churches themselves. Finally, Bacon considered the alternative of having administrators and executive committees report annually to general assemblies of members and the interested public. The problem here, in Bacon's view, was that such gatherings tended to be forms of public entertainment, not forums for the conduct of the serious business of "free inquiry and debate."

The one form of accountability that Bacon believed could ensure the accountability of administrators was a true working board of trustees, in which each member retained a sense of individual responsibility for the activities of the organization. Bacon's conception of what made a good board was amazingly prescient, showing a remarkable sensitivity both to group dynamics and to issues of organizational boundaries—the mechanisms for defining the borders between organizations and society at large. More significantly, however, it proposed a way of preserving the efficacy of individual moral agency in large, complex organizations by properly structuring and functionally differentiating the various components of governance and operations. Even more important, it addressed issues of organizational legitimacy and authority in a democracy by suggesting that these, rather than proceeding from electoral or political accountability, proceeded from the fiduciary responsibilities imposed on trustees as managers of the property of others. These involved both religious elements of stewardship and formal legal elements based on the equitable relationship of trustees to donors and beneficiaries, living and dead.

The notion that there could be legitimate forms of authority that co-existed with democratic authority founded in the popular will and also nurtured and were crucial to sustaining it was a bold assertion with important implications for completing the then still embryonic and fragmentary rationale for the existence of voluntary organizations. When Bacon's article was written, the Jeffersonian and Jacksonian animus against voluntary organizations was still very much alive. Most states outside of New England either forbade or strictly limited the activities of private commercial and eleemosynary corporations—a situation that would persist until the last decade of the nineteenth century, when an aggressive effort to promote New England–style civil privatism would transform the institutional cultures of New York, Pennsylvania, and the midwestern states.[30]

Although Bacon modestly concluded that he had "proposed no revolutionary changes, no new constitutions, no rash experiments," and assured his readers that his proposed remedy involved "nothing violent, nothing revolutionary," just "very simple changes . . . in great establishments," it was clear that he realized that he had achieved an important conceptual breakthrough. "We will not pursue the subject any farther at present," he mildly asserted, "for the discussion which we have opened is one which is likely to be taken up in other quarters, and which we may therefore have occasion to resume, hereafter."[31]

It is no exaggeration to call Bacon's essay the first serious study of nonprofit management and governance. His analysis of the dimensions and dilemmas of governance is remarkably penetrating. And even though he does not use terms such as "contract failure," "bureaucratization," or "the iron law of oligarchy," he describes them with such astonishing clarity that his essay is relevant not only to the problems of organizational accountability and, more specifically, of board–staff conflict as they existed in the 1840s, but equally so to those problems as we perceive them today.

"Yale men, who got their training here, and are as able to manage its affairs as Rev. Mr. Pickering, of Squashville, who is exhausted with keeping a few sheep in the wilderness": Stakeholders Demand a Voice

There had been stirrings of change in America's colleges since the 1820s. But the real transformation of higher education began only in the 1860s, when alumni at both Harvard and Yale moved to demand a voice in university governance. Although these struggles took place at elite institutions, they commanded national attention: the effort by "Young Yale," led by prominent New York businessmen and lawyers, produced dozens of articles in the leading New York newspapers, many of which were reprinted elsewhere; letters for and against the proposed reforms dominated the letters columns for months in such national periodicals as the *Nation*; and "serious" journals such as the *New Englander* and the *North American Review* carried essays that argued for one view or the other.

The extraordinary amount of national attention given the issues of governance at Yale between 1868 and 1871 suggests that the public—or at least the journalists who presumed to serve the public—perceived that the struggle was far more than a parochial matter of institutional control. On one level, it was acknowledged to be a showdown between the clergy and the laity for control of the central institutions of American culture. On another, it took the measure of the emergent business class as a national leadership group. At the same time, both the contenders and journalistic bystanders seemed to be aware of the extent to which the struggle involved an attempt to articulate a new rationale for the privatization of important domains of American life.

The uprising of Yale's lay alumni began innocently enough. It was sparked by an account in the *New Englander* written by Yale's president, Theodore Dwight Woolsey, of an address on the reform of Harvard's charter delivered to a meeting of alumni in July of 1866, the text of which had appeared in the *Atlantic* in September of that year.[32] In the address, Harvard professor Frederic H. Hedge had detailed the history of Harvard's relationship to the state, presenting Josiah Quincy's highly partisan account, which demeaned the state's contributions to Harvard and exaggerated the contributions of private donors. This was by way of justifying recent changes in the college's charter, which substituted for *ex officio* Overseers representatives elected by the alumni.

Woolsey's critique of Hedge's address, while observing the important differences between Harvard's and Yale's governance structures (Harvard having two boards, the Fellows and the Overseers, and Yale having one, the Corporation) and criticizing Hedge's advocacy of curricular and disciplinary innovations (Hedge favored a broadening of curricular offerings, an elective system, and a system of discipline that placed the burden on students' sense of honor), commented favorably on the substitution of alumni representatives for state officials and suggested that the Yale Corporation would do well to consider instituting such a change.[33]

After reviewing what he considered to be long-standing defects in Harvard's governance, Woolsey turned his thoughts to Yale—specifically the question of "whether a similar plan of graduate election, can be engrafted on its charter with advantage."[34] While asserting that the 1792 inclusion of eight *ex officio* government officials as members of the corporation had worked to the benefit of the college, he criticized the bylaw which required that a quorum of the board be based on the attendance of all nineteen members. Because the *ex officio* members attended meetings irregularly, it made it difficult for the corporation to do its work. "In this state of things," Woolsey mused,

> we cannot but feel that the connexion between the College and the State is, as far as the deputation from the Senate is concerned, a mere form—a form which does no harm to the College that we know of, but which adds nothing to the efficiency and dignity of its corporation. Men are wanted in that place who will feel it their duty to be present, but it is idle, we conceive, to expect punctuality from the Senators, as the Senate is at present constituted. They change every year, so that the same man rarely reappears in the council of the College. They have no time to learn what duties are expected from them, nor to become acquainted with the condition and wants of the institution. They are in some cases men who take very little interest in the higher seminaries of learning, or perhaps even question their utility altogether. Neither sympathy then, nor knowledge, nor power to uphold a permanent policy belongs to them to any great extent.[35]

Then came the shocker: "Let the voters be all masters of arts and graduates of a higher, or an equal rank, together with Bachelors of all the Faculties of five years standing," Woolsey suggested, and

> let that part of the Board now elected from the Senate of the State give place to graduates, who shall hold their offices for at least six or eight years, and be reeligible, when their term expires; let the elections be held not every year, but every other year, or even less frequently;—will not the result be greater interest, punctuality, knowledge, sense of responsibility, and devotion to the welfare of the institution on the part of the new members; will they not, if well elected, be a new strength of their Alma Mater; will they not bring with them views at once enlightened and conservative?[36]

Woolsey's comments galvanized Yale's alumni, who, as they anticipated the president's retirement (he had served since 1846), began pushing actively both for a change in the college's charter and for curricular reforms akin to those proposed at Harvard (abandoning the prescribed classical curriculum for an elective system). Alarmed, Yale conservatives, led by Rev. Noah Porter, Professor of Mental and Moral Philosophy, began to mobilize against the laity and their supporters within the faculty.

The battle was fully joined in January of 1869, with the first meeting of the Yale Alumni Association of New York at Delmonico's, one of the city's most elegant restaurants. Chaired by U.S. Attorney General William Maxwell Evarts (a graduate of 1837) and attended by such notables as inventor

S. F. B. Morse (Class of 1810) and President Theodore Dwight Woolsey, along with some 250 other wealthy and successful alumni, the tumultuous conclave received national attention and was covered by reporters from the *New York Tribune* and the *New York Times*. "We have come here to-night," Evarts declared,

> to consider the prosperity and the prospects of the College. How much this College has done for us and how little we have done for it! How much this College has done for the country, and how much some of our countrymen, for whom personally the College has done nothing, have done for the College—SHEFFIELD, of New-Haven, and PEABODY, of London. [Cheers.] Among the sons of Yale who have benefited the country, I will mention WHITNEY, whose cotton gin has done so much for our comfort, by giving us cheap cloth, and MORSE, [cheers.] who has put it in the power of the poor man to send messages and receive information which kings and armies could not have collected before. . . . [Three cheers for Prof. Morse.] And we must not forget those who, without earning fame, have spread the influence of learning through the country—the common soldiers of learning. [Cheers. . . .] To keep alive the interest of graduates different alumni associations must be represented in the college government, as the President has suggested. [Cheers.] Nothing is required but a statute of the State of Connecticut, and now we come to a tract—no, a song—no, a treat. . . . "Yale College"—our college, of whom the President a hundred years ago said: "Esto perpetua, Alma Mater Yalensia."[37]

President Woolsey, with a clear awareness of the political storm breaking around him, responded to Evarts's rousing speech with a cautious affirmation of his confidence in the corporation as then constituted. The proposal to place alumni on the corporation did not originate in any want of confidence in the present board, he declared:

> So far as the management of the finances of the College is concerned and the proper exercise of their powers, perfect reliance is to be placed in the corporation of Yale College. They never have lost a single cent—that is to say, every dollar ever given to that College is now in their treasury. Here is a body which has such confidence in the faculty that it never undertakes anything affecting the practical working of the College without its having been previously discussed by the faculty and by a committee of the corporation.[38]

Still, he suggested, the disadvantages of having nearly half the board made up of men who took little or no interest in the college—and seldom even bothered to attend meetings—needed to be weighed against the advantages of knowledgeable and committed trustees. Nonetheless, Woolsey pointed out, the strength of the alumni's commitment was far from obvious. "The graduates have never done much for the college," he lamented. Only thirty-six graduates have ever given it over $5,000; and a gentleman here present, not a graduate, has given more than all put together. Is it likely, then, we asked ourselves, that we can move our College, and provide suitable buildings for it, and that endowments can be raised which are more important than brick or marble?[39]

Without demonstrating their commitment, changing the constitution of the college to include alumni appeared likely to be "a thing impracticable."

The gathering forces of "Young Yale" elicited ever more vehement responses from faculty conservatives. An unsigned essay in the *New Englander* in April of 1869, reviewing the meeting of the New York alumni, detected more than a little anticlericalism in the comments of those in attendance. Many alumni evidently wanted to go beyond merely replacing the eight elected officials who served *ex officio* on the Corporation—and were pushing for opening the whole board to the laity.

The conservatives' most coherent and concerted response to the alumni came in a series of articles by Professor Noah Porter, who defended the old order in a series of articles, "American Colleges and the American Public," which appeared in the *New Englander* in 1869 and were published in book form the following year under the epigraph "it is not necessary that this should be a school of three hundred or one hundred and fifty boys, but it is necessary that it should be a school of Christian gentlemen."[40] In response, faculty moderate Timothy Dwight published a series of essays, "Yale College—Some Thoughts Respecting Its Future," which welcomed the transformation of Yale into a university.[41]

Porter's most vehement remarks were reserved for the proposal to admit alumni to the Yale Corporation. His arguments could not have been more inflammatory: he suggested that alumni lacked the necessary knowledge to govern a college, and that allowing them to elect trustees would set loose the worst kinds of partisan excesses; he even rejected the idea that trustees should be elected from outside the state of Connecticut—since the college was, preeminently, a Connecticut institution. Porter stalwartly denied that the ministers who composed the board were financially incompetent: he claimed the board had never lost a cent—conveniently forgetting the Eagle Bank debacle of forty years earlier, in which Yale had lost nearly all of its endowed funds in an ill-advised bank speculation involving President Dwight and a coterie of relatives (including President Woolsey's father, bank speculator William Walton Woolsey). And he denied that the ministers' competence as financial managers had anything to do with the reluctance of alumni to contribute money to the school.

Porter's defense of the old order deserves to be taken seriously, for it engages the most fundamental issues surrounding trustee governance: Who owns an eleemosynary institution? Who has standing to demand a voice in its affairs? Porter's arguments against the alumni drew on the trusteeship-as-stewardship doctrines developed in the 1840s by his colleague Leonard Bacon, and pointed toward the special claims that professionals would be making in the future—that expertise made them more qualified than laymen to make decisions in their special areas of competence. As a member of the faculty, Porter also seemed to be advancing—through his repeated use of the term "we"—special claims for the professoriate as a constituency with superior standing to the alumni.

Porter's contentious disquisition bears a striking contrast to the open and cosmopolitan spirit of Charles W. Eliot's articles on the "New Education"—the series of essays, published by the *Atlantic Monthly* in 1869, that paved the way for the young reformer's election as president of Harvard—and to the reorganization of the college as the first genuine American university.[42] In a remarkably resonant way, Porter's essay reveals the defensive state of mind of the clerically dominated colleges as they faced the challenge of an educated national secular elite, determined to remake the world in its own image.

Porter's arrogant and insulting response to the alumni provoked predictable outrage. At commencement at the end of June 1870, when hundreds of graduates assembled in New Haven for their annual alumni dinner, their anger boiled over. One speaker, William Walter Phelps, a graduate of the Class of 1860, candidly expressed the feelings of the younger alumni. Phelps was no minor player: the only son of John Jay Phelps, co-founder of the Phelps–Dodge copper fortune, and son-in-law of Joseph Earl Sheffield, Yale's greatest single benefactor, Phelps was a successful corporate lawyer and Republican politician. "I speak for the Class of 1860," Phelps began:

> We are gathered from country and city, north and south; we are lawyers and clergymen, physicians and capitalists, judges and editors, representing all the interests of the varied civilization, from whose fiercest current we step for the moment aside. We are here to testify to our love for each other, and our interest in Yale College.

"We have a message," he declared, "the message of young Yale to old Yale, it is what the graduates of the last fifteen years think and say to each other; what they have not yet had opportunity nor courage to say to you." And then he took off his rhetorical gloves:

> The younger alumni are not satisfied with the management of the college. They do not think that in any thing, except scholarship, does it keep progress with the age. They find no fault with the men; they find much fault with the spirit of the management. It is too conservative and narrow. . . . The college wants a living connection with the world without—an infusion of some of the new blood which throbs in every vein of this mighty

Republic—a knowledge of what is wanted in the scenes for which Yale educates her children—this living connection with the outer world—this knowledge of the people's wants, can be acquired only from those who are in the people, and of the people. This great want can be supplied only by the Alumni. Put them into your government. Get them from some other State than Connecticut—from some other profession than the ministry. Call them, and they will gladly and eagerly come—call them, and with the reform will pass away every appearance of alumni coldness and indifference. . . . Believe me, men who sit on the Supreme bench, who control the cabinet of the executive—who in all moral and intellectual reforms are the leaders of their countrymen; Yale men, who got their training here, and are as able to manage its affairs as Rev. Mr. Pickering, of Squashville, who is exhausted with keeping a few sheep in the wilderness, or Hon. Mr. Domuch, of Oldport, who seeks to annul the charter on the only railway that benefits his constituency.[43]

Very much in the brash competitive spirit of Gilded Age entrepreneurialism, Phelps suggested that the clergy's otherworldly resistance to change placed the college at a decided competitive disadvantage, pointing to the decisions by the sons of Lincoln and Grant to attend Harvard rather than Yale. "Don't let Harvard, our great rival, alone have the benefit of it," Phelps demanded.

[L]et Yale condescend to be worldly wise. The son of a President is a young gentleman about to enter college. Yale says—it is worldly to secure him. We will make no effort to secure him. Saintly Yale folds her arms in true dignity of saintliness, and young Vicksburg goes to Harvard. The press, in a telegram carries the fact to hamlet and prairie, and the fame of Harvard enters a thousand households, for the first time. . . . Harvard takes great poets and historians to fill its vacant professorships—Yale takes boys, who have proved their qualifications by getting their windows broken as tutors.

At this open challenge to the conservatives, all civility dropped away. The debate over Yale's governance became a national issue—the subject of newspaper editorials and endless letters in national periodicals. The attention devoted to the issue is not surprising; the stakes involved nothing less than the question of who should control American culture—the ministers who had reigned basically unchallenged since the establishment of the first colleges, or the emergent class of businessmen and professionals who, as alumni, felt closely tied to the colleges and, as the people being asked to support them, felt that they were owed a voice in them. Moreover, Yale held a particularly important place in the American institutional imagination because so many colleges throughout the South and West had been founded by Yale graduates, and because the college's widely dispersed alumni tended to be the leaders of benevolent ventures of every sort in cities, towns, and villages outside of New England. The outcome of the struggle at Yale would serve as a paradigm both for the control of higher education in America and, more broadly, for a redefinition of the boundaries between the public and private domains.

The resolution of the struggle for control of Yale was a less than satisfactory compromise. The corporation agreed to seek a charter revision from the legislature, which, while retaining the governor and lieutenant-governor as *ex officio* members, would replace the senators with six trustees elected by the alumni and serving six-year terms. The ten "successor trustees"—the self-perpetuating part of the board—were opened in theory to the laity, but laymen would not succeed in achieving a majority on the board until 1910. The price the alumni paid for this concession was the election of conservative leader Noah Porter as president, which ensured continuing resistance to the curricular changes that were already transforming Harvard from a sleepy sectarian college into America's leading university.

But the laity took revenge in 1871, when Yale initiated a major fund drive. Reassured by Porter's confident claims that Young Yale represented only a handful of self-seeking troublemakers, the college sought to raise $500,000. The effort was an abysmal failure: only $172,452 was subscribed. Quite clearly Young Yale, outraged by the conservatives' maneuverings, had closed its pocketbooks to the college. In marked contrast, Harvard's newly enfranchised alumni celebrated the election of Charles W. Eliot—the university's first lay president—by giving $2.2 million in a single year.[44]

The conservatives' grip gradually loosened. After a decade and a half, Porter stepped down and was succeeded by the younger Timothy Dwight, who had taken a moderate position in responding to Young Yale's demands. The graduates greeted his election by organizing the Yale Alumni University Fund, one of the first annual fund drives to be launched by an American university. But only when Yale took on a business-oriented president, with the election in 1899 of railroad economist Arthur Twining Hadley, did the university finally gain the full confidence of its more worldly-wise graduates. They rewarded the corporation's shift by raising a fund of $1.1 million to celebrate Yale's 1901 bicentennial.

The displacement of clergymen from controlling positions in higher education and charity was a hallmark of American institutional life after 1870. While ministers and denominational groups continued to hold sway over many smaller colleges and eleemosynary organizations, by the turn of the century all the other major universities and most of the national associational enterprises had come under lay control. The final blow was Andrew Carnegie's offer to fund pensions for college and university faculty—on condition that their institutions sever their religious ties. Laicization was more than anticlerical, however. It was, more centrally, an effort to replace guild-like forms of professional self-government with decision making by "disinterested" businessmen and their allies. As such, it can be seen as an effort to create a new kind of public accountability—accountability not to the public as represented by government or by professional authority, but to the public as represented by the most economically successful.

By the end of the nineteenth century, three mechanisms of accountability had emerged from Americans' experiments with the governance of voluntary associations: a fiduciary standard, which concerned itself primarily with financial management and devolved responsibility on laity; a professional standard, which conceded to experts authority in their domains of expertise; and a stakeholder representation standard, which acknowledged, in the absence of ownership, an organization's obligations to the constituencies that supported or were significantly affected by its activities. The largest nonprofits—hospitals, universities, and museums—were already moving toward differentiated, mixed governance modes, which allocated authority to various groups, with lay-controlled governing boards linked to major external constituencies making fiduciary (fundraising, budgetary, and major policy) decisions, and internal committees, made up largely of professional specialists, exercising authority in appropriate domains of expertise. The activities of these groups were increasingly mediated by growing cadres of administrative specialists who carried out the policies of these decision-making bodies.

Mixed governance of this kind was, at best, an uneasy compromise, especially after the establishment of the great grantmaking foundations—the General Education Board, the Carnegie endowments, and the Rockefeller Foundation—which served to amplify enormously the influence of business across a wide range of cultural, educational, health, and human services institutions.[45] The rise of the foundations rekindled the debate of the 1870s over institutional accountability: the congressional Commission on Industrial Relations (1913–1916), as well as a host of academic critics, inveighed against the emergent power of business leaders—broadening their critique beyond Noah Porter's defense of clerical prerogatives in governance to a fully articulated assertion of the authority of experts not only in institutions, but over society itself.[46]

Social critic Thorstein Veblen, in his 1916 essay *Higher Learning in America*, identified the difficulty of clearly distinguishing fiduciary and professional authority.[47] Lay control of university budgets, in Veblen's view, created a situation in which "men of affairs" were able to decide "what the body of academic men that constitutes the university may or may not do with the means in hand; that is to say, their pecuniary surveillance comes in the main to an interference with the academic work, the merits of which these men of affairs on the governing board are in no special degree qualified to judge."[48] Moreover, he argued, lay trustees did not bring their business acumen to bear on the actual day-to-day management of university finances—a task increasingly delegated to the growing cadre of administrators. "These governing boards of businessmen commonly are quite useless to the university for any businesslike purpose," Veblen grumbled. "Their sole effectual function is to interfere with the academic management in matters that are not of the nature of business, and that lie outside their competence and outside the range of their habitual interest."[49] Rejecting the claim that administrative intermediaries, particularly strong presidential leadership, could effectively balance the fiduciary authority of the lay trustees and the professional authority of faculties and other experts, Veblen argued that business-dominated boards were likely to "create an academic head in its own image."[50]

Veblen did not view stakeholder accountability—through the election of alumni to governing boards—as a significant counterforce to the power of business. "It follows as an inevitable consequence of the current state of popular sentiment," he wrote,

> that the successful businessmen among the alumni will have the deciding voice, in so far as the matter rests with the alumni; for the successful men of affairs assert themselves with easy confidence, and they are looked up to, in any community whose standards of esteem are business standards, so that their word carries weight beyond that of any other class or order of men. The community at large, or at least that portion of the community that habitually makes itself heard, speaks to the same effect and on the same ground, viz., a sentimental conviction that pecuniary success is the final test of manhood. Business principles are the sacred articles of the secular creed, and business methods make up the ritual of the secular cult.[51]

The result was that business trustees invariably delegated academic leadership to "one of their own kind"—"a businesslike 'educator' or clergyman, some urbane pillar of society, some astute veteran of the scientific demimonde."[52]

"Government by People outside of Government": Accountability in the Era of Corporate Liberalism, 1920–1960

As all domains of production and service—economic, social, and cultural—became more dependent on expertise, the authority of the laity came increasingly into question. Some critics, including Veblen himself, moved toward the political fringes, advocating government by engineers and other experts. Others of a more conservative bent, such as management innovator Frederick Winslow Taylor and his followers, promoted the reorganization of the workplace in ways that would place engineers and other experts in control of industrial enterprise. A third, more moderate set of proposals was advanced by the emergent cadre of professional corporate managers, many of whom combined credentialed expertise with high positions in large business firms:

> Espousing a general theme of cooperation, social harmony, and economic and political order, they stood in opposition to socialism, on the one hand, and the anarchy of unrestrained competition, on the other. These "corporate liberals," as they have been called, sought above all to reconcile traditional democratic notions of individualism, self-reliance, free enterprise, and anti-statism with corporate capitalist and scientific-technological demands for order, stability, and social efficiency. Emphasizing first one, then the other, they worked to regulate the corporate economy through the agencies of government, through private associations like chambers of commerce, and trade organizations, and through such research agencies as the National Bureau of Economic Research, the Brookings Institution, and the National Industrial Conference Board. Through reform bodies like the National Civic Federation, they promoted social welfare legislation in order to reduce the burdens and antagonism of working people, and strove to enlist the labor unions as voluntary partners in the corporate industrial system, thereby hoping to substitute orderly and predictable negotiation for industrial warfare.[53]

This kind of thinking, with its stress on the public responsibilities of corporate leadership and its willingness to act through large-scale organizations, cut across conventional political divisions and affected all realms of activity, from social work and government to business.[54] The First World War lent impetus to these corporate leaders. The war mobilization was an experiment in public-private partnership, as industrial production, transportation, food, finance, and other crucial domains were coordinated by quasi-public boards staffed by "dollar-a-year men"—volunteers from big businesses. On the civilian front, corporate managers took charge of new charitable vehicles such as the Community Chest and the Red Cross and displaced the clergy and other traditional community leaders from positions in older social welfare institutions such as the charity organization societies.

The most articulate spokesman for this new style of leadership was Herbert Hoover, a millionaire mining engineer turned public servant, who gained international prominence as administrator of European food relief during and after the war. Hoover's 1922 book, *American Individualism*, set forth his vision of a "New Era," and summarized the previous half-century of social thought by business reformers.[55] Acknowledging the "great inequalities and injustices" caused by modern industry, Hoover sought to frame a new conception of "progressive individualism" which would reconcile traditional democratic and Christian values to the realities of advanced

capitalism. Hoover recognized that inequality was an inevitable consequence of industrialism, but he believed that equality of opportunity, combined with an ethos of service and cooperation that acknowledged the interdependence of all Americans, could lead to a new social and economic
order. Hoover believed that this new order was evolving from the changing nature of capitalism itself: domination of big business by a few rapa-
cious individuals was being replaced by public ownership (in the form of
widely disseminated stock ownership) and public-spirited professional management.[56] The new ethos of management drew as much on idealism as on
the pragmatic realities of an economy based on mass production and distribution, which, to succeed, required economic empowerment of the masses
through high wages, educational opportunity, and ample leisure.

Central to the success of this "associative state" was a new conception
of public life based on new kinds of "organizations for advancement of
ideas in the community for mutual cooperation and economic objectives—
the chambers of commerce, trade associations, labor unions, bankers,
farmers, propaganda associations," each of which served as a locus for
the "realization of greater mutuality of interest, service, and public responsibility."[57] In this system, organizations promoting economic cooperation
worked closely with other kinds of "voluntary organizations for altruistic
purposes"—associations for advancement of public welfare, improvement,
morals, charity, public opinion, health, the clubs and societies for recreation
and intellectual advancement—to combine self-interested pursuits with the
higher values of cooperation and public service. Accepting the post of secretary of commerce from President Harding, Hoover strove through the 1920s
to implement his vision of "self-government by the people outside of government" and based on "voluntary co-operation within the community."[58]

Hoover's efforts not only helped to familiarize the mass of Americans
with board governance, but also democratized and disseminated its use as
a mechanism for public and private decision making. In towns and cities
around the country, citizens, working through chambers of commerce,
trade associations, service clubs, organized charities, and a host of public
boards and commissions, worked to solve problems in such fundamental
areas of public life as city planning, education, public health, and recreation.[59]

Perhaps the most compelling evidence for the impact of New Era social
philosophy on governance is the emergence, beginning in the mid-1920s,
of focused efforts to educate trustees and to improve board performance.
On the eve of the war, stimulated by congressional investigations of philanthropy and finance by the Walsh and Pujo committees and the writings of
reformers such as Louis Brandeis, press coverage had directed public attention to abuses of corporate boards by robber baronial figures such as Carne-

gie, Morgan, and Rockefeller, who allegedly used interlocking directorates to control the American economy.[60] These efforts raised a host of concerns about the responsibilities of directors to the public and to stockholders, focusing on such issues as accountability, conflict of interest, fiduciary prudence, and the duty of loyalty.

After the war, there was a pronounced shift in the focus of writing about boards and board governance toward concerns about the governance of private social service agencies and libraries—hybrid organizations which, like many of the components of Hoover's "associative state," straddled the public–private boundary. Between 1921 and 1930, ten articles on board governance appeared in such general-circulation periodicals as the *Saturday Evening Post* ("Directors Who Direct"), *Survey* ("Institute of Trusteeship," a piece announcing the formation of training programs for board members of public health nursing organizations), *Delineator* ("Trusting the Trustee"), and *Social Work* ("The Board Member: What Is He? What Are His Responsibilities? How Can He Be Made Efficient?")—along with a host of pieces on public library boards in *Library Journal* ("Library Trustee"), *Public Libraries* ("Responsibilities and Duties of Library Trustees"), and *Libraries* ("What the Librarian Can Do to Make the Trustee's Meeting Profitable" and "Why Library Trustees?").[61]

During the 1930s, dozens of articles appeared, most of them focusing on social service agency and library boards—and one announcing the formation of an annual conference of college and university trustees.[62] But this increased attention from general-interest periodicals barely suggested the virtual explosion of interest in governance in specialized journals, at professional conferences, and within community agencies. In 1936, the New Haven Council of Social Agencies—a consortium of representatives of the Community Chest, the Connecticut Society for Mental Hygiene, the Family Society, Farnam Community House, New Haven Hospital, the Visiting Nurse Association, and the YMCA—published *The Board Member: A Guide for the Discharging of Administrative Responsibilities for Social Work*.[63] This volume was clearly intended to help train not only local trustees, but also a national constituency, since the council worked closely with leading academics in Yale's School of Nursing and the Medical School's Department of Public Health—the nation's leading educator of public health professionals. (The chair of the council committee that produced the volume, who served as president of New Haven's Visiting Nurses Association, was the wife of Charles-Edward Amory Winslow, the university's senior professor of public health.) *The Board Member* contained an extensive bibliography, listing more than seventy publications on various aspects of organizational governance, all of them published in the previous six years. A 1938 volume, *Social Agency Boards and How to Make them Effective*, published by Harper & Brothers, listed nearly two hundred books and articles on board governance—all but a handful published after 1924.[64]

The major themes of these publications would sound familiar to a board member of the 1990s. Describing the public health nurses' newly formed "Institute of Trusteeship" in an article in the *Survey* in May of 1927, Annie R. Winslow (wife of Yale's C.-E. A. Winslow) listed "the three outstanding problems which confront the members of a board of management in any field of social activity": "1. How shall the necessary funds be raised?" (fundraising); "2. What kind of a nurse shall the board employ?" (hiring an executive director); "3. Having raised the funds and chosen the technical expert, what else has the board to do?" (dividing organizational responsibilities between board and staff). Cross-cutting the answers to these questions were themes of effectiveness, efficient use of resources, and accountability.[65]

The board training activities described in the article had a similarly contemporary character. The first institute, which met in New Haven in April of 1927, attracted two hundred participants from twelve states, representing ninety local VNAs and twelve national organizations and educational institutions. It featured plenary sessions with speakers representing the concerns of major stakeholders ("board members, the public health nurse, and the physician or the community") and small group discussions which "gave opportunity for intimate, informal discussion of the subjects . . . [and] their application of communities of different sizes." Topics addressed included "the organization of the board and its relation to the professional staff," "the function of board members," "mobilizing public support for public health nursing," relationships between social agencies, and "education of board members."[66] "The essential importance of these meetings," Winslow concluded,

> lay in their expression of the recognition by board members of their need for fitting themselves to meet their increasing responsibilities, both inside their own associations and in their outside contacts with allied agencies in their communities. The American tendency toward the development of large and important voluntary associations, rendering public service with private funds, demands a new and enlightened type of administration from the volunteer servants who direct their activities. The New Haven Institute has perhaps its message for the public-spirited citizen in other fields of social activity.[67]

The Board Member, which Annie Winslow took the lead in producing nine years later, further broadened the range of concerns, with chapters on the conduct of meetings, committee structure, the management of professional staff and volunteers, financial management and responsibility, planning, marketing, public relations, and collaborative activities.

Winslow's comment about the message of her efforts "for the public spirited citizen in other fields of social activity" proved prophetic. After 1940, concerns about governance and formal efforts to educate boards broadened to include public and private colleges and universities, boards of education, independent schools, hospitals, and grantmaking foundations. The debate over the role and responsibilities of the boards of business corporations was also rekindled. But despite the increasing inclusiveness of coverage of governance issues, educational efforts also displayed a curious narrowing of focus. Through the 1920s, those writing about—and educating—trustees and directors expressed deeply felt concerns about community welfare and the interrelationship of public and private power; after 1930, board literature and education focused increasingly on issues of technique and framed concerns about vitality, efficiency, and harmony within particular firms. In the decades after World War II, emphasis on the stewardship/self-policing dimensions of governance was replaced by conflicting agendas, one featuring regulatory frameworks imposed by government, the other stressing the perspectives and methods of managerial professionalism.

"That tax-exempt organizations . . . recognize an obligation to be responsive to changing viewpoints and emerging needs and that they take steps [toward] such a broadening their boards and staffs to ensure that they are responsive": Board Governance in the Era of Big Government, 1960–1990

The years following the Second World War witnessed an explosion in the number of organizations seeking charitable tax-exempt status from the Internal Revenue Service. They were estimated by the IRS commissioner to number some fifty thousand in 1950; by the mid-1960s, more than a quarter-million were registered, and by the mid-1980s, more than a million nonprofits were operating in the United States.[68] This extraordinary growth contradicted conventional wisdom about eleemosynary organizations, which had assumed that the growth of government would lead to a diminution of private initiative.

Conventional wisdom, as it turned out, had failed to grasp the unique nature of the American welfare state. Rather than being based on the elaboration of vast central government bureaucracies, it operated as an allocative mechanism, which—while centralizing the gathering of tax revenues (chiefly through the universalization of the income tax) and the formulation of policy—delegated the implementation of federal programs to states and localities and, through tax incentives that encouraged charitable giving, to private nonprofit organizations.[69] Growing direct (grants and contracts) and indirect (tax-exemption and deductibility) subsidies of nonprofits increased the need for trained managers, skilled in meeting the complex demands of external funders.

The impact of these changes in government policy was dramatic. In some industries, such as health care—where most services had been provided by governmental or proprietary firms—eligibility for government funding encouraged conversions to nonprofit forms of ownership. In others, such as arts and culture—which had been almost entirely proprietary—the advantages of charitable tax-exempt status combined with the increasing availability of government dollars and funding from foundations and corporations sparked both conversions of ownership and the establishment of thousands of new nonprofit museums, theaters, and schools. The number of conversions was sufficiently alarming to cause Congress to hold hearings on the subject as early as 1947.[70]

As their numbers increased, so too did regulatory scrutiny. By the early 1950s, Congress began tightening federal surveillance of tax-exempt entities, particularly foundations and nonprofits that controlled profit-making enterprises. By the 1960s, these concerns broadened to include the rapidly growing universe of charitable tax-exempt donee organizations. After a series of acrimonious hearings in 1969, Congress passed a tax reform bill which, in enacting rigorous registration, reporting, and accountability requirements, further stimulated the need for skilled management. With the increasing sophistication and intensity of marketing and soliciting by professionally managed nonprofits, many states increased their regulatory attention to these enterprises. These policies fundamentally altered the character of nonprofits. By the 1980s, traditional nonproprietary organizations supported by donations and governed by volunteers were rapidly being supplanted by professionally staffed "commercial nonprofits," supported by grants, contracts, and earned income, and governed by insider boards.[71] And the shift in this direction was being reinforced by increasingly professionalized and entrepreneurial management, which proved adept at mastering the turbulence in the funding and policy environments.

Among the most powerful forces transforming board governance were changes in the fundamental laws that had given American nonprofits their uniqueness as private corporations serving the public interest.[72] The most important of these legal changes was the Model Nonstock Corporation Statute, drafted by the American Bar Association in 1964 in an effort to bring the statutory treatment of nonprofits into line with the main body of corporate law. It permitted the establishment of nonprofits for any legal purpose—rather than restricting them to the charitable, educational, and religious uses mentioned in the Elizabethan Statute of Charitable Uses and its Americanized equivalents, thereby freeing nonprofits to engage freely in business activities, as long as these ultimately served eleemosynary objectives. Further, the model statute shifted criteria of prudence and probity from a strict trust standard to a more flexible corporate director standard. Under trust standards, self-dealing and other forms of conflict of interest had been strictly prohibited; under the corporate director standard, such transactions were permissible as long as the board as a whole was fully informed and they were not demonstrably contrary to the best interest of the nonprofit firm.

The adoption of the model statute by many states went a long way toward eliminating the distinctions between for-profit and nonprofit enterprise. Nonprofits could do anything for-profits could do—except distribute their surpluses in the form of dividends. Although private inurement was prohibited, in practice it became virtually impossible—except in instances of outright theft—to prevent it. While boards remained invested with an aura of public-mindedness, the standards by which these could be measured and defined became harder to enforce. The transformation of nonprofit law created an ironic situation in which for-profit corporations—with accountability to stockholders and to customers—were more amenable to standards of ethical conduct than nonprofit corporations. As one scholar put it in the late 1980s, the nonprofit sector had become "an ethical black hole" in which the professed high purposes of charitable tax-exempt firms had become a cover for activities that would not be tolerated in the world of business.

These trends had profound impacts on governance. As nonprofit organizations proliferated and their purposes expanded beyond traditional charitable, educational, and religious activities, the pool of trustees came increasingly to include men and women with no previous board experience and, more often than not, ideas about organizational and community leadership that differed significantly from those of the Protestant elites who had historically dominated nonprofit governance.[73] Increasing dependence on government funding in certain nonprofit industries—by 1980, more than half the revenues of nonprofits in the human services were derived directly from government—created a demand for board members who could span the boundaries between entrepreneurial organizations and influential constituencies, which had come to include government agencies, foundations, corporations, and client groups.[74]

At the same time, increasingly professionalized management downplayed the importance of trusteeship: schooled in business models of management in which insider boards rubber-stamped the decisions of executives, career-minded administrators were likely to regard independent-minded trustees as an obstacle to organizational effectiveness.

The convergence of these forces stimulated widening perception of a crisis in nonprofit governance, which was greeted first by a trickle, then by a deluge, of books and articles on boards and their responsibilities. Not surprisingly, the first scattered efforts centered on governance in higher education and grantmaking institutions—two industries that had experienced extraordinary growth and been the focus of particular attention from the press and regulatory bodies during the 1960s. Much of this work was sponsored by trade groups such as the Council on Foundations, the Foundation Center (and its predecessor, the Russell Sage Foundation), and the Association of Governing Boards of Colleges and Universities.

The real tidal wave of interest emerged in the early 1980s—when the number of publications about governance surged from two or three a year to dozens. Generally written by consultants, these books and articles appeared in a host of new newsletters, including *Grassroots Fundraising Journal*, *Board Letter*, *Voluntary Action Leadership*, *Nonprofit Executive*, and *Grantsmanship Center News*—publications that focused on defining the responsibilities of boards, particularly as fundraisers and representatives of stakeholder groups. The chronology of interest, with 1982 marking the steepest rise in the number of publications, suggested that they represented the response of nonprofits to the major cuts in government spending proposed by Ronald Reagan the previous year. Interestingly, little if any of this work was produced by scholars or by national industry groups such as INDEPENDENT SECTOR, suggesting that the pinch of government austerity was being felt primarily on the local agency level, where managers were desperately trying to activate their boards, while at the same time ensuring that boards did not become inappropriately empowered.

By the mid-1980s, concern about board governance had spread to academia and national trade groups, and the range of issues dealt with began to include such topics as effectiveness, director liability, committee structure, the interpretation of mission, and the division of responsibilities between board and staff.[75] The last of these signaled the eruption of highly publicized conflicts between boards and executive directors in organizations throughout the country, and these were followed by a series of notable scandals (Covenant House, the "televangelists," United Way) that called attention to the increasingly problematic nature of nonprofit governance and increasing confusion about the role of nonprofit boards of directors.[76] By the late 1980s, the National Center for Nonprofit Boards was formed in response to the increasing call for governance information by nonprofits of every kind.

Accountability in the Postliberal Era

The conservative ascendancy, which began with the election of Ronald Reagan in 1981, served to highlight the increasingly ambiguous character of nonprofits and the problems of holding them accountable. Reagan, evoking a Tocquevillian vision of the possibilities of private voluntary action, proposed massive cuts in federal spending in the belief that, unconstrained by government red tape, the private sector, families, and communities would be freed to "take up the slack" in service provision. Forced to consider the likely impact of Reagan's budget cuts, liberal policy scholars discovered that the nonprofit sector, rather than being donative and voluntary, had become so massively subsidized by government that the cuts, if exacted, would devastate nonprofits providing education, health, and human services—between a third and two-thirds of whose annual revenues consisted of direct subsidies from federal agencies and programs.[77]

The conservatives' response to this was contradictory. On the one hand, they aggressively promoted further privatization of health and human services—joining liberals in efforts to dismantle state institutions caring for the disabled and replace them with privately run systems of community-based treatment and care, which they proclaimed to be both less expensive and more flexible and responsive to client needs. On the other hand, they continued to reiterate their old suspicions of nonprofits as instruments of special interests by trying to limit their ability to earn commercial income (unrelated business income) and to engage in advocacy (the Istook Amendment).

More significantly, the devolutionary thrust of conservative policies shifted the arena of debate over accountability from the federal to the state and local level. Jurisdictions that had once unquestioningly accepted federal tax-exemption as a criterion for granting exemptions from state and local taxes began taking a closer look at whether exempt organizations were providing benefits commensurate with the privileges they received, and whether their subsidized activities constituted unfair competition with for-profit businesses offering the same services.

With increasing success during the 1980s and 1990s, localities challenged the exemptions of nonprofits, compelling their boards to consider—as the law no longer did—the important differences between charitable and commercial activities and the regulatory and tax consequences of how they struck the balance between the two. Some industries, notably health care, responded by abandoning the nonprofit form and converting to for-profit ownership. Others, such as group homes serving disabled populations, sought statutory relief by having themselves redefined by law as families and obtaining a variety of immunities from local regulatory oversight.[78] Still others sought affiliation with faith-based groups, in the hope that First Amendment protections, still enjoyed by religious and religiously tied enterprises, would provide a credible defense against government monitoring and oversight.

At the same time, Congress has begun notching up accountability mechanisms in ways likely to affect boards with particular force. Responding to the succession of scandals involving large nonprofits—Covenant House, United Way, New Era Foundation—in which the failure of boards to exercise their oversight responsibilities was particularly egregious, Congress in 1997 passed "intermediate sanctions" regulations.[79] Rather than holding organizations to account for impermissible transactions, these regulations focus on the actions of individuals, holding them accountable for organizational lapses. Perhaps the most interesting aspect of intermediate sanctions regulations is their requirement that all charitable tax-exempt entities make their annual reports to the IRS (their 990s) available to any member of the public who requests them. There is already evidence that public interest groups concerned about nonprofit accountability intend systematically to monitor these documents to target organizations operating on the margins of the sector.[80]

Finally, the legal standing of stakeholders seems to be undergoing significant redefinition. For nearly two centuries, courts have held that the fundamental character of a charitable trust hinged on the idea that it could not benefit any particular person—and have reasoned from that to deny beneficiaries legal standing to challenge the management of charitable trusts. The 1996 Adelphi University case, though not brought by beneficiaries, was initiated by them—and resulted in the ouster of the institution's president and board. More recently, dissident faculty, students, and alumni of Yale's Divinity School have been granted standing to challenge the university's management of the school's endowment—only the second time in American legal history that such standing has been granted. If the suit is successful, it seems likely that it will transform our understanding of trustee accountability. At the same time, court decisions, particularly in the area of tort liability, are increasingly likely to find boards and their members liable for failure to act prudently—discarding long-held doctrines of charitable immunity and limited liability.

In sum, historic trends of organizational autonomy—which granted to private groups substantial authority to act for and on elected government officials—seem to be in a process of being reversed. Viewed from this perspective, the shifting of responsibilities from government to private sector actors appears to be accompanied by legal and regulatory changes that, in substantially increasing the accountability of nonprofits, substantially answer Jefferson's concern that in permitting eleemosynary institutions too much autonomy, the courts and legislatures were promoting "the idea that institutions, established for the use of the nation, cannot be touched or modified, even to make them answer their end, because of rights gratuitously supposed to be in those employed to manage them in trust for the public." Devolution and privatization, rather than actualizing the Tocque-villian vision of a nation that did its public business through "associations of a thousand kinds," may actually, in tilting the balance between voice and equality toward the latter ideal, be diminishing the capacity of private citizens and citizens' groups to act in what they define to be the public interest.

Notes

The research on which this paper is based was supported by the AAFRC Trust for Philanthropy, Aspen Institute's Nonprofit Sector Research Fund, the Lilly Endowment, the National Center for Nonprofit Boards, and the Program on Non-Profit Organizations (PONPO), Yale University. I am grateful to Rikki Abzug, Avner Ben-Ner, Evelyn Brody, Bradford Gray, John H. Langbein, Robert Wood Lynn, Melissa Middleton Stone, Harry Stout, and Miriam Wood for conversations that helped to inform my understanding of the evolution of board governance. I am especially grateful to Pam Greene, Claire Gillis and Phuc (Jerry) Tran, who provided invaluable assistance in compiling a nearly definitive collection of publications on boards as part of the work of PONPO's Project on the Changing Dimensions of Trusteeship.

1. Sidney Verba, Kay Schlozman, and Henry Brady, *Voice and Equality: Civic Voluntarism in American Politics* (Cambridge: Harvard University Press, 1996), 1–14.

2. Alexis de Tocqueville, *The Old Regime and the French Revolution*, trans. Stuart Gilbert (New York: Doubleday & Co., 1858/1955), 163.

3. See James Madison, "Federalist #10," in *The Federalist Papers* (New York: New American Library, 1961), 77–84. See also Thomas Jefferson's comments on the Society of the Cincinnati in "Answers and Observations for Demeunier's Article on the United States in the Encyclopedie Methodique, 1786," in Thomas Jefferson, *Public and Private Papers* (New York: Vintage Books/Library of America, 1990), 256–62.

4. Aedanus Burke, *Considerations on the Society or Order of Cincinnati Lately Instituted* (Charleston: Printed for A. Timothy, no. 100, Meeting-Street, 1783).

5. On the democratic societies and the controversies they occasioned, see Noble E. Cunningham, *The Jeffersonian Republicans: The Formation of Party Organizations, 1789–1801* (Chapel Hill: University of North Carolina Press, 1957); W. N. Chambers, *Political Parties in a New Nation: The American Experience, 1776–1809* (New York: Oxford University Press, 1963); Richard Hofstadter, *The Idea of a Party System: The Rise of Legitimate Opposition in the United States, 1780–1840* (Berkeley: University of California Press, 1968); Philip S. Foner, ed., *The Democratic-Republican Societies, 1790–1800: A Documentary Sourcebook of Constitutions, Declarations, Addresses, Resolutions, and Toasts* (Westport, Conn.: Greenwood Press, 1976); and J. F. Hoadley, *Origins of American Political Parties, 1789–1803* (Lexington: University of Kentucky Press, 1986).

6. George Washington, "Farewell Address: The address, and resignation of His Excellency Geo. Washington Esq. President of the United States of America" (Lansingburgh: Printed by Luther Pratt, & Co., 1796).

7. Richard J. Purcell, *Connecticut in Transition, 1775–1818* (Middletown, Conn.: Wesleyan University Press, 1963).

8. Thomas Jefferson, "Letter to Governor William Plumer," 21 July 1816, in Saul K. Padover, ed., *The Complete Jefferson* (New York: Modern Library, 1948).

9. James Sullivan, "Opinion of the Attorney General of Massachusetts on the Life

of the Corporation, 1802," quoted in Oscar and Mary Flug Handlin, *Commonwealth: A Study of the Role of Government in the American Economy, 1774–1861* (Cambridge: Harvard University Press, 1969), 254–61.

10. John H. Langbein, "The Twentieth Century Revolution in Wealth Transmission," *Michigan Law Review* 86, no. 7 (1988): 723–50; Peter Dobkin Hall and George E. Marcus, "Why Should Men Leave Great Fortunes to Their Children? Class, Dynasty, and Inheritance in America," in Robert K. Miller and Stephen J. Williams, eds., *Wealth and Inheritance in America* (New York: Plenum Publishing, 1997), 141–72.

11. "Harvard College and Massachusetts General Hospital versus Jonathan and Francis Amory, Trustees," *Pickman's Reports* 446–465 (1829).

12. John H. Langbein and Richard A. Posner, "Market Funds and Trust Investment Law," *American Bar Foundation Research Journal* 42, no. 1 (1976): 1–33; John H. Langbein and Richard A. Posner, "The Revolution in Trust Investment Law," *American Bar Association Journal* 62 (1976): 887–91; Bevis Longstreth, *Modern Investment Management and the Prudent Man Rule* (New York: Oxford University Press, 1986).

13. Lizbeth Moody, "State Statutes Governing Directors of Charitable Corporations," *University of San Francisco Law Review* 18, no. 3 (1984): 749–61; Howard Oleck, *Nonprofit Corporations, Organizations, and Associations*, 6th ed. (Englewood Cliffs, N.J.: Prentice Hall, 1988); Evelyn Brody, "Agents without Principals: The Economic Convergence of the Nonprofit and For-Profit Organizational Forms," *New York Law School Law Review* 40 (1996): 457–536.

14. William Ellery Channing, "Remarks on Associations," in *The Works of William E. Channing, D.D.* (Boston: American Unitarian Association, 1900), 138–58.

15. Francis Wayland, *The Limitations of Human Responsibility* (New York: D. Appleton & Co., 1838).

16. Ibid., 98–99.

17. Ibid., 109–10.

18. Ibid., 112–13.

19. Ibid., 114–17.

20. Ibid., 118.

21. Clifford S. Griffen, *Their Brothers' Keepers: Moral Stewardship in the United States, 1800–1865* (New Brunswick, N.J.: Rutgers University Press, 1960), 79–80.

22. On Bacon, see H. C. Kingsley, Leonard J. Sanford, and Thomas B. Trowbridge, Jr., *Leonard Bacon: Pastor of the First Church in New Haven* (New Haven: Tuttle, Moorehouse, & Taylor, Printers, 1882). For an evaluation of his place in the evolution of board governance, see Peter Dobkin Hall, "Religion and the Origin of Voluntary Associations in the United States," PONPO Working Paper #213 (New Haven: Program on Non-Profit Organizations, Yale University, 1994).

Bacon served at one time or another on the boards of Yale, the Domestic Missionary Society of Connecticut, the American Bible Society, the American Tract Society, the American Board of Commissioners of Foreign Missions, the Congregational Home Missionary Society, the Society for Promoting Collegiate and Theological Education at the West, and the American College and Education Society—as well as on numerous denominational boards and commissions and as a director of local charitable and educational enterprises.

23. Bacon's concerns were not entirely disinterested: his increasing commitment to abolitionism and his frustration in his efforts to persuade the national organizations with which he was involved to take principled stands on the issue of slavery had kindled his awareness that the chief obstacle to his efforts was the tendency of the management of great charitable enterprises to "slide into the hands of the executive"—with an "almost

irresistible" impulse to sacrifice commitment to fundamental principles to administrative convenience and efficiency. Leonard Bacon, "Responsibility in the Management of Societies," *New Englander* (1847): 62.

24. Ibid., 28.

25. Ibid., 29–30.

26. Ibid., 33.

27. Ibid.

28. Ibid., 34.

29. Ibid.

30. On this, see Peter Dobkin Hall, "Inventing the Nonprofit Sector," in Hall, *Inventing the Nonprofit Sector and Other Essays on Philanthropy, Voluntarism, and Nonprofit Organizations* (Baltimore: Johns Hopkins University Press, 1992), 20–31, 36–41; and Hall and Marcus, "Why Should Men Leave Great Fortunes to Their Children?"

31. Bacon, "Responsibility," 35.

32. Frederic H. Hedge, "University Reform: An Address to the Alumni of Harvard, at Their Triennial Festival, July 19, 1866," *Atlantic*, September 1866, 296–307.

33. Theodore Dwight Woolsey, "Dr. Hedge's Address to the Alumni of Harvard," *New Englander* 25, no. 4 (October 1866): 695–711.

34. Ibid., 699.

35. Ibid., 700–701.

36. Ibid., 701.

37. "Yale Alumni Dinner—A Pleasant Gathering at Delmonico's—Speeches of Hon. Wm. M. Evarts and Others," *New York Tribune*, 30 January 1869.

38. Ibid.

39. Ibid.

40. Noah Porter, "American Colleges and the American Public," *New Englander* 28, no. 2 (1869): 272–91.

41. Timothy Dwight, "Yale College—Some Thoughts Respecting Its Future," *New Englander*, July 1870–October 1871.

42. Charles W. Eliot, "The New Education," *Atlantic* 23 (February 1869): 203–20; 24 (March 1869): 348–57.

43. "Speech of William Walter Phelps," *The College Courant*, 23 July 1870, 71–72.

44. For comparative statistics on giving to Harvard and Yale, see Jesse B. Sears, *Philanthropy in the History of American Higher Education* (Washington, D.C.: Government Printing Office, 1922). For more detailed numbers on Yale, see "Yale's Larger Gifts," *Yale Alumni Weekly* (1910): 607–609, 634–37; S. R. Betts, "Alumni Gifts to Yale," in G. H. Nettleton, ed., *The Book of the Yale Pageant* (New Haven: Yale University Press, 1916). On Harvard, see Seymour Harris, *The Economics of Harvard* (New York: McGraw-Hill, 1970), 270. For a superb qualitative overview of these issues, see Merle Curti and Roderick Nash, *Philanthropy in the Shaping of American Higher Education* (New Brunswick, N.J.: Rutgers University Press, 1965).

45. See Abraham Flexner, *Medical Education in the United States and Canada*, Bulletin no. 4 (New York: Carnegie Foundation for the Advancement of Teaching, 1910), and Stephen Wheatley, *The Politics of Philanthropy: Abraham Flexner and Medical Education* (Madison: University of Wisconsin Press, 1988).

46. For criticism of increasing business domination of eleemosynary institutions, see Commission on Industrial Relations, *Industrial Relations: Final Report and Testimony*, 64th Congress, 1st Session, Senate Document no. 415 (Washington, D.C.: U.S. Government Printing Office, 1916); Scott Nearing, "Who's Who among College Trustees," *School and Society* 6 (8 September 1917): 297–99; Upton Sinclair, *The Goose-Step:*

A Study of American Education (Pasadena: Published by the Author, 1923); Earl J. McGrath, "The Control of Higher Education in America," *Educational Record* 17 (April 1936); Harold J. Laski, *The Dangers of Obedience and Other Essays* (New York: HarperCollins, 1930).

47. Veblen, *Higher Learning in America* (New York: B. W. Huebsch, 1916).

48. Ibid., 47.

49. Ibid., 48.

50. Ibid., 59–60.

51. Ibid., 61.

52. Ibid.

53. David N. Noble, *America by Design: Science, Technology, and the Rise of Corporate Capitalism* (New York: Oxford University Press, 1977), 61.

54. On this, see Robert M. Wiebe, *The Search for Order* (New York: Hill & Wang, 1967); Louis Galambos, "The Emerging Organizational Synthesis in Modern American History," in Edwin J. Perkins, ed., *Men and Organizations: The American Economy in the Twentieth Century* (New York: G. P. Putnam's Sons, 1977), and "Technology, Political Economy, and Professionalization: Central Themes of the Organizational Synthesis," *Business History Review* 57 (1983): 471–93; M. J. Sklar, *The Corporate Reconstruction of American Capitalism, 1890–1916* (New York: Cambridge University Press, 1988).

55. Herbert C. Hoover, *American Individualism* (New York: Doubleday, Doran and Co., 1922).

56. Ibid., 39.

57. Ibid., 41–43. See also Ellis W. Hawley, ed., *Herbert Hoover as Secretary of Commerce: Studies in New Era Thought and Practice* (Iowa City: University of Iowa Press, 1974), and "Herbert Hoover, the Commerce Secretariat, and the Vision of an 'Associative State,'" in Edwin J. Perkins, ed., *Men and Organizations* (New York: G. P. Putnam's Sons, 1977), 131–48.

58. Hoover, *American Individualism*, 4–5.

59. For examples, see Peter Dobkin and Karyl Lee Hall, *The Lehigh Valley: An Illustrated History* (Woodland Hills: Windsor Publications, 1982); Peter Dobkin Hall, "Philanthropy as Investment," *History of Education Quarterly* 22, no. 2 (1982): 185–91. For a superb account of service clubs in this period, see Jeffrey A. Charles, *Service Clubs in American Society: Rotary, Kiwanis, and Lions* (Urbana: University of Illinois Press, 1996).

60. See Louis D. Brandeis, *Other People's Money and How the Bankers Use It* (New York: Frederick A. Stokes Co., 1914), and "Interlocking Directorates; Why They Should Be Abolished," *Annals of the American Academy* 57 (January 1915): 45–49; "Directors and Their Trust," *Nation* 97 (September 25, 1913): 296; F. H. Dixon, "The Economic Significance of Interlocking Directorates in Railway Finance," *Journal of Political Economy* 22 (December 1914): 937–54; "Responsibility of Directors," *Worlds Work* 29 (March 1915): 493–94; "Changes in Boards of Directors," *Independent* 85 (January 24, 1916): 136; Scott Nearing, "Who's Who among College Trustees," *School and Society* 6 (September 8, 1917): 297–99.

61. "Directors Who Direct," *Saturday Evening Post*, December 8, 1928, 28; Annie R. Winslow, "Institute of Trusteeship," *Survey* 58 (May 15, 1927): 218–19; A. Wilcox, "The Board Member: What Is He? What Are His Responsibilities? How Can He Be Made Efficient?" *National Conference of Social Work* (1921): 406–10; F. P. Hill, L. E. Denny, and R. R. Bowker, "Library Trustee," *Library Journal* 51 (March 15, 1926): 279–83; "Responsibilities and Duties of Library Trustees," *Public Libraries* 29 (April 1924): 157–69; J. W. Hale, "Why Library Trustees?" *Libraries* 35 (January 30, 1924): 5–7.

62. "Second Annual Conference of College and University Trustees, Lafayette College," *School and Society* 43 (April 11, May 23, 1936): 503, 713–16.

63. New Haven Council of Social Agencies, *The Board Member: A Guide for the Discharging of Administrative Responsibilities for Social Work* (New Haven: Yale University Press, 1936).

64. Clarence King, *Social Agency Boards and How to Make Them Effective* (New York: Harper & Brother Publishers, 1938).

65. Winslow, "Institute of Trusteeship," 218. See also E. K. Davis, "Board Education: The Public Health Nurses Start Something," *Survey* 67 (February 15, 1932): 548.

66. Winslow, "Institute of Trusteeship," 219.

67. Ibid.

68. For statistics on nonprofit establishments, see Burton Weisbrod, *The Nonprofit Economy* (Cambridge: Harvard University Press, 1989), and Hall, *Inventing the Nonprofit Sector and Other Essays on Philanthropy, Voluntarism, and Nonprofit Organizations*.

69. See Carolyn Webber and Aaron Wildavsky, *A History of Taxation and Expenditure in the Western World* (New York: Simon & Schuster, 1986), and Lester M. Salamon, "Partners in Public Service," in W. W. Powell, ed., *The Nonprofit Sector: A Research Handbook* (New Haven: Yale University Press, 1987), 99–117. See also Lester M. Salamon, *Partners in Public Service: Government-Nonprofit Relations in the Modern Welfare State* (Baltimore: Johns Hopkins University Press, 1996).

70. See *Hearings before the Committee on Ways and Means, House of Representatives, 80th Congress, 1st Session, on Proposed Revision of the Internal Revenue Code*, Part 5, December 2–12, 1947 (Washington, D.C.: Printed for the Use of the Committee on Ways and Means, 1947).

71. Henry Hansmann, "Economic Theories of Nonprofit Organization," in Powell, *The Nonprofit Sector*, 27–42.

72. Henry Hansmann, "Reforming Nonprofit Corporation Law," *University of Pennsylvania Law Review* (1981): 129; Lizbeth Moody, "State Statutes Governing Directors of Charitable Corporations," *University of San Francisco Law Review* 18, no. 3 (1984): 749–61. Howard Oleck, *Nonprofit Corporations, Organizations, and Associations*, 6th ed (Englewood Cliffs, N.J.: Prentice Hall, 1988); J. J. Fishman, "The Development of Nonprofit Corporation Law and an Agenda for Reform," *Emory Law Journal* 34 (Summer 1985): 617–83; Avner Ben-Ner, "Who Benefits from the Nonprofit Sector? Reforming Law and Policy toward Nonprofit Organizations," *Yale Law Journal* 104 (1994): 731–62; J. J. Fishman and S. Schwartz, *Nonprofit Organizations: Cases and Materials* (Westbury: Foundation Press, 1995); Evelyn Brody, "Agents without Principals: The Economic Convergence of the Nonprofit and For-Profit Organizational Forms," *New York Law School Review* 40 (1996): 457–536.

73. Miriam M. Wood, "The Governing Board's Existential Quandary," PONPO Working Paper #143 (New Haven: Program on Non-Profit Organizations, Yale University, 1989); Peter Dobkin Hall, "Cultures of Trusteeship in the United States," in Hall, *Inventing the Nonprofit Sector and Other Essays on Philanthropy, Voluntarism, and Nonprofit Organizations*, 135–206; Rikki Abzug, "Variations in Trusteeship: A Six City, Comparative Historical Study of the Evolution of Nonprofit Boards" (Ph.D. dissertation, Department of Sociology, Yale University, 1994).

74. On funding relations between government agencies and nonprofit groups, see Lester M. Salamon and Alan Abramson, *The Federal Budget and the Nonprofit Sector* (Washington, D.C.: Urban Institute Press, 1982); Kirstin Gronbjerg, *Understanding Nonprofit Funding: Managing Revenues in Social Service and Community Development*

Organizations (San Francisco: Jossey-Bass Publishers, 1994). On board members as boundary-spanners, see Melissa Middleton, "Nonprofit Boards of Directors: Beyond the Governance Function," in Powell, *The Nonprofit Sector*, 141–53.

75. For examples of this approach, see Cyril O. Houle, *Governing Boards* (New York: Association Press, 1960); Brian O'Connell, *The Board Member's Book* (New York: Council on Foundations, 1982); R. D. Herman and J. Van Til, eds., *Nonprofit Boards of Directors: Analyses and Applications* (New Brunswick, N.J.: Transaction Press, 1989); Cyril O. Houle, *Governing Boards* (San Francisco: Jossey-Bass Publishers, 1989); John Carver, *Boards That Make a Difference: A New Design for Leadership in Nonprofit Organizations* (San Francisco: Jossey-Bass Publishers, 1990); Richard P. Chait, Thomas P. Holland, and Barbara E. Taylor, *The Effective Board of Trustees* (New York: Macmillan, 1991); Dennis R. Young, Robert M. Hollister, Virginia A. Hodgkinson, and Associates, *Governing, Leading, and Managing Nonprofit Organizations* (San Francisco: Jossey-Bass Publishers, 1993).

76. See Miriam M. Wood, *Nonprofit Boards and Leadership: Cases on Governance, Change, and Board-Staff Dynamics* (San Francisco: Jossey-Bass Publishers, 1995).

77. Salamon, "Partners in Public Service," 104–105.

78. Peter Dobkin Hall, "There's No Place Like Home: Contracting Human Services in Connecticut, 1970–1995," PONPO Working Paper #236 (New Haven: Program on Non-Profit Organizations, Yale University, 1996); Melissa M. Stone, "Competing Contexts: The Evolution of an Organizational Governance Structure in Competing Environments," PONPO Working Paper #185 (New Haven: Program on Non-Profit Organizations, Yale University, 1993); and Melissa M. Stone and Barbara Bigelow, "Re-examining the Contractual Ideal: Organizational and Political Reality," PONPO Working Paper #194 (New Haven: Program on Non-Profit Organizations, Yale University, 1993).

79. See Bruce R. Hopkins and D. Benson Tesdahl, *Intermediate Sanctions: Curbing Nonprofit Abuse* (New York: John Wiley & Sons, 1997).

80. Harriet Bograd, "Nonprofit Cyber-Accountability—Why?" paper presented to the Panel on Cyber-Responsibility, Annual Conference, Association for Research on Nonprofit Organizations and Voluntary Action, New York City, November 7, 1996.

2 | Foundations in the American Polity, 1900–1950

David C. Hammack

F OR NEARLY TWENTY YEARS, historians and other scholars have been discussing the development of the American "polity," referring broadly to the arrangements and institutions, state, local, and national, both private and public, through which Americans are governed.[1] Philanthropic foundations—indeed the entire nonprofit sector of American society—have received less attention than one might have expected in these discussions.[2] How should we view foundations, especially the largest foundations that have pursued national agendas, as participants in the American polity?

One of the most influential assertions about the nineteenth-century American polity is Stephen Skowronek's:

> The state of courts and parties emerged triumphant from the politics of Reconstruction. As the extraordinary institutional machinery of the Civil War was swept aside, American government resumed its normal mode of operations.[3]

I would amend Skowronek's formulation: the nineteenth-century American polity consisted of courts, parties, and corporations. Among the corporations were both business firms devoted to profit-making and eleemosynary corporations—private institutions devoted to the "public good" as seen by their boards and by the legislatures that chartered them. The eleemosynary corporations of the nineteenth-century United States provided significant human and cultural services, making up the equivalent of what since the 1970s has been called the "nonprofit sector" in American society.[4] The distinction between "private" and "public" has, of course, been neither absolute nor stable over time. Public governments charter and regulate private nonprofits, and government-collected tax money has paid for some of the facilities that nonprofits use, and for many of the services they have provided. But the distinction is important: nonprofits remain much more independent from direct political influence than government agencies and are controlled by small boards that can emphasize concerns too narrow to dominate legislatures.[5]

In the first third of the twentieth century, foundations came to play an important role in the organization, management, and support of eleemosynary corporations; that fact, even more than the recent attempts to shape government policy that are emphasized in most of the essays included in this volume, makes foundations important to the American polity.

Here I will focus on the fairly small group of "general purpose foundations" that broadly seek to "improve the welfare of mankind."[6] Unlike other active nonprofit organizations these general purpose foundations do not themselves provide services. A foundation has no specific mission; it is neither school, research institute, library, hospital, clinic, home for orphans or the elderly, nor a museum.[7] As Dwight Macdonald famously described the Ford Foundation, a foundation is simply "a large body of money completely surrounded by people who want some."[8]

Because active nonprofit organizations have clearly defined purposes we can fairly easily discuss ways of determining how well they are doing, despite the inevitable debates about "real" purposes and about the motives of leaders.[9] General purpose foundations, by contrast, can shift their programs without worrying about continuing commitments to staff and or constituents. Because they lack clearly stated purposes, foundations are difficult to evaluate. If it is hard to define the purpose of, or to evaluate, particular foundations, what can we say about the field in general?[10]

Historians have been moving toward a better understanding of America's general purpose foundations. We have been learning about their purposes not only by studying the private and public statements of their donors and managers, but also by looking at their actions, at their interactions with other forces in American society, and at the means they have adopted.

Broadly speaking, foundations have sought to use six distinct approaches in their efforts to improve "the welfare of mankind." Foundations have:

- Provided direct support for scientific and scholarly research;
- Sought to shape public opinion by supporting studies that highlight particular problems and devise and advance particular policies;
- Supported and honored those whose actions they consider exemplary;
- Helped devise and promote specific government policies;
- Purchased services from (or subsidized the supply of services by) nonprofit and governmental agencies that provide health care, social welfare, educational, or cultural services;
- Sponsored the creation of new, or the reorientation and reorganization of existing, service providers.

Merle Curti, Roderick Nash, Roger Geiger, Robert Kohler, and many other scholars have extensively examined direct support for research, the foundation activity that is most directly relevant to the scholarly community.[11] This is a large, complex, and contested area, but historians agree that a small group of foundations, led by the Rockefeller Foundation, played a central role in adding research to the agenda of American universities, in creating the twentieth-century American research university, and in focusing university research on practical matters of broad public interest and on empirical research methods, and away from theory and speculation. Private donors and the federal and state governments also played important roles, of course, and charismatic scientists and university leaders often influenced the foundations. The funders—private individuals and business firms as well as foundations and government agencies—have certainly had a good deal to say about the great expansion of scientific research, about many research agendas, and about the preference for empirical research methods in all disciplines, but historians disagree about the degree to which funder preferences and the internal logic of the disciplines have shaped the development of knowledge. The histories of individual disciplines often emphasize internal logic to the exclusion of funder preferences, and have thus neglected one of the roles of foundations in the polity. The federal government dominated research funding in the United States after World War II, leaving a more modest role for foundations, many of which reshaped their programs to influence the federal research policy over time. Foundation-supported research has influenced the polity most by establishing the idea that scientific research was both valuable to the nation and an activity that belonged in major research universities. Once established, this idea affected both the development of the flagship campuses of state university systems and the expansion of federal funding for scientific research.[12]

A much smaller number of historians has sought to assess foundation efforts to shape public opinion through studies designed to call attention to particular problems and to advance the discussion of possible solutions. Ellen Condliffe Lagemann has used the phrase "technologies of influence" to characterize the sponsorship of large-scale studies designed to provide authoritative policy guides to both private and public agencies. Examples of such projects include the Carnegie Corporation's support for Gunnar Myrdal's *American Dilemma* and the Twentieth Century Fund's support of Jean Gottmann's *Megalopolis: The Urbanized Northeastern Region of the United States*.[13] The development of such a study is distinct from its implementation, as Steven Wheatley's *Politics of Philanthropy* demonstrates.[14] Several of the essays in this volume consider postwar studies of this kind, including the more recent efforts of foundations to promote change by supporting social movements rather than institutions.

Still fewer historians have seriously studied foundation efforts to support and honor people whose views or qualities they hope others will emulate. The most famous are not American: Britain's Rhodes Scholars and Sweden's Nobel Prizes. But many American examples exist, from Andrew Carnegie's early "Hero Funds," through the John Simon Guggenheim Foundation's grants to scientists, scholars, and creative artists, the Danforth Foundation's graduate school scholarships for young people of virtuous character, and the W. K. Kellogg Foundation's current leadership development program. Foundation managers are well aware that the recognition that comes with an individual grant or prize is often more valuable than the money. To the extent that they change the distribution of recognition, prestige, and honor, foundations promote public agendas. Surprisingly, no cultural historian has yet sought to evaluate foundation awards to individuals.[15]

Stimulated particularly by the suggestions of sociologist Edward Shils and by the pioneering work of Barry Karl and Stanley Katz, historians and political scientists interested in the power of the state, in the rise of the U.S. federal government, or in the fate of liberty and democracy in America, have also written about foundation efforts to influence—directly through studies of alternative policies and indirectly through efforts to influence public opinion—the federal government.[16] Karl and Katz argue that a few large national foundations have helped Americans make up for their fragmented government's inability to respond as effectively as European governments to problems arising from the early-twentieth-century industrial development. Foundations certainly provided a new setting for the work of policy specialists after World War I: in the late nineteenth century there had been no foundations to employ such specialists. But policy specialists had existed—in law offices, on the staffs of periodicals and trade associations, in universities and other operating nonprofits, in religious organizations, and occasionally in the agencies of local and state government or supporting themselves out of accumulated wealth.[17] Many factors shape government policies, and a satisfying, detailed account of foundation influence has proved difficult to produce.[18] The paths of influence are often indirect; Alice O'Connor's essay in this volume notes, for example, that federal officials concerned with economic stability provided key support for the antipoverty and community development policies promoted by the Ford Foundation's "Gray Areas" program. Government agencies have, on occasion, shaped foundation policies more than the foundations have shaped them. Preoccupation with the national government, moreover, has led to neglect of foundation attempts to influence state and local governments—although the papers of Gregory Raynor, William McKersie, and Lucy Bernholz in this volume go far to remedy that neglect for recent decades.[19]

Direct support for research, attempts to shape public opinion, the conferring of money and honor on individuals, and direct attempts to influence government policy constitute four of the six approaches to "improving social and living conditions in the United States" that foundations have utilized.[20] But historians and other scholars—including contributors to this volume—have rather neglected the foundations' fifth and sixth approaches, which involve intervention in the markets for nonprofit services. Yet these are the approaches that general purpose foundations have favored.

Many foundation grants directly increase the supply of nonprofit services, either by paying for such services or by expanding a nonprofit organization's facilities, enabling it to increase its supply of services without raising—and perhaps even while reducing—the price it must charge. These grants affect the general polity only at the margins, by helping in small ways to increase the already large role of nonprofit organizations in the United States. Most foundation grants, like most donations from wealthy people in general, fall into this category.

More strategically, during the first half of the twentieth century a select group of foundations intervened in nonprofit markets by creating new groups of service providers and reorganizing markets. In doing so, these foundations went beyond the mere support of nonprofit organizations to play the role of what Ellis Hawley and others have called "private governments" in American life.[21] These foundation actions had the most important impact on how the United States is governed.

The Limited Resources of Foundations

Countless foundation officals have restated John D. Rockefeller's assertion that "there is not enough money for the work of human uplift and . . . there never will be."[22] No foundation has ever been able to do much directly to improve "social and living conditions in the United States" or to "improve the welfare of mankind."

Agencies of all kinds—for-profit businesses, governments, and nonprofit, nongovernment agencies—claim to advance the general welfare in the United States. Rockefeller himself argued that "the best philanthropy" is "the investment of effort or time or money, carefully considered with relation to the power of employing people at a remunerative wage." In the United States, most of the performing and visual arts, nursing home care, medical care, and vocational education have always been provided by profit-seekers.[23] Donations even as large as Rockefeller's amounted to a small part of the total economy; the billion dollars he is estimated to have given away over more than forty years was less than one percent of the U.S. national income during a single year of the 1920s.[24] Rockefeller's donations were also tiny in relation to the scope of government. Before the 1960s local governments provided most elementary education and public health, most poor relief, and much medical care.[25] Local government accounted for five percent of the Gross National Product in 1902 and has risen steadily throughout the century.

Government Expenditures as Percentage of Gross National Product in the United States, 1900–1990[26]

Year	State & Local Expenditures as % of GNP	Federal Expenditures as % of GNP
1900		3
1902	5	
1910		2
1913	6	
1920		7
1927	8	
1930		4
1932	14	
1940	11	10
1950	10	15
1960	12	18
1970	15	20
1980	16	22
1990	19	24

Collectively, nonprofit organizations also dwarfed such great fortunes as those of Rockefeller and Carnegie. We do not yet have precise estimates for the period before the 1970s, but we have good clues to the order of magnitude. In the mid-1890s, private, nonprofit organizations provided most secondary education in New York City (which did not have a free public high school until after 1900), most of its higher education and its libraries, much of its hospital care, many of its social services (especially care of orphans and the aged), and nearly all of its museums and orchestras; similar patterns prevailed in Boston, Philadelphia, Chicago, and St. Louis.[27] Most small towns and rural communities lacked these facilities except when they could be supplied by individual families.

In Cleveland, Ohio, nonprofits continued to provide more higher education, health and hospital care, specialized social services, and "high" culture than government through most of the twentieth century. Between 1960 and 1990 Cleveland's nonprofits more than tripled their share of the region's wages and salaries, while nationally local government was only growing by just over fifty percent.

Expenditures of Nonprofit Organizations as a Share of Wages and Salaries Cuyahoga County, Ohio (Cleveland), 1930, 1960, 1990

Year	Hospitals	Social Services	Higher Education	Arts	Total
1930	1.0	1.3	0.7	0.3	3.3
1960	2.2	0.6	0.9	0.2	3.9
1990	11.5	1.3	2.0	0.5	15.3

Nonprofits have not owed their growth to private philanthropy. In 1930 Cleveland's private hospitals and colleges—which together account for nearly three-quarters of the nonprofit sector—already depended more on payments by patients and students than on private contributions. By 1990 the combined contributions of private gifts, the United Way, and endowment accounted for just three percent of the income of Cleveland's nonprofit hospitals and only one-sixth of the income of its private social service agencies and colleges. Almost all nonprofits earn most of their income through the sale of services to individuals and to governments.

Private Contributions and Endowment as Sources of Income for Private Nonprofit Organizations by Subsector, Cuyahoga County, Ohio, 1930, 1960, 1990

Year	Hospitals	Social Services	Higher Education
1930	38	70	42
1960	11	58	40
1990	3	16	17

If the largest private foundations have always been too small to increase significantly the supply of services devoted to the "general welfare," they have been forced to intervene strategically if they were to make an impact. The most effective strategies have reorganized and redirected the activities of nonprofits.

The Nonprofit Sector in the American Polity, 1776–1900

Foundations did not create the nonprofit sector. Americans have relied on private, nongovernment, nonprofit organizations to supply much of their educational, health care and social services, and many of their arts and civic activities since the days of the early Republic. Political debates in early America produced a federal government whose ability to raise taxes and undertake programs was limited by many checks and balances, by the separation of powers, and by federalism. Early American political debates also led to the separation of church and state at the federal level. The same political debates affected individual states, whose forms of government limited action in the same ways as the federal government. Following the Revolution all states ended tax and other support for established churches. The Anglican church lost support immediately; Connecticut disestablished the Congregational Church in 1819; Massachusetts followed suit in 1833.[28]

During the colonial period most education, health care, and social care and service had been provided by fee-charging individuals, by town governments, or by established, tax-supported religious organizations—Congregational in New England, Anglican almost everywhere else. The new constitutional regimes for both the federal government and the states retained colonial exemptions from property tax, but forced religious charities and congregations to seek new sources of support. The First Amendment, which separated church and state, also guaranteed to citizens the rights of free speech, assembly, and petition. The First Amendment can thus be seen as the basis for nonprofit organizations, which—it might be said—allow Americans not only to assemble as they like and to petition governments, but to put their ideas into practice. Nonprofit organizations obtained an additional key constitutional basis in the Supreme Court's decision in *Dartmouth College,* which confirmed and expanded the powers of nonprofit boards of trustees, including their independence from state governments once they had obtained their charters, their ability to hold property, and even certain immunities from lawsuits.[29]

In the American polity, then, aspects of sovereignty are lodged not only in "the people" and in the states, but also in chartered corporations. The nineteenth-century federal government carried the fragmentation of sovereignty to extraordinary extremes. During the Civil War the federal government used a private corporation to provide sanitary and hospital services to the Union Army, and after the war Congress gave the private Society for the Suppression of Vice the right to open the U.S. mail in its campaign against abortion and birth control.[30]

In nineteenth-century America nonprofit corporations obtained through religious campaigns many of the resources they could not get from taxes. Especially important were the voluntary contributions for denominational schools and other institutions of what historian Ray Billington has called the "Protestant Crusade"; as the nineteenth-century went forward, increasingly successful efforts to establish Jewish and Catholic institutions were also important.[31] To a significant but not yet measured extent, nineteenth-century nonprofits also obtained resources from governments, chiefly county and municipal governments. Local governments provided land as well as tax exemption for schools, hospitals, museums, and libraries.[32] Local governments also paid private nonprofits for the full, or nearly full, cost of most of the charitable services they provided, from the care of orphans and the elderly poor to hospital care for the poor and secondary-school educations for town scholars at private academies.[33] And, of course, nineteenth-century nonprofits relied to a considerable extent on payments for services from those who hoped to benefit from the services: the vocabulary included such terms as "tuition," "admissions fees," "subscriptions," and "hospital charges."

Bolstering the Nonprofit Sector: Foundations *in* the Market

Throughout the twentieth century most foundations have simply contributed to the ongoing programs of nonprofit organizations. Responding to requests from institutions, most foundations have supported educational, medical, and social services and literary and artistic activities. In his influential critique, Waldemar Nielsen argued that most foundations, including many of the large ones, were merely "passive, ameliorative institutions." Rather than make active use of their resources, they simply offered "the multitude of useful nonprofit organizations in American life . . . 'another door to knock on.' "[34]

It is also true that when foundations purchase services from nonprofits or enable nonprofits to increase the supply of the services they offer, they affirm and support the role of private, nongovernmental organizations in the American polity. In this sense, even passive foundation expenditures in the markets for the services provided by nonprofits go largely to support the nongovernmental parts of the American polity. By adding resources to eleemosynary institutions that date from the nineteenth century and to new institutions created in the twentieth century, foundations have played a role in sustaining the nonprofit sector. But governments have provided far more funds, even before the 1960s, and fees paid by those who use their services have always constituted the largest source of nonprofit income.

Those who created the great foundations did, of course, support the nonprofits they favored by giving money directly to them. Mrs. Russell Sage, for example, inherited about $75 million from her husband in 1902; she put only $15 million into the Russell Sage Foundation and gave the rest directly to a wide variety of colleges and universities, health care and social service organizations, and churches. Carnegie, Rockefeller, Harkness, Rosenwald, Mellon, and most other creators of notable general purpose foundations acted in similar ways. Foundations have also made gifts directly to instutitions, but they have been most useful in reorganizing or transforming old institutions and in creating new ones.[35]

Reinventing the Nonprofit Sector after 1900

From their first appearance shortly after 1900 foundations have played their most important roles as reinventors of the nonprofit sector, as reshapers of nonprofit institutions, as organizers of new nonprofit institutions. Carnegie and Rockefeller criticized the nonprofits of their day, and Rockefeller famously insisted that the large donor "must add service in the way of study, and he must help to attack and improve underlying conditions."[36] Rockefeller's language has led many commentators to emphasize the commitment of the large foundations to scientific research and the creation of the twentieth-century research university.[37] More impressive were their efforts to assemble significant expertise and to establish connections with key groups of leaders in specific fields, and then to make strategic investments in the design of institutions. These actions enabled their foundations to play central roles in the reorganization of each part of the nonprofit sector before World War II. As several of the other essays in this volume suggest, foundations have also worked to reorganize the nonprofit sector and its subsectors during the Cold War and in the thirty years since the Great Society transformed American social policy in the mid-1960s.

One of the chief rationales for the nonprofit sector in the American polity has been the argument that it institutionalizes and defines the separation of church and state, making it easier for Americans to manage the inevitable conflicts produced by religious diversity.[38] Because private, nongovernmental, nonprofit organizations provided most educational, health care, and social services in nineteenth-century America, governments could avoid many conflicts. Governments could pay for services to meritorious scholars or needy patients but allow the institutions that provided such services (the care of orphans and the aged, secondary education) to remain under sectarian control. The potential for religious and cultural conflict increased with the arrival of many adherents of the Catholic, Eastern Orthodox, and Jewish traditions from southern and eastern Europe at the end of the nineteenth century.[39] The Carnegie, Rockefeller, and kindred foundations helped nonprofits find ways to respond.

Congregationalists, Presbyterians, Episcopalians, Methodists, and Baptists effectively supervised most nineteenth-century nonprofits through formal governing arrangements, through informal processes for evaluating leaders, by directing students and patients to the doors of particular institutions, and by mobilizing volunteers and donors. By 1900 conflicts among competing Protestant sects as well as opposition to science by some of them seemed to Carnegie, Rockefeller, and like-minded donors to have grown beyond all bounds. Further, the massive immigration of Catholics, Jews, and Orthodox Christians challenged Anglo-Saxon Protestant dominance.[40] The result was what Thomas Haskell has called a late-nineteenth-century "crisis of authority."[41]

Liberal Protestantism had already produced important interdenominational, nondenominational, and scientific social service, health care, and moral uplift societies long before the end of the nineteenth century. They ranged from New York Hospital and the University of Pennsylvania through the American Bible Society to the Perkins School for the Blind to the late-nineteenth-century Boston Museum of Fine Arts, the Johns Hopkins University, to the many charity organization societies. Religious belief also became in some ways less salient to the public as the nineteenth century wore on.[42] But most "nonsectarian" institutions were Protestant, and nearly all local schools, poverty-relief organizations, clinics, and hospitals drew their support through religious networks.[43]

Foundations—not government agencies or the courts—played the leading role in responding to the late-nineteenth-century crisis of Protestant authority. They did this by providing significant funds outside the channels of the religious establishments, enabling many nonprofits to shift from a Protestant denominational (or inter- or nondenominational) basis to nonsectarianism and science.[44] They also created key opportunities for discussions of new institutional arrangements. The result was a thoroughgoing reorganization of the nonprofit sector early in the twentieth century and the creation of a new set of nonsectarian coordinating organizations for nonprofits.

Thomas Haskell suggested that one result of the nineteenth-century crisis of authority was a loss of influence and legitimacy for the liberally—and often theologically—educated men who ran so many private (and public) asylums, hospitals, clinics, and other institutions and who comprised the leaders of the American Social Science Association (ASSA). As Haskell points out, the new, specialized, professional disciplinary associations in economics, political science, sociology, and statistics displaced the ASSA. But the disciplinary associations replaced only some ASSA functions, those that had to do with evaluating scientific and scholarly research. The ASSA had also provided a forum for debates about the operations and policies of private institutions and government agencies among the generalists who served as managers and trustees. Early in the twentieth century much of this debate moved into the leading national foundations.

The roles of foundations in reorienting the nonprofit sector and in developing new, nonsectarian arrangements for coordinating nonprofit activities and setting standards can be seen clearly if we take each of the largest nonprofit subsectors in turn. In recent years nonprofit health care organizations have accounted for about half the expenditures of all nonprofits; colleges and universities have accounted for about one-quarter of the expenditures; social service and civic organizations have accounted for about one-sixth.[45] Scholars have paid more attention to higher education.

Higher Education

Several scholars have shown how the shift to nonsectarian, cosmopolitan, scientific research occurred in the colleges and universities. Central to the process was the new emphasis on research, especially scientific and medical research. As Merle Curti and Roderick Nash, Ronald Geiger, Robert Kohler, and Mark Smith have demonstrated, foundations—Rockefeller above all—made possible the rise of the American research university.[46] After explicit consideration of the question, the senior staff and the boards of the Rockefeller, Carnegie, and Russell Sage foundations all decided after World War I that research should be located in universities rather than in independent institutes, hospitals, or research bureaus.[47] Nineteenth-century American universities had not emphasized research, and they did not initiate the change.[48] Instead, a small group of foundation leaders believed that science was producing real advances: they provided the necessary buildings and laboratories, funded many of the research professorships and more of the operating expenses of university research institutes, and even set up entire research units within universities. Foundations also supported research through competitive programs of research grants and fellowships.[49] And the large national foundations—again, Rockefeller above all—provided essential support for the scholarly and scientific intermediary organizations, especially the National Research Council and the Social Science Research Council, that provide the critical arenas in which competing researchers debate research agendas and seek to establish scientific reputations.[50] In all these activities, as Ellen Condliffe Lagemann, Steven Wheatley, Donald Fisher, and others have shown, the Rockefeller, Carnegie, and other foundations provided more than money: their own offices also provided tables around which advocates of research could define strategies.

For all the international significance of the rise of the American research university, only a few universities developed significant research activity. More important for the reorientation of the American system of higher education as a whole was Andrew Carnegie's college teacher retirement fund. This fund eventually evolved into the Teacher's Insurance and Annuity Association, TIAA, which today provides a large share of American college faculty and staff with retirement arrangements. Through a process which Lagemann has shown was shaped as much by the foundation's leaders and by discussions among college presidents as by Carnegie himself, the retirement fund accepted only professors from four-year colleges that had separated themselves from denominational control and that accepted as students only those who had completed a comprehensive four-year high school course. To make their faculties eligible for Carnegie pensions, many colleges ended their formal relationship to a Protestant denomination. Frederick Rudolph, a historian of American colleges and universities, wrote dramatically that "the Carnegie Foundation and the General Education Board tried to weaken further and kill off the weaker denominational colleges."[51] They did not entirely succeed, but they certainly accelerated the rise of the nonsectarian college and university at a time when the federal government had almost nothing to do with higher education.

Lagemann has also traced the story of Carnegie support for the development of the College Board, the Educational Testing Service (a private, nonprofit corporation), and their standardized college admissions tests.[52] Again, it is certainly true that the idea of nationally standardized examinations for college admissions predated the College Board: Harvard's President Charles W. Eliot had offered such examinations in several cities as early as the 1870s. But it was through the College Board that university leaders worked out a single national standard for the evaluation of applicants to private colleges—a standard that came to be used for certain purposes by state universities as well. By the 1940s the College Board and the Educational Testing Service it created were able to relieve individual colleges from responsibility for devising tests, for listening to protests against biases the tests may have contained, and for reevaluating tests in the light of criticism.[53] As in the case of TIAA, the effect has been to help transform not one organization but many, in effect to reshape the market for college education.

In many ways the entire story of American foundations begins with the efforts of several Protestant denominations and of the Peabody, Slater, and Daniel Hand funds (and later the Anna T. Jeanes Fund, the General Education Board, and the Rosenwald Fund) to support educational institutions for African Americans in the former slave states.[54] Because these institutions faced continuing harassment and threats of supression from segregationist local and state governments, donors provided funds through intermediary funds rather than through direct gifts to endowment. Like the later general purpose foundations, these funds promoted institutional innovation, seeking not to establish individual schools but to create an entirely new set of organizations that could win continuing support in the relevant markets—and that would bring a standard set of American institutions into the segregated South.

Health Care

Medical research not only supported the rise of the research university and the creation of new knowledge, it also transformed the organization of health care services. As Steven Wheatley and others have shown, the Carnegie, Rockefeller, and other foundations played key roles in creating the university-based medical center that combines the education of physicians with hospital care and scientific research. The foundations were not alone in promoting university medical schools as superior to apprenticeship to private physicians, and university hospitals as superior to small church- and community-sponsored institutions. They intervened strategically in a larger process, at what Wheatley describes as the opportune "Flexnerian moment" when doctors, institution builders, and community leaders needed both outside funds and the authority of highly regarded laymen.[55]

Foundations also played an important but less fully explored role in the replacement of small, parochial, denominational clinics and hospitals by large, professional, scientifically based medical centers. David Rosner has provided the best overall account of this change for a single city. Rosner does not focus on foundations, but it seems certain that the Rockefeller Foundation, the Commonwealth Fund, the Milbank Memorial Fund, and a few others played important roles.[56] Vanessa Northington Gamble has shown that the Rosenwald, Duke, and Rockefeller foundations contributed significantly to the development of modern hospitals for segregated African Americans.[57] In Cleveland, one locale that Gamble studied in detail, foundations provided little of the money required to create the University Hospitals complex, but the Flexner Report, an evaluation of Cleveland's hospitals by Haven Emerson, and the recommendations of the Cleveland Foundation-supported Community Fund were central to the process through which such private donors as Samuel Mather and Edward Harkness decided to take the lead in supporting that large effort.[58] As in the case of research universities, foundations provided money, expertise, and credibility that helped establish a new set of institutions—institutions which then flourished because they successfully offered their services to students, to paying patients (and later their insurance companies), and to governments.

Social Welfare

Foundations also played an important and underappreciated role in the reorientation of social welfare nonprofits from narrow denominationalism to a nonsectarian, scientific basis. Although they have been ignored in comparison with universities and hospitals, private social service organizations employed more people and spent more money than hospitals in the first third of the twentieth century.[59] In 1900, a religious denomination or faith tradition sponsored virtually every social service organization. By 1930 professional social workers and nonsectarian organizations dominated social welfare.[60]

Although it lacked the wealth of the Rockefeller and Carnegie foundations, the Russell Sage Foundation provided leadership as well as money for this transformation. Just as university presidents and rising medical and scientific reformers played key roles at the Carnegie and Rockefeller funds, Russell Sage brought together some of the most influential and strategically placed experts, administrators, and civic leaders in the field, providing them both with funds for research and with the opportunity to develop authoritative statements of practice. Mrs. Sage had identified herself closely with the charity organization societies of New York City and Brooklyn, with societies for the blind, and with the campaign to control tuberculosis. Her chief advisor, the railroad attorney Robert W. deForest, served for several decades as the president of the New York Charity Organization Society. In selecting other board members Mrs. Sage and deForest made a conscious effort to embrace organized charity up and down the east coast—and from the beginning they made a point of working with Jewish as well as Protestant leaders.[61]

The early Russell Sage Foundation did not seek to advance academic social science: it was resolutely practical. One of its early specialties was convening experts to propose national standards for the state laws and private arrangements that regulated workers' compensation, pensions, collective bargaining, housing, sanitation, public health, consumer credit, public health, and city planning.[62] Russell Sage also sought to establish standards for the management of social case work, for workers' compensation legislation, for the hours and working conditions appropriate to women, for housing, sanitation, and zoning, for the measurement of the cost of living, for consumer credit, and for state facilities for juvenile delinquents.[63] It promoted the creation of new professional, nonsectarian foundations and other nonprofit institutions.[64] And it promoted the professionalization of social work, creating the New York—now Columbia University—School of Social Work, maintaining a leading research library, producing texts, and housing and subsidizing social work's professional associations until the late 1940s.[65]

The famous *Pittsburgh Survey*'s six large volumes on the steel city's social and living conditions launched this effort, established the credibility of the social survey, and started *The Survey*, a periodical that, with $328,000 in Russell Sage subsidies, served as a source of credible information for social work professionals and trustees of social service nonprofits from the 1910s to the 1940s.[66] Between the early 1920s and 1947 Russell Sage invested nearly $2 million both to create the multivolume *Regional Plan of New York and New Jersey* and to establish the Regional Plan Association of Greater New York as a permanent, nongovernmental agency for the study and control of urban development in the vast three-state metropolitan region whose outer borders are marked by New Haven on the north and Princeton on the south.[67] In all these activities Russell Sage Foundation leaders worked not only with professionals and civic leaders in the relevant fields but also with individual donors and other foundations.

The institutions of organized charity and professional social work for which the Russell Sage Foundation served as a center worked with community chests and community foundations as key elements in the new nonsectarian, "scientific" arrangement of the nonprofit sector after 1900. Community chests set standards for the agencies that shared in the funds they raised—and the standards always included both nonsectarianism and the separation of social service from religious proselytization.[68] During the 1910s and 1920s midwestern community foundations, developed from many donors, serving specific geographical areas, and controlled by boards representing the community, worked with community chests and national general purpose foundations to promote nonsectarian, comprehensive, science-based service by private and public agencies.[69] All of these agencies sought to reorganize formerly sectarian social services—including the teaching of English as a second language, rehabilitation from severe injury, job training, family counselling—into a form that would make them acceptable to the Catholics and other non-Protestants who became such a large part of the industrial labor force by 1910. The Carnegie, Rockefeller, and Russell Sage foundations paid close attention to—although they did not initially promote—the community chests and community foundations. As the new community institutions became established in many cities, local foundations did use them as channels for much of their support of local social service organizations, even making special contributions to sustain the chests during such periods of crisis as the Great Depression.[70] Critics have objected that such foundation grants failed to "make a difference." Perhaps, however, they did make a difference by supporting through depression and World War II the nonsectarian institutions that replaced the long-dominant Protestant-dominated charity organization societies.

Conclusion

What do these several cases tell us about foundations in the American polity? Foundations have participated in the polity by promoting basic research, by seeking to confer honor and authority on selected individuals, by conducting studies of social problems and possible solutions, and by promoting discussions of specific government policies. But most foundations have merely participated in the markets for nonprofit educational, health care, social welfare, and cultural activities and have done nothing to transform those markets.

During the first half of the twentieth century, however, a few general-purpose foundations, including some regional foundations as well as a number that addressed the entire nation or even the world, played key roles in the reorganization and governance of America's nonprofit organizations. In some cases—higher education before the 1960s, the evaluation of college applicants, education for African Americans in the segregated South, establishing the teaching hospital-medical school complex in the 1920s and 1930s, creating the institutions of nonsectarian private social welfare between 1905 and 1930—foundations played a more important role than federal or state governments, the courts, religious denominations, or other previously existing organizations.

Foundations made their greatest impact in these fields not simply through grants, but by connecting with and helping to organize key groups of leaders. Using not only money but also the expertise, the capacity to convene definitive discussions, and the credibility and authority provided by the foundations, these leaders set up new patterns of activity that won support over the long run through the markets for payments for service, government contracts, and to a small extent through annual private donations. This small group of foundations also provided a new locus of employment for policy specialists. Late in the nineteenth century policy experts worked in law firms, in universities, in religious organizations, in social service organizations sponsored by churches and universities, and in a few civic organizations.[71] In the twentieth century foundations provided policy specialists with salaries, research funds, and access to networks of professionals that helped them to define and advance particular research, programmatic, and public and private policy agendas.

The small group of nationally and regionally influential general-purpose foundations supported several interrelated trends early in the twentieth century. They favored the creation of nonsectarian agencies and the subordination of denominationalism among Protestant-sponsored agencies (meanwhile, of course, other foundations, including the Duke Endowment and the Lilly Endowment, directed significant support to explicitly religious purposes). They favored universalism and professionalism in the provision of services and the development of uniform standards for service delivery. They favored programs that advanced scientific research or that were based on science rather than on religious dogma. They emphasized self-sufficiency and self-help for individuals. And for nonprofit organizations they emphasized nonprofit activity that could become self-sustaining through the markets for fees, government contracts, and private donations, small as well as large.[72]

As most of the other papers in this volume show, since World War II the most influential general purpose foundations have pursued several other agendas. The stockmarket crash and the Great Depression reduced the resources of many foundations. Impressed by the enormous expansion of the federal government in the New Deal, World War II, and the Great Society, most historians have assumed that foundations, and nonprofits in general, faded after 1932. But that did not happen. New foundations, several of them very large indeed, continued to arrive. Community chests, transformed into United Way; community foundations; and the other private coordinating institutions of nonsectarian, "scientific" social service, health care, and education, all remain active.

In what some see as a paradox, the great expansion of government spending has led not to a decline in the size and vitality of the "nonprofit sector," but in its great expansion. The role of the Ford Foundation and a few other foundations in promoting the expansion of government activity has often been noted and criticized, though it has just come under serious historical scrutiny. But as Lester Salamon and his associates have established, much of the federal money has been spent on the services provided by nonprofits.[73] Those who study foundations in the mid- and late twentieth century might ask: to what extent did foundation leaders shape the arrangements that directed federal funds through nonprofits during the Great Society and after?

Notes

For comments that have greatly improved this essay I am indebted to Stanley N. Katz, Robert Lynn, Peter Dobkin Hall, Ellen Condliffe Lagemann, Richard Magat, and Steven Wheatley, and to my students in the Social Policy History Ph.D. Program at Case Western Reserve University (especially Qiusha Ma, Michael FitzGibbon, Martha Gibbons, and Brian Ross), and in CWRU's Mandel Center for Nonprofit Organizations.

1. Among the books that launched this discussion and carried it forward are Morton Keller, *Affairs of State: Public Life in Later Nineteenth-Century America* (Cambridge, Mass.: Harvard University Press, 1977); Stephen Skowronek, *Building a New American State: The Expansion of National Administrative Capacities, 1877–1920* (New York: Cambridge University Press, 1982), and Theda Scocpol, *Protecting Soldiers and Mothers: The Political Origins of Social Policy in the United States* (Cambridge, Mass.: Harvard University Press, 1992). For a thorough, penetrating, and balanced discussion of much of this literature, see Ellen M. Immergut, "The Normative Roots of the New Institutionalism: Historical Institutionalism and Comparative Policy Studies," in Arthur Benz and

Wolfgang Seibel, eds., *Beitrage zur Theorieentwicklung in der Politik-und Verwaltung-swissenchaft* (Baden-Baden: Nomos Verlag, 1996), available (in English) on the World Wide Web. A parallel literature of longer lineage exists on the relation between government and private corporations in American history; for an excellent recent overview see Ellis W. Hawley, "Introduction to the 1995 Edition," in Hawley, *The New Deal and the Problem of Monopoly: A Study in Economic Ambivalence.* 2nd ed. (New York: Fordham University Press, 1995), xvii–xxxvii.

2. But see Robert Wuthnow, ed., *Between States and Markets: The Voluntary Sector in Comparative Perspective* (Princeton: Princeton University Press, 1991), and Walter W. Powell and Paul DiMaggio, *The New Institutionalism in Organizational Analysis* (Chicago: University of Chicago Press, 1991).

3. Skowronek, *Building a New American State,* 39.

4. That many social and cultural services are provided by municipal corporations and school districts in the United States reinforces this argument, even as it makes it more complicated.

5. On the relative autonomy of nonprofits in American society, see Henry Hansmann, "Economic Theories of Nonprofit Organization," in Walter W. Powell, ed., *The Nonprofit Sector: A Research Handbook* (New Haven: Yale University Press, 1987), 27–42; Gabriel Rudney, "The Scope and Dimensions of Nonprofit Activity," ibid., 55–65; John G. Simon, "The Tax Treatment of Nonprofit Organizations: A Review of Federal and State Policies," ibid., 67–98; Peter Dobkin Hall, *Inventing the Nonprofit Sector and Other Essays on Philanthropy, Voluntarism, and Nonprofit Organizations* (Baltimore: Johns Hopkins University Press, 1992), ch. 1; David C. Hammack and Dennis R. Young, "Perspectives on Nonprofit Organizations in the Marketplace," in David C. Hammack and Dennis R. Young, ed., *Nonprofit Organizations in a Market Economy* (San Francisco: Jossey-Bass, 1993); and Lester M. Salamon, *America's Nonprofit Sector: A Primer* (New York: Foundation Center, 1992).

6. The mission of the Commonwealth Fund.

7. There are, of course, "operating foundations" that maintain active programs of research or service; and there are foundations whose charters focus or limit their donations to specific fields. But these exceptions prove the rule: they are special kinds of foundations, combining the grant-making activities of all foundations with the research institute or other activities of an operating nonprofit. It is also true that some nonprofits that are not "foundations" in the general sense use the term in their names (the "Cleveland Clinic Foundation") and that most substantial nonprofit organizations have endowments that serve in a sense as in-house foundations. In this essay I will follow common usage and define a "foundation" as strictly a grant-making entity, ordinarily one whose funds come from an endowment but which in some cases, especially in the case of corporate foundations, obtains its funds on an annual or other periodic basis from a current donor or donors.

8. Dwight Macdonald, *The Ford Foundation: The Men and the Millions* (New York: Reynal, 1956), 3.

9. David A. Sills, *The Volunteers: Means and Ends in a National Organization* (Glencoe, Ill.: Free Press, 1957); Rosabeth Moss Kantor, "Doing Well While Doing Good: Dilemmas of Performance Measurement in Nonprofit Organizations and the Need for a Multiple-Constituency Approach," in Powell, ed., *The Nonprofit Sector,* 154–66; Robert K. Merton, "Manifest and Latent Functions," in *Social Theory and Social Structure* (Glencoe, Ill.: Free Press, 1957).

10. Overviews of the field by "insiders" include Warren Weaver, *U.S. Philanthropic Foundations: Their History, Structure, Management, and Record* (New York: Harper &

Row, 1967); Waldemar A. Neilsen, *The Big Foundations* (New York: Columbia University Press, 1972); Merrimon Cuninggim, *Private Money and Public Service: The Role of Foundations in American Society* (New York: McGraw-Hill, 1972); and F. Emerson Andrews, *Foundation Watcher* (Lancaster, Penn.: Franklin and Marshall College, 1973). See also Harold M. Keele and Joseph C. Kiger, eds., *Foundations* (Westport, Conn.: Greenwood Press, 1984), and Hall, *Inventing the Nonprofit Sector*, 62–80.

11. Among the most comprehensive assessments are Roger L. Geiger, *To Advance Knowledge: The Growth of American Research Universities, 1900–1940* (New York: Oxford University Press, 1986), and *Research and Relevant Knowledge: American Research Universities since World War II* (New York: Oxford University Press, 1993); Robert E. Kohler, "A Policy for the Advancement of Science: The Rockefeller Foundation, 1924–29," *Minerva* 16 (1978): 480–515, and *Partners in Science: Foundations and Natural Science, 1900–1945* (Chicago: University of Chicago Press, 1991). Notable studies of the impact of foundations on specific fields include Robert A. McCaughey, *International Studies and Academic Enterprise: A Chapter in the Enclosure of American Learning* (New York: Columbia University Press, 1984); Martin Bulmer, *The Chicago School of Sociology: Institutionalization, Diversity, and the Rise of Sociological Research* (Chicago: University of Chicago Press, 1984); Donald Critchlow, *The Brookings Institution, 1916–1952: Expertise and the Public Interest in a Democratic Society* (DeKalb: Northern Illinois University Press, 1984); and Mark C. Smith, *Social Science in the Crucible: The American Debate over Objectivity and Purpose* (Durham: Duke University Press, 1994).

12. Before we give too much credit to the foundations, however, we need to recognize the influence both of the German and French examples of national support for science and of earlier American experience with the Coast and Geodetic Survey and with agricultural research.

13. Ellen Condliffe Lagemann, *Private Power for the Public Good: A History of the Carnegie Foundation for the Advancement of Teaching* (Middletown, Conn.: Wesleyan University Press, 1983); Jean Gottmann, *Megalopolis: The Urbanized Northeastern Region of the United States* (New York: Twentieth Century Fund, 1961); Jean Gottmann, Oral History Interview with David C. Hammack, Columbia University Oral History Office, 1986. See also Guy Alchon, *The Invisible Hand of Planning: Capitalism, Social Science, and the State in the 1920s* (Princeton: Princeton University Press, 1985).

14. Steven C. Wheatley, *The Politics of Philanthropy: Abraham Flexner and Medical Education* (Madison: University of Wisconsin Press, 1988).

15. Cuninggim, *The Role of Foundations in American Society*, 181–82; on foundation grants to individuals, see Gerald Freund, *Narcissism and Philanthropy: Ideas and Talent Denied* (New York: Viking, 1996). For a detailed and careful authorized account of the early years of the W. K. Kellogg Foundation, see Horace B. Powell, *The Original Has This Signature: W. K. Kellogg* (Battle Creek, Mich.: W. K. Kellogg Foundation, 1956, 1989).

16. Barry D. Karl and Stanley N. Katz, "The American Private Philanthropic Foundation and the Public Sphere, 1890–1930," *Minerva* (1981): 236–70; Ellen Condliffe Lagemann, *The Politics of Knowledge: The Carnegie Corporation, Philanthropy, and Public Policy* (Chicago: University of Chicago Press, 1992); Robert F. Arnove, ed., *Philanthropy and Cultural Imperialism: The Foundation at Home and Abroad* (Bloomington: Indiana University Press, 1982); John F. McClymer, *War and Welfare: Social Engineering in America, 1890–1925* (Westport, Conn.: Greenwood Press, 1980); Peter Dobkin Hall, "Inventing the Nonprofit Sector," in Hall, *Inventing the Nonprofit Sector*, 41–80; James A. Smith, *The Idea Brokers: Think Tanks and the Rise of the New Policy Elite* (New York:

Free Press, 1991); Gloria Garrett Samson, *The American Fund for Public Service: Charles Garland and Radical Philanthropy, 1922–1941* (Westport, Conn.: Greenwood Press, 1996); Mary Anna Culleton Colwell, *Private Foundations and Public Policy: The Political Role of Philanthropy* (New York: Garland, 1993).

17. David C. Hammack, *Power and Society: Greater New York at the Turn of the Century* (New York: Russell Sage Foundation, 1982).

18. Wheatley, *The Politics of Philanthropy*, is a notable exception. Apart from studies of higher education and civil rights, accounts of policy innovations in social welfare fields from the 1880s to the New Deal say little about foundations; see, for example, Roy Lubove, *The Progressives and the Slums: Tenement House Reform in New York City, 1890–1917* (Pittsburgh: Pittsburgh University Press, 1962); Edward Berkowitz and Kim McQuaid, *Creating the Welfare State: The Political Economy of Twentieth-Century Reform* (New York: Praeger, 1980); Daniel M. Fox, *Health Policies, Health Politics: The British and American Experience,1911–1965* (Princeton: Princeton University Press, 1986); Michael B. Katz, *In the Shadow of the Poorhouse: A Social History of Welfare in America* (New York: Basic Books, 1986).

19. Cuninggim, *Private Money and Public Service*, notes the regional focus of the Duke Endowment and several other foundations but does not evaluate their influence. On the Russell Sage Foundation and state legislation see John M. Glenn, Lilian Brandt, and F. Emerson Andrews, *Russell Sage Foundation, 1907–1947* (New York: Russell Sage Foundation, 1947), and David C. Hammack and Stanton Wheeler, *Social Science in the Making: Essays on the Russell Sage Foundation, 1907–1947* (New York: Russell Sage Foundation, 1994). For a preliminary discussion of Andrew Carnegie's demands for local tax support of libraries, see Abigail A. Van Sylke, *Free to All: Carnegie Libraries and American Culture, 1890–1920* (Chicago: University of Chicago Press, 1995).

20. The mission of the Russell Sage Foundation.

21. Ellis W. Hawley, "Herbert Hoover, the Commerce Secretariat, and the Vision of an 'Associative State,' 1921–1928," *Journal of American History* 45 (1974): 117.

22. John D. Rockefeller, "The Difficult Art of Giving," in Brian O'Connell, ed., *America's Voluntary Spirit* (New York: Foundation Center, 1983), 114.

23. Ibid., 110.

24. Albert F. Schenkel, *The Rich Man and the Kingdom: John D. Rockefeller Jr. and the Protestant Establishment* (Minneapolis: Fortress Press, 1995); Andrew Carnegie, "The Gospel of Wealth," in O'Connell, *America's Voluntary Spirit*, 105.

25. Theda Scocpol emphasizes the two important exceptions: the Civil War veterans' pensions and the less important but notable Sheppard-Towner Act; see Scocpol, *Protecting Soldiers and Mothers*.

26. The data can be found in *Historical Statistics of the United States* and in the *Statistical Abstract of the United States*. Compare Robert Higgs, *Crisis and Leviathan: Critical Episodes in the Growth of American Government* (New York: Oxford University Press, 1987); and Ballard C. Campbell, *The Growth of American Government: Governance from the Cleveland Era to the Present* (Bloomington: Indiana University Press, 1995), 34.

27. Albert Shaw, "The Higher Life of New York City," *The Outlook*, 25 January 1896, 132–39; Everett P. Wheeler; "The Unofficial Government of Cities," *Atlantic Monthly* 86 (1900): 370–76. On education in late-nineteenth-century New York City, see David C. Hammack, *Power and Society*.

28. Sydney E. Ahlstrom, *A Religious History of the American People* (New Haven: Yale University Press, 1972), 380.

29. I develop these arguments at length in *Nonprofit Organizations and American Democracy: Documents and Interpretations* (Bloomington: Indiana University Press, forthcoming).

30. George Fredrickson, *The Inner Civil War* (New York: Harper & Row, 1965); Heywood Broun and Margaret Leech, *Anthony Comstock: Roundsman of the Lord* (New York: Literary Guild of America, 1927).

31. Ray Allen Billington, *The Protestant Crusade, 1800–1860* (New York: Macmillan, 1938); Peter Dobkin Hall, *The Organization of American Culture, 1700–1900: Private Institutions, Elites, and the Origins of American Nationality* (New York: New York University Press, 1984); Clifford S. Griffen, *Their Brothers' Keepers: Moral Stewardship in the United States, 1800–1965* (New Brunswick, N.J.: Rutgers University Press, 1960); Robert Baird, *Religion in the United States of America* (1844; reprint, New York: Arno Press, 1969). On Catholic institutions see Jay Dolan, *The Immigrant Church: New York's Irish and German Catholics, 1815–1865* (Baltimore: Johns Hopkins University Press, 1975); James W. Sanders, *The Education of an Urban Minority: Catholics in Chicago, 1833–1965* (New York: Oxford University Press, 1977); Susan Scharlotte Walton, *To Preserve the Faith: Catholic Charities in Boston, 1870–1930* (New York: Garland Press, 1993).

32. In New York City, for example, the Metropolitan Museum of Art, the American Museum of Natural History, the New York Historical Society, and the New York Public Library all stand on city land, in buildings built largely with city money, and to this day benefit from municipal support for their utilities and custodial services. Similar arrangements were made in Boston, Philadelphia, Cleveland, and other cities.

33. On the sometimes considerable payments by nineteenth-century municipal governments to private nonprofits, see Carl F. Kaestle, *Pillars of the Republic: Common Schools and American Society, 1780–1860* (New York: Hill and Wang, 1983), 119; David Rosner, *A Once Charitable Enterprise: Hospitals and Health Care in Brooklyn and New York, 1885–1915* (Princeton: Princeton University Press, 1982), 49–50; Amos G. Warner, *American Charities* (New York: Thomas Y. Crowell, 1908), ch. 17.

34. Nielsen, *The Big Foundations*, 274.

35. Merle Curti and Roderick Nash, *Philanthropy in the Shaping of American Higher Education* (New Brunswick, N.J.: Rutgers University Press, 1965), ch. 10.

36. Carnegie, "The Gospel of Wealth," 105; Rockefeller, "The Difficult Art of Giving," 112.

37. Geiger, *To Advance Knowledge*.

38. Merle Curti, "American Philanthropy and the National Character," in O'Connell, *America's Voluntary Spirit* 167, originally published in *American Quarterly* 10 (Winter 1958): 420–37; David C. Hammack, "Putting the Nonprofit Sector into Practice: A Historical Perspective on the Nonprofit Sector in the United States," in Virginia Hodgkinson, ed., *Selected Papers from the 1996 Independent Sector Spring Research Forum* (San Francisco: Jossey-Bass, forthcoming).

39. The classic account of increasing religious conflict in late-nineteenth-century America is John Higham, *Strangers in the Land: Patterns of American Nativism, 1860–1925.* 2nd ed. (New Brunswick, N.J.: Rutgers University Press, 1988). To emphasize the late-nineteenth-century crisis is not to downplay the significance of early-nineteenth-century bigotry and strife, as documented many years ago in Ray Allen Billington's *The Protestant Crusade, 1800–1860* (New York: Macmillan, 1938).

40. Higham, *Strangers in the Land;* Ahlstrom, *A Religious History of the American People.*

41. Thomas L. Haskell, *The Emergence of Professional Social Science: The Ameri-*

can *Social Science Association and the Nineteenth-Century Crisis of Authority* (Urbana: University of Illinois Press, 1977).

42. Charles Rosenberg, *The Cholera Years: The United States in 1832, 1849, and 1966* (Chicago: University of Chicago Press, 1962).

43. This topic deserves far more exploration than it has yet received, but see, for example: Griffen, *Their Brothers' Keepers*; Carroll Smith Rosenberg, *Religion and the Rise of the City: The New York City Mission Movement* (Ithaca: Cornell University Press, 1971); Higham, *Strangers in the Land*; John Webb Pratt, *Religion, Politics, and Diversity: The Church-State Theme in New York History* (Ithaca: Cornell University Press, 1967); and James M. McPherson, *The Abolitionist Legacy: From Reconstruction to the NAACP* (Princeton: Princeton University Press, 1975).

44. Albert Schenkel makes the related argument that John D. Rockefeller played a dominant role in funding the nonsectarian and interfaith religious organizations that came to constitute what Schenkel calls the "Protestant Establishment"; see Schenkel, *The Rich Man and the Kingdom*.

45. Lester M. Salamon, *The Nonprofit Sector: A Primer* (New York: Foundation Center, 1992), 24; Virginia A. Hodgkinson et al., *Nonprofit Almanac 1992–1993: Dimensions of the Independent Sector* (San Francisco: Jossey-Bass, 1992).

46. Curti and Nash, *Philanthropy in the Shaping of American Higher Education*, ch. 10; Geiger, *To Advance Knowledge*; Kohler, *Partners in Science*; Bulmer, *The Chicago School of Sociology*; Smith, *Social Science in the Crucible*.

47. Geiger, *To Advance Knowledge*; Hammack, "The Road Not Taken: The Independent Research Institute," in Hammack and Wheeler, *Social Science in the Making*.

48. Laurence R. Veysey, *The Emergence of the American University* (Chicago: University of Chicago Press, 1965); Haskell, *The Emergence of Professional Social Science*; Dorothy Ross, *The Origins of American Social Science* (New York: Cambridge University Press, 1991).

49. Geiger, *To Advance Knowledge*; Robert E. Kohler, "A Policy for the Advancement of Science" and *Partners in Science*; Bulmer, *The Chicago School of Sociology*.

50. Donald Fisher, *Fundamental Development of the Social Sciences: Rockefeller Philanthropy and the United States Social Science Research Council* (Ann Arbor: University of Michigan Press, 1993); Geiger, *To Advance Knowledge*, 169.

51. Lagemann, *Private Power for the Public Good*, ch. 3; Frederick Rudolph, *The American College and University: A History* (New York: Alfred A. Knopf, 1962), 430–34; see also Curti and Nash, *Philanthropy in the Shaping of American Higher Education*, 220–22; Wall, *Carnegie*, 869–78; Frederick Rudolph, *The American College and University: A History* (New York: Alfred A. Knopf, 1962), 432.

52. Lagemann, *Private Power for the Public Good*; for a thorough discussion of the impact of standardized testing on college admissions practices in large state universities as well as in Ivy League colleges, see Harold S. Wechsler, *The Qualified Student: A History of Selective College Admission in America* (New York: Wiley, 1977).

53. For an account of the explicitly anti-Semitic purposes of some early users of standardized tests, see Wechsler, *The Qualified Student*.

54. On the Slater and Peabody Funds see McPherson, *The Abolitionist Legacy*; the most extensive and penetrating recent discussion is James D. Anderson, *The Education of Blacks in the South, 1860–1935* (Chapel Hill: University of North Carolina Press, 1988); recent and more moderate studies of foundation aid to southern education include Jerry Wayne Woods, "The Julius Rosenwald Fund School Building Program: A Saga in the Growth and Development of African American Education in Selected West Tennessee Communities" (Ed.D. thesis, University of Mississippi, 1995); Jayne Rae Beilke, "To

Render Better Service: The Role of the Julius Rosenwald Fund Fellowship Program in the Development of Graduate and Professional Educational Opportunities for African Americans" (Ph.D. dissertation, Indiana University, 1994); and Courtney Sanabria Woodfaulk, "The Jeanes Teachers of South Carolina: The Emergence, Existence, and Significance of Their Work" (Ed.D. thesis, University of South Carolina, 1992).

55. Wheatley, *The Politics of Philanthropy*; A. McGehee Harvey and Susan L. Abrams, *"For the Welfare of Mankind": The Commonwealth Fund and American Medicine* (Baltimore: Johns Hopkins University Press, 1986); Qiusha Ma, "The Rockefeller Foundation and Modern Medical Education in China, 1915–1951" (Ph.D. dissertation, Case Western Reserve University, 1995); Frederick T. Gates, "Address on the Tenth Anniversary of the Rockefeller Institute," Gates Papers, Rockefeller Archive Center. I am indebted to Dr. Qiusha Ma for calling my attention to this document. Scientific medicine, Gates argues, was "as universal in its scope as the love of God . . . and as beneficial in its purpose."

56. Rosner, *A Once Charitable Enterprise,* cites the role of Russell Sage Foundation-funded charities and of the Charity Organization Society in calling attention to key problems in New York's hospitals pp. 49, 69, 136). John Duffy, *History of Public Health in New York City, 1866–1966* (New York: Russell Sage Foundation, 1974), refers repeatedly to the role of the Milbank Memorial Fund in opening and reorganizing clinics in the city during the 1920s and 1930s. See also C.-E. A. Winslow, *A City Set on a Hill: The Significance of the Health Demonstration at Syracuse, New York* (Garden City, N.Y.: Doubleday, Doran, 1934).

57. Vanessa Northington Gamble, *Making a Place for Ourselves: The Black Hospital Movement, 1920—1945* (New York: Oxford University Press, 1995).

58. Mark Gottlieb, *The Lives of University Hospitals of Cleveland: The 125-Year Evolution of an Academic Medical Center* (Cleveland: Wilson Street Press, 1991), 140–156.

59. See Steven Anthony Agoratus, "The Core of Progressivism: Research Institutions and Social Policy, 1907-1940" (D.A. thesis, Carnegie-Mellon University, 1994).

60. Roy Lubove, *The Professional Altruist: The Emergence of Social Work as a Career, 1880–1930* (Cambridge: Harvard University Press, 1965); Walter I. Trattner, *From Poor Law to Welfare State: A History of Social Welfare in America.* 3rd ed. (New York: Free Press, 1984); James Leiby, *A History of Social Welfare and Social Work in the United States* (New York: Columbia University Press, 1978); John H. Ehrenreich: *The Altruistic Imagination: A History of Social Work and Social Policy in the United States* Ithaca: Cornell University Press, 1985).

61. Hammack, "A Center of Intelligence for the Charity Organization Movement: The Foundation's Early Years," in Hammack and Wheeler, *Social Science in the Making,* ch. 1; Charles Lewis Bland, "The Emergence of State Level Welfare Supervision in New York, 1867-1898" (Ph.D. dissertation, State University of New York at Buffalo, 1988); Stephanie Wallach, "Luther Halsey Gulick and the Salvation of the American Adolescent" (Ph.D. thesis, Columbia University, 1989); Lee K. Frankel and Miles M. Dawson, *Workingmen's Insurance in Europe* (New York: Russell Sage Foundation, 1910).

62. Hammack, "A Road Not Taken: The Independent Social Research Institute," in Hammack and Wheeler, *Social Science in the Making,* 44–52.

63. Glenn, Brandt, and Andrews, *Russell Sage Foundation, 1907-1947*; Hammack, "The Regional Plan of New York and Environs: A Plan and a Planning Service," in Hammack and Wheeler, *Social Science in the Making,* ch. 3.

64. Glenn, Brandt, and Andrews, *Russell Sage Foundation, 1907-1947*; Hammack, ch. 1, 2, and 3, in Hammack and Wheeler, *Social Science in the Making*; Bertha F. Hulse-

man, *American Foundations for Social Welfare* (New York: Russell Sage Foundation, 1938); Shelby M. Harrison and F. Emerson Andrews, *American Foundations for Social Welfare* (New York: Russell Sage Foundation, 1946); F. Emerson Andrews, *Foundation Watcher.* Compare Hall, *Inventing the Nonprofit Sector,* ch. 8.

65. Glenn, Brandt, and Andrews, *Russell Sage Foundation, 1907–1947;* Hammack and Wheeler, *Social Science in the Making;* John F. McClymer, *War and Welfare: Social Engineering in America, 1890–1925* (Westport, Conn.: Greenwood Press, 1980); Guy Alchon, *The Invisible Hand of Planning;* Celestine C. Tutt, "Library Service to the Columbia University School of Social Work, 1898 — 1979 (D.L.S. thesis, Columbia University, 1983); Margaret Tillson Pittman-Munke, "Mary Richmond and the Wider Social Movement: Philadelphia, 1900–1909" (Ph.D. dissertation, University of Texas at Austin, 1985); Stephanie Wallach, "Luther Halsey Gulick and the Salvation of the American Adolescent" (Ph.D. dissertation, Columbia University, 1989); Sarah Henry Lederman, "From Poverty to Philanthropy: The Life and Work of Mary E. Richmond" (Ph.D. dissertation, Columbia University, 1994).

66. Clark Chambers, *Paul U. Kellogg and the Survey: Voices for Social Welfare and Social Change* (Minneapolis: University of Minnesota Press, 1971); Hammack, "A Road Not Taken," in Hammack and Wheeler, *Social Science in the Making,* 37–38, ; Allen Eaton and Shelby M. Harrison, *A Bibliography of Social Surveys: Reports of Fact-Finding Studies Made as a Basis for Social Action; Arranged by Subjects and Localities* (New York: Russell Sage Foundation, 1930); Glenn, Brandt, and Andrews, *Russell Sage Foundation,* vol. 2, 685.

67. Hammack, "The Regional Plan of New York and Environs: A Plan and a Planning Service," in Hammack and Wheeler, *Social Science in the Making,* ch. 3.

68. Brian Ross, "The New Philanthropy: The Reorganization of Charity in Turn-of-the-Century Cleveland" (Ph.D. dissertation, Case Western Reserve University, 1989); David C. Hammack, "Philanthropy," *Encyclopedia of Cleveland History.* 2nd ed. (Bloomington: Indiana University Press, 1996); Peter Dobkin Hall, *Inventing the Nonprofit Sector,* 144–70. Compare Eleanor Brilliant, *The United Way: Dilemmas of Organized Charity* (New York: Columbia University Press, 1990).

69. Hammack, "Community Foundations: The Delicate Question of Purpose," in Richard Magat, ed., *An Agile Servant: Community Leadership by Community Foundations* (New York: The Foundation Center, 1989), 23–50.

70. Ibid.; Diana Tittle, *Rebuilding Cleveland: The Cleveland Foundation and Its Evolving Urban Strategy* (Columbus: Ohio State University Press, 1992), 74–78.

71. David C Hammack, *Power and Society: Greater New York at the Turn of the Century* (New York: Russell Sage Foundation, 1982).

72. If these foundations helped transform the American "establishment," their emphasis on sustainability in the market for services gave that establishment remarkable staying power. The definitive analysis of the "establishment" is Richard H. Rovere, "The American Establishment," in *The American Establishment and Other Reports, Opinions, and Speculations* (New York: Harcourt, Brace, & World, 1962), 3–21. Critics from Eduard C. Lindeman to Robert Arnove and William Domhoff have insisted that foundations simply advance the interests of the wealthy; see Lindeman, *Wealth and Culture* (New York: Harcourt, Brace, 1936); Arnove, *Philanthropy and Cultural Imperialism;* William G. Domhoff, *The Power Elite and the State: How Policy Is Made in America* (New York: de Gruyter, 1990). Recent contributions to this debate include Teresa Odendahl, *Charity Begins at Home: Generosity and Self-Interest among the Philanthropic Elite* (New York: Basic Books, 1990), and Francie Ostrower, *Why the Wealthy Give: The Culture of Elite Philanthropy* (Princeton: Princeton University Press, 1996). The wealthy

donors who create large foundations have their own agendas and advance them as best they can. But wealthy donors have never needed foundations for such purposes: in the nineteenth-century United States rich men and women gave funds to individuals, non-profit organizations, and even governments from their own offices or the offices of their attorneys and bankers, and through religious agencies and civic associations; see, for example, Kathleen D. McCarthy, *Noblesse Oblige: Charity and Cultural Philanthropy in Chicago, 1849–1929* (Chicago: University of Chicago Press, 1982), and Nathan Huggins, *Protestants against Poverty: Boston's Charities, 1870–1900.* (Westport, Conn.: Greenwood Publishing Corp., 1971) If the great general purpose foundations made a major difference between 1900 and 1950, it is because they provided a new institution through which donors could work with specialists and managers to develop new ways to provide services and to promote both scientific research and the rise of "scientific," "independent," "ethical" professions. This enterprise has attracted considerable skeptial attention in recent years, both from academic historians and sociologists—see, for example, Magali S. Larson, *The Rise of Professionalism: A Sociological Analysis* (Berkeley: University of California Press, 1977); Andrew Abbott, *The System of Professions: An Essay on the Division of Expert Labor* (Chicago: University of Chicago Press, 1988); for a more positive view, see Burton J. Bledstein, *The Culture of Professionalism: The Middle Class and the Development of Higher Education in America* (New York: Norton, 1976), and Samuel Haber, *The Quest for Authority and Honor in the American Professions, 1750–1900* (Chicago: the University of Chicago Press, 1991)—and from the conservatives of the religious right—see Marvin Olasky, *The Tragedy of American Compassion* (Washington, D.C.: Regnery Gateway, 1992), which suggests that it is a noteworthy achievement.

73. Lester M. Salamon, "Partners in Public Service: The Scope and Theory of Government-Nonprofit Relations," in Walter W. Powell, ed., *The Nonprofit Sector: A Research Handbook* (New Haven: Yale University Press, 1987); see also Peter Dobkin Hall, *Inventing the Nonprofit Sector,* and Steven Rathgeb Smith and Michael Lipsky, *Nonprofits for Hire: The Welfare State in the Age of Contracting* (Cambridge, Mass.: Harvard University Press, 1993), ch. 3.

3 Private Foundations as Public Institutions

Regulation, Professionalization, and the Redefinition of Organized Philanthropy

Peter Frumkin

Drawing on their tremendous resources and independence, foundations have over the years shown a willingness to attempt projects that government and business are either unwilling or unable to carry out for political or financial reasons. Foundations can perform a distinctive role in society because they are free from the influence of organized constituencies and shareholders. If successful, foundations can serve as laboratories for experimentation where new and controversial ideas can be put to the test. While foundations have the capacity to play a critical role in providing venture capital for social experimentation, they have themselves quietly undergone profound change and reinvention over the past two and a half decades. This study of the evolution of private foundations begins with a question: Given their financial strength and independence, why did foundations in the 1970s move to reinvent philanthropy, embrace an ethos of openness, and attempt to professionalize grant making? To frame this question more fully, it may be useful to start with two snapshots of private philanthropic foundations.

In the first snapshot, dating from around the turn of the century to 1960, private foundations appear to be uncomplicated institutions with minimal administrative staffs. The early foundations were dominated by the leadership of a small cadre of donors who set the standards for large-scale philanthropy. Private foundations often operated discreetly, avoided public controversy, and had as their mission the pursuit of the private philanthropic interests and values of wealthy donors. Trustees charged with running the foundation and eventually carrying on the donor's philanthropic mission were mostly Ivy League graduates who enjoyed careers in business, law, government, and higher education.[1] With small or nonexistent administrative staffs and little concern with public accountability, foundations used their tremendous resources however they saw fit.

In the second snapshot, dating from the 1970's and beyond, large private foundations appear dramatically transformed. Gone is the simple administrative structure that enabled early foundations to act quickly and decisively. In its place is a complex administrative bureaucracy staffed by a new cadre of foundation professionals, often with multiple approval levels through which grant decisions must travel. More important than staffing changes, however, is a conceptual shift in the understanding of the foundations' place in society. Foundations emerge as profoundly public institutions, open and accountable to all, that work hard to build better relations with grant applicants and the public. Far from shying away from publicity, the new public foundation actually seeks out opportunities to explain and advertise its work to anyone who will listen.

This research attempts to ascertain how and why foundations transformed themselves from private institutions guided by the values of the donor into public institutions governed by grantmaking professionals. My answer ultimately focuses on the effects of government regulation on organizational behavior and culture. A traumatic encounter with Congress culminating in the passage of new regulations on private foundations propelled these organizations to increase their accessibility and to professionalize their field. In an effort to defend philanthropy from further government investigation and regulation, foundations strategically recast themselves as public trusts to be governed by public purposes and brought in a new class of foundation professionals to manage external relations. In this sense, government regulation was the direct trigger to the paradigm shift that occurred throughout organized philanthropy starting in the 1970s.

My discussion of the recent transformation of American philanthropic foundations proceeds in four broad steps. First, I discuss the immediate response and the early organizing efforts of foundations after the passage of the Tax Reform Act of 1969. In a second section, I chart the strategic emergence of a new understanding of foundations as public trusts. In a third section, I look at changing foundation practices and early efforts at professionalization stemming from the newly defined public responsibilities. Finally, I conclude by sketching the implications of this analysis for the future study of private foundations.

Regulations and Early Foundation Organizing Efforts

In the early 1960s, private foundations were under siege from a number of different fronts. Financial abuses at a few small foundations and highly politicized grants by some of the larger foundations brought increased public and congressional scrutiny. In 1961, Congressman Wright Patman, a populist from Texas, launched what would become an eight-year inquiry into the grantmaking and management practices of foundations. After extended hearings and negotiations in the House and Senate, Congress settled on a package of regulations designed to bring foundations under greater oversight. Although Congress had considered as punishment a requirement that all foundations expend all assets in forty years and go out of business, this proposal and others that were deemed too onerous were ultimately left out of the bill. The Tax Reform Act of 1969 (TRA 1969) set in place the following major regulations on foundations: a four-percent annual excise tax on net investment income, prohibitions against self-dealing, a six-percent annual payout of assets, a twenty-percent limitation on ownership of any corporation, and various disclosure requirements.

Writing in 1970, Carnegie Corporation president Alan Pifer reflected on philanthropy's encounter with government and the imposition of regulations:

> It was a period during which foundations were kicked in the shins and had their noses bloodied, and consequently we who work for them tend now to harbor an understandable sense of injustice. We resent the unfairness and shortsightedness of some of the features of the legislation and the extra administrative burden these will cause us. We resent the irrational emphasis placed by the Congress on a few uncharacteristic instances of administrative caprice in foundations and the excessive attention given to a few egregious cases of real abuse, while the overall positive record of foundations in American life was ignored. We resent the impression left with the public as a result of the legislation, that foundations were simply indicted, tried, found guilty and punished.[2]

In the months following the passage of TRA 1969, foundations went through a period of extensive self-examination. As Luce Foundation vice president Martha Wallace noted at the time: "Suddenly we realized we were not the conscientious, silent do-gooders we thought we were, but a vast array of extremely diverse organizations—with little or no constituency to come to our collective defense. Even more eye opening was the sudden realization that we needed defense—and needed it badly."[3] What could be done to improve the positions of foundations after the embarrassment of 1969? Foundation leaders ultimately pulled closer together to defend philanthropy from any further outside intrusion. They did so by pushing a two-pronged strategy: First, through an aggressive campaign mounted by their national association, private foundations abandoned any claim to privacy and recast themselves as public institutions that were open and accountable to all; second, they took important steps to professionalize foundation work as part of a quest for greater legitimacy.

Soon after the TRA 1969 was enacted on December 31, 1969, foundation magazines and newsletters were awash in recriminations and dire predictions of the impending decline of charitable giving. In the midst of general confusion, conferences were hurriedly organized to discuss the implications of the new regulations. One official of the Council on Foundations, who helped explain the new regulations to foundations in 1970, recalled the mood of the time:

> There was an atmosphere of terror. There was great fright and lack of understanding by most of the foundations that had not been closely involved with the legislative process. Most foundations around the country had not stayed close to the process. They'd read about it in the newspapers, and the descriptions there had been very frightening. The whole thrust of the publicity about the bearing of this legislation on foundations was that it's terrible, foundations are at least an endangered species, and they may well be on their way to extinction. The mood was almost one of panic.[4]

What could be done in light of the unfortunate precedent set by TRA 1969? In February 1970, only two months following the passage of TRA 1969, the Council on Foundations, the Foundation Center, and the National Council on Philanthropy moved to set up a special Committee on the Foundation Field. The mission of the committee was to "delineate and examine in light of present circumstances those services that need to be provided to the foundation field, and to recommend an organizational structure for the field most appropriate thereto."[5] The Committee was chaired by John Gardner, the former Secretary of the the U.S. Department of Health, Education, and Welfare, and included three foundation officials and the dean of Harvard University's John F. Kennedy School of Government. With three weak and ineffectual membership and service organizations vying for control of the field, the committee faced a difficult charge.

The Committee nevertheless was able to see that "the fragile position of foundations" called for action. The Committee urged change on seven fronts: (1) increased reporting and information dissemination by foundations; (2) support of independent research and publications on foundations; (3) continuation and extension of library services for the general public; (4) improved government relations; (5) development of voluntary standards of good practice; (6) provision of a central clearinghouse and forum to facilitate the exchange of information and cooperation among foundations; and (7) development of a public relations strategy for the field as a whole.

The Committee also proposed a major organizational change for the field. It urged the merger of the Council on Foundations, the largest foundation trade association, and the Foundation Center, the clearinghouse and reference library serving the entire nonprofit sector. While these two organizations shared a floor in a New York office building for some time, the arrangement never suited the parties. The Foundation Center saw its primary role as an information broker for all organizations in the sector, with a particular focus on the need of nonprofit organizations for assistance in researching funding sources. The Council, on the other hand, sought to define for itself the role of spokesman for organized philanthropy. These two missions—and their different constituencies—made collaboration difficult.

While the proposed merger never took place, the Committee on the Foundation Field nevertheless highlighted the need to eliminate some of the competing voices within the sector. The Council on Foundations eventually moved to Washington, D.C., where it could have more direct access to Congress, the Treasury Department, and the Internal Revenue Service. As the Council's visibility and membership grew, the rival National Council on Philanthropy declined. The Committee's recommendation that philanthropy organize itself around a single association was realized when the National Council on Philanthropy was merged with the Coalition of National Voluntary Organizations to form Independent Sector, a new national organization representing all nonprofits.[6] By January 1980, the Council on Foundations became the prime spokesman for foundations.

The Council on Foundations emerged as the main voice for the field by mounting a sustained effort to expand its membership in the years after TRA 1969. The Council brought in new members each year by moving its national meeting to different sites around the country, each time attracting non-member foundations from the host city. During the 1970s, the annual meetings also began featuring well-known speakers designed to draw in new grantmakers to the Council's work. Speakers included Ramsey Clark, Daniel Bell, Bill Moyers, Ralph Nader, and other figures from politics, the arts, and the media.

Annual Meetings of the Council on Foundations

Date	Location	Registrants
1970	San Francisco	550
1971	Montreal	550
1972	New York	600
1973	St. Paul	550
1974	San Antonio	600
1975	Chicago	625
1976	Atlanta	720
1977	St. Louis	820
1978	Washington, DC	1150
1979	Seattle	1200

Source: *Foundation News* 1970–1980

In the aftermath of 1969, the Council on Foundations filled a huge gap. Foundation administrators were confused and frightened and needed help understanding the implications of the legislation. Senior staff at the Council, including president David Freeman, chairman Robert Goheen, and vice president Gene Struckhoff, traveled extensively around the country to dozens of cities where foundation administrators met to hear about the new regulations and about what measures needed to be taken to bring foundations into compliance. Foundation executives were particularly confused and concerned about "expenditure responsibility" as defined in the legislation, which forced foundations to be more careful in documenting the recipients of their grants. As a result of its outreach efforts during the early 1970s, the Council cemented its position as the main spokesman and organizer of the field.

One of the main battles that the Council aimed to fight was against philanthropic timidity. Avoiding capitulation and retreat after 1969 was a recurrent theme in many of the Council's meetings with foundation administrators during its national tour. One official at the Council on Foundations observed: "Many tax lawyers and accountants were counseling everybody to do only the most obviously safe things. There was a great tendency on the part of foundations to let their accountants and their tax lawyers make their charitable judgments for them. The Council was saying don't do that. You are the people who are the experts in your field."[7] The effort to keep foundations from becoming too cautious was significant because it necessitated a broader effort to place foundation management in the hands of a budding class of professionals. In the decades ahead, these philanthropic experts would not just make safe grants to private universities and hospitals, but instead push the frontiers of charitable giving into new areas corresponding to new social needs.

Throughout the 1970s, the Council on Foundations thus defined for itself two important missions. First, the Council sought to define a new understanding of the place of foundations within society, one that defined foundations as public trusts, open and accountable to all, and, most importantly, operated for public purposes. This first mission was vital because Patman's populist anti-foundation crusade was founded on the notion that foundations were only tax dodges for the wealthy and a way to pursue their private agendas without accountability. Second, the Council sought to reform foundation management practices and eliminate those practices that had brought the entire field before Congress for scrutiny and criticism.

In the end, the Council's two missions, to create a professional culture within organized philanthropy and to reposition foundations as public institutions, fit well together. For as foundations slowly embraced their new public responsibilities, they naturally sought to expand their professional staff to improve relations with the public, including most importantly the myriad of grant seeking organizations in the broader nonprofit sector. At the same time, the new foundation managers wholeheartedly embraced the new public trust conception of foundations because it coincided with their own beliefs and sanctioned their new careers.

Public Trust Conception of Foundations

Acting strategically, the Council's principal concern following TRA 1969 was to open up foundations to the public and to instill in foundation workers the belief that foundations were really public trusts to be operated for public purposes. One of the first and most important goals of the field was therefore to increase the visibility and accessibility of foundations through improved reporting. As the former communications director of the Ford Foundation remarked about the move towards accountability:

> Foundations have adopted communications programs after hewing to an ethic of privacy for years. They decide to "go public" for a variety of reasons. They may be swayed by the example of other foundations, persuaded by the accountability effort of the Council on Foundations, or impelled by crisis. Many foundations took the step as a result of the Tax Reform Act of 1969, in the realization that each had a vital stake in dispelling mystery and myth about the field as a whole.[8]

For many foundations, the first step in "going public" was the publication of an annual report, a move that the Council enthusiastically endorsed.

Improving Foundation Reporting

One area where almost everyone agreed that there existed room for improvement was in the publication of annual reports. In the years immediately following TRA 1969, numerous articles in *Foundation News* trumpeted increased foundation accountability through greater reporting. Some foundations issued their first annual reports, while others held "town meetings" at which grant seekers could ask questions and express concerns. In a 1974 editorial, the Council informed its members that "to paraphrase the New Hampshire state motto, foundations are going to have to learn to 'Communicate Freely, Or Die.' "[9]

Failure to report adequately was a main complaint of the Congressional investigators, with one member of the Senate Finance Committee commenting during the hearings that he deplored "the concealment of foundation activities." The Senate staff charged with assembling data on foundations was also frustrated by the lack of reporting, noting that only 140 foundations issued annual reports and that thousands did not even respond to a request for information. Even though foundations were beginning in 1970 to see the need to change their ways, the information flow within philanthropy was uneven. Many of the smaller foundations had yet to follow the urgings of Council leadership being voiced in *Foundation News*. One foundation worker noted in 1970 that foundations could be divided into four groups:

> For reporting purposes we can divide foundations into four groups. The first includes the 140 who issue annual reports plus those who unquestionably take the public into their confidence through newsletters or reporting on a different time basis and are definitely on the right side of the blanket.
>
> The second, typified by the Pew Memorial Trust, we can call "the public be damned" group. Typical was the comment of the head of the Pew Trust who told a *Fortune* reporter last spring that it was the Trust's "announced purpose to remain as anonymous as possible."
>
> The third group is a very small one whose members are engaged in a free-wheeling variety of abuses, and they are well aware of it. Not much chance for reporting here, not willingly that is.
>
> The fourth category is much the largest and is composed of the many foundations, most small, who have never been made to realize the threat they constitute to the entire foundation field by their refusal to adequately communicate their activities to the public. . . . Some say that if they reported they would call attention to themselves and invite requests that they neither want to consider nor have the staff to answer. Their comments have at least a dash of "the public be damned" and are liberally laced with the "it's my foundation, so it's my money."[10]

One idea for addressing the reporting problem discussed at some length in the 1970s involved the creation of a "Foundation Press," which would assist smaller foundations produce and publish annual reports. If greater public disclosure was needed by all foundations, the argument went, then the philanthropic community as a whole had a responsibility to join together and help the smaller foundations find ways—even with their limited staffs—to be open and accountable. As the head of the Twentieth Century Fund noted: "All of us should endorse and practice the principle of full disclosure. Every form of cronyism and self-dealing should be banned."[11]

Typical of the response to the new call for openness was the Field Foundation's public promulgation of new principles guiding the Foundation's operation. Chief among these was a pledge to improve public information and accessibility:

> [Foundations] should be open to public scrutiny, making public reports at reasonable intervals and constantly sharing information and ideas with other persons and groups, including other foundations, active in the same areas. They should conduct their deliberations and reach their decisions by established and non-arbitrary procedures made known to all who seek their assistance.[12]

Resistance to this trend toward openness was not met kindly. As one foundation executive put it: "Foundations not yet ready to assume their responsibilities [for reporting] should perhaps rethink their role in the foundation picture. It has been said that 'it is easy to dodge our responsibilities, but it is impossible to dodge the consequences of dodging our responsibilities.' "[13] The Council of Foundations also began the practice of surveying its members on their reporting in 1971. By 1975, 275 members of the Council—72 percent of the membership—were issuing annual reports. At the same time, the number of foundations producing a newsletter increased from 3 in 1969 to over 40 in 1984.[14]

Although the campaign to open up foundations through increased reporting started in 1970, it has continued in various forms ever since. For example, the Council launched an awards program in the 1980s to recognize the best-produced annual reports by its members. Even in 1979, the first item on the Council's "Checklist for Foundations" emphasized the continued need for openness: "We must be open, honest and candid about what we do. . . . Disclosure is no longer an option; it is a necessity. Annual reports by foundations are a minimum form of disclosure that far too many foundations still do not use."[15] Disdain for secrecy in foundation management was also fueled by a desire to build relations with outside constituencies, which would assist philanthropy in future skirmishes with government. As John Nason, a consultant to the Council on Foundations, observed in 1977: "If we maintain a high wall of secrecy around ourselves, we invite people to suspect us. If we refuse to tell people what we do, we cannot expect to have friends in time of need. If we refuse to respond to inquiries, we shall make enemies rather than friends."[16] For many leaders in philanthropy, increased reporting was a first and critical step in building a strong defense for the field.

Joining Givers and Receivers

As part of the effort to open themselves up to the public and appear more engaged, foundations began to rethink their relationship with their grantees. Instead of seeing themselves simply as the purveyors of funds, anonymous check-writers supporting worthy causes, foundations began to assert for themselves a more direct relationship with their grantees. A new relationship with, and responsibility to, nonprofit projects was thought to offer the best chance of affecting the recipient organization on a long-term basis. Foundations in the 1970s were urged to be team players, which meant encouraging other funders to join in projects and coordinating the involvement of outside parties. This new role would entail "indemnifying, recruiting, and providing technical assistance to the funded organization"—not just sending a check.[17]

Instead of seeing the nonprofit grantseeker as a burden to be dealt with either by rejecting or approving their grant request, many foundations—

particularly those involved in the Council's work—reconceived their relationship with grantees in more collaborative terms. The strategic value of the repositioning was obvious. As long as foundations were seen as partners in the nonprofit sector, working side by side with community organizations and social service agencies of all sorts, charges of elitism and detachment would be more difficult to support.

Reflecting on the question "Is There a New Grantor-Grantee Relationship?" Basil Whiting, a Ford Foundation program officer, typified the new philosophy:

> The passage of the Tax Reform Act of 1969 has prompted foundations to examine themselves and the ways they have traditionally operated. Not surprisingly, some consternation is apparent . . . because of the extra care with which grants must now be made seems to do violence to some aspects of the prevailing view that philanthropy has come to have of itself during the last century. This is a view of legitimacy and honor.[18]

Whiting went on to note that the regulations, though only "a signal" that a reassessment of foundations was overdue, were leading foundations to rethink their relationship with grantees. The traditional view within philanthropy held that once a grant is made, "the relationship between foundation and grantee should be characterized by mutual trust and a hands-off attitude on the part of the foundation."[19] In place of this detached style, Whiting argued that foundations were moving toward a more engaged grantmaking style in which grantees are closely monitored in their work and foundations offer support and resources to those carrying out programs.

One of the most dramatic attempts to make this shift was undertaken by the Cummins Engine Foundation immediately following TRA 1969. At a time when urban racial strife was increasing, Cummins announced its intention to focus all of its philanthropic energies on urban problems. Cummins soon announced with some fanfare its hiring of four black program officers to administer the program. The goal of this reorientation was threefold: First, Cummins hoped to make its grant making more socially relevant and direct it to the most needy; second, the program was a step toward opening up grant making to disadvantaged populations; and third, the new staff would work hand in hand with community groups in a new way.

Other notable efforts to improve foundation relations with the nonprofit community included a series of "open houses" held across the country in the 1970s. At these philanthropic town meetings, nonprofit organizations were invited to come and ask questions about the operation of foundations to local foundation trustees and professional staff. One such meeting that attracted national press attention in 1976 was hosted by the

Bush Foundation in Minnesota, which drew over 400 representatives from the local nonprofit community. Because it had encouraged increased reporting, the Council on Foundations supported these public meetings through a series of editorials and reports.

As in other areas, the Council also played a leadership role by clearly defining proper foundation policy in the area of grantee relations. Soon after taking over as president of the Council, James Joseph focused on the importance of including grant recipients in the operation of foundations. Joseph argued that the grant recipient could be the most effective defender of the charitable sector—when properly cultivated. To ensure that the donee would be a proponent rather than opponent of foundations, Joseph advocated three measures: 1. Donees must be treated as if they are important to the foundation's mission; 2. Donees must be allowed to provide input on the foundation's priorities; 3. Donees must be made to feel that they have a stake in the continued health and well-being of foundations (Joseph, 1982).

Evaluation

To increase openness and accountability, foundations turned their attention to evaluating their own programs. Frederick Bolman of the Esso Education Foundation noted in 1970 that foundations operate with few defined standards:

> Public and private distrust of foundations may arise in part because these tax-favored organizations neither police themselves nor visibly exert themselves for renewal of purpose and performance. The professions— law, medicine, architecture, teaching, and the like—all have established minimum standards. Not so group philanthropy, despite a half-century of existence.[20]

After acknowledging the aborted effort by the Foundation Center to set up an accrediting system for foundations, Bolman argued that outside approval of philanthropy was ultimately no panacea: "For foundations, as for colleges and universities, such accreditation is really the lowest rung on the ladder of excellence. Even more important is that foundations develop the skill of constant self-improvement."[21] Because foundations enjoy tax exemption, they have responsibilities to the public that flow from these privileges: "[The public] therefore has a right to know that the purpose and performance of foundations are under constant surveillance. . . . Foundations must come to realize that theirs is a goldfish bowl existence."[22]

Bolman's position on foundation performance and evaluation was typical of foundation thinking in the aftermath of 1969. With increased public scrutiny and regulation, foundations began to realize that there was indeed a need for more sophisticated techniques for building public confidence and addressing government's concerns. Indeed, foundations were criticized during the congressional hearing for failing to follow up on certain grants, particularly those to individuals. As a consequence, TRA 1969 legislation included an "expenditure responsibility" provision, which required foundations to review and report on what was done with certain grants. The provision required that a private foundation institute reasonable procedures to insure that grants to organizations that are not registered charities are spent for the intended charitable purposes.

John Labovitz, who studied the impact of TRA 1969 on foundations for the American Bar Foundation, noted:

> This provision probably led to more foundation paperwork than any other in the law; one official of a large foundation described it as "a dog-gone hassle and a lot of hooey." Foundations were given two options with regard to expenditure responsibility: either stop making grants to individuals and non-certified organizations or institute new post-grant evaluation procedures to comply with the requirement.[23]

Most of the smaller foundations undoubtedly simply restricted their grants to IRS certified organizations, while the larger foundations were forced to track their grants more carefully. By 1976, the vice president of the Robert Wood Johnson Foundation reported on the "consciousness raising" in philanthropy since TRA 1969 with regard to evaluation: Foundations must conduct evaluations of their own programs because they have a responsibility to "account for how they spend the dollars they hold in trust."[24] Increased evaluation and concern over effectiveness were cornerstones in the new public-trust conception of foundations, on which a new code of ethics would eventually be built.

A Code of Conduct

One of the most significant moments in the emergence of a profession is the propagation of a code of ethics, governing the behavior of professionals.[25] In philanthropy, the adoption of a code of ethics represented the final step toward instilling a new ethos of openness. A code of ethics was slow in coming for two reasons: First, the Council did not want to impose a code unilaterally too soon after 1969 for fear of alienating its new and growing membership; and second, foundation officials prided themselves on their independence and were generally resistant to outside parties seeking to influence a foundation's policies. However, many foundation officials felt there was a need for some kind of statement from the field as a whole, which would outline acceptable foundation practices and demonstrate to the public that foundations were capable of self-governance and self-regulation.

The Council made a first effort after TRA 1969 at laying down operating principles for foundations in 1973 when it published "Some General Principles and Guidelines for Grantmaking Foundations: A Policy Statement of the Directors of the Council on Foundations."[26] The principles were non-binding and generally sought to reinforce the notion that foundations must make special effort to be open and accountable. Included in the principles was a clear reference to TRA 1969 as a lesson not to be forgotten:

> Despite the "overkill" contained in these provisions—which one must hope will prove open to Congressional adjustment as working experience with the effects of the Tax Reform Act of 1969 become clearer—the act's forceful reminders that foundations exist for the public benefit and must be so directed have to be recognized as necessary and for the good.[27]

The policy pronouncements of 1973 set in place the cornerstone on which a more ambitious effort to develop operating principles for foundations was built six years later.

In 1979, the board of directors of the Council on Foundations took the first step toward creating an ethics code by appointing a special committee. Meeting often over the course of a year, the committee worked through numerous drafts and presented them at meetings of various regional gatherings and at the annual meeting of the Council in Dallas. The Council was clear about the purpose of the code: "The purpose of the statement is to provide practical counsel to new foundations just establishing their operating guidelines and to existing foundations and other donor organizations that may be re-examining their policies and procedures."[28]

The statement of Recommended Principles and Practices for Effective Grant Making also served an important public relations function. In the aftermath of regulation, the Council went to considerable lengths to help its members increase their public profile and improve relations with recipient organizations. The code fit well into this plan. The Council noted that "It draws heavily on the experience and insights of foundation executives and corporate giving administrators and is couched in terms of what has proved useful in the successful handling of grants and in the maintaining of good relations with the various publics with which grantmakers must be concerned."[29]

The eleven principles and practices amounted to complete endorsement of the view that private foundations have important public responsibilities and must be governed in the public interest. The first three principles urged foundations to establish a set of policies that clearly define fundamental objectives, appoint a board of directors committed to implementing these objectives, and set up processes for receiving, examining, and deciding on grant applications. These first three principles all focused on the importance of clear objectives, policies, and procedures. The forth, fifth, sixth, and seventh principles focused on accountability and accessibility. The Council urged that foundations recognize public responsibilities to a broad range of constituents, including recipient organizations, state government, and the IRS. Open communication with the public and grantseekers was recommended, including prompt and honest responses to all grant requests and the publication of an annual report. These ideas flowed directly from the experience of foundations during the 1960s, when an inability to communicate the good work of foundations opened the door for congressional attacks. The ninth, tenth, and eleventh principles supported common-sense measures aimed at improving foundation performance. The Council recommended the periodical evaluation of foundation programs, the careful avoidance of any transactions that might appear self-interested, and active participation in the Council, regional associations, and organizations representing the entire nonprofit sector.

Ten of the eleven principles and practices were uncontroversial and predictable in that they pushed the Council's accountability and openness agenda, while seeking to ensure that foundations continue to improve and professionalize grant making practices. One of the eleven principles did, however, cause some controversy and provoke some resistance: The eighth principle urged foundations to professionalize their staffs and rely on affirmative action in their hiring:

> It is important that grantmakers be alert and responsive to changing conditions in society and to the changing needs and merits of particular grantseeking organizations. Responses to needs and social conditions may well be determined by independent inquiries, not merely by reactions to requests submitted by grantseekers. In response to new challenges, grantmakers are helpful if they use the special knowledge, experience and insight of individuals beyond those persons, families or corporations from which the funds originally came. Some grantmakers find it useful to secure ideas and comments from a variety of consultants and advisory panels, as well as diversified staff and board members. In view of the historic under-representation of minorities and women in supervisory and policy positions, particular attention should be given to finding ways to draw them into the decision making processes.[30]

Three years after the Council on Foundations propounded its principles and practices, it required all member foundations to agree in writing to follow these guidelines as a condition for membership in the association. Although most foundations were already hiring women and minorities in significant numbers, a few more conservative members of the Council did not like the political tone of the eighth clause, nor did they share the Council's conception of foundations as public trusts. Because philanthropy has always prided itself on the plurality of visions and approaches that it encompasses, the Council's attempt to impose a single set of operating principles was naturally met with resistance by some foundations.

Many observers have interpreted the schism caused by the Council in purely political terms, seeing in the Council's endorsement of affirmative action the cause of the departure of a block of more conservative foundations from the Council's ranks. In reality, the dispute embodied more than just politics. It pitted two fundamentally different perceptions of the nature of philanthropy: The minority view believed foundations did not need an outside party looking in on the internal affairs of private foundations; the majority view embraced the new openness and welcomed the Council's input.

The alienation of a small number of Council members in 1983 was a small price to pay for having a large and influential number of private foundations publicly endorse the Council's ethics code. Ten years after the move to require Council members to subscribe to the Principles and Practices, the Council noted: "The fact that the vast majority of our members had, indeed, affirmed the statement on principles and practices was not lost on our elected officials. No public presentation by the Council or other witnesses was as effective as this demonstration of commitment to responsible foundation practices in making the case for less government regulation."[31] For the Council, the passage of a code of conduct was a momentous event. Not only did it signify that foundations were serious about patrolling their own ranks, but it also demonstrated that the Council's leadership could govern the field and successfully spread its vision of foundations as public institutions. Looking back at the process of creating and propagating the Principles and Practices, the Council noted: "The attempt to identify and affirm principles and practices constitutes a marriage of private and public values." The development of a code of conduct was a critical public relations coup and a triumph of the Council's public agenda: "This union [of public and private values] preserves the social contract between private philanthropy and American society and protects the legal charter which makes each foundation a trustee of the public good."[32] For Joseph, the passage and acceptance of the principles and practices represented the most important step in positioning foundations: "It is our 'public purpose' commitment which is the most persuasive in convincing critics and public policy makers that we should be permitted to hold philanthropic resources in trust for perpetuity."[33]

For Joseph and the Council on Foundations, the acceptance of the Principles and Practices was an event of signal importance. It not only marked a significant moment in the move to professionalize philanthropy, but also confirmed the view that foundations were indeed public trusts to be operated for public purposes. With a set of common principles and standards and a strong national association, foundations were moving decisively to cement into place a new normative order, one that began in the early 1970s with the Council on Foundations' proclamation: " 'Not our money, but charity's' should be the key principle guiding each act of foundation donors, trustees, and managers, whether in earning money or giving it away."[34]

Professionalization and New Practices

With the Council on Foundations leading the way, foundations began to change their management structures and hiring practices. Most significantly, the new open and accountable foundations of the 1970s and 1980s discovered that they needed new staff to manage their increasingly complex external relations. It is therefore not surprising that one of the most obvious changes within private foundations in the 1970s occurred on the balance sheet: The new regulations drove up administrative costs. Indeed, looking at the administrative expenses of foundations after TRA 1969, one observer at the time remarked:

> For foundations that attempted to adapt their procedures to the new restrictions, a lengthy review process was required. The day-to-day involvement of legal counsel in the operation of foundations increased dramatically—hardly an unmixed blessing. Many foundations began to ask their lawyers to review each grant they were considering and sought opinion letters on a wide variety of other transactions. . . . Legal fees paid by foundations have almost certainly increased since 1969; the paperwork the lawyers recommended has led to higher clerical costs and has in some instances required additional staff.[35]

The implementation costs of the new regulations are evident when one considers changes in foundation administrative expenses between 1966 and 1972. Administrative expenses include all costs related to the operation of a foundation, excluding grant outlays. During this six-year period administrative expenses as a percent of grant outlays increased from 6.4 percent to 14.9 percent. This increase was a significant change from the trend during the previous decade, when administrative costs were dropping.

Foundation administrative expenses as a percent of grant outlays: 1957–1989

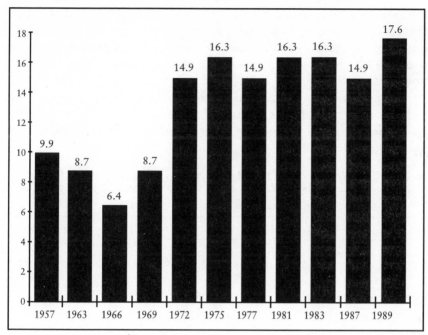

Source: Foundation Center and Margo (1990)[36]

To some foundation managers, the increasing administrative costs were simply a requirement of the new regulations. The increase in administrative costs immediately after TRA 1969 was an early indication of what would be a broader trend in the field toward more staffing.

> The foundation of the seventies will be far more professionally staffed than has been the case to date. . . . It will no longer be possible to operate a foundation out of a banker's pocket. The new legislation regarding private foundations—the possible stiff penalties, the danger of personal liability for each and every officer and trustee, the more extensive reporting and auditing requirements, expenditure responsibility for particular grants—all lead inevitably to the conclusion that someone had best be on duty full-time, minding the store.[37]

To fill the new openings within private foundations with a cadre of professional grantmakers, foundations began to change their recruiting in the 1970s.

Seeking Philanthropic Expertise

A key element in the emergence of any profession is the recognition of the salience of specialized expertise. Throughout the 1970s and 1980s, foundations clearly began to recognize philanthropic expertise as a qualification for foundation work and to seek it out. No longer interested in outsiders from higher education and government who could come to foundation work without preconceived ideas, many foundations began to look favorably on previous professional experience in philanthropy. To illustrate and document the growing salience of professional expertise and experience, I have collected data on the hiring practices of foundations over the past two decades.[38]

Previous Employment of All Foundation Professional Staff: 1970–1989

	Foundation	Nonprofit	University	Government	Other	Total
1970–74	15.8%	18.7%	38.1%	18.7%	8.6%	100%
	(22)	(26)	(53)	(26)	(12)	(139)
1975–79	22.7	18.0	31.7	14.4	13.2	100
	(38)	(30)	(53)	(24)	(22)	(167)
1980–84	26.5	15.0	21.1	21.1	16.3	100
	(39)	(22)	(31)	(31)	(24)	(147)
1985–89	41.6	21.0	18.2	12.0	7.2	100
	(87)	(44)	(38)	(25)	(15)	(209)
Total	28.1	18.4	26.4	16.0	11.0	100
	(186)	(122)	(175)	(106)	(73)	(662)

Two significant trends in hiring can be seen. First, there has been a substantial increase in the hiring of foundation staff with previous grant making experience. This increase confirms that the move to professionalize foundation work was not merely rhetorical and that philanthropic expertise was valued. The second trend is a steady decline in recruitment from higher education over the past two decades. As foundations began to recruit staff with foundation and nonprofit experience, the number of academics within philanthropy declined. The large number of foundation workers recruited from colleges and universities in the 1970s coincided with a general decline in the academic job market, a decline that pushed many Ph.D. recipients into nonacademic professions. By the 1980s, however, as philanthropic experience began to trump disciplinary expertise and training, the numbers of foundation workers recruited from colleges and universities decreased by more than half, from 38 percent in 1970–74 to 18 percent in 1985–89.

When the data on foundation hiring is broken down into two separate tables, one for executive directors and the other for program staff, additional trends emerge.

Previous Employment of Foundation Executive Directors: 1970–1989

	Foundation	Nonprofit	University	Government	Other	Total
1970–74	33.3%	16.7%	6.7%	26.7%	16.7%	100%
	(10)	(5)	(2)	(8)	(5)	(30)
1975–79	35.3	17.6	10.3	17.6	19.1	100
	(24)	(12)	(7)	(12)	(13)	(68)
1980–84	45.4	14.6	7.3	25.4	7.3	100
	(25)	(8)	(4)	(14)	(4)	(55)
1985–89	47.8	14.7	13.3	15.4	8.8	100
	(65)	(20)	(21)	(18)	(12)	(136)
Total	42.9	15.6	11.8	18.0	11.8	100
	(124)	(45)	(34)	(52)	(34)	(289)

Among executive directors, hires with foundation experience have climbed from 33.3 percent in 1970–74 to 47.8 percent in 1985–89. Between 1970 and 1989, a large part of the hires of executive directors—48 percent—can be attributed to an increase in promotions from within foundations, as a growing number of senior program staff were promoted to leadership positions.

The data on hiring patterns of program staff reveal a slightly different trend than that on executive directors. The percentage of staff hires from other foundations is about half that for executive directors. However, program staff have been increasingly recruited from nonprofit organizations over the past 25 years.

Previous Employment of Foundation Program Staff by Categories

	Foundation	Nonprofit	University	Government	Other	Total
1970–74	11.0%	19.3%	46.8%	16.5%	6.4%	100%
	(12)	(21)	(51)	(18)	(7)	(109)
1975–79	14.1	18.2	46.5	12.1	9.1	100
	(14)	(18)	(46)	(12)	(9)	(99)
1980–84	15.2	15.2	29.4	18.5	21.7	100
	(14)	(14)	(27)	(17)	(20)	(92)
1985–89	30.1	32.9	23.3	9.6	4.1	100
	(22)	(24)	(17)	(7)	(3)	(73)
Total	16.6	20.6	37.8	14.5	10.5	100
	(62)	(77)	(141)	(54)	(39)	(373)

Between 1980 and 1990, the percentage of program staff coming from non-profit organizations was twice that for executive directors. This difference reflects the fact that foundations often hire staff from recipient organizations to build ties to the field, train them in grant making for a number of years, then watch them move on to serve as executive directors of other foundations or promote them to executive positions from within. As was the case with executive directors, higher education has declined as a port of entry for program staff into the field of philanthropy.

Several key foundation appointments in recent years highlight the importance attached to philanthropic expertise. In 1990, the Henry J. Kaiser Foundation chose as its new president, the director of the health program at the Pew Charitable Trusts. In 1991, the Pew Charitable Trust selected as its deputy director a senior program officer from the Robert Wood Johnson Foundation. In 1992, the McCormick-Tribune Foundation selected as its new vice president a program officer from the Joyce Foundation in Chicago. The MacArthur Foundation has hired frequently from other foundations: From 1990 to 1995, MacArthur hired staff from the Rockefeller Foundation, the Ford Foundation (two program officers), and the Rockefeller Brothers Foundation. The Minneapolis Foundation selected a Ford Foundation program officer as its president in 1993. In 1994, a former Ford Foundation program officer, who had moved on to be program director at the MacArthur Foundation, assumed a key position at the Northwest Area Foundation.

The growing salience of philanthropic expertise was made most clear in 1996 when the Ford Foundation selected its new president. For the most visible and important position in the entire field, no national search was launched. Instead, without much fanfare and as many observers had predicted, Susan Berresford, a 25-year Ford Foundation veteran who had begun work at the Foundation soon after graduation from college, was elevated from vice president to president. The significance of this move was twofold: First, it confirmed once and for all that philanthropic expertise was one of the key qualifications for foundation work; and second, it made clear that work in philanthropy was indeed a legitimate professional career in and of itself.

In addition to the move to seek out professional expertise, another trend within the field is manifest: A field-wide move toward affirmative action has led to the steady increase of women and minorities in professional positions within foundations. While women and minorities began to enter philanthropy in significant numbers in the 1970s, only in the 1980s and 1990s did they reach proportions that surpass those in other professions. In 1992, for example, one major survey of foundation demographics revealed that fully 61 percent of all foundation program officers were women and 28 percent were minority group members.[39] These numbers are particularly significant when one considers that in the broader economy minorities represented in 1993 only 14.3 percent of all professionals and only 10.8 percent of all managers. Similarly, on a national level in 1993, women constituted 50.2 percent of all professionals and 29.9 of all managers.[40] That foundations managed in a period of only two decades to increase both minority and female employment well beyond national averages is a clear sign of the field's interest in creating an open, inclusive, and legitimizing workplace. The trend toward increased diversity dovetails with the trend noted earlier toward hiring more program staff from the nonprofit sector, where many of the health and social service organizations have traditionally employed substantial numbers of women and minorities. By making foundations look more like the broader nonprofit sector, foundations managed simultaneously to improve relations with recipient organizations and counter charges of elitism.

The events of 1969 made it clear that the costs of professional staffing were minor in comparison to the costs of appearing unresponsive and unaccountable. In the early years, only the larger foundations had full-time grant-making staff. However, two decades of encouragement by the Council on Foundations changed this situation dramatically. In recent years, the majority of Council members have come to accept the need for professional staff.

**Percentage of Private Foundation Members
of the Council on Foundations with Paid Staff in 1994**

Type of staff	Private Foundations (N=419)
Any Paid Staff	79%
Paid Professional Staff	
Full Time	55
Part Time	32
Total	74
Paid Support Staff	
Full Time	40
Part Time	41
Total	64

Source: Council on Foundations (1994)

Training Programs

In the early 1970s, foundation administrators had little literature to draw upon in their efforts to improve foundation management. Not only was there no practitioner's manual on how to operate a foundation, but there was also little understanding of what good foundation management actually entailed. After 1969, "black letter" standards for proper philanthropic management were all too clearly spelled out in the new regulations, which prohibited various self-interested transactions and certain investments. All that was needed was for the legal requirement to be melded with practical tips into a real foundation operating manual.

In 1972, the Cleveland Foundation convened a group of representatives from eighteen major foundations to discuss the state of the art in foundation administration. A year later, the result was a 250-page administrative manual for the Cleveland Foundation, which included eleven chapters on everything from budgeting, grant making, personnel selection, and portfolio management to financial administration. Although this "Staff Reference Manual" was originally intended for internal use only, it soon began to circulate in the foundation world, particularly among small and midsized foundations. The Cleveland Foundation made copies available to any interested foundation and the manual was a point of departure for many foundations to discuss their own administrative policies.[41]

Appreciating the need identified by the Cleveland Foundation, the Council on Foundations stepped up its own publication program. Over the course of the 1970s and 1980s, the Council published several books about foundation management. The most important of these books was the *Handbook on Private Foundations*, which in addition to focusing on the art of grant making in some detail, gave step by step instructions for setting up a foundation from scratch.[42] Most importantly, the *Handbook*, authored by Council president David Freeman, represented a very visible sign that the Council was taking steps to lay down standards and norms for the field.

The creation of manuals on foundation administration was coupled with a move to develop training programs for the new personnel entering philanthropy. A variety of professional training programs emerged in the 1980s, designed to teach newcomers the profession of grant making. Many of the regional associations began holding two or three-day "institutes" for new grantmakers, at which experienced practitioners would give talks and answer questions. At the same time, some of the larger foundations began to consider in-house preparation and training programs.

Because it employs the largest number of professional staff and has a steady turnover in its ranks, the Ford Foundation has led the way in developing professional training programs for its new staff. The Ford program, which has evolved over the years, includes the following components: philanthropic goals and strategies; case studies illustrating issues such as collaboration, capacity building, and failing projects; a workshop on racial and sexual diversity; a lecture on the field of philanthropy and private foundations; and a discussion of grantor-grantee relationships. The Ford Foundation training program has attracted the attention of many of the other large foundations in recent years. Foundation managers from across the country have attended the training program to learn more about it, including representatives from the MacArthur Foundation and Pew Charitable Trusts. These managers returned to their institutions with the complete training materials where they were shared more broadly.

These efforts to build training programs were part of the move to professionalize grant making and build credibility for the field. Having well-trained, experienced staff was no longer a luxury to be enjoyed by the largest foundations. As one foundation manager observed, professional staffing was nothing short of survival strategy in the 1970s:

> I believe that the rapid development of a cadre of foundation executives capable of advancing the enlightened interested of foundations is a matter of organizational survival. Foundation executives are yet to be included in any current listing of the professions. However, they do have a vocation requiring specialized knowledge and substantial academic preparation. One only has to look back at the events leading to the TRA 1969 to see the results of the paucity of leadership and how thinly spread was whatever existed.[43]

By the early 1980s, the Council on Foundations declared that "professional development has become one of the Council's highest priorities."[44] Professionalizing foundation work was critical because it was essential that the judgment of foundation workers have legitimacy and hold up to scrutiny. As James Joseph, president of the Council on Foundations, noted: "Despite an endless list of contributions to the public good—meeting a wide variety of human needs, feeding the hungry and housing the homeless, articulating social values and a sense of civic culture—private foundations are periodically forced to engage in a subtle form of competition for legitimacy."[45] Improving training and professional development programs was thus an obvious direction for philanthropy in the 1970s and 1980s.

New Funding Practices

In philanthropy, organizational form did not follow function, but rather the opposite occurred. The organizational transformation of American philanthropy brought new grantmaking practices: With new professional staff appearing within many foundations, trustees could no longer justify simply making decisions based on personal connections. Grantmaking decisions were in large measure handed over to the new staff, as boards gravitated more toward a policy and planning role. As foundations became more heavily staffed, they began to change the way grants were made. No longer content to simply write unrestricted checks based on the overall reputation of a grant-seeking organization, foundations began requiring more convincing and more details before they would agree to provide a grant.

Beginning in the 1970s and continuing on during the next two decades, the grants nexus would undergo profound changes. Back in the 1950s and 1960s, the best way to land a grant was to have a personal connection to a trustee who would secure the requested funds in a time-honored process of log-rolling, which allowed all trustees to fund their favored charities. The professionalization of foundations challenged this trustee-centered system and eventually displaced it with a new, more legitimate grantmaking process that placed detached professionals at the center of grantmaking decisions.

Professionalization also brought about a shift from "general operating grants" to what came to be termed "project grants," restricted to specific purposes defined in advance of the awarding of a grant. Foundation staff, imbued with new responsibilities, needed to find ways to judge grant requests beyond simply relying on the reputation of the grant seeker. In the quest for a more objective and more legitimate basis for evaluating grant requests, many foundations reformulated their grantmaking guidelines to reflect a new focus on project requests. Under the new system, grant seekers would no longer simply submit a letter requesting support, but instead would outline a specific program or project within their organization that needed support. As one grantmaker noted in 1971: "Once a professional staff develops, you can be pretty sure of an even stronger inclination toward project funding and a predominance of foundations which feel it is vital to develop their own program thrust—and locate projects which meet certain defined objectives. This is very different from the foundation of the sixties, which merely served as a conduit for the donor's giving program."[46]

As a consequence of this shift, grant requests to foundations became longer and more detailed throughout the 1970s and 1980s. Proposals began to describe not just charitable missions and programs, but also outcomes and expectations. To meet the requirements of foundation professionals, grant seekers began tailoring requests to individual foundations, offering each a different funding opportunity. What was gained by the shift away from general operating to project and program support? For foundations, the new system brought through the doors more detailed proposals, which in turn allowed foundation staffers to argue that their judgments were based on a set of objective criteria grounded in the content of proposals.

The shift also justified the cost and administrative burden brought on by the introduction of professional workers into foundations. Quite simply, for the new foundation decision makers to remain occupied both before and after recommending a grant, proposals needed to become narrower in their scope.

For nonprofits, the shift meant more fund-raising effort and more post-grant work. After specifying how funds would be expended in great detail, discussing these plans with a foundation staffer, submitting to a site visit, and writing a report on the project, nonprofit organizations found themselves increasingly burdened by the new foundation procedures. The shift also necessitated the recruitment and training of development directors and program staff who would know how to handle foundation professionals and the new rigors of securing grants.

The natural inclination toward accountability of the foundation profession fit well with the move toward more restricted project giving. Instead of having to make a subjective decision based on the overall quality of a grant seeker — always a difficult and subjective process — foundation staff sought more "objective" and measurable standards. They began to base their decisions on receiving detailed information about how grant funds would be expended and expect a more thorough accounting after the grant period was over. Project giving thus brought with it a heightened ability to judge, oversee, and evaluate grant requests — features that foundation professionals embraced in the name of openness and accountability.

Conclusion

The decade of the seventies was a turning point in the development of modern philanthropy. The changes ushered in during this period did have clear precedents, however. Early philanthropic leaders, like the Carnegie Corporation's Frederick Keppel, had urged increased openness in the 1930s. Similarly, the Russell Sage Foundation advocated early on the improvement of foundation administrative practices. However, it took a regulatory shock to the field in the 1970s and the strengthening of the Council on Foundations for philanthropy's two major transformations to take root among a broad range of foundations.

First, foundations embraced a new self-understanding of their status as public trusts that were to be operated for public purposes. With the Council pushing for greater reporting and better relations with grantees, foundations fundamentally redefined their work. Gone was the tendency toward secrecy and aloofness. In its place was a new sense of the public responsibilities of foundations. The seventies ushered in a whole new conception of private foundations as public trusts, open and accountable to all. A second major transformation took place in the administrative practices of foundations. New staff entered foundation work to fulfill philanthropy's new public mission. If foundations were to be open, accessible, and responsive, new professionals had to be brought in to meet these new objectives. Although administrative expenses soared at many of the larger foundations, no price was too high to defend philanthropy from further attack and from further government encroachment.

These two transformations—in beliefs and practices—were, of course, mutually reinforcing and overlapping. Yet it would be a mistake to see the two phenomena as causally related. The new conception of foundations as public trusts, open and accountable to all, may have begun to emerge earlier than the move to increase staffing, but both developments unfolded over a period of years and each reinforced the other. After all, newly hired foundation staff had a vested interest in pushing forward the new ethos of openness. Selling the idea that foundations must increase visibility and external relations created the very conditions under which professional staff entered the field of philanthropy in large numbers. As more and more staff entered the field, it was only natural they in turn would embrace and promulgate the principle of openness that made professionalism possible in the first place.

In the long run, the opening up of foundations holds both promise and danger. On the positive side, securing information about the grantmaking activities of major foundations is now easier than it has ever been. Access to foundation directories, annual reports, and foundation staff have simplified the initial identification of possible funding sources—though actually getting grants remains fraught with difficulty. New foundation staff, a strong national association, and a growing literature on foundations have also increased the general public's understanding of philanthropy. On the negative side, the new ethos of openness has obscured to some extent serious critical evaluations of foundation performance. With their tremendous resources directed outward, foundations now control their image more fully than ever before.

In the end, openness and professionalism hardly guarantee that foundation resources are being used effectively and creatively. The new ethos of openness and the introduction of a new cadre of foundation professionals have, however, successfully lulled some into assuming that foundations are now better managed and making a greater contribution to society than ever before. What is needed at this juncture is a greater body of critical literature on the actual performance of foundations, one that cuts through the aura of openness and professionalization to look at results and outcomes. In this sense, independent voices within the foundation field are actually needed now more than before foundations made the strategic decision to professionalize and open themselves up to the public.

Notes

1. F. Emerson Andrews, *Philanthropic Foundations* (New York: Russell Sage Foundation, 1956). Eduard C. Lindeman, *Wealth and Culture: A Study of One Hundred Foundations and Community Trusts and Their Operations during the Decade 1921–1930* (New Brunswick, N.J.: Transaction Publishers, [1936] 1988).

2. Merrimon Cuninggim, *Private Money and Public Service: The Role of Foundations in American Society* (New York: McGraw-Hill, 1972), 211.

3. Martha R. Wallace, "The Foundation Meets the Fund Raiser," *Foundation News* 12, no. 1 (1971): 1.

4. Jack Shakely, "Tom Troyer Appraises the Tax Reform Act of 1969," *Foundation News* 21, no. 3 (1980): 22.

5. Committee on the Foundation Field, *Report of the Committee on the Foundation Field.* (Manuscript on file at the Foundation Center, 1970.)

6. Brian O'Connell, *Powered by Coalition: The Story of Independent Sector* (San Francisco: Jossey-Bass Publishers, 1997), 35–54.

7. Jack Shakely, "Tom Troyer Appraises the Tax Reform Act of 1969," 24.

8. Richard Magat, "Out of the Shadows," *Foundation News* 25, no. 4 (1984): 26.

9. Council on Foundations, "On Communication," *Foundation News* 15, no. 3 (1974): 56.

10. Mary J. Tweedy, "How Can Foundations Be Strengthened?" *Foundation News* 11, no. 2 (1970): 57.

11. M. J. Rossant, "Where Do We Stand Now?" *Foundation News* 11, no. 5 (1970): 190.

12. Council on Foundations, "Five Practices: The Field Foundation," *Foundation News* 12, no. 3 (1971): 101.

13. Mary J. Tweedy, "How Can Foundations Be Strengthened?," 58.

14. Richard Magat, "Out of the Shadows."

15. Council on Foundations, "Reducing Confusion: A Checklist for 1979," *Foundation News* 20, no. 1 (1979).

16. Dennis P. McIlnay, "The Public Accountability of Foundations: Private Organizations in the Public Interest," *Philanthropy Matters* (Spring Edition, 1994): 14.

17. Louis B. McCagg, "A New Dimension for Foundations," *Foundation News* 11, no. 2 (1970): 49.

18. Basil Whiting, "Is There a New Grantor-Grantee Relationship?" *Foundation News* 11, no. 4 (1970): 173.

19. Ibid., 174.

20. Frederick Bolman, "The Need to Evaluate a Foundation," *Foundation News* 11, no. 1 (1970): 20.

21. Ibid.

22. Ibid., 21.

23. John R. Labovitz, "1969 Tax Reform Reconsidered," in *The Future of Foundations*, ed. Fritz Heinman (Englewood Cliffs, N.J.: Prentice Hall, 1973), 117.

24. Margaret E. Mahoney, "Evaluation Can Help Make the Manager's Life Easier," *Foundation News* 17, no. 6 (1976): 29.

25. Harold L. Wilensky, "The Professionalization of Everyone," *American Journal of Sociology* 70 (1964): 134–58.

26. Council on Foundations, *Some General Principles and Guidelines for Grant-Making Foundations* (Washington: Council on Foundations, 1973).

27. Ibid., 3.

28. Council on Foundations, "Recommended Principles and Practices for Effective Grantmaking," *Foundation News* 21, no. 5 (1980): 8.

29. Ibid., 8.

30. Ibid., 9.

31. *Principles and Practices for Effective Grantmaking* (Washington: Council on Foundations, 1990).

32. Ibid.

33. James A. Joseph, "Why the Concern with Principles?" *Foundation News* 24, no. 6 (1983c): 64.

34. Council on Foundations, "Private Foundations and the 1969 Tax Reform Act," in *Research Papers*, sponsored by the Commission on Private Philanthropy and Public Needs (Washington, D.C.: U.S. Department of the Treasury, 1977).

35. John R. Labovitz, "1969 Tax Reform Reconsidered," in *The Future of Foundations*, ed. Fritz Heinman (Englewood Cliffs, N.J.: Prentice Hall, 1973), 105.

36. No data is available for 1970 and 1985.

37. Martha R. Wallace, "The Foundation Meets the Fund Raiser," 4.

38. This data was culled from two main sources: (1) the hiring announcements in *Foundation News*; and (2) the appointments column in the *Ford Foundation Letter*. In addition, some supplementary data was gathered from the newsletters of regional associations of grantmakers and books on foundations. The database contains information on the foundation that the individuals joined, the position assumed there, the organization from which the individual came, and the previous position of the worker. The limitations of these data are clear: By considering only the most recent position held prior to entrance to the foundation field, the data do not always capture the breadth of experience brought to the field by the new entrants. Another limitation of the dataset is its focus on large foundations. Small foundations may not be fully represented in the sample because they are less likely to be members of the Council on Foundations, the publisher of *Foundation News*, and because they are less likely to be in the habit of sending hiring notices to the foundation press. While large foundations do the bulk of all hiring in what is a small job market, these institutions do not convey a comprehensive picture of the vast array of foundations that populate the philanthropic scene.

39. Council on Foundations, *Foundation Management Report* (Washington, D.C.: Council on Foundations, 1994).

40. Charity Anne Dorgan, ed., *Statistical Handbook of Working America* (New York: ITP, 1995).

41. Timothy D. Armbruster, "Foundation Administration Moves into a New Era," *Foundation News* 15, no. 6 (1974).

42. David F. Freeman, *The Handbook on Private Foundations* (Washington, D.C.: Seven Locks Press, 1981).

43. Robert Bonine, "One Part Science, One Part Art," *Foundation News* 12, no. 6 (1971): 244.

44. James A. Joseph, "Professional Development: New Questions for a New Era," *Foundation News* 24, no. 5 (1983B): 48.

45. James A. Joseph, "1969–1983: From Abuses to Access—A Different Spotlight," *Foundation News* 24, no. 4 (1983a): 43.
46. Martha R. Wallace, "The Foundation Meets the Fund Raiser," 4.

Bibliography

Andrews, F. Emerson. *Philanthropic Foundations*. New York: Russell Sage Foundation, 1956.

Armbruster, Timothy D. "Foundation Administration Moves into a New Era." *Foundation News* 15, no. 6 (1974).

Bolman, Frederick. "The Need to Evaluate a Foundation." *Foundation News* 11, no. 1 (1970).

Bonine, Robert. "One Part Science, One Part Art." *Foundation News* 12, no. 6 (1971).

Committee on the Foundation Field. *Report of the Committee on the Foundation Field*. Manuscript on file at the Foundation Center, 1970.

Council on Foundations. "Five Practices: The Field Foundation." *Foundation News* 12, no. 3 (1971).

——. *Some General Principles and Guidelines for Grant-Making Foundations*. Washington: Council on Foundations, 1973.

——. "On Communication." *Foundation News* 15, no. 3 (1974).

——. "Private Foundations and the 1969 Tax Reform Act." In *Research Papers*, sponsored by the Commission on Private Philanthropy and Public Needs. Washington, D.C.: U.S. Department of the Treasury, 1977.

——. "Reducing Confusion: A Checklist for 1979." *Foundation News* 20, no. 1 (1979).

——. "Recommended Principles and Practices for Effective Grantmaking." *Foundation News* 21, no. 5 (1980).

——. *Principles and Practices for Effective Grantmaking*. Washington, D.C.: Council on Foundations, 1990.

——. *Foundation Management Report*. Washington, D.C.: Council on Foundations, 1994.

Cuninggim, Merrimon. *Private Money and Public Service: The Role of Foundations in American Society*. New York: McGraw-Hill, 1972.

Dorgan, Charity Anne, ed. *Statistical Handbook of Working America*. New York: ITP, 1995.

Foundation Center. *The Foundation Directory*. New York: Foundation Center, 1994.

Freeman, David F. *The Handbook on Private Foundations*. Washington, D.C.: Seven Locks Press, 1981.

Joseph, James A. "The Donee as a Philanthropic Stakeholder." *Foundation News* 23, no. 6 (1982).

——. "1969–1983: From Abuses to Access—A Different Spotlight." *Foundation News* 24, no. 4 (1983a).

——. "Professional Development: New Questions for a New Era." *Foundation News* 24, no. 5 (1983b).

———. "Why the Concern with Principles?" *Foundation News* 24, no. 6 (1983c).

Labovitz, John R. "1969 Tax Reform Reconsidered." In *The Future of Foundations,* ed. Fritz Heinman, 101–31. Englewood Cliffs, N.J.: Prentice Hall, 1973.

Lindeman, Eduard C. *Wealth and Culture: A Study of One Hundred Foundations and Community Trusts and Their Operations during the Decade 1921–1930.* New Brunswick, N.J.: Transaction Publishers, [1936] 1988.

Magat, Richard. "Out of the Shadows." *Foundation News* 25, no. 4 (1984).

Mahoney, Margaret E. "Evaluation Can Help Make the Manager's Life Easier." *Foundation News* 17, no. 6 (1976).

Margo, Robert A. "Foundations." In *Who Benefits from the Nonprofit Sector?,* edited by Charles Clotfelter, 207–334. Chicago: University of Chicago Press, 1990.

McCagg, Louis B. "A New Dimension for Foundations." *Foundation News* 11, no. 2 (1970).

McIlnay, Dennis P. "The Public Accountability of Foundations: Private Organizations in the Public Interest." *Philanthropy Matters,* Spring Edition, 1994.

Pifer, Alan. *Philanthropy in an Age of Transition: The Essays of Alan Pifer.* New York: Foundation Center, 1984.

Rossant, M. J. "Where Do We Stand Now?" *Foundation News* 11, no. 5 (1970).

Shakely, Jack. "Tom Troyer Appraises the Tax Reform Act of 1969," *Foundation News* 21, no. 3 (1980).

Tweedy, Mary J. "How Can Foundations Be Strengthened?" *Foundation News* 11, no. 2 (1970).

Wallace, Martha R. "The Foundation Meets the Fund Raiser." *Foundation News* 12, no. 1 (1971).

Whiting, Basil. "Is There a New Grantor-Grantee Relationship?" *Foundation News* 11, no. 4 (1970).

Wilensky, Harold L. "The Professionalization of Everyone." *American Journal of Sociology* 70 (1964): 137–58.

PART II

Case Studies in Early-Twentieth-Century Foundation Philanthropy

4 Constructing a New Political Economy

Philanthropy, Institution-Building, and Consumer Capitalism in the Early Twentieth Century

Meg Jacobs

In the increasingly vast literature on foundations, scholars seem close to reaching a consensus on the origins and evolution of philanthropic organizations in the twentieth-century United States. As Barry Karl and Stanley Katz explained in an early and important article on philanthropic foundations at the turn of the century, "Foundations came into existence because American society was unable to maintain a social order which corresponded to its passionately held localist ideals." More recently, organizational historian Guy Alchon has explored the way "private bodies . . . assume[d] larger public responsibilities," emphasizing "the public role of private institutions in the rise of the managed society." Social feminist scholars like Linda Gordon also point out how, in the absence of a national welfare state, philanthropic foundations played an important part in constructing an organized system of aid that would later shape parts of the New Deal state. Essentially, these scholars argue, both the structure of the American polity and the nation's antistatist political culture necessitated the development of private organizations to fill in the lacunae of the nation's federalist system of government and facilitate the modern "search for order."[1]

In many of these studies, the rise of what Ellis Hawley has labeled the "associative state" necessarily or inevitably coincided with the decline of popular democracy and public participation in policy making. As philanthropic organizations made the transition from agents of ameliorative relief to centers of social-scientific investigation, they helped to spawn the birth of a new technocratic elite culture. These experts then participated in the designing of an administrative state far removed from electoral politics and popular participation. Though scholars debate the aims and objectives of philanthropic giving, they seem to share the same working assumption about the nature of an increasingly passive citizenry. At most, in their early years, foundations attempted to educate an enlightened citizenry and arouse public opinion. One is left with the impression of a public sphere expanded only grudgingly and then simply as the product of private plans grafted onto public policy through the workings of experts. Thus in the histories of foundations, the public tends to fall from view both historically and historiographically.[2]

In truth, a crucial part of the history of early foundations involved an important debate over the definition and reconceptualization of the "public." Foundations emerged, as Karl and Katz explained, at a moment when the nation's ruling elite felt least certain about how to confront the many social problems that accompanied industrialization. But philanthropic organizations were more than simply a functional response. Scholars of the Progressive Era continue to discover permutations of reform.[3] And the world of foundations proved no exception. Reexamining the early history of foundations reveals the existence of competing visions of political economy and of the public. Indeed, as this chapter begins to demonstrate, the Twentieth Century Fund, founded by department-store magnate Edward A. Filene, stood in contrast to other early foundations by articulating the need for and promotion of a transformed and enlarged activist public. According to Filene, foundations should not only engage in "preventive" actions but should also sponsor the creation of new institutions that energize the populace by redistributing political and economic power. Rather than being detached and disengaged, experts should be linked organically to the fostering of new social movements, mostly among the laboring classes.[4] The Twentieth Century Fund sought to build state-sanctioned local institutions, such as credit and trade unions, that would revitalize the nation's citizenry, restructure its political economy, and, in the process, redistribute income to create a new all-inclusive consuming public.

We can compare two distinct approaches to turn-of-the-century problems such as the "labor question" through a microcosmic look at attitudes toward working-class credit. In the early twentieth century, the ability to obtain credit became central to the emerging mass-consumption economy. In the modern marketplace of automobiles and appliances, the need for credit expanded to include middle-class consumers as well as businesses. Working-class Americans also came to rely on loans for doctors' bills and burial costs. Yet, in an era that predated the creation of personal-loan departments at commercial banks, very few means existed for the loaning of money to those of small income. While middle-class consumers could purchase consumer durables on time, working-class Americans could not obtain credit for their cash needs. Such a deficiency resulted in the rise of "loan-sharking" and other forms of usurious money lending.[5] Early on, credit and its concomitant counterpart, indebtedness, attracted the attention of philanthropic organizations because the notion of "independence" had long constituted a central ingredient in Americans' political identity.

Two leaders on this issue were the Russell Sage Foundation and the Twentieth Century Fund.[6] Both believed in preventive action and the need to ameliorate conditions of the modern industrial society. And both utilized social-science expertise and cultivated a professional-public policy nexus. But these two foundations embodied differing visions of American political economy. They diverged on what they saw as the causes and solutions to the problem of working-class credit. For the Russell Sage Foundation, wage-earners' debt constituted a "social problem" and threatened the moral order of the community. Social stability could be preserved only by rehabilitating and freeing what they saw as a dependent "borrowing public" through raising public awareness about loan sharking. State legislation would regulate commercial lending institutions that, in turn, would make "character loans" and supervise the personal finances of the laboring classes. This conception bespoke a greater fear about working-class debt and consumption as profligate and dangerous. By contrast, Filene saw an incipient working-class consumption and the pursuit of higher standards of living as the core of American democracy. He and the organizations he supported thought of credit as fundamentally an economic problem. A prolific thinker about mass consumption, Filene maintained that mass production required a more equitable distribution of national income and affordable access to credit. He believed that only an empowered "consuming public" operating through self-supporting democratic institutions such as credit unions could effectively restructure the nation's political economy. Whereas the Russell Sage Foundation had a backward outlook that sought to accommodate change while preserving the existing social order, the Twentieth Century Fund looked ahead to the construction of a new political economy of consumer capitalism.

These two competing visions—a borrowing public and a consuming public—reflected a broader debate about American political economy. The Russell Sage Foundation's formulation suggests the power of the "long nineteenth century" characterized by a producer citizenship rooted to the moral economy of the household and regulated by the local community.[7] Their understanding of a dependent borrowing public in need of help by licensed moneylenders complemented the ideals of a voluntary social reform movement led by trained experts and supported by paternalistic welfare capitalists. In contrast, the Twentieth Century Fund's positive view about credit reflected a shift to a consumer citizenship defined by mass participation in the national marketplace and premised on a redistribution of political and economic power to the working classes. The Fund would play a key role in drafting the National Labor Relations Act (1935), which would enable workers to enhance their purchasing power through collective bargaining. Thus, by examining attitudes about credit, we can see the significance of foundations in building institutions and we can track the debate between the ideals of the independent local producer and the empowered national consumer as the basis of American political culture. In doing so, we can recover competing influences on what eventually became different parts of the New Deal state.

The Russell Sage Foundation and the Evils of Debt

Following the death of her wealthy husband, Russell Sage, in 1906, Margaret Olivia Sage received roughly 60,000 letters of personal solicitation for charity. After consultation with leaders in the field of social work, Mrs. Sage established a philanthropic foundation dedicated to "the improvement of social and living conditions in the United States of America." Moving beyond individual charity, the Russell Sage Foundation devoted itself to the "preventive science" of seeking the causes of pauperism. Out of the obligations of wealthy Christian society, the Foundation would work toward the "social betterment" of the working classes, whose stability and morality were key to the social order of the larger community. In keeping with its mission statement and the Board of Trustees' backgrounds in education, charity, and research, the Russell Sage Foundation's initial grants included studies on tuberculosis, "child-saving" through recreation and playgrounds, and charity organization. They also sponsored the Pittsburgh Survey and other social surveys as tools of community improvement.

Out of the thousands of personal requests for help Mrs. Sage had received, many came from those in the debt of loan sharks.[8] Under the guidance of Sage's legal adviser Robert W. de Forest, the Foundation turned to the social-work community and commissioned the young social-work student Arthur Ham to investigate the field of small loans, including philanthropic societies, small-loan companies, and chattel mortgage lenders. In October 1910, the Russell Sage Foundation created the Division of Remedial Loans under Ham's direction and dedicated itself to eradicating loan sharking and "salary buying" as a "social problem" that undermined the moral order of the community. Support came from the Provident Loan Society, the "philanthropic pawnshop" that de Forest had helped to organize after the depression of 1893–1894. In 1909, there were only fourteen remedial institutions that lent money at reasonable rates on chattel mortgages or pledges of personal property. They joined together to form the National Federation of Remedial Loan Associations, and, beginning with his appointment at the Foundation, Ham also served as the Federation's de facto executive director.[9]

From the heights of the Russell Sage Foundation, Ham sought to bring the evils of loan sharking to the attention of the social-work community. In 1916, at the National Conference of Charities and Correction in Indianapolis, Ham pointed to "the lack of thrift in American families" as one of the greatest "obstacles that lie in the path of the modern program for the improvement of social and living conditions." Forced to turn to professional moneylenders as a result of "unthrifty" behavior, wage earners risked becoming further enmeshed in a net of debt. At this time, there were about 300 chattel-loan and salary-loan lenders in New York City acting in violation of usury laws, charging interest rates as high as 20 percent per month. Ham denounced the "parasitic character of the loan shark," who preyed on vulnerable borrowers. He warned, "[T]hereby begins a chain of transactions which, except in rare instances, leads to greatly increased distress and often to theft, family desertion and suicide." Conjuring images of social decline and decay, Ham explained the fate of Postal Telegraph employees who "for years had been paying tribute to the loan sharks." He continued, "Many operators were driven to do things they never would have thought of doing had they been free from this curse and they became roving, unstable workmen. Afraid to walk in and out of the front doors of the offices, they dodged through rear entrances, drew their faces into all sorts of shapes so that they could not be recognized, —even changed their names when asking for employment after being dismissed."[10] When social worker W. Frank Persons had sifted through Mrs. Sage's requests for personal charity, he segregated the letters written from those in the "grasp" of moneylenders. He deplored the fate of the thousands who were "earnestly desirous of being self-respecting and self-supporting" but presumably could no longer be because they had sold their salaries and had become the "victims of loan sharks."[11] According to this world view, usurious money lenders threatened to engulf workers in a downward spiral of debt and dependency that then threatened to bring moral decline.

The Russell Sage Foundation's understanding of credit was embodied in the notion of "the borrowing public."[12] This was the segment of the population who, by reasons of personal failings, had become dependent on loan sharks. The dependency of this population then challenged the social and political stability of the local community. In a classically Progressive fashion, the Foundation aimed to bring loan-sharking practices to the attention of the public. A study commissioned by the Russell Sage Foundation asserted that it was necessary to expose these practices because "the entire success of the salary loan business depended upon their ability to keep the general public uninformed as to their methods."[13] Publicity would then pave the way for new lending laws and the creation of remedial institutions. Under public regulation, the borrowers would be restored and the community would be saved.

Between 1909 and 1914, the Russell Sage Foundation spearheaded a crusade against the evils of loan sharking. Ham appealed to the Retail Dry

Goods Association to support their employees in their disputes against loans sharks by not firing them or handing over assigned wages. The Foundation sponsored and funded the creation of the Chattel Loan Society of New York as an institution that would make loans on household furniture. Ham also attempted to reach a wider audience in a publicity campaign that included the production and release of a motion picture, *The Usurer's Grip* (1912). By 1914, the major newspapers no longer accepted advertisements of illegal moneylenders. The District Attorney of New York County established a bureau for the prosecution of usury cases.

Acknowledging that moneylending was inevitable, Ham sought to regulate the practices of small-loan lenders by bringing them under public supervision. Because small-loan companies did not accept deposits, they had to capitalize all their loans, and in order to attract the necessary funds, they had to promise a profit. Thus, Ham sponsored uniform small-loan legislation that allowed for interest rates of 3.5 percent a month, or 42 percent annually. Though substantially higher than the rate for commercial loans, this proposal encountered much opposition from unregulated moneylenders, who were accustomed to charging at least five times that amount and, if necessary, using coercive means to collect. However, once state legislatures had begun to pass regulatory laws over their protests, many of the big firms did a classic about-face and recognized that legislation could provide a legitimizing influence. These newly licensed and legitimated moneylenders then formed the American Association of Small Loan Brokers in April 1916. They now declared themselves the self-appointed protectors of the borrowers, promising "to standardize, dignify, and police the small loan business." Representatives of these 325 companies told their more philanthropic counterparts, the National Federation of Remedial Loan Associations, "We are as much opposed to loan sharks or unfair and oppressive moneylenders as is the National Federation." Thereafter, they joined forces with Ham and the Federation to draft and gain passage of uniform small-loan laws in all states.[14]

Though Ham devoted most of his energies toward cleaning up the small-loan business, he recognized that commercial loan companies did not fill the needs of all classes of borrowers. Ham turned his attention to credit unions. Credit unions first made their appearance in England and Germany, and then in Canada. Growing out the need for small loans, these cooperative institutions offered credit at low rates. Typically, membership required a nominal initiation fee and a five-dollar share, payable in installments. Members could then borrow and repay at annual interest rates no higher than 6 percent. These "people's banks" allowed for one vote per member regardless of the number of his shares. Ham sponsored a credit-union law in New York in May 1913. By 1917, New Yorkers had established thirty-nine credit unions.[15]

Ham's thinking about credit unions brings to light his fundamental mistrust of working-class credit. Essentially, Ham sponsored credit unions as agencies that could maintain the social order of communities by providing escape from the commercial economy, instead making members reliant on each other. He regarded these community institutions as "one of the most potent moral, educational, and social forces in the enrichment of the life of the common people."[16] Ham hoped they would provide a stabilizing influence. Large employers such as American Express shared Ham's expectation and encouraged the establishment of credit unions among their employees. As Vice President H. K. Brooks put it, "Everyone knows that workers who are involved in irregular financial transactions are less efficient than those who are in fairly easy circumstances. An employee caught in the net of a loan-shark . . . is not in a frame of mind to attend strictly to business." The loans, Brooks explained, were "for any righteous emergency or productive use."[17] In concrete terms, that meant loans restricted to repaying of debts, home ownership, perhaps furniture, and expenses relating to sickness and death.

At that time, there was a distinction in popular discourse between "consumptive borrowing" and "productive borrowing."[18] In Ham's view, credit unions should make loans "only for productive purposes, and purposes that will effect a saving or supply an urgent need."[19] Rather than supplementing installment credit, Ham regarded that type of financial transaction as deplorable, the product of "the wasteful and uneconomic use of income by American families."[20] He regarded credit unions as an antidote to "the installment purchasing evil." By contrast, credit unions would "facilitate loans for legitimate purposes."[21]

The most legitimate purpose was of course to pay off other debts, a process laden with moralism. "Credit unions," Ham explained, "are simply associations by means of which men combine to establish local, self-governing institutions of credit to meet their requirements, relying on their own efforts and initiative to work out their own salvation."[22] In 1916, the creation of the Federal Employee Credit Union for government employees in New York reflected similar sentiments. The idea was "to rescue customs employees from the exactions of 'loan sharks' and credit agencies generally." Credit unions would enable these men to begin "conserving their own resources . . . that will be of mutual aid in times of stress."[23] The narrative was one of the fall from grace, enslavement, and redemption. As the *Saturday Evening Post* put it, "[W]hen every man is his own Shylock there is no reason why he should fall into the clutches of money lenders." Credit unions offered escape for the "working forces from the morale-shattering effects of peonage to salary buyers."[24] Another *Saturday Evening Post* account of Lowe's Grove Credit Union in Durham County, North Carolina reflected this notion that a community could free itself. As the reporter put it, "Step by step the [citizens of Durham County] emancipated themselves through this Credit Union by pooling of their own little resources." Reporter Samuel Crowther continued, "Instead of a countryside of listless, shiftless, poor whites, not knowing just why anything was or should be, we now have a community of alert, independent men." As result of their credit union, "these men became their own masters."[25]

Absent in these narratives was a discussion about low wages. In the popular formulation, borrowers were forced to borrow out of "urgent needs." As the decennial report of the Division of Remedial Loans explained, "The essence of the loan shark business was of course the urgent need of the borrowers. . . . Only this made it possible to develop the business into an institution of human exploitation." Of course the assumption was that the borrower did not have enough money but whether this was because he did not earn enough or because he squandered his income was not mentioned. Most likely the Russell Sage Foundation thought the latter, explaining in its report that the lack of "systematic saving and thrift . . . constituted the backbone of the whole pernicious structure of the loan shark's business."[26] In fact, Ham believed that installment agencies were to blame in part by "enticing people to purchase unnecessary articles . . . thus becoming an important contributing cause of poverty and distress."[27]

For Ham and the many social workers who shared his perspective, thriftiness represented the ideal value for workers. Thus credit unions were seen not only as vehicles to provide for the escape from loan sharks, but also, and perhaps even primarily as institutions "to encourage thrift." In explaining the justification for credit unions being tax exempt, Ham argued that "If the State exempts a thrift agency from taxation it does so because it considers thrift to be a desirable quality deserving encouragement among its citizens."[28] Though participation in a credit union introduced members to "business methods," in fact, these institutions provided protection, if not escape from the modern commercial economy. As an institution constituted by a body of peers, credit unions made loans to a member on the basis of "intimate knowledge of his personal habits and of his financial and domestic situation." As Ham explained, "The borrower's solvency which plays such a large part in commercial credit plays but a small part in the determination of credit by a credit union." Initial membership relied on "good moral character—reputation for honesty, sobriety and industry."

Such an institution could subject members to the moral tenets of an insular community and could presume that all members defined their interests similarly; thus the penalty of default became all the more personal. Regarding close moral scrutiny as this new institution's virtue, Ham instructed the social-work profession that "This community of interest enables the credit union to loan with safety upon character alone, for the moral responsibility of repayment is great when a man knows that by violating his obligation he not only withholds money of a fellow-worker or associate, but invites social ostracism."[29] Ham feared that the obstacles to establishing credit unions would be "inherent lack of thrift, lack of homogeneity; mobility of population; strong individualism." In this case, mutualism could serve to tie members to a community and define community in terms of homogeneity.[30] In addition, Ham's understanding about credit comported with contemporary notions of the family-wage ideal with the male breadwinner. He believed that loans were for the benefit of men, for example, "the [telegraph] operator and his family." The way in which the Division helped to structure small-loan legislation also reinforced the family-wage ideal, as evidenced by the stipulation that the assignment of wages should be subject to notification of the employer and the consent of the borrower's wife.[31]

Russell Sage Foundation's sponsorship of institutions to encourage thrift did not occur in a vacuum. In fact, interest in small loans in the first three decades of the century coincided with an explosion of consumer credit. By 1926, consumers purchased roughly $5 billion of goods on time, half of which were automobiles. According to political economist E. R. A. Seligman, six of every ten cars were sold on the installment plan.[32] It was in this context that the Russell Sage Foundation supported institutions that it thought would shield workers from the unregulated market. Indeed, in 1927, the Massachusetts Credit Union League voted to recognize the birthday of Benjamin Franklin, that great "apostle of thrift," as National Credit Union Day.[33]

The Twentieth Century Fund and the Promise of Working-Class Credit

Thrift in and of itself did not appear to all credit unions members as a terminal goal. Whereas small-loan societies clearly comported with an ethos of welfare capitalism, in fact, credit unions served as harbingers of consumer capitalism. The original sponsors of the Massachusetts Credit Union League that lionized Benjamin Franklin included many prominent Boston merchants and retailers. These businessmen saw credit unions as vehicles that would allow wage-earners to save not simply for emergencies nor for the values that such saving promoted, but rather in order to spend. This dualism between thriftiness and buying captures American society at a moment of transition, an awkward moment that both valorized saving and sponsored spending. The promotion of spending by credit unions makes more sense if we point out that many regarded Edward A. Filene, founder of Filene's Basement and leading thinker on merchandising and consumption, as the true leader of the credit-union movement in the United States.

Unlike Arthur Ham and the Russell Sage Foundation, Filene advocated credit unions as an integral part of the new consumer economy. Rather than an escape from the market, credit unions would enable workers to participate in the newly emerging national economy. He believed that the American economy would prosper and grow only if wage earners had enough income to consume all the goods that the nation's manufacturers were capable of producing. Credit unions would not increase the real wages of workers, but they would enhance the workers' purchasing power. In this way, through greater access to credit, workers would join the rest of the "consuming public," the great "masses who alone are numerous enough to provide an adequate market to insure prosperity in this machine age."[34]

Filene first encountered credit unions in India in 1907. Upon his return to Boston, he devoted his time and money to the passage of the Massachusetts Credit Union Law, the first general statute for the incorporation of credit unions in the U.S. Success came in April 1909. The movement lagged, and then in January 1914 Filene and other wealthy businessmen in the wholesale and retail trades formed the Massachusetts Credit Union League. By 1915, though, there were only roughly fifty credit unions throughout the state. In 1920, Filene launched a renewed effort to establish credit unions. He hired public accountant and lawyer Roy Bergengren to head the Credit Union National Extension Bureau. Filene and Bergengren agreed that the National Extension Bureau should dedicate itself to passing state credit-union laws, setting up new unions, and forming an independent national association to promote credit unionism. Until then, the money would come from the Twentieth Century Fund, a philanthropic foundation funded by Filene.[35]

Set up in 1919, the Twentieth Century Fund represented Filene's attempt to devise national solutions to the country's industrial and economic problems. Originally constituted as the Cooperative League, its mission was to promote "the investigation and study and providing instruction as to economic and industrial questions and aiding and improving the relations between employers and employees." In 1922, Filene and the Board adopted the Twentieth Century Fund as its new name and changed its charter to "the improvement of economic, industrial, civic and educational purposes." This expansion reflected Filene's shift in attention from the workplace to the larger economic system as a whole. He regarded the Fund as a research laboratory akin to those of General Electric and AT&T. His laboratory, however, would study the new consumer economy and try to devise methods to institute a high-wage, low-price economy to stimulate mass consumption. There his economists studied issues such as the national debt, waste in distribution, and health care, all aiming toward developing a science of consumption. Throughout, these reports underscored the centrality of mass purchasing power to the economic and political health of the country. By subjecting the nation's entire systems of mass production and mass distribution to fact-finding research, the Fund sought to demonstrate the economic rationale for redistributing income to the working classes. To the extent that democratic institutions such as credit unions contributed to such redistribution, philanthropic aid would become unnecessary.[36]

Throughout the 1920s, the Credit Union National Extension Bureau and the Division of Remedial Loans were constantly at odds with one another. Roy Bergengren essentially blamed the staff at the Russell Sage Foundation for hindering the growth of credit unions in New York and nationally. By supporting legislation for both small-loan companies and credit unions, the Russell Sage Foundation split the political capital available for this issue. Indeed, the strongest opposition to credit-union legislation quite often came from the American Association of Small Loan Brokers, the organization of commercial lenders that Arthur Ham had helped to establish. In 1928, Bergengren told Louis Robinson, the new director of the Russell Sage Foundation Division of Remedial Loans, "[W]e feel that the credit union is the only solution in sight of the wage workers small loan problem if the wage worker is ever to be able to get credit at anything approaching bank rates. . . . We have come to feel that every possible effort should be concentrated on the credit union development as the fundamental thing."[37] Bergengren saw credit unions as the "right sort" of lending institutions, explaining to Filene, "There is no business, large or small, in the United States which could operate on 42% credit. . . . There is no worker in the United States who can afford . . . to pay 42% credit."[38] Bergengren charged that their higher rates and probing inquiries made small-loan institutions less attractive than credit unions.

Known popularly as "poor men banks," credit unions appealed to growing numbers of those who had no access to other forms of credit. The roster included a wide array of groups from the McComb Business Women's Club in Mississippi to the teachers of Detroit to employees of New England Telephone and Telegraph and the Rock Island and Pacific Railroad in Chicago. In addition, many public employees formed credit unions.[39] As director of the Department of Service Relations of the United Stated Post Office, Henry Dennison, a liberal manufacturer and member of the Board for the Twentieth Century Fund, sponsored credit unionism among postal employees. By 1927, in just five years, there were eighty-three postal credit unions in major cities with assets of over $1 million and loans of $3 million.[40] (A common joke held that becoming a postal worker required having one's name on the moneylender's books.) Just before the holiday season in 1924, the Boston Post Office Employees Credit Union urged workers to "Save Something Systematically . . . Join Your Credit Union Now!" Their ads sold the idea of credit unions as a way to build up personal capital and, presumably, to have more spending money. "Start an account and save something every week or every month and watch your money grow." "What will you have a year from today?" it asked.[41]

Filene was an unflagging proponent of mass consumption. In contrast to Arthur Ham's moralizing condemnation of working-class consumption, Filene believed that all Americans had "the right to buy things." In his political economic vision, a newly constructed economic citizenship as manifested in credit unions would benefit both the individual and the nation. He constantly emphasized the need to transform workers into consumers by increasing their wages and their access to credit. As he put it, "Consumption must be financed if there is to be general prosperity."[42] Urging his countrymen to shed their nineteenth-century world views, he explained in a national radio broadcast, "The sooner we get over the idea that people should not become involved in debt. . . . the sooner we are likely to have a credit arrangement suitable to the needs of the society in which we live."[43]

And yet for Filene, credit unions were more than necessary props of capitalist expansion. For Filene and Bergengren, the credit union movement helped to forge a new democracy based on economic citizenship. As Bergengren put it, credit unions would "result in a better citizenship" by "educat[ing] great numbers of our people in the management and control of money." Fearful that indebted workers would be "the sort of raw material out of which bolshevism is manufactured," Bergengren believed "the credit union system will prove to be a bridge—over which, as a people, we may travel to a more perfect, a sound and a permanent democracy." Hence he named the Credit Union National Extension Bureau newsletter *The Bridge*.[44]

Filene shared Bergengren's faith in the democratizing potential of credit unions. As he saw it, credit unions stood as a democratic alternative to commercial lenders and installment agencies such as the General Motors Acceptance Corporation, which, incidentally, charged interest at least four times as great as credit unions. Credit unions would not only lend at affordable rates but would also expose workers to the managing of their own financial resources. These institutions were "democratic agencies of self-help," allowing for "democratic management and control of the economy." According to Filene, economic democracy would reinforce political democracy.[45]

This conflation of economic and political democracy makes more sense when placed in the context of Filene's other projects. Within his department store, he had established the Filene Cooperative Association, an employee union that the industrial-reform community hailed as a model of worker representation. Moreover, Filene introduced a profit-sharing plan, which he intended to result in worker ownership. In 1928, the year that workers were to take over, the rest of the store's management, including Edward's younger brother Lincoln, voted to eliminate both this plan and Edward Filene's active involvement in store policies. From his "outside office" which he retained, Filene continued his support of the League of Women Voters, minimum wage laws, and numerous other labor-liberal reforms. His main interest focused on the Credit Union National Extension Bureau and the Twentieth Century Fund.[46]

Though credit unions were slow to establish themselves as an important cog in the emerging consumer economy, Filene was not discouraged. Likening the advent of "mass credit" to mass production, Filene saw credit unions as the natural adjunct of a consumer economy. "Henry Ford popularized the automobile. The credit union has begun to popularize banking. . . . Twenty years ago it was as unheard of for workingmen to own and operate banks of their own as it was for them to own and operate their own automobiles." By 1930, there were over one thousand credit unions, with assets of $45 million and annual loans of $60 million.[47] Still small in number, these institutions were firmly established. In 1935, the Twentieth Century Fund ended its funding of the Credit Union National Extension Bureau, which had now become self-supporting. Under Bergengren's direction, the Bureau set up permanent headquarters in Madison, Wisconsin.

From Moral Economy to Consumer Economics

The conflict between the Credit Union National Extension Bureau and the Division of Remedial Loans was, of course, in part personal and in part strategic, a typical turf war. But in back of that lay fundamental differences. Comparing these foundations' attitudes about credit reveals a debate about the basis of American citizenship. The Russell Sage Foundation's conception of political economy stemmed from its commitment to a nineteenth-century moral order in which credit was only a means to bolster economy and thrift, bringing stability to communities across the country. For them, the independent moral producer represented the bulwark of American democracy against the evils of debt and decline. In contrast, Filene and the Twentieth Century Fund were engaged in constructing a new political economy that promoted consumption as a means to national prosperity, social integration, and renewed civic participation. They saw the independent, prosperous consumer as heralding a shift in American political culture from economy to economics.

More generally, these foundations had radically different conceptions of the public. The Russell Sage Foundation's understanding was confined to the boundaries of the "community" defined as those among whom one lived. These social workers were dedicated to improving living and working conditions as they affected the social stability and moral order of the community. Within any given community, there were members of the borrowing public whose ability to save and, in effect, be saved depended on and determined the welfare of the general public. In her original donation letter, Mrs. Sage had in fact stipulated that a substantial portion of the funds be spent on New York. Perhaps the more radical Mary Van Kleeck and her Division of Industrial Studies provided an obvious exception, although she too spoke in the language of community. As Van Kleeck remarked at an annual meeting of the Taylor Society in 1924, she thought that Taylorism could "make industry and all its results in human lives harmonize with our ideals for the community."[48]

Filene by contrast set his sights on the entire nation. Early on, Filene had begun to shift his political consciousness from the immediate community to the industrial workplace. As he told the Merchants Association of Massachusetts in 1909 while serving as state chairman of the Committee on Industrial Relations, "We spend the greatest part of our conscious lives with the people with whom we work and owe far more to them, whether we employ them or are employed by them, than the people whose homes happen to be in the same street as ours." In this way, Filene began to reconceptualize the political economic landscape. At the same time as he supported industrial democracy, Filene also sought to bring more organization to industry. He helped to set up the United States Chamber of Commerce and the International Chamber of Commerce, institutions he would later renounce. Finally, at the Twentieth Century Fund, Filene sought to harmonize the clashing interests of workers and employers by redefining the nation's citizenry into a collective consuming public.[49]

These two alternatives, one bounded and steeped in moralism and the other national and linked to consumerism, would ultimately shape different parts of the New Deal state. Through its influence on social work and the case-study method, the Russell Sage Foundation helped to structure Social Security's Aid to Dependent Children. Here social welfare became defined as private charity writ large.[50] At the same time, Filene and the Twentieth Century Fund participated in the drafting of the National Labor Relations Act, which gave workers the right to organize and bargain collectively. Employing the language of purchasing power, this measure justified and linked workers' rights in the nation's factories, mills, and offices to their roles in the marketplace.[51] These radically different public policies—social welfare and industrial democracy—suggest the importance of understanding the political economic visions out of which they grew and the history of the foundations that supported them.

Notes

I would like to thank Ellen Condliffe Lagemann for encouraging and supporting my interests in the history of philanthropic organizations. Special thanks also to Susan Kastan and Richard Magat, and to the other participants at the Philanthropy in History Conference, Indianapolis, 26 September 1997, where I first presented this chapter.

1. Barry D. Karl and Stanley N. Katz, "The American Private Philanthropic Foundation and the Public Sphere, 1890–1930," *Minerva* 19 (Summer 1981): 236–70; Guy Alchon, "Mary Van Kleeck and Social-Economic Planning," *Journal of Policy History* 3 (1991): 1–23; Linda Gordon, *Pitied but Not Entitled: Single Mothers and the History of Welfare* (Cambridge, Mass.: Harvard University Press, 1994).

2. On the rise of a technocratic elite, see Ellis Hawley, "Herbert Hoover, the Commerce Secretariat, and the Vision of an 'Associative State,' 1921–1928," *Journal of American History* 61 (1974): 116–40; Louis Galambos, "Technology, Political Economy, and Professionalization: Central Themes of the Organizational Synthesis," *Business History Review* 57 (Winter 1983): 471–93; and Guy Alchon, *The Invisible Hand of Planning: Capitalism, Social Science, and the State in the 1920s* (Princeton: Princeton University Press, 1985).

3. On progressivism see Richard Hofstadter, *The Age of Reform* (New York: Vintage, 1955); Robert H. Wiebe, *The Search for Order, 1877–1920* (New York: Hill and Wang, 1967); David P. Thelen, *The New Citizenship: Origins of Progressivism in Wisconsin, 1885–1900* (Columbia: University of Missouri Press, 1972); Richard D. McCormick, "The Discovery That Business Corrupts Politics: A Reappraisal of the Origins of Progressivism," *American Historical Review* 86 (1981): 247–74; Daniel T. Rodgers, "In Search of Progressivism," *Reviews in American History* 10 (1982): 113–32. For two more recent works that have shaped my thinking on the reconceptualization of American political economy at this time, see James T. Kloppenberg, *Uncertain Victory: Social Democracy and Progressivism in European and American Thought, 1870–1920* (New York: Oxford University Press, 1986); and Mary O. Furner, "Knowing Capitalism: Public Investigation and the Labor Question in the Long Progressive Era," in Mary O. Furner and Barry Supple, eds., *The State and Economic Knowledge: The American and the British Experiences* (Cambridge: Cambridge University Press, 1990), 241–86.

4. This idea of reconciling expertise and democracy received support from leading philosophers and reformers sympathetic to the idea of pragmatism. For an excellent example that saw a natural, necessary union between science and social movements, see Walter Lippmann, *Drift and Mastery* (New York: Mitchell Kennerley, 1914). Kloppenberg elaborates on this point in *Uncertain Victory*. See also David A. Hollinger, "Science and Anarchy: Walter Lippmann's *Drift and Mastery*," *American Quarterly* 39 (1977): 463–75; and Hollinger, "The Problem of Pragmatism in American History," *Journal of American History* 67 (1980): 88–107.

5. Although the rise of credit was a key component in the emergence of mass consumption, there are few scholarly treatments. A thorough analysis is Martha L. Olney,

Buy Now, Pay Later: Advertising, Credit and Consumer Durables in the 1920s (Chapel Hill: University of North Carolina Press, 1991). The best treatments were actually written at the time that reformers came to be aware of "the small loan problem." See Clarence W. Wassam, *The Salary Loan Business in New York City* (New York: Russell Sage Foundation, 1908); Arthur H. Ham, *The Chattel Loan Business* (New York: Russell Sage Foundation, 1909); Louis N. Robinson and Maude E. Stearns, *Ten Thousand Small Loans* (New York: Russell Sage Foundation, 1930); David J. Gallbert, Walter S. Hilborn, and Geoffrey May, *Small Loan Legislation: A History of the Regulation of the Business of Lending Small Sums* (New York: Russell Sage Foundation, 1932); Evans Clark, *Financing the Consumer* (New York: Harper & Brothers, 1933); Louis N. Robinson and Rolf Nugent, *Regulation of the Small Loan Business* (New York: Russell Sage Foundation, 1935); Charles O. Hardy, ed., *Consumer Credit and Its Uses* (New York: Prentice-Hall, 1938); and Rolf Nugent, *Consumer Credit and Economic Stability* (New York: Russell Sage Foundation, 1939). For statistics that demonstrate the lack of working-class participation in the consumer durable market in the first several decades of the twentieth century, see Frank Stricker, "Affluence for Whom?—Another Look at Prosperity and the Working Classes in the 1920s," *Labor History* (Winter 1983).

6. For the general history of the Russell Sage Foundation, see the two-volume history of the foundation by John M. Glenn, Lilian Brandt, and F. Emerson Andrews, *Russell Sage Foundation, 1907–1946* (New York: Russell Sage Foundation, 1947). See also David Hammack, "Russell Sage Foundation," in Harold Keele and Joseph Kiger, eds., *Foundations* (Westport, Conn.: Greenwood Press, 1984), 373–80; and Sheila Slaughter and Edward T. Silva, "Looking Backwards: How Foundations Formulated Ideology in the Progressive Period," in Robert Arnove, ed., *Philanthropy and Cultural Imperialism: The Foundations at Home and Abroad* (Boston: G. K. Hall, 1980), 55–86. On the Twentieth Century Fund, see Adolph A. Berle, *Leaning against the Dawn* (New York: Twentieth Century Fund, 1969); Kim McQuaid, "An American Owenite: Edward A. Filene and the Parameters of Industrial Reform, 1890-1937," *American Journal of Economics and Sociology* 35 (January 1976): 77–94; and James Allen Smith, *The Idea Brokers: Think Tanks and the Rise of the New Policy Elite* (New York: Free Press, 1991), 84–86, 290–91.

7. I am grateful to the other contributors to this volume and to the discussion at the Philanthropy in History Conference, Indianapolis, 26 September 1997, particularly the comments by Peter Dobkin Hall, for reinforcing this notion of a long nineteenth century.

8. Robinson and Nugent, *Regulation of the Small Loan Business*, 85.

9. Glenn, Brandt, and Andrews, *Russell Sage Foundation*, vol. 1, 66.

10. Arthur Ham, "People's Bank," Address Delivered before the National Conference of Charities and Correction, 15 May 1916, pp. 3, 5, 12, Edward A. Filene Papers (hereafter EAF Papers), Credit Union National Association, Madison, Wisconsin (hereafter CUNA). Glenn, Brandt, and Andrews, *Russell Sage Foundation*, vol. 1, 138.

11. Robinson and Nugent, *Regulation of the Small Loan Business*, 85.

12. Decennial Report of the Division of Remedial Loans, Series 3, Box 25, Folder 123, p. 5, Russell Sage Foundation Papers (hereafter RSF Papers), Rockefeller Archives Center, North Tarrytown, New York (hereafter RAC).

13. Robinson and Nugent, *Regulation of Small Loan Business*, 89.

14. Glenn, Brandt, and Andrews, *Russell Sage Foundation*, vol. 1, 144–46.

15. The most thorough treatment on the credit-union movement is J. Carroll Moody and Gilbert C. Fite, *The Credit Union Movement: Origins and Development, 1850-1970* (Lincoln: University of Nebraska Press, 1971).

16. Ham, "Take the Credit and Let the Cash Come," *Outlook*, 17 September 1924, 78.

17. H. K. Brooks, "Our *Workers* Organize a Credit Union," *System*, September 1925, 299–301.

18. For a discussion of this distinction, see Robinson and Nugent, *Regulation of the Small Loan Business*, 32–35. See also Hardy, ed., *Consumer Credit and Its Uses*, 1–12. As the latter work points out, the distinction between producers' credit and consumers' credit remained hard to pinpoint because a loan to purchase a car, for example, could be considered as belonging to either type depending on whether the borrower intended to use the car for pleasure, to enhance his income, or both.

19. Ham, "People's Bank," 9.

20. Ibid., 4.

21. Ham, "Object of the Credit Union," *New York Times*, 7 May 1916, II, p. 12.

22. Ham, "People's Bank," 13.

23. "Federal Employees Get Credit System," *New York Times*, 21 May 1916, VII, p. 4.

24. "Every Man His Own Shylock," *Saturday Evening Post*, 2 July 1927, 26.

25. Samuel Crowther, "You Can Start a Poor Men's Bank," *Saturday Evening Post*, 30 September 1922, 14.

26. Decennial Report of the Division of Remedial Loans, Series 3, Box 25, Folder 123, p. 6, RSF Papers, RAC.

27. Ham, "People's Bank," 4.

28. Ham, "Object of the Credit Union," 12.

29. Ham, "People's Bank," 7–10.

30. Ham, "The Credit Union and the Cooperative Store." Address delivered at the Conference of the Eastern Cooperative Societies, Cooperative League of America, 1917, reprinted by Russell Sage Foundation, pp. 3, 7, EAF Papers, CUNA.

31. Glenn, Brandt, and Andrews, *Russell Sage Foundation*, vol. 1, 143. For an excellent discussion of the family wage ideal and its influence on social workers in this period, see Gordon, *Pitied But Not Entitled*, 51–59.

32. Edwin R. A. Seligman, *The Economics of Installment Selling: A Study in Consumers' Credit with Special Reference to the Automobile* (New York: Harper & Brothers, 1927).

33. Roy Bergengren to E. L. Field, n.d. January–May 1927, Correspondence and Records of E. L. Field, Box 24, Virginia Credit Union League Papers (hereafter VCUL Papers), Alderman Library, University of Virginia, Charlottesville (hereafter UVA).

34. Edward A. Filene, "The Problem of Consumer Credit," Economic Series Presentation, no. 20, University of Chicago Press, 8 April 1933, p. 11, EAF Papers, CUNA.

35. Moody and Fite, *The Credit Union Movement*, 26–53.

36. Filene gave thousands of public lectures and published his opinions in hundreds of articles. A few of his books capture his ideas about mass consumption, the need to reform the processes of distribution, and the importance of industrial democracy as a check to industrial autocracy. Collectively, he referred to his ideology as one geared toward discovering and implementing what he called the "next step forward." See Edward A. Filene, "What Can a Rich Man Do?" *Collier's*, 21 July 1922, 5–6; Filene, *The Way Out* (Garden City, N.Y.: Doubleday, Page, 1924); Filene, *Successful Living in This Machine Age* (New York: Simon and Schuster, 1932); Filene, *Next Steps Forward in Retailing* (Boston, 1937); and Filene, *Speaking of Change: A Selection of Speeches and Articles* (New York, 1939).

37. L. N. Robinson to Roy F. Bergengren, 29 August 1924; Bergengren to Robinson,

2 September 1924; Bergengren to Robinson, 9 September 1924; Robinson to Bergengren, 10 September, 1924; Series 3, Box 26, Folder 200, RSF Papers, RAC. For continuing evidence of a clash between the Foundation and Bergengren, see Leon Henderson to John Glenn, 28 April, 1928, re: Proposed Plan of Bergengren to Organize Credit Unions in New York State, Series 3, Box 24, Folder 187, RSF Papers, RAC. Henderson warns that Bergengren's plan "runs so strongly contrary to our concept of the State's needs," and "I cannot see that we can do anything but definitely break with Bergengren if he comes to New York."

38. Bergengren to Filene, 4 November 1931 as quoted in Moody and Fite, *The Credit Union Movement*, 143.

39. "An Organized Front against Fakers," *Collier's*, 13 October 1923; Roy Bergengren, "E Pluribus Unum Banking," *Survey*, 15 February 1925, 567–70; Bergengren, "Riding the Credit-Union Circuit," *Survey Graphic*, November 1930, 137–41.

40. Moody and Fite, *The Credit Union Movement*, 113.

41. Boston Post Office Employee Credit Union poster, 1923–24, Correspondence by E. L. Field, Box 24, VCUL Papers, UVA.

42. "The Right to Buy Things," *Philadelphia Record*, 1 November 1930; Edward A. Filene, "The Spread of Credit Unions," *Survey* 65 (1 November 1930): 180–81, as quoted in Moody and Fite, *The Credit Union Movement*, 140.

43. Edward A. Filene, "The Problem of Consumer Credit," Economic Series Presentation, no. 20, University of Chicago Press, 8 April 1933, p. 3, EAF Papers, CUNA.

44. Moody and Fite, *The Credit Union Movement*, 98, 109.

45. Evans Clark, Report of the Director to the Executive Committee of the Board of Trustees of the Twentieth Century Fund; Edward A. Filene to Evans Clark, 20 October 1930; Evans Clark, Memorandum on Mass Credit, 22 October 1930; Twentieth Century Fund Papers (hereafter TCF Papers), Twentieth Century Fund Archives, New York, New York.

46. For a good overview of Filene's different interests, see Gerald W. Johnson, *Liberal's Progress: Edward A. Filene, Shopkeeper to Social Statesman* (New York: Coward-McCann, 1948). For information on the Filene Cooperative Association, see W. Jett Lauck, *Political and Industrial Democracy* (New York: Funk & Wagnalls, 1926), 209–12, 266–67, 273; and Mary La Dame, *The Filene Store: A Study of Employees' Relation to Management in a Retail* Store (New York: Russell Sage Foundation, 1930).

47. Edward A. Filene, "The Spread of Credit Unions," *Survey,* 1 November 1930, 180–81.

48. Alchon, "Mary Van Kleeck and Social-Economic Planning," 6.

49. Edward A. Filene, Chairman, First Report of the Committee on Industrial Relations, Presented to the Boston Merchant Association, 17 February 1909, Box 7, EAF Papers, CUNA. Filene's involvement in the Chambers of Commerce is well documented in his papers.

50. Linda Gordon, *Pitied but Not Entitled*, 220.

51. Edward A. Filene to Evans Clark, 20 December 1933; Filene, Memo: Labor Unions Project for the Twentieth Century Fund, 30 January 1934, TCF Papers; Steve Fraser, *Labor Will Rule: Sidney Hillman and the Rise of American Labor* (New York: Free Press, 1991).

5 Selling the Public on Public Health

The Commonwealth and Milbank Health Demonstrations and the Meaning of Community Health Education

Elizabeth Toon

IN THE MID-1920S, readers of the Sunday *Syracuse Post-Standard* would encounter a regular health column, usually in the form of a dialogue between an imaginary Mrs. Wise and her neighbor, Mrs. Smith. One week, Mrs. Smith asked Mrs. Wise a question that, given the city's recent onslaught of parades, newspaper pieces, exhibits, and lectures devoted to health, real Syracuse residents might well have asked: "What is a Health Demonstration?"

> When I don't understand anything—and there are heaps of things I don't—[responded Mrs. Wise] I think to myself, "What did the good Lord put a tongue in my head for if it wasn't to ask questions?" . . . Now this Syracuse Health Demonstration . . . was started a little over a year ago in our city to demonstrate the fact that a lot of sickness can be prevented. . . . A lot of the babies could be saved if people were as intelligent on health subjects as they are on fashions. . . . [1]

In the 1920s, several philanthropic foundations hoped to do just that— to save babies and eliminate a variety of sociomedical ills by creating an active, cooperative public "intelligent on health subjects." Two prominent foundation sponsors of public health work, the Milbank Memorial Fund and the Commonwealth Fund, pursued this task with special fervor. In communities as varied as Syracuse, New York and Salem, Oregon, the Milbank and the Commonwealth organized "health demonstrations," ongoing projects expected to "demonstrate" the value of preventive health services. Assured that, in the influential words of one public health leader, "public health is purchasable,"[2] the Milbank and the Commonwealth sought to show the nation and the world the returns certain to accrue on a typical community's investment in prevention. In order to prove that public health was purchasable, the Milbank and the Commonwealth found themselves trying to "sell" demonstration communities on their visions of public health. To do this, foundation executives and demonstration advisors looked to community health education. Educating the public about health, they agreed, meant more than persuading individuals to adopt healthier habits; it was also a means for convincing communities to demand and support the preventive services introduced under foundation guidance—a demand that, in the end, would be measured in dollars and cents.

Education's Role in the Demonstrations

The roots of these health demonstrations lay in late-nineteenth-century charity organization work and turn-of-the century social surveys, but their more direct antecedents were two landmark public health projects in the 1910s. First, in the early 1910s, the Rockefeller Sanitary Commission's campaign to eradicate hookworm disease in the South showed public health workers the enormous organizational resources philanthropy could contribute to public health.[3] Second, in the later 1910s, the Metropolitan Life Insurance Company's Framingham Health and Tuberculosis Demonstration, seemed to prove that public health was indeed purchasable.[4] Encouraged by these projects and, in general, by the possibilities for social progress and efficiency that seemed to flow naturally from preventive health services, the Commonwealth and Milbank got into the demonstration business in the early 1920s.[5] Their goal, as one chronicler of the Milbank's demonstrations later explained, was to "test out the claims of the public health experts on a sufficiently large scale to determine what could actually be done in the way of adequate community health organization, how it could best be done, what it would cost, and what concrete results could be attained."[6]

Foundation executives and technical experts at both the Commonwealth and Milbank planned to focus on especially visible health problems, and to use such work to undergird the organization of more comprehensive health services adapted to the needs of different types of communities. The Milbank's New York state demonstrations were originally concerned most with tuberculosis control and prevention. Leaders at the Milbank chose areas for the demonstrations representative of three community types: Cattaraugus County, a rural upstate county dotted with small towns and villages; Syracuse, a bustling mid-sized city; and Manhattan's Bellevue-Yorkville district (including much of the Lower East Side), where demonstration organizers planned to take on "complex metropolitan health problems that had previously defied solution."[7] The Commonwealth Fund, eager to determine the value of county-wide health organization in improving child health, began seeking out "typical" communities in 1922. As Peter

Buck has shown, Commonwealth staff leaned especially toward those communities which seemed to boast cooperative local professionals and civic leaders as well as the beginnings of an "intelligent," "wide-awake" citizenry.[8] The final choices were the smallish Midwestern city Fargo, North Dakota; Clarke County, Georgia, home to a college town (Athens); impoverished Rutherford County, Tennessee, "the least developed" of the four, in terms of public health infrastructure;[9] and Marion County, Oregon, which contained Salem and many small agricultural villages.

Having selected the demonstration communities, the experts selected by the foundations began their work by cumulating a statistical portrait of the demonstration communities, surveying local organization for health and welfare, and using this information to assess the communities' strengths, weaknesses, and pressing needs. They then usually sought to add personnel to local health departments in keeping with their newly established priorities. For instance, they often funded part or most of the salary for public health nurses and school health education experts. Demonstration organizers also sought to work through existing community networks as much as possible, enlisting the area's voluntary institutions (such as anti-tuberculosis leagues) and official agencies (such as county boards of education). With whatever "forward-thinking" local support they could muster, demonstration organizers and workers set up child and/or neighborhood health clinics and health education programs in the schools. They also used newspapers and other publicity media to build public awareness of the new services offered by these expanded health departments.[10]

Organizers intended for these demonstrations to use education as a primary tool for improving the public's health and local public health organization. Children were thought to be a particularly efficient focus for health education efforts, and several of the demonstration communities, especially the Fargo and Cattaraugus County demonstrations, invested heavily in the development of school health education programs.[11] These programs often followed the lines urged by experts in the newly revitalized field of school health education, such as curricula focused on the formation of health habits and the measurement and charting of children's growth; demonstration organizers and school health education experts also encouraged closer connections between public clinic work, home nursing, and school teaching.

In other demonstration communities, perhaps most notably in Syracuse and in the Bellevue-Yorkville district, organizers made educating the public a central task. By the 1920s, what had been called health publicity had developed into a specialized field known as public health education or community health education. Practitioners of this art combined publicity know-how, advertising tactics, Chautauqua-style education, and techniques drawn from mass amusement and public relations. In Syracuse, residents were surrounded by a combination of publicity, boosterism, and "fretting about health" that would have been familiar to readers of Sinclair Lewis's *Arrowsmith* (1925) or *Babbitt* (1922).[12] Children paraded through the streets at lunchtime, dressed as vegetables and expressing scorn for bad health habits. When the health department and demonstration officials decided to campaign for diphtheria immunization, they recruited the Alaskan dog-sled team that had recently been anointed "health heroes" for carrying needed anti-toxin to Nome to parade through Syracuse's streets at midday. Newspapers carried regular columns on health subjects, usually written by the health commissioner or taking the form of "real-life" dialogues such as that between Mrs. Wise and Mrs. Smith. In Bellevue-Yorkville, community health education emanated from the district's health center. The health center hosted clinics, lectures, exhibits, and meetings, and provided area residents with centralized access to social service agencies and representatives.[13] Health center workers organized educational programs that would reach neighborhood residents through their workplaces, through media of interest to the largely immigrant population, through visiting nurses, and even through the Metropolitan Life Insurance Company agents who resided in the neighborhood. Movies on smallpox, influenza, and diphtheria (again, funded by the Metropolitan) offered residents health advice and guidance, as did radio programs, pamphlets, newspaper features, and the demonstration's own semi-monthly "tabloid," *Health News*.[14]

These campaigns and attempts to "educate the public about health," however, were intended to do more than encourage individuals to adopt healthier personal habits. When health officers wrote columns for the local papers, they not only provided the usual health hints about refrigeration, nutrition, and child-rearing, but also sought to interpret improvement in the community's local statistics and offer anecdotal evidence of the good works done by the demonstration and the newly strengthened health department. Public health nurses sought out residents in their homes and attempted to persuade them of the clinic's value. And demonstration officials encouraged residents to form neighborhood committees, which were meant to serve simultaneously as "the eyes, ears, and tongue of the community in watching, understanding, and interpreting the health program" and as an index of public opinion.[15] This was necessary, demonstration organizers and workers argued, if the "cooperative" relationships envisioned for local officials and voluntary agencies were to work. Physicians, teachers, local leaders and opinion-makers, and, most important, voters and taxpayers would have to adopt the mission of prevention and support the reorganized webs of local services engineered by the demonstration committees. The "most thoughtful interpreters of education in health," Dinwiddie explained, saw it not simply as a matter of disseminating facts about health or advertising the health department's services, but rather understood it to be

> the leading of individuals, singly or in groups, out of attitudes or ways of living that run counter to their own or the community's health into attitudes or ways that make for health. If this leading is educational in the highest sense the changes of attitude that result must be based on the inner conviction of the person led, as the end product of sound reasoning. . . . The fruits of this sort of education are not academic data stored in some dusty attic of the mind but a sane understanding of what makes for healthy living and an intelligent support of reasonable public policies.[16]

The demonstration, with this broad definition of community health education, would work to "[encourage and stimulate] the greatest possible local demand for a well proportioned public health program coupled with a real sense of proprietorship in it," and, in order to assist other communities interested in the same process, could "throw some light [on] the extent to which citizen participation may be secured in the actual promotion and development of local health services."[17]

Assessing the Results of Community Health Education

If the goal was to "develop a popular understanding of public health aims so that future progress in the demonstration communities will be intelligently supported by public opinion,"[18] demonstration organizers and workers needed to assess how effectively they had encouraged public sentiment, "citizen participation," "intelligent" support, and "a real sense of proprietorship." Ideally the results of community health education, like the results of the demonstrations themselves, would be measured in the most quantifiable way possible. The development of public sentiment and of a sense of proprietorship, however, was difficult to quantify, as were the results of the demonstrations themselves. The measure most often used to evaluate the demonstrations' success was the improvement in each community's score on the American Public Health Association's appraisals of local health work. Outside evaluators rated community performance based on the service provided in branches of public health work such as vital statistics and tuberculosis control, and by the late 1920s, the demonstration communities boasted two- and three-fold increases in appraisal scores.[19] Technical advisors and demonstration personnel also tried to assess community performance relative to that of neighboring, similar counties which could serve as rough "controls," or, alternatively, tried to compare the communities' mortality and morbidity rates to estimates extrapolated from the pre-demonstration period.[20]

Demonstration organizers and advisors made few concerted attempts to quantify the success of their efforts in community health education. In part, this was because proponents and practitioners of public health education generally had little insight regarding evaluation of their efforts. In the 1920s and well into the 1930s, popular health education was most often evaluated in terms of how widely and thoroughly material had been disseminated, and the demonstration personnel and local health officials followed the same lead, noting carefully how many people had attended a movie screening or a lecture, how many column-inches health topics received in newspapers, or how many copies of a particular pamphlet had been distributed. When pressed to assess what *effect* the material's contents had had, advocates of public health education often turned to anecdotal evidence—stories of particular individual attitudes changed—to establish that disseminated material had led to concrete improvement in community health. This they backed up with their own sense of the community feeling regarding public health matters, often noting an impressively positive regard for health work.

Aware that these were crude instruments for evaluating success, foundation personnel and advisors also turned to measures of public sentiment that grew naturally out of the idea that "public health is purchasable": increases in budgets and tax assessments for the demonstration communities' health departments. These increases were offered as one measure, however inexact, of community consciousness of health, for they signified to demonstration organizers that citizens had indeed become forward-thinking and had learned to participate intelligently in community affairs. For instance, by the end of its five-year demonstration, Rutherford County, Tennessee had managed to improve its health services and facilities dramatically, and the community's fiscal investment in public health served as an index of its "active interest" in building a better county:

> It should not be inferred from this that money alone has accomplished this, it was but one factor. There was the active interest of local people stimulated by a carefully planned educational program over a period of five years. There was the will to succeed, a cooperative spirit which encouraged citizens to take full advantage of the opportunities offered them. Once the usefulness of this health work became apparent to citizens through personal experience, their willingness to support through taxes was soon made manifest.[21]

But in several of the demonstration communities, the cooperative spirit suffered some setbacks; organizers and workers faced local indifference, even on the part of public officials and local professionals, or, as one account gingerly explained, demonstration-sponsored health work simply "did not always get full cooperation."[22] In 1926 and 1927, for instance, members of the Cattaraugus County Medical Society suddenly embarked on a publicity campaign of their own, attacking the demonstration and, in general, what they considered to be the pernicious "interference" of lay groups. This attack gained attention from public health leaders and representatives of organized medicine, and the Cattaraugus County demonstration became grist for national debates about the provision of preventive health services. Nevertheless, the Cattaraugus experience was later judged successful because of "the County's readiness, despite the bickering mentioned, to continue the expanded work."[23] Likewise, as the demonstrations came to their conclusion, organizers and advisors publicly expressed their sense that the demonstrations had been successful: the demonstration communities seemed to be "sold" on public health. As Milbank advisor and public health leader C.-E. A. Winslow concluded in his account of the Bellevue-Yorkville demonstration, "You cannot take away enlarged visions and widened horizons. Ignorance and superstition, once set aside, do not return to haunt us."[24]

Despite enlarged visions and widened horizons, when the time came for the demonstration communities to take over the work and expense associated with expanded preventive services, several could not or would not. Foundation executives and demonstration directors understood that there would be some slippage in community health services below demonstration levels in the years immediately afterward. The Depression exacerbated already bad conditions in rural areas, and a great many of the demonstration communities made extensive cuts in their health department budgets. Annoyed with and worried about this push for "false economy," Commonwealth Fund executive director Barry C. Smith again made recourse, now less gracefully, to the need for community health education in the demonstration communities. In a statement revealing of how foundation officials sometimes perceived the communities they sought to aid, he directed his staff to find out more about "educational lines in the way of seeing to it that the general public has rubbed under its nose the tangible results of the health work, the reasons for those results, and the importance of adequate expenditure to maintain it."[25]

Conclusion

For the Commonwealth and the Milbank, then, teaching the people how to live healthier lives and creating a public appreciative and supportive of public health work were mutually reinforcing goals. The foundations and their advisors often alluded to a greater goal, as well: the building of better communities. The message sent by the demonstrations, said one observer of the Commonwealth's work in Fargo, was that "the successful demonstration . . . is based on common sense organization and administration and the

Golden Rule applied to public relationships."[26] Milbank advisor Winslow, in a chapter titled "The Gospel of the Good Neighbor," concluded that good district health service was actually a form of "organized neighborliness."[27] In the rationally organized community, where needs and priorities were determined by scientific evaluation and met through expert assistance and local cooperation, improved public health was but one manifestation of better times to come.

The foundations' drive to educate communities about health and about the nature of community is not surprising, given foundations' attempts to encourage what they casually referred to as "intelligent" civic participation in the many other aspects of public life. Just as they expected communities to use the building of new schoolhouses as a spur to further enlightened action in support of public education, they expected demonstration communities to take heed and then take initiative in the pursuit of public health. Or as Syracuse's model citizen Mrs. Wise explained to her not-yet-wise neighbor Mrs. Smith: "It's up to you and me to get acquainted with the doctors and nurses, visit [the demonstration's] offices, read everything written about it, and ask questions. . . . "[28] But no matter how firmly the Commonwealth encouraged residents of Fargo, Salem, and the other demonstration communities to take responsibility for local health services, and no matter how earnestly Milbank workers reminded themselves not to impose their ideas on the locals, these "educational" experiments in civic enlightenment were meant to be just that: enlightenment. This cooperative partnership was still a hierarchical relationship, the success of which depended on the locals' recognizing the inherent wisdom of cooperation. When the demonstration communities seemed prepared to embark on measures of "false economy," foundation sponsors and demonstration experts sought to promote their idea of public health through education yet again—to "sell" communities (and by implication a nation of observers) once again on the wisdom of an investment in prevention.

The natural question for us might be whether there were alternatives to this hierarchical relationship that also could have helped improve public health. Advocates of community health education continued to struggle for a long time (as they do today) with the hierarchical relationship between expert educators and their publics. As the Cattaraugus County debates suggested, there certainly were alternative visions of *prevention* available besides those being "sold" by demonstration organizers, supporters, and workers. When the Commonwealth's and the Milbank's cadre of experts and community-builders sketched plans for health promotion and the provision of preventive services, they had a very particular ideal community in mind. Here an enlightened local citizenry (meaning middle- and upper-middle class) would be led by cooperative professionals and "wide-awake" civic leaders and—through an integrated network of lay, voluntary, and unofficial agencies and with the aid of receptive local physicians—would support the work of an expanded health department; this ideal health department's efforts to reach individuals would be channeled largely through clinics, schools, public health nurses, and publicity materials, and its persuasive, neighborly authority would show the working- or lower-class residents of the community the immediate virtues of prevention. While many public health leaders agreed on the basic contours of this ideal, others committed to prevention did not. The American Medical Association, for instance, had a different view of how preventive health services might be organized. Their vision put the individual private practitioner and the medical profession's leadership at center stage, and they tenaciously sought to defend that physician-centered vision. The debates about these visions of prevention and the role of community health education in them would grow only more strident in the decade that followed.

Notes

This paper is a revised version of a paper I gave at the Center for the Study of American Culture and Education, New York University, June 1995. My thanks to the audience at that workshop and to Jennifer Gunn, Charles Rosenberg, and Janet Tighe for their questions, comments, and suggestions, some of which I have addressed in this version. This paper also summarizes the research and conclusions that form part of Chapter Five of my dissertation, "Managing the Conduct of the Individual Life: Public Health Education and American Public Health, 1910–1940" (University of Pennsylvania, 1998).

1. "What Is a Health Demonstration, Mrs. Wise?" *Syracuse Post-Standard*, n.d., mid-1920s, as cited in Louise Franklin Bache, *Health Education in an American City: An Account of a Five-Year Program in Syracuse, New York* (Garden City, N.Y.: Doubleday, Doran, 1934), 104–105.

2. "Public health is purchasable. Within natural limitations a community can determine its own death-rate." This phrase, coined by New York City Health Commissioner and elder statesman of public health Hermann M. Biggs, appeared on the October 1911 issue of the New York City Health Department's *Monthly Bulletin*. It became the Department's motto and was widely quoted by other health officers, workers, and writers. C.-E. A. Winslow, *The Life of Hermann M. Biggs, M.D., D.Sc., LL.D., Physician and Statesman of the Public Health* (Philadelphia: Lea & Fabiger, 1929), 230–31.

3. John Ettling, *The Germ of Laziness: Rockefeller Philanthropy and Public Health in the New South* (Cambridge, Mass.: Harvard University Press, 1981); also William A. Link, *The Paradox of Southern Progressivism, 1880–1930* (Chapel Hill: University of North Carolina Press, 1992), 142–59.

4. The Metropolitan Life Insurance Company undertook the Framingham Demonstration with the National Tuberculosis Association. Louis I. Dublin, *A Family of Thirty Million: The Story of the Metropolitan Life Insurance Company* (New York: Metropolitan Life Insurance Company, 1943), ch. 20, and Marquis James, *The Metropolitan Life: A Study in Business Growth* (New York: Viking, 1947), ch. 13. Framingham was

not the Metropolitan's only demonstration, although it certainly received the most press. The company also funded demonstrations in Thetford Mines, Quebec and Kingsport, Tennessee. The Commonwealth Fund and the Rockefeller Foundation also invested in Kingsport; see Peter Buck, "Why Not the Best? Some Reasons and Examples from Child Health and Rural Hospitals," *Journal of Social History* 18 (1985): 423–25.

5. The Milbank's programs were apparently more directly influenced by Framingham than were those of the Commonwealth. Not only did accounts of the Milbank demonstrations cite Framingham as the demonstrations' most notable antecedent, but three of the Metropolitan's leaders who were crucially involved in the Framingham demonstration (Lee K. Frankel, Louis I. Dublin, and Donald B. Armstrong) were on the Milbank's Advisory Council for its demonstrations. The Metropolitan also lent assistance to the Commonwealth's and the Milbank's demonstration activities, often by volunteering its agency force for local activities; see below.

6. C.-E. A. Winslow, *A City Set on a Hill: The Significance of the Health Demonstration at Syracuse, New York* (Garden City, NY: Doubleday, Doran, 1934), 62. The Milbank's *Annual Report* for 1923 described the demonstrations' purpose as being "To demonstrate by cooperation with three typical communities, embracing a population of half a million people, whether, by intensive application of known health measures, the extent of sickness in the United States can be further and materially diminished and mortality rates further and substantially reduced, and whether or not such practical results can be achieved in a relatively short period of time and at a per capita cost which communities will willingly bear." Quoted in *Milbank Memorial Fund: Thirty-Five Years in Review* (New York: Milbank Memorial Fund, 1940), 15.

7. Clyde V. Kiser, *The Milbank Memorial Fund: Its Leaders and Its Work, 1905–1974* (New York: Milbank Memorial Fund, 1975), 36.

8. Buck, "Why Not the Best?" 415–17.

9. A site visit report from the middle 1920s was typical: "My general impression of the demonstration was that it is doing thorough work under pretty good organization, but from my brief observation the difficulties seem almost insurmountable." [Barbara Quin?], "Memorandum re: Visit to Murfreesboro Child Health Demonstration," [n.d., probably 1925], p. 4, in Folder 39, Box 3, Child Health Demonstrations Series, Commonwealth Fund Archives, Rockefeller Archive Center, North Tarrytown, New York (hereafter RAC).

10. There is a substantial primary literature describing the demonstrations. Besides the large numbers of journal articles that came out of the demonstrations and the segments of the foundations' annual reports devoted to the demonstrations, both the Commonwealth and the Milbank chronicled and assessed each demonstration experience in books. On the Commonwealth's demonstrations, see *Five Years in Fargo: Report of the Commonwealth Fund Child Health Demonstration in Fargo, North Dakota* (New York: Commonwealth Fund, 1929); *A Chapter of Child Health: Report of the Commonwealth Fund Child Health Demonstration in Clarke County and Athens, Georgia, 1924–1928* (New York: Commonwealth Fund, 1930); Harry S. Mustard, *Cross-Sections of Rural Health Progress: Report of the Commonwealth Fund Child Health Demonstration in Rutherford County, Tennessee, 1924–1928* (New York: Commonwealth Fund, 1930); Estella Ford Warner and Geddes Smith, *Children of the Covered Wagon: Report of the Commonwealth Fund Child Health Demonstration in Marion County, Oregon, 1925–1929* (New York: Commonwealth Fund, 1930); and Courtenay Dinwiddie, *Child Health and the Community: An Interpretation of Cooperative Effort in Public Health* (New York: Commonwealth Fund, 1931). The Milbank asked Demonstration Advisory Council member, long-time demonstration advocate, and noted public health leader C.-E. A.

Winslow to write accounts of its demonstrations, and he produced *Health on the Farm and in the Village: A Review and Evaluation of the Cattaraugus County Health Demonstration with Special Reference to Its Lessons for Other Rural Areas* (New York: Macmillan, 1931); *A City Set on a Hill*; and with Savel Zimand, *Health under the "El": The Story of the Bellevue-Yorkville Health Demonstration in Mid-Town New York* (New York: Harper, 1937).

11. On children as an efficient focus for educational/preventive work, see the *Second Annual Report of the Commonwealth Fund* (New York: Commonwealth Fund, 1920), 15 and the *Eighth Annual Report of the Commonwealth Fund*, (New York: Commonwealth Fund, 1926), 17. See also Dinwiddie, *Child Health and the Community*. On school health education in Fargo, see Maud Brown, *Teaching Health in Fargo* (New York: Commonwealth Fund, 1929); also Sally Lucas Jean to Courtenay Dinwiddie, 13 April 1927, p. 6, in Folder 19 ("Child Health Demonstration Committee"), Box 1, Sally Lucas Jean Papers, Southern Historical Collection, Wilson Library, the University of North Carolina at Chapel Hill. Jean, a noted health-education consultant (to the Metropolitan Life Insurance Company and several other agencies) and Commonwealth Fund Demonstration Committee member, pronounced the Fargo school health program "the best one I have had the privilege of witnessing. . . . " For Cattaraugus County's health programs, see Ruth E. Grout, ed., *Handbook of Health Education: A Guide for Teachers in Rural Schools* (Garden City, NY: Doubleday, Doran, 1936), a widely lauded textbook based on health teaching and curricula developed in Cattaraugus County under Milbank sponsorship.

12. *Arrowsmith* features a sharp parody of early-twentieth-century public health education, describing how Almus Pickerbaugh, health officer of Nautilus, "started in January with a Better Babies Week, and very good Week it was, but so hotly followed by Banish the Booze Week, Tougher Teeth Week, and Stop the Spitter Week that people who lacked his vigor were heard groaning, 'My health is being ruined by all this fretting about health.'" Sinclair Lewis, *Arrowsmith* (New York: Penguin, 1980), 214.

13. George Rosen, "The First Neighborhood Health Center Movement: Its Rise and Fall," in Judith Walzer Leavitt and Ronald L. Numbers, eds., *Sickness and Health in America*, 2nd ed., rev. (Madison: University of Wisconsin Press, 1985), 483–84. Rosen notes that the Bellevue-Yorkville Health Demonstration was one of the successful programs (the East Harlem Health Center was another) that spurred New York City's adoption of the district health-center plan.

14. The Metropolitan Life Insurance Company's extensive cooperation with both the Milbank's and the Commonwealth's demonstrations owed much to the company's long-standing commitment to public health work, as well as the concrete relationships between both foundations and Metropolitan executives Lee K. Frankel, Louis I. Dublin, and Donald B. Armstrong. See, for example, "Bellevue-Yorkville Health Demonstration," Box 11, Lee K. Frankel Papers, American Jewish Historical Society, Waltham, Massachusetts.

15. Dinwiddie, *Child Health and the Community*, 48. On the strategies used in specific demonstration communities, see Dinwiddie, *Child Health and the Community*, ch. 4 ("The Demonstrations and Public Opinion"); Bache, *Health Education in an American City*; and Winslow, *Health on the Farm* (esp. ch. 16), *City Set on a Hill* (esp. ch. 12), and Winslow and Zimand, *Health under the "El"* (esp. ch. 8).

16. Dinwiddie, *Child Health and the Community*, 46.

17. *Eighth Annual Report of the Commonwealth Fund*, 24 and 25.

18. *Eleventh Annual Report of the Commonwealth Fund* (New York: Commonwealth Fund, 1929), 31.

19. The Appraisal Form for City Health Work and the Appraisal Form for Rural Health Work, prepared and revised by the American Public Health Association's Committee on Administrative Practice, were commonly used in the 1920s and 1930s.

20. On the Milbank demonstrations, see Winslow, *Health on the Farm*, ch. 14 ("Statistical Results of the Demonstration") and ch. 16 ("Psychological Reactions to the Demonstration"); *City Set on a Hill*, ch. 17 ("The Balance Sheet") and ch. 18 ("Is It Worth While?"); *Health under the "El"*, ch. 11 ("Costs and Results"); on the Commonwealth demonstrations, see for instance Dinwiddie, *Child Health and the Community*, 29–31 and ch. 4.

21. W. F. Walker, "Survey of Public Health Activities, Rutherford County, Tennessee, 1923–1928," p. 3 and insert, Folder 48, Box 3, Child Health Demonstrations Series, Commonwealth Fund Archives, RAC.

22. Kiser, *The Milbank Memorial Fund*, 38–39.

23. Ibid., 33. When demonstration advisor and advocate C.-E. A. Winslow prepared his account of the Cattaraugus demonstration, he grouped a summary of the 1927 crisis, a study of the local press's health coverage, the "impressions" of experts and participants, and a brief (five question) survey of taxpayers' attitudes toward the demonstration in a final chapter called "Psychological Reactions to the Health Demonstration." His conclusion was that although Cattaraugus County taxpayers were conservative, they had been sold on the demonstration; the activities of the local physicians in 1927, he suggested, were perhaps a result of psychological resistance and resentment. Winslow, *Health on the Farm*, ch. 16.

24. Winslow, *Health under the "El,"* 198.

25. Barry C. Smith to Barbara Quin, 10 August 1932, p. 2, in Folder 37, Box 3, Sub-series 1 (General Files, Part 2), Series IV4B4.Ph (Division of Public Health), Commonwealth Fund Archives, RAC.

26. Review of *Five Years in Fargo*, p. 3, in Folder 30, Box 2, Sub-series 1 (General Files, Part 2), Series IV4B4.Ph (Division of Public Health), Commonwealth Fund Archives, RAC.

27. Winslow, *Health under the "El,"* 155.

28. "What Is a Health Demonstration, Mrs. Wise?" as cited in Bache, *Health Education in an American City*, 104–105.

6 Constructing the Normal Child

The Rockefeller Philanthropies and the Science of Child Development, 1918–1940

Julia Grant

In an address to the Conference on Research in Child Development in 1927, Leslie Ray Marston speculated: "In the very success of the childward movement is the grave danger that the demand from various quarters . . . will so far exceed the supply provided by the slow processes of research that the movement will escape the bounds of fact and wander off into the alluring jungle of easy generalization and over-confident dogmatism. Science is asked to point the way where as yet there is no way."[1] The slow process of accumulating knowledge about children in contrast with the proliferation of child welfare and parent education programs troubled both child developmentalists and foundation professionals alike. Child psychologist Robert Sears acknowledged the social origins of his profession in 1975, when he asserted, "Child development is a product of social needs that had little to do with science qua science."[2] The emergence of child development as a research specialty, claiming grant monies and institutional housing in universities, was due in part to the lobbying efforts and activities of mothers, educators, and social reformers, who demanded that information be created and disseminated that would assist parents in raising healthy, law abiding, and well-adjusted citizens. However, while reformers of the 1920s assumed that the creation and dissemination of knowledge about children could be accomplished simultaneously, child researchers and foundation executives of the 1930s became increasingly skeptical about the aim of dissemination and instead focused on the more narrowly defined aim of basic research in child growth and development.

What follows is an account of the role of the Rockefeller philanthropies in contributing to the creation of the profession and science of child development during the 1920s and 1930s. The history of the Rockefeller's philanthropic activities in this arena sheds light on the emergence of child development as a science, the relationship of science to reform, and the trajectory of child welfare reforms. The foundation's initial interest in children may be categorized under the term "child welfare," a major reform movement during and after World War I that focused on improving the health and well-being of American children. The second emphasis, parent education, was a central feature of the charity's agenda during the 1920s, when widespread angst about the problems of parenting spurred many educational ventures. The first two phases of the foundation's work were directly related to the grassroots reform activities of club women and other advocates of social change. During the third and final phase of this work during the 1930s, foundation officials focused on supporting basic research in child growth and development and were less enthralled with the notion of utilizing knowledge for the purposes of societal reform.

From Amelioration to Prevention: The Laura Spelman Rockefeller Memorial

The child development program was housed in three separate Rockefeller philanthropies during the course of its existence. From its founding in 1918 through 1929, the Laura Spelman Rockefeller Memorial (LSRM)—one of five independent corporations under the rubric of the Rockefeller Foundation—was the unit charged with funding child study and welfare programs. With the brilliant Beardsley Ruml and Lawrence K. Frank orchestrating the unit's activities and with a clear mission to advance and disseminate knowledge about children, the LSRM provided the institutional support and structures essential to establishing the profession of child development. The LSRM was dismantled in 1929 and existing programs continued to be supported by the Spelman Fund, which gradually diminished its commitments to child study during the 1930s. From 1931–36, the General Education Board continued to sponsor research in child growth and development, under the leadership of Lawrence Frank. Frank resigned from the Foundation in 1936, and the program in child growth and development was terminated in 1940. By this time, child development had obtained respectability as a subject of academic inquiry but was no longer singled out for special attention by the Rockefeller philanthropies.[3]

The LSRM's child development program was guided by two remarkable men who were both sharply attuned to the latest trends in social scientific research and adept at converting fashionable ideas into permanent institutions. Hired as director of the LSRM 1921, Beardsley Ruml had a Ph.D. in psychology from the University of Chicago, where he had studied under pioneer psychologist James Angell. As the new director, Ruml's task was to discern how best to utilize funds that had previously been dispensed haphazardly in order to achieve long-lasting results in social welfare. He determined that ameliorative programs, aimed at treating the symptoms of social problems, were shortsighted at best. What was needed, Ruml hypothesized, was a science of social welfare that might point the way to the prevention of social problems in the future. He argued, "All who work toward the general end of social welfare are embarrassed by the lack of that knowledge which the social sciences must provide." Ruml aimed to utilize foundation monies in the service of establishing a science of society, which would be as impartial and respectable as that of engineering or physics.[4] Toward this end he moved the LSRM in the direction of sponsoring university-based research in the social sciences and assisted in the establishment of such institutions as the Social Science Research Council. That the LSRM's efforts were instrumental in bringing the social sciences into the mainstream of university research was attested by University of Chicago's chancellor Robert Hutchins, who claimed in 1929: "The LSRM in its brief but brilliant career did more than any other agency to promote the social sciences in the United States."[5]

Shortly after he had taken over the directorship of the LSRM, Ruml hired Lawrence Frank as his second-in-command. Frank had studied economics at Columbia University, where he had his first encounter with social problems when he conducted a study of mortality in the Lower West Side of New York. Although Frank did not have an advanced degree in the social sciences, he was widely read, had a probing mind, and was a close friend of a number of leading intellectual figures, including the progressive educator Lucy Sprague Mitchell and anthropologist Margaret Mead. Frank spent the remainder of his life advancing the cause of utilizing social-science research toward the betterment of human existence. Frank was somewhat of an intellectual gadfly, and his academic passions were usually in sync with the advance guard of progressive thinkers in the social sciences. However, Frank was not only an idea person; he had the ability to initiate and sustain institutional structures to support his visions. When Ruml asked Frank how the LSRM might expend approximately $1 million on behalf of children, Frank went to work at devising a multi-faceted program of child study and parent education.[6] During the term of his leadership at the philanthropy, Frank proved his ability to sniff out intriguing lines of inquiry; court and mentor talented social scientists, educators, and reformers; and bring together diverse constituencies to forge a new interdisciplinary field of endeavor.

The achievements of the LSRM in the arena of child development were substantial. The philanthropy provided funds and direction for all of the major institutes of child research, including the Iowa Child Welfare Research Station, the University of Minnesota Child Welfare Research Station, the Institute of Child Welfare at Teachers College, the Yale Clinic of Child Development, the Merrill-Palmer Motherhood and Home Training School, and the University of California Child Welfare Institute; funded the newly established Society for Research in Child Development; granted fellowships to graduate and post-graduate students in child development and parent education; and inaugurated the popular *Parents' Magazine,* to name a few of its more enduring achievements. Frank was also responsible for constructing a broad-based program of parent education in conjunction with the research programs and institutions that the Memorial sponsored. During the period of the LSRM's largesse, historian of psychology Emily Cahan notes, child development was transformed into a full-fledged profession, "complete with professional societies, journals, and university-based research and training centers."[7]

Organized in 1918 and named after the late wife of John D. Rockefeller, the LSRM's initial mission was to fund programs related to the needs of women and children. During the early years of the organization, "child welfare" dominated the philanthropic agenda—which, in this context, referred to reform movements aimed at improving children's health and well-being. Among the initial organizations funded were the East Harlem Health Center, the Maternity Center Association of Manhattan, and the American Child Health Association. These organizations were participants in a nationwide child health campaign directed at reducing infant mortality and improving the physical condition of the nation's poor children. Drawing on the volunteer work of cadres of club women, the campaign promoted birth registrations, well-baby health examinations, maternal instruction in infant care, and the distribution of bacteria-free milk through milk stations. Clinics were also established to diagnose and correct children's nutritional deficiencies, and visual and hearing impairments, and to provide intelligence and psychological testing when necessary. The child health movement was bolstered by reports that American army recruits for World War I were in terrible physical and mental condition. The campaign was also inspired by the need to diagnose and treat young children's physical and mental impairments so that they would be more easily integrated into the expanding public school system.[8]

By the mid-1920s, foundation workers were having doubts about the fruitfulness of the programs they had been funding. Upon assuming leadership of the LSRM, Ruml had decided to restrict funding for social welfare programs that merely addressed the symptoms of social problems and to instead focus on attacking the underlying causes of such problems through systematic and impartial research. Ruml requested that Frank examine the programs for children that the LSRM had been funding with this end in mind. Frank's review of the programs suggested that few were able to show any concrete achievements. A document on "child welfare" circulated in 1925 noted that many of the foundation's child-saving efforts thus far had consisted of diagnosing and remedying children's "handicaps" and "defects," many of which might "be attributed to the parents who, through ignorance, misunderstanding, timidity and neglect have failed to give their children that wholesome regime, the lack of which makes necessary these many child welfare programs."[9]

Thus it was parents who did not discharge their duties responsibly who were to blame for many child welfare problems. It was not enough to fund child welfare clinics if the mothers did not carry through with the instructions dispensed by pediatricians and nutritionists.[10] Frank and Ruml hypothesized that a joint program of child study and parent education could serve the purpose of both creating and disseminating the knowledge that was essential to good parenting. While acknowledging that existing knowledge on child development was "fragmentary . . . inaccessible and in some measure unintelligible to the average parent," they intended to fund organizations to prepare accessible materials on child care for parents, and promote educational activities for mothers in the form of groups and classes in parent education.[11] In time, Frank and Ruml hoped that the "home as a child welfare agency will tend increasingly to reduce this need for specialized remedial services." Imbued with the scientific utopianism that many of their peers in the social sciences shared during this era, the two program officers envisioned that child study and parent education might eliminate the need for child welfare entirely in the future.[12]

Yet parents could not apply knowledge of child development to their work in the home if accurate information did not yet exist. Thus, Frank put in place a two-tiered program of child study and parent education that both supported basic research in children's growth and development and simultaneously sought to involve university-based researchers, public educators, and club women in the task of disseminating child care knowledge to American parents. His aim was to pursue the "advancement of research" and the "diffusion of knowledge" concurrently.[13] With the financial support of the LSRM and state and federal tax monies, the child welfare institutes inaugurated at Teachers' College, Yale University, University of Minnesota, University of Iowa, and the University of California at Berkeley, provided institutional spaces for furthering the new science of child development.

The tension between the aims of research and diffusion were apparent from the very beginning, however. While LSRM-sponsored research was expected to contribute to improved parenting practices in the home, researchers commonly tried to put some distance between their work and the betterment of society. As a means of furthering scientific research on children, for instance, the LSRM funded the Committee on Child Development in 1925, which was initially an outgrowth of the National Research Council's Division of Anthropology and Psychology. The first professional organization for child developmentalists, the Committee would resurface as the Society for Research in Child Development in 1934. According to historian Alice Boardman Smuts, organizers tried valiantly to dissociate the work of the organization from anything which might smack of "child welfare or parent education activities." The head of the Iowa Child Welfare Institute and one of the original committee members, Bird Baldwin, insisted, "We are concerned with a scientific analysis of the fundamental scientific problems underlying childhood rather than with formulating remedial measures or outlining methods of training." Yet in his role as leader of the Institute, Baldwin was also responsible for administering parent education programs. Baldwin's plight mirrored that of many other researchers in child development who owed their jobs and grant monies to those who wished them to put their research in the service of reform. But the scientific imperative of impartiality remained a seductive ideal that would continue to infuse the research being carried out in such venues.[14]

Normalcy and Nursery Schools:
Child Development Research in the 1920s

While Progressive Era social scientists had been fixated on "abnormal" children—whether they were juvenile delinquents, mentally retarded, disabled, or suffering from the effects of poverty—Frank and his colleagues agreed that the time had come to accumulate knowledge of the so-called normal child and child rearing. They planned to determine which child-rearing practices were most effective in producing normal children, to provide the resources to craft what Ruml termed a "coordinated technique of child nurture." Ruml stated the objective of the program in these terms: "This is a scientific program which appeals to the research workers because at present available data on child growth are based on children who come with all the sins of their parents' omission and commission. No one knows therefore what norms of wholesome development may be so that these studies will be pioneer work. . . . Here is indeed a remarkable case where the objective of scientific research coincides with the needs and desires of the people generally."[15] That is, the children who had been the subject of previous child welfare efforts were, for the most part, suffering from poverty, and could not provide physicians and pediatricians with guidelines for normal development. The needs and desires of which the memo spoke were those of the broad middle class of American parents who sought greater knowledge about how to care for and assess the development of their children. These children could only be evaluated against the standard of a child who was not suffering from environmental or physical handicaps. Therefore, the vast majority of research studies inaugurated at this time took their bearings from the concept of the "normal" child.

The primary venue for the study of normal children was in scientific nursery schools, which were organized in tandem with the child welfare institutes and university child study programs that the LSRM funded during the 1920s. While there were few widely accepted theories of childhood at this time, all of the major theories—from psychoanalysis to behaviorism—suggested that the first six years of life were most critical in contributing to children's physical and emotional well-being. More concrete studies of young children were needed in order to test such theories and to provide data on the growth, development, and behavior of young children. Educational reformers had been returning from England with stories of the positive impact of philanthropic nursery schools on young children. Researchers and educators in child development seized on the concept of the nursery school as a venue for studying children in conjunction with child welfare institutes.[16]

Thus most early nursery schools were formulated expressly for the purpose of serving as laboratories for child development research. The Iowa Child Welfare Research Station claimed that its preschool was established "primarily for the purpose of bringing together for scientific study groups of normal children between the ages of two and five years, to be observed under controlled conditions. Coincidentally, an attempt is made to offer a favorable environment for maximum development of the child."[17] Although nursery school proponents soon began to testify to the educational and social benefits that children gained in such settings, research remained a central rationale for university-based nursery schools. In scientific nursery schools researchers observed, measured and tested children, seeking to generate data with which they might test theories about children and construct norms of child development. At the same time, through their educational practices, teachers tested techniques for rearing and caring for children.

In nursery schools, researchers aimed to acquire data about the development of "normal" children; however, researchers had a priori notions of what constituted a normal child.. The Iowa nursery school contended that "Only children of normal development are accepted," even before they had accurate knowledge of the parameters of normal development, based on a more random sample than nursery school attendees, who were overwhelmingly white, middle-class, and native born.[18] Children were carefully screened for developmental abnormalities prior to admittance, and most schools would not accept children who were diagnosed as having a low IQ or a physical disability. The educators of the Merrill-Palmer Institute nursery school in Detroit claimed that they would admit "any child who can walk and who is moderately well trained for the toilet . . . provided he is approximately normal mentally and physically." But they also refused to accept African-American children and had a quota for Jewish children.[19]

Almost all of the nursery schools affiliated with the institutes were limited to children of the middle and upper classes, since the hours were not structured to accommodate the needs of working mothers and a fee was often involved. While the LSRM provided lavish funding to set up university and college-based nursery schools, it did not extend financial assistance to day nurseries. Although day nurseries had the potential to provide many resources for research, day-nursery children were considered to be outside the bounds of normalcy by virtue of the fact that they came from family situations that were defined as abnormal. Just as importantly, day nurseries were considered to be service institutions and were judged to be remedial rather than preventive. Any research to be accomplished in such a setting would be secondary.[20]

Bringing Science to the People: Parent Education in the Early Years

It is clear from the new direction of the Memorial's programs that Frank and his peers were becoming more interested in children's mental hygiene than in children's physical health. As children's health improved, problems of children's behavior began to occupy an increasingly prominent place in many parents' minds during the 1920s. Middle-class parents struggled to rear their children in the context of increased geographic mobility, smaller families, and the expanding influence of the schools, motion pictures, and peer culture on their children. Because medical science was instrumental in improving the physical well-being of American children, many intellectuals believed that psychology as a science could do much to ensure children's healthy emotional development. The behaviorist approach to psychology, particularly as espoused by the infamous John Broadus Watson, had much to do with investing the discipline of child psychology with scientific credentials. Watson sought to prove that psychology had the potential to be as "scientific" as the natural and physical sciences. He argued that behavior was elicited primarily by external stimuli and thus was easily controllable once it was clear which stimuli elicited desirable forms of behavior.[21] Although Watson's voice was not the only one to be heard in the emerging discourse of child development, the idea that psychology was on the threshold of transforming the art of parenting into a science was an overarching paradigm. This paradigm guided the vision of Frank and his colleagues during the 1920s as they dispensed funds dedicated to both constructing the science of child psychology and simultaneously disseminating the researchers' findings to American parents.[22]

Frank sought to enlist the aid of existing women's associations in order to disseminate child development expertise to parents. Clearly he believed that women—as professionals, club women, and homemakers—should be at the forefront of what he perceived to be a social movement of the greatest magnitude. There is ample evidence that American club women of the 1910s and 1920s were already "child-centered." Club women had agitated for the establishment of the U.S. Children's Bureau, lobbied for the Sheppard-Towner Act, and flocked to organizations such as the PTA, which placed children at the center of its efforts. Even an organization that had been founded on the notion of gaining women access to the classical education traditionally reserved for men—the American Association of University Women—elevated child study to an important place in its platform during the 1920s. That many mothers experienced a felt need for assistance in child care is suggested by the voluminous correspondence directed to the officials of the U.S. Children's Bureau, where poor urban, rural, and middle-class women alike spoke of the dearth of services, information, and support for the work of mothering. Unsure as to how to raise their children in a rapidly changing society, many women sought answers to the complex problems of mothering in professional expertise. The growing numbers of women who had received college educations contributed to the appeal of parent education, as many women sought to combine their intellectual interests with their everyday pursuits as mothers.[23]

Frank was quite cognizant of the growing appeal of parent education for middle-class mothers. He theorized that club women would eagerly participate in parent education activities and would be a positive force in their communities by furthering the "gospel of child development," in historian Steven Schlossman's apt terminology. With this in mind, he met with numerous leaders of women's organizations—such as the Child Study Association of America, the American Association of University Women, the PTA, and the American Home Economics Association of America—in order to discuss funding their organizations for work in parent education. The leaders were distinctly enthusiastic and with the use of the LSRM's monies conducted campaigns for parent education from within their organizations, developing popular reading materials for parents, organizing conferences on parent education, and setting up numerous clubs and classes for mothers throughout the nation. Although Frank's ostensible aim was to improve the well-being of children, he was also conscious of filling a need for women to find an accommodation between their increasing levels of education and their work as mothers in the home.[24]

Frank was not content, however, to place parent education solely in the hands of unpaid and presumably inexpert club women. He foresaw the possibility of utilizing the federal funds provided by the Smith-Lever (1914) and Smith-Hughes (1917) acts for extension work in home economics as a means of disseminating child development expertise to American families. This legislation mandated that educational funds that had been traditionally earmarked to educate primarily male farmers would also be utilized to educate rural women. Frank was especially intrigued by the possibility of making use of the rapidly growing network of home-demonstration agents working in rural areas with the Agricultural Extension Service. Several of the major LSRM-funded child welfare institutes—California, Iowa, and Minnesota—also had well-developed networks of extension educators working at the universities where the institutes were housed. Cornell University, whose College of Home Economics also received substantial funding from the LSRM, already had an active extension program associated with the College. The agents were engaged in organizing and educating local homemakers and dispensing information about a variety of female enterprises from sewing to gardening. With proper training, Frank reasoned, they could also function as parent educators. By providing seed money for child development projects in states with major land-grant universities and established extension services, the LSRM might ensure parent education's future sponsorship by state educational institutions.[25] Such a plan provided obvious benefits for home economists, who envisioned greater professional possibilities and societal influence for themselves as leaders in parent education.

Unlike many scientists involved in the creation of the institutes, Frank saw a distinct role for home economists in distributing knowledge about children to American homemakers. However, the growing interest of home economists in child development was met with skepticism by male academics who were reluctant to ally themselves with such an undeniably female discipline. Some of the male psychologists who staffed the child research institutes feared that the association of parent education with home economics would subvert their efforts to elevate the prestige of child development research. Bird Baldwin at the Iowa Child Welfare Research Station was said to have complained to his colleagues, "Why are the Home Economics people trying to break into this field of child study and parent education?" And Harold Jones, an important behavioral psychologist at the California Institute of Child Welfare, complained to Frank that they were "getting a little too much cooperation from Household Science."[26]

Child developmentalists were still struggling to be recognized as legitimate scientists within the disciplines of psychology and medicine, and they feared that connections with a gendered discipline such as home economics would "taint" their efforts. Home economists, on the other hand, stood to gain prestige by affiliating with disciplines consisting primarily of men. However, they knew of the fears of their male colleagues in the social sciences, and in their exchanges with them underscored that home economists were primarily to be the disseminators rather than the producers of information in the behavioral sciences. Flora Rose, who jointly directed Cornell's College of Home Economics with Martha Van Renssalaer, addressed the concerns of social and behavioral scientists that home economists might be encroaching on their professional turf: "Just as physics, chemistry or economics are taught in other departments at the university and application made in home economics, so also application is made in the College of Home Economics with reference to environmental conditions in the governing of family life with special reference to children."[27] Thus, as a tactic to ensure themselves a place in the burgeoning child development movement, home economists yielded to the growing division of labor between the producers of knowledge, who were generally male, and those who applied it, who were most often women.

Although the alliance between home economics and child development was not without problems, home economists were successful in their efforts to provide educational opportunities for rural and small town mothers in states such as Minnesota, Iowa, New York, and California. Parent education leaders were constantly complaining that they could not begin to meet the demand of mothers' groups for leaders, speakers, and reading materials. But while both home economics extension workers and child welfare institute personnel could agree on the need to develop and disseminate information about children, inevitably tensions arose between researchers and disseminators, and producers and consumers of knowledge. As child development became increasingly professionalized, there was an emerging division of labor between the producers of child development expertise and those applying professional expertise. In this gendered division of labor, the scientists increasingly gained the upper hand and the research dollars. For scientists seeking to make a name for themselves in this new study of the child, the decentralization of knowledge advocated by the Frank and extension educators was somewhat problematic, given that they were not yet on sure footing in their knowledge of the child and had to contend with the intrinsic difficulties of ensuring that those who were not scientists themselves were imparting the "correct" child-rearing advice. Frank acknowledged these concerns in a memo written in 1926, the early part of the experiment: "The situation has all the dangers of boom over-enthusiasm and probably disillusioned deflation, because it is impossible to meet the public demand for knowledge and instruction. The knowledge in large measure remains to be discovered and the teachers are yet to be trained."[28] Yet while child developmentalists benefited from the research dollars afforded them at the new institutes and the study of children began to acquire some real scientific moorings, parent education progressed as well, although its actual benefits were not very closely tied to the research work being carried on at the various institutes.

Perhaps what was most significant about these programs was the philosophy of progressive education that informed them, the ways in which the participants commingled their everyday experiences as parents in the home with the expertise that was supplied to them. Because the extension service was decentralized and lacked sufficient numbers of trained personnel, lay women were responsible for organizing and directing most groups. As a result, women developed their leadership skills and groups served the purpose of assessing, rather than merely disseminating, expert advice. The participants frequently expressed their gratitude for the opportunity to utilize their intellects in a setting where women's work was taken seriously and which allowed for critical reflection on both personal child-rearing practices and the professional literature. As Lilian Diane Madigan, a member of the long-lasting Bennett Study Club, phrased it: "The greatest benefit to me has been through the knowledge that every two weeks I would meet and be able to *discuss* . . . problems which were pertinent to my job!" For women who suffered from the tedium and isolation that often accompanied rural homemaking, the clubs also offered a welcome respite. A leader of a group from Hilton County, New York, wrote to a home economics instructor at Cornell who was responsible for coordinating extension education: "My furniture never was so shabby, my wardrobe so nearly exhausted nor I so happy as I am now. At one time I felt as though I was stagnating. All I seemed able to talk about was housework and babies. Child guidance was the turning point for me. Studying and reading books on psychology has given me an entirely different slant on life. My time is so occupied with worthwhile things that I don't have time to be small and petty. Things which used to make me fume and rage don't even sink under my new armor plate."[29] The volunteers who led the groups repeatedly expressed their appreciation for the training they received in leadership, the contact with other women, and the chance to do extensive reading and studying.

However, educators had not predicted the degree to which study club members would take matters into their own hands and measure expert recommendations against the yardstick of common maternal practices. A remark made by a secretary of a Cornell home bureau study club was not unrepresentative: "The comment oftenest voiced is 'Have these writers had experience with children?' The methods are so different from our former knowledge of dealing with children that some are slow to accept them."[30] Another group secretary noted that the members of her club quite staunchly clung to their own opinions when discussing the common childhood problems of nail-biting, thumb-sucking, and bedwetting: "I'm afraid it's one subject we each had our own opinions on and that we each had met the situation in the best way possible, whether or not it conformed with the text." The language of this sentence, which stresses that mothers met their problems "in the best way possible," implies that groups could serve the function of reinforcing mothers' decisions, regardless of whether or not they conformed with expert advice.[31] While undoubtedly many mothers were convinced to at least try out expert theories of child rearing as a result of club participation, members were as apt to critique as to praise expert advice, and in many cases they were able to garner support for their point of view from other club members. Thus, in practice parent education did not achieve what it had initially promised: the transformation of parenting according to new scientific principles.

Parent education had originally been based on the pedagogical premise that there was a science of child rearing to be communicated to the nation's mothers. The benefits women may have gained by participating in mothers' meetings, wherein they were accorded a venue to dissect expert recommendations and discuss their own child rearing strategies, were neither easily verifiable nor quantifiable. And few studies were able to measure the benefits that children may have derived from their parents' participation in parents' classes. More importantly, scientists and educators began questioning the shaky intellectual edifice upon which these educational programs were built. Maturationists such as Arnold Gesell challenged the behavioristic model of development by the early 1930s, suggesting that many of children's behavior problems could be attributed to their developmental stage rather than poor socialization.[32] Studies began appearing that claimed that children raised according to Watsonian premises were displaying troubling behavioral problems. An emerging clinical perspective suggested that the parents' adjustment was far more important for a child's well-being than parent education. In short, both child development and parent education were becoming increasingly pluralistic, and it was by no means clear what the content of parent education programs should be.[33] A comment by one of the committee responsible for reviewing the LSRM's child study program is suggestive of the skepticism that began to infuse parent education programs: "Do we know enough about what is desirable human behavior to instruct parents on how to produce it? Are not our own limitations through lack of knowledge so great that any program for parent education must be of elementary, fragmentary character? If we say we must know more from the social sciences before we promote active programs for improving human society, from what sanction do we derive our confidence in active promotion of parent education?"[34] With such uncertainty about the purposes and results of parent education, foundation officials gradually ceased funding educational programs. However, this did not put a halt to child study or mothers' clubs, many of which continued to flourish under the rubric of the Agricultural Extension Program, the PTA, and in other less formal venues during the interwar years.

Back to Basics: The General Education Board and Child Studies

Questions about the direction of parent education led foundation officials to increasingly focus their attention on the needs of basic research in child growth and development rather than on the more controversial program of seeking to transform parenting practices. If researchers could not yet prescribe how parents should behave, at least they could describe "normal development," with the hope that such research might have practical applications in the future. In 1936, the program in child study, now sponsored by the General Education Board, defined its work as being limited to "a few research centers to study child development at the level of infancy and prenatal development and at adolescence with the intention of tracing the various developmental sequences through the application of the different life sciences techniques."[35] But it was medicine that played the primary role in shaping the direction of the favored studies of the period, with its emphasis on distinguishing between the diseased and the healthy, and between normal and abnormal development. The major studies being supported aimed to observe the development of a representative group of children at specific intervals over a period of time in order to discern the path of normal childhood. Reams of data on children's physical, cognitive, and personality growth were collected at regular intervals by teams of researchers representing diverse disciplines, such as pediatrics, anatomy, psychology, and psychiatry. Preconceived theories of behaviorism, psychoanalysis, and learning theory were abandoned in these studies; instead, researchers sought unbiased "facts" about children's physical, emotional, and cognitive development.[36]

The longitudinal studies sponsored by the General Education Board (some of which began at the LSRM) proved to be one of the philanthropy's most long-lasting legacies to child development. Elizabeth Lomax has credited Frank with doing more to initiate longitudinal studies than any other individual.[37] Frank was deeply committed to these studies, and engaged in constant conversations with grantees to ensure that research teams were truly interdisciplinary and that researchers maintained a broad conception of the "whole child," rather than focusing on narrowly defined research questions which might yield them greater numbers of publications. He encouraged grantees to limit their publications until they had had time to come to conclusions based on a greater knowledge of the multiple dimensions of child development over time. He pleaded the cause of the Berkeley

Growth and Guidance Studies, the Denver longitudinal studies, and the Harvard Study of Child Development to foundation officials long before it was clear that concrete results would be forthcoming. The studies were expensive and time-consuming, yet Frank was optimistic that the studies would ultimately yield information that would guide pediatric and parenting practices in the future.

One of the major purposes of the studies was the establishment of norms of children's growth that would enable pediatricians to assess children's development. Frank expressed his sense of the purpose of these studies: "The differentiation between normal variations and incipient disease, or abnormal development, cannot be accurately defined until further knowledge is acquired."[38] Thus the studies were essentially descriptive and normative, but Frank hoped that they might ultimately yield predictions about the future developmental status of the children being studied. Historian of the California Institute of Child Development John A. Clausen has discussed the predictive purpose of the Berkeley growth studies in these terms: "Would early competence in handling their bodies and manipulating objects predict later verbal intelligence?" Although ostensibly seeking to discern the linkages between early childhood problems and later adult maladjustment and disease, the studies simultaneously sought to include only healthy, seemingly "normal" children in their studies as they mapped the developmental trajectory of childhood.[39]

Those conducting the studies made no secret of the fact that their conception of the "normal" child was limited by race, class, and culture, although this acknowledgment did not lead them to question the validity of the data they acquired. For instance, the architects of the Harvard Study of Child Development claimed that they would recruit "only mothers who speak English; white and native educated mothers, or [mothers who] have adjusted to American customs."[40] A report on the Denver longitudinal studies, conducted by Alfred H. Washburn, stated that the studies comprised a "rough cross-section of our Denver population with the exclusion of the lower social strata." Similarly, in a report of the Berkeley Growth Study in 1938, the authors admitted that when the study was begun in 1928, the families selected comprised only "white, English-speaking parents" who were permanent residents of Berkeley.[41]

Frank at least recognized that there were important gaps in researchers' knowledge about children due to the limited character of the research samples upon which these studies were based. Thus he attempted to establish a center for research on African-American children at Atlanta University. But in his mind and the minds of his colleagues, African-Americans were cast as other than the "normal child" that child developmentalists were constructing. In a memo on the child study program, it was noted, "Comparative investigations of different children of different racial stocks and living under different cultural conditions will be of immense value in helping to provide *contrasting material* [emphasis mine]." Research on African-American children was meant for purposes of comparison only, rather than for the purpose of providing a more inclusive conception of normalcy. In the same memo, a plea was made to establish a research center for African-American children at Atlanta University "because the pattern of growth and the rate of growth of Negroes is known to be different than that of whites." The attempt floundered, and it would be years before solid research on African-American children would enter the mainstream of child development literature.[42]

The child study work that the Rockefeller philanthropies supported had come a long way from the LSRM's initial interest in child welfare. Beginning with their support for the child health movement of the 1910s, they had next given their support to the middle-class parent education movement of the 1920s, before lending their substantial resources to the seemingly apolitical science of the normal child in the 1930s. Frank's and Ruml's belief that dissemination of knowledge to parents would have immediate and significant consequences for social welfare quickly dissipated as they discovered how much scientists did not yet know about children and parenting. In their move "back to basics" they sought to retreat from the world of reform in order to find a firmer ground upon which to stand in any educational efforts. In so doing, however, they neglected to take account of the advantages for parents in having an opportunity to assess the expert knowledge that was bombarding them in the mass media, the schools, and their physicians' offices. In fact, as we can see from the perspective of the 1990s, there is little "expert" knowledge about children and parenting that is free from ideological biases. Parent education, rightly understood, should provide opportunities for parents to evaluate professional expertise, rather than merely to imbibe it, and to instruct experts in the perspectives, philosophies, and practices of those actively engaged in parenting. Rather than fearing the consequences of the decentralization of knowledge, professionals might have benefited from the educational opportunities that parent education might have afforded *them*, in addition to allowing parents (mostly mothers) the opportunity to engage in critical thinking about their parenting practices and expert recommendations.

The loss of scientific utopianism in parent education was accompanied by a less utopianistic attitude toward the aims of research in child development. But researchers and foundation officials alike were fooling themselves when they claimed that basic research in child development was value-free. There have been significant social consequences of this research, as the norms of child development found their way into pediatricians' textbooks and the parenting manuals that were increasingly adorning the typical middle-class home. But the normal child, whose development was charted in the baby books, was the optimal child, one with an enriched home life who did not suffer from environmental and familial handicaps and who shared the racial background of the dominant class. Even middle-class white parents, for whom the science of the normal child was ostensibly created, have been haunted by the phantom of the normal child when their little darlings do not talk or walk on schedule. We continue to contribute to the discourse of the normal child when we judge the development of young children by the standards of the privileged classes. Providing medical labels for children who do not meet these standards is one way of evading the human consequences of inequality.

Notes

I am grateful for the assistance of a Spencer Postdoctoral Fellowship in completing the research for this essay.

1. Leslie Ray Marston, "Present Tendencies in Research in Child Development," paper presented at the Second Conference on Research in Child Development, Washington, D.C., 5–7 May 1927, series 3, box 31, file 328, Laura Spelman Rockefeller Memorial Papers, Rockefeller Archive Center [hereafter referred to as LSRM].

2. Robert R. Sears, "Your Ancients Revisited: A History of Child Development," *Review of Child Development Research*, vol. 5, ed. E. Mavis Hetherington (Chicago: University of Chicago Press, 1975), 4.

3. Emily D. Cahan, "Science, Practice, and Gender Roles in Early American Child Psychology," in *Contemporary Constructions of the Child: Essays in Honor of William Kessen*, ed. Frank S. Kessel, Marc H. Bornstein, and Arnold J. Sameroff (Hillsdale, N.J.: Lawrence Erlbaum Associates, 1991), 231–33. On the General Education Board's role in child development, see Raymond B. Fosdick, *Adventure in Giving: The Story of the General Education Board* (New York: Harper & Row, 1962), 259–65.

4. Raymond B. Fosdick, *The Story of the Rockefeller Foundation* (New York: Harper & Brothers, 1952), 194.

5. Fosdick, *The Story of the Rockefeller Foundation*, 200.

6. Cahan, "Science, Practice and Gender Roles," 232.

7. Steven L. Schlossman's work on the Memorial and parent education has been invaluable, especially "Philanthropy and the Gospel of Child Development," *History of Education Quarterly* 21 (Fall 1981): 275–99; "Before Home Start: Notes toward a History of Parent Education in America," *Harvard Educational Review* 46 (August 1976): 436–67; and "The Formative Era in Parent Education: Overview and Interpretation," in *Parent Education and Public Policy*, ed. Ron Haskins and Diane Adams, (Norwood, N.J.: Ablex, 1983), 7–38. Another important overview of parent education is Hamilton Cravens, "Child-Saving in the Age of Professionalism, 1915–1930" in *American Childhood: A Research Guide and Historical Handbook*, ed. Joseph Hawes and Ray Hiner (Westport,

Conn.: Greenwood, 1985), 415–81. See also Judith Sealander's chapter on the Memorial in *Private Wealth and Public Life: Foundation Philanthropy and the Reshaping of American Social Policy from the Progressive Era to the New Deal* (Baltimore: Johns Hopkins University Press, 1997). For an important history of the Iowa Child Welfare Research Station, see Hamilton Cravens, *Before Head Start: The Iowa Station and America's Children* (Chapel Hill: University of North Carolina Press, 1993).

8. For a detailed account of the infant health movement see Richard A. Meckel, *Save the Babies: American Public Health Reform and the Prevention of Infant Mortality 1850–1929* (Baltimore: Johns Hopkins University Press, 1990). See also, Sydney A. Halpern, *American Pediatrics* (Berkeley: University of California Press), 85; William J. Breen, *Uncle Sam at Home: Civilian Mobilization, Wartime Federalism, and the Council of National Defense, 1917–1919* (Westport, Conn: Greenwood, 1984), 127–28; Alisa Klaus, "Women's Organizations and the Infant Health Movement in France and the United States, 1890–1920," in *Lady Bountiful Revisited: Women, Philanthropy, and Power*, ed. Kathleen D. McCarthy (New Brunswick, N.J.: Rutgers University Press, 1990), 157–73; Marilyn Irvin Holt, *Linoleum, Better Babies and The Modern Farm Woman, 1890–1930* (Albuquerque: University of New Mexico Press, 1995), 114.

9. "Child Welfare," 17 September 1925, series 3.5, box 30, #315, LSRM; "Parent Training," 3 September 1924, series 3.5, box 30, #315, LSRM.

10. Lawrence K. Frank, "Parent Training," 26 March 1924, series 3.5, box 30, #315, LSRM.

11. Lawrence K. Frank, "Child Study and Parent Education," [n.d.], series 3.5, box 30, #316, LSRM.

12. "Child Welfare," 17 September 1925. On scientific utopianism, see Fred Matthews, "The Utopia of Human Relations: The Conflict-Free Family in American Social Thought, 1930–1960," *Journal of the History of the Behavioral Sciences* 24 (October 1988): 343–62.

13. Frank, "Child Study and Parent Education."

14. Alice Boardman Smuts, "The National Research Council Committee on Child Development and the Founding of the Society for Research in Child Development, 1925–1933," in "History and Research in Child Development," *Monographs of the Society for Research in Child Development* 50, ed. Alice Boardman Smuts and John W. Hagen (1986): 112.

15. "Child Study Program," [circa 1924], series 3.5, box 30, #315, LSRM.

16. For the fullest discussion of the history of the nursery school, see Barbara Beatty, *Preschool Education in America: The Culture of Young Children from the Colonial Era to the Present* (New Haven: Yale University Press, 1995).

17. "The State University of Iowa, Iowa City: The Preschool Laboratories, 1931," (Iowa City: State University of Iowa, 1931), 5, pamphlet in Merrill-Palmer Archives, Wayne State University Library, Detroit, Michigan.

18. "The State University of Iowa, Iowa City: The Preschool Laboratories, 1931."

19. "Annual Report—The Nursery School, 1922," box 64, file 1, Merrill-Palmer Institute Papers, Archives of Labor and Urban Affairs, Wayne State University, Detroit, Michigan. In an oral history interview of Ethel Childs Baker, the Merrill-Palmer Institute's first African-American student, she states that the first African-American child was not admitted to the nursery school until 1947. See "Oral History Interview of Ethel Childs Baker by Louise L. Brown," 25 March 1988, Archives of Labor and Urban Affairs.

20. On the nursery school movement, see Beatty, *Preschool Education in America*. On the Merrill-Palmer Institute see the organization's records at the Walther Reuther Ar-

chive of Labor and Urban Affairs, Wayne State University, Detroit, Michigan. A discussion of the unrepresentative character of the Merrill-Palmer nursery school is included in Charles A. Wilson et al., "The Merrill-Palmer Standards of Physical and Mental Growth" (Detroit: Merrill-Palmer Institute, 1930), where the authors also admit that the standards they derive from their studies are "optimal" rather than average. On day nurseries, see Elizabeth Rose, *A Mother's Job: The History of Day Care, 1890–1960* (Oxford: Oxford University Press, 1998).

21. The most influential of John B. Watson's works include *Psychological Care of Infant and Child* (New York: W. W. Norton, 1928) and *Behaviorism* (New York: W. W. Norton, 1924). On Watson and behaviorism in the 1920s, see John. M. O'Donnell, *The Origins of Behaviorism: American Psychology, 1870–1920* (New York: New York University Press, 1985); Lucille C. Birnbaum, "Behaviorism in the 1920s," *American Quarterly* 1 (Spring 1955): 15–30; and Kerry W. Buckley, *Mechanical Man: John Broadus Watson and the Beginnings of Behaviorism* (New York: Guilford Press, 1989).

22. Sealander sees behaviorism as the predominant, if not the only, paradigm guiding the Memorial's work in child study. While I agree that behaviorism's view of psychology as a "science" was central to these programs, I have found many other competing streams of psychological thinking to have been operating in parents' classes. Behaviorism, for instance, was always in tension with the developmentalism advocated by G. Stanley Hall and John Dewey, which was also featured in class curricula.

23. On the "maternalist" concerns of American club women, see especially Molly Ladd-Taylor, *Mother-Work: Women, Child Welfare, and the State, 1890–1930* (Urbana and Chicago: University of Illinois Press, 1994). On the letters to the Children's Bureau, see Molly Ladd-Taylor, *Raising a Baby the Government Way: Mothers' Letters to the Children's Bureau, 1915–1932* (New Brunswick, N.J.: Rutgers University Press, 1986).

24. On the women's club movement's role in parent education, see chapter two in my book, *Raising Baby by the Book: The Education of American Mothers, 1800–1960* (New Haven: Yale University Press, 1998). See also, Schlossman, "Before Home Start."

25. I am indebted to Steven Schlossman's "Philanthropy and the Gospel of Child Development" for this terminology. See also Schlossman's essay, "Before Home Start"; Cravens, "Child-Saving in the Age of Professionalism, 1915–1930"; and Christine Mary Shea's dissertation, "The Ideology of Mental Health and the Emergence of the Therapeutic Liberal State: The American Mental Hygiene Movement, 1900–1930" (Ph.D. diss., University of Illinois at Urbana, 1980), 294–96; Lawrence K. Frank to Mrs. Clifford Walker, 6 June 1924, series 3, box 44, #458, LSRM.

26. Lawrence K. Frank to Anna E. Richardson, 26 March 1927, series 3, box 26, #274, LSRM; Lawrence K. Frank, memo of interview with Dean Anna Richardson of School of Home Economics at Iowa, 2 March 1925, series 3, box 32, #341, LSRM; Harold Jones to Lawrence K. Frank, 28 September 1928, series 3, box 43, #452, LSRM.

27. Confidential Report of the Home Economics Conference in Albany—21 November 1929, box 2, folder 2, College of Home Economics Archives, Division of Rare and Manuscript Collections, Cornell University Library.

28. Lawrence K. Frank, "Child Study and Parent Education," 23 December 1926, series 3.5, box 30, #316, LSRM.

29. Jennie Bernhard to Margaret Wylie, 21 September 1943, in Bennett Study Club Records, Kenmore—1940–45, Margaret Wylie Collection, Cornell University Library, Division of Rare and Manuscript Collections, Cornell University Library; Mrs. Walter Quinn to Margaret Wylie, 17 November 1933, Margaret Wylie Collection.

30. School #65 PTA Child Study Club Report, 6 January 1932, Buffalo, Erie County, Margaret Wylie Collection.

31. Coldwater Child Study Club Report, 13 April 1936, Monroe County, Margaret Wylie Collection.

32. See especially Frances Ilg and Arnold Gesell, *Infant and Child in the Culture of Today* (New York: Harper & Brothers, 1943).

33. For a discussion of the changes in parent education during the 1930s, see chapter six of my *Raising Baby by the Book*.

34. S. H. Walker, "Committee on Review—Child Study and Parent Training," 10 March 1927, series 3.5, box 30, #316, LSRM.

35. Memo, Lawrence K. Frank to A. G., 3 March 1936, series 1, box 369, #3849, General Education Board.

36. Elizabeth M. R. Lomax, *Science and Patterns of Child Care* (San Francisco: W. H. Freeman, 1978), 153–54.

37. Lomax, 153.

38. "Child Study Program," 31 October 1936, series 1, box 369, #3849, General Education Board.

39. On the longitudinal studies conducted at the Institute of Child Welfare, California, including the Berkeley Growth Studies, see John A. Clausen, *American Lives: Looking Back at the Children of the Great Depression* (New York: Free Press, 1993), 30. The book is based on an analysis of the children who were the subjects of the original studies and looks at how the assessments of their personalities as children and adolescents predicted their later adult development. What is worrisome about this book is that there is no attempt made to explain or evaluate the limitations of the original studies.

40. "Purpose and Prospectus of Consecutive Study of Children in Early Life," 12 December 1930, box 372, #3881, series 1, General Education Board, Rockefeller Archive Center.

41. "Opportunities for a Liaison Between Psychiatry and Pediatrics in a Child Research Institute," Afred H. Washburn, 5 June 1935, series 1, box 370, #3857, General Education Board; Institute of Child Welfare, University of California, "The First Berkeley Growth Study," 1 May 1938, box 37, #3916, General Education Board.

42. "Child Study Program," 31 October 1936, series 1, box 369, #3849, General Education Board.

7 | Mary van Kleeck of the Russell Sage Foundation

Religion, Social Science, and the Ironies of Parasitic Modernity

Guy Alchon

"It is my prayer that every girl in college may long to say . . . 'To me to live is Christ.'"

—Mary van Kleeck, 1903

"Religion . . . is a machine for scaring."

—H. L. Mencken, 1930

"While we are quite ready, as secularists, to share in Freud's view of religion, and to treat its zealotries with contempt and disdain, almost everything Freud had to say about religion *is now true of secularism itself,* . . . partaking of precisely the same arrogance, the same irrationality and passion for certainty, the same pretense to unquestioned virtue against which its powers were once arrayed."

—Peter Marin, 1995[1]

T ODAY, NOT MUCH ATTENTION is paid to that student of American associational enthusiasm, H. L. Mencken. What Tocqueville might have been had he had a sense of humor and a taste for lager, Mencken possessed an ability to distill national truth from local detail. He found Americans an endless inspiration, and administered spankings proportionate to pretensions. Evidently still in experimental trials, "Democracy in America" was an instructive parade of frauds, half-wits, and sanctimonious "wowsers." Professors, then as now having among their number adepts of lifeless disputation, were a favorite target. Little excited Mencken more, however, than the spectacle of Americans in religious earnest. And at the close of *Treatise on the Gods,* his survey of the world's religions, he testified to the essential blessings of life among so devout a people. "As an American," he concluded, "I naturally spend most of my time laughing."[2]

A fount of reliable amusement, religion was also an elemental conspiracy against human happiness, and Mencken's rude burlesque part of the larger "modern revolt" against the dead hand of civilization. The modern insurgency, in turn, owed much to the "progress" already wrested from fate by Darwinism and the storm of material achievement that had capped the nineteenth century. The first decades of the new century roiled with a generic urge to "face facts," an enthusiasm for the real and the frank variously expressed in the birth control, scientific management, mind cure, social survey, divorce reform, and eugenic movements of the day. These and other trends apparently symbolized the displacement, the defeat, of an older genteel culture, and the emergence of a more mature, sophisticated, more modern America.[3]

This, at least, was the view once promoted by partisans, and over the intervening decades it became the predominant perspective, the self-evident "origin myth" of the American passage into modernity. The polemic against religion was an important subdivision of this story. Its chief targets were the large and still-muscular armies of evangelical Protestantism, and against them the party of the future usually framed the struggle in the stark, Manichean terms that to this day remain typical and influential.

Against the palpable achievements of science and progress, Christianity had been rendered obsolete and ridiculous, "a machine for scaring," "an organized and unquestioning belief in the palpably not true." Between tradition and progress, between the consolations of revealed faith and a world yielding to human will and mastery, little common ground was discernible. In the twentieth century, it now seemed certain, the future would liberate the present from the encumbrances of the past.[4]

Overdrawn and exaggerated, a mix of the tactical and the principled, such zero-sum formulations are perhaps best understood as promotional. The campaign for American modernity, in other words, constituted a "machinery for scaring" in its own right, the marketing of a new cultural regime, its "urgent calls for sweeping reform" announcing the triumphal entrance of a new status quo.[5]

Of course facts and urgencies are usually more stubborn and complicated than advertised. In the countercultural revolt of the early twentieth century, people were conflicted, and partisans, even Mencken, sometimes changed their minds. The story is further complicated by the sort of "parallel insurgency" launched by women such as the Russell Sage Foundation's Mary van Kleeck. Van Kleeck's life and her career in social science and at the Sage Foundation were defined not by the revolt against tradition but by an insistence upon the essentially spiritual affinities between Christian and social-science idealism. Only by synthesizing these totems of the old and the new could the material and psychic challenges posed by modernity be addressed.[6]

Van Kleeck invites, then, further consideration of things and people we thought we already knew—reform, philanthropy, and the religious heritage of social science; and besides Mencken, Willa Cather, Scott Fitzgerald, Mary Antin, and Henry James. She also invites consideration of people and matters we've never much attended to—the Christian Socialist (and van Kleeck's mentor) Vida Scudder, for example. Scudder viewed modernity as a test of character, and her belief in the salvific potential of Scientific Management, or Taylorism, would be taken up by van Kleeck, eventually underwriting the Russell Sage Foundation's version of industrial sociology.[7]

Which, then, was the more daring, the more radical, the more lasting subversion: the cultural liberationism that Mencken helped to promote, or the more decorous social scientism of van Kleeck? Ultimately, such a question bears even upon us, upon the matter of our cultural parentage, upon the relative weight of these different bloodlines in our makeup. What is the relative mix of these ancestries in our lives today, as social scientists and philanthropoids, as members of late modernity's New Class?[8]

"A new order . . . pressing toward the control of the industrial causes of poverty and misery . . . [is] well within the bounds of possibility. . . . "

—Mary van Kleeck, 1915[9]

Although she is hardly remembered today, from her graduation from Smith College in 1904 to her retirement from the Russell Sage Foundation in 1948, Mary van Kleeck was the fountainhead of some of the vital streams and events of the twentieth century: the campaign to fit the worker and the immigrant within the American frame; the fetish for social facts, for their presumed power to elevate life by subordinating it to reason's discipline; and the insurgency of the New Woman and her installation within a New Class of expert, managerial authority.[10]

As the first and only director of the Sage Foundation's industrial-studies program, for more than fifty years van Kleeck operated seamlessly between the YWCA's Industrial Work program and the Scientific Management movement, between Vida Scudder's quasi-ascetic sisterhood, the Companions of the Holy Cross, and the hidden-in-plain-sight subterfuge that was Communist fellow-traveling. To an unusual degree, she personified the promise and agony of a particular type of New Woman: the evangelical Christian as social scientist and social savior. Twenty years before, Jane Addams and Scudder, among others, had pointed the way, but it would be van Kleeck who embraced the technical hubris of her day, making it completely her own. This was the critical addition, the quality that made her life, and its otherwise unremarkable conflation of religious faith and socialist ideals, so distinctive. In a way classically American, then, van Kleeck was an entrepreneur of the self; her life, a delicate highwire balance of forces, her primary achievement.[11]

In an interview several years ago, a distant cousin of van Kleeck's captured an essential truth about this elusive woman. In doing so, Barbara Roberts also captured something essential about the religious ancestry of American social science, a genealogy once literally visible, as in the case of van Kleeck, within some nineteenth-century families. According to Roberts the van Kleecks were "a family of many ministers," and "just because a daughter wasn't a minister didn't mean she didn't preach."[12]

Stubborn, correct, and intellectually imposing, according to some accounts van Kleeck occasionally lapsed into know-it-all sanctimony. But cousin Roberts meant no criticism, only that whatever Mary van Kleeck's failings in this regard, as a minister's daughter she came by them honestly. Roberts's remark, in any case, is more interesting as a succinct allegory, a quick sketch of the northeastern or midwestern high-church "family of many ministers," and for its suggestion of a daughter, dutiful, alert, and destined for a pulpit of her own.

For a time around the last turn-of-the-century, and largely through the medium of the women's colleges and the YWCA, many of these daughters did achieve ministries of a sort. Encouraged by the sororal enthusiasms of college life, more than a few consecrated themselves to lives of devotional "service" and unforced chastity, establishing settlement houses and staffing the once vast domains of domestic and foreign missions.[13]

We've long known of these daughters, the secular "brides of Christ" from among the first and second generations of New Women. Their formulation of the "Social Question" resonated with the radical challenge of Christian idealism. The test of how to live in right relation to a disordered world, to the material wonders and human wreckage of industrialism lay in the essential simplicity: "What would Jesus do?" Within these terms, many fashioned new lives, professions, and forms of authority. Some, such as Vida Scudder, Grace Coyle, and Miriam Van Waters, actually had clergymen fathers. But many who did not, among them Jane Addams, Emily Balch, Florence Simms, and Ida Tarbell, belong here, too.[14]

Respectable pioneers and decorous rebels, they were unlikely to be taken for sex radicals, birth controlers, or salon bohemians, notwithstanding the proto–lipstick lesbianism of their "Boston marriages." By temperament they were instead constituents of what Rochelle Gurstein, borrowing from Agnes Repplier, has termed the "party of reticence," one of the larger factions of "tradition" and one engaged in the great modern quarrel over the ingredients and boundaries of public life. Yet, as progressives, Taylorites, and social scientists, these women employed a "poetical language" of scientism similar to that favored by the "party of exposure" in its campaign against convention, the clarion of an age of "scientific" social reconstruction.[15]

The twentieth century opened upon a world hopeful of modernity's benign fulfillment, but one also shaken by a sense of historical discontinuity, as if history had broken apart and hope itself were threatened. This theme, and this heightened degree of historical self-consciousness, was a favorite of writers. Virginia Woolf, for example, famously asserted that the snap could be heard on or about a certain month in 1910. For Ford Madox Ford, "January 1896 marked the division between an irrevocably lost past and our own perpetually changing present." And later, in 1936, Willa Cather denominated "1922 or thereabouts" as the great pause in which "the world broke in two. . . . " Others, among them Henry James, Agnes Repplier, and Jane Addams, felt the "shuddering plunge" and wrote movingly of the derangement.[16]

The sense of fracture resonated especially for younger Americans, "early awakened and made observant" by what Alfred Kazin long ago called "those dark years of the 1880s and 1890s, when all America stood suddenly between one moral order and another." For the more sensitive sons and daughters of the middling classes, the intensity of the impending change was "oppressive in its vividness." Somehow they understood that modernity would require of them an "inexpressible moral transformation," and that "the drama of the future" would require a moral response, "an effort at moral history."[17]

Vida Scudder reminds us that these challenges were met, at least by some, with poise and zest. "[A] shuddering plunge into new social experiences awaits our generation," she wrote in her book of 1912, *Socialism and Character*. "The magnitude of the changes may well daze us. . . . " Opening with a summary judgment against the "incredibly wasteful, impossibly cruel" nineteenth century, Scudder set out to plumb the subjective changes underway, "the interesting things happening to our souls." The first "sharp shock of waking contact" with the "deformities of modern life," its squalor and human wreckage, had stunned the mid-Victorian sensibility. Suddenly, civilization assumed an aspect "so complex and seemingly inevitable . . . that the mind was forced to accept as necessity what revolted the heart as monstrosity." By the century's close, "the Social Problem was before us, and life had begun."[18]

This last note of romantic readiness hints at the generational drama then unfolding within the fading world of an older, Protestant, America: the higher education of its daughters, and their mobilization for the crossing into the twentieth century. Against the "Social Problem," they would aim a refurbished Christian idealism, a Christianity socialized and scientized. "Life to be found," ran Scudder's gloss, "must be lost in the whole of humanity's well-being." And in the intensifying contest between capitalism and socialism, in the great reorganization and repopulation of America already underway, college women by the thousands rose to a challenge as much spiritual as material, and were transformed.[19]

Whatever its objective weight, Scudder averred, modern change also pulsed for good and ill within the individual, a subjective force pressing against human character. And "what happens to the individual soul," to character, "is the only matter of real consequence. . . . " In its radical simplicity this was an essential Christian assertion; it was also for a brief historical moment an essential modern one, as technical and productive powers suddenly combined to generate wealth sufficient to free humanity from soul-crushing material poverty. From this late-nineteenth-century "discovery of abundance" would arise much of the early twentieth century's ferocious utopianism. The ancient dream of the "cooperative commonwealth" might soon be realized, it seemed, and the "New Order" would make possible the "new man."[20]

None of this seemed certain, however. Unhinged by a disorienting mix of migrations, labor sinks, and new ways of life, the world of the late nineteenth century had moved to a tipping point, and from its rural precincts poured a transforming diaspora, much of it, so Henry James noted, "ingurgitated" at "terrible little Ellis Island."[21]

Of the multiple anxieties he suffered upon his tour of New York City in 1905, James was especially troubled by the rapid shedding of old manners and ancient deferences by the millions of newcomers. Anything but superficial, these "positive properties" seemed to him the stuff of character, and he wondered if they could be "extinguished in an hour," or "do they burrow underground, to await their day again?—or in what strange secret places are they held in deposit and in trust?"[22]

Willa Cather suffered no such worries, and answered James through the character and grace of Antonia Shimerda, "early awakened and made observant by coming at a tender age from an old country to a new." Having grown up "in the first bitter-hard times," she and the many like her had sacrificed for their families, especially for their younger siblings who, despite their "advantages," never seemed "half as interesting or as well educated." In their vitality and physical presence, Cather noted, they had risen into young adulthood, "almost a race apart."[23]

James understood that this human flood would overwhelm the older American civilization that had shaped him, opening as never before the question of American character and its purpose. He also understood that even its impending doom did not release the America of his childhood from its world-historical duty. Like Jane Addams and Vida Scudder, James understood that the times demanded an extraordinary combination of selfless courage and intelligently selfish calculation. In order to maintain both self-respect and some claim to the future, "we, not they, must make the surrender. . . . We must go *more* than halfway to meet them," the aliens destined to become Americans.[24]

Led by the likes of Addams, Scudder, and many others, this, then, would be the task of the thousands of daughters who increasingly personified the merger of the "scientific attitude" and the Social Christian commitment. Whatever its ultimate results, their gamble would lead them more than halfway into new relations of generosity and authority in the new America.

For them, as for such newcomers as Mary Antin, the Social Question had subdivided into a "great ethnic question," and that, in turn, into matters of first principle. As James had formulated the matter, "Who and what is an alien"? "Which is the American"? "What meaning . . . can continue to attach to such a term as the 'American' character"? The answer, of course, rested with the children. These "millions of little transformed strangers" would become the new American. "*They*, wrote fussy, convoluted Henry James, are the stuff of whom brothers and sisters are made."[25]

Mary van Kleeck's commitment to living "the Christlife" meant engagement with these brothers and sisters, the sweated bookbinders, milliners, and artificial-flower makers of New York City. Following her Smith College graduation in 1904, van Kleeck began her studies of women workers at New York's College Settlement, a Lower East Side enterprise founded by Vida Scudder and several Smith graduates. Her first investigations helped to make the case for protective legislation and led to the beginning of her career with the Russell Sage Foundation. With the entry of the U.S. into World War I, van Kleeck was soon managing much of the nation's women war workers, a job which led to her becoming the first director of the new Women's Bureau of the Department of Labor, in June 1919. She soon resigned this post, however, to return to New York City, her dying mother, and the postwar task of turning her Russell Sage Foundation department into a force for technocratic social investigation.[26]

During the interwar years, van Kleeck emerged as a leader of the movements for scientific management, national planning, and interfaith social justice. She was one of the first women members of the Taylor Society, the chief American organization for the promotion of scientific management and national planning, and she devoted her mature career to the merger of the Christian socialist's demand for a "just materialism" with Taylorism's promise of abundance through planning. This pursuit of what she later termed "Social-Economic planning" animated her defense of protective legislation for women against the Equal Rights Amendment, her alliance with Herbert Hoover's macroeconomic planning efforts, and even her efforts to help the thousands of Hollywood movie "extras" through the creation of the Central Casting Corporation in 1926.

By the late 1920s, van Kleeck's interests had turned decisively "internationalist." She had begun, first, a life-long union with the charismatic Dutch labor reformer Mary "Mikie" Fledderus. Together they devoted the interwar years to building the International Industrial Relations Institute (IRI), a Euro-American association of women personnel managers, progressive employers, Protestant and Catholic socialists, modernist architects, Theosophists, and Taylorites committed to international economic planning. By the late 1920s she had become, secondly, the object of a considerable "courtship" by Soviet authorities, who were apparently eager to draw a woman of such independent and authoritative reputation into their orbit. The implicit messianism of Stalin's first Five-Year Plan could not have been better designed to do just that, appealing as it did to fundamental aspects of her Christian socialist and Taylorite faiths. And with the advent of the Great Depression, van Kleeck felt simultaneously confirmed in her disillusionment with Christian and social-science gradualism, and freed to embrace the most militantly salvationist of the mutually reinforcing elements within the Social Christian, Taylorite, and Stalinist religions.

Throughout the 1930s, then, van Kleeck played an unusual role in public debate. She was the only prominent American who could claim, for better or worse, a simultaneous and leading reputation in the worlds of social science, Christian social action, and Communist fellow-traveling. And she lent her energy and reputation, then and through her retirement in 1948, to an array of enterprises. She was, for example, a member of the original editorial board for the *Encyclopedia of the Social Sciences*; an ally of the American Communist Party in its struggles to win diplomatic recognition for the Soviet Union and to shape the National Labor Relations and Social Security Acts; and a leading figure, together with Vida Scudder, in that remarkably influential sisterhood of Episcopal women, the Society of the Companions of the Holy Cross.

Her prominence in these areas brought her into alliance and combat with a range of people, including John Dewey, Sidney Hook, Earl Browder, Will Hays, Elizabeth Gurley Flynn, Otto Neurath, D. H. Lawrence, Beatrice Webb, and Anna Louise Strong. Throughout, she refused to countenance criticism of the Soviet Union, defending Stalin well into the 1950s. By then she had retired from her "unusual and blessed destiny" to a house she shared with Mikie Fledderus in Woodstock, New York. There, among a few friends and with occasional visits from the FBI, she would live until her death in 1972.[27]

Van Kleeck's life was riven by an irreconcilable devotion to skeptical reason, on the one hand, and the claims of a progressive hope always tending toward the utopian, on the other. Perhaps more intensely than other women of her generation, she was continually in transit between worlds, between the sensibilities of tradition and the aspirations of scientism. She was raised in an explicitly religious framework, one which "privileged" self-sacrifice and bearing witness, a way of life most of us are glad to be rid of. Yet, like us, van Kleeck embodied the New Class claim to technique as authority. Science, even social science, would make transparent both truth and the future, or so many serious people once proclaimed. If no longer quite a proclamation, this is still the ruling claim, the essential assertion, of the enlightened and credentialed.[28]

Like so many of us, then, van Kleeck's investment in progressive hope lived in tension with her commitment to skepticism. Creative, it was also unsustainable, and eventually it undermined even her capacity for introspection. Toppled into a swamp of self-righteousness, her skeptical powers withered as her sense of embattlement deepened in the 1930s and 1940s, and not until her final years did she begin to recover her balance.

No one can yet tell us all that F. Scott Fitzgerald meant when he said that 'there are no second acts in American lives,' or why we have been so oppressed by the sense of time, or why our triumphs have been so brittle. We can only feel the need of a fuller truth than we possess.

—Alfred Kazin, *On Native Ground*[29]

At a time when "social workers" meant something closer to "social engineers," Vida Scudder hailed them as "masters of the future," the "destined leaders of the cooperative commonwealth" to come. Scudder was more prophetic than she knew. The swollen ranks of credentialed experts, including even we professors, indicates as much. Rather less confident than Scudder would have predicted, we nonetheless occupy the higher reaches of a world made largely by and for the technocratic idealism of social science. For better or worse, we personify the triumph of this singular American radicalism.[30]

But as the mid-century "Golden Age" of expanding economies and material affluence recedes, we find ourselves in the 1990s unmoored, as if cut loose from historical time itself. One intriguing measure of this is the difficulty we have in imagining the future. For at least thirty years, it has been hard to picture the future with anything resembling the richness, depth, and anticipation that once was so characteristic, especially among Americans, as recently as the 1940s and 1950s.[31]

Perhaps the future doesn't claim our attention because we are convinced that the trend lines are all wrong, because from whatever angle today the future looks more like a threat than a promise. It seems already a long time, after all, since such modern totems as socialism and capitalism had a purchase on the imagination, since the gospels of science, technology, and progress possessed transcendental allure. No matter their considerable contributions to human welfare, all have been fatally compromised by their complicity in the organized horrors that have defined modern times.[32]

The modern revolt against tradition would thus weaken before history's rebuke, the astonishing and murderous twentieth century. The United States, of course, has enjoyed a fortunate twentieth century. But even this distinction, the emblem of American exceptionalism, is fast disappearing. The watershed of 1973, the year in which real incomes, wages, and productivity growth began their slow decline, marked the winding down of the American imperium. It also signaled the unwinding of the American middle class, a disintegration apparently still underway. Its progress thus checked in a way not seen since the 1930s, the American sovereign self has metamorphosed, in Juliet Schor's telling phrase, into the "overworked American."[33]

As the dense weave of modern life frays, its yearnings and terrors grow only more insistent, especially within the redoubts of love and family. Overworked citizens of a declining empire, Americans since the early 1970s have responded with characteristic zeal by launching campaigns of improvement. Pandemic enthusiasms, whether for mass divorce, sport-utility vehicles, or the aesthetic mutilations of cosmetic surgery—are brave, or desperate, attempts to refute Fitzgerald's dictum, to shake free of time, to secure a lasting triumph, to possess a fuller truth.[34]

Americans, as we have seen, have felt a similar anxiety before, a sense of history off the tracks, and yet the future, the tracks, remained somehow within reach. In the passage into the twentieth century, however, there was, as Leon Wieseltier reminds us, the crucial difference that not the future but "the past was the danger":

> The past stifled with all its dictates and demands, all its presumptions upon the present; and so it came to be defined as a "burden" that had to be resisted.

Out of reason, science, and progress, and with the encouragement of H. L. Mencken, among so many others, we Americans fashioned a liberating resistance. And "we are still living," says Wieseltier, "in the culture of that resistance." If he is right, then we might wonder whether or how much a "culture of resistance" still suits us in the 1990s. We might even wonder whether that totem of social science, the idea of "cultural lag," finally makes a wicked kind of sense, if it is we moderns who are now "violently out of harmony with the new conditions of life."[35]

More than thirty years ago, Donald Meyer made a passing observation that bears upon these questions. The modern reform impulse, he wrote, is best understood as "the social gospel unconscious of its religious debts."

Meyer's invocation of "unconscious indebtedness" suggests that in attempting to understand modern America—its philanthropic, social science, and reform history—we might wish to consider the parts played by ignorance compounded by ingratitude. We might wish to consider the unacknowledged debt that modernity, and we, might owe to traditions long ago subordinated or forgotten.[36]

Now more than a century into the thing, in other words, we are better able to grasp the essential parasitism of modernity, its heedless dependence upon reserves of "moral capital" that it is incapable of replenishing. As we seem increasingly to realize, modernity is presumptuous; it presumes the perpetuity of such things as families and the individual's capacity for trust, kindness, and conviction. These are the essential ingredients of "character," and without them liberal society is, literally, unimaginable. Products of centuries of shame, sacrifice, awe, love, and faith, the elements of "moral capital" are also the burdens and constraints that we moderns have tried so hard to escape.[37]

Matters we know to be essential seem to depend, then, upon larger traditions that the modern revolt definitionally rejects and whose collapse we are now, to our astonishment, beginning to regret. To be sure, most of us, most of the time, are glad to have secular modernity. Most of us are glad to be rid of that older America steeped in maudlin religiosity and overhung with counsels of duty and self-sacrifice. That it was also an America animated by depths of hope and a vivid sense of location within history— attributes we seem to have misplaced—is, we'll admit, interesting. But we New Class professionals, skilled in the art of authoritative contempt, are nothing if not "well-defended" and can usually paper over any temptation toward regret or even wistfulness with the labels of "false consciousness" or "nostalgia."[38]

Modernity has been a powerful and indiscriminate solvent, corroding not only historical continuity but the very sources of solidarity—the capacities for selfless love, constancy, and independent judgment—without which modernity itself is inconceivable. To an extent that we have scarcely realized, the liberal-managerial culture that the foundations helped to build has been necessarily, if irrationally, parasitic, simultaneously undermining and living off the defeated traditions of an older world of smaller scale and mournful faith. In the length of one lifetime the scientific managerial culture has apparently drawn down stocks of the older moral capital that took many generations to accrue. The cleavages of wealth, condition, individual competence, and social trust, so pronounced today, reflect this emptying of accounts, making plain the severity of our predicament and suggesting how little we really understand of the "moral history" of our times.

In a striking case of unintended consequences, the enthusiasm for the scientized society played an unusually potent part here, as did one of its apostles, the redoubtable Mary van Kleeck of the Russell Sage Foundation.[39]

Notes

1. Mary van Kleeck to Frances Bridges, 13 September, 1903, in the author's possession; H. L. Mencken, *Treatise on the Gods* (New York: Knopf, 1930, 1946), 290; and Peter Marin, *Freedom and Its Discontents* (South Royalton, Vt.: Steerforth, 1995), 202.

2. Mencken, *Treatise on the Gods*, 293; "Adventures of a Y.M.C.A. Lad," in *Heathen Days* (New York: Knopf, 1943), ch. 3. Also, Fred Hobson, *Mencken, A Life* (Baltimore: Johns Hopkins University Press, 1994); and Alistair Cooke, "An Introduction to H. L. Mencken," *The Vintage Mencken* (New York: Random House, 1955).

3. That modern man still needs such consolations is no more than proof that the emancipation of the human mind has just begun. . . . Once he attains to anything approaching a genuine mastery of his environment they will become as irrational to him as the old belief in ghosts. . . . Religion, in fact, is already a burden . . . , [it] afflicts him with moral ideas . . . violently out of harmony with the new conditions of life that his own immense curiosity and ingenuity have set up." Mencken, *Treatise on the Gods*, 290.

Also, Hutchins Hapgood, *A Victorian in the Modern World* (New York: Harcourt, Brace, 1939), especially part 2, "Youth"; George Moore, *Memoirs of My Dead Life* (New York: Boni & Liverwright, 1920); Van Wyck Brooks, *The Confident Years, 1880-1915* (New York: E. P. Dutton, 1952); Henry F. May, *The End of American Innocence: A Study of the First Years of Our Own Time, 1912-1917* (Chicago: Quadrangle, 1959, 1964); Christopher Lasch, *The New Radicalism in America, 1889-1963: The Intellectual as a Social Type* (New York: Knopf, 1965); Ann Douglas, *Terrible Honesty: Mongrel Manhattan in the 1920s* (New York: Farrar, Straus & Giroux, 1995); and David E. Shi, *Facing Facts: Realism in American Thought and Culture, 1850-1920* (New York: Oxford University Press, 1995).

4. Mencken, *Treatise on the Gods*, 289-91.

5. Much the same point was first made by Christopher Lasch in *Haven in a Heartless World: The Family Besieged* (New York: Basic, 1977), 75.

6. Mencken's change of heart is examined in Rochelle Gurstein, "Reticence Restated," in *The Repeal of Reticence: A History of America's Cultural and Legal Struggles over Free Speech, Obscenity, Sexual Liberation, and Modern Art* (New York: Hill & Wang, 1996), chap. 8.

7. Scudder's autobiography, *On Journey* (London: J. M. Dent, 1937), is still the best introduction to her life and thought. On the Sage Foundation, see David Hammack and M. Stanton Wheeler, *Social Science in the Making: Essays on the Russell Sage Foundation, 1907-1972* (New York: Russell Sage Foundation, 1994).

8. On the idea and significance of the New Class, see Alvin W. Gouldner, *The Future of Intellectuals and the Rise of the New Class* (New York: Seabury, 1979); Steven Brint, *In an Age of Experts: The Changing Role of Professionals in Politics and Public Life* (Princeton: Princeton University Press, 1994); B. Bruce-Briggs, *The New Class?* (New Brunswick, N.J.: Transaction, 1979); Daniel Bell, *The Cultural Contradictions of Capitalism* (New York: Basic, 1976); Barbara Ehrenreich, *Fear of Falling: The Inner Life of*

the Middle Class (New York: Pantheon, 1989); and Charles Derber et al., *Power in the Highest Degree: Professionals and the Rise of a New Mandarin Order* (New York: Oxford University Press, 1990).

9. Van Kleeck, "Industrial Investigations of the Russell Sage Foundation," September 17, 1915, p. 4, in Box 13, Folder 28, Mary van Kleeck/Russell Sage Foundation Collection, Reuther Library, Wayne State University (hereafter, MvK/R).

10. Van Kleeck (1883–1972) is the subject of several biographical essays; see for example, that by Eleanor M. Lewis, in Barbara Sicherman and Carol Hurd Green, eds., *Notable American Women: The Modern Period* (Cambridge, Mass.: Belknap, 1980), 707–709; see also the entry by Jan Hagen in *Biographical Dictionary of Social Welfare in America*, ed. Walter Trattner, (Westport, Conn.: Greenwood, 1986) 725–28; and one by the present writer, in *American National Biography*, ed. John Garraty (New York: Oxford University Press, 1999).

11. David Danbom has written perceptively on the continuities between what he terms Christian and Scientific Progressives. Nonetheless, and like most students of the subject, he emphasizes their fundamental incompatibility. But in Mary van Kleeck we see a remarkable conflation of the two categories. See David B. Danbom, *"The World of Hope": Progressives and the Struggle for an Ethical Public Life* (Philadelphia: Temple University Press, 1987). See also Harriet Anderson, "Moral Feminism" and "The Legacy of Visionary Feminism," in *Utopian Feminism: Women's Movements in Fin-de-Siècle Vienna* (New Haven: Yale University Press, 1992), ch. 13 and conclusion.

12. Barbara Steven Roberts, Stockbridge, Massachusetts, July 10, 1990.

13. David F. Noble, *A World without Women: The Christian Clerical Roots of Western Science* (New York: Knopf, 1992), chs. 1, 3; Patricia Ann Palmieri, *In Adamless Eden: The Community of Women Faculty at Wellesley* (New Haven: Yale University Press, 1995). Florence Simms, "Milestones in YWCA Industrial Work," p. 107, Box 24, Folder 1, National Board of the YWCA Records, Sophia Smith Collection, Smith College.

14. Jean Bethke Elshtain, "A Return to Hull House: Reflections on Jane Addams," in *Power Trips and Other Journeys: Essays in Feminism as Civic Discourse* (Madison: University of Wisconsin Press, 1990); Ellen Condliffe Lagemann, *A Generation of Women: Education in the Lives of Progressive Reformers* (Cambridge, Mass.: Harvard University Press, 1979); and Sheila M. Rothman, "The Protestant Nun," in *Woman's Proper Place: A History of Changing Ideals and Practices, 1870 to the Present* (New York: Basic, 1978).

15. Agnes Repplier, "The Repeal of Reticence," *The Atlantic Monthly* 113 (1914); Gurstein, *The Repeal of Reticence*, chs. 2–4. Also, Constance M. Chen, *"The Sex Side of Life": Mary Ware Dennett's Pioneering Battle for Birth Control and Sex Education* (New York: New Press, 1996); and Charlotte Perkins Gilman, *The Living of Charlotte Perkins Gilman* (Madison: University of Wisconsin Press, 1935, 1991).

16. Vida Scudder, "The Modern Adventure," the opening section of *Socialism and Character* (Boston: Houghton Mifflin, 1912); Margaret Halsey, "The Upward Step," in *The Folks at Home* (New York: Simon & Schuster, 1952), chap. 1; Rebecca West, *1900* (London: Weidenfeld & Nicolson, 1982); and Hermione Lee, *Virginia Woolf* (New York: Knopf, 1997).

Virginia Woolf, *Mr. Bennett and Mrs. Brown* (London, 1924) p. 4; Ford, *A History of Our Own Times* (Bloomington: Indiana University Press, 1988), p. 11; Willa Cather, *Not under Forty* (New York: Knopf, 1936), Prefatory Note. On James's startled and sympathetic meditation upon the shock that was modern America, see his passages on New York City in *The American Scene* (New York: Harper & Brothers, 1907), chs. 2–3. Also,

Robert Morss Lovett, *All Our Years* (New York: Viking, 1948); Agnes Repplier, "The Virtuous Victorian," in *Eight Decades: Essays and Episodes* (Boston: Houghton Mifflin, 1937); and Jane Addams, *Democracy and Social Ethics* (New York: Macmillan, 1902).

More recent ruminations on this large subject include Hillel Schwartz, *Century's End* (New York: Doubleday, 1996); John Lukacs, *The End of the Twentieth Century and the End of the Modern Age* (New York: Ticknor & Fields, 1993); Hans Koning, "Notes on the Twentieth Century," *The Atlantic Monthly* 280, no. 3 (September 1997): 90–100; John Ralston Saul, *Voltaire's Bastards* (New York: Vintage, 1992); Leszek Kolakowski, *Modernity on Endless Trial* (Chicago: University of Chicago Press, 1990); Robert Skidelsky, *John Maynard Keynes—Hopes Betrayed, 1883-1920* (New York: Viking Penguin, 1986, 1994) 26–31, 400–402; Paul Berman, *A Tale of Two Utopias: The Political Journey of the Generation of 1968* (New York: Norton, 1996), 339.

17. "Drama of the Future" is attributed to the young Freda Kirchwey by her biographer, Sara Alpern, in *Freda Kirchwey: A Woman of the Nation* (Cambridge, Mass.: Harvard University Press, 1987), 18. "Early awakened . . . " is from Willa Cather, *My Antonia* (Boston: Houghton Mifflin, 1918; New York: Dover, 1994), 96. Alfred Kazin, *On Native Grounds* (New York: Harcourt, Brace, 1942), viii, x.

18. Scudder, *Socialism and Character*, 9, 3. Also, "The Christian Attitude toward Private Property," *New Tracts for New Times*, no. 11 (October) (Milwaukee: Morehouse, 1934), 13.

19. Scudder, *Socialism and Character*, 8. Henry F. May, *Protestant Churches and Industrial America* (New York: Harper, 1949), part 4.

20. Scudder, *Socialism and Character*, 3. Scarcity's defeat by a new age of "abundance" was a favorite theme of Simon N. Patten. See "The New Civilization," in *A New Basis of Civilization*, ed. Daniel M. Fox (Cambridge, Mass.: Belknap, 1968), chap. 9. Also, Daniel M. Fox, *The Discovery of Abundance: Simon N. Patten and the Transformation of Social Theory* (Ithaca, N.Y.: Cornell University Press, 1967); Richard T. Ely, *Ground under Our Feet: An Autobiography* (New York: Macmillan, 1938); John R. Commons, *Myself: The Autobiography of John R. Commons* (Madison: University of Wisconsin Press, 1963); Christopher Lasch, "The Idea of Progress Reconsidered," in *The True and Only Heaven*, chap. 2; and Guy Alchon, "Managerialism," in *A Companion to American Thought*, Richard W. Fox and James T. Kloppenberg, eds. (Cambridge, Mass.: Blackwell, 1995). On modern American character as a historical problem, see Warren I. Susman, "Personality and the Making of 20th Century Culture," in *Culture as History: The Transformation of American Society in the Twentieth Century* (New York: Pantheon, 1984), chap. 14.

21. James, *The American Scene* (New York: Harper, 1907), 66; Eric Wolf, *Europe and the People without History* (Berkeley: University of California Press, 1982); and Patricia Hampl, *A Romantic Education* (New York: Houghton Mifflin, 1990).

22. James, *The American Scene*, 66–67, 95–98.

23. Cather, *My Antonia*, 96–97.

24. James, *The American Scene*, 66–67, 95–101.

25. James, *The American Scene*, 92–98; Mary Antin, *The Promised Land* (Boston: Houghton Mifflin, 1912).

26. Van Kleeck's life after college is treated more fully in my "Mary van Kleeck and Social-Economic Planning," *Journal of Policy History* 3, no. 1 (1991): 1–23.

27. "Unusual and blessed destiny" is from van Kleeck to Margaret Grierson, first director of the Smith College Women's History Archive, December 10, 1957, in the Margaret Grierson Papers, Sophia Smith Collection, Smith College.

28. Isaiah Berlin long ago noted this tension and the illiberal tendencies "of the heirs of the radicals, rationalists, 'progressives' of the nineteenth century" in "Political Ideas in the Twentieth Century" (1949), reprinted in *Four Essays on Liberty* (New York: Oxford University Press, 1969), 33–39.

29. Kazin, *On Native Grounds*, x.

30. Vida Scudder, *Socialism and Character*, 311. Also, Walter Lippmann, *Drift and Mastery* (New York: Mitchell Kennerly, 1914); Edwin L. Earp, *The Social Engineer* (New York: Eaton & Mains, 1911); and Guy Alchon, "Policy History and the Sublime Immodesty of the Middle-Aged Professor," *Journal of Policy History* 9, no. 3 (1997): 358–74.

31. Our predicament, as David Gelernter suggests in his meditation on the 1939 New York World's Fair, *1939: The Lost World of the Fair* (New York: Avon, 1995), is that we find ourselves in the supremely fortunate and uncomfortable position of *living in the future*. By the 1960s and the climax of the post-1945 "Golden Age," as Eric Hobsbawm terms the epoch, Americans had finally achieved the widespread material prosperity and security that for so long constituted the core of civilizational hope. Hobsbawm, *The Age of Extremes: A History of the World, 1914–1991* (New York: Random House, 1994, 1996).

32. Alain Destexhe, *Rwanda and Genocide in the Twentieth Century* (New York: New York University Press, 1994, 1995); Richard Rubenstein, *The Cunning of History* (New York: Harper, 1975).

33. Juliet Schor, *The Overworked American: The Unexpected Decline of Leisure* (New York: Basic, 1994); Wallace Peterson, *Silent Depression: Twenty-Five Years of Wage Squeeze and Middle-Class Decline* (New York: Norton, 1994); Katherine Newman, *Declining Fortunes: The Withering of the American Dream* (New York: Basic, 1993); and Arlie Russell Hochschild, *The Time Bind: When Work Becomes Home and Home Becomes Work* (New York: Metropolitan, 1997).

34. Walter Russell Mead, *Mortal Splendor: The American Empire in Transition* (Boston: Houghton Mifflin, 1987); Alan Ehrenhalt, *The Lost City: The Forgotten Virtues of Community in America* (New York: Basic, 1995); Gorman Beauchamp, "Dissing the Middle-Class: The View from Burns Park," *The American Scholar* 64, no. 3 (Summer 1995): 335–49; and Lewis Lapham, "In the Garden of Tabloid Delight: Notes on Sex, Americans, Scandal, and Morality," *Harper's* 295, no. 1767 (August 1997): 35–43.

35. Leon Wieseltier, "After Memory," May 3, 1993, in *The New Republic Reader*, ed. Dorothy Wickenden (New York: Basic, 1994), 169 (emphasis added); Mencken, *Treatise on the Gods*, 290. Also, George W. Stocking, Jr., "The Ethnographic Sensibility of the 1920s and the Dualism of the Anthropological Tradition," in *Romantic Motives: Essays on Anthropological Sensibility* (Madison: University of Wisconsin Press, 1989), 208–76; and Alan Wolfe, "Realism and Romanticism in Social Criticism," in *Marginalized in the Middle* (Chicago: University of Chicago Press, 1996), chap. 3.

36. Donald Meyer, *The Protestant Search for Political Realism, 1919–1941* (Middletown, Conn.: Wesleyan University Press, 1960, 1988), 3.

37. Jean Bethke Elshtain, *Democracy on Trial* (New York: Basic, 1995); Christopher Lasch, *The True and Only Heaven: Progress and Its Critics* (New York: Norton, 1991); Alan Wolfe, "Modernity and Its Discontents" and "The Dubious Triumph of Economic Man," in *Whose Keeper: Social Science and Moral Obligation* (Berkeley: University of California Press, 1989), Introduction and chap. 1; and Peter Marin, *Freedom and Its Discontents*.

38. Christopher Shannon, *Conspicuous Criticism: Tradition, the Individual, and Culture in American Social Thought from Veblen to Mills* (Baltimore: Johns Hopkins Uni-

versity Press, 1996); and Kenneth Anderson, "Illiberal Tolerance: An Essay on the Fall of Yugoslavia and the Rise of Multiculturalism in the United States," *Virginia Journal of International Law* 33, no. 2 (Winter 1993): 385–431, and "Heartless World Revisited," *Times Literary Supplement*, no. 4825 (September 22, 1995), 3–4.

39. Guy Alchon, "The 'Self-Applauding Sincerity' of Overreaching Theory, Biography as Ethical Practice, and the Example of Mary van Kleeck," in *Engendering Social Science: The Formative Years*, ed. Helene Silverberg (Princeton: Princeton University Press, 1998).

PART III

Foundations and Recent Social Movements

8 | The Ford Foundation and Philanthropic Activism in the 1960s

Alice O'Connor

In the late 1950s and early 1960s, the Ford Foundation was the principal sponsor of a series of community-based experiments designed to combat juvenile delinquency and deteriorating conditions in the so-called "gray areas" of U.S. central cities. Based on ideas drawn from sociology and urban planning, these experiments combined institutional reform, citizen participation, and social scientific planning in an attempt to develop models for comprehensive, coordinated social intervention in poor urban communities.[1] Long recognized as inspiration for community action in the War on Poverty, these local experiments also represented a new, more activist phase in the philanthropic quest for social relevance and policy influence. Taking the experience of the Gray Areas program as an example, this essay examines the Ford Foundation's turn to philanthropic activism and its significance in the attempt to forge a new relationship between private philanthropy and an expanding liberal state.

The Ford Foundation was by no means the first or only major philanthropy to take an active interest in shaping government policy. From their very beginnings in the early twentieth century, the "big foundations" such as Rockefeller and Carnegie had been claiming to serve the "general welfare" in their efforts to cultivate and mobilize scientific expertise on policy matters ranging from industrial relations, public health, and agricultural modernization to the organization of government itself.[2] At the same time, they were careful to maintain their own identity as "private" philanthropies even as they relied on government to maintain their tax status as "public" trusts. More important, these "private" tax-preferred institutions looked to the national government to define and justify their sense of national purpose. By mutual agreement, the foundations would do what, as Stanley Katz and Barry Karl put it, government "did not, or could not, or should not do." In reality, the distinctions between "public" and "private" were constantly blurring, a situation to which philanthropy readily adapted by concentrating its resources on funding the network of quasi-public institutions that provided government agencies with expert knowledge, advice, and, frequently, personnel throughout the 1920s and beyond.[3] Both partners stood to gain from this "associational" arrangement: the foundations, a venue for assuming public purpose outside the channels of political accountability; the government, a way of expanding its administrative functions without seeming to violate the private-sector preserve; and, particularly important in light of the vast private fortunes that funded the philanthropic enterprise, a way of maintaining America's commitment to limited state intervention and "free market" capitalism as the prevailing norms in the political and economic system.[4]

The terms of the associational arrangement were rapidly changing in the late 1940s and early 1950s, however, when the Ford Foundation burst onto the scene with more money, and less sense of direction, than either of its two major philanthropic rivals. On the one hand, the rise of the U.S. as a world economic and military power greatly expanded the frontiers for liberal philanthropy, merging with the political and ideological exigencies of the Cold War to make international peace, "third world" development, and the behavioral and economic sciences central to the preservation of the "national interest" the foundations had always set out to serve. At the same time, the federal government was continuing to encroach on traditional philanthropic territory, assuming vast responsibility for social welfare provision in the wake of the Depression, and escalating its support for university-based research through the National Science Foundation, the National Institute of Mental Health and other agencies.[5] The arrival of Ford, described by one contemporary as "the fat kid in the boat," only contributed to the sense of flux in the foundation world.[6] Adding to the uncertainty was the ever-present threat of a Congressional crackdown on foundation tax exemptions, much of it spurred by the kind of McCarthyite suspicion of "un-American activities" featured in back-to-back investigations conducted by Representatives Cox and Reece in 1952 and 1954.[7] It was thus as much a concern for self-preservation as for meeting new national needs that led Ford and other foundations to seek out a different kind of relationship with the federal government, one that would secure the continued legitimacy and relevance of private philanthropy within an expanding, dynamic public sphere. At the Ford Foundation, this effort reached its height in the grant-making strategies developed in the Gray Areas and related community experiments, strategies that put the Foundation in the role of "change agent," demonstration station, and policy incubator for an administration willing to embrace the cause of liberal social reform.

The Ford Foundation was a study in unevenness when it began its tentative entry into the urban gray areas in the mid-1950s. Guided by such lofty goals as "the establishment of peace," "strengthening democracy," and "improved scientific knowledge of individual human behavior and human relations," the young Foundation had built up a substantial international grant portfolio and a strong overseas presence within a few short years, owing in large part to the efforts of its first, briefly tenured president, businessman and Marshall Plan administrator Paul Hoffman.[8] It also enjoyed close ties to Washington's foreign policy establishment, here again thanks to the credentials of staff members such as Hoffman, and trustees like John J. McCloy, the former Assistant Secretary of War and High Commissioner of Germany who later became chairman of the Chase Manhattan Bank.[9] The picture was much different on the domestic side, however, where the "interlocking" networks linking the Foundation to Washington were not as strong, and where chronic staff/trustee conflicts had taken their toll. Having "retired" its first two presidents after relatively brief tenures, the trustees were also less than satisfied with the third, educator Henry T. Heald, whose main emphasis in domestic programs was on building educational excellence.[10] Meanwhile, the Foundation's Public Affairs program had been largely neglected and was being run without a permanent staff. Complicating matters further was the trustees' own skittishness when it came to involving the Foundation in certain "hot button" issues such as civil liberties and school integration.[11] No issue was more "off limits" than race, which was kept off the Foundation's agenda by a combination of intimidation—the Ford Motor Company was regularly threatened with boycotts by white groups wary of potential Foundation interventionism—and indifference. In comparison to the international arena, then, where the staff enjoyed considerable autonomy and close contact with government agencies, the Foundation's domestic policy presence seemed weak, directionless, and unable to take on the major issues of the day.[12]

This domestic disarray would change over the next five years, as newly recruited staff members worked to reconstruct the Public Affairs program, bringing to it a focus on urban social problems while also managing to work within the often unspoken norms that kept highly controversial issues, and especially race, off limits as explicit targets for intervention. It was here, in the reconstructed Public Affairs program, that the staff introduced the activist style of grant making that would make the Foundation a voice for urban reform, and for an expanded federal presence in the nation's poor communities. The new approach was more concerned with direct social action than with detached academic research, and featured demonstration projects; applied, pragmatic expertise; a search for "strategic" points of intervention; and the kind of labor-intensive networking that would bring notice in federal policy circles. It also called for a particular kind of program officer, the skilled, politically astute negotiator rather than the "philanthropoid" with academic credentials. Finally, it revolved around a distinctive, well-articulated reform vision that sought to position the foundation as a "catalytic force" for social change.

The vision underlying what would later become the community action experiments emerged out of the Foundation's early work in the areas of juvenile delinquency and metropolitan governance. Delinquency was fast becoming a national obsession in the 1950s, leading to a wave of congressional hearings, social welfare agency experiments, and attempts to pass federal legislation that would remain stalled in Congress for much of the decade.[13] Drawing on a theoretical framework first developed by "Chicago-school" sociologists in the 1920s, Foundation program officers rejected the psychologized "individual pathology" diagnosis that prevailed at the time and started to experiment with neighborhood- or community-based solutions instead. Delinquency, in this view, was a product of community, not individual "disorganization," and called for neighborhood-based, "indigenous" programs of community renewal and reorganization in response.[14] Revised and expanded by sociologists Richard Cloward and Lloyd Ohlin in the early 1960s, these ideas became the basis of the "opportunity theory" of delinquency, which traced its causes to a broader systemic failure—of schools, social welfare agencies, political institutions, indeed, of society itself—to provide legitimate avenues of success for youth in poor neighborhoods.[15]

Although developed along a separate track, the Foundation's program in metropolitan governance was coming to a parallel set of conclusions about the state of the traditional urban "system." The municipal form of government simply did not have the power or the jurisdiction to cope with the industrial decentralization, middle-class suburbanization and large-scale in-migration of poor minorities occurring in major American cities after World War II, in the view of Public Affairs staff members.[16] The city was caught up in a "crisis of metropolitanization" that only a new, more metropolitan form of government could resolve.[17] Among their recommendations to the trustees was a program to build "new knowledge," with a more "action-oriented" program of research and programs to train a rising generation of urbanologists and administrators in new ways of doing business.[18] Together with the turn toward community-based intervention in juvenile delinquency, these ideas formed the core of the Foundation's experimental urban reform strategy, which sought to bring about comprehensive systems reform through a combination of institutional reorganization, citizen participation, and applied social scientific expertise, or action research.

Acting as the catalytic agent in this strategy was none other than the Foundation itself, which was there to provide the vision and the outside "leverage" for change.

Just as they imagined taking the Foundation in untried directions, the Public Affairs staff members shaping this emerging reform vision saw themselves as challenging the tradition of philanthropic detachment that seemed to prevail in other program areas. They were also well aware of the constraints established by the controversy-shy trustees, however, even as they worked indirectly to get around them. No one was more adept at pushing the boundaries from within than Public Affairs director and Gray Areas program architect Paul N. Ylvisaker, who joined the staff in 1955 to help breathe some life into its urban program. The son of a Lutheran minister from St. Paul, Minnesota, Ylvisaker liked to remind his colleagues that he was an unlikely urbanologist, having trained to follow his father into the ministry at Bethany Lutheran College and Mankato State University in Minnesota. And yet Ylvisaker combined the personality with the training and experience of what many felt to be the ideal urbanologist: he was a generalist with broad, interdisciplinary interests and an occasionally philosophic bent; he felt comfortable in academic circles but was himself more of an activist; though passionate in his convictions, he was not an ideologue, and proved himself a pragmatic, tireless coalition builder throughout his career. Ylvisaker also built his early career in ideal training grounds for a liberal urban activist. After attending Harvard for a masters of public administration in 1945 and a Ph.D. in political economy and government in 1948, he became an aide to Philadelphia reform Mayor Joe Clark, who had run on an anti-machine, good-government platform, believed in the virtues of public service, rational planning, and executive-centered government, and was successful in his pursuit of federal urban renewal funds. After Clark was elected to the U.S. Senate in 1954, Ylvisaker began his own campaign for national urban policy from the somewhat unlikely platform provided by the Ford Foundation. There, he honed his already considerable political skills in building internal support for his ideas and in laying the groundwork in select urban areas for a program of foundation experimentation.[19]

Ylvisaker started gradually, with an emphasis on urban redevelopment and metropolitan governance, and a "frankly experimental," mostly disappointing effort to create "urban extension" units at several state universities.[20] By the late 1950s, frustrated by the unwieldy nature of metropolitan government schemes, Ylvisaker had begun to turn more attention to what he referred to as "people problems," shifting attention away from a focus on "bricks and mortar and power structures" and toward the problems of race and poverty in the inner cities.[21] Still aware of the unspoken racial "embargo" established by the trustees, he turned instead to the presumably more neutral concepts of the "gray areas"—here referring to deteriorating inner-city slums—and migration—here referring to the swelling ranks of black, Latino, and white Appalachian "newcomers" arriving from rural areas to the south—as the framework for an urban program.[22] The problem of the "gray areas," Ylvisaker told the trustees in an analysis reminiscent of the Chicago school, was essentially sociological: Slum neighborhoods were no longer serving as a "staging grounds" for assimilation and upward mobility, as they had for an earlier generation of European immigrants. Abandoned by industry and the white middle class, cities were left to "those who are even more rural and backwoods in their culture than we: Negroes from the rural South; mountain folk from the Ozarks and Appalachians; Puerto Ricans from their island villages." In light of their high birth rates, he informed the trustees, the migrants "will continue to provide the Gray Area with an expanding population, the more so as their escape into better jobs and neighborhoods is slowed by the depressed conditions they live in or by the color they were born with."[23] The solution, which Ylvisaker saw as effectively sidestepping the "*verbotens* of race relations and so forth," was to "perfect the process" of assimilation to make these culturally backward new migrants into "first-class citizens."[24]

Ylvisaker felt he had made a real "intellectual breakthrough" in pinpointing the gray areas and the migration process as the themes that would unify Public Affairs' various urban concerns. Less apparent, perhaps, was the extent to which the new unifying themes took the foundation's urban program in a narrower direction. The urban problem was now being defined in terms of a very traditional philanthropic concern: changing the culture and behavior of the poor.

Now pinpointing the fragmented array of educational and social welfare services as the best "point of entry" for an urban reform program, Ylvisaker started to look for opportunities to test his ideas in actual city bureaucracies. He got his chance unexpectedly when in 1959 the Foundation's Education Program received a request for help from a 14-member coalition of big-city school superintendents headed by Chicago's Benjamin Willis. The cities were faced with a "crisis situation" as their underfunded school systems tried to cope with an influx of poor children from economically depressed rural areas, according to the superintendents, and they needed outside assistance to identify solutions. Distrustful of the Education Program, which until that point had paid little attention to the needs of poor and educationally disadvantaged groups, Ylvisaker decided he wanted in on the grant negotiations.[25] At the cost of what he later described as a "tremendous confrontation" between the Education and Public Affairs programs, Ylvisaker went directly to Foundation President Henry Heald for permission to start an inner-city school improvement initiative that would force the educational establishment to work together with city hall to make schools the "point of contact" for a more comprehensive array of family and social welfare services for the "culturally disadvantaged" migrants.[26]

In 1960 the Foundation launched the Great Cities School Improvement program as a joint Education/Public Affairs initiative, with one-year grants to ten cities for curricular revision, teacher training and program development. Equally significant was the elaborate process of "constant evaluation," cross-site conferences and frequent site visits that accompanied the grants, for it was here that Ylvisaker began to mobilize support for a more ambitious phase of urban experimentation. Broadening the local constituency beyond the educational establishment, workshops were set up to encourage cooperation among urban educators, social workers and police officials and to school them in the Foundation's analysis of the gray areas problem. One such workshop brought urban bureaucrats to Berea College in Kentucky, where they were meant to learn first-hand about the Appalachian origins of the migrants' educational "handicaps." Ylvisaker also brought in outside consultants to help with evaluation, choosing experts on each of the major migration "streams" to reinforce the program's thematic unity.[27]Meanwhile, in his own internal reports on the progress of the schools experiment, Ylvisaker was making a case for a more fully developed program of action and reform.[28] The key, he wrote in a memo to Heald, was to find an entry point that would enable the Foundation to "encourage broader-than-school approaches to the human problems of our urban Gray Areas." In a subsequent memo to Heald reflecting on these efforts, Ylvisaker admitted that this was "destined by its nature to be a search for the Holy Grail," for the target was not just one institution, but the whole tangled network of agencies responsible for housing, social services, and employment for the poor. In fact, the staff was by this time convinced that the answer would require creative new institutional forms. "'Where is the author, and where the brainpower that can provide a coordinated and leavening force?'" Ylvisaker asked rhetorically. "Neither presently exists. . . . " The situation, as he wrote to the trustees, required "the stimulus of new ideas and the catalytic action of an outside force such as philanthropy" to "activate" community resources behind change.[29]

Ylvisaker's search for the "holy grail" was based on his belief that traditionally organized municipal bureaucracies were both too limited in jurisdiction and too fragmented to provide the comprehensive services demanded by gray area residents. Just as they had for an earlier generation of Progressive reformers, good government, better planning, and applied expertise would provide answers to the problems of immigration and urban decay. Nor did he have much faith in political mobilization as a way to make the system work, here again echoing themes from the older Progressive tradition of municipal reform. And yet Ylvisaker was convinced that the urban problem required action beyond what earlier generations of philanthropists had pursued. More than a source of expertise or even direct provision, the Ford Foundation had to be willing to put itself out on the urban "firing line," and to create the new institutional forms that would make government work. Increasingly, beginning with the multi-site Gray Areas program, the Foundation would look to what only later became known as "intermediary organizations" to carry out its reform agenda. In the case of the Gray Areas program, these organizations were established with foundation support as private, non-governmental agencies, albeit with governing boards that included elected officials as well as constituency representatives from the community at large, to act as coordinating, planning and fundraising bodies for the local initiatives. Again reflecting the blurred boundaries between public and private responsibility, they were designed to channel the funding and programs from existing agencies into a more comprehensive, coherent approach to intervention. Thus, with the creation of quasi-public organizations such as Community Progress, Inc., in New Haven, Action for Boston Community Development, the Philadelphia Council for Community Advancement, and the United Planning Organization in Washington, DC, the Ford Foundation had found a new way to do what government "could not, should not, or would not" do on its own: reform the way it delivered social services.

But the forces to be "activated" and coordinated were not contained within city limits; to make a difference, Ylvisaker knew, the experimental organizations would have to attract federal dollars and attention and, eventually, operate as intermediaries between federal government and local need. Their programs would have to demonstrate "national significance" and act as models for what could be done in cities nationwide.[30] Equally important, and with active assistance from the Foundation, city administrators would need to cultivate the grantsmanship skills to tap into the "scores of grant and demonstration funds available" within the federal bureaucracy. The grants were there, according to Ylvisaker, but they remained "unknown, wrapped in a discouraging amount of red tape, inconsistent in their objectives and effects, or ineffective if used singly rather than in combination." Accordingly, the Foundation sponsored workshops with local administrators on how to shape programs and write proposals that would be responsive to federal grant requirements, and even tried to coordinate its own grant decisions with federal agency schedules. Foundation staff members lobbied on behalf of the demonstration sites with government grant administrators, promising the seed money that would help local administrators put federal dollars to innovative uses. In public appearances and speeches, they promoted the basic ideas behind their reform program, such as community action, systems reform and opportunity theory, for select audiences. And, taking advantage of the spirit of government activism embraced by the Kennedy administration, Ylvisaker and his colleagues also began seeking out opportunities for direct collaboration with government officials, many of them former staff members or grantees who now held key administrative positions. When the administration made its call for action and change, the Foundation and its local intermediaries would be prepared to show the way.

The Foundation's most visible domestic policy impact was on the emerging Kennedy administration initiative against juvenile delinquency. Thanks in large part to the efforts of Public Affairs program staff member David Hunter and Foundation Vice President Dyke Brown, Cloward and Ohlin's opportunity theory was gaining widespread attention as the most promising new approach in the field. As one of the program's senior staff members and a representative from one of the single largest sources of grant money, Hunter actively promoted opportunity theory in speeches to social-work groups and other groups around the country. In its own program guidelines, the Foundation also encouraged grantee organizations to embrace the approach. Opportunity theory, it seems, had an appeal beyond its persuasiveness as a diagnosis of the problem: It offered a concrete set of institutional targets for intervention and a way to tap into job training and related sources of federal funding. Most important, the Foundation proved willing to throw its weight behind the idea with a pledge of support for Mobilization for Youth (MFY), a demonstration project on New York's Lower East Side created by a coalition of settlement houses, local service agencies and the Columbia University School of Social Work, with central involvement from Cloward and Ohlin. Although the actual grant represented only a small part of MFY's initial start-up budget, the Foundation's imprimatur was instrumental in persuading New York City and federal government officials to provide the $2 million to launch MFY as a full-scale demonstration project. So, too, were Foundation officials eager to lobby Washington on its behalf. In 1961, just after President Kennedy established the Committee on Juvenile Delinquency (PCJD) by executive order, Hunter and Brown met with PCJD Executive Director David Hackett, armed with a background paper describing opportunity theory, the MFY initiative, and the principal theorists behind them. Hackett, who had been struck most of all by the lack of coordination among existing federal anti-delinquency initiatives, was impressed with the theory's coherence and its emphasis on institutional coordination and reform. He subsequently recruited Lloyd Ohlin away from his post as MFY research director to help in developing the new federal initiative, making Ohlin the "key architect" of the PCJD "philosophy" and the legislation that accompanied it.[31] Foundation staff member

Richard Boone, a former police commissioner in Chicago's Cook County, also joined the PCJD staff. The Committee's enabling legislation, passed in the fall of 1961, explicitly recognized "limited opportunity" as a central cause of delinquency, and authorized funding for a number of demonstration projects across the country. Soon afterwards, the President's Committee announced that MFY would be its first major project, with collaborative support from New York City, the National Institute of Mental Health, and the Ford Foundation. By then, the PCJD was a virtual extension of the Foundation's Public Affairs program, with Lloyd Ohlin providing intellectual leadership, former program officer Richard Boone on staff, and Gray Areas program consultant Clifford Campbell on the review committee designated to screen proposals from local applicants. This connection would later prove instrumental in funneling ideas into the War on Poverty.[32]

The Foundation's efforts to establish a direct federal connection were equally intensive in the case of the Gray Areas experiments. Drawing once again on well-placed former consultants and staff members, Ylvisaker organized monthly briefing sessions in the offices of former Gray Areas consultant Robert C. Weaver, then head of the Housing and Home Finance Administration (HHFA), whom Ylvisaker had endorsed for the post only months before.[33] These sessions were attended by a wide range of agency officials, often including former Foundation staff member and Budget Bureau economist Kermit Gordon, and Department of Defense analyst Adam Yarmolinsky, who had briefly served as a Foundation consultant before becoming one of Robert McNamara's "whiz kids," and who in early 1964 was appointed deputy to the task force charged with planning the War on Poverty.[34] Noting an essential "consistency" between Foundation and federal agency purposes, Ylvisaker asked these and other program administrators to think of Gray Area cities as "pilot communities" for "experiments of consistent and critical impact" where federal resources could be concentrated.[35] Too big and unwieldy to manage the experiments on its own, government could nevertheless provide the funding to make them significant, and, in the process, gain a source of social learning that the Foundation was in a unique position to offer. That these efforts paid off is indicated by the degree of overlap between Foundation and federal government demonstration grants: the PCJD made grants to four of the five Gray Areas cities for juvenile delinquency prevention projects; Department of Labor grants went to Philadelphia, New Haven and Boston for employment and training programs. All told, nearly $30 million in combined federal and foundation funding was going into or designated for the local demonstration projects that Ford had helped to create by late 1962. And, thanks to the efforts of what was now clearly a well-established "interlocking" network of contacts, the idea of community action had a presence in Washington. Its main institutional base within the Administration, the PCJD, was under the direct authority of Attorney General Robert Kennedy, assuring at least some access to the White House. It was "a beautiful running time," Ylvisaker recalled, "[W]hen the world wanted to solve the problems, when the Ford Foundation was golden, when Kennedy was in office and you could talk about the experimental programs that would go into governmental programs."[36]

And yet, before long the demonstration projects began to encounter some major problems and inconsistencies within the underlying vision of systems reform and community action as a strategy for change.[37] To begin with, local planning proved more time-consuming and more political than even the most seasoned of the Foundation and PCJD "advance men" anticipated. "Oakland has available to it, at long last, an instrument for social planning, staffed by competent professionals who are prepared to move forward," a Foundation reviewer concluded blandly—three years after the initial grant had been made.[38] Boston suffered from persistent interagency conflict and jealousies, engaging ABCD executive director Joseph Slavett in a longstanding struggle with Boston Redevelopment Agency chief Ed Logue for control over federal government funds. "Basically, we have two strong men, Ed and Joe, vieing [*sic*] with each other for a position of power," wrote evaluator Clifford Campbell to Ylvisaker following a site visit to Boston.[39]

Resident participation turned out to be a more explosive problem, revealing both vagueness and ambivalence at the heart of community action thinking. As soon became apparent, community action theory could accommodate several different approaches to citizen participation. In the more radical tradition inspired by community organizer Saul Alinsky and adopted by Mobilization for Youth, resident participation meant political organizing and local autonomy—and suspicion of the motives of "outside groups" seeking to impose their own reform expertise on poor neighborhoods.[40] Alinsky's approach also acknowledged the conflicting interests among different class and ethnic groups and sought to exploit them for the purposes of building cohesive political organizations. At MFY, the program to "Organize the Unaffiliated" was willing to embrace confrontational tactics such as rent strikes, school boycotts and mass demonstrations, progressively alienating its city agency and settlement house sponsors. Eventually, MFY's organizing activities provoked red scare tactics, drawing accusations of Communist Party affiliation from the New York *Daily News*, and charges of radical liberal reformism from disaffected poverty warrior Daniel P. Moynihan.[41]

An alternative, more elite or "executive-centered" approach was to define the principle of resident participation much more narrowly, on the assumption that gray area neighborhood residents were too apathetic or uneducated to have a meaningful say in program planning.[42] This stance, too, proved highly controversial, immediately embroiling the Gray Area experiments in the increasingly polarized racial politics that Ylvisaker hoped to avoid. In one bitter, highly publicized conflict, New Haven's CPI was accused of trying to squelch grassroots black leadership when Executive Director Mitchell Sviridoff refused to support community efforts to organize the defense for three young black men accused of raping a white nurse. Taken up as a cause by local civil rights leaders and Yale law students, the case became a symbol of unequal justice in the black community and CPI was on the wrong side: Given the chance to organize local residents in the cause of racial justice, legal services lawyer and former CPI staff member Jean Cahn charged in a widely disseminated *Yale Law Review* article, CPI had instead undermined "incipient" leadership in the black community, in the interest of assuring its own political survival.[43] PCCA in Philadelphia also drew public redress for its racial politics, this time at the hands of journalist and *Fortune* magazine editor Charles Silberman. Troubled from the start by rifts within its coalition of sponsors, PCCA had been organized by a group of academics at Temple University without the endorsement of local civil rights groups and without any participation from the predominantly black constituency it was meant to serve. "[T]he people being planned for in a $1.7 million Ford Foundation project are hardly even mentioned, let alone represented," Silberman wrote of the PCCA planning document. "The notion that citizens conceivably might want to speak for themselves obviously never occurred to the academicians, government officials, and 'civic leaders' who drew up the document," he added in a rebuke to the presumptions of program architects, "as if the residents of a Negro slum needed to be told what their problems are!"[44] In an ironic twist, the situation led one influential black leader to use a tactic earlier employed by southern white citizens' councils fearful that the Foundation would interfere in local race relations: He threatened a boycott of Philadelphia-area Ford Motor Company dealerships unless the foundation withdrew its funding.[45]

Silberman's critique, issued in his book *Crisis in Black and White*, was especially damaging because it cut to the heart of the program's conceptual framework. Nor did it help that Silberman was writing with funding from Ford's Public Affairs program, and with "complete freedom" from Ylvisaker, as he acknowledged, "to bite the hand that fed me."[46] Calling the Gray Areas program a "grandiose fusion of paternalism and bureaucracy," he criticized the Foundation for fleeing "the really hard and controversial issues that lie at the heart of the Negro problem—issues that involve the most fundamental conflict of interests between Negroes who want jobs and white trade unionists reluctant to surrender their job monopolies; between Negro tenants and white landlords; between Negro homeowners and white universities seeking land for expansion, and so on."[47] Silberman was equally damning in his critique of the "white liberal" assumptions underlying Gray Areas, and above all the analysis that "makes no distinction between the problems faced by Negroes and those faced by other contemporary migrants."[48] The expectation that blacks would be assimilated just like past and current generations of white ethnics ignored "the central fact," Silberman wrote. "The Negro is unlike any other immigrant group in one crucial regard: he is colored." For Silberman, this "central fact" pervaded every one of the interrelated problems the Gray Areas projects were trying to address. "Nothing less," he wrote, "than a radical reconstruction of American society is required if the Negro is to be able to take his rightful place in American life."[49] As a starting point, he offered an Alinsky-influenced community-based organization called The Woodlawn Organization (TWO) as an example of community action that could work.

While the issues of race and participation were being raised with growing intensity by outside critics, community action insiders were also growing frustrated with the systemic and structural barriers they faced once the experiments got under way. Bureaucratic resistance to coordination and change was rampant, as the many turf wars over funding suggest. A more basic problem plagued the experiments with employment and training services, when even the most successful projects found they could not deliver actual jobs. As analyses by economist Ray Vernon and others had shown, the same structural economic changes that were drawing manufacturing industries outside the central cities were making it harder for low-skilled Gray Area residents to find local employment—with devastating impact on the black working class. Partly as a result, the local employment and training programs favored already-skilled or previously employed applicants—for whom success rates were higher—over more disadvantaged applicants.[50]

Nor was the process of learning and evaluation as easy or straightforward as the logic of demonstration projects suggested. To some degree the problems were methodological, as evaluators grappled with the issue of how to arrive at concrete measures of success for programs that were by definition interactive, process-oriented, and subject to unanticipated "midcourse" changes.[51] But the real barriers to evaluation were institutional and political. With the exception of Boston's ABCD, few of the Gray Areas grantees showed much inclination to integrate scientific evaluation into their action programs, and indeed program administrators came to resent the social scientists' insistence on theoretical rigor and consistency when it appeared that flexibility and ongoing revision were in order. The fact was, in many instances, that social scientists and practitioners had different needs and conflicting expectations of what research could provide: the scientists, a test of theory, a replicable result, a precise measure of the concrete impact an intervention was having; the practitioners, immediate feedback, suggestions for change, a measure of accountability that could be used for sponsors and program participants. "The action-oriented professional has regularly lambasted the ivory tower, whose inhabitants supposedly spend all their time gathering data aimed not at solving concrete human problems, but at building bigger and better theories to be discussed at stuffy conferences and debated in unreadable journals," wrote one Gray Areas program research director. "The researcher, for his part, is often heard belittling the action-oriented practitioner for his failure to conceptualize clearly, for his inability to think in terms of systems; for his tendency to act on the basis of subjective whims or impressions; . . . and for his apparent fear of evaluation on the grounds that it might call his own actions into question."[52] Even had the demonstration projects been subjected to the most scientifically rigorous type of evaluation, however, it is doubtful that the Foundation had the capacity to absorb and act on the lessons emerging from experience. From trustees and government officials alike, the political demand was for quick and visible results, and against too direct an involvement with controversial issues. As program staff kept their sights on gaining notice in Washington, community action's success would be measured more on its visibility and degree of innovation than on its long-range capacity to effect change.

The local demonstration projects, then, posed challenges to some of the basic beliefs and assumptions behind community action and the form of philanthropic activism it represented. Visions of cooperative, rational planning ran up against the realities of political in-fighting and bureaucratic resistance. Resident participation was racially charged, difficult to achieve within the limited framework of orderly bureaucratic reform, and highly unpredictable. The belief that race could be addressed within the "neutral" context of migration was quickly shattered by the experience of racial conflict and resistance, while structural economic conditions raised the question of whether systems reform alone was enough to change the "opportunity structures" for Gray Area residents. Finally, community action's experimental idealism—its belief that change could be achieved in a rational sequence of scientifically informed planning, experimentation, assessment, and eventual adoption by the federal government—was being challenged by tensions between scientists and practitioners and by the difficulties of getting federal agencies to break out of their fragmented, categorical approaches to funding. Meanwhile, community action strategists were themselves beginning to feel constricted within the confines of the problem areas they had set out to work in; juvenile delinquency and Gray Areas, it appeared, were really symptoms of a more fundamental social problem that was then beginning to get a name. In the spring of 1963, actively searching for a new conceptual and institutional base for their reform efforts, community action proponents found the answer in an emerging new administrative initiative: the federal attack on poverty.

Community action's turn to poverty came amidst a more general groundswell of popular, social scientific and pressure-group concern that, building sporadically since the late 1950s, finally began to gain momentum within the administration in the early months of 1963. In January, a review essay by social critic and Ford Foundation biographer Dwight Macdonald appeared in the *New Yorker* which drew attention to several recent studies documenting the shocking but "invisible" reality that the world's most affluent society still harbored substantial numbers of poor people.[53] Among the works featured in Macdonald's essay were scholarly documentations by economists Robert Lampman, Gunnar Myrdal, and by a team of researchers at the University of Michigan, but its real impact was to draw attention to Michael Harrington's passionate call to action, *The Other America*. Other popular accounts, including a television documentary in late 1962 and a September 1963 *New York Times* series on the Appalachian poor that reportedly prompted hundreds of phone calls to the White House, helped to convince President Kennedy and his political advisers that poverty held potential as a campaign issue for the upcoming election year. Pressure was also coming from the organizers of the Civil Rights March on Washington that was being planned for August, which took employment and economic well-being as central themes. In June, Kennedy authorized Council of Economic Advisers (CEA) chair Walter Heller to establish an informal interagency task force to conduct preliminary investigations into the poverty problem. Meanwhile, community action planners had also come to the conclusion that poverty should be their main target point. "In order to prevent and control delinquency, it is necessary to . . . [r]educe poverty," MFY announced in a revised mission statement issued in June, and to "change social conditions so that new economic opportunities are created."[54] In September, Ylvisaker announced that "poverty, and the vicious cycle of poverty" would become the "label" for the "essential concerns" of the Ford Foundation's Public Affairs program."[55] Community action proponents were therefore prepared when, in late October 1963, President Kennedy gave the CEA poverty task force a go-ahead to move to the next stage of planning. With PCJD Executive Director David Hackett leading the way, they mobilized their networks and successfully introduced their ideas into the policy pipeline. Within weeks community action had become, as one memo described it, "the basic concept" defining the impending poverty program.[56]

Hackett's proposal to the Administration's poverty task force showed little recognition of the problems being encountered in the demonstration sites—after all, most of the experiments were themselves just getting underway. Indeed, his proposed plan was an elaboration on the core community action themes of rational planning, institutional reform, citizen participation, and applied learning. "What we are proposing is continuous planning on a national scale to make better use of Federal resources in programs which more effectively serve the poor," he wrote to Attorney General Robert Kennedy.[57] It was also an approach "that would encourage a dramatic approach to the problems," he added in a memo to task force chair Walter Heller. The plan proposed to begin with an additional series of task forces "to study the large pockets of poverty in the nation . . . and to approach the problems of the poor first by consulting the people themselves, examining their life conditions, then looking through them at the institutions which are attempting to assist them." Based on these inquiries, the task forces would make recommendations for legislation, for new "administrative arrangements in the Federal Executive departments," and for a few—no more than five—comprehensive demonstration projects that would be mounted with interagency support. The investigative task forces would remain in existence to evaluate the demonstrations and continue research and planning. The "central focus" of all this activity would be "on that poverty which is passed on from one generation to the next."[58]

For the economists in charge of the CEA poverty task force, the community action idea held considerable appeal: It kept program responsibility out of the hands of any single one of the "old line" federal agencies, it offered a way to cut through bureaucratic inefficiencies, it had an attractive air of localism while asserting a strong federal role in community change, and it would not require major new spending.[59] It also seemed innovative, a major selling point as the administration tried to construct its domestic program in the aftermath of President Kennedy's assassination—and to come up with something distinctive for President Johnson to propose. In late December the new idea—without the encumbrance of Hackett's elaborate task forces, and expanded well beyond the original provision for a "limited number" of experiments—appeared on White House aide Theodore Sorenson's desk as the core of the CEA's anti-poverty proposal. In his January 1964 State of the Union address, Johnson announced that he would soon be presenting a major new package of legislation to lead an attack on poverty; later that month, he announced that Kennedy in-law R. Sargent Shriver would be leading a new task force to put the program together.[60]

Suddenly community action, only recently a relatively obscure and experimental concept harbored by Ford and the PCJD, was caught up in the whirlwind of politics and planning that led to the passage of the Economic Opportunity Act in August 1964. The impact on the local demonstration projects was immediate. No longer works-in-progress with room for experimentation and change, they were now touted as model programs, subject to an "influx" of federal visitors eager to witness the new idea in action. New Haven, the Gray Area showcase, even established a separate public information office to handle the rush of inquiries. Local directors were much in demand for advice, as were the Foundation program officers in charge. Ylvisaker became an even more tireless promoter, ever on hand to plug community action when enthusiasm seemed to be waning within the Shriver task force. Hackett, Richard Boone and other members of the PCJD staff formed the core of a committee designated to draft the community action title of the Economic Opportunity Act. With the Act approved and the Office of Economic Opportunity (OEO) just underway, the Foundation sponsored a major conference in Puerto Rico in December 1964, gathering OEO officials and Gray Area grantees to discuss "the kinds of problems and questions that arise in organizing and executing community action programs of the type contemplated by the new Economic Opportunity Act."[61]

And yet it was also with a sense of loss and trepidation that those most directly engaged in the Foundation's community action experiment saw it become caught up in the momentum of, and eventually taken over by the War on Poverty. For in the process of being discovered and taken up as the latest weapon against poverty, the local projects had lost the shield of experimentation and the luxury of testing their assumptions about the possibility of informed, rationally planned social change. They had no room, let alone time, for absorbing and acting on the lessons from experience. Hackett's initial task force proposal to the contrary, community action had been transformed from experimentation to action before complete evaluations had been done. "In a sense, the promoters of community action had succeeded too well," wrote evaluators Peter Marris and Martin Rein a few years later. "Their ideas became fashionable before they were proved."[62] The local projects were also subject to a whole new level of political pressure with the availability of millions of dollars in federal anti-poverty funds: Suddenly, the stakes were much higher and the competition fiercer for local program control. Now responsible for administering much larger influxes of federal money, Gray Areas evaluator Clifford Campbell warned, the local projects were also apt to lose sight of their original goals. The Foundation had a "continuing interest in maintaining for posterity the integrity of programs already launched . . . ," he wrote not long after the poverty program had gotten underway.[63] Coordination, too, was an even more daunting challenge than in the past, especially in light of the "at least 42 federal government programs under 6 separate federal government agencies dealing directly with the problems, causes and cures of poverty," as the staff noted in composing the letter of invitation to the Puerto Rico conference.[64] But there was also a more basic, mostly unspoken question to answer: What would happen when community action, unproved as a method for the more

limited goals of combating juvenile delinquency or promoting systems reform, was expected to "break the cycle of poverty"?

Such reservations aside, the Gray Areas experiment was deemed a re-
sounding success within the Foundation. "[T]he community action section of the poverty program builds heavily on the experiments of the Gray
Areas project," Ylvisaker reported to the trustees, noting that New Haven's
Mitchell Sviridoff and North Carolina's George Esser "had quite a hand in
drafting and shaping it." In addition to embracing the essential reform principles the Foundation had been endorsing, the new poverty bill included
provisions for funding private, quasi-governmental community action agencies along the model of the intermediaries the Foundation had created in
Gray Areas cities. This was a major triumph, too, for the new style of grantmaking—more hands-on, less academic, ready to step up to the "urban
firing line"—that Ylvisaker was trying to cultivate in domestic programming. Passage of the Economic Opportunity Act of 1964, and the Foundation's role in it, was the Public Affairs program's "proudest achievement,"
and clear evidence of Gray Area's success.[65]

The political triumph of community action helped to usher in an era
of stepped-up engagement with federal officials, and established Ylvisaker's
Public Affairs program as the leading edge of liberal philanthropic activism. Once skeptical of Ylvisaker's grantmaking style, Foundation President
Henry Heald now made an attempt to capitalize on its success. In fact, evidently aware that Ylvisaker had gotten out ahead of him, Heald quickly
made a thinly disguised move to consolidate control over "relations with
government programs" within his own office. Borrowing a bureaucratic
feature from Robert McNamara's Department of Defense that would soon
be adopted in all domestic agencies, Heald created a centralized office of
Policy and Planning at the Foundation, and included among its charges the
responsibility for establishing a regular liaison with "key officials of government charged with activities and objectives shared by private philanthropy."
Chief among its responsibilities was to set up regular seminars, informal
dinners and monitoring activities to keep each side apprised of what the
other was doing. The new Policy and Planning office would also serve to
monitor staff contacts with federal officials, albeit in the name of centralized coordination. Some thought was also being given to creating a special
position in the Budget Bureau specifically designated to maintain founda-
tion/government relations, Heald informed his staff in the spring of 1965.[66]
Heald by then had already inaugurated the new relationship by setting up a
meeting at Washington's Sheraton Carlton Hotel, where he and Foundation
vice-president for Policy and Planning McNeil Lowry were joined by Budget
Bureau director Kermit Gordon, Commissioner of Education Francis Kep-

pel, OEO director Sargent Shriver, Secretary of Labor Willard Wirtz, and Vice President Hubert H. Humphrey, among others. Ylvisaker was conspicuously absent, but his legacy was not. Welcoming the prospect of regular collaboration, Shriver noted that the Gray Areas program was a stellar example of how the new relationship should work. It was politically impossible for the federal government to conduct experimental programs in a limited number of jurisdictions, he and others agreed, but such demonstrations were the key to solving society's most pressing social ills.[67]

Despite the hubris attending Heald's efforts, for the Foundation this was as much a defensive as an activist move. "One of the factors complicating the policies and plans of the Ford Foundation in 1965 is the expansion of Federal, and therefore also of state and local, activities in so many areas in which the Ford Foundation and other private foundations have worked," he wrote to Foundation officers following the meeting with federal officials. Without indicating a "slackening in the efforts of the Ford Foundation to maintain its own independence and autonomy as a private philanthropic organization," he continued in ponderous foundation-ese, it would be necessary to acknowledge the "difficulty of carrying out long-range planning for the Ford Foundation without an awareness both by the Foundation and by the Government of the particular programs each is desirous of carrying out."[68] Heald was also very conscious of renewed legislative attempts to regulate private philanthropic activities. Once again under fire from the populist Texas congressman and long-time foundation foe Wright Patman, the philanthropic sector had just come through a period of extended anxiety over the outcome of a Treasury Department investigation of tax-exempt foundations, which was expected to propose potentially inhibiting regulations on asset accumulation and spending patterns. Although the report and eventual regulations were far less onerous than feared, Heald was eager to show just how vital the independent philanthropic sector was to carrying out the public purpose. It was no longer possible to maintain a rigid separation between public and private responsibilities, he told federal officials, but government still needed private philanthropy for the very functions it could not carry out on its own. For this very reason, it was also in the government's interest to protect philanthropy from the kind of state intrusion that would threaten its independence.[69]

It was not until former Kennedy/Johnson advisor McGeorge Bundy took over as president, however, that the logic of the Foundation's philanthropic activism reached its peak. The ultimate establishment insider, with his Ivy League credentials and government connections, Bundy had little hesitation about blurring the lines between foundation and government business, even after the Foundation had suffered the embarrassment of public scandal over its "study grant" awards to former members of Robert F.

Kennedy's staff in 1969. Stung as well by charges that one of its grantees had improperly used funds for a voter-registration drive in Cleveland's black neighborhoods, the Foundation was also subject to tighter legislative restrictions on what could be construed as improper political activities. Bundy's tenure also coincided with a period of trustee belt-tightening, declining annual income and political backlash against Great Society liberalism. These developments did not bode well for an increase in philanthropic activism. Nevertheless, Bundy pushed the Foundation much further into the forefront of liberal social reform, positioning himself as an advisor to Mayor John Lindsay during New York City's school decentralization controversy and announcing that the Foundation would forthrightly commit itself to solving the racial problem. He doubled the size of the Public Affairs program, now renamed National Affairs, and, passing over Ylvisaker, appointed former Gray Areas grantee and Lindsay administration official Mitchell Sviridoff to take charge.

By the mid-1970s, the Foundation was sounding a far more cautious note about its ability to take on the country's social dilemmas, but its partnership with the federal government had never been more extensive or secure. Sviridoff, characterizing "the constructive impact of our work on government policy," reported that the National Affairs program was involved in a large number of demonstration projects, most of them planned and funded in direct cooperation with the federal government. The program had also expanded the practice of establishing various kinds of intermediary organizations that were being used to implement, evaluate, manage, and otherwise smooth the operations of federal social programs. Decidedly more modest than their predecessors in their aspirations for social change, these new intermediaries prided themselves on their non-partisan professionalism and technical proficiency; their role was to work within, not challenge, the status quo.[70] "We and government act together as *bona fide* partners rather than competitors or adversaries" in demonstration projects, Sviridoff assured Bundy. If anything, the relationship had grown increasingly interdependent: Without assurances that federal agencies would co-sponsor and eventually take over, the rationale for the projects—and for much of the National Affairs program—would essentially disappear.[71] The Ford Foundation had secured the position it sought in the Gray Areas program. Meanwhile the domestic policy agenda was changing all around it. Welfare, not poverty, had become the target of social reform.

There was at least one major problem with the "partnership" arrangement that developed in the 1970s: It would not last. Indeed, it left the Foundation ill-prepared to deal with the arrival in 1980 of a new administration that was openly hostile to government planning, to liberal philanthropy, and to the welfare state itself. Having accommodated the ideological shifts of the post–Great Society political order, the Foundation was unable to offer, or to mobilize, a coherent response to the more fundamental ideological challenge that the advent of the Reagan Administration represented. Instead, it remained on the sidelines, insisting on its own ideological neutrality, as newly ascendant conservative foundations mobilized intellectual and popular support behind their own agenda for social change.

In retrospect, it is not difficult to find flaws in the Gray Areas vision, with its too-narrow focus on social-service systems reform and its naïve hope that it could sidestep the problem of race. Ylvisaker himself, having not long before been a peacemaker in violence-torn Newark, New Jersey, looked back on the program as a "period piece" in the 1970s.[72] But the Gray Areas vision was also flawed in its assumption that a smooth-running foundation-government partnership would—or should—displace political struggle, ideological conflict, and grass roots organizing as a means of influencing social policy, and this is the lesson that Ford and other liberal foundations seem to have learned least of all. Indeed, Gray Areas continues to represent a kind of "golden age" in foundation lore, the "smooth running time," as Ylvisaker called it, when Ford could feed its experimental programs directly into federal government action. And yet in its concern with getting its programs adopted by the federal government, and in its subsequent efforts to maintain policy relevance, the Foundation was giving up the potential it might have had as a critical and independent voice for social change. Shifting their frame of reference in response to changing administration objectives, foundation demonstration projects continually narrowed their objectives, focusing on what appeared to be politically safe, ideologically acceptable targets for change. Perhaps, then, the Gray Areas experience is better remembered not as a model of the way philanthropic activism ought to work, but as a lesson in the dangers of working within rather than challenging the boundaries established by federal government policy.

Notes

1. For a more detailed discussion of the Gray Areas program and its vision of urban reform, see Alice O'Connor, "Community Action, Urban Reform, and the Fight against Poverty: The Ford Foundation's Gray Areas Program," *Journal of Urban History* 22 (July 1996): 586–625.

2. Waldemar Nielson, *The Big Foundations* (New York: Columbia University Press, 1972) features Rockefeller, Carnegie, and Ford most prominently in his "gallery of portraits." On foundations and their efforts to influence policy through expertise, see Barry D. Karl and Stanley N. Katz, "The American Private Philanthropic Foundation

and the Public Sphere 1890–1930"; Ellen Condliffe Lagemann, *The Politics of Knowledge: The Carnegie Corporation, Philanthropy, and Public Policy* (Middletown, Conn.: Wesleyan University Press, 1989); Kenneth Prewitt, "Social Sciences and Private Philanthropy: The Quest for Social Relevance" (Indianapolis: Indiana University Center on Philanthropy, 1995). On knowledge and policy more generally, see Michael J. Lacey and Mary O. Furner, eds., *The State and Social Investigation in Britain and the United States* (Washington, D.C.: Woodrow Wilson Center Press, 1993).

3. Karl and Katz, "The American Private Philanthropic Foundation," 262.

4. Russell Marks, "Legitimating Industrial Capitalism: Philanthropy and Individual Differences," in Robert F. Arnove, ed., *Philanthropy and Cultural Imperialism: The Foundations at Home and Abroad* (Boston: G. K. Hall, 1980), 87–122. On the "associative" state, see Ellis Hawley, "Herbert Hoover, the Commerce Secretariat, and the Vision of an 'Associative State,' 1921–1928," *Journal of American History* 41 (June 1974): 116–40.

5. On the role of post–World War II federal agencies in research funding in the behavioral, especially psychological, sciences, see Ellen Herman, *The Romance of American Psychology* (Berkeley: University of California Press, 1995), 126–28.

6. Quote in Donald K. Price Oral History Transcript, Ford Foundation Archives, 6.

7. For discussions of these and other hearings, see Thomas C. Reeves, ed., *Foundations under Fire* (Ithaca: Cornell University Press, 1970).

8. Francis X. Sutton, "The Ford Foundation: The Early Years," *Daedalus* 16 (Winter 1987): 41–91.

9. Kai Bird, *The Chairman: John J. McCloy, the Making of the American Establishment* (New York: Simon & Schuster, 1992).

10. Sutton, "Early Years," 64–87; Richard Sheldon Oral History Transcript, FFA, 82; Ford Foundation, *Annual Report* (New York, 1957), 9–10.

11. In fact, the Foundation did not avoid these issues entirely, but did manage to create a distance by establishing separate operating funds: the Fund for the Republic and the Fund for Education. While enjoying a greater degree of freedom than direct Foundation programming would allow, the Funds themselves became lightning rods for conservative attack, and were eventually ended.

12. Donald David, Oral History Transcript, FFA, 8–9; Richard Magat, Oral History Transcript, FFA, 7; Special Committee, "Evaluation of Public Affairs Program, 1950–1961 and Statement of Current Objectives," December 1961, Report # 004736, FFA. For examples of the Foundation's involvement with government agencies in international affairs, including its problematic relations with the CIA, see Bird, *The Chairman*, 426–29.

13. On the emergence of juvenile delinquency as a national issue in the post-war years, see James Gilbert, *Cycle of Outrage: America's Reaction to the Juvenile Delinquent in the 1950s* (New York: Oxford University Press, 1986). Sheldon Glueck and Eleanor T. Glueck, *Delinquents in the Making: Paths to Prevention* (New York: Harper, 1952) reflects the work of two of the most influential social psychologists of the time. The Gluecks' work, which was for a short time funded by the Foundation, is discussed extensively in Robert J. Sampson and John H. Laub, *Crime in the Making:Pathways and Turning Points through Life* (Cambridge, Mass.: Harvard University Press, 1993).

14. The classic statement of the Chicago School interpretation of delinquency is in Clifford R. Shaw, *Delinquency Areas: A Study of the Geographic Distribution of School Truants, Juvenile Delinquents, and Adult Offenders in Chicago* (Chicago: University of Chicago Press, 1929).

15. Richard Cloward and Lloyd Ohlin, *Delinquency and Opportunity: A Theory of Delinquent Gangs* (Glencoe, Ill.: Free Press, 1960).

16. The interrelated processes of industrial restructuring, technological change, and migration patterns in the post–World War II years have been well documented in Mark Gelfand, *A Nation of Cities: The Federal Government and Urban America, 1935–1965* (New York: Oxford University Press, 1975), ch. 5; Arnold R. Hirsch, *Making the Second Ghetto: Race and Housing in Chicago, 1940–1960* (New York: Cambridge University Press, 1983); Kenneth T. Jackson, *Crabgrass Frontier: The Suburbanization of the United States* (New York: Oxford University Press, 1985); Thomas Sugrue, "The Structures of Urban Poverty: The Reorganization of Space and Work in Three Periods of American History," in Michael B. Katz, ed., *The "Underclass" Debate: Views from History* (Princeton: Princeton University Press, 1993), 85–117; Leonard Wallock, "The Myth of the Master Builder: Robert Moses, New York, and the Dynamics of Metropolitan Development Since World War II," *Journal of Urban History* 17 (1991): 339–62. For more contemporary views of the "crisis," see William H. Whyte et al., eds., *The Exploding Metropolis* (Garden City, N.Y.: Doubleday, 1958).

17. The Foundation's entry into issues of metropolitanization is announced in a staff report entitled "Public Affairs Program," 1953, Report #010656, FFA.

18. "Metropolitan Affairs," December 1955, Report #012030, FFA. The report and recommendations reflected the thinking of a special committee of consultants, which met during the summer of 1955 to discuss "the most urgent problems arising in metropolitan areas." The committee members were Coleman Woodbury, John T. Howard of the MIT School of Architecture and Planning, Joseph Fisher of Resources for the Future, Walter Isard of the MIT Center for Urban and Regional Studies, former Chicago alderman and Assistant to the Director of the Bureau of the Budget Robert Merriam, Oberlin economist and former State Department official Robert Tufts, and Foundation staff member Frank Sutton.

19. Joseph F. Clark Oral History Transcript, John F. Kennedy Library.

20. The various urban extension grants are discussed in Grant File PA62-29, FFA.

21. Paul Ylvisaker Oral History, FFA, 20–23.

22. The term "gray areas" was borrowed from economist Raymond Vernon, and referred to what Chicago school theorists had earlier described as the "zone of deterioration": the neighborhoods between the central city business district and the suburb which housed new urban immigrants while they were trying to gain a foothold in an unfamiliar environment. Ylivisaker, Oral History Transcript, 23; Raymond Vernon, "The Changing Economic Function of the Central City," in James Q. Wilson, ed., *Urban Renewal:The Record and the Controversy* (Cambridge, Mass.: MIT Press, 1966), 3–23.

23. Ylvisaker, "Planning in a Period of Change," speech before the American Institute of Planners, New York, October 27, 1958 (a version of the speech appeared as "The Deserted City," *Journal of the American Institute of Planners*, February 1959); "The University in a Changing Environment," speech before the Annual Meeting of the Association of Urban Universities, November 3, 1958; docket excerpt, March 1961, FFA.

24. Dyke Brown, "Public Affairs: Proposed Activities Concerned with Problems of Migration," December 23, 1959, FFA Report # 005055; Ylvisaker, Oral History Transcript, 58; speech before the 50th Anniversary Luncheon of the Philadelphia Housing Association, December 3, 1959, Speech File, FFA.

25. Clarence Faust, Oral History Transcript, FFA, 182. The major exceptions had been a substantial grant in 1953 to fund New York City's Puerto Rican Study, a curriculum/language training program to respond to the educational needs of Puerto Rican

192 | Alice O'Connor

migrant children, and support for research by social psychologist Martin Deutsch on early childhood education.

26. Ylvisaker, Oral History Transcript, 24–25.

27. Information on the Great Cities projects is in grant files to the individual city school systems, only some of which are open for review. Coordination and evaluation of the program as a whole was conducted under a Foundation Administered Project (FAP) which provided funding for consultants, workshops and conferences, Grant Files PA60-200, PA61-268, FFA. On the migration theme, and its links to concepts of "cultural deprivation" and poverty, two reports written by staff member Henry Saltzman are helpful, "Compensatory Education," Report #010238 and "The Invisible Schools," Report #002264, as is a grant to Berea College in Kentucky for a workshop to give urban service providers first-hand exposure to the problems faced by rural migrants, Grant File PA590-0212, all in FFA.

28. Ylvisaker, Memo to Henry Heald, "Status of the 'Gray Areas'-Great Cities School Improvement' Program," January 4, 1961, Henry Heald Office Files, Box 9, FFA; see also Peter Marris and Martin Rein, *Dilemmas of Social Reform: Poverty and Community Action in the United States* (New York: Atherton, 1967), 7–32.

29. Ylvisaker to Heald, "Status and Future of Great Cities-Gray Areas Program," October 24, 1961, Heald Office Files, Box 9; "Public Affairs: Gray Areas Program," September, 1964, Report #002845, FFA; Ylvisaker, "Community Action: A Response to Some Unfinished Business," speech to the Citizen's Conference on Community Planning, January 11, 1963, Speech File, FFA.

30. Ylvisaker to Heald, October 24, 1961.

31. David Hackett Oral History Transcript, October 21, 1970, John F. Kennedy Library, 66–73.

32. Marris and Rein, *Dilemmas of Social Reform*, 20–25. Clifford Campbell, former Deputy Commissioner of Planning in Chicago, was hired as a foundation consultant to evaluate the Gray Areas program.

33. Ylvisaker to Senator Willis Robertson, (Chairman of the Senate Banking and Commerce Committee), February 3, 1961. Heald Papers, Box 12, Folder 150, FFA.

34. Ylvisaker to Heald, October 24, 1961. An economist who had written widely about black segregation and ghetto formation in the 1940s and 1950s, Weaver was one of the "migrant streams" consultants for urban programs. He later became the first black cabinet official when he was appointed Secretary of Housing and Urban Development by Lyndon B. Johnson. Gordon was on the Foundation's Economic Development Program staff while on leave from Williams College in the mid-1950s and again in 1960, before going to the Bureau of the Budget in 1961. Kermit Gordon, Oral History Transcript, FFA.

35. Ylvisaker to Heald, October 24, 1961. Ylvisaker and others began to push for the idea of concentrating resources in a few "demonstration cities" in the early 1960s, an idea that would later be realized in the form of the Model Cities program.

36. Ylvisaker, Oral History Transcript, 28.

37. The Gray Areas evaluation consisted mostly of a relatively informal but consistent process of observation, site visits, and conferences. Although many staff members and outside consultants were involved in this process, the two principal evaluators were former Deputy Commissioner of Planning for Chicago Clifford Campbell and Peter Marris. Though hardly "scientific" according to the norms applied to evaluation today, the results of these observations, conveyed in letters, memos and discussions, were invaluable to the learning process that accompanied Gray Areas and contain insights about community change efforts that are still relevant. Campbell's reflections are chronicled in a series of letters to Ylvisaker, Grant File PA62-29. See also Marris and Rein, *Dilemmas of Social*

Reform. For the Foundation's more official view of the programs, see "Gray Areas Review."

38. Clifford Campbell to Paul Ylvisaker, May 28, 1964, PA 62-29.

39. Campbell to Ylvisaker, May 2, 1964, PA 62-29.

40. Saul D. Alinsky, "Community Analysis and Organization," *American Journal of Sociology* 46 (1941): 801.

41. Daniel P. Moynihan, *Maximum Feasible Misunderstanding: Community Action in the War on Poverty* (New York: Free Press, 1969), 102–105.

42. These divergent approaches to resident participation are discussed in Frances Fox Piven, "Participation of Residents in Neighborhood Community Action Programs," *Social Work* 11 (January 1966): 73–80; Howard W. Hallman, "Planning with the Poor: A Discussion of Resident Participation in the Planning of Community Action Programs," paper prepared for a Ford Foundation conference on community Action, December 1964, PA 62-29.

43. Campbell to Ylvisaker, May 28, 1964, PA 62-29; Edgar S. and Jean C. Cahn, "The War on Poverty: A Civilian Perspective," *Yale Law Journal* 73 (July 1964): 1317–52; Marris and Rein, 171–77.

44. Charles E. Silberman, *Crisis in Black and White* (New York: Random House, 1964), 352–53.

45. Marris and Rein, 105–107; "Gray Areas Review," Report # 002845, FFA.

46. Silberman, *Crisis*, xi.

47. Silberman, *Crisis*, 351–54.

48. Silberman, *Crisis*, 37.

49. Silberman, *Crisis*, 10.

50. Marris and Rein, *Dilemmas of Social Reform*, chs. 3–5; Mitchell Sviridoff, "The Manpower Problem: A View from a Bridgehead," remarks delivered to the Conference on Community Development, San Juan, Puerto Rico, December 1964.

51. Alice O'Connor, "Evaluating Comprehensive Community Initiatives: A View from History," in James P. Connell et al., eds., *New Approaches to Evaluating Community Initiatives* (Washington, D.C.: Aspen Institute, 1995).

52. Michael P. Brooks, "The Community Action Program as a Setting for Applied Research," *Journal of Social Issues* 21 (January 1965): 37; Marris and Rein, 199–202.

53. Dwight Macdonald, "Our Invisible Poor," *The New Yorker*, January 1963.

54. Quoted in Daniel Knapp and Kenneth Polk, *Scouting the War on Poverty: Social Reform Politics in the Kennedy Administration* (Lexington, Mass.: Heath Lexington, 1971), 109.

55. Ylvisaker, "Social Bargaining and Community Welfare," *Economic and Business Bulletin* (September 1963), 8. Ylvisaker also noted that the poverty label "can be restrictive. Many of the problems of the urban newcomers go beyond poverty; discrimination is one example." Nevertheless, as Marris and Rein point out, "breaking the cycle of poverty" became the catch-phrase of the Gray Areas programs. *Dilemmas of Social Reform*, ch. 2.

56. Memo to Cabinet members from Kermit Gordon and Walter Heller, "Outline of a Proposed Poverty Program," January 6, 1964. Wilbur Cohen Papers, Box 149, Folder 6, Wisconsin State Historical Archives.

57. Hackett to Kennedy, November 6, 1963. This memo is included with the background materials for a 1973 Conference on "Poverty and Urban Policy" held at Brandeis University, JFK Library.

58. Hackett to Heller, "Attack on Poverty," December 1, 1963, LBJ Library, Legislative Background, Economic Opportunity Act of 1964, Box 1.

59. James L. Sundquist, "Origins of the War on Poverty," in Sundquist, ed., *On Fighting Poverty* (New York: Basic Books, 1969), 21–25; Carl M. Brauer, "Kennedy, Johnson and the War on Poverty," *Journal of American History* 69 (June 1982); 95–119.

60. Memo to Theodore Sorenson, December 23, 1963, Legislative Background, Economic Opportunity Act of 1964, LBJ Library, Box 1.

61. Materials related to the Puerto Rico conference are included in PA 62-29, FFA.

62. Marris and Rein, 211.

63. Campbell to Ylvisaker, December 2, 1964, PA 62-29.

64. These issues are raised in the planning documents for the Puerto Rico conference, in PA 62-29.

65. "Gray Areas Review," 17.

66. Henry Heald to Foundation Officers, "Relations with Government Programs," May 4, 1965, Heald Papers, Box 12, folder 152, FFA.

67. Report #010581, "Summary of Ford-Foundation-Government Meeting," April 7, 1965, FFA.

68. Heald, "Relations with Government Programs."

69. Various memos concerning the Patman investigations and the Treasury Department report are in Heald Papers, Folder 154, FFA.

70. One example of such an intermediary is the Manpower Demonstration Research Corporation (MDRC), created by Ford in cooperation with the Department of Labor to administer and evaluate work and training demonstration projects for various segments of the poor population.

71. Sviridoff to Bundy, March 7, 1978, Bundy Papers, Series II, Box 18, folder 228, FFA.

72. Ylvisaker, Oral History Transcript, 29. Ylivsaker was later praised for his personal intervention to stop heavily armed National Guard contingents from conducting house to house weapons searches in the aftermath of the Newark riots in 1967. *New York Times*, March 20, 1992, A21.

9 | The Ford Foundation's War on Poverty

Private Philanthropy and Race Relations in New York City, 1948-1968

Gregory K. Raynor

THE FORD FOUNDATION emerged as a national force in the decade following the death of Henry Ford in 1947. The legendary automobile manufacturer had chartered his foundation in 1936, but only as an accounting mechanism to ensure ownership of the Ford Motor Company for his heirs. Before 1950 the Foundation was never in a position to grant much more than a million dollars in any given year and it pursued a relatively limited agenda in and around Detroit, Michigan. Only after the death of Henry Ford and his son Edsel (1943) did the philanthropy bearing their name transform itself into the largest, most influential, and most controversial foundation in the United States.[1]

Endowed with Ford Motor Company assets approaching $500 million in 1950, the Ford Foundation immediately dwarfed the Rockefeller Foundation and Carnegie Corporation to become the largest private philanthropic foundation in the United States. Ford's enormity was not the only attribute that made it influential. The activated Foundation drew members of its board and staff from the upper echelons of the nation's corporate, governmental, and university establishments. Ford Foundation officials, with links to the Truman and Eisenhower administrations, advocated for educational reform and and the advancement of the social sciences as nonmilitary means to strengthen the United States in its conflict with the Soviet Union. They assumed that America had to achieve a modicum of improvement in domestic race relations in order to protect its international image and secure its place as leader of the free world. Ford and its leading subsidiaries laid the institutional and ideological foundations of the War on Poverty in the 1950s through this liberal human resource agenda for the Cold War.[2]

When the War on Poverty in New York City is viewed within the broader postwar history of the Ford Foundation and its satellite organizations, we see that this reform movement was more than a decade in the making. The dynamics of board governance, policy planning, and coalition building by Ford, its Fund for the Advancement of Education (FAE), and Mobilization for Youth (MFY) directly influenced ongoing social movements on Manhattan's Lower East Side in the fifteen years preceding President Lyndon B. Johnson's Great Society. Although scholars have long been interested in MFY, no studies to date appreciate that FAE's work with the Lower East Side's public schools and settlement houses in the 1950s initiated the local community organization project that Ford and the Kennedy Administration later institutionalized as MFY. Analysts also depict the demise of MFY at the hands of a red-smear campaign as a historical aberration. On the contrary, McCarthyite political attacks, punitive audits, and Congressional hearings against Ford, its subsidiaries, and its grantees continued throughout the 1950s and the 1960s.

Race, McCarthyism, and the Ford Foundation's FAE

In 1950, a professional staff of attorneys, scholars, and professional philanthropists expanded the Ford Foundation's charter and reorganized it to pursue a diversified program of social, educational, and public affairs reform. H. Rowan Gaither, Jr., a California attorney, veteran of the civilian wing of the military establishment, and chairman of the Rand Corporation, headed the reorganization team. Gaither and his colleagues produced what probably remains the most exhaustively researched and explicitly stated blueprint for a foundation's operations. Gaither's team wrote Ford's commitment to desegregation in public education into its mission statement of 1950 (Gaither Report): "Even in this country persons of all races and colors do not have equal access to education. The advantages of education are also walled off behind economic barriers. . . . The poorer families, and those composed of members of our minority groups, are the ones most urgently requiring educational opportunity to improve their economic and cultural status. Yet they are the very ones against whom these educational barriers loom highest, and in consequence their cultural and economic inequalities tend automatically to be inherited."[3] Ford policy makers established an intellectual linkage between race, inequality of educational opportunity, and poverty in America. A major priority of Ford's domestic agenda was to subsidize the reform of public schools serving substantial numbers of immigrant and minority children. In this manner, the Foundation wedded reform of education and social services into a broader conception of social-welfare policy. Ford experimented with this approach in the 1950s before developing it as the basis for the Kennedy administration's nascent antipoverty agenda. Lyndon B. Johnson put race and education at the center of his ambitious legislative agenda, applying this Ford-inspired model on a national scale through the federally sponsored War on Poverty.

Ford President Paul Hoffman and his close associate Robert Maynard Hutchins were most responsible for creating FAE as an independent organization. Hoffman had complemented his successful career as CEO of Studebaker Corporation by serving in various capacities under Herbert Hoover and Franklin D. Roosevelt. He achieved his greatest renown in the Truman administration as the chief executive of the Marshall Plan in Europe, a position in which he allocated billions of dollars for the reconstruction of war-ravaged western Europe. Hoffman was also a close friend, confidant, and political advisor to Dwight Eisenhower. He personified the bipartisan rapprochement among leaders of America's Cold War state. Hoffman hired former University of Chicago Chancellor Robert Maynard Hutchins, with whom he had become acquainted as a trustee of the University, as an associate director at Ford.

Together, Hoffman and Hutchins had spent more than a decade trying to bring scholars and corporate professionals into the policy-making process at the national level. Hutchins was particularly successful at Chicago in bringing disparate specialists together to address pragmatic policy issues. The Gaither Report expressed the shared faith among American policy makers in large-scale social and political engineering: "In the modern world large scale and complicated arrangements are needed to provide the social and economic and political conditions under which human freedom may be assured and human welfare advanced. This is not to say that political institutions in and of themselves can assure human welfare—or even constitute democracy. Undemocratic institutions may be found in a free, democratic society. Majority rule alone does not guarantee democracy. What distinguishes a democratic society is the respect for others which makes men unwilling to be either slaves or masters. When the democratic spirit is deep and strong it animates every phase of living—economic, social, and political relations among groups and nations, as well as personal relations among men."[4]

The democratic rhetoric in this passage captured the essential paradox embodied in philanthropic foundations. Like its predecessors, Ford tried to gear a top-down, centrally administered organization to pursue what it viewed as democratic ideals. The great potential of the Foundation rested in its leaders' executive authority to make grants and create new institutions without public oversight or bureaucratic second-guessing. Given this freedom of action, the quality, commitment, and values of Ford leaders determined the Foundation's relative ability to realize its potential for the betterment of race relations. A set of peculiar historical circumstances concerning the donor family further mitigated the Foundation's reform agenda and increased the relative power of the staff to set policy.

Until his death, Henry Ford remained an outspoken critic of private philanthropy and therefore neglected his Foundation. The added fact that his son Edsel, an able philanthropist and manager, died prematurely in 1943, resulted in a complete vacuum of authority at the board level of the reorganized Ford Foundation. Henry Ford II overcame his playboy reputation as a Yale dropout by effectively overseeing the reorganization of the struggling Ford Motor Company, but as the Foundation's chairman he devoted much less time, interest, and ability. This lack of executive authority undermined any theoretical benefits of the Gaither Report. There simply was no common rationale or ethos to integrate the Foundation, because the enlarged board did not have substantial ties with the Ford family or the staff. Also, the reconstructed Ford charter arbitrarily divided the staff into five departments and did not preclude the creation of semi-independent subsidiary organizations. Exacerbating each of these problems were tax-law provisions that pressured Ford to spend the bulk of its massive yearly income. The result was an unwieldy organization divided within itself, unable to control the spontaneous proliferation of intermediaries, and led by a detached staff of policy entrepeneurs.

In 1951, Paul Hoffman and Robert Hutchins controverted the Gaither Report's warnings about the premature creation of intermediaries to push Ford to delegate its education reform agenda to an independent FAE. Endowed with upwards of $50 million in Ford money in the age of the *Brown v. Board of Education* decision, FAE matched the Foundation's bold pronouncements with a program of research, networking, and action. FAE's support for desegregation became apparent as it established its own board in 1952. No individual personified this commitment more than trustee Ralph Bunche. Bunche was a primary researcher for the Carnegie Corporation-sponsored Myrdal Study on race relations in America. Published in 1944 as *An American Dilemma*, that study firmly established Bunche as a leading scholar, black leader, and "philanthropoid." Largely due to the Myrdal Study, a cottage industry of academic research on race relations emerged in the 1950s. With financial aid from organizations like the National Association for the Advancement of Colored People (NAACP) and the National Jewish Congress, scholars began more thoroughly to explore the social, psychological, and moral implications of racism in America. When Thurgood Marshall and his legal colleagues sought to convince the Supreme Court to overturn past decisions that upheld Jim Crow laws, they could draw upon a corpus of social science research on racial discrimination.[5]

Bunche joined FAE shortly after he was appointed Undersecretary of the United Nations and accepted the Nobel Peace Prize in 1950 for negotiating the Palestinian-Israeli Peace Accord on behalf of the United Nations. He opened his 1951 address to the Forty-Second Annual Conference of the NAACP in Atlanta, Georgia, by arguing that events on the world stage shed greater light on the "incessant struggle against great odds to win for the Negro citizen the simple rights to which the Constitution of his own country entitles him. This is the Negro's burden and the nation's shame. . . . This leads me to say that the problem of race relations in this country is a national problem. So long as it persists, it is the responsibility of every American citizen, North, South, East and West. The fight against racial prejudice, therefore, must be nation-wide and must continue, and will continue, until the society is completely purged of this evil."[6] FAE clearly established its intent to spearhead private philanthropic support for minority education by naming Ralph Bunche as a trustee. More than any individual in the field of race relations, he enjoyed the respect of both black and white leaders. His contacts in government, in the philanthropic community, and among African-Americans were unparalleled.

During its first full year of operations, FAE granted funds to extend the work of the Phelps-Stokes Fund in southern communities. Among its grantees was the Southern Regional Council, a reporting service for black leaders and organizations to exchange information and strategies for desegregation campaigns. FAE also helped cultivate an educated African-American leadership through the National Scholarship Service and Fund for Negro Students. The nationwide talent search of this college scholarship organization placed heavy emphasis on public service and community organizing. The staffs of the Southern Regional Council and the National Scholarship Service and Fund for Negro Students took dangerous risks along with their clients by intervening in southern communities ruled by white supremacy. They challenged the prevailing view that blacks were incapable of learning and threatened to end blacks' dependency on white employers. A follow-up report on the scholarship fund found that blacks who initially scored poorly on standardized aptitude tests dramatically improved their scores and generally caught up quickly with average college freshman and sophomores.[7]

By 1952, Ford and FAE aroused serious opposition from southern communities, elected officials, and Ford Motor Company dealerships. Segregationists boycotted Ford products and threatened a broader political reaction against Foundation- and FAE-sponsored desegregation experiments. As that year's presidential elections approached, congressional conservatives, professional anticommunists, and southern segregationists raised the specter of a shadow government of liberal elites in conspiracy with foreign nationals and domestic subversives. Fulton Lewis, Jr., used his nightly radio broadcasts to spread fear of communist infiltration of the foundations. Syndicated columnists Westbrook Pegler and George Sokolsky made Ford and FAE special targets of attack and the American Legion encouraged members of its local affiliates to write and telephone their elected officials.[8] Writing in the *American Legion Magazine* in August 1952, William Fulton argued that the names of Ford, Rockefeller, Carnegie, and Rosenwald were synonymous with capitalism, but that in some mysterious manner millions of dollars left by such capitalists had fallen into strange hands: "These foundations are huge pools of capital created by industrial tycoons and merchant princes. . . . Their large tax-exempt income is dipped into by outright communists, fellow travelers, socialists, do-gooders, one-worlders, wild-eyed Utopians, and well-meaning dupes."[9]

Congressional leaders took advantage of this mood of fear and paranoia in 1952, convening an investigation of Ford and the nation's other large philanthropies. Chaired by Representative Eugene Cox (D-Georgia), the Select Committee to Investigate Tax-Exempt Foundations charged that America's largest private philanthropic foundations had been infiltrated by communists who funded subversive activities. The list of forty witnesses who testified before the committee included some of the nation's wealthiest corporate leaders and philanthropists, suggesting the specious nature of the charges—Chester Barnard, Vannevar Bush, John W. Davis, Charles Dollard, Marshall Field, Henry Ford II, Paul Hoffman, John D. Rockefeller, Jr., Dean Rusk, Alfred Sloan, and Donald Young, to name a few. Nonetheless, the publicity surrounding the Cox Committee hearings of 1952 placed foundations under greater scrutiny than ever before. Few Americans outside the nonprofit community even knew that foundations existed; even fewer knew of their elusive functions in the formulation of public policies. Few of the charges leveled at the major foundations had merit and the Cox Committee lost momentum as the fervor surrounding the election of 1952 subsided. The investigation produced no punitive legislation against foundations, but the congressional inquiry exposed internal divisions within the Ford Foundation and exacerbated growing tensions between Ford and FAE.

Because of the power vaccum at the top of the Foundation, the Cox Committee hearings precipitated a series of high-level firings and board realignments. A board coalition centered around Donald David, Dean of the Harvard Business School and trustee of the Foundation and the Ford Motor Company, actively criticized Hoffman and Hutchins for delegating controversial operations to FAE. Henry Ford II was relatively indifferent about the substance of Ford and FAE's programs, but had become increasingly annoyed with Hoffman's absence and Hutchins's unabashed disrespect for the trustees. Hoffman had become less and less active in Ford deliberations due to the failing health of his wife and his active role in Dwight Eisenhower's presidential campaign. Hutchins' transgressions were rooted mostly in his unparalleled intelligence, arrogance, and competitiveness. The fallout from these conflicts forced Hoffman and Hutchins from their leadership positions at the Foundation in early 1953. Shortly thereafter, the board appointed H. Rowan Gaither, Jr., as Ford's second president since its reorganization in 1950.[10]

Conceiving a National Urban Policy

In 1953, the Supreme Court heard arguments against segregation in public education, lending important momentum to the civil rights movement and legitimizing philanthropic activism. FAE sponsored a major study of the legal history and empirical dynamics of institutional racism in American public education. It hired Harry S. Ashmore, a widely respected commentator on race relations and executive editor of the *Arkansas Gazette*, to direct the study. Published on the eve of the Supreme Court's 1954 *Brown v. Board Of Education* decision, *The Negro and the Schools* (Ashmore Report) crystallized FAE's mission and helped nationalize the race debate. Former Supreme Court Justice Owen Roberts, a trustee on FAE's board, wrote that "The Fund soon came, as many a philanthropy before it, to the peculiar problems involved with the schooling of the American Negro. And there, in the late spring and early summer of 1953, the Fund's officers found unanimous agreement among educators they consulted—white and Negro, Southern, and non-Southern—that there was an urgent need for a new and comprehensive look at the structure of bi-racial education in the United States."[11] The Ashmore Report was actually a compilation of field studies of desegregation campaigns in the South, in border states, and in the North. In addition to funding the research of more than forty scholars and journalists, Ashmore deployed his staff to provided advice to local coalitions that wanted to press for racial integration of their public schools. In many cases, their field reports stemmed from ongoing extension work with schools, churches, and social agencies. Civil rights advocacy thus merged with social research, journalistic reporting, and minority scholarships.

Ashmore cautioned that many communities would resist outside support for school desegregation, for, as he wrote: "Interest in the schools is universal, and it is an interest that directly involves not only the taxpayer but his family, and therefore his emotions. Those who are indifferent to all other community affairs tend to take a proprietary interest in the schools their children attend, or will attend, or have attended. . . . No other public activity is so closely identified with local mores."[12] A series of successful regional conferences on race relations in education convinced the FAE board to support the Southern Education Reporting Service, a nonprofit news service created to provide timely and accurate information about developments in desegregation and school reform. The service brought together southern journalists who covered race relations in their respective communities.[13]

The Ashmore Report did not portray institutional racism in education as an isolated southern problem. It concluded that the migration of millions of blacks from the South to northern cities in the previous decades made segregation a national issue. FAE officials were aware that in many of these receiving cities, teachers and school officials viewed the rural poor and racial minorities as inferior and incapable of learning. They failed or expelled minority youths who exhibited problems with learning or classroom discipline. In addition to indicting Jim Crow in the South, FAE saw the need for a national urban policy to aid metropolitan areas undergoing stresses and strains associated with the in-migration of racial minorities.

Also in 1953, FAE planned a pilot project in conjunction with the New York City Board of Education to speed the city's adjustment process in the "New Age of Migration." The findings of the enterprise presumably would be applied in cities like Philadelphia and Cleveland where migrations of Puerto Ricans and other racial minorities altered the demographic and social makeup of urban communities. FAE officials conceived race relations in education in terms of immigration policy and social assimilation: "If those who move are 'different' in race, creed, color or other noticeable characteristics from those in their new neighborhoods, the newcomers will have troubles and they will cause troubles. This is especially true if newcomers are poor and are starting on the bottom rung of the occupational ladder. Since most of the migration is from 'underdeveloped areas' of the U.S.; e.g., the South and Southwest and Puerto Rico, the newcomers are generally poor."[14] In keeping with the assumptions of the Ford Foundation, FAE officials believed that educational and social-service institutions had to play a vital and cooperative role in reducing community frictions and individual suffering caused by the Great Migration. The goal of FAE's research and action initiative was to push the Board of Education to improve school-community relations by drawing upon the talents of social workers, mental hygiene specialists, clinical psychologists and psychiatrists, and public health experts. The enterprise developed unevenly over a period of four years and resulted in the publication of *The Puerto Rican Study*, a technical volume on race relations, education, and ancillary social services, in 1958.[15]

FAE conceived this minority assimilation initiative as a broad based, multi-disciplinary endeavor that brought a range of local institutions into alliance with selected local public schools. FAE chose four high schools and three junior high schools for experimental study and programming. Six schools were in Manhattan and one was in the Bronx. *The Puerto Rican Study* sponsored assimilation programs focused on bilingual education and the development of cross-cultural curricula at Public School 61 and Junior High School 65, both racially mixed schools located in the heterogeneous public housing neighborhoods of the Lower East Side. FAE officials viewed the community as an ideal test site because it typified impoverished multi-racial neighborhoods blighted by white flight, destabilized by urban renewal, and besieged by rural migrants and minorities.[16]

Following World War II, state and federal housing policies of unprecedented scale dramatically changed this traditionally white ethnic slum community. Unlike thoroughly established African-American or Puerto Rican communities such as those in Harlem or across the Williamsburg Bridge in Brooklyn, the Lower East Side contained few minority-owned businesses and established social institutions to welcome and support newcomers based on ethnic, racial, or kinship ties. In spite of these conditions, the area's low-income public housing projects were among the few plausible residential options for those families forcibly relocated by government-sponsored slum clearance or for rural migrants from the South and Puerto Rico.[17]

Eighty percent of the Lower East Side's population resided in decrepit old-law tenements or one of the massive public housing projects constructed along the East River between 1945 and 1958. One hundred red brick, low-income high-rise apartment buildings stretched from the Brooklyn Bridge northward past the Williamsburg Bridge and beyond Fourteenth Street. These unadorned, densely clustered monoliths were the architectural products of multi-billion dollar public policies that concentrated immigrants, racial minorities, and the poor in inner cities while subsidizing suburban development as a refuge from the problems of race, crime, and poverty.[18]

Many of the newcomers to the Lower East Side were rural migrants displaced by the collapse of the southern sharecropping system under the weight of mechanization and the consolidation of large-scale agribusinesses. More of them had fled poverty and unemployment on the island of Puerto Rico. FAE and the Board of Education relied heavily on settlement houses in the community to reach out to newly arrived minority families who faced fear and hostile resistance from white residents. As settlement houses witnessed their host communities changing around them, they either had to relocate to follow their mobile clientele or reestablish themselves among their new neighbors. A self-analysis conducted in 1953 by twenty-six affiliates of United Neighborhood Houses of New York, Inc. (UNHNY), showed that New York's settlement movement was in dire financial condition. Every one of the participating organizations reported an annual operating deficit at some time between 1951 and 1953. Half were in the red all three years.

Nearly a third received no capital investments for five years or more and had expended their endowments.[19] Amidst the McCarthyite groundswell of the 1950s, few elite patrons or elected officials of any political stripe were willing to step forward for the settlements or their new minority neighbors. The FAE public school initiative represented a ray of hope to UNHNY leaders who feared disastrous racial conflicts and the financial demise of their organizations. Yet, congressional conservatives soon reminded FAE, the Ford Foundation, and settlement activists that reform came with political risks, especially in the overlapping arenas of education, social welfare, immigration, and urban race relations.

Representative B. Carroll Reece (R-Tennessee) convened a second Select Committee on Tax-Exempt Foundations in late 1954. It renewed the attacks on Ford and FAE in particular, charging them with fostering domestic subversion through their undue influence over the educational system. The Reece Committee gave greater latitude to McCarthyites and political opportunists. They cast aspersions on a host of educational and extra-university planning councils which they termed "accessory agencies" to the communist plot within the foundation and academic communities. The Reece Committee pressured the American Council of Learned Societies, the National Research Council, the American Council on Education, the National Education Association, the Progressive Education Association, the John Dewey Society, the American Historical Association, and the League for Industrial Democracy.[20] Only the latter organization could be considered socialist or significantly leftist. Nonetheless, the formal power of the Congressional committee sent a chill through New York's educational and social-welfare establishments. The Reece Committee staff produced a blacklist that included the National Negro Congress, leaders of New York's settlement house establishment, and a host of civil rights organizations.[21]

For nearly a year the Reece Committee kept the staffs of Ford and FAE busy responding to punitive congressional audits and official questionnaires. Faced with a seemingly endless stream of attacks through 1954 and 1955, Ford president H. Rowan Gaither, Jr., initiated an internal screening process that restricted further activities with New York City's settlement houses or traditional welfare councils. Ford officials based this reversal of FAE practice on a policy review of the Rockefeller Foundation, Carnegie Corporation, and Chase Manhattan Bank. Each of these institutions viewed local contributions to traditional charity organizations as antithetical to their national orientation.[22]

The Reece Committee did not place a formal check on Ford's activities. However, congressional pressure pushed the Foundation to reabsorb FAE and discontinue its equally controversial Behavioral Sciences Program. Associate director and vice-president William McPeak, a liberal activist with a background in New Deal agricultural policy, described the board's reaction against FAE as follows:

> The experience of the Ford Foundation, like that of other foundations in the past, is that the relationships with semi-independent intermediaries, however sound their programs and their accomplishments, are unsatisfactory because the relationships are, at bottom, administratively unworkable. . . . It is the conviction of the officers of the Foundation that the maintenance of flexibility in operations and of the Trustees' control of program requires new relationships between the Foundation and the Funds on more workable administrative lines. While supporting both the accomplishments of the Funds established by the Foundation and the purposes for which they were established, the Foundation's officers believe that alternatives to the present organization must be sought.[23]

This internal discussion outwardly centered around the idea of improved flexibility. In fact, too much flexibility and independence on FAE's part was the underlying problem as perceived by Ford officials. The proposed restructuring would dissolve FAE's strong, liberal, and independent board to restore Foundation control over its educational agenda:

> Theoretically, a foundation is entirely free to reject proposals from a subordinate intermediary, but the experience of foundations over the past half century shows that such freedom is merely technical. A foundation can discourage an idea or a tentative proposal from its own staff without embarrassment to anyone. If a proposal from a subordinate intermediary has been approved by its own board of trustees, however, the parent foundation has less freedom to discourage it. Such a proposal will ordinarily have received so much attention that its rejection would be seriously embarrassing to many people. By the same token, if the staff of the subordinate intermediary seeks encouragement about a particular proposal from the foundation itself, the intermediary risks putting its own board of trustees in the role of a rubber stamp.[24]

In addition to restoring central control over FAE, Donald David and the ascendent Ford board coalition directed the Foundation staff to make a half billion dollars in unassailable grants to private universities for business administration, engineering, medical research, and private hospitals in 1955–56. There were merits in this $500 million flurry, but it clearly took place within the context of a thoroughgoing review of Ford's public relations. Ford later contracted an opinion poll that showed that the campaign worked. The overwhelming number of people surveyed who knew of the Foundation had a positive impression of it, mostly stemming from its support for higher education and hospitals. Ford had survived the congressional investigations, but the board relieved besieged Ford president Gaither of his duties, which by this time consisted mostly of defending the Foundation against outside criticism.[25]

The Foundation's retreat from controversy may have secured its reputation, but it raised political barriers between Ford, university-based social scientists, and liberal reformers who protested the state-subsidized ghettoization of minorities and immigrants in northern slums with virtually no investment in their education and assimilation. Ford's failure in 1955–1956 to use the Regional Planning Association's twenty-fifth anniversary celebration as a forum to critique regional transformations that exacerbated racial inequality completely nullified FAE's educational reform activities. Outgoing New York University president Henry Heald took part in the ceremonial event just before accepting his appointment as the third president of the postwar Ford Foundation.[26] The lack of a balanced urban policy ensured that the spatial, demographic, and architectual parameters of the urban crisis became entrenched by the late 1950s. In the same year that the New York Board of Education published *The Puerto Rican Study* (1958), Ford dissolved FAE and absorbed its operations into the Foundation-proper. All the while, grass-roots pressure for education and social-service reform grew and racial tensions continued to mount in New York. Settlement house leaders capitalized on this public ferment.

The Negro and the Schools and *The Puerto Rican Study* initiated a process of contested reform within the New York City school system and in the social-service community. FAE inspired a major settlement-led community organization enterprise on the Lower East Side of Manhattan in conjunction with the experimental public school programs. Historians have previously failed to recognize that Ford through FAE inspired this original community organization program at the heart of MFY. The settlement movement's preliminary findings suggested that the Board of Education and the schools were wholly unprepared, and perhaps unwilling, to educate an entire generation of Spanish-speaking youths from underdeveloped agricultural regions. They also questioned the city establishment's willingness to deal with the problem of racial gangs in any other way than to hand it off to the police. A consortium of settlements published a study in 1955 that foreshadowed social stress and potential violence stemming from the city's inability to respond constructively: "Our position has been taken with the conviction that unless something constructive is done, an already bad situation will deteriorate into utter chaos, hurting not only the Puerto Rican people, but the people of the City of New York and the whole nation as well."[27]

The Origins of Mobilization For Youth

On Wednesday, August 8, 1956, escalating youth gang fighting on the Lower East Side of Manhattan threatened to ignite a citywide gang war.

Allied groups of approximately 150 African-American youths battled a Puerto Rican gang of about seventy-five members. Through five days and nights of intensifying clashes, City Youth Board officials, the police, and local settlement houses attempted to quell the street fighting. Shortly before midnight on Monday, August 13, Henry Street Settlement (HSS) and Youth Board officials mediated a cease-fire, which received national attention. It was later termed the "Truce of '56."[28]

Many Americans perceived the escalation of interracial youth gang violence on the Lower East Side of Manhattan as the crest of a wave of juvenile delinquency sweeping the nation in the 1950s. Parents, educators, religious leaders, and social workers joined politicians and law enforcement officials in a heated debate over the adolescent crisis supposedly threatening social order. Intense worry focused on the allegedly pernicious generation of urban youths who spoke an underground language and lived outside the dominant social and moral order.

Significant legislative and law enforcement responses accompanied the media storm surrounding juvenile delinquency. In addition to Senate hearings, there were as many as 300 bills pending in Congress between 1954 and 1960 concerning juvenile delinquency. The Attorney General's Committee on Juvenile Delinquency and the Federal Bureau of Investigation raised the specter of rampant delinquency and urban disorder, encouraging local law enforcement agencies to crack down on misbehaving adolescents and youth gangs. Many communities passed ordinances that held parents legally liable for their children's crimes.[29]

The fear of an independent and potentially hostile youth culture indicated America's anxieties over the ability of traditional institutions like the family, the community, and the public schools to withstand the pressures of rapid economic change and the racialization of northern cities. On the Lower East Side, the outbreak of gang warfare pushed religious and community leaders to shape new institutional responses to the social problems of a once predominantly Jewish and white ethnic slum community being dramatically transformed by the migration of thousands of African-Americans and Puerto Ricans.

Because of and in spite of McCarthyite congressional pressure, HSS director Helen Hall skillfully transformed the public outrage over interracial youth gang violence into support for antidelinquency enterprises at settlement houses throughout New York. She lobbied on behalf of UNHNY and the Lower East Side Neighborhoods Association (LENA), a community council representing over 90 settlements, churches, synagogues, civic organizations, social agencies, parent-teacher's associations, local business, and labor unions. Although LENA conducted community organization programs related to education, recreation, housing, and summer employment, its increased public notoriety stemmed from its political support of successful HSS cease-fire negotiations. Helen Hall took full advantage of HSS's central role in the gang truce of 1956 by campaigning in support of the LENA Gang Leadership Project and the HSS Pre-Delinquent Gang Project. These two programs represented the earliest manifestation of MFY. HSS officials hoped to reinvigorate New York's struggling settlement houses by leading them across the color line.

HSS institutionalized its investigation of the warring gangs in the form of the LENA Gang Leadership Project. The purpose of the project was to understand and modify the behavior of youths at important decision-making levels of gang leadership. Staffed by street workers from the settlements, local churches, and the City Youth Board, the Gang Leadership Project applied generic case-work skills within a street-corner context. It reflected the social work maxim to work with clients "where they are." Their aim was to seek out the gang leaders and parents who held in their hands the balance between social conformity and antisocial aggression. The Gang Leadership Project's notion of an indigenous leadership referred to those teens and parents who spoke out against the gangs and willingly assimilated into mainstream community activities.[30]

Ministers of African-American and Puerto Rican Pentecostal churches were among the most visible leaders in the LENA community organization project before 1956. Shortly thereafter, however, they withdrew their support from the community council. According to Helen Hall, "They were obviously the best known leaders in the early days, but we found them too involved in building their own churches to take on anything else." Preliminary evidence suggests the opposite—that ministers and lay leaders of the local minority communities felt that HSS, its sister settlements, and LENA only sought to further their own institutional interests and political authority. They had even less confidence that the public schools or the police would change their racist perceptions of minorities. African-American and Puerto Rican parents argued that the notion of juvenile delinquency was used by school officials as a barely veiled justification for expelling their children.[31]

The goals and methods of the HSS Pre-Delinquent Gang Project further demonstrate how HSS perceived the links between juvenile delinquency and supposedly dysfunctional minority families. Settlement leaders viewed juvenile delinquency as a psychological pathology that threatened discipline and order within the settlements, the public schools, and on the streets. Run in affiliation with the Mental Hygiene Clinic at HSS, the Pre-Delinquent Gang Project focused attention on groups of boys between the ages of 8 and 12 who were beginning to show early signs of disruptive and violent behavior at school. As was typical in the 1950s, the program applied the Glueck Scale of clinical juvenile delinquency diagnosis. Harvard social psychologists Sheldon and Eleanor Glueck developed this diagnostic scale with the help of over $300,000 in grants from the Ford Foundation's Behavioral Sciences Program. According to the Glueck Scale, a series of environmental and behavioral factors measured through psychiatric casework techniques could predict the development of antisocial personalities in young children. Even when loosely applied by settlement caseworkers, this approach reinforced the assumption that younger siblings of gang members were predisposed to follow a similarly destructive path—thus the program's term "pre-delinquent."[32] Despite this potential prejudice, the HSS Pre-Delinquent Gang Project and other extension programs began focusing on younger and younger children who exhibited signs of impoverishment. Early childhood development and daycare became special foci of settlement programming in the ensuing years. This trend in the broader social-service community had an enduring impact on War on Poverty programming, informing the future Head Start program.

Despite their stated clinical approach, psychiatric casework techniques only partially penetrated HSS practices. Granted, two psychiatric social workers remained on call for the Pre-Delinquent Gang Project. However, HSS delivered the cognitive and behavioral training at the core of the program in the form of remedial education and traditional settlement practices. Like most of the settlements, HSS provided basic recreational and educational programming as after-school activities. What differentiated programming for so-called delinquents was the fact that they were sequestered from normal settlement activities so as to prevent disruption of classroom authority and discipline. HSS conceptions of juvenile delinquency as an individual pathology echoed popularly held assumptions about the moral and cultural depravity of poor and nonwhite families: "Our experience shows small chance of real change unless we are equipped to give these groups special time, leadership, skills and imagination. This in addition to the regular programs being conducted for the great majority of children who are in no way caught up in the distortion of values which have captured the minds and spirits of the groups we are discussing."[33]

Helen Hall and her close friend and ally Helen Harris, the executive director of UNHNY, created a Foundations Committee to head a capital drive in support of the HSS-LENA community organization project. If the antidelinquency campaign won significant funding, it would replenish the depleted UNHNY joint fund. Hall, Harris, and liberal Republican City Councilman Stanley Isaacs, the director and chairman of UNHNY for thirty years, headed an ad hoc committee on the Ford Foundation.[34] Despite the relative success of HSS's antigang campaign, its proposals to extend the enterprise as an ancillary service to additional public schools were denied by both public and private funding agencies. The Ford Foundation turned down UNHNY official solicitations in 1958.[35] Settlement officials were unaware that Helen Hall and Helen Harris had been blacklisted by the Reece Committee and the House Committee on Un-American Activities.[36] Although Ford grantmakers did not officially acknowledge such warnings, past experience favored prudence.

HSS also received mixed signals from the National Institute of Mental Health (NIMH). NIMH had funds and was actively reassessing its commitment to the community mental hygiene movement. As evidenced by the HSS Pre-Delinquent Gang Project, the clinical approaches to juvenile delinquency embodied in community psychiatric programs produced limited results. NIMH had nearly $100 million in unallocated funds for these programs and was looking to invest in alternative models of delinquency prevention.[37]

At the forefront of this reevaluation was Russell Sage Foundation sociologist Leonard Cottrell. Trained under Ernest Burgess at the University of Chicago school of sociology and recruited to NIMH in the mid-1950s, Cottrell helped shift the agency's emphasis from individual-centered antidelinquency measures to community-based enterprises.[38] Following up on his 1955 book *Identity and Interpersonal Competence*, Cottrell helped recast family and youth policies toward the development of "interpersonal competence." He contended that individual spouses, parents and children operated within a series of familial processes that tied them together through their relative abilities to communicate, cooperate and identify with each other. Instead of emphasizing the diagnosis and treatment of an individual family member's psychiatric problems, he suggested that social research and service be refocused toward the improvement of these interpersonal skills. Intervention on the functional level of the family arguably would produce a cascading effect that then might change previously unalterable individual personalities.[39]

Cottrell transposed his model of the interactive family to the broader framework of urban community relations, suggesting that existing institutions and interest groups were not effectively communicating, identifying, and interacting with each other. It followed that gang violence and escalating juvenile delinquency occurred because local institutions could no longer perform their organic function of social control. Cottrell and his foundation colleagues argued that organizations and human resources had to be reorganized to restore and sustain order. Just as interpersonal competence could be instilled in a family, Cottrell argued that the establishment of "community competence" should be the objective of future social and educational policies.

Unfortunately for New York's settlement movement, this sociological schema reinforced the belief within foundations and public policy circles that settlements were culturally antiquated, professionally obsolete, and alienated from the local constituencies they proposed to serve. New instrumentalities had to exhibit heightened awareness and sensitivity to the needs, opinions, and demands of local minority families and lay leaders. From Cottrell's perspective, community competence would be measured by the relative ability of social agencies and schools to include local residents in the reform process in a substantive and meaningful way. The new constituency largely consisted of disenfranchised poor whites, racial minorities, and rural immigrants who were previously neglected by mainstream institutions like the social settlements. Cottrell's commitment to citizen participation acknowledged the swelling revolt among poor and minority residents against the right of professionals in the "agency establishment" to make decisions that determined the course of their lives. The form of the revolt ranged from militant protests against slum clearance projects to threats to boycott the public schools.[40]

Although Cottrell's NIMH panel rejected the initial MFY proposal, it did not summarily dismiss HSS lobbyists. They knew that the gang wars of the Lower East Side had created a great deal of publicity concerning juvenile delinquency and urban disorder, making the community an ideal location for an experimental program. The Ford Foundation, in particular, was interested in launching a nationwide urban program by sponsoring demonstration projects in selected cities. Despite his view that settlement houses were incapable of dealing with the delinquency problem, Cottrell also recognized that the HSS Board retained much of its pre–World War II political cachet. Throughout the mid- and late 1950s, congressional pressure on the foundations forced NIMH to downplay its collaboration with the Ford Foundation and the Social Science Research Council. Cottrell and his Ford counterparts hoped that HSS could provide political cover for the MFY initiative through its strong ties with local elites and elected officials.[41]

Through extended political, philanthropic, and social service networks, HSS exerted an influence on New York City politics far outweighing the sum of the services it provided to families of the Lower East Side. Dozens of political figures, philanthropists and notables sat on HSS's board of trustees through World War II and the Great Society, including: Newbold Morris (served 1936–1966), Fiorella La Guardia's parks commissioner and career Manhattan Burrough president; Nicholas Kelley (served 1937–67), son of Progressive reformer Florence Kelley and chief executive officer of the

Chrysler Corporation; and representatives of the Schiff, Vanderbilt, and War-
burg families (served 1934–68). Far more than a neighborhood-based voluntary association, HSS was a locus for elite New York philanthropic activities, a political front for aspiring Democratic, Fusion and Reform Party
politicians, and the chief broker of private social-welfare resources on Lower
Manhattan.

The most crucial HSS official in the MFY enterprise was Board President Winslow Carlton. Carlton's father had been the CEO of Western Union
and invested extensively with German Jewish banker Jacob Schiff, the
founding patron of HSS in 1893. After he graduated in Harvard's class of
1929 and finished his graduate training at Columbia School of Business,
Carlton joined Henry Hopkins's Federal Emergency Relief Administration
in California. During the 1940s, he served as the CEO and sole employee
of Group Health, Inc., one of America's pioneering health maintenance organizations. This range of experiences earned him the presidency of HSS and
the National Welfare Assembly—a twenty-member national board that allocated funds for the American Red Cross and the United Neighborhood
Houses. Carlton took full advantage of the contacts he developed over this
long career of social-welfare entrepreneurship, assuming the Board Chair-
manship of MFY in 1959.[42]

Through the Washington lobbyist of his long-time friend Mary Lasker,
a chief philanthropic patron of the American Cancer Society, Winslow
Carlton gained access to the political keepers of NIMH. He arranged a
meeting with Representative John Fogarty (D-Rhode Island), the chairman
of the House Appropriations Committee, who had authority over NIMH
funding. Carlton brought Fogarty to New York to visit with the top Democratic officials. He arranged for the congressman to speak before several
prominent political clubs and wined and dined him at a series of dinner
receptions with local philanthropists. The large New York congressional
delegation also played a significant role in the courtship. By the time of the
presidential election in November 1960, MFY had won the crucial support
of the Appropriations Committee chairman. In short, NIMH and Ford officials used the HSS board to bridge the organizational gaps created by the
McCarthyite investigations of the 1950s.[43]

After Carlton secured this political support, Leonard Cottrell and his
NIMH panel referred HSS to the group of theoretical sociologists at the
Columbia University School of Social Work for a revision of the MFY pro-
posal, which lacked a requisite theoretical model for research and evalu-
ation. The HSS board retained sociologists Lloyd Ohlin and Richard
Cloward to take over the project through a grant to the Research Center of
Columbia's School of Social Work. The board of directors of the nascent
MFY enterprise, previously comprising HSS, LENA, and UNHNY of-

ficials, expanded to include representatives from the administration of the school.[44]

Like Cottrell, Lloyd Ohlin earned his Ph.D. at the University of Chicago as a student of Ernest Burgess. He sat on Chicago parole boards for most of the 1950s and established close ties with delinquency and corrections consultants to the Ford Foundation. Ohlin's Columbia colleague, Richard Cloward, was a doctoral student of theoretical sociologist Robert Merton. Merton carried the standard for Columbia sociology, the most renowned program in the country. He is most famous for his theory of the middle range, but it was his adaptation of Durkheim's concept of *anomie* that directly informed Cloward and therefore MFY. Through the idea of *urban anomie*, Merton argued that the chaos and violence in large cities resulted because disenfranchised residents had no stake in mainstream society and therefore did not adhere to its prevailing social mores.[45]

In 1959, Cloward and Ohlin prepared to publish *Delinquency and Opportunity: A Theory of Delinquent Gangs*, their theoretical reinterpretation of juvenile delinquency, which combined the renowned field work tradition of Chicago sociology with Merton's concept of *urban anomie*. Through their *opportunity theory*, they argued that antisocial behaviors like gang formation were rational responses to foreclosed opportunities in an inequitable capitalist system characterized by institutional racism.[46] They identified structural inequality as the source of delinquency rather than individual psychological problems, completely overturning the Glueck diagnostic approach. In turn, Cloward and Ohlin debunked the notion that antidelinquency campaigns should focus on individual gang members and misbehaving children.

On its face, the Columbia sociologists' concept of the opportunity system echoed traditionally held American ideals of democratic individualism. From this perspective, even the poorest residents of urban ghettos could supposedly achieve success via legitimate means because of unlimited American bounty. However, neither MFY nor the other Gray Areas projects had a comprehensive plan to reverse the trend of public and private divestment from interracial urban communities. While they used the language of economic opportunity, the purview of the program was limited to educational and social reforms. They identified the settlements, the public schools, and the city government as the targets of change:

> In this view, the individual is defined as being located in a structure of human relationships which inhibits or facilitates the realization of his goals. It is in this sense that we view the community as the primary target of change. Where in the past attention has been focused upon the individual delinquent, or the gang, or the parents of the delinquent, or upon some other aspect of the total problem, we argue for an approach which

seeks to alter the basic structure of the community. By changing the defeating conditions which confront the young, we expect that basic changes in their behavior and orientation will also occur. And we argue further that the immensity of the task ought not to deter us from mounting a major effort to achieve this end.[47]

In all likelihood, few officials in the emerging MFY coalition actually read Cloward and Ohlin's redrafted proposal. Had they done so, they might have recognized it as a radical critique of American capitalist society and the New York City government—a leap few Ford, HSS, or political officials were prepared to make. Richard Cloward, in particular, saw a need to challenge and alter the very structure of community life on the Lower East Side in order to create legitimate opportunities for the poor and racial minorities. Cloward and Ohlin's structuralist explanation for delinquency argued that gangs resulted from the oppression of racial minorities and immigrants at the hands of white institutions. They echoed civil rights leaders' claims that the economic inferiority of blacks stemmed primarily from white racism.

In the months prior to and following the 1960 presidential election, public discourse over national urban policies more openly addressed the problems associated with the urban renewal program and the Great Migration. Speaking at a pre-election gathering of Detroit settlement house leaders, Helen Hall for the first time referred explicitly to issues of race as the primary challenge facing the settlement movement and MFY: "Neighborhoods change rapidly—the Puerto Ricans move into the Irish community and the Italians move into a predominantly Negro neighborhood. The settlement worker has to bring the two elements together. We achieve this by bringing the parents together. We told them we would give their children special help if they would work with us."[48] Hall maintained that settlement houses were the proper arbiters of racial cooperation, despite the obvious rift between HSS and its minority neighbors. Despite Hall's declaration, the Ford Foundation's Public Affairs Department formulated MFY and the Gray Areas Projects as independent alternatives to the supposedly antiquated and establishment-oriented settlements.

Leonard Cottrell, Lloyd Ohlin, and Richard Cloward represented an ascending generation of sociologists who adapted their theoretical conceptions to social policy making. In the process, they advanced an explicit critique of the settlement movement and the urban political establishments upon which it depended. Within months of the publication of *Delinquency and Opportunity*, Cloward became co-director of MFY and Ohlin joined the President's Committee on Juvenile Delinquency and Child Crime (CJD), the executive branch commission that linked Ford's Public Affairs Department to the Kennedy Administration. The Foundation's intervention altered the leadership of MFY in an attempt to push forward the social and educational reforms initiated in New York by FAE.

Foundations of the War on Poverty in New York City

Between 1960 and 1962, a mid-level Ford official named Paul Ylvisaker emerged as one of the most influential planners of New Frontier education and social welfare policy. A Harvard-trained political scientist, Ylvisaker gained significant municipal government experience as the chief aide to the mayor of Philadelphia. After suffering a heart attack at the young age of 33, he decided to take a position at Ford rather than continue his career in politics. Ylvisaker attracted an impressive group of city planners, youth policy experts and career civil servants to the Foundation's Public Affairs Department to formulate more coordinated community approaches to urban reform. Public Affairs officials negotiated the now renowned Gray Areas Projects in Oakland, Boston, Philadelphia, Washington, D.C., Pittsburgh, and a statewide undertaking in North Carolina. Like Harry Ashmore at FAE, Ylvisaker balanced the Foundation's commitment to the reform of race relations with a deep respect for the power of reactionary forces. Against the warnings of some his Public Affairs colleagues, he championed controversial components of the Gray Areas Projects, such as legal aid to the poor. Still, he selected municipal regimes that promised moderation, accountability, and political stability.[49]

Ylvisaker did not negotiate the MFY contract, however. An independent subsection of Public Affairs was given the responsibility to develop a federal antidelinquency demonstration project for CJD in New York City. A career civil servant named David Hunter headed Ford's Office of Juvenile Delinquency. A self-described European-style social democrat, Hunter served in the administration of the Marshall Plan in West Germany before heading the United Nations Children's Emergency Relief Fund's Latin American office. He joined Ylvisaker at Ford in 1959 and went on to run the Stern Foundation after MFY's federal charter in 1962.[50]

David Hunter established a close relationship with Richard Cloward and Lloyd Ohlin during the planning phase of MFY, committing the organization to an aggressive desegregationist stance and to active lay participation in service formulation and delivery. Whereas Paul Ylvisaker negotiated the Gray Areas contracts in close cooperation with city agencies, elected officials and local elites, Hunter and Cloward viewed those forces as the targets of change. They believed that institutional discrimination against minorities formed the root of America's urban problems. For eighteen months, MFY's new leadership put together a 300-member staff of professional social workers, educators, gang specialists, and scholars. By 1962, MFY had undergone a complete transformation from its HSS origins. Instead of embracing the traditional values of assimilation that typified the settlements and the public schools, MFY became a powerful agent for the radical social movements of the 1960s. From a tactical perspective, New York's settlement houses favored moderate reforms that would not completely alienate city hall and the board of education. In contrast, MFY prepared to mount an aggressive political offensive against the urban establishment.

After losing executive control of MFY in 1960, HSS and UNHNY recovered by winning a $1 million grant from the recently activated (1959) Vincent Astor Foundation for antidelinquency campaigns in nine New York settlement house communities. The male-dominated circles of policy makers at Ford and CJD ridiculed Brooke Astor, Helen Hall, and the mostly female leadership of UNHNY as the "ladies bountiful," despite their crucial role in developing MFY.[51] Brooke Astor, Vincent Astor's widow, rejected this chauvinist critique, making the UNHNY-Astor Project the first in a long line of bold grants in her philanthropic career. This grant effectively split the original MFY coalition along two tracks. MFY aligned itself with Ford and the federal government against recalcitrant city agencies while the settlements retained their ties to city hall, the board of education, and local philanthropic foundations.

On June 1, 1962, Attorney General Robert Kennedy joined New York City Mayor Robert Wagner, Jr., at a City Hall news conference to publicize the creation of MFY, President Kennedy's three-year, $13-million federal demonstration project for community action. They celebrated the organization as an unprecedented alliance between, federal, state, municipal, and private resources. Its immediate goal was to curb the rise in gang violence and juvenile delinquency that erupted on the Lower East Side of Manhattan in the late 1950s. Its broader agenda was to address the persistent problems that prevented poor and minority families from raising themselves from poverty.

Robert Kennedy championed MFY in a high-profile fashion, cultivating a reputation as a friend to the poor and racial minorities. His conspicuous support of the program, coupled with Ford's close collaboration with CJD, reflected how Democratic control of the White House had changed political dynamics since the Cox and Reece investigations of the foundations. However, in his eagerness to ride the changing political tide Kennedy failed to appreciate the underlying ideological divisions inherent in the evolving MFY coalition. He also underestimated the hostility the program might evoke from elected officials and existing social and educational organizations.

MFY began operations over the summer of 1962 at storefront facilities throughout the Lower East Side. The use of storefront space reflected a conscious effort to disassociate the organization from traditional social agencies increasingly viewed by the minority communities as hostile and interloping institutions. Reformers historically viewed the physical structures of settlement houses as examples of the "better life" that was open to hard-working and upwardly mobile slum residents. MFY rejected this stance, opting for more accessible and less pretentious facilities. In addition to this architectural and spatial departure, MFY deviated from the geographic target populations of HSS's proposed plan. Storefront agencies located themselves in predominantly African-American and Puerto Rican neighborhoods rather than mixed settlement neighborhoods. The staff encouraged residents of the surrounding neighborhoods to walk right in for consultations about their problems with landlords, social agencies, the public schools, and the police and welfare departments.[52]

In 1962 and 1963, MFY employed a broad range of social-service and educational practices, many of which were found at traditional social agencies. These included remedial education, mentoring programs, arts and music programs, student tutoring, cognitive and behavioral training, family counseling, employment services, home economics, drug addiction intervention, and extensive referrals. The staffs of the storefront facilities also provided immediate relief in the form of small loans, escort services, and child care. Many of these services are worthy of independent analysis and receive thorough treatment in existing evaluation studies. I am primarily concerned with their collective impact on educational and social-welfare governance in the months preceding the formal declaration of the War on Poverty.

MFY was unique because it operated as a multifaceted reform organization, pressuring public and private institutions to be more responsive to racial minorities and the poor. It consistently advocated minority community positions, standing against the white establishment that its leaders viewed as the source of poverty, delinquency and hopelessness.[53] The flexible and enthusiastic responses of MFY staffers represented a broader assault on the symptoms of poverty than its settlement predecessors. Rather than promising an ephemeral ideal of upward mobility and middle-class stability, they aimed to deal with the concrete, everyday problems associated with life in the slums and ghettos.[54]

As later described by Richard Cloward and Frances Fox Piven, MFY staffers placed telephone calls to countless city and state functionaries and often accompanied families to see officials in person: "They argued and cajoled; they bluffed and threatened. 'When I go to welfare,' one staff member declared, 'I don't wait around for the stall. If I don't get treated with respect, I start hollering for the supervisor, and then I threaten legal action. Any way you cut it, they are the enemy.'"[55] A primary goal of MFY was to fight the administrative red tape that characterized many welfare agencies and the public schools. Perhaps the organization's most enduring contribution was its widespread introduction of legal aid for the poor. As procedural complaints multiplied, public agencies found it easier to grant clients' demands than to embark on cumbersome, undesirable lawsuits. Few of the cases were actually litigated because organizations ordinarily preferred to settle out of court. The practice of using litigation to reform welfare bureaucracies expanded under the provisions of the Economic Opportunity Act of 1965.[56]

As time passed, however, storefront staff members became frustrated with the same repetitive administrative and service-delivery grievances. They began to think more about collective action as a vehicle for their racial and class critiques of urban institutions. They reasoned that fifty clients and staffers protesting together would be far more effective at coercing recalcitrant agencies than individual bargaining. MFY's turn to collective action sought to empower indigenous minority groups, consciously confronting what they perceived as an internal colonial order of racial and class exploitation. MFY pushed the settlements to conduct seminars on sensitivity training and class reorientation. MFY pushed the UNHNY leadership, in particular, to reevaluate and reform their purportedly middle-class assumptions about educational and social-welfare programming.[57]

During 1963 and 1964, the MFY agenda increasingly took on the appearance of a Maoist struggle for the allegiance and grass roots support of Lower East Side minority residents. Fueled by the momentum of the civil-rights movement, the MFY staff sponsored sit-ins and rent and labor strikes, and took part in racial demonstrations against the police and welfare departments and city hall. In late 1963, the MFY staff helped spark a staff strike and picket line at HSS, virtually shutting the organization down through the winter. The academic critique of HSS and the settlement movement burgeoned into a frontal assault on its governance and personnel policies. MFY criticized HSS and its sibling settlements for the lack of racial minorities and indigenous residents on their staffs, and their failure to adequately pay lay volunteers from the neighborhood.[58]

Leaders of the settlements and other traditional social agencies complained about MFY tactics to city, Ford, and CJD officials. Paul Ylvisaker chose his words carefully to avoid making an outright repudiation of traditional social-service agencies. Nonetheless, he expressed the prevailing view among Foundation and federal officials that the settlements were insufficient instruments for New Frontier social-welfare policies: "There is some feeling that this decision to establish new instrumentalities is an attack on the present system of community health and welfare councils. If so, it came not by intent nor with malice, but as a commentary on the gap that exists between the job to be done and the capacity of our urban communities as presently structured to accomplish it."[59]

Despite the increasing public criticism of Ford's adventuresome satellite, MFY staffers continued to take part in the demonstrations of their clients. Activist staffers cooperated with representatives of the Congress On Racial Equality (CORE) and other New Left and civil rights organizations. The Lower East Side Civil Rights Committee, comprised partly of minority religious leaders who left the LENA coalition in the late 1950s, joined civil rights forces who advocated a boycott of the New York City public school system in January of 1964. The organization wrote Winslow Carlton to ask for a formal endorsement from MFY: "In our community, at least 65% of the school children are behind in reading, with a large percentage two to four years behind. Probably 70% of our present enrollment will drop out of school before the end of high school, and form a part of the unemployable social dynamite of our city. Despite the efforts and money expended by institutions such as yours to meet this alarming situation, no reversal of this serious trend is in sight. City Hall and the Board of Education have failed to match their alleged commitment to quality-integrated education with corresponding action."[60] Carlton and the MFY board turned down the civil rights organization's request for an official endorsement, but many dissident staffers supported the boycott. Minority activists and their MFY allies took their case to the community: "The Boycott of Schools is set for February 3rd!! Parents want the end of segregated schools with bad equipment and bad attitudes! Leaflets are being given out at schools and supermarkets and door-to-door!! Children will be told where to spend that day . . . safe and cared for and given their lunches!! No parent needs to worry about his child. Most of all, every parent can be proud to keep a child out of school because this is the way to fight for what we believe in!!"[61] The threat was very real and few local officials took heart from the fact that the planned February action never took place. Talk of a future school boycott continued. Over the summer of 1964, racial animosities that had been temporarily channeled into non-violent political activism gave way to frustration and violence.

On Thursday, July 16, 1964, a fifteen-year-old African-American boy was shot and killed en route to a remedial reading course typical of settlement and federal antipoverty demonstration programs. Word spread among New York's minority communities that the assailant was a white off-duty police lieutenant. Two days of vitriolic protests ensued. When the sun set on a tense CORE rally on Saturday, rioting broke out on the streets of Harlem. Two nights following those skirmishes, violence, looting, and vandalism spread to the Bedford-Stuyvesant area of Brooklyn. After three nights of rioting, police made 276 arrests, and 22 serious injuries and 556 incidents of property damage had occurred.[62]

City Hall and law enforcement officials suspected that MFY had had a hand in the protests leading up to the riots. Mayor Wagner promised a New York City Investigation Department probe of the protests, the ensuing riot, and the organizations suspected of fostering the unrest. By week's end, City Council President Paul Screvane launched a public broadside at MFY. He leaked to the *Daily News* that "communists and other leftists have infiltrated the organization and are fomenting subversive activity."[63]

MFY's unabashed threats to city agencies and the public schools invited sharp bureaucratic discipline from the local political establishment. The public smear campaign broadened into a year-long investigation concerning MFY's administrative practices and budgetary accountability. Federal officials froze the organization's funding while awaiting the completion of probes by the FBI, the Justice Department and Congress. The ensuing legal and administrative battles forced the resignation of two of the organization's program directors and caused the retrenchment of its community-action funding. Following the investigation, recently elected Mayor John Lindsay and the city council stripped MFY of its authority over antipoverty funding. Months before President Johnson formally declared the federal War on Poverty, reactionary local forces undermined its celebrated demonstration project. Whether or not the organization had a direct hand in the events of July 1964 mattered little. The Bedford-Stuyvesant race riots enabled local political officials and the anti-communist press to paint MFY with a broad red brush: "Mobilization for Youth, Red- and violence-tinged welfare organization for fighting juvenile delinquency, gets an enthusiastic whitewash from a group of top-flight social workers headed by Secretary Leonard Cottrell of the Russell Sage Foundation. MFY's encouragement of rent strikes, school boycotts, marches on Washington and other activities can all too easily slop over into violence."[64]

UNHNY officials withdrew their support from MFY in early 1965. UNHNY executive director Helen Harris, a close ally of Helen Hall, resigned from her post as chairman of the City Council's Planning and Coordinating Board for antipoverty projects. She protested the newly created Office of Economic Opportunity's subsidization of groups hostile to existing public and private agencies: "It is always a clear day in Washington and by some God-given extrasensory perception, Office of Economic Opportunity staff can see what is needed in New York City, which individual or group is best able to provide it and which project should be processed first."[65] Hall also criticized MFY's guerilla actions against UNHNY-Astor Project affiliates: "No one on the MFY staff seemed to realize that the so-called 'target population' does not exist in a vacuum. They are woven into the fabric of community life, however tenuously, into relationships with the school system, with the police, with landlords, with local and city politicians, and with local churches and other agencies of all kinds."[66] What began as an organizational split in the nonprofit antidelinquency coalition had widened into a vitriolic ideological battle between supposedly allied reformers. Tens of millions of dollars of federal antipoverty funding hung in the balance while MFY board chairman Winslow Carlton, Ford's Public Affairs Department and newly elected New York Mayor John Lindsay attempted to reconstitute the antipoverty coalition through a series of leadership changes.

Reaching a Settlement

The leaders of New York's fractured antipoverty coalition institutionalized the political reaction against MFY. Between 1965 and 1967, a series of leadership and organizational realignments took place within New York City government and MFY, as well as within HSS and the Ford Foundation. Each helped reconstitute the nonprofit coalition at the heart of MFY by moderating the organization's militancy. The most obvious changes occurred within MFY itself. Although the MFY board spared Richard Cloward, it forced the organization's administrative and program directors to step down. In their place the board hired the more moderate Bertram Beck, a leading figure in the National Association of Social Workers and a member of the CJD Advisory Committee, which had just audited MFY. Beck brought to the organization a stabilizing professional force on which government and Ford Foundation officials could rely. Reportedly, he was fond of saying that "MFY must be above reproach, like Caesar's wife" as a way of expressing his willingness to work with the mayor, the city council, the settlements, and their traditional welfare councils. Humor aside, Winslow Carlton used Beck's reputation as a moderate as a foil against the steady public onslaught against the organization. He diverted funds away from more confrontational political activities to traditional educational, social, and vocational services. Any hopes for further government backing of MFY hinged on this change in leadership and orientation.[67]

The HSS role in the MFY coalition came full circle in 1967 when Beck accepted Winslow Carlton's request that he succeed the retiring Helen Hall as HSS director. The city compensated HSS for its original investment in MFY through a block grant and recommended that additional federal antipoverty funds be allocated to UNHNY affiliates through subcontracts. Beck served as director of both MFY and HSS for two years. During his ensuing ten-year tenure at HSS, he implemented many of the reforms envisioned by Hall and innovated at MFY. Although some of his critics viewed him as an apologist for "the establishment," he helped transform HSS into a more responsive agency that reflected the needs and demand of its heterogeneous neighbors. HSS underwent substantial turnover in its staff, with racial minorities assuming greater responsibility for youth programming and the overall settlement agenda. Beck's commitment to education and social reform helped sustain Lower East Side school reforms initiated by FAE, carried forward by MFY and the HSS-LENA coalition, and institutionalized by the Ford Foundation after 1967.

The restoration of city, HSS, and LENA authority over local social-welfare policy created heated animosity among spurned MFY activists. Referring to Helen Hall as "the dowager empress of traditional social work on the Lower East Side," MFY sympathizer Susan Brownmiller captured the essence of the political conflict in a 1968 *Village Voice* article. "The powerful, elitist Miss Hall was both a sponsor of the original MFY and a dedicated enemy of MFY's community organizing program," she charged. A decade after McCarthyites labeled her a communist sympathizer and civil rights agitator, New Left activists accused Hall of selling out the cause.[68]

The crippling of MFY stunned and embarrassed Ford Foundation officials. MFY represented the most radical departure from the sustainable local reform models envisioned by most Ford officers and trustees. They scrambled to repair New York's antipoverty and desegregation coalition by drawing from the Foundation's national roster of urban reformers. Other gray areas projects had faced similar political problems. The director of Ford's New Haven, Connecticut program, Community Progress Incorporated (CPI), proved especially adept at maintaining sound ties with municipal authorities. Mitchell Sviridoff, CPI's director, had previously served as the director of the Connecticut United Auto Workers and later as chairman of New Haven's board of education. His historical anti-communist labor stances and progressive educational reform record made him suitable Foundation-officer material in the eyes of many Ford trustees. In a much-publicized racial controversy in New Haven, he distanced CPI from the minority community position and retained close ties to New Haven's mayor.[69] Sviridoff parlayed the points he had won as a moderate in that controversy into increased authority within urban policy circles. Ford officials strongly recommended Sviridoff as Lindsay's chief social policy consultant in the wake of the MFY debacle.

Backed by the Foundation's recommendation and the mayor's executive order, Sviridoff directed the creation of the New York City Human Resources Administration (HRA), a bureaucratic agency charged with oversight of community development, manpower and career services, social policy, public assistance, and educational extension programs.[70] Sviridoff and analysts at the Institute of Public Administration conceived HRA as an agency that would strike a better balance between the trend toward decentralized community control and the Mayor's need for more political accountability than had been present in the MFY experiment. Sviridoff's policy team recommended that nonprofit corporations be chartered in impoverished neighborhoods to ensure that community development policies would be effectively sustained. In order to avoid offending its minority supporters, the Lindsay administration set up its own storefront facilities to coordinate local service delivery.[71] In effect, HRA co-opted and bureaucratized many of the functions carried out by the independent MFY experiment, adapting many of its service practices but rejecting grass-roots community authority over social and educational programming.

Shortly after he was elected senator of New York in 1964, former Attorney General and MFY sponsor Robert Kennedy joined forces again with the Ford Foundation to support a relatively new model for urban antipoverty programs, the community development corporation. Built atop the wreckage of the Bedford-Stuyvesant race riots of 1964, the Bedford-Stuyvesant Restoration Corporation (BSRC) eschewed the radicalism of MFY and rejected the poor people's democracy envisioned in the community action movement. BSRC focused more on job development and environmental restoration of the dilapidated ghetto. Therefore, one of today's dominant forms of urban social welfare governance—the community development corporation—was born out of Ford's reaction against community action.

In contrast, education reform once again cast Ford and HSS into the heart of heated controversy. Both organizations sided with minority community activists against city hall, the board of education, and the teachers' unions in the school decentralization crisis of 1967–1968. A citywide school boycott and the subsequent teachers' strike deteriorated into a pitched battle between minority community action activists and the predominantly Jewish and white ethnic school establishment. Amid this racial polarization, resilient HSS, LENA, and Ford officials successfully expanded FAE's original experimental program with two Lower East Side schools into the larger Two Bridges Experimental School District, an organizational cousin to the renowned Ocean Hill-Brownsville Experimental School District. Thus ended more than a decade of policy planning and coalition building, in which cold-war politics exacerbated conflicts between reformist and radical strategies and limited the successes of the Ford Foundation's War on Poverty in New York City.

Epilogue

Recent events cast renewed attention on the role of private foundations in shaping public policy. The end of the cold war in 1989 pushed Americans to once again reconsider the federal government's role in organizing our society. Congressional Republicans' victory in the midterm elections of 1994 then raised the stakes of this debate, as the new congressional majority called for the devolution of federal power to the states and a return to America's traditions of voluntarism and private charity. The challenges of federal devolution are already upon us, yet we are only beginning to develop the historical background necessary to discuss the complex issues this entails. In the coming years, foundations will shape new models for governance and provide leaders that will implement those models in the process of federal devolution. Therefore studies of Ford and other foundations are timely and relevant for public policy makers, nonprofit practitioners, academicians, and laypeople.

I have derived three conclusions about studying foundations from my ongoing historical analysis of Ford and its subsidiaries. First, a great deal more attention must be paid to the role of board governance in the creation of foundation policies and the building of philanthropic coalitions. Trustees' self-conscious ethic of fiduciary responsibility represents a formal link between the corporations that accumulate massive philanthropic trusts and the foundations that administer them. In most cases boards set the broad parameters of foundation action without intervening in daily operations.[72] As demonstrated by the Ford Foundation in the 1950s, however, shifting board coalitions and conflicts undermined individual grants, inspired broader organizational reforms within the Foundation, and facilitated significant changes in its executive leadership. These internal dynamics destabilized Ford's urban-affairs agenda and exposed conflicts within New York City's antipoverty coalition.

My second general conclusion is that study of congressional regulation of private philanthropic foundations is central to our understanding of how external forces shape and constrain these unique nonprofit institutions. Public regulation of foundations was and is part of a continuous battle among national leaders for control over government agencies, national policy commissions, the major political parties, and extra-university planning councils. Disputes within the two major political parties over the role of foundations and the federal government in domestic race relations inspired the punitive investigations of Ford in 1952, 1954, and 1969. Although there are important differences between each of these national commissions and the local red-smear campaign that destroyed MFY, they are part of an identifiable history of political influence on private philanthropy. Since there surely will be future congressional inquiries into the role of foundations in American life, a better understanding of Ford's history as a lightning rod has contemporary importance for scholars, nonprofit practitioners, and public policymakers.

My third working assumption about thorough research of foundations is that a comprehensive notion of political history is necessary to capture their complex and often hidden role in public policy. Foundations have to be viewed within the context of the political party system, all three branches of government, and the complex interaction of local, regional, and federal levels of government. However, this level of policy analysis is at its best when complemented by critical social research of policy implementation. Ford's disordered institutional development in the 1950s clearly demonstrates that organizational realignments, personal competitions, and ideological conflicts had consequences, often tragic ones, for the local communities that the Foundation was committed to serve. Thus, I have tried to unite the interests of scholars and practitioners by combining an evaluation of discrete reform models, an institutional history of Ford, and a local political history of New York City.

Notes

1. On Henry Ford's early charitable endeavors, see William Greenleaf, *From These Beginnings: The Early Philanthropies of Henry and Edsel Ford, 1911–36* (Detroit: Wayne State University Press, 1964); Waldemar Nielsen, *The Big Foundations* (New York: Columbia University Press, 1971), 78–98; on the expansion and reorganization of the Ford Foundation after 1950, see Francis X. Sutton, "The Ford Foundation: The Early Years," *Daedalus* 116 (Winter 1987): 42–91.

2. Ellen Condliffe Lagemann, in *The Politics of Knowledge: The Carnegie Corporation, Philanthropy, and Public Policy* (Middletown, Conn.: Wesleyan University Press, 1989), 207–209, acknowledges the mutual influence of Ford and Carnegie on the national education agenda. Ford established a niche as a leading organizer and financial supporter of demonstration projects; Joel Spring, *The Sorting Machine: National Educational Policy since 1945* (New York: David McKay, 1976). Spring showed that Presidents Truman and Eisenhower justified their national human-resource policies and federal educational reforms through national policy commissions geared to fight the cold war.

3. H. Rowan Gaither, ed., *Report of the Study for the Ford Foundation on Policy and Program* (Detroit: Ford Foundation, 1949), 3.

4. Ibid., 1.

5. Ben Keppel, *The Work of Democracy: Ralph Bunche, Kenneth B. Clark, Lorraine Hansberry, and the Cultural Politics of Race* (Cambridge, Mass.: Harvard University Press, 1995), 1–96.

6. Ralph Bunche, "NAACP Convention Address (1951)," in Charles P. Henry, ed., *Ralph J. Bunche: Selected Speeches and Writings* (Ann Arbor: University of Michigan Press, 1995), 240.

7. Paul Woodring, *Investment in Innovation: An Historical Appraisal of the Fund for the Advancement of Education* (Boston: Little, Brown and Company, 1970), 174–77; National Scholarship Service and Fund for Negro Students, *Service to Local Communities in Talent Searching Projects: A Prospectus for the NSSFNS Role in the Early Identification and Educational Stimulation of Promising Students*, 2 January 1957, 3, FAE, box 41, folder 231, Ford Foundation Archives (FFA).

8. Nielsen, *The Big Foundations*, 84.

9. William Fulton, *Let's Look at Our Foundations* (New York: Guardians of American Education, 1952), 1, as the *American Legion Magazine*, August 1952.

10. Nielsen, *The Big Foundations*, 78–79.

11. Foreword by Owen J. Roberts in *The Negro and the Schools*, Harry S. Ashmore, ed. (Chapel Hill: University of North Carolina Press, 1954), i.

12. Ibid., 82.

13. Ashmore, *The Negro and the Schools*, 83; Woodring, *Investment in Innovation*, 174–77.

14. Fund for the Advancement of Education, *Suggestions for a Project to Ease and Speed the Adjustment Process in the New Age of Migration*, 1, FAE, box 43/4, folder 238, FFA.

15. J. Cayce Morrison, ed., *The Puerto Rican Study, 1953–57: A Report on the Education and Adjustment of Puerto Rican Pupils in the Public Schools of the City of New York* (Board of Education of the City of New York, 1958), FAE, box 43/4, folder 238, FFA.

16. Dora Tannenbaum, Sara McCaulley and H. Daniel Carpenter, *The Puerto Rican Migration* (Hudson Guild Neighborhood House, Colony House and the Grand Street Settlement, 1955), FAE, box 43/4, folder 238, FFA.

17. Lower Eastside Neighborhoods Association (LENA), *Survey of Population, Housing, Education and Health on the Lower East Side, 1950–1958*, 7, Henry Street Settlement Papers (HSS), box 77, folder 6, University of Minnesota Social Welfare History Archives (SWHA); Anthony Jackson, *A Place Called Home: A History of Low Cost Housing in Manhattan* (Cambridge, Mass.: MIT Press, 1976), 226.

18. LENA, *Survey, 1950–1958*; Robert Caro, *The Power Broker: Robert Moses and the Fall of New York* (New York: Vintage Books, 1975), 879–82, 964–68.

19. United Neighborhood Houses of New York, Inc., *Statement of Need and Proposed Plan to Work Toward Joint Supplemental Fund Raising for Non-Financially Federated Settlements, June 1954*, United Neighborhood Houses of New York, Supplemental Papers (UNHNY Papers), box 29, folder 3, SWHA.

20. Norman Dodd, *A Report from Norman Dodd, Director of Research, Covering His Direction of the Staff*, report prepared for the Special Committee of the House of Representatives to Investigate Tax-Exempt Foundations and Comparable Organizations, 83d Cong., 2d sess., 1954, Files of Waldemar Nielsen, Assistant to the President of the Ford Foundation (Nielsen files), box 3, folder 34, FFA.

21. Norman Dodd, *Report to the Select Committee to Investigate Tax-Exempt Foundations, April 1953*, 83d Cong., 2d sess., 1954, Nielsen files, box 3, folder 34, FFA. This so-called research report was a recycled 1947 blacklist compiled by two former FBI agents for the House Un-American Activities Committee.

22. Joseph M. McDaniel, Jr., memorandum to members of the Ford Foundation Program Committee concerning local community contributions, 16 June, 1954, Files of William McPeak, Associate Director/Vice President of the Ford Foundation (McPeak files) box 1, folder 29, FFA.

23. W. McNeil Lowry, internal memorandum, "The Foundation's Relation's with Intermediaries," 26 January, 1954, 7, Report #010838, FFA. See also accompanying program staff correspondence in McPeak files boxes 1–2.

24. Ibid., 4.

25. Quigg Newton, "Public Relations Problems and Policies," 1 June 1956. Report #002670; American Institute of Public Opinion, "Knowledge of and Attitudes toward the Ford Foundation," August 1956, Report #010593, FFA.

26. Regional Plan Association, *Metropolitan in the Making: The Next Twenty-Five Years in the New York Metropolitan Region* (New York, 1955).

27. Tannenbaum, McCaulley and Carpenter, *The Puerto Rican Migration*, 2.

28. Clayton Knowles, "4th Gang Assents to East Side Pact: Police to Study Delinquency Policy Anew Tomorrow," *New York Times*, 15 August 1956.

29. James Gilbert, *A Cycle of Outrage: America's Reaction to the Juvenile Delinquency in the 1950s* (New York: Oxford University Press, 1986), 136–37, 153–54; Harrison Salisbury, *The Shook-Up Generation* (New York: Harper, 1958), 45–50.

30. Milton Yale, *Lower Eastside Neighborhoods Association Gang Leadership Project Report, 1958*, 24, HSS Papers, box 76, folder 10, SWHA.

31. Helen Hall, *LENA—How It Began: Report for the United Neighborhood Houses Conference*, 5 November 1955 HSS Papers, box 79, folder 1, SWHA; Frances Low, ed., *The Puerto Ricans Study News Exchange, No. 6* (Board of Education of the City of New York, 21 April 1955), FAE, box 43, folder 237, FFA.

32. Helen Hall and Ruth Tefferteller, *Annual Report of the Pre-Delinquent Gang Project, 1957*, 2, HSS Papers, box 66, folder 3, SWHA; Sheldon Glueck and Eleanore T. Glueck, *Delinquents in the Making: Paths to Prevention* (New York, 1952).

33. Hall and Tefferteller, *Annual Report of the Pre-Delinquent Gang Project, 1957*, 1.

34. Helen Harris, memorandum to Ad Hoc Committee on the Ford Foundation, 29 May 1957, HSS Papers, box 31, folder 12, SWHA.

35. John J. McCloy, letter to Frederick P. Greenman, 23 September 1958, HSS Papers, box 31, folder 12, SWHA.

36. Dodd, *Report to the Select Committee to Investigate Tax-Exempt Foundations, April 1953*, 20–21.

37. Daniel Knapp and Kenneth Polk, *Scouting the War on Poverty: Social Reform Politics in the Kennedy Administration* (Lexington, Mass.: Heath Lexington, 1971), 25–27.

38. This policy shift at NIMH continued the historical fluctuation of prevailing social-service methodologies between individual- and community-centered perspectives. See John Ehrenreich, *The Altruistic Imagination: A History of Social Work and Social Policy in the United States* (Ithaca: Cornell University Press, 1985).

39. Nelson N. Foote and Leonard Cottrell, Jr., *Identity and Interpersonal Competence: A New Direction in Family Research* (Chicago: University of Chicago Press, 1955), v–vi; Knapp and Polk, *Scouting the War On Poverty*, 28.

40. Knapp and Polk, *Scouting the War On Poverty*, 9, 25.

41. Joseph Helfgot, *Professional Reforming: Mobilization For Youth and the Failure of Social Science* (Lexington, Mass.: D. C. Heath, 1981), 27–29.

42. Wolfgang Saxon, "Winslow Carlton, Official of Agencies and Fund Chief, Dies at 86," *New York Times*, 8 December 1994, B22; Winslow Carlton, unpublished essay on the "Beginnings of Group Health, Inc.," 1–2, personal papers of Winslow Carlton.

43. Helfgot, *Professional Reforming*, 28; Helen Hall, "A Note on the Inception and Impact of Mobilization For Youth," 1, attachment to the *Minutes of the Henry Street Settlement Board of Directors Meeting, March 13, 1967*, HSS Papers, box 80, folder 4, SWHA.

44. Hall, "A Note on the Inception and Impact of Mobilization for Youth," 2.

45. Robert Merton, *On Theoretical Sociology: Five Essays, Old and New* (New York: Free Press, 1957), 39–73; Robert Merton, *Social Theory and Social Structure* (New York: Free Press, 1957), 131–132.

46. Richard Cloward, James McCarthy and Lloyd Ohlin, *Mobilization For Youth: A Demonstration Action Research Project for the Prevention and Control of Juvenile Delinquency and Youthful Crime in an Urban Neighborhood, September 8, 1959*, 42, HSS Papers, box 79, folder 11, SWHA.

47. Ibid., 45.

48. Pauline Sterling, "The World Has Turned to the Neighborhood," *Detroit Free Press*, 5 November 1959.

49. Peter Marris and Martin Rein, *Dilemmas of Social Reform: Poverty and Community Action in the United States* (New York: Atherton Press, 1967).

50. Marris and Rein, *Dilemmas of Social Reform*, 21, 28.

51. Nicholas Lemman, *The Promised Land: The Great Black Migration and How It Changed America* (New York: Vintage Books, 1991), 121.

52. Richard Cloward and Frances Fox Piven, *Regulating the Poor: The Functions of Public Welfare* (New York: Vintage Books, 1971), 290–293.

53. Ibid., 294–295.

54. Harold H. Weissman, ed., *Individual and Group Services in the Mobilization for Youth Experience* (New York: Association Press, 1969).

55. Piven and Cloward, *Regulating the Poor*, 290.

56. Ibid., 295.

57. Helen Harris, memorandum to the Board Presidents and Executive Directors of UNHNY affiliates concerning Class Values and settlement Practice, 1 February 1964, UNHNY Papers, box 19, folder 8, SWHA.

58. "Lower East Side Residents Form Committee to Help Settle Strike," *New York Times*, 26 March 1964, sec. 9, 2.

59. Paul Ylvisaker, speech before the Citizen's Conference on Community Planning, Indianapolis, Indiana, January 1963. Segment of quotation in James L. Sundquist, *Politics and Policy: The Eisenhower, Kennedy and Johnson Years* (Washington, D.C.: Brookings Institution), 125.

60. Reverend Michael Allen and Reverend Richard Johnson, letter to Winslow Carlton, 7 January 1964; Winslow Carlton, letter to Reverend Michael Allen and Reverend Richard Johnson, 31 January 1964, HSS Papers, box 119, folder 1, SWHA.

61. Lower East Side Civil Rights Committee, *Community News*, January 1964.

62. Jack Newfield, *Robert Kennedy: A Memoir* (New York: E. P. Dutton, 1969), 90–109.

63. "Wagner, City Council President Screvane Confirm Probe," *New York Times*, 16 August 1964, sec. 2, 78.

64. *Daily News*, "Whitewash for MFY," 18 November 1964.

65. "Casualty of the War on Poverty," *New York Times*, 15 January 1965.

66. Helen Hall, *The Inception and Impact of Mobilization For Youth*, 5, HSS Papers, box 80, folder 4, SWHA.

67. Susan Brownmiller, "MFY: Six Candles on a Stale Cake," *Village Voice*, 24 October 1968, 13.

68. Ibid.

69. Marris and Rein, *Dilemmas of Social Reform*, 172.

70. Mitchell Sviridoff, *Report to the Mayor on the Establishment of a City Human Resources Administration* (New York: Institute of Public Administration, 1966), 9.

71. Ibid., 11–13.

72. Peter Dobkin Hall, *A History of Nonprofit Boards in the United States* (Washington, D.C.: National Center for Nonprofit Boards, 1997); Donald R. Young and Wilbert E. Moore, *Trusteeship and the Management of Foundations* (New York: Russell Sage Foundation, 1969), 11–14.

10 Grassrooting the System?

The Development and Impact of Social Movement Philanthropy, 1953–1990

J. Craig Jenkins and Abigail Halcli

IN THEIR ANALYSIS OF philanthropic elites, Althea Nagai, Robert Lerner, and Stanley Rothman contend that foundation elites are politically polarized, with the major liberal foundations increasingly funding "action" projects to bring about social change. Funding social movements, either directly or through nonprofit surrogates, has become a significant and perhaps major part of this foundation giving. In her recent *Money for Change*, Susan Ostrander traces the development of the Haymarket Fund, an "alternative" foundation that has pioneered the use of community funding boards to bridge the social gap between wealthy donors and grassroots movement groups. In earlier work, we portrayed social movement philanthropy as a tiny yet highly leveraged section of institutional philanthropy that has channeled social movements by funding the professionalization of social movement organizations and facilitating the implementation of gains secured by indigenous protest.[1]

These portraits raise several important questions. First, how large and institutionalized is the social movement sector of American philanthropy? Is social protest an essential element in the growth of social movement philanthropy? If so, how has it fared during the 1980s with the rise of the "new right" and relative tranquility on the left? Second, what are the priorities of movement funders? The channeling thesis argues that movement funders respond to grassroots protest by funding professionalized projects. Has this held over the past four decades? Third, what is the impact of social movement philanthropy? Does it fuel social change by strengthening social movements, or is it a cooptative force that weakens and blunts the impact of movements?

We begin by tracing trends in social movement philanthropy over the past four decades, comparing giving patterns from the early 1950s through 1990. These indicate a significant growth and overall persistence of social movement philanthropy with a growing emphasis on "middle-class" movements, professionalized projects, and avoiding unruly protest groups. At the same time, a new type of alternative philanthropy has developed which emphasizes grassroots projects and community control of funding. We also show that, despite considerable turnover among social movement funders during the 1980s, funding priorities have persisted and total funding has grown, which we interpret as indicating that social movement philanthropy has become institutionalized. Finally, we examine the consequences of recent social movement philanthropy, showing that it has been largely reactive and that, as earlier, it has contributed to the implementation of the gains created by indigenous mobilization.

The Growth of Social Movement Philanthropy, 1953–1990

By a "social movement," we mean a collective attempt to organize or represent the interests of a previously unorganized or politically excluded group. Social movement philanthropy, then, centers around foundation grants to social movement projects, whether these go to grassroots movement groups, to professional advocacy and service organizations, or to institutionalized organizations such as churches and universities that are sponsoring movement work. These donations constitute "surplus wealth" in that they are charitable donations largely from wealthy donors whose income surpasses that needed for a comfortable living. These foundations may be legally chartered as private, corporate, community, or operating foundations as well as grant-giving public charities.

As Table 10.1, shows, social movement philanthropy has grown steadily since the early 1950s. In the early 1950s, there were only three social movement funders: the Field Foundation of New York, and the Emil Schwartzhaupt and Wiebolt Foundations, both of Chicago. In 1953, the Field Foundation began supporting the legal office of the National Association for the Advancement of Colored Persons, which had since the mid-1940s success-

Table 10.1. Foundation Grants for Social Movements

	Current $	Constant $ (= $1982–84)	% Total Foundation Giving	Number of Funders	Number of Grants
1953	$85,700		.00001	3	4
1960	259,000	873,709	.036	10	21
1970	10,973,000	28,281,229	.578	65	311
1980	22,863,000	22,747,532	.814	109	1,235
1990	88,070,000	67,383,643	1.128	146	3,418

fully used test-case litigation to attack racial discrimination.[2] In the same year, the Schwartzhaupt and Wiebolt Foundations initiated funding for two pivotal projects: Saul Alinsky's Industrial Areas Foundation to launch the Community Service Organization in California, a Mexican-American civil rights organization that provided the basis for the United Farm Workers Union in the 1960s; and the Highlander Center to initiate voter education projects in the deep South, thereby encouraging an approach that would later make Highlander into a "movement halfway house" for the civil rights movement, providing leadership training and tactical advise to the Southern Christian Leadership Council (SCLC) and the Student Nonviolent Coordinating Committee (SNCC).[3] In 1953, there were only four social movement grants totaling $85,700.

Social movement philanthropy grew steadily over the 1950s with the addition of nine funders: the William C. Whitney, New York, Norman, New World, Taconic, and Ottinger Foundations in New York; the Huber Foundation of New Jersey; the Institute for World Order, a New York public charity promoting world peace and disarmament; and the New York Community Trust, a community foundation. By 1960, these foundations provided twenty-one movement grants totaling over $259,000, with the largest recipient being the NAACP. The only foundation to withdraw was the Wiebolt Foundation, which ceased funding the movements until 1966. The early stirrings of the civil rights and student movements caught the attention of wealthy donors such as Stephen and Audrey Currier (Taconic Foundation), David Heyman (New York Foundation), and Andrew Norman (Norman Foundation), who funded voter registration, community organizing and litigation by the NAACP, the SCLC, and the SNCC, as well as civil-rights projects of the National Student Association. It was an appealing combination: a grassroots social-protest movement centered in the Deep South and challenging Jim Crow racism through nonviolent protest and a general "rights" framework to legitimize a bid for political and social integration into mainstream American society. These foundations and a legion of others over the next decade funneled major funding into this civil-rights effort.

Over the course of the 1960s, the upsurge of new social movements and the urban riots coupled with the continued growth of foundation assets spurred rapid growth in movement philanthropy. By 1970, there were sixty-five foundations actively making social movement grants, almost $11 million in funding, and 311 grants. Controlling for inflation, this was over thirty-two times the movement funding in 1960. There were also an additional eleven funders who were active at some point during the 1960s. Table 10.2 charts the turnover in movement funders, identifying funders active during each decade, new funders, funds that died (ceased operations), and those that withdrew (ceased funding movements while continuing to give

Table 10.2. Growth in Social Movement Funders, 1953–1990

	Active Funders	New Funders	Deceased Funders	Withdrawal Funders	Mortality Rate	Withdrawal Rate	Birth Rate
1953	3	–	–	–	–	–	–
1953–1960	12	9	0	1	0%	8.3%	75%
1961–1970	76	65	1	1	1.3	1.3	85.5
1971–1980	133	56	6	10	4.5	7.5	42.1
1981–1990	186	68	13	15	7.0	8.1	36.6

grants). Of the seventy-six funders active during the 1960s, sixty-five were new funders that had not been active before 1961. Only two ceased funding movements: the Schwartzhaupt Foundation paid out all of its assets, and the Benton Foundation withdrew. Typically, a foundation that began sponsoring movements remained active in the area with funding growth coming primarily from the entry of new funders. Although the majority of the funders were located in New York (forty-four of the seventy-seven, or 58 percent), there were movement funders in San Francisco; Columbus, Indiana; Albuquerque; Washington, D.C.; Clearwater, Florida; and Cleveland.

Rapid growth in movement philanthropy was fueled partially by the entry of large establishment foundations such as the Ford Foundation, the Carnegie Corporation, the Rockefeller Foundation, the Sloan Foundation, and the Lilly Endowment. Under McGeorge Bundy's leadership, the Ford Foundation funded all of the national civil-rights organizations and, almost single-handedly, launched a set of new advocacy organizations, such as the National Council of La Raza to serve as the "NAACP for Mexican-Americans," the Mexican-American Legal Defense Fund to serve as the equivalent of the NAACP Legal Defense and Education Fund, and an array of public-interest law firms in the areas of the environment, consumer protection, and women's rights. The Carnegie Corporation granted Ralph Nader $55,000 to create the Center for the Study of Responsive Law, John Gardner $20,000 to launch Common Cause, and $10,000 to launch the National Committee Against Discrimination in Housing.

There was also a tremendous growth of funding from smaller family foundations. Several New York–based foundations—such as the Norman, Taconic, and the New York Foundations (which had earlier supported the NAACP's litigation efforts)—supported the emerging black student sit-in protests by providing bail money, legal support, and stipends for protest organizers. Under the prompting of Robert Kennedy, Attorney General in the Kennedy administration, these foundations created the Council for United

Civil Rights Leadership (CUCRL) to coordinate funding for voter registration by the SNCC and SCLC. These projects were also supported by the Stern Family Fund, which also funded a variety of community organization projects, union democracy efforts, and the United Farm Workers Union in California. In 1965, Midas Muffler magnate Nate Sherman used his GBS Foundation to fund Ralph Nader to create the Center for Auto Safety and to support several civil rights projects. Shortly afterwards, the Irwin-Sweeney-Miller Foundation of Columbus, Indiana, began supporting civil rights and community organizing in small and medium-sized towns throughout the Midwest. General Motors heir Stewart R. Mott created the small Spectamur Agendo fund to contribute to the National Abortion Rights Action League's campaign to legalize abortion, SANE's nuclear disarmament efforts, the launching of Amnesty International's human-rights monitoring effort, and the anti-war projects of the Fund for Peace and the Indochina Peace Campaign. Novelist Kurt Vonnegut donated book royalties to the Rosewater Foundation, which funded Ralph Nader's Agribusiness Accountability Project, Campaign GM, and related efforts. Finally, the Field Foundation, which had earlier funded the civil rights struggle, expanded its mandate by supporting the Fund for Peace's Center for Defense Information so that retired Rear Admiral Gene LaRocque could monitor the military and intelligence communities, and by funding the Center for National Security Studies directed by Morton Halperin to monitor government surveillance and intelligence-community abuses.

There were also several corporate funders of movements, such as Cummins Engine (Columbus, Indiana), which focused on civil rights and community organizing; the Borg Warner Foundation (Chicago), which targeted racial discrimination in housing and employment; and the George E. Johnson Foundation (Chicago), the lone African American foundation, which funded the civil rights movement.

There was also new public charity funding. In 1963, several wealthy New Yorkers created the Joint Foundation Support as a public charity to provide technical support for their tax-deductible charitable contributions. In 1970 Ralph Nader used the settlement from his successful suit against General Motors to create the Public Safety Research Institute, which launched Nader's Raiders and an array of public-interest accountability projects. In San Francisco, a small group of peace activists created the Agape Foundation, a public charity funded by small contributors and by benefit concerts by Joan Baez and Gordon Lightfoot, to promote the philosophy of nonviolence and related social-protest efforts. During the 1970s, recipients included the War Resisters League, the Catholic Worker Movement, the Central Committee for Conscientious Objectors, the United Farm Workers Union, the Abalone Alliance, and the Stop the B1 Bomber Campaign.

Recognizing the tension between the democratic philosophy guiding this funding and the privileged control of wealthy donors, Agape experimented with diversifying the funding board by bringing social movement activists into the decision making.

The 1980s proved complex. In terms of active foundations, social movement philanthropy grew steadily, reaching 109 active funders in 1980 and another twenty-four funders who were active at one point or another during the decade. In terms of total funding, more than $22.8 million was donated to social movement projects in 1980, but, controlling for inflation, this represented an almost twenty percent drop in effective funding (Table 10.1). Although there were 1,235 grants in 1980, the mean size of these grants dropped significantly (from $25,283 in 1970 to $18,513 in 1980 in current dollars), reflecting a significant decline in the resources and interest of the larger foundations. Mapped in terms of yearly change, the peak of movement philanthropy came in 1977, when over $24.1 million was available, but funding then declined to $22.9 million in 1980. Despite the addition of fifty-six new funders, there were sixteen that dropped out, six due to foundation deaths and ten that withdrew from funding movements (Table 10.2). With the sharp drop off in mass protests in the early 1970s and the election of Jimmy Carter in 1976, foundation interest in social movements appeared to wane. In addition, inflation seriously eroded the assets of the larger foundations, cutting their giving programs and ability to initiate new projects. Yet, despite this decline in real funding, social movement grants increased from roughly 0.5 percent of total foundation giving in 1970 to over 0.8 percent in 1980. Movement funding proved persistent even if minuscule.

Alongside these trends was the rise of a new set of alternative foundations modeled on the Agape experience. First was the Vanguard Foundation, a public charity organized in San Francisco in 1972 by Obie Benz and several young, wealthy inheritors who had been active in the antiwar and civil-rights movements. Within a few years, six additional alternative foundations had been launched: Haymarket People's Fund in Boston; Liberty Hill Foundation in Venice, California; the McKenzie River Gathering in Portland, Oregon; Liberty Hill in Santa Monica, California; Bread & Roses in Philadelphia; and North Star in New York. Chartered as public charities, these alternative foundations created community funding boards of local activists and, for donors who wished to select the recipients of their grants, a donors' board. Typically donors were allowed to make specified donations through the donor board as long as they contributed a base amount to the community funding board. Most of these grants were in the $200 to $1,000 range, and directed at local organizing efforts, such as rape crisis centers, tenant organizing, prisoners' rights, protests against nuclear power, and community advocacy for the homeless and disabled movements. In

1979, they banded together to create the Funding Exchange as a technical-resource center to promote the alternative foundation effort.

The early 1970s also witnessed the creation of public charities among movement communities. In San Francisco, the Genesis Church created the Third World Fund to link domestic minority struggles with those in the Third World, funding projects from the American Indian Movement and the Leonard Peltier Defense Committee, to the boycott against South African apartheid, and the U.S. Committee on Central America. On Long Island, the North Shore Unitarian Church created the Veatch Foundation, which funded peace, women's rights, hunger, and Third World advocacy. In New York, the Ms. and Astrea Foundations were organized among women's movement supporters to fund women's rights projects. In Boston, the A. J. Muste Memorial Institute contributed to legal defense for conscientious objectors, antiwar organizing, and training in pacifism. In Philadelphia, the People's Fund supported transit worker union organizing, the nationalist Puerto Rican Socialist Party and the Venceremos Brigade to promote change in U.S.-Cuba relations.

The 1980s witnessed the renewed growth of social movement philanthropy. In 1990, there were 146 foundations, which invested a total of nearly $88.1 million in movement projects. Although this represented but a tiny portion of total foundation giving, its continued growth—up to 1.1 percent of total foundation giving—indicated that social movement philanthropy had become an institutionalized factor (although a tiny one) in American society. Mean grant size increased to $25,767, and the number of grants mushroomed to 3,418. Adjusted for inflation, this represented an increase of almost 2.5 times the amount of movement funding a decade earlier. Over the course of the 1980s, there were 186 foundations involved in supporting movements with sixty-eight new funders—only twenty-eight of which became inactive, thirteen of which closed and another fifteen that simply withdrew from movement funding. As Table 10.2 shows, this maturation of movement philanthropy entailed increased organizational mortality and withdrawal rates alongside a declining organizational birth rate. Indicating the further geographic spread of movement philanthropy, only a third of these foundations were headquartered in New York with movement funders in places like Austin, Boulder, Seattle, Atlanta, Dayton, and Oakland. The Funding Exchange expanded to eleven members, and there were an additional twelve public charities based in social movement communities.

What is perhaps most remarkable about this growth and institutionalization of social movement philanthropy is that it occurred during the conservative onslaught of the rise of the "new right" and the conservative policies of the Reagan and Bush administrations. During the first Reagan administration, the Internal Revenue Service conducted a harassing audit campaign targeted at several movement recipients, contending that they were commercial ventures that did not warrant nonprofit status, or that they were significantly involved in political lobbying.[4] They also audited several movement funders, such as the Rosenberg Foundation in San Francisco, attempting to intimidate movement funders to withdraw. Although there was little direct success in forcing withdrawals, it seems likely that this campaign slowed the growth of movement philanthropy. Yet the number and resources of social movement funders increased, thereby boosting the overall size of the funding base for social movements. If anything, the threat of a conservative administration with several well-known "new right" figures in prominent decision-making positions spurred liberal and progressive funders to invest more heavily in social movements. There were also new protest movements, such as the gay/lesbian and animal rights campaigns, which spurred new funding. But, as we show below, this was not central to the growth in movement philanthropy. This growth should also be kept in perspective. Although "new right" funding has yet to be fully mapped, it undoubtedly dwarfed this "new left" funding base. Nonetheless, this conservative challenge did little to reverse and may well have spurred greater support for social movement causes.[5]

Table 10.3 provides a more complex picture of these funding trends in terms of the types of foundations. We distinguish between four types of movement funders: family foundations, institutional foundations, the alternative foundations, and the movement community–based public charities. *Family foundations* are private, endowed foundations in which the donor or family members still sit on the board of directors and thus guide giving priorities. Most of these are small, operating with only one or two permanent staff, and with donors and family members directly involved in the grant-giving process. They constitute between forty and sixty percent of the social movement funders, increasing during the rapid build up of the 1960s and then slowly declining as movement-based public charities and alternative foundations entered the field during the 1980s. In terms of the number of grants and grant dollars, they give a smaller proportion of movement grants, reflecting their smaller size and tendency to combine movement giving with more conventional philanthropy. Their average grant is less than half of that for the institutional foundations and, in total giving, they had declined slightly by 1990 from their peak in 1980.

Institutional foundations are those in which donors and family members are no longer present and control has shifted to business associates, social notables, community leaders, and professional experts. Generally they are controlled by business leaders involved in community and public affairs; these leaders are tapped because of their social prominence, political judg-

Table 10.3. Types of Foundations and Their Grants, 1960–1990

	1953		1960		1970		1980		1990	
	Number	Percent	Number	Percent	Number	Percent	Number	Percent	Number	Percent
Number of Foundations										
Family	1	33.3	4	40.0	44	67.7	66	60.6	90	61.6
Institutional	2	66.7	5	50.0	17	26.2	26	23.9	34	23.3
Movement Charity	0	0.0	1	10.0	4	6.2	9	8.3	10	6.8
Alternative	0	0.0	0	0.0	0	0.0	8	7.3	12	8.2
Total	3	100.0	10	100.0	65	100.0	109	100.0	146	100.0
Number of Grants										
Family	1	25.0	6	30.0	183	58.8	552	44.7	1,541	45.1
Institutional	3	75.0	13	65.0	114	36.7	234	18.9	747	21.9
Movement Charity	0	0.0	1	5.0	14	4.5	103	8.3	555	16.2
Alternative	0	0.0	0	0.0	0	0.0	346	28.0	575	16.8
Total	4	100.0	21	100.0	311	100.0	1,235	100.0	3,418	100.0
Grant Dollars (Current $)										
Family	1,000	1.2	34,447	13.3	2,227,519	20.3	9,876,816	43.2	34,259,230	38.9
Institutional	84,700	98.8	221,445	85.5	8,646,724	78.8	10,837,062	47.4	40,336,060	45.8
Movement Charity	0	0.0	3,108	1.2	98,757	.9	1,600,410	7.0	11,977,520	13.6
Alternative	0	0.0	0	0.0	0	0.0	548,712	2.4	1,497,190	1.7
Total	85,700	100.0	259,000	100.0	10,973,000	100.0	22,863,000	100.0	88,070,000	100.0
Mean Grant Dollars (Current $)										
Family	1,000		5,742		12,172		17,893		22,232	
Institutional	28,233		17,034		75,848		46,312		53,997	
Movement Charity	0		3,108		7,054		15,538		21,581	
Alternative	0		0		0		1,586		2,604	
Total	21,425		12,333		35,283		18,513		25,767	

ment, and social ties. We also include in this category eight corporate foundations, six community foundations, and one operating foundation which made social movement grants over the past four decades. They are directed by corporate leaders and community elites and hence closely resemble the institutional private foundations. Most have large endowments and a significant permanent staff with formalized grant-giving procedures. They have been significant actors in the social movement arena throughout this period, declining with the rapid growth of family foundations in the 1960s and the inflationary squeeze of the 1970s. Nonetheless, their grants are consistently three to four times the size of those of the family foundations. If a social movement project requires an expensive professional staff, the large institutional foundations are the primary funders to which bids must be addressed.

The *alternative foundations* are public charities that raise money from wealthy donors, but assign control over grants to community funding boards. Responding to the conflict between inherited wealth and ideological commitments to a progressive ideology of popular empowerment, many younger wealthy inheritors decided to entrust decision making over grants to a community funding board made up of local movement activists. As Pillsbury Flour Company heir George Pillsbury argued in *Robin Hood Was Right* (a booklet for progressive-minded inheritors published by the Funding Exchange), a community board has a better sense of movement priorities and eliminates the guilt associated with inherited wealth.[6] These alternative foundations have also maintained a separate donor's board through which donors may assign grants to a designated recipient but are required to maintain a basic commitment to the community board. Haymarket, for example, gave $175,000 in donor-advised grants in the early 1990s while granting $430,000 through the General Fund. This has led to complex debates about relations between wealthy donors and the staff, but has allowed these alternative foundations to mobilize a much larger resource base.[7] Nonetheless, these alternative foundations constitute only a tiny portion of social movement funding with a mean grant size of between $1,500 and $2,500. They represent only two to three percent of total social movement philanthropy.

Fourth are the *movement community–based public charities*, which mobilize support from a large number of small donors. Typically these are based on fundraising appeals to a social movement community, such as the peace and women's movements. Examples are the Institute for World Order, which established "Peace Money" in 1959 to fund international peace and disarmament, the Astrea Foundation, launched in 1979 to fund the women's movement, and Ralph Nader's Public Safety Research Institute discussed above. As Table 10.3 shows, these grew significantly in the 1980s, constituting almost fourteen percent of movement grants, with mean grants comparable to those by family foundations.

The Changing Priorities of Social Movement Philanthropy

The growth of movement philanthropy has entailed significant changes in the priorities guiding movement funding. Table 10.4 charts these in terms of the major constituencies receiving movement support. In the 1950s and early 1960s, social movement philanthropy was almost exclusively focused on civil rights, especially the battle against Jim Crow laws and the effort to bring African Americans and other racial minorities into the mainstream of American society. Projects such as the litigation program of the NAACP and the NAACP Legal Defense and Education Fund ("the Inc. Fund") received the bulk of the funding. Of all movement philanthropy in 1953, forty percent went to African Americans and the other sixty percent to Mexican Americans. In 1960, African American advocacy received over half of all funding, with comparable efforts by Native Americans and Mexican Americans receiving another quarter. Some money went to community organizing in the big cities, chiefly Saul Alinsky's Industrial Areas Foundation, and to general public-interest advocacy. Reflecting the indigenous origins of these movement groups and the importance of protest in triggering these grants, forty percent of this funding went to movement organizations with a history of participation in direct action protests.

The upsurge of social protest during the 1960s dramatically altered these priorities. Although civil rights and the problems of African Americans continued to receive over a third of all funding in 1970, the field had become more diverse. First, there was the broadened definition of the groups qualifying for support. Building on the general civil-rights framework used by the African American advocates, there was a new array of movements claiming comparable protection. In addition to racial minorities, Appalachian whites, Puerto Ricans, women, children, prisoners, and the disabled received attention. Second, the definition of these "rights" expanded to include political and social rights such as voting and political representation, as well as economic security and equal access to education and public services. In the modern welfare state, full citizenship expanded to include this broader set of political and social rights. Most of these movement projects were organized around professional advocacy groups, such as the Children's Defense Fund, which monitored government programs and lobbied for social programs to protect children, the Pension Rights Center, which served as a watchdog for beneficiaries of corporate pension funds, the Center for Economic Alternatives, which advocated legal changes to promote employee ownership and cooperative enterprise, and the Federa-

Table 10.4. The Changing Priorities of Social Movement Philanthropy, 1953–1990

	Percent of Grant Dollars				
	1953	1960	1970	1980	1990
Social Movement Projects					
Racial/Ethnic Minorities					
African Americans	40.49	50.85	33.95	13.36	5.74
Mexican Americans	59.51	11.52	5.35	4.08	4.64
Native Americans	—	14.89	0.00	2.34	2.50
Puerto Ricans	—	—	0.23	2.37	0.30
Hispanics	—	—	—	—	2.48
Asian Americans	—	—	—	0.25	0.35
Jews	—	—	—	—	0.28
Appalachians	—	—	1.15	0.96	0.45
White Ethnics	—	—	—	0.03	—
Minorities in General		—	9.40	5.22	3.86
Total	100.00	77.26	50.08	28.61	20.60
Economic Justice					
Urban Communities	—	17.13	26.64	16.13	17.27
Rural Communities	—	—	—	—	3.83
Total	—	17.13	26.64	16.13	22.05
Other Groups					
Women's Rights	—	—	0.34	16.44	12.50
Children's Advocacy	—	—	1.21	8.03	3.90
Prisoner's Rights	—	—	1.55	3.11	1.14
Disabled Rights	—	—	0.09	1.00	0.27
Aged Advocacy	—	—	—	0.21	0.36
Gay/Lesbian Rights	—	—	—	0.24	1.12
Animal Rights	—	—	—	—	0.00
Total	—	—	3.19	29.03	19.29
Peace and World Order					
Student Movement	—	—	1.09	0.00	0.15
Peace Movement	—	—	2.87	2.16	5.28
Third World Advocacy	—	—	0.00	0.31	5.02
Veteran's Rights	—	—	—	0.02	0.00
Total	—	—	3.97	2.49	10.45
Public Interest Movement					
Environmentalism	—	—	6.88	12.64	17.75
Consumer Rights	—	—	6.35	4.30	0.78
General Public Interest	—	5.61	2.89	6.80	9.08
Total	—	5.61	16.12	23.74	27.61
Total All Grants	100.00	100.00	100.00	100.00	100.00

tion of Southern Coops, which promoted economic cooperatives among small African American farmers in the South.

Third was the emergence of strong middle-class reform movements promoting a broader definition of citizenship rights to environmental protection, consumer rights, and governmental accountability. By 1970 environmental advocacy organizations such as the Environmental Defense Fund, the Natural Resources Defense Council, the Wilderness Society, and the Sierra Club Foundation received almost seven percent of the money. Ralph Nader launched a new set of research and advocacy organizations, ranging from the Center for Auto Safety and the Center for the Study of Responsive Law to the various Public Interest Research Groups (PIRGs), which operated as "people's attorney generals" in pressing for public disclosure, open hearings, and campaign finance reform. Reinforced by an array of new public-interest groups focused on problems of governmental secrecy, regulatory accountability, and freedom of information, consumer protection and governmental accountability received almost ten percent of the funding. Student and antiwar organizing received another four percent of the money. Most of these new movement organizations were professionalized, relying on litigation, public education efforts, and lobbying to press for changes. As a consequence, funding to groups with a protest history dropped to only twenty-one percent of the total funding.

The 1970s witnessed a further growth in the movements making claims for support, while, treated in real terms, the amount of movement philanthropy declined. By 1980, social movement philanthropy in constant dollar terms had declined by almost twenty percent. This produced heightened competition and an effective transfer of funding from African Americans and the racial minority movements to the middle-class reformers. The major loser was the African American movement, which lost in absolute as well as relative terms, receiving in 1980 less than fifteen percent of all funding and, in constant dollar terms, suffered a decline to less than a third of its 1970 funding level. On the growth side, the major winners were the women's movement (which garnered sixteen percent of the funding), children's advocacy (eight percent), prisoners' rights (three percent), and the middle-class environmentalists, consumer rights, and public-interest efforts (almost a quarter of the funding). There were also new campaigns on behalf of the aged, gay/lesbian people, and veterans, especially the victims of Agent Orange during the Vietnam War. Following the earlier trend, funding for groups with a protest history declined further to eighteen percent of movement funding.

By 1990, the rise of the "new right" and the Reagan and Bush presidencies had spurred a backlash among social movement funders. Overall, this growth in movement philanthropy followed the basic outlines of earlier funding. African Americans and racial minorities continued to lose ground relative to the middle-class movements. In constant dollar terms, funding for African American advocacy grew slightly, as did that for minorities generally. A new category of Hispanic advocacy developed alongside Jewish advocacy against anti-Semitic attacks. Community organizing in urban areas was complemented by rural organizing, especially in areas affected by the farm crisis of the 1980s. The movement for women's rights lost some of its centrality, along with advocacy for children and other disadvantaged groups, while funding for environmentalism, peace, and Third World issues increased. The latter benefitted from increased public awareness of the contradictory foreign policies of the Vietnam era and before, targeting foreign-policy support for death squads and racist regimes abroad. There was also a small outpouring of support for animal rights. Reflecting the further professionalization of movement politics, funding for protest groups declined further to only fourteen percent of total funding.

Overall, there was remarkable stability in the field of projects receiving support. To investigate this further, we split the "new" and "old" funders in 1990 to see if they supported different projects. The old funders were slightly more likely to be institutional foundations, especially corporate and community foundations, while the new funders were alternative foundations and social movement public charities. The assets of the new funders were significantly smaller ($40.1 million vs. $148.4 million for the old funders) as was the size of their grants ($18,172 mean grant vs. $30,866 for the old funders). There were also some differences in their funding priorities. The new funders were less interested in the problems of racial minorities, investing only ten percent of their funds in these projects as compared to a quarter of the old-funder money. New funders were also more concerned about international affairs, investing more in peace (eleven percent of their funding) and Third World advocacy (six percent). They also favored environmentalism, investing twenty-six percent of their funds in these efforts (vs. fourteen percent for old funders). The new funders were more responsive to new movement issues and to the middle-class movements. Yet overall, the funding priorities were remarkably similar. This suggests that the new funders largely mimicked the old funders by adopting similar priorities. As for the old funders, their priorities had largely been set earlier and persisted. The growth of professional networks, such as the National Network of Grantmakers, Women in Philanthropy, and the Association of Black Foundation Executives encouraged these new movement funders to adopt priorities similar to those of the older funders, producing what Paul DiMaggio and Walter Powell call institutional isomorphism.[8]

This social movement philanthropy was organized around a general "rights" framework emphasizing the need for equal political representation and social protection. Drawing on what Theodore Lowi has called the ideology of "interest group liberalism," these funders have assumed that the public interest is best served by allowing interest groups to make public policy.[9] Identifying the key problem in American society as the underrepresentation of disadvantaged and unorganized groups in the political process, these foundations have funded various advocacy and organizational efforts to insure that all groups have at least some political representation. Hence we have advocacy on behalf of children, the disabled, prisoners, and animals. It also represents a deepening of the underlying conception of citizen rights. Drawing on T. H. Marshall's argument about the growth of citizenship in the modern welfare state, these foundations have responded to a broadening quest for protection in civil and political affairs as well as a search for social protection.[10] Hence we can see these movements and their patrons as pursuing an enlarged definition of citizenship as their central goal.

The Impact of Social Movement Philanthropy

Past discussions have focused largely on the impact of social movement philanthropy, debating whether this external assistance fuels social movements or blunts and coopts them. Radical critics have argued that foundation patronage has "a corrosive influence on democratic society . . . by serv[ing] as 'cooling out' agencies, delaying and preventing more radical, structural change"[11] In a more sophisticated formulation, Herbert Haines and Doug McAdam have argued a "social control" thesis that social protest is the major spur to foundation patronage and that, due to a "radical-flank effect," this protest legitimizes moderate movement leaders, thus directing most of the money toward the less militant projects, thereby demobilizing grassroots protest.[12] Refining this social-control thesis, my earlier work on the African American movement showed that foundation patronage is overwhelmingly reactive to indigenous protest activism and that the major recipients are professional social movement organizations (or SMOs), especially professional advocacy projects.[13] This advanced a *channeling thesis*—that movement-based philanthropy tended to professionalize indigenous-movement groups and to create new professional-movement organizations, thus channeling movements into institutionalized actions. This trend does not eliminate grassroots protest or organizing but does strengthen the professional components of social movements. Social movement philanthropy is also credited with providing critical resources for implementing social movement gains. Although most of these advances stemmed from grassroots organizing and protest (e.g. the Civil Rights Acts of 1964 and 1965), professional advocacy was essential to converting these legal changes into actual changes in practices. Hence, instead of describing a simple cooptation process, the channeling argument contends that professionalization and the associated movement philanthropy may provide the means for implementing major movement gains.

How does this channeling argument fare generally? We lack the space for a full analysis of the political effects of social movement philanthropy across all of these movements, but we can trace the allocation, temporal development, and impact of movement philanthropy on five of the major challenges of this period. We examine the origins and impact of social movement philanthropy on three indigenous or grassroots-based movements—the African American, peace/antiwar, and women's movements— as well as two largely professionalized efforts—environmentalism and the consumer-protection/government-accountability movements. We address three questions. First, what types of movement groups received foundation funding? Second, how was this funding related to indigenous mobilization and protest? Finally, what role did this funding play in the successes of these movements?

In examining the allocation of movement funding, we look at funding for four types of movement groups: indigenous or "grassroots" movement groups; professional advocacy organizations; technical support organizations; and institutionalized organizations. *Indigenous movement groups* are those with a chapter membership or that mobilize resources directly from the official beneficiaries of their major projects. The NAACP, the SNCC, the Sierra Club, and Friends of the Earth are prime examples of this type of classical grassroots-movement group.

In discussing *professional advocacy organizations,* we draw on John McCarthy and Mayer Zald's idea of professional social movement organizations based on paid professional staff who "represent" or "act on behalf" of groups. Resources come largely from institutions and "conscience constituents" who do not have a direct stake in the issues being addressed.[14] Such professional SMOs typically have a paid permanent staff which controls decision-making and operates programs with little input from official beneficiaries. The Children's Defense Fund, for example, does not organize children but rather mobilizes support from foundations and wealthy donors and uses its professional staff to act on children's behalf. Some professional SMOs are closely allied with indigenous groups, such as the NAACP Legal Defense and Education Fund, which was originally the legal office within the NAACP until the IRS threatened in 1955 to revoke the tax-exempt status of the NAACP, thereby forcing the Legal Defense and Education Fund to incorporate legally as a separate 501-(c)3 tax-exempt organization. Similarly, the NOW Legal Defense and Education Fund operates as the legal office of the National Organization for Women. Others are only loosely associated with grassroots groups, such as Ralph Nader's Public Citizen and the Natural Resources Defense Council, both of which are staff-dominated advocacy organizations that raise their money from foundations, government agencies, wealthy donors, and direct-mail appeals.

A second type of professional SMO is the *technical support organization*, such as the Center for Community Change and the Youth Project, which provide technical services to grassroots and professional advocacy projects. Services range from financial and fund-raising to media development, training in community organizing, and assistance in securing 501-(c)3 tax-exempt status. Because of their grassroots ties, foundations often view technical support centers as an efficient device for funding grassroots efforts.

Finally, some movement philanthropy goes to *institutionalized organizations* such as churches and universities that are sponsoring movement projects. Although sometimes this is a pass-through arrangement until a movement organization secures tax-exempt status, it also occurs because foundations wish to buffer themselves against controversy by assigning responsibility to a legitimized church or educational institution.

Table 10.5 charts the overall trend in funding of these organizations. Combing professional advocacy and technical support organizations, professional SMOs have been the largest recipients, receiving between half and three-fourths of movement philanthropy. In the early period, institutional recipients were favored, with almost half of the money going to churches and universities. Indigenous groups received only four percent of the money, with the assumption apparently being that these had grassroots volunteers and hence did not need significant grants. With the upsurge of social protest during the 1960s, contributions to indigenous groups grew significantly, rising to fifteen to twenty-one percent of funding in 1970 and 1980. Professional advocacy and technical support centers gained slightly over this same period. The major shift was away from institutions to indigenous groups, as movement funders became more willing to deal directly with grassroots groups. The 1980s witnessed a reversal, with indigenous funding dropping by 1990 to only fourteen percent and professional advocacy rising to nearly sixty percent of the funding. Institutions also reemerged as a significant recipient of movement philanthropy.

To tap the interaction between these movements and philanthropic support, Figures 10.1–10.5 trace the annualized funding for the five major movements of this period—the African American, peace/antiwar, women's, environmental, and consumer/governmental-accountability movements—and the count of social movement protests and total movement actions as reported in the *New York Times* for the period 1953–1980. In four of these movements, sustained movement actions emerged a year or more before the

Table 10.5. Priorities of Social Movement Foundations, 1953–1990

	1953		1960		1970		1980		1990	
	% Grants	% Grant $	% Grants	% Grant $	% Grants	% Grant $	% Grants	% Grant $	% Grants	% Grant $
Type of Donee Organization										
Indigenous	25.0	22.9	10.0	4.1	19.3	15.4	25.9	21.4	21.3	13.9
Professional Advocacy	0.0	0.0	40.0	34.9	36.7	38.9	30.0	40.1	50.2	58.0
Technical Support	0.0	0.0	20.0	14.8	31.8	34.6	38.7	33.0	19.9	19.3
Institutions	75.0	77.1	30.0	46.2	12.2	11.1	4.6	5.5	8.6	8.7
Total	100.0	100.0	100.0	100.0	100.0	100.0	100.0	100.0	100.0	100.0

infusion of the first movement grants. Only in the consumer-rights movement did funding precede movement actions, indicating that the professional movement entrepreneurs and foundation sponsors were central to initiating mobilization. In the other movements, movement activity for at least two successive years emerged first, indicating that foundations were responding to movement activity. When examining the overall relation between movement action and funding, the upsurge in movement actions led the way for the upsurge in movement philanthropy with a five- to six-year lag between the peak in actions and that for funding. The consumer movement was again the exception, where funding growth preceded growth in movement actions. A closer look at the development of each of these movements will make this pattern clearer.

We begin with the master movement of the period: the African American civil-rights movement. Black protest first emerged in 1953 with the Baton Rouge bus boycott, which demonstrated the ability of African Americans to mobilize for collective action, and the Montgomery bus boycott of 1955–1956, which created both the Montgomery Improvement Association and the Southern Christian Leadership Conference (SCLC) and proved that Southern black communities could effectively mobilize to secure change (Figure 10.1). A second protest wave erupted in 1960 with the student sit-ins at lunch counters throughout the South, which had been prefigured by sit-ins in Oklahoma during 1957–1958 but which did not receive news coverage.[15] In 1961 a third protest developed with the "freedom rides" in which protestors boarded public buses in desegregated areas and headed South, challenging the segregation line. Finally in 1963–1964 came the mass community campaigns focused on voting rights and a second round in 1965–1966, which opened the way for more systematic voter registration across the South.[16]

Although there were small grants to the NAACP in the early 1950s, the early protests were centered in the South among new indigenous groups such as the SCLC and SNCC, which were centered in the local churches and community organizations of the South. By contrast, foundation support was initially targeted at the NAACP, which was virtually non-existent in the South, having been outlawed in several states and persecuted by White Citizens Councils and local police. In other words, movement organizing was centered among indigenous local groups, but foundation funding went to support the litigation effort of the NAACP in the North. The first significant foundation grants to the grassroots organizations came in 1960 and 1961, when several New York–based foundations funded voter registration drives in response to the sit-in and freedom-ride victories. Movement philanthropy was essential, providing bail money and lawyers to keep the protestors active. Without this support, the protests would have been

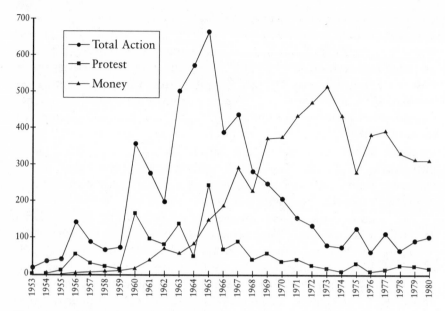

Figure 10.1. African American Movement

weaker and enforcement of many court rulings would have never occurred. The major growth of movement philanthropy came after the 1964 and 1965 Civil Rights Acts, which provided a legal basis for protecting the civil and political rights of Southern blacks. With major funding for voter registration, black voting turnout in the South began to approach that of whites. Movement philanthropy peaked, however, in 1973 and declined as the African American movement became embroiled in more contentious issues such as school integration and busing conflicts, open-housing fights, and attempts to enforce affirmative action in higher education and employment. The urban riots of the late 1960s also led some foundation trustees to associate the movement with violence and radical claims. Although this initially spurred a growth in funding, it also reduced long-term sympathies. The field of movement philanthropy also became more competitive with newer causes, such as environmentalism, women's rights, and the consumer movement.

What was the impact on the movement? Although black protest and overall movement action did decline in the late 1970s, protests persisted through the end of the decade and continued on a low level through the 1980s. In the early years, grassroots groups with a protest history received over half of the funding and, between 1953 and 1980, roughly equal thirds went to grassroots, advocacy, and technical support organizations. Founda-

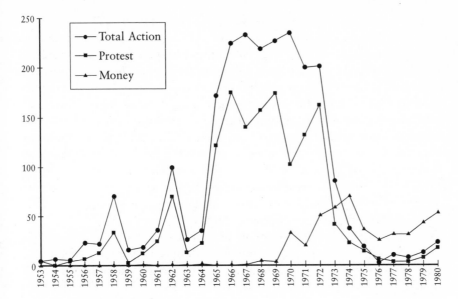

Figure 10.2. Peace Movement

tion patronage professionalized the civil-rights movement, building new professional advocacy and service organizations and professionalizing the existing indigenous groups, such as the NAACP and SCLC. This may have reduced the incentive for movement leaders to engage in grassroots organizing and thus blunted the impact of the movement. Yet, given the importance of these legal and political resources for the civil rights of African Americans and for implementing the legal victories of the movement, this movement philanthropy was also critical to the implementation of movement successes.

The mobilization of the peace movement follows a similar pattern with less than a tenth of the foundation funding. Centered among religious dissenters and middle-class radicals, early ban-the-bomb protests emerged in 1948–1949 in response to the escalating nuclear testing in the Nevada range and the Pacific. By 1949, the Soviet Union announced that it had an operational nuclear bomb, setting off the nuclear arms race and creating the stage for the Cold War. Movement philanthropy, however, did not emerge in this arena until 1956, when the first foundations grants were given to the Fund for Peace and the American Friends Service Committee to promote public understanding of the United Nations and to provide legal protection for conscientious objectors (Figure 10.2). Despite another round of grassroots anti-nuclear arms protest in 1962–1963, the foundations ignored these efforts. Questioning the national security state was too politically controversial, and the foundations decided to ignore these concerns. With the Vietnam buildup in 1964, campus protests mushroomed, leading eventually to violent confrontations and the growth of radical student groups committed to an underground struggle against "the system." In 1968–1969, this movement finally spurred an outpouring of funding for student organizing, including a campaign to lower the voting and drinking age to eighteen, and, after the first revelations about Federal infiltration of antiwar groups in 1971, the foundations began to fund research and advocacy on the problems of security abuses and governmental surveillance. With Vietnamization and the withdrawal of U.S. ground troops from Vietnam in 1973, the antiwar protests largely subsided, but funding for peace and the antinuclear movement continued to grow, facilitating protests against nuclear arms production and nuclear power plants in the late 1970s. In contrast to the civil rights movement, over half of all peace funding went to existing institutions, primarily pacificist churches and universities, which sponsored student organizing and efforts to legally protect conscientious objectors. Although mass protest played a major role in creating the withdrawal from Vietnam, this was a grassroots effort that received virtually no foundation support. Foundation support has been overwhelmingly reactive and largely non-existent, having relatively little impact until the late 1970s, when several family and alternative foundations sponsored the anti-nuclear campaigns.

As a "late riser" movement that built off the mobilization and political opportunities created by these earlier challenges, the women's movement mobilized much more quickly, thus bringing philanthropic support more quickly into the movement. With the founding of the National Organization for Women (NOW) in 1966 and its growing militancy after being rebuffed by the Johnson Administration over enforcement of the sex-discrimination clauses of the Equal Employment Opportunity Act, NOW joined the emerging radical "younger branch" of the women's movement in a series of protests in 1967. Spectamur Agendo, a new foundation created by Stewart Mott, provided a $100,000 grant to further the women's rights campaign. In contrast to the African American movement, women's movement funding grew steadily through the end of the 1970s (Figure 10.3) and by 1990 had experienced only a slight decline. Movement philanthropy created a new set of professional advocacy and service centers, such as the Women's Legal Defense Fund and the Women's Law Fund, which engaged in legal advocacy and lobbying to eliminate sexual discrimination barriers and to protect access to abortion. Despite this massive influx of foundation patronage, feminist protest persisted through the early 1980s, peaking again during the final battles over the Equal Rights Amendment in 1982 and 1983. In this case, movement philanthropy has been essential in providing the

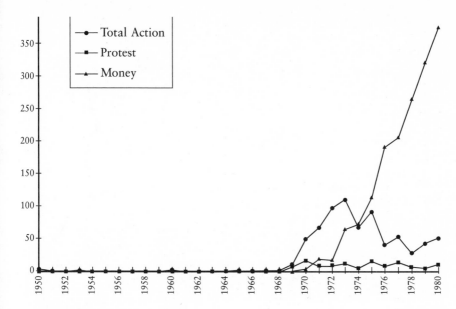

Figure 10.3. Women's Movement

legal and technical resources to secure legal changes and ensure their enforcement. Yet, as Anne Constain has argued, movement philanthropy and professionalization have also reduced the incentive for movement leaders to engage in time-consuming grassroots organizing, which has blunted the movement and thus reduced its impact.[17]

Although the environmental movement today is largely professionalized, its origins bespeak a grassroots middle-class radicalism that adopted professional methods of movement work. In the early 1960s, heavy smog in the Los Angeles basin stirred citizen protests in 1962 and 1963 (Figure 10.4). In the early 1960s, Rachel Carson at the Audubon Society recognized the damage of DDT and other pesticides to birdlife, and her *Silent Spring* caught the attention of ecological scientists. In 1966, a group of natural scientists banded together to found the Environmental Defense Fund, which launched suits against Suffolk County, New York to bar DDT. In 1968, a group of New York University law students and professors decided to join forces with wealthy landowners opposing the Storm King Power Plant on the Hudson River, forming the Natural Resources Defense Fund, which received founding support from the Ford and other New York area foundations. In both cases, professionals whose practices dealt with environmental problems recognized the possibilities of using the new idea of nonprofit public-interest law firms to assemble legal and natural-science teams that

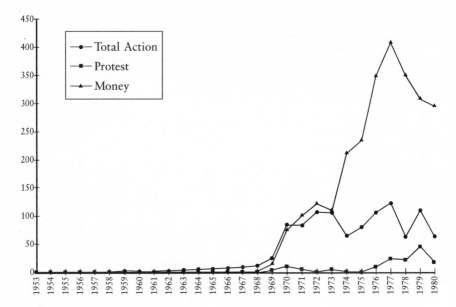

Figure 10.4. Environmental Movement

could litigate against polluters. Foundation patronage was critical to each of these projects and thus to the enforcement of the new environmental legislation. In contrast to the earlier movements, the environmental movement entailed little protest. Except for a flurry of protests around Earth Day in 1970 and another upsurge in the late 1970s centered around nuclear power plants and other environmental hazards, protest events were rare (Figure 10.4). Over seventy percent of the funding went to advocacy organizations with less than seven percent going to grassroots groups. Movement philanthropy was essential to launching these organizations and enabling them to carry out their program of environmental protection. More recently these professional SMOs have become involved in localized protests linked to the siting of hazardous waste dumps and similar environmental problems. Here they have provided invaluable technical support, assisting grassroots local groups in their efforts to combat environmental damage.

The consumer/governmental-accountability movement has been the most professionalized, organized around a set of public-interest law firms and advocacy organizations. In contrast to the other movements, foundation patronage preceded the emergence of sustained movement organizing, spurring its development. In 1965 Ralph Nader published *Unsafe at Any Speed*, an exposé on the hazards of General Motors' Corvair. The following year, it surfaced in Congressional testimony that GM had hired private investigators to undermine Nader's credibility. Nader promptly sued, winning a libel victory in 1967, which legitimized the effort. The next year, the Carnegie Corporation provided $55,000 to found the Center for the Study of Responsive Law, which began producing reports on weaknesses in Federal regulatory agencies and monopoly power in industry. In 1969, John Gardner, a moderate Republican and former Secretary of Health, Education, and Welfare in the Johnson administration, tapped wealthy donors and several foundations for support to create Common Cause, a public-interest lobby that developed a grassroots volunteer structure and focused on governmental secrecy, campaign-finance reform, and Congressional procedural reform. Social protest on this front was non-existent and grassroots involvement has been relatively limited, typically confined to responding to direct-mail solicitations, but the movement has still secured significant legal and administrative victories, such as new consumer-protection laws, open-hearing requirements in administrative rule-making, and greater access to governmental records. By the end of the 1970s, there were over fifty advocacy organizations associated with Ralph Nader and an equal number of public-interest law firms and research centers throughout the country. Sixty percent of all funding went to advocacy organizations, with only three percent going to indigenous groups and the rest to technical support centers. Although the grassroots links of this movement has been weak, the Nader and other public-interest organizations have attempted to forge alliances with local civil rights, women's, and environmental groups, thus forming "progressive" coalitions. Overall, this movement is the most financially dependent on foundation patronage and, in terms of impact, the most reliant on legal advocacy and related types of efforts.

Conclusion

Social movement philanthropy has become institutionalized as a significant force in American society. Although representing but a tiny portion of institutional philanthropy, it constitutes a highly leveraged form of "risk capital" philanthropy, having major impact on most of the social movements that have developed in the past four decades. It has fueled these movements in that it has provided needed technical resources and created new organizations that have been vital to securing and implementing movement gains. However, at the same time, it has also reduced the pressure on movement leaders to engage in costly and time-consuming grassroots organizing, thus potentially blunting the impact of these movements.

Let us speak first to the overall trend in movement philanthropy. As we have seen, foundation funding for social movements has grown rapidly since the early 1950s, becoming a small institutional force in American poli-

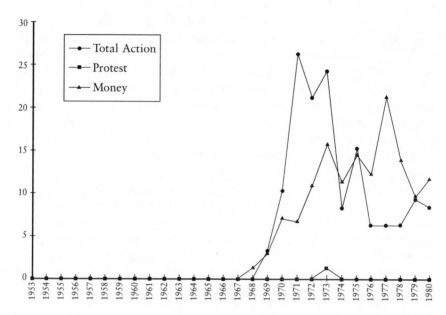

Figure 10.5. Consumer Movement

tics. Social protests and the entrepreneurial work of movement leaders has spurred foundations to fund social movements, thus creating new organizations and projects and strengthening the implementation capacities of movement groups. Despite significant turnover among the foundations involved, the total pool of funding has increased and displayed relatively stable patterns in terms of total funding and priorities. There has also been a significant growth in movement-based public charities and alternative foundations, which have been more likely to fund grassroots and unruly protest groups. Overall, social movement philanthropy has been guided by a general "rights" framework that emphasizes the importance of political representation and the extension of civil, political, and social rights to all groups. In a sense, it has attempted to realize the model of a pluralistic democracy where all groups and interests are politically represented. This has created and incorporated a variety of previously excluded and unorganized groups, thus "grassrooting" the system.

Yet much of this new political representation has been professionalized and has often had only a limited grassroots basis. The civil-rights and peace/antiwar movements had the lowest proportion of funding going to professional SMOs and, for the former, the highest proportion going to indigenous groups. This reflected both the grassroots nature of the movement, which mobilized mass protests and local campaigns throughout the South, and its generally moderate assimilative goals, which facilitated funding. By comparison, the women's, environmental, and consumer movements were more professionalized, both in terms of movement activity and foundation funding. This has led many critics to question the usefulness of this representation, arguing that it is cooptative and demobilizing or, at best, weaker than grassroots organization.

Does professionalization work against the grassroots mobilization and success of movements? In some arenas, such as child advocacy and the rights of the disabled, indigenous mobilization is not feasible. For such constituencies, professional representation has no alternative. In other areas, indigenous mobilization interacts with professionalization. Here the record is complex. In terms of addressing legal and political advocacy, professionalization and the movement philanthropy in which it is rooted have provided resources which have helped implement and ensure enforcement of many of the changes secured initially by grassroots protests. In this sense, movement philanthropy has helped to grassroot the system and to make it more responsive to unorganized and excluded interests. At the same time, movement philanthropy has also provided alternative resources to movement leaders, thus reducing the incentive for engaging in time-consuming and costly grassroots organizing. It also appears to have encouraged the development of more centralized movements dominated by professionalized organizations and, in this sense, has perhaps weakened the competitive stimulus for movement innovation and growth. In this sense, movement philanthropy may also have dampened the development of movements and blunted the long-term impact of their efforts.

Notes

This chapter has benefitted by the critical comments of Bob Bothwell, Susan Ostrander, Terry Odendahl, Mary Anna Colwell, Jean Entine, and Sarah Priestman, as well as the cooperation of the Washington D.C. Foundation Center staff, who helped track down information on foundation giving. We also benefitted from the financial help of the National Committee on Responsive Philanthropy, along with support for an earlier study from the National Endowment for the Humanities and the Russell Sage Foundation.

1. Susan Ostrander, *Money for Change: Social Movement Philanthropy at the Haymarket People's Fund* (Philadelphia: Temple University Press, 1995); J. Craig Jenkins. "Foundation Funding of Social Movements," in J. Shellow, ed., *The Grant Seeker's Guide*, 2nd ed. (Washington, D.C.: National Network of Grantmakers, 1985), 7–17; J. Craig Jenkins and Craig Eckert, "Channeling Black Insurgency: Elite Patronage and the Development of the Civil Rights Movement," *American Sociological Review* 51 (December 1986): 812–30; J. Craig Jenkins, "Non-Profit Organizations and Policy Advocacy," in

Walter Powell, ed., *Non-Profit Organizations: A Handbook* (New Haven: Yale University Press, 1986) 296–318; J. Craig Jenkins, "Foundation Funding of Progressive Social Movements," in J. Shellow, ed., *The Grant Seekers Guide*, 3rd ed. (Mt. Kisco, N.Y.: Moyer-Bell, 1986), 1–13; J. Craig Jenkins, "Social Movement Philanthropy and American Democracy," in Richard Magat, ed., *Philanthropic Giving: Studies in Varieties and Goals* (New York: Oxford University Press, 1989), 292–314.

2. Richard Kruger, *The Trumpet Shall Sound* (Cambridge, Mass.: Harvard University Press, 1972), 260–84; and Steven Lawson Lawson, *Black Ballots: Voting Rights in the South, 1944–1969* (New York: Columbia University Press, 1976), 37–42.

3. Aldon Morris, *The Origins of the Civil Rights Movement* (New York: Oxford University Press, 1984); and Carl Tjerandsen, *Education for Citizenship* (Santa Cruz: Emil Schwarzhaupt Foundation, 1980).

4. Angus MacKenzie, "When Auditors Turn Editors," *Columbia Journalism Review* 9 (1981): 29–34.

5. For an earlier picture, see J. Craig Jenkins and Teri Shumate, "Cowboy Capitalists and the Rise of the New Right," *Social Problems* 33 (December 1985): 130–45.

6. George Pillsbury, *Robin Hood Was Right* (New York: The Funding Exchange, 1982).

7. Susan Ostrander, *Money for Change: Social Movement Philanthropy at the Haymarket Peoples' Fund* (Philadelphia: Temple University Press, 1995), 94, 81–130.

8. Paul DiMaggio and Walter Powell, *The New Institutionalism in Organizational Theory* (Chicago: University of Chicago Press, 1991).

9. Theodore Lowi, *The End of Interest Group Liberalism* (New York: Norton, 1979).

10. T. H. Marshall, *Class, Citizenship, and Social Development* (New York: Cambridge University Press, 1979).

11. Robert Arnove, *Philanthropy and Cultural Imperialism* (Boston: G. K. Hall, 1980); and Joan Roelefs, "Foundation Influence on Supreme Court Decision-Making," *Telos* 62 (1983): 59–87, and "Do Foundations Set the Agenda? From Social Protest to Social Service," unpublished paper, Department of Political Science, Keane University, Keane, N.J., 1986.

12. Doug McAdam, *Political Process and the Development of Black Insurgency* (Chicago: University of Chicago Press, 1982); and Herbert Haines, *Black Radicals and the Civil Rights Mainstream, 1954–1970* (Knoxville: University of Tennessee Press, 1988).

13. J. Craig Jenkins and Craig Eckert, "Channeling Black Insurgency: Elite Patronage and the Development of the Civil Rights Movement," *American Sociological Review* 51 (December 1986): 812–30.

14. John McCarthy and Mayer Zald, *Social Movements in an Organizational Society* (New Brunswick, N.J.: Transaction, 1987).

15. Aldon Morris, *The Origins of the Civil Rights Movement* (New York: Free Press, 1984), 17–40, 192–94.

16. Doug McAdam, "Tactical Innovation and the Pace of Black Insurgency," *American Sociological Review* 48 (March 1983): 735–54.

17. Anne Costain, *Inviting Women's Rebellion* (Baltimore: Johns Hopkins University Press, 1992).

11 | When Grantees Become Grantors

Accountability, Democracy, and Social Movement Philanthropy

Susan A. Ostrander

QUESTIONS ABOUT PUBLIC accountability of private philanthropy in a democratic society arose almost as soon as foundations were established in the United States. Often "public accountability" has meant accountability to government as the agent of public trust. This includes requiring foundations to complete and make publicly available the Internal Revenue Service 990 return with information on income, expenses, assets, grants, and liabilities.

In contrast to this focus on government, my focus here is on the accountability of foundations to grantees, both current and potential. In relation to this kind of accountability, I have recently explored possibilities for re-organizing the typically hierarchical social relations between grantor and grantee by increasing the participation of grantees in grant-making decisions. This participation both makes grant making more accountable to grantees, and makes philanthropy more democratic by being more open and accessible to grantees.

Based on my field research from 1991 to 1993 at Haymarket People's Fund—a small, social-change public foundation that had already been functioning in Boston for over two decades—I argued in my book *Money for Change* that grantee participation in grant-making decisions can transform and re-organize the typical hierarchical social relations of philanthropy.[1] In these typical relations, grantors retain power over grant money. In the case of the Haymarket Fund, grantees have actually become grantors and have thus greatly increased their power over money.

My focus is on foundations engaged in some kind of social-movement activity, a collective effort that empowers and improves the circumstances of historically marginalized or excluded constituent groups and redistributes wealth and power in a more equalitarian way. The reason for this focus is that, given their ultimate goals of empowerment and inclusion of historically marginalized groups, foundations engaged in social-movement philanthropy may exhibit alternative practices that can inform the more widespread adoption of democratic and accountable foundation practices generally. The Haymarket Fund exhibits a most unusual philanthropic practice whereby grantees, who are also social-movement constitutents, make the decisions about grants.

My aim in this chapter is to anchor my previous research in more historical terms. I begin with a review of how democracy and accountability of U.S. foundations is currently being discussed in the writing of both scholars and practitioners, and I allude to how this discussion has (and has not) changed over time. Then, I summarize the aspects of my research on the Haymarket Fund that are most relevant to this chapter, and make an initial attempt to trace Haymarket's practices in relation to the history of social movement philanthropy. I suggest the possibility of an established legacy for this way of doing philanthropy.[2]

Past and Present Discussions of the General Issue of Foundations, Democracy, and Accountability

Accountability of foundations has historically been talked about in the context of debates about the role of philanthropy in a democratic society, pointedly formulated as a question about "the power of money in a democracy."[3] Accountability has also long been discussed in relation to debates about the privileged and publicly granted tax-exempt status of charitable foundations, a status established and regulated by the state as the main legitimate agent of public trust.

Indicative of the tensions between democracy and philanthropy, only three years after the establishment of the Rockfeller and Carnegie foundations, the Congressionally appointed Walsh Commission began an investigation in 1914 with these issues as their main concerns. A central question at that time was "the implications for democracy of the inordinate concentration of wealth and power in an elite group of professional philanthropists tied to corporate industrial interests."[4]

In another well-known historical example—in 1961, following on the heels of McCarthy-era right-wing charges that foundations were conspiring to support progressive social change—Congress began to investigate the tax privileges of charitable foundations. Congressman Wright Patman was spurred on by concerns about the Ford Foundation making grants to support voter-registration campaigns. Such efforts on the part of a conservative administration to curb foundation support for citizen participation and advocacy continue into the present. The Patman hearings resulted ultimately in the Tax Reform Act of 1969, which placed a number of limitations on foundation funding, especially forbidding them to use their money to directly influence legislation or elections.[5]

Current examples of ongoing concern about the place of foundations in a democratic society and the issue of public accountability include a plenary at the 1993 annual meeting of the Association for Research on Nonprofit Organizations and Voluntary Action (ARNOVA) called "Crisis in Regulation." Historian Peter Dobkin Hall organized the panel for scholars to respond to and debate a series published in the *Philadelphia Inquirer* under the title "Warehouses of Wealth: The Tax-Free Economy." The series charged, among other things, that most large nonprofit organizations—including foundations—were not operating for the public good, and their privileged tax-exempt status was therefore unwarranted in many cases.

Another example of current concern about foundations and the accountability issue is an article in *Nonprofit and Voluntary Sector Quarterly* that states unequivocally that "Few charitable organizations have escaped public examination as much as America's 30,000 foundations, whose poor record of public accountability deserves public scrutiny."[6] Derek Bok echoed this sentiment in the context of a review of a book on foundations: "Of all the institutions in America, philanthropic foundations are surely among the least accountable."[7]

A question closely related to the accountability of foundations is whether these charitable organizations are public or private. Those who define them as private argue that foundations need not be publicly accountable either to government as an agent of "the public" or to the "public" that makes up its grantee constituency, because they are "private organizations created by private citizens using private money."[8] In contrast, those who see them as public argue that their privileged (and publicly granted) tax-exempt status demands that they serve the public interest, and democratic principles require that their economic power be restrained through some measure of public accountability. Some have extended the tax-exempt argument to suggest that public citizens can legitimately demand accountability of foundations because taxpayers "must bear an additional financial burden to compensate for the taxes that foundations and their sponsors avoid."[9]

Calling into question any historically based argument for foundations as private organizations, historians Barry Karl and Stanley Katz have argued that the "claim to privacy among foundations" is largely a matter of historical accident. Karl and Katz show how early founders such as John D. Rockefeller actually sought to leave their money as public trusts in the form of a governmental corporation, with trustees named as a Public Council appointed by the states.[10]

Some social scientists (including myself) have argued that conceptualizing public and private as distinct and separate spheres, sectors, or institutional realms in society—and then attempting to locate nonprofits within or between them—is not the most useful way to understand nonprofits. Foundations, like all non-governmental nonprofits, are outside both the "public" state and the "private" market. In this sense they are neither public nor private, but—as some have argued—located in some "third sector" that spans, connects, or mediates the other two.

Building on the work of others—especially feminist scholars who have re-conceptualized public/private relations—I have suggested another way of thinking that is not about sectors at all. I have argued that nonprofits can perhaps best be seen as differentially located along a continuum containing aspects of both "public" and "private."[11] In this way of thinking, the question becomes how—and to what extent—foundations are public and/or private. This *how* question refers not to where foundations are located in some pre-defined societal sector or sphere—first, second, or third—but rather to where they are located on a continuum of being more or less receptive to accessibility and influence by varying "publics," including grantees.

Using this kind of definition of public and private, I would argue that foundations should be "private" to the extent they are governed by a trustee board of private citizens, not by the public state. On the other hand, while it may be legitimate for foundations to "privately" define their specific grantmaking focus and their own priorities and guidelines for grantmaking, foundations should be "publically" more open, accessible, and influenced by and answerable to the constituencies and communities they serve. That is a large part of what the debates concerning accountability and democracy are about.

While there are several aspects of "public" accountability that have been subject to debate, foundations' accountability specifically to grantee groups or potential grantee groups merits greater attention. The National Committee for Responsive Philanthropy (NCRP) and the National Network of Grantmakers (NNG) are among those who have long been interested in this kind of accountability. NCRP has criticized community foundations for their lack of accessibility to grantees and for their resistance to providing information about their grant-making priorities and procedures.[12] NNG has developed an assessment tool for foundations to use so they can become more accountable and open in their relation to grantees.

Some have suggested that greater foundation accountability in this regard, especially more grantee involvement in the grant-making process, would help foundations to be more effective in achieving their larger social goals. This claim is based in part on the belief that grantees could—if the philanthropic process allowed for it—bring their own critical knowledge about community problems and solutions into foundation policies and practices, including setting criteria and priorities for funding. An article in *The Economist*, for example, claims, "[Foundations] would have better programs if they sought independent assessment of their work and encouraged their grantees, under a guarantee of anonymity, to comment on the work of programme officers."[13] If this claim of greater effectiveness proved correct, it would be a compelling reason indeed to alter the grantor/grantee relationship from its more traditional historical form, in which the power to decide what projects to fund lies solely with grantors—either in the form of original donors or foundation staff and boards.

Concerns about the hierarchically structured relationship between grantors and grantees are by no means new. Nearly a century ago, settlement-house founder and progressive social scientist Jane Addams criticized what she called the "charitable relation . . . between benefactor and beneficiary" for its fundamental contradiction with democracy.[14] This contradiction lies in Addams's view of the charitable relation as one where benefactors give in accordance with their own interests, without the involvement of recipients in determining for themselves their major needs and interests. Addams explicitly labels this relation as hierarchical. Benefactors, she claims, retain superiority and power. The charitable relation takes place at the benefactor's discretion, with the benefactor retaining the right to decide who is worthy of help and what kind of help is needed, without consulting the beneficiary.[15]

Anthropologist Marcel Mauss, writing in the 1920s, was apparently the first scholar to systematically study gift exchange in societies around the world. Like Jane Addams, Mauss stated explicitly that relations created by gift giving and receiving are hierarchical and asymmetrical. They create an involuntary relationship of subordinance, dependence and obligation on the part of the receiver toward the giver. In this way, "charity wounds him who receives."[16]

In more recent years, a few scholars have begun exploring the possibility of reconstructing or transforming the social relations of philanthropy so they are less hierarchical, more reciprocal, and, in this way, perhaps more democratic. In a 1990 paper, Paul Schervish and I argued that there might be certain conditions under which donors and recipients could create a more symmetrical relationship.[17] We argued that philanthropy at its best is a reciprocal relationship where all parties give and get, where all bring something of value to a mutually shared interest, and where there is a common commitment to some cause or concern in the community. Some recent guiding principles for fundraising have been formulated consistent with this way of thinking.[18]

Beginning in 1990, I set out to explore a foundation that appeared to be organized along these lines. The story of Haymarket and the tracing of its historical lineage have implications for our thinking about the social relations between grantors and grantees, and the possibilities for transforming those relations.

The Case of Haymarket People's Fund

Anthropologist, critic of mainstream philanthropy, and Executive Director of the progressive National Network of Grantmakers, Teresa Odendahl has called the Haymarket Fund "a democratically representative alternative that is close to the kind of philanthropy that might truly be for the public good."[19] Nonprofit scholar Michael O'Neil has called Haymarket "the prototype of the alternative funds."[20]

At the Haymarket Fund, the typically hierarchical relation between grantors and grantees is reorganized in a way that is both more democratic and more accountable. Haymarket democratizes the decision making about grants by opening them up to social groups who have historically been marginalized, and holds the organization accountable to grantee constituencies by locating decisions in their hands. Supporting my argument that this practice changes the social relations of philanthropy, the balance of power over where the money goes is shifted from grantor to grantee and institutionalized in the form of grantee-based funding boards. These boards are the sole and final authority on which community organizations get a grant.

At the Haymarket Fund, the grantors who make the decisions about who gets the money—who, therefore, hold power over this money—are drawn from a local constituency of grantees who are also social-movement activists. These individuals are most often members of past, occasionally present, and sometimes future grantee organizations. They are the grantmakers. Reports suggest that some of the relatively new women's funds also operate in this way, with at least some grantee representation on funding boards.[21]

Since most of the social-movement activity that Haymarket funds is directed at constituencies of low-income people, people of color, and often women, most of the people on the grantee-based funding boards also come from these groups. Transforming social relations of philanthropy in this context thus also means transforming relations of class, race, and gender.

While much more needs to be known about how foundations select their grantees and whose voice holds sway when these selections are made, Haymarket's practice appears to be profoundly different from how most foundations make grant decisions. Most decide through a board of trustees made up largely of people from the business and professional communities, with little, if any, representation of people of color or white women. Professional foundation staff apparently have a substantial degree of influence over the decisions made by these boards. While staff are likely to be women, they too are most often white and middle to upper income.[22] In social terms, then, those who hold the power over grants in foundations are much closer to their donor base—even one from decades ago in the case of private foundations—than to their grantee base.

Relations of class, race, and gender in the U.S. overall are, of course, highly strained; and democracy is, as they say, a messy business. Any organization attempting to alter social relations of class, race, and gender is therefore taking on a difficult project indeed. Even limited success is worthy of celebration. It is not surprising, then, that strains along lines of class, race, and gender were evident during the years of my field research at Haymarket. Rather than viewing these as problems, the organization took them as an integral part of what they did.

There were, for example, tensions among a racially diverse staff about how to raise money. (Recall that Haymarket is a public foundation and so raises its own funds annually.) Staff of color tended to want to make more "political" appeals that (in their view) were more reflective of Haymarket's progressive social goals. Whites—especially white women—emphasized more "personal" appeals, saying they raised more money for the Fund, and that donors initially brought in this way could be gradually moved to a more political way of thinking about their giving. Sometimes gender- and race-based disagreements arose among funding-board grantee-activists about whether a grantee group was engaged in the kind of progressive social-movement activity they wished to fund, or whether the activity was more social service than social change. This arose, for example, about battered-women's shelters, which women—especially women of color—defined as clearly social-change work; and men, and some white women, saw more as service.

There were also class-based tensions specific to donors. Some donors (mostly wealthy and virtually all white) felt that funding-board grantee-activists (nearly all low income, with many people of color) held negative stereotypes of people with wealth. There was also the ongoing possibility that wealthy donors might seek to make their own decisions about which grantee organizations to give to, turning from the Haymarket Fund's bedrock commitment to grantee-based grant making. This has occurred there (as elsewhere in foundations) in the mid 1990s with an increase in donor-advised grants, where the donor retains power over where her or his money goes.

Another concern at Haymarket that is closely connected to issues of democracy and accountability is that—while funding boards based in the communities from which grantees come represent a significant democratizing of the more common hierarchical grantor-grantee relation—these funding boards can themselves become a self-perpetuating elite. Given that they function as gate-keepers to obtaining a grant, these boards could—however constructed—simply produce another kind of hierarchy between some grantees who had access and other grantees who did not.

Various measures were in place at Haymarket People's Fund during the years of my research to mitigate these undesirable consequences. These measures included an open application process for new funding-board members, and conflict-of-interest rules about board members not participating in decisions about grants to organizations of which they were a member. Still, funding-board members expressed concern to me that some grantees were successful because they knew the right language to use in their proposals, and conformed to a particular kind of organizing that appealed most to funding-board members but that some suspected of containing an implicit race or class bias.

While a study of the history of social-movement philanthropy remains to be done, my reading of existing accounts suggests that foundations like Haymarket can be traced back at least to the Rosenwald Fund (established by Julius Rosenwald in 1917, it closed its doors in 1948);[23] and to the Stern Fund (established by Rosenwald's daughter in 1936 and closed in 1986).[24] The importance of this historical tracing is to suggest a strong historical tradition, albeit a small one, for social movement philanthropy in U.S. foundations of a sort that led very slowly to more involvement of grantees in grant making.

Tracing the Historical Path to Haymarket People's Fund

Julius Rosenwald made his fortune from Sears, Roebuck, and Company in the early decades of the twentieth century. He was said to be "embarrassed to have so much."[25] Eleven years after establishing his foundation, Rosenwald requested that its "entire income and principal be expended within twenty-five years after my death," citing a concern for "tendencies toward bureaucracy and a formal or perfunctory attitude toward the work which almost inevitably develops in organizations which prolong their existence."[26] Influenced by his reading and then meeting in 1911 with Booker T. Washington, Rosenwald made "the cause of Negroes his chief philanthropy" for the foundation he established in 1917. Initially, the Fund supported improvements in separate educational and training facilities for African Americans, like Tuskegee Institute, and health and medical services. The establishment of the Rosenwald Fellows program was part of "raising the status" of African Americans, and its recipient list reads like of a Who's Who of American Blacks in the 1930s and 1940s. It included Kenneth Clark, St. Clair Drake, E. Franklin Frazier, W. E. B. DuBois, Langston Hughes, Katherine Dunham, and Marian Anderson.

Later "it became increasingly evident that raising the status of Negroes was not enough," so "the Fund turned its attention squarely to the problem of segregation."[27] It made grants to the National Association for the Advancement of Colored People (NAACP), and the National Urban League, as well as various religious organizations involved in the emerging civil-rights movement.

General literature on foundations refers briefly, though consistently, to Rosenwald and the foundation he established. Waldemar Nielsen notes that the Rosenwald Fund was "one of the great foundations of the past that deliberately spent themselves out of existence."[28] He cites Rosenwald as having "an authentic and powerful new perspective on philanthropy," and he calls founder Julius Rosenwald "one of a handful of truly great philanthropists in American history."[29] Education historians James D. Anderson and Edward Berman, in a less positive reference, consider Julius Rosenwald an early supporter of a kind of education for African Americans that served largely to keep them in a subordinate status.[30] Sociologists J. Craig Jenkins and Craig Eckert, looking at a later period in history, report that "the NAACP Legal Defense Fund was originally launched in 1935 with a grant by the Rosenwald foundation."[31] Writer and progressive philanthropy activist Alan Rabinowitz cites the Rosenwald Foundation as one of the early funders of the Highlander Center, a training center for union organizers in the South in the 1930s.[32]

Researchers have simply not done sufficient work on the Rosenwald Fund to come to firm conclusions about its role, though we can say more about two of its grantees: the NAACP and the Highlander Center. The importance of the NAACP in the civil-rights movement is unquestioned, though not all would see it in exactly the same way. The Highlander Center continues to this day to be an important force in training political organizers for a wide variety of social-movement groups. It can be said with certainty that the Rosenwald Foundation did engage, to at least some small degree, in social-movement funding toward the end of its tenure and in response to a rising movement for the civil rights of African Americans.

The Stern Fund was established in 1936 by Julius Rosenwald's daughter, Edith Stern, and her husband, Edgar. Following Rosenwald's path of purposefully spending out their assets, the Stern Fund opened in 1936 and closed in 1986. According to a 1992 book from the Institute for Media Analysis on the Stern Fund, the fund did not begin focusing on social-movement funding until 1964, twenty-eight years after it was founded, and (I would add) some twenty years after Edith Stern's father, Julius Rosenwald, had begun funding social-movement groups active in civil rights for African Americans. When Executive Director David Hunter came to Stern from the Ford Foundation in 1963, Edith Stern directed him at the outset to concentrate on funding racial justice. The delay in moving to this kind of funding is attributed in large part to Edgar Stern, Edith Stern's conventional New Orleans husband, who died in 1960 and who preferred more traditional grants, for example, to the local Community Chest, two local universities, and the city's symphony orchestra.

In an early effort to involve members of potential grantee groups, the Stern Fund sought advice from civil-rights leaders about how the Fund might best contribute, making clear its preference for systemic change over "charitable services." Hunter's guidelines stated, "The Stern Fund chooses to support institutional or social change in an attempt to get at and correct the root cause of social pathology and foster a more humane and egalitarian society."[33] His practice was also to have potential grantees give in-person presentations to the board—not nearly the same as having grantee-based decisions about grant making, but arguably a step in that direction.

While about a quarter of Stern Fund grants during its last two decades (1964–1981) went to local New Orleans organizations, including some quite conventional ones, national grants by 1970 included "groups that questioned economic arrangements under the status quo," such as Ralph Nader's Project on Corporate Responsibility, Barry Commoner's efforts to create alternative forms of energy, and the anti-nuclear movement in the form of a grant to the Clamshell Alliance. Grants averaged around $20,000. Women's-rights groups were added in 1972, including the National Women's Political Caucus and the NOW Legal Defense Fund. Students for a Democratic Society (SDS) and CORE were grantees, as were Mobilization for Survival, the National Congress of Neighborhood Women, and the Center for Third World Organizing.[34]

Overall, the 1992 book on the Stern Fund concludes that the Fund considered itself a "social movement funder," and "played a vital role in legitimizing systemic social change as a proper role for charitable foundations."[35]

Sociologist Herbert H. Haines is among the other writers who mention the Stern Fund and its also oft-mentioned counterpart, the Field Foundation.[36] Haines writes, "Certain progressive foundations—small to medium-sized ones for the most part, such as the Stern Family Fund and the Field Foundation—began [in the 1950s] to make occasional grants to civil rights organizations with integrationist leanings."[37] Jenkins notes the significance of "the early grants in 1961 from the Marshall Field Foundation to the Southern Christian Leadership Conference (SCLC) to transfer a citizenship training program from the Highlander Institute to the SCLC, paving the way for SCLC's move into voter registration."[38] Historian Peter Dobkin Hall notes that the grants made by the Stern foundation to support voter-registration drives in the South "had disproportionately great effects."[39]

Sociologist Mary Anna Culleton Colwell refers to a Field Foundation grant in 1975 for a project to protect political activists from surveillance by the United States government. Colwell calls this "the far left" of all the foundation grants she studied, even though the group that was funded (the Center for National Security Studies) was in her view, "moderate and legalistic ... certainly not a radical group."[40] She characterizes Field as "the most liberal of all the foundations in [her] sample," and she cites it to illustrate how "a relatively small foundation that concentrates its grants ... may have a disproportionate impact."[41] Colwell also notes the difficulty that foundations such as Stern and Field have had in influencing other foundations to follow in their path.[42]

One key individual from the Stern Fund, David Hunter, Executive Director from 1963 to 1986, and another, Leslie Dunbar from the Field Foundation, apparently had a significant impact on the future of social-movement funding by some of the new public foundations, including Haymarket People's Fund. Writer Alan Rabinowitz says that "by the early 1960's the stage was set for the emergence of a network of progressive social change philanthropies." He calls attention to the critical role played by David Hunter and Leslie Dunbar in influencing wealthy individuals and some foundations to support social-change groups.[43] Rabinowitz calls David Hunter the "dean of progressive funders."[44]

Hunter's influence is said to have been especially critical for Obie Benz and George Pillsbury, the founders of the radical San Francisco social-change fund, the Vanguard Foundation, and its East Coast Boston counterpart, Haymarket People's Fund. In further support of this connection, the 1992 book on the Stern Fund states that, "Hunter's most lasting contribution to philanthropy may be ... the strong, supportive role he played ... with young people with inherited wealth who ... wanted to fund institutional change and ... to democratize the grant-making process by involving those whom the funds were supposed to help."[45] Given this brief sketch of the historical lineage of Haymarket People's Fund, it seems possible to suggest a long history of social-movement philanthropy that eventually played a part in bringing grantees into foundation decision making.

Conclusion

Past and present efforts to involve grantee constituencies in foundation grantmaking bring in "the public" as active participants in deciding where the money goes. These efforts may prove useful in answering critics who question how well foundations today are doing in serving and in answering to the public good, which critics often see as a condition for retaining tax-exempt status. The stable and successful leadership exercised by grantee-based funding boards in foundations such as the Haymarket Fund issues a challenge to foundations overall. The challenge is to narrow the gap between grant makers and grant seekers, increase the representation of community constituents on foundation boards, and give grantees as members of the larger community more of a voice in criteria and priorities in grant making and grant decisions. This means institutionalizing new more accountable and more democratic social arrangements that increase the amount of power that grantees have over grant decisions. I believe this can be usefully conceptualized as reorganizing the social relations between grantors and grantees by moving grantees closer to established positions as grantors.

Notes

1. Susan A. Ostrander, *Money for Change: Social Movement Philanthropy at Haymarket People's Fund* (Philadelphia: Temple University Press, 1995).

2. Susan A. Ostrander, "Charitable Foundations, Social Movements and Social Justice Funding," in *Research in Social Policy: Social Justice Philanthropy*, vol. 5 (Greenwich, Conn.: JAI Press, 1997), 169–90.

3. Dennis P. McIlnay, "The Privilege of Privacy: Twenty-five Years in the Public Accountability Record of Foundations," *Nonprofit and Voluntary Sector Quarterly* 24, no. 2 (Summer 1995): 119.

4. Barbara Howe, "The Emergence of Scientific Philanthropy, 1900–1920: Origins, Issues and Outcomes," in *Philanthropy and Cultural Imperialism: Foundations at Home and Abroad*, ed. Robert F. Arnove (Bloomington: Indiana University Press, 1980), 35–36.

5. Robert Bremner, *American Philanthropy* (Chicago: University of Chicago Press, 1988), 182. John A. Edie, "Congress and Foundations: Historical Summary," in *America's Wealthy and the Future of Foundations*, ed. Teresa Odendahl (New York: Foundation Center, 1987).

6. McIlnay, 117.

7. Derek Bok, "Mute Inglorious Wizards: A Plea for Foundations to Devote Their Money to Finding Talent," *New York Times Book Review*, November 17, 1996, 43.

8. McIlnay, 119.

9. Jacek Titenbrun, "Ownership of Philanthropic Foundations," *Science and Society* 55, no. 1 (Spring 1991): 96.

10. Barry D. Karl and Stanley N. Katz, "Foundations and Ruling Class Elites," *Daedalus*, Winter 1987, 11–13.

11. Susan A. Ostrander, Stuart Langton, and Jon Van Til, eds., *Shifting the Debate: Public/Private Relations in the Modern Welfare State* (Rutgers, N.J.: Transaction Press, 1987), 1, 128. Susan A. Ostrander, "Feminism, Voluntarism, and the Welfare State: Toward a Feminist Sociological Theory of Social Welfare," *American Sociologist* 20, no. 1 (Spring 1989): 29–41.

12. National Committee for Responsive Philanthropy, *Community Foundations at the Margin of Change: Unrealized Potential for the Disadvantaged* (Washington, D.C.: National Committee for Responsive Philanthropy, 1989).

13. "Charitable Foundations: Philanthropy, Meet Controversy," *The Economist*, January 13, 1990, 30.

14. Jane Addams, *Democracy and Social Ethics* (Cambridge, Mass.: Harvard University Press, 1964; orig. 1902), 18.

15. Ibid., 154.

16. Marcel Mauss, *The Gift: Forms and Functions of Exchange in Archaic Societies* (1925; reprint, New York: W. W. Norton, 1967), 58, 63, 72.

17. Susan A. Ostrander and Paul G. Schervish, "Giving and Getting: Philanthropy as Social Relation," in *Critical Issues in American Philanthropy*, ed. Jon Van Til and Associates (San Francisco: Jossey-Bass, 1990).

18. Kathleen Kelly, *Fundraising and Public Relations: A Critical Analysis* (Hillsdale, N.J.: Lawrence Erlbaum, 1991). Joseph Mixer, *Principles of Professional Fundraising: Useful Foundations for Successful Practice* (San Francisco: Jossey-Bass, 1993).

19. Teresa Odendahl, *Charity Begins at Home: Generosity and Self-Interests among the Philanthropic Elite* (New York: Basic Books, 1990), 184.

20. Michael O'Neil, *The Third America: The Emergence of the Nonprofit Sector in the United States* (San Francisco: Jossey-Bass, 1989), 148.

21. Suzanne Messing, "Women's Funds Take Chances," *Social Policy* 20 (Fall 1989): 55. Marcy Murnighan, "Women and Philanthropy: New Voices, New Visions," *New England Journal of Public Policy* (Spring/Summer 1990): 253.

22. John A. Edie, "Congress and Foundations: Historical Summary," in *America's Wealthy and the Future of Foundations,* ed. Teresa Odendahl (New York: Foundation Center, 1987), 43–64. Teresa Odendahl, "Foundations and the Nonprofit Sector," in *America's Wealthy*, 27–42.

23. Edwin R. Embree and Julia Waxman, *Investment in People: The Story of the Julius Rosenwald Fund* (New York: Harper Brothers, 1949).

24. Instititute for Media Analysis, *The Stern Fund: The Story of a Progressive Family Foundation* (New York: Institute for Media Analysis, 1992). The book has an apparently unclaimed authorship, though Philip Stern's Preface attributes much of the writing to Judy Austermiller. Sterns called the book a "less-than-complete history, since the foundation's files were dispersed before the final research and writing could be done" (viii).

25. Embree and Waxman, 13.

26. Ibid., 31.

27. Ibid., 180.

28. Waldemar A. Neilsen, *The Golden Donors* (New York: E. P. Dutton, 1988), 10.

29. Ibid., 111, 265.

30. James D. Anderson, "Philanthropic Control Over Private Higher Education," in *Philanthropy and Cultural Imperialism: Foundations at Home and Abroad*, 168. Edward Berman, "Educational Colonialism in Africa: The Role of American Foundations, 1910–1945," in *Philanthropy and Cultural Imperialism*, 180.

31. J. Craig Jenkins and Craig M. Eckert, "Channeling Black Insurgency: Elite Patronage and Professional Social Movement Organizations in the Development of the Black Movement," *American Sociological Review* 51 (December 1986): 827.

32. Alan Rabinowitz, *Social Change Philanthropy in America* (New York: Quorum, 1990), 44.

33. Institute for Media Analysis, *The Stern Fund*, 41, 43.

34. Ibid., 77, 78, 81, 86.

35. Ibid., 128, 132.

36. The University of Texas library in Austin told me they have a very large collec-

tion of materials on the Field Foundation that has remained largely unanalyzed. I obtained sections of an uncompleted manuscript based on this collection from former staff member Kathy Schwarzchild. Since I was unable to ascertain either its status or its authorship, I have not used material from it here.

37. Herbert H. Haines, *Black Radicals and the Civil Rights Mainstream, 1954–1970* (Knoxville: University of Tennessee Press, 1988), 114.

38. J. Craig Jenkins, "Social Movement Philanthropy and American Democracy," in *Philanthropic Giving: Studies in Varieties and Goals*, ed. Richard Magat (New York: Oxford University Press, 1989), 301.

39. Peter Dobkin Hall, *Inventing the Nonprofit Sector, and Other Essays on Philanthropy, Voluntarism, and Nonprofit Organizations* (Baltimore: Johns Hopkins University, 1992), 93.

40. Mary Anna Culleton Collwell, *Private Foundations and Public Policy: The Political Role of Philanthropy* (New York: Garland, 1993), 130.

41. Ibid., 130–31.

42. Ibid., 206.

43. Rabinowitz, 44–46.

44. Ibid., xviii.

45. Institute for Media Analysis, *The Stern Fund*, 123.

12 | The Ford Foundation and Women's Studies in American Higher Education

Seeds of Change?

Rosa Proietto

THE PAST TWENTY-FIVE years have witnessed the emergence of women's studies as the "educational arm" of what was initially called the women's liberation movement, but has more recently been reconceived as the women's or feminist movement.[1] Between 1970 and 1990, women's studies academic programs were established at 621 (19 percent) of the approximately 3,300 four-year post-secondary educational institutions in the United States. Beginning in the late 1970s, formal curriculum integration projects were initiated to bring the results of feminist scholarship into university-wide curricula. The basic strategy behind a curriculum integration project was the re-education of faculty from disciplines other than women's studies. The projects were typically funded by private foundations, such as Carnegie, Rockefeller, or Ford. Since 1978, approximately two hundred projects have been carried out in U.S. universities.[2]

Although the spread of women's studies courses and programs has been called a 'movement,' and despite a massive scholarly literature on women's studies from within the ranks of its own participants, these phenomena have not been studied as a social movement.[3] Conceiving women's studies as a movement allows us to understand seemingly disparate actions as part of a collective course of strategic conduct to transform the resources available to women within the university and, more generally, the nation.[4] This perspective also allows for an understanding of the development of personal and professional identities of the participants, on the one hand, and a collective identity of the movement as a collective social actor, on the other.

Defining women's studies as a social movement not only enables us to see specific phenomena as examples of social action and hence as meaningful, but, in particular, allows us to explore this action in relation to a specific institutional social system. It thus provides an arena within which particular relations of structure and agency may be examined. This is not to imply that "structure" is to be identified with the university and "agency" with the movement; rather, the structure–agency relation is constitutive of the movement, of the university, and of the social system they jointly form. In other words, agency and structure are analytic categories, whereas the "university" and the "movement" are here meant as descriptive categories.

In this chapter, I will focus on the influence of the Ford Foundation on the development and directions taken by the U.S. women's studies movement. I chose the Ford Foundation as a case study not because it is a typical foundation but because, in the eyes of many, it is a leading foundation— a pathbreaker and trendsetter. It is the largest private foundation by any measure, highly professionalized and differentiated in its staff and program organization, with a worldwide reach. Its predominant political philosophy could be characterized as liberal mainstream. The following analysis is based on archival research and in-depth interviews with Ford personnel.

Theories of the Relation of American Foundations to Social Movements

Progressive Leadership and Innovation

In the 1960s and early 1970s social scientists, federal politicians, and officials in government agencies shared a conception of foundation activity as progressive, innovative, and useful in creating pilot programs that could become models for progressive social legislation. A good example of this is the Community Action Programs initiated by the Ford Foundation in the 1960s and later implemented by the federal government's Office of Economic Opportunity. This view was expressed by Irving Horowitz and Ralph Horowitz, who wrote that foundations acted in an "innovative role . . . in contrast to the more established role of the government—the cautious partner." They argue that foundation activity liberalizes public policy and can do so because of its more liberal constituency. Richard Magat, a Ford Foundation insider, wrote in 1979, "In the United States . . . we [at Ford] have consciously and deliberately worked to affect public policy."[5] Others agree that foundation activity is fundamentally friendly to and supportive of progressive and radical social movements. This position is shared by conservatives, who seem to agree that most foundations are in fact liberal and that they support the aims of progressive, left-wing, and radical movements.[6] These writers are, of course, characterizing a relationship between foundations and the state.

Social Control and Channeling Models of Foundation Influence

A second group of writers has cast serious doubt upon the validity of such a perspective. Nelson Pichardo's review of the literature suggests that elites may choose to provide sponsorship in order to deradicalize a movement's goals or actions.[7] This position constitutes a social control model of movement-elite relationships. The idea here is that a movement is appropriated to achieve or maintain elite interests. In a study of 142 United States foundations from 1953 to 1980, Craig Jenkins found that foundations were "rather conventional in their approach to social movement giving," preferring to play a reactive role rather than instigating collective action or promoting new or controversial values. He suggests that foundations play the role of political "gatekeepers," selecting social movements that have effectively transformed themselves into professional advocacy groups influencing public policy. Here we have an image of foundations providing sponsorship only to those movements whose goals and forms of organizations are, in fact, most similar to elite interests.[8]

Craig Jenkins and Craig Eckert, focusing on the civil rights movement, show that major funding was forthcoming only after the upsurge in protests.[9] Jenkins argues that interest group liberalism appears to be the general guidepost to social movement philanthropy. He argues that the effect of foundation funding has been to channel the movement into more organized and more professional structures of administration and governance. This channeling model of influence implies a "neo-corporatist system of political representation."[10] In other words, elites are able to expand regulation over the representation of social stakes. This entails consequences for a social movement: a less radical political tenor and weaker ties between professional advocacy organizations and local grassroots groups. This critical perspective represents an advance in the understanding of social movement–foundation relations. Its proponents, however, have adequately specified neither the mechanisms whereby channeling takes place nor the differential employment of channeling by specific types of funding sources such as the state and private foundations.

Both models—social control/cooptation and channeling—advance our understanding of relations between elites and social movements. However, they do not adequately specify the mechanisms whereby cooptation or channeling take place. Also, should we assume that the influence of elite sponsorship will be the same in all its forms? Do specific types of funders respond differently to a movement's grievances and demands? Furthermore, these models typically conceive of social movements as existing independently of state and other elite institutions, conceiving movements as challenging these from below. Examples of antagonistic social movement actors in tense or negative relations with elites abound in the sociological and related literatures. William Gamson, in an extensive survey of social movement mobilization in the U.S., devotes an entire chapter to the use of violence and disruption by collective actors.[11] By contrast, the interest of this chapter is to explore the *collaborative tension* between social movements and elite institutions—specifically through a case study of Ford's sponsorship of the women's studies movement.

Elements of Ford Sponsorship of Women's Studies

By the late 1960s the women's studies movement and its scholar-activists had not only produced innovative and at times radical ideas, but had begun to constitute institutions to house, preserve, and disseminate those ideas. These included archives, libraries, newspapers, newsletters, journals, publishing companies, films, tapes, and academic curricula and programs. As Catharine Stimpson, acting as a consultant to Ford, wrote in 1982, "Ford has done more than to respond to this institution-building. It has actively influenced the directions it would take."[12] That influence developed in five relatively distinct, nonsequential phases.

Fellowship Program

The Ford Foundation began its involvement with women's studies with a three-year program of funding individual women's scholarships in 1972. These grants, to both faculty and graduate students, served to support individual scholars, and the applications provided Ford with valuable information as to the existing ideas of emerging women studies scholars. The program also served to legitimate feminism as a ground of inquiry.

Research Centers

By the mid-1970s, the results of Ford's experience sponsoring individual scholars led it to shift its emphasis to institutional, rather than individual, support. The goal was to create research centers and thereby to develop an institutional base to support feminist scholarship. The first grant was made to Stanford University in 1974 to establish the Center for Research on Women. At the same time, the Carnegie Corporation funded a Center for Research on Women at Wellesley College. These two centers provided models for a rapidly expanding system of research centers spread across the United States. By 1992, Ford had funded fifteen such centers.[13] Earlier, Ford had funded the creation of two policy-oriented centers: the Center for the American Woman and Politics, a unit of the Eagleton Institute of Politics at Rutgers, in 1971, and the Center for Women Policy Studies in Washington, DC, in 1972.

National Institutions

Beginning in 1975 Ford supported a series of initiatives designed to facilitate the establishment of women's studies institutions on the national level. The first of these was the journal *Signs,* published by the University of Chicago Press, under Stimpson's editorship. Special issues were subsequently funded by Carnegie, Rockefeller, and the Lilly Endowment. Ford funded the organizing meetings that led to the establishment of the National Women's Studies Association (NWSA) in 1977. In 1981, Ford granted $100,000 to the National Council for Research on Women (NCROW) in New York. Founding president Mariam Chamberlain had earlier been a program officer at Ford from 1956 through 1981. These developments were meant to constitute the institutional basis for women's studies as an independent area of study. The explicit function of these three institutions is to create an integrated system: *Signs* links individual scholars, NWSA links women's studies academic programs, and NCROW links research centers.

Mainstreaming Projects

In 1976, Ford sponsored a study of the extent to which women's studies had changed the general college curriculum. The study, conducted by a group of women's studies faculty at Princeton University, concluded that little or no attention was given to women in the mainstream curriculum. Since that time a large number of mainstreaming projects have taken place. A mainstreaming project (also known as a curriculum-integration or curriculum-transformation project) typically attempts to introduce the results of feminist scholarship, including elements of feminist pedagogy, into areas of the university curriculum external to women's studies academic programs proper. The typical device is a series of faculty workshops during which faculty in other disciplines are educated by women's studies faculty. Ford's efforts have been concentrated in its "Mainstreaming Minority Women's Studies" project, which sought throughout the 1980s to integrate knowledge about minority women into university curricula.[14]

Finally, in 1993, Ford funded a national Curriculum Integration Clearinghouse at Towson State University. This grant represented, as one program officer told me, the institutional "enshrinement" of Ford's national curriculum-reform program. No further mainstreaming or clearinghouses are planned. Overall, Chamberlain and Bernstein estimate that Ford has contributed about $22 million of the total of $36 million in philanthropic funds spent on women's studies since 1972.[15]

Internationalization of Women's Studies

The most recent program initiative, begun in the late 1980s, has fostered the establishment of women's research centers in a growing number of non-Western countries (in places such as Indonesia, India, Kenya).[16] The goal has been to improve the condition of women as a sine qua non for political and economic development. It is also an attempt to diversify a movement that, in the opinion of one Ford executive, has become too "U.S.-focused." Beginning with the United Nations Mid-Decade Conference for Women in Copenhagen in 1980, Ford supported the development of a world-wide network of women's studies scholars which has continued to meet every three years to the present.

Effects of Ford Sponsorship of the Women's Studies Movement

Ford's influence can be characterized as 1) atomizing the movement and indirectly creating competition; 2) institutionalizing the movement at both the individual and organizational levels; 3) creating a knowledge base; 4) creating a national two-tier hierarchy (first decade); 5) democratizing the movement (second decade); 6) diversifying the movement (third decade).

The effect of Ford's faculty and dissertation fellowships was to atomize the movement as opposed to developing collective action in, for example, grassroots organizations. As one Ford executive told me:

> It's very easy to give fellowship support. It's not very politically transformative, however, because all you're doing is intervening in the lives of people who probably would have done it anyway. It's a very conservative philanthropic strategy.[17]

For instance, Ford did not fund a women's studies committee, or any of the collectives that later led to the development of women's studies academic programs. Neither did Ford give support to any established program. The indirect effect of its program of individual scholarships was to create competition between women's studies scholars with the result that a "star" system separated successful competitors from unsuccessful ones. The idea of women's studies as a collective endeavor was superseded by conventional academic conduct. With the funding of research centers, Ford continued to channel women's studies in a conventional academic way, that is, into pre-existing structures of organization. A Ford administrator explained part of the reason for this approach:

> [F]unding research centers is a very comfortable category for philanthropy because it does not have the kind of action-orientation of teaching and learning. So, when you're starting out with a new field, a pretty conservative strategy, or strategy that doesn't shake people up too much, is individual fellowships and research centers. Things begin to get more complicated when those research centers are generating new knowledge which then should transform the canon for undergraduates—and that's when the battles began.

The foundation had followed a similar procedure in the development of foreign area-studies (e.g., Latin American, Asian, Middle Eastern studies) and business administration. Ford was continuing its tradition of funding scientific/academic, rational approaches to social problems, thus establishing an academic tradition in women's studies while solidifying and legitimating women's studies as a field of inquiry.

Cumulatively, these first two steps—giving individual fellowships and supporting research centers—transformed the movement in significant ways. The women's studies movement at its inception had created a new form of knowing, a form of collective consciousness and a process through which collective consciousness could develop and new individuals could come to participate in it. This was known as "consciousness raising"— probably the most innovative element of the women's movement in general, and of women's studies in particular.

I would argue that Ford's funding of the fellowship program and research centers transformed the processes of consciousness raising into the processes of constructing academic and scientific information. It did so specifically by changing the base of consciousness from personal experience to objects of observation, from experiential awareness to objective knowledge. At the same time, it transformed the locus of consciousness from the collective to the individual scholar. So, no more is it what "we" know, it is what "I" know. In this way, consciousness became a commodity represented by certificates and diplomas, and one could now become a socially certified aware person. Ford's intent was to build a national infrastructure for women's studies scholarship, which it would support for six to eight years, with the hope that by then each center would become self-supporting. Ford was employing a pre-existing organizational form (the research center or institute) to organize and advance a new social movement.

Herbert Haines's "radical flank hypothesis" suggests that elite sponsors support the moderate branches of a radical movement in order to enable those moderate forces to become hegemonic in the movement and hence channel the movement into courses of conduct and forms of organization that support elite interests.[18] A concrete instance is Ford's limiting competition for grants under its mainstreaming minority women program to only those research centers affiliated with NCROW. This device of "limited competition" contrasts sharply with the strategy of universal competition employed by state agencies and favored by academic norms of scholarship and science. Limited competition created a two-tier hierarchy—both for individual scholars and for research centers—which institutionalized the original configuration of women's studies at elite schools and contained the movement within that environment for about a decade. With the introduction of Alison Bernstein, formerly with the Fund for the Improvement of Postsecondary Education (FIPSE), as program officer for the women's studies portfolio at Ford, a new series of programmatic initiatives began. The first of these attempted to democratize women's studies by extending it beyond Ivy League and major research universities to second-tier and two-year colleges. At the same time, women's studies was extended into university curricula more broadly. As one person at Ford put it:

> By about '85, '86 one of the concerns many of us had . . . was that the people running these programs, the people who were studied in these programs, the people who took these courses were overwhelmingly white and we sort of turned our attention to the issue of diversity in women's studies. . . . And, maybe, I think, there, Ford was really in the vanguard of pushing that issue a bit, not just with money, but the bully pulpit helps a lot too. And when a major foundation says . . . ,"We need to pay more attention to the diversity of women and not just presume white women are the measure," people pay attention.

The most recent initiative to internationalize women's studies can be seen as continuing the general project of diversification globally.

Organizationally, Ford's sponsorship led to the formalization of social relationships, decision-making mechanisms and development of institutional linkages within the movement:

1. Ford's grant programs consistently institutionalized existing roles: The scholarship program clearly designated who in women's studies was a scholar. The research centers all had a formal role-structure with a designated head and specified affiliates. The curriculum-integration projects likewise had designated heads, specialized consultants, and named participants. Many also designated and financially rewarded specific faculty in development seminars.

2. Ford's grant programs consistently led to formalization of decision-making mechanisms within recipient organizations. The creation of research centers, national institutions, and curriculum-integration projects exhibited formal decision-making mechanisms. In no case did Ford fund a women's studies collective. In all instances a structure of officers, a stipulated succession mechanism, a budget, an internal committee structure, and an explicit mission statement were features of the funded organizations.

3. Finally, institutional linkages were created—with NWSA linking the women's studies academic programs, NCROW linking research centers, *Signs* linking individual scholars, and the curriculum-integration clearinghouse linking past and potential curricular-reform initiatives. Ford's sponsorship helped to create a system of functionally differentiated, rationally organized institutions.

Strategically, Ford's sponsorship established a set of incentives to promote a shift of the strategic orientation of women's studies. Before Ford's involvement, the typical model for movement action in women's studies was grassroots insurgence, where local, relatively informally organized groups of university women (both faculty and students) disrupted or threatened to disrupt university routine unless demands were satisfied by administrators. Beginning with Ford's scholarship program, strong financial and status incentives encouraged individuals to submit formal applications in support of research. Success with these applications was in the interest of both the applicant and university administrators, now giving them a common interest. The resulting entrepreneurial alliance involved the collaboration between movement participants and elites, specifically, university administrators and foundation officials. With this, the insurgent model of action rapidly passed into history. Ford's subsequent introduction of research centers and curriculum-integration projects further solidified this pattern around not only much larger financial stakes, but also around the growing public reputation of women's studies within the academic community.

Overall, Ford's effect on the women's studies movement has been that the movement increasingly resists reliance upon strategies and actions which risk alienation or stigmatization. In the U.S., women's studies became part of the universe of special interest groups in competition with other interest groups vying for representation in the university curriculum. That this earlier focus was extended to include minority women was logical. The point here is that as women's studies acquired the institutional accoutrements or paraphernalia of institutional success, it began to act more on behalf of its institutional constituency and less on behalf of its earlier vision of a broad societal transformation.

Ideologically, an important effect of Ford's interventions has been to promote a change in the form of ideological discourse. In place of an older, politicized, emotionalized, personalized, and urgent articulation of grievance and demand, movement participants have come to articulate their ideological positions in terms of the norms and canons of academic scholarship. This has had the indirect effect of splitting or fragmenting the movement between its more activist and more scholarly wings.

Increasingly, commitment to women's studies is evidenced by the possession and display of documentary credentials rather than the display of a personal history of participation in movement actions (demonstrations, strikes, marches, and the like) or a display of personal militancy. Collective identity has become more professionalized insofar as the Ford Foundation helped to generate the institutional apparatuses of a profession (e.g., an area of study, a national association, recognized research centers, a widely respected journal, and a set of local organizational structures which increasingly reproduce those of other units within the university). With the funding of a multi-institution curriculum-integration project in 1989, Ford helped to diversify the movement ethnically and racially.

Foundations as Avant-Garde? Conventional Wisdom Challenged

My data do not support the popular and even academic conception that the primary role of foundations in relation to state agencies (such as the NEH, NEA, and FIPSE) is to be on the cutting edge, a pathbreaker and trend-setter. Specifically, successful model programs are not emulated on a larger scale by the greater resources of the state as often as anticipated. As early as 1976 a Ford-funded survey based at Princeton University revealed that the results of feminist scholarship had made virtually no impact on the mainstream curriculum in United States universities. One year later, a major review of foundation and government grant making for women's issues (a study conducted by Rosabeth Moss Kanter and commissioned by Ford) revealed to Ford a consensus among women scholars that the time for supporting individual research projects, and academic research in general, had passed. The highest priority was given to action projects intending to change institutions, specifically, the university.[19] The first major externally funded curriculum-integration project was launched at the University of Arizona with support from the National Endowment for the Humanities in 1981. Two years later, Ford gave the same university over $400,000 to extend the integration activities to surrounding universities and community colleges. The implication that I draw from this is that Ford was not able to identify curriculum integration as a fundable project of the women's studies movement, despite having been informed of both the need for it and the relative consensus within the field that institutional change initiatives had become a clear priority. Ford apparently needed the example of a state-funded agency to lead the way.

Perhaps a stronger example of Ford's responsiveness to federal initiatives is provided by the timing of Ford's creation of a Woman's Program, which coincided with the passing of the Title IX Amendment to the Elementary and Secondary Education Act in June 1972. This Amendment prohibited sex discrimination in higher education as well as in public schools. Two Ford program officers, Terry Saario and Mariam Chamberlain, in a March 1978 Information Paper, wrote that "The Ford Foundation's response [to Title IX] was to launch a major program on sex discrimination and equality of opportunity for women in education in 1972." Twenty-three percent of the Woman's Program budget was devoted to support of monitoring and litigation efforts pursuant to Title IX.[20]

Kanter's comparative review of major foundation and government-agency funding casts further doubt on the primary role of foundations in social movement sponsorship during the formative period of the women's studies movement; specifically, from 1972 to 1976. For example, during this period, foundations devoted a larger share of their giving to education (58 percent by value, 52 percent by number of grants) than did federal agencies (26 percent by value, 33 percent by number).[21] However, federal agencies devoted a slightly larger proportion of their educational dollars to women's studies (12 percent by value, 22 percent by number) than did foundations (10 per cent by value and by number).[22] From 1972 to 1976, calculating from Kanter's data, total foundation giving to women's studies was $2,136,000, whereas federal giving was $1,095,000. While the foundations gave more to women's studies, the federal agencies gave a slightly higher proportion of their education budgets overall, reflecting a difference in programmatic priority. (These figures include only grants of $5,000 or more.)

These data support two basic points. First, that the conventional characterization of the state as a "lethargic leviathan" and the foundation as a "nimble innovator" is doubtful. Ford programs officers and administrators illustrate this point in the following comments:

- There's a difference between someone who scores the points and someone who makes the assist. Philanthropy makes the assist. It doesn't score the points. The people in the field, who care about it from the beginning, are the ones who make the transformation happen. Philanthropy just assisted in that process.
- I think it's open to new ideas and innovations, but I wouldn't call Ford a cutting-edge organization.
- I don't think philanthropy's role is a cutting-edge one. I think people are cutting-edge. You could say that often we are willing to back people who have new ideas and fresh ways of looking at things, but the organization itself is what I would call mainstream progressive. . . .
- The Ford Foundation supports innovation but is also very conservative, so you need to do progressive things in conventional ways.

Second, the state may be more responsive to movement pressure, while the autonomy of foundations permits them a luxury of deliberation. Given this, the question becomes one of why foundations respond to movements since they are under no obligation to do so. In the case of Ford, key individuals in critical positions acted as advocates on behalf of the movement and educated their superiors—particularly those who were perceived to be open-minded. One Ford administrator outlined the process:

A good program officer is much more about thinking programmatically than about making grants . . . you attempt to define priorities for the foundation—programmatic priorities . . . then you make grants to . . . serve these purposes: First, you want to do things that have a positive effect [for the target population]. Second, to contribute to institutional change. Good grants lead to entire institutions changing themselves.

> Third, attempt to affect the field itself. . . . I think we care more about affecting the field than contributing to individual institutions changing or helping individual [members of target populations].

In the case of one program officer this process was more complex in that her immediate superior was not sympathetic to or impressed by women's studies. The program officer was nonetheless able to fund many important women's studies projects by going around her superior and receiving direct support from a sympathetic female higher in the administration. Kanter also notes that having women in positions of power is of critical importance to foundations' support of women's projects.[23] One Ford employee made the following observation:

> When X was here she was the only woman [program officer]. I think she got the women's studies portfolio because she was interested in women and I think nobody would have done it. I also think she wanted to do it. It wouldn't have happened had she not been interested in it.

Evaluation and Elite Accountability

The total amount of Ford's grant allocations from January 1972 through September 1981—the entire life span of Education and Public Policy Program grants relating to equality of opportunity for women in higher education—was $9,231,750, of which $13,065 was spent for evaluation studies (.0014 percent). This miniscule commitment to evaluation suggests that Ford's concern was not to obtain demonstrable, substantive results.

As one program officer put it to me, "I guess, evaluation just isn't sexy enough." This statement, I think, reflects not so much the absence of sexiness in evaluation work, but more importantly, the low priority attached to evaluation specifically, and accountability generally. While this paper does not include equivalent data from a government agency, it would be incredible to suggest that any agency could spend a smaller proportion of its funds on program evaluation. Moreover, political pressures for accountability impel state agencies not only to seek substantive results for their grant making, but also to conduct such evaluation studies as are necessary to demonstrate those results. This has direct implications for the scope, specificity, and focus of programs and their relation to particular projects.

Conclusion

One implication of elite sponsorship is that social movements become projects through a process which I term "programmatic alienation." The movement is disaggregated into conventionalized elements that can then be

treated as the objects of funding programs. A consequence of this is deradi-
calization. This suggests that the process of cooptation involves the extrac-
tion of dynamic elements of a movement through the funder's ability to
privilege that element by providing funds, legitimacy, and other resources,
with little or no reference to the whole political or social revolutionary vision. One consequence is that the movement becomes disembodied and conventionalized. Another consequence is that the movement acquires resources and political salience it might not have enjoyed otherwise, thereby
increasing the probability of making social change, even if that change
might not be what movement members have visualized initially.

Although I claim that social movements are differentially influenced
by the specific character of sponsorship, it is important to recognize that
neither the state nor private foundations are totalizing in their effect. For
instance, critical factors such as the generation of a movement's symbols,
language, and the way in which a movement's discourse affects the general
population, a particular institution, the state, or public policy, are not always predictable or containable. In other words, channeling of movements
cannot determine their outcomes, though it may continuously influence
them. Collective movements at their peak have a certain volatile character
which, sometimes, makes almost anything possible.

Notes

1. Florence Howe and Carol Ahlum, "Women's Studies and Social Change" in
Academic Women on the Move, ed. Alice S. Rossi and Ann Calderwood (New York:
Russell Sage Foundation, 1973), 393–423.
2. National Women's Studies Assocation, *NWSA Directory of Women's Studies
Programs, Women's Centers, and Women's Research Centers* (Washington, D.C.: NWSA,
1990). See also *A Report to the Profession: Liberal Learning and the Women's Studies
Major* (Washington: NWSA, 1991).
3. Sheila Tobias, "Women's Studies: Its Origins, Its Organization and Its Prospects," *Women's Studies International Quarterly* 1 (1978): 85–97. Cf. Marilyn J. Boxer,
"For and about Women: The Theory and Practice of Women's Studies in the United
States," *Signs* 7 (1982): 661–95. For a more recent appraisal see also Constance Black-
house and David H. Flaherty, eds., *Challenging Times: The Women's Movement in Canada and the United States* (Kingston: Queens University Press, 1992).
4. Jo Freeman, "A Model for Analyzing the Strategic Options of Social Movement
Organizations," in *Social Movements of the Sixties and Seventies*, ed. Jo Freeman (New
York: Longman, 1983), 193–210.
5. Irving Horowitz and Ralph L. Horowitz, "Tax-Exempt Foundations: Their
Effects on National Policy," *Science* 168 (1970): 227. For an "insider" discussion of foundation activity, see Richard Magat, *Ford Foundation at Work: Philanthropic Choices,
Methods, and Styles* (New York: Plenum, 1979).
6. James Douglas, "Political Theories of Nonprofit Organization," in *The Non-*

profit Sector: A Research Handbook, ed. Walter W. Powell (New Haven: Yale University Press, 1987). See also Althea K. Nagai, Robert Lerner, and Stanley Rothman, *Giving for Social Change: Foundations, Public Policy, and the American Political Agenda* (Westport, Conn.: Praeger, 1994).

7. Nelson Pichardo, "Resource Mobilization: An Analysis of Conflicting Theoretical Variations," *Sociological Quarterly* 29 (1988): 105. Cf. Douglas McAdam, *Political Process and the Development of Black Insurgency* (Chicago: University of Chicago Press, 1982), and Joan Roelofs, "Foundations and the Supreme Court," *Telos* 62 (1984/85): 59–87.

8. J. Craig Jenkins, *The Politics of Insurgency: Farm Workers' Movement in the 1960s* (New York: Columbia University Press, 1985), 9.

9. J. Craig Jenkins and Craig Eckert, "Channeling Black Insurgency: Elite Patronage and Professional Social Movement Organizations in the Development of the Black Movement", *American Sociological Review* 51 (December 1986): 812–29.

10. Jenkins, *The Politics of Insurgency*, 311.

11. William Gamson, *The Strategy of Social Protest*, 2nd ed. (Belmont, Calif.: Wadsworth, 1990).

12. Catharine R. Stimpson, *Consultant's Report To: Ford Foundation Program on Education and Culture*, #011359 (November 1982), 20.

13. Mariam Chamberlain and Alison Bernstein, "Philanthropy and the Emergence of Women's Studies," *Teachers College Record* 93 (Spring, 1992): 559.

14. Carol Musil, ed., *The Courage to Question: Women's Studies and Student Learning* (Washington, D.C.: Association of American Colleges, 1992). See also "Special Report: Mainstreaming Women's Studies," *Ford Foundation Letter* (New York: Ford Foundation, 1986), 2–3.

15. Chamberlain and Bernstein, "Philanthropy and the Emergence of Women's Studies," 566.

16. For an overview of this recent development, see *Women's Studies, Area and International Studies Curriculum Integration Project* (New York: National Council for Research on Women, 1996).

17. Semi-structured, in-depth interviews with Ford Foundation executives and program officers were conducted during the summer of 1994 while I was a Rockefeller fellow at the Program on Non-Profit Organizations at Yale University. Since the total number of interviewees is relatively small, special care needs to be exercised in order to preserve their anonymity. Henceforth, excerpted portions of interview transcript appear without attribution.

18. Herbert H. Haines, *Black Radicals and the Civil Rights Mainstream, 1954–1970* (Knoxville: University of Tennessee Press, 1988).

19. Rosabeth Moss Kanter, "Review of Grant-Making for Women's Issues in the 1970s: Past Patterns and Future Priorities," *A Report to the Coordinating Committee on Women's Programs of the Ford Foundation*, #003505 (April 1977), 176–83.

20. Terry N. Saario and Mariam K. Chamberlain, "The Education and Research Division's Program on Sex Discrimination and Equality of Opportunity for Women," *Information Paper for the Education Committee*, #004136 (March 1978): 2.

21. See Table X-a in *A Report to the Coordinating Committee on Women's Programs of the Ford Foundation*, #003505 (April 1977).

22. See Table XI-a in *A Report to the Coordinating Committee on Women's Programs of the Ford Foundation*, #003505 (April 1977).

23. Rosabeth Moss Kanter, "Review of Grant-Making for Women's Issues in the 1970s: Past Patterns and Future Priorities," *A Report to the Coordinating Committee on Women's Programs of the Ford Foundation*, #003505 (April 1977), 149.

13 Going for Broke
The Historian's Commitment to Philanthropy

Barry Dean Karl

I HAVE BEEN INVOLVED with the history of American philanthropic foundations for a large part of my career as a historian. In the earlier years of that involvement, that is in the late 1950's and through most of the 1960's, it was something of a struggle, but a peculiar one. Like Jacob wrestling with his angel, it seemed to take place in darkness, with shapes that never really identified themselves and beat up on me for purposes that might or might not be sinister, depending on how I interpreted the silences. To be frank about it, I didn't even see the ladder. I was writing histories of government programs and social science research that at first seemed to depend only incidentally on foundations, so I really didn't feel the lack of sources, only the vague mystery of the combat.

My lack of interest could be explained in part by the character of the documentation itself. Unlike today, scholarly communication depended entirely on correspondence, cheap postage, ill paid but obediently efficient secretaries, typewriters that lasted at least one lifetime, carbon copies stapled to the letters to which they were responses, and drafts with penciled corrections that revealed the careful rethinking and adventitious self-interest that underlay the structure of argument. Old-fashioned correspondence had a ballet-like character that made it possible to see the motion of ideas as well as their content. One could see connections from point to point and watch the subtleties of change in arguments that none of the participants ever expected to see the light of day, let alone fall under the eye of another scholar. While long-distance telephone calls were no longer restricted to emergencies, as they had been in my childhood, the noncompetitive Ma Bell was costly for long-distance purposes, and local communication was conducted at leisurely lunches in faculty clubs at universities and the equally exclusive city clubs of New York, Chicago, Boston, and Washington, D.C. The very few conferences that were convened brought together small groups of participants who traveled back and forth in the comfort of roomettes on trains with names like the Twentieth Century and the Capitol Limited, the latter wending its way through the hilly landscape of Virginia while one break-fasted from china atop heavy white linen with coffee served from plated silver weighted to withstand the side-to-side motion of the dining car.

I learned of foundations through their letterheads in the files that faculty members had opened to me. The quality of the stationery alone stood out. The few universities who allowed access to their archives placed fifty-year limits on availability. In 1958, Pendleton Herring, then President of the Social Science Research Council, turned me down when I asked to see the papers there of Charles Merriam, the Council's founder and first president. His reason: they were a private corporation and did not grant such requests. That restriction was overcome at least in part by the availability of faculty papers, giving me one side of the argument on crumbling yellow second sheets, the other side being the foundation originals. The University of Chicago gladly shipped the papers (all seventy-seven file drawers of them) of Charles Merriam to me, then a Harvard graduate student with limited space lent by the then Dean of the Littauer Center, Don. K. Price. They were cluttering up the hallways of the Social Science Building at Chicago. The only debate was over who would get the cabinets, the old green metal cases, some of which went back to the First World War.

Even though Merle Curti of the University of Wisconsin and F. Emerson Andrews of the Russell Sage Foundation had begun the history of foundations and philanthropy, they, too, juggled for sources and came up, as had I, with shadows that made Plato's cave seem positively luminescent. The article that Curti published in the *American Historical Review* in 1957 was the first announcement to the historical profession of the importance of research in foundation philanthropy.[1] That was ten years after Andrews and his associates at Russell Sage had published their two-volume history of that foundation, a process that decimated the foundation's archives by leaving in place only those papers that had been used in the preparation of the history. Their reasoning had nothing to do with protection, only the releasing of space, like Chicago's concern over the bulk of the Merriam papers. When I first saw the filing cabinets in the Sage offices, they were so tightly packed that one feared damaging them by attempting to remove even one folder. There they stood, like a papal tomb in St. Peter's, ceremonially and efficiently sealed, their opening awaiting the Last Judgment.

Where one marks the change to greater openness is a bit difficult for me to pinpoint. Stanley Katz and I had been introduced to the Carnegie Corporation papers by Florence Anderson. She was spending her retirement as Secretary to the Corporation cleaning up the Corporation's papers in preparation for their transfer to, as it turned out, Columbia University. While not a historian, she was sympathetic to history and generous in her willingness to show us whatever we wanted to see. Her chief utility to us was her extraordinary memory not only for subject matter of projects Carnegie had invested in but for the exact titles given those subjects in the Carnegie lexicon of the previous half-century. One could ask her a relatively general question and get six folders with often totally unrelated titles which actually concerned the general issue we had raised. Race, for example, was rarely the term used to describe an interest in Negroes, and the relation between the Negro and poverty was at times awkward and clumsy. Still, the file cabinets were on another floor of the building, and we were never allowed direct access to them to search on our own. In between work sessions we lunched with her at the Waldorf. Her meals, as I recall, consisted chiefly of the cigarettes she chain-smoked, entertaining us between relightings with tales of her coming to Carnegie as a new graduate of Mount Holyoke, her career in the WAVES, and then her fight to gain the vaunted position of Secretary to the Corporation on her return, when it was clear that she would be passed over for the next male on the list if she didn't threaten to leave. Florence was not one to make idle threats. Her memory was acute, and her knowledge of the Corporation covered the inside, the outside, and the underside in glorious, often comic, and sometimes sad detail.

Similarly, the Rockefeller family archives were stored in the nether regions of Rockefeller Center in the very early 1970s. Plans were underway for the opening of the Archive Center at Pocantico Hills, but we were helped by Joe Ernst, who dusted off a table for us and brought us whatever we could think to ask for. By 1975, all of that had begun to change with the opening of the Rockefeller Archive Center in the former home of Martha Baird Rockefeller, the second Mrs. Rockefeller Jr., and its effective rebuilding as a modern and super-efficient archive that rivals, even excels, presidential archives and in some ways the National Archives itself.

The subsequent creation of philanthropic studies centers around the country was a consequence of the Filer Commission, a project that was again Rockefeller sponsored in an important sense by the interests of John D. Rockefeller 3rd. The battle over the Tax Reform Act of 1969 had helped re-stimulate a concern over the justification and defense of foundations just as the previous attacks had the work of Russell Sage and the setting up of the Foundation Library and Center in New York. In this latter endeavor, it may be reasonable to say that historians were replaced by economists in an effort to show that private investment in public policy was more efficient, more effective, and certainly less expensive than public investment. "Volunteer" had begun to take on a meaning different from the one it had developed after World War I. There was a sense of permanence and an essential character that term hadn't quite had before. The arguments in favor of discussing Third and Independent Sectors and the growing interest in the value of nonprofit and volunteer activities was initially based on what I would call an economic defense, and unpaid service was given a numerical value that stood firmly, if somewhat fantastically, against all the traditional rules of labor, supply, and demand. While this had a political resonance that was only beginning to be felt in the 1970s, the perverse presidential support of the philanthropic sector that began with the Reagan administration in 1981 triggered enthusiasms and energies that came to involve history and historians, but in a way that I would argue was not beneficial to either one. Even that is a puzzling statement to have to make–at least puzzling to me. Let me pause to enlighten non-historians about current debates in the historical profession, debates that have nothing to do with philanthropy and may try those whose patience with seemingly meaningless abstraction is limited. Without intending to, these debates feed into the problems historians have with foundations. I hope I can do this without committing an injustice to either side of the debate.

There is in the historical profession today a significant group of intellectuals who argue that traditional historical writing is the artificial construction of historians who have interests to exploit and who use narrative and assemblage of facts to exploit them. The more extreme thinkers in this camp argue that the function of the historian now is to deconstruct this exploitative history in order to reveal its purposes. This argument can then be extended to say that all history is essentially exploitative of some purpose and that what traditional historians have thought of as real or even scientific history is an impossibility, if not a manipulative and dishonest subterfuge. This is an idea that may seem at first to have little to do with foundations until one looks at the idea of institutional order that the term "foundation" itself implies. There is an underlying assumption that there is enough resemblance among institutions called foundations to make generalizations possible. Those generalizations will be helpful for understanding how foundations work, but only to the extent that these general notions bear a close relation to the real world in which foundations operate. Such an overview can be useful if it tells us something about the steps to be taken to make our understanding of foundations part of a practical world that includes foundations as instruments of human improvement. If the history of foundations has no useful meaning, we are in trouble.

Again, without getting too deeply into metaphysics, I would say that the basic ideas involved are not as new as some of their proponents think. The philosopher Immanuel Kant distinguished three kinds of reasoning—pure, practical, and aesthetic—in order to make similar divisions among ways of knowing the world. His view of pure reasoning was that it was based on categories that human beings used to interpret the reality of the world around them and was not inherent in that world except insofar as human thinking put it there simply in order to be able to talk about it. Time and numbers, for example, are in reality our methods of understanding the world, not because things in the real world count or measure themselves in order to be or to act. From that perspective, scientific history is an imposition of order on the world in much the same way that physics is, and just as much in need of reordering as our understanding of facts and principles changes. This idea was picked up by philosophers, including David Hume in Great Britain, who questioned whether human understanding ever really got to the real world. It might be worth noting that Robert Lucas's Nobel Prize in Economics was based on writing that said much the same about economic theory and its relation to economic reality. Economists, he wrote, were not very good at predicting the future with accuracy or affecting public policy with results that fitted their intentions. The implication that economics and the actors in the economic world were similarly out of touch with one another was a logical consequence of his argument as well as a warning to economists who fancied themselves policy-makers. For my purposes here, it could be extended to argue that all policy ideas are questionable tools in the political marketplace. Since foundations have been funding such ideas virtually from their beginnings as policy institutions in American life, the extensions are potentially threatening.

What has this to do with foundations and philanthropy, you might ask, and my answer would have less to do with either of them *per se,* but a great deal to do with what we understand of their histories. Ever since Curti and Andrews opened the field, there have been two separate but related histories. One has tried to find out what actually happened in the world of philanthropy, the other has tried to defend or attack what has happened as a result of that world. As is unfortunately the case in most historical writing, the second tends to be more interesting than the first, chiefly because it arouses more exciting debate. It is, after all, potentially good theater, and the relation between history and theater has been well known, at least since the Greeks, and certainly since Shakespeare. But then Aeschylus did not have to convince Agamemnon of the truth of his interpretation or Shakespeare Richard III. They certainly didn't have to depend on them for financial support. They had audiences who were more than willing to applaud their efforts and after centuries they are still good box office. The same is true, relatively speaking, of what I might call "attack history."

One could say that history that generates debate still pays, but there the history of philanthropy will have to remain an exception. Or at least a partial exception. One can make a living as a historian by attacking politics or by criticizing the social order. These days, in particular, negative history sells. There are many historians both in and out of the profession who have been able to raise attention by attacking foundations. Foundations, in turn, have been moderately forthcoming in funding historians who will sing their praises, or at least help protect them from harm. They will also give temporary support to their critics, just to prove that their skins are tough, they can stand the pain, and the blood is really catsup.

The chief stumbling block in either case is the fact that Curti's exhortations of 1957 have not convinced many history departments that philanthropy and foundations constitute subject matter worth tenure. Virtually all of us who have invested our time in our histories of the subject got tenure chanting other lays as we climbed the ladder of academic success. I myself have been my department's chief political historian. Not until my retirement and benefitting from the generosity of Harvard's Kennedy School have I had the opportunity to devote my full attention to the history of philanthropy. Needless to say, I approach this apparent reprieve from senescence with a mixture of dread and delight, eager to play my new role, but uncertain, as all of us end up being, whether the curtain will drop before the play ends.

If one puts it in its most extreme form, historians of foundations and philanthropy can find themselves trapped between foundations that don't want to fund them and history departments that, for very different reasons, don't want to hire them (I must necessarily except the research groups such as the Aspen Institute and Independent Sector, which have helped me, and a number of others); but still, history is less interesting than those quantifiable subjects that will prove consequences and expand that chimera of chimeras in the philanthropic field, evaluation. In these days of fascination with all sorts of new histories—ethnic studies, racial history, gender history, and gay and lesbian history—foundation history may stand alone as the history nobody wants.

I'm sure it's at this point that I'm supposed to ask, "Why is that?"—so I will ask it: "Why is that?" I'm also supposed to say, "The answer is most complex," but that, in my judgment, is not the truth. It isn't very complex at all, just a bit messy. There is, I must say, a dilemma, but it's a real dilemma, that is, it's built on very recognizable parts that don't fit together, not on mysteries or imaginative bits and pieces that don't connect, which is the way dilemma has sometimes come to be used today. Dilemma was originally a form of logical syllogism in which two major premises were connected by a minor premise that made a choice between them impossible. It came to mean, in normal discourse, a choice between two equally undesirable outcomes. I will try to construct the classical original, since I think the question of desirability is what makes the whole business so messy. We want what this syllogism is supposed to produce, even if, logically, we can't get it. Let's take the premises.

First premise: Foundations are sources of funding for new truths.

Second premise: New truths are the products of educated elites whose processes of thinking are not bounded by the regulations of the state or the priorities set by religious commitment.

Middle term: The American concept of a democratic society is committed to the intuitive beliefs of individuals dedicated to the right to meet their own needs as long as they do no harm to anyone else—and dedicated as well to the rejection of governing elites.

I don't think it takes long hours of cogitation to see how impossible it is to fit those three propositions together. Indeed, as one examines the history of foundations, one sees the first proposition concerning the search for truth forever being moderated (if not altogether butchered) by the third, as foundations seek to make the search for truth useful by limiting themselves to topics that will either meet the desires of the American public or avoid the ones the public finds offensive. Hence, the search for truth becomes the search for some kinds of truth. And insofar as the government can use its authority over foundations to set barriers, foundations will have to face the consequences, often unpleasant, of the critical attacks that result.

The incompatibility of the second proposition may seem more obvious on its face than it really is. The governing of American society rejects elites, or at least it tries to, often with limited success. Yet science and technology require the presence of educated specialists who may cost us a good bit less than movie stars or basketball players but are still a good bit pricier than the majority of other occupations. Unfortunately, the public can get its revenge on school teachers, perhaps because they are closer to home in our precious system of local control of schools, but not without complaining about the quality of education their children receive. On the whole, however, educated elites are not acceptable, and educated elites are what most foundations depend on, produce, and attempt to fit into the necessary pigeon holes that constitute the knowledge establishment in our society.

That, then, is the dilemma spelled out according to the most ancient of logical techniques. Like a true dilemma, it has no solution. The syllogism is simply impossible to resolve. It is there, and it must be lived with. While I may be wrong, or may be becoming more wrong in today's world, American society has had more trouble living with dilemmas of this kind than societies that have been able to develop social and managerial structures that avoid what I suppose I must call the pitfalls of democracy. Americans, by contrast, revel in them, although the sounds of revelry have a din-like character that seems much more like pain to those of us who prefer rational debate. Americans sometimes seem to become more disillusioned with their government when it does what they have told it to do than when it doesn't. There is another dilemma, but let's not go into it.

That leaves us, then, with the question of foundation history and its historians, why there seem so many points of disjunction between those who do it and those who pay them to do it. The answer lies not only in the dilemma as I have tried to lay it out, but in the fact that foundation history, in my opinion, stands at the center of irresolvability in twentieth-century

American history. As the demands for democracy and democratic inclusiveness have expanded in this century, the role of truth and the elites who search for it has become more troublesome. For if, as I would insist, foundation history is a branch of political history, it is inherently the most anachronistic of its branches. By depending upon knowledge and the logical distribution of it, foundation history violates the commitment to disorder that is one of the virtues we most demand of our political system. For that is precisely what popular control does to political order. Responsiveness is the key to democratic order and to political disorder, make of it what you will. We want government to meet our most immediate needs, not tell us that we must wait our turn, let alone that we do not deserve to have those needs met.

It would be easier if one could argue that foundations serve public purposes best when they persist in promoting long-range analyses for long-range problems, but that is not as easy as it may sound. The drama of short-range issues, particularly those with long-range effects, generates pressure on all non-governmental funding sources for action. Foundations operate in the world of public problems, where reasonable human beings differ regarding solutions to be sought and approaches to be determined. Like all of the public and private groups committed to dealing with such issues, they have their own score cards, and their records for wins and losses is no better than those of any of their contemporaries in the public or private worlds. Yet the perception of foundations as operating with a special public benefit in the form of the tax exemption puts the burden on them to produce better records, regardless of how absurd such an idea might be. That burden has led them into self-defenses that are essentially indefensible, though sometimes in response to attacks that are essentially unjustifiable. They find themselves in the unenviable position of having to defend themselves for doing no better than the best of public agencies and at least as well as their contemporaries in the private, nonprofit world. That role has led them into temptations that go back to the early years of foundations and the hiring of Ivy Lee by the Rockefellers to improve their public image. In so volatile a world, no image at all would often seem better than one so deliberately designed to present an image of good intentions in a universe of uncertain consequences. And no image at all is precisely what foundations have sought from time to time.

The introduction of research into the foundation world in the late 1960s was taken as a major step in being both public and private at the same time. Published research and the funding of such research were a way of being successfully public. The effort to make that research usefully supportive of foundations, not only in the process but in the outcomes of the process, meant that foundations could benefit from research that was also proof of the significance of foundations. Critical attacks on foundations could be countered. Yet there was a problem that was at that very moment being enhanced by the emergence in the foundation world of new institutions committed to taking ideological stances on previous foundation research. When I used a book review to point out the inherent futility of such a stance, I was roundly condemned for having somehow demeaned what had seemed to me a curious form of research, that is, research designed to prove the good of research by virtue of its private source of funding. Research is a major issue in the world of social policy, and foundations play a special role when they enter that world. That the freedom they have may also be a freedom to suffer criticism seemed to me part of the logic of foundation research, particularly when foundations enter the field of critical historical study.

Foundation history in particular and philanthropic history in general can serve as a window on that side of the American political mind that seeks stability in the understanding of the instability we crave. To do that, both historians and the foundation world would have to acknowledge their place in the order of American politics. Unfortunately, influencing politics is precisely what political critics persistently accuse foundations of trying to do, what foundations just as persistently deny doing, what historians critical of foundations happily distort by applying inapplicable ideological constructs to foundation activity, and what the field of history itself ignores, perhaps with some justification, given the fact that foundation history thus far has tended to fudge the relationship by substituting metaphors for hard facts. Greeting-card phrases such as "the welfare of mankind" do not tell us what we need to know. A better understanding of the role of foundations in our political system might do at least part of the job.

If we could see foundation history as political and social history combined, and acknowledge its impact on public policy, we might not find ourselves unemployed. And if foundations could admit their function and ask us to demonstrate both its benefits and its defects, we might not find ourselves broke. But then there's that dilemma. The Greeks had a word for it. It just might not be one that American foundations find satisfying. If historians take the same stance, albeit for different reasons, the outcome can scarcely mean anything genuinely significant for the future of historical research on foundations.

Note

1. Merle Curti, "The History of American Philanthropy as a Field of Research," *American Historical Review* 62 (1957): 352–63.

14 | In Search of the Ford Foundation

Richard Magat

SHORTLY BEFORE HIS retirement in 1979, McGeorge Bundy, the fourth president of the Ford Foundation as a national institution, expressed the hope that some scholar might be stirred to write a full-scale history of the Foundation.[1] Seventeen years after the installation of his successor, Franklin A. Thomas, the call for a scholarly history of the world's largest philanthropy has yet to be answered. This essay speculates on the reasons for this lacuna in the literature of philanthropy. Along the way, it attempts to answer the questions, *What do we know about the Ford Foundation?* and *How do we know it?*

Critics have accused foundations of "maintaining an obsession for privacy."[2] A conference of scholars concluded, "Philanthropy has been neglected by historians partly because it has been regarded, at least in its private phases, as a confidential matter, most meritorious if kept secret. Facts and statistics in the field are therefore not easy to assemble."[3]

Nonetheless, there is no dearth of histories of individual foundations. The pioneering Peabody Education Fund was chronicled, albeit uncritically, as early as 1898 by the Fund's second executive director.[4] Unlike the majority of foundations in the twentieth century, Peabody was unusually forthcoming, publishing six volumes of the proceedings of its trustees (1867–1914). The other great nineteenth-century foundation, the Jeanes Fund, was also the subject of a history, financed, interestingly, by another foundation, Carnegie Corporation.[5] And the early collective self-consciousness of foundations is suggested by *Seven Great Foundations*, a 79-page report published by the Russell Sage Foundation in 1911.

Historical treatments of prominent foundations established around the turn of the century have also appeared, but many of them were authorized accounts written by people who worked for them. Among them is the two-volume history of the Russell Sage Foundation, virtually a compilation of forty years' worth of annual reports, but barren of scholarly analysis.[6] One of the co-authors himself, F. Emerson Andrews, acknowledged years later:

> I am less convinced that the history of an institution is best produced by staff. The advantages of superior access to records and intimate personal

knowledge must be balanced against a tendency, which is even more dangerous if it is unconscious, to magnify success and overlook or omit failure.[7]

The Rockefeller Foundation, to say nothing of other Rockefeller philanthropies, has been the focus of a shelf-full of histories. Peter Dobkin Hall
has characterized most of these as tainted: "Even if other scholars were willing to overlook the fact that [Allen] Nevins was on the family payroll, without access to the family papers the work could never be judged as other
scholarly volumes were."[8] One history of the Rockefeller Foundation was
written by a former president, Raymond B. Fosdick (1936–1948), yet thirty-
seven years after its publication an independent scholar, Steven C. Wheatley,
deemed it the most comprehensive guides to the activities of the Foundation
before 1950. "Although Fosdick only glancingly deals with issues of power,
politics and authority," Wheatley wrote, "none of the historians now laboring in libraries and foundation archives have, so far, assayed to revise or
extend Fosdick's first draft of institutional history. . . . Although it falls
short of our present standards for institutional history, it is a much rarer
contribution: an institutional autobiography, or at least as close to that
imaginary species as we are likely to get."[9]

Peter Dobkin Hall has observed that the Rockefeller family itself had
doubts about the value of authorized encomiums: "At best they kept alive
public suspicions of the family and its motives. At worst, they prevented
both the public and the Rockefellers themselves from ever really understanding their role in American history."[10] On the other hand, unauthorized
biographies, such as Peter Collier and David Horowitz's, deeply upset the
family, not only for its revelations, but also for its alleged distortions, such
as John D. Rockefeller 3d's shortcomings. In part to do justice to JDR 3d,
the family commissioned a major account of the family's philanthropy by
family employees.[11] Although Hall points to several weaknesses and errors
in this massive work, he terms it "the first fully informed and reasonably
dispassionate portrayal of the activities and interests of the Rockefeller
brothers." Other critics have applauded its candor.

Although not so exhaustively chronicled as the Rockefeller philanthropies, important accounts of the Carnegie foundations abound, ranging from
Carnegie's autobiography to Joseph Wall's authoritative 1970 biography.[12]
But the towering histories of Carnegie philanthropy are Ellen Condliffe
Lagemann's.[13] Even so skeptical a critic as Hall lauds them, and a review in
the *Bulletin of the Atomic Scientists* says her first volume "combines fidelity
to narrative exposition with a sophisticated sense of historiographical issues" and treats her subject "with balance and acuity."[14]

Other foundations enshrined between hard covers include Z. Smith
Reynolds, Milbank Memorial, Rosenwald, and Baron de Hirsch. Several

foundations are covered at length in books about their founding families, for example, the five Guggenheim foundations, Jessie Ball du Pont, Mellon, Kellogg, Charles Stewart Mott, Phelps Dodge, Commonwealth, Bollingen, and, most recently, Ewing M. Kaufman.[15] Knowledge of individual foundations may also be gleaned from memoirs of foundation staff members, biographies of them by others, and in some cases, biographies of philanthropists by other philanthropists, for example, Flexner's biography of Carnegie's president, Henry Pritchett.[16] The literature of foundation history has been admirably covered in Lagemann's bibliographic essays in her two Carnegie books and by Joseph Kiger.[17]

So what of the Ford Foundation?

Except for its first decade and a half, when it remained in obscurity as a family philanthropy, the Foundation has been quite visible.[18] Its journey into the front rank of philanthropy was accompanied by fervent acclaim, stormy controversy, and the continuous glare of public attention. In its infancy, the Foundation drew media attention because of controversial grants by its spin-off, the Fund for the Republic; the departure of the Foundation's president, Paul Hoffman, in 1953 to work on the Eisenhower Presidential campaign; the iconoclastic pronouncements by Robert Hutchins, then one of the Foundation's associate directors; and the scrutiny of two Congressional investigations into allegations of foundations as hotbeds of subversion. Although the Foundation emerged unscathed and indeed with enhanced credit from the Cox Committee hearings—where Henry Ford, Hoffman, and Hutchins made effective appearances—and the Reece Committee collapsed in discredit, anxieties over the Foundation's reputation subsided slowly.

On the heels of the investigations the Foundation decided in 1955 to make the first sale of Ford Motor Company stock to the public, followed by a record-breaking half-billion dollars in grants to colleges, universities, hospitals, and medical schools. When the Foundation again changed leaders (1956), Henry T. Heald appeared on the cover of *Time* magazine. During the Bundy years, spotlights were trained on the Foundation's role in New York City's stormy school decentralization issue and on Congressional assaults of the 1960s.

Given the turbulent seas through which the Foundation sailed in the 1950s, it is hardly surprising that it was jittery about its image. The Foundation for several years commissioned polls of public knowledge of and attitudes toward the institution. And, given that segregationists and others upset by certain Foundation activities launched boycotts of Ford Motor Company vehicles, it is not surprising that the Foundation's public relations were handled by Earl Newsom and Company, guardian of the company's fair name.[19]

Therefore, when Dwight Macdonald notified the Foundation that he was at work on a *New Yorker* profile of the institution, alarm bells went off. Macdonald, after all, had quit *Fortune* because of a conflict with its editor over a series he had written that criticized the U.S. Steel Corporation. As Francis X. Sutton notes in his introduction to a reissued edition of the book based on the magazine profile, Macdonald had drifted leftward—to the *Partisan Review*, Trotskyism, anarchism, and pacifism.[20]

Porter McKeever, the Foundation's in-house public relations director, saw only two courses of action—refuse to cooperate or "do our darndest to get him better acquainted with the whole operation, hoping that a more positive attitude would result." McKeever tried feverishly to feed Macdonald material that would divert him from a negative viewpoint. The book "shows how he waffled back and forth between his desire to kick the Foundation in the groin and the perhaps reluctant necessity of acknowledging the good things the Foundation was doing." Although many of his colleagues were unhappy about the book, McKeever concluded that "the society needs Dwight Macdonald, and I think the Ford Foundation needs Dwight Macdonald."[21] Macdonald devotes a substantial part of his book to a discussion of the history and operations of foundations other than Ford. The *Saturday Review* noted, "What U.S. scholarship needs, and is not getting by courtesy of foundation funds, is precisely the sort of clear, original, analytical work that Mr. Macdonald's book typifies."[22]

Curiously, full-length histories have been written of two satellites of the Ford Foundation, the Fund for the Advancement of Education[23] and the Fund for the Republic. The latter, because of its traffic in controversy, acquired the nickname "wholly disowned subsidiary." It was the subject of two well-researched analytical works that prominently examine the key role of Robert Maynard Hutchins, *enfant terrible* who headed the Fund and raised gooseflesh among trustees of the parent foundation.[24] Hutchins himself is the subject of three biographies, one of which, Milton Mayer's, provides an account of Hutchins's relations with the Ford Foundation, its short-term president Hoffman, the controversy-plagued Fund for the Republic, and Henry Ford II.[25] But other important actors in the Foundation's history (Bundy, Heald, and Alvin Eurich, for example) have been ignored by biographers. The late Paul N. Ylvisaker, a towering, inspirational figure in philanthropy, has been recognized within the field, but not in a biography, though a collection of his speeches and writing is in preparation. Douglas Ensminger, a midwestern agronomist who presided over the Foundation's far-flung program in India and was close to the inner circles of the Nehru government, is little known outside the annals of Ford lore. W. McNeil Lowry, who brought the Foundation into the arts (and was offered the first directorship of the National Endowment for the Arts), has been mentioned in articles, but is only treated in a book as one of nine men who have greatly influenced American culture.[26] Besides an interesting personal and professional portrait of Lowry, the author provides intimate details of politicking and decision-making in the Foundation. The literature is full of substantive material published by the Foundation itself on some of its major projects, to say nothing of popularized reports.[27]

Independent scholars have analyzed parts of the Foundation, such as its business education program and its international cultural activities.[28] Some 200 doctoral dissertations deal with activities in which it has been involved, but the vast majority are microviews of particular projects, such as a Hagerstown, Maryland, instructional television project, ethnic inclusion strategies for a World Affairs Council in California, student work programs in three liberal arts colleges, and an Icelandic social sciences curriculum. A Foundation staff member, Walter Ashley, wrote a generally complimentary dissertation on the Foundation's international activities.[29]

A penetrating view of personalities and conflict within the Foundation is given in a dissertation about the Foundation's role in one of the formative projects in the war on poverty, reforming the New Haven public schools.[30] Drawing heavily on the Foundation's oral history and interviews with non-Foundation participants, the author, Daniel C. Humphrey, analyzes the tensions and hopes in a major instance of "strategic philanthropy." Among the sources from which he draws is a modest yet highly influential analysis of the Foundation's role in antipoverty theory and practice.[31]

Several academic analysts view the Foundation from a left perspective. Peter Seybold, for example, attributes to the Foundation a "revolution" in which "the whole foundation of political science was altered as behavioralists came to dominate the major journals and departments. . . . The Foundation sought to restructure the discipline to serve the interests of the corporate elite." Seybold claims that Ford's strategy was based on fears of social instability.[32]

Mary Anna Culleton Colwell sampled Ford and three other foundations and said her findings "raise questions about whether the third sector operates as it has been described and about accountability for public policy in a democracy."[33] Among prominent critiques by other radical academics are Edward H. Berman's and various chapters in a volume edited by Robert F. Arnove.[34]

At the opposite end of the ideological spectrum are works like *The Tax-Exempt Foundations*, by William H. McIlhany II, one-fourth of which is devoted to Ford.[35] The drift of his argument may be glimpsed from the following:

[T]he Ford Foundation has been the leading supporter of practically every scheme to increase the power of government in the United States, as well

as the development of a world-government system internationally. . . .
Ford has promoted many areas of left activism, from the profit and advantage awarded to former political associates to grants for a myriad of
pressure groups openly engaged in partisan lobbying efforts.

Among the hysterical analyses of foundations that have found their way
into print is a book by Rene Wormser, worth noting only because he was
general counsel to the Reece Committee.[36] Devoting about a third of the
book to the Ford Foundation, he complains about its alleged ultraliberalism
and sympathy with the Soviet Union, and its funding of such threats to the
social order as the behavioral sciences program, the Fund for the Republic,
and the Social Science Research Council. B. Carroll Reece provides a preface in which he reminds readers that the predecessor Cox Committee paid
more attention to foundations' words than their deeds. In contrast, his
Committee addressed the grave unanswered question, "To what extent, if
any, are the funds of the large foundations aiding and abetting Marxist tendencies in the United Sates and weakening the love which every American
should have for his way of life?"

The perception of foundation officers as behind-the-scenes, if not face-
less, personalities, is borne out by the small number who have written about
the institution to which they devoted major parts of their professional lives.
One is Francis X. Sutton, a veteran of the Foundation's behavioral sciences
and international divisions. In addition to his introduction to the new edition of Dwight Macdonald's book, Sutton has written a long, insightful essay on the Foundation's formative years.[37] Beginning with a lovely meta-
phor, he describes the very dilemma that this paper explores:

[Institutions'] origins and youth attract curiosity that can be gratified in
coherent and smooth-textured narration. Later they become like great
trees with proliferating branches and foliage that blinds the sight. So it
has been with the Ford Foundation. Its beginnings have been told several
times, and some of the branches followed, but the canopy remains largely
undescribed.

For the last several years Sutton has been writing a history of the Foundation's international activities. [38]

A candid view of the Foundation's extensive role in the population field
is offered by Oscar Harkavy, who ran the program for thirty years. This
account, which examines the population activities of foundations as far
back as the 1920s, also touches on such matters as the role of wives of Ford
Foundation trustees in bringing the subject of population to action and the
high-flying activities of a major (and very effective) grantee who wound up
in jail.[39] The Foundation's wide-ranging work in conservation and environmental programs over four decades was analyzed in a 7,000-word article by
Marshall Robinson, a former Foundation vice president, and a history of its

work in India was written by Eugene Staples, former head of the Foundation's office there.[40] Sutton's extensive history of the Foundation's international activities, in process, is available in the Foundation Archive.

Waldemar Nielsen, another former staff member, has sought to provide intimate profiles of the Ford Foundation in two books about the nation's largest foundations, written a dozen years apart. Nielsen talks of "the reluctance—even fear—of individuals in the tight little world of philanthropy to talk about the inner working and problems of foundations." Describing Ford as "an adolescent that has had great trouble growing up," Nielsen nonetheless gives it high marks for its willingness to tackle controversial issues, but he concludes that its scale seems to have contributed to sloppy grant-making and impaired its leadership capacity. He recommended that it be broken into three or four smaller units.[41] His second volume renders a generally positive judgment on the Bundy administration despite highly visible mishaps. On the Thomas administration, Nielsen sketched a shaky, in some respects traumatic, start but concluded that, "If [he] can combine his pragmatism and strong sense of social purposes with improved skills as a manager and leader, it is possible that he may achieve even greater results than Bundy did."[42]

Ben Whitaker, an English lawyer and Labour government minister, devoted considerable attention to Ford in a readable and informative work. Emphasizing his freedom from strings and the perils of subsidies, the jacket of the book bears the subtitle "An Unsubsidized Anatomy of the Burden of Benevolence."[43] "If I had not taken a decision at the outset that I would not seek or accept any grant for the work for this book," Whitaker declares, "it might have taken me less than the six years it has to complete."

Urbane and witty, Whitaker's book is an Oxford echo of Dwight Macdonald: "The Ford Foundation's anatomy of decision-making resembles a private State Department, with hawks and doves among its officers competing for power." Whitaker cites actual or threatened boycotts of Ford company products by Afrikaners as a result of the "cautiously liberal character" of the Foundation because of its support of the South African Institute of Race Relations, by the Portuguese because of a grant to an antigovernment institute in Mozambique, by Catholics because of support for family planning, and others.

The one occasion when a full scholarly history of the Foundation was attempted was marked by attenuated institutional indecision and shabby treatment—if not betrayal—of a scholar.

In October 1955, William Greenleaf, a young historian at Colorado State University, was given a dual mission by the Foundation—to compile a bibliography of documents gathered in the course of the proceedings of the Reece Committee and to write a monograph on the personal philanthropies of Henry Ford, his wife Clara, and his son Edsel. Greenleaf had been a research associate of Allan Nevins on his three-volume history of the Ford Motor Company,[44] and he was recommended for the task by Professor Richard Morris of Columbia University. Morris called Greenleaf "one of the outstanding graduate students in American history in recent years," and Prof. Henry Steele Commager said he made a brilliant record in his seminar.[45]

Greenleaf completed the manuscript of the monograph in August 1956. The following year, the Foundation engaged him to write its history from 1936 through 1956. Greenleaf's enthusiasm is indicated by the fact that he chose the assignment over an offer from Nevins to continue work on a Ford family history. The fee, for a thirteen-month period, was $8,000. Ironically, in light of what eventually happened, Greenleaf said, "It will be a pleasure to resume my association with The Ford Foundation, the more so in view of the complete freedom with which I was permitted to work as an independent scholar during the preparation of the manuscript on the early Ford philanthropies."

Greenleaf proposed to write a non-technical history: "Over my back hovers the hypothetical lay reader, the fellow who has perhaps heard of The Ford Foundation, but does not know precisely what it is and does, and who would be hard pressed if he were asked to tell us about foundations as a whole."

Midway through the assignment, Adolph Suehsdorf, director of the Foundation's Office of Reports, which administered the project, suggested that Greenleaf carry the book one year further, to cover the first year of the administration of Henry T. Heald as president. To end at the beginning of the Heald incumbency, Suehsdorf said, would leave out "several important evolutionary steps . . . the return of the Fund (for the Advancement of Education) to the Foundation, the conclusion of the Behavioral Sciences program . . . and the enormous and specific commitment to education as our *raison d'être*."[46]

Greenleaf was even-tempered and obliging, but signs of strain began appearing two months before the deadline for delivery of the manuscript. Through no fault of his own, he wrote, he was unable to see most of the people he had intended to interview during the summer of 1957, and in one instance where he had expected to have at least an hour's interview, he was given only twenty minutes. This episode referred to H. Rowan Gaither, Heald's predecessor, with whom he had a difficult time obtaining an appointment at all. Gaither said he had to catch a plane and invited Greenleaf to come along. Greenleaf declined. Even in the short interview, Greenleaf said, Gaither was guarded and not frank.[47] "Thus, if I seem to bear down too hard on the Gaither regime, it may be because I didn't get a rounded picture from the people who might have helped. . . . If there is a strong case to be made out for the Gaither regime's performance, I would certainly appreciate having the research materials. Obviously, until any or all parties concerned write their memoirs or make available their diaries or day log-books, if any, the data will have to come by way of the interview method." He said several others in the Foundation had not been frank out of solicitude for Gaither's feelings.

Stressing the need for the writer in such a project to maintain his integrity, Greenleaf said he would want the manuscript sent to several people for opinion and criticism. Five months after he delivered the manuscript, Harvey B. Matthews, Jr., assistant to Heald, recommended that the book not be published "at this time." Although Greenleaf's book would give "a more objective and favorable image of us" than Dwight Macdonald's, he argued, "the Heald regime has had insufficient time to supplant previous ones in the direction and substance of Foundation history." Matthews also worried about the portrayal of Hutchins as the dominant personality in the Greenleaf work: "Why should we put out a sponsored book to resurrect a ghost!" He recommended that the manuscript be updated and published to mark the tenth anniversary of the emergence of the Foundation as a national philanthropy and the twenty-fifth year of its establishment.[48]

I urged Matthews two years later to reopen the subject with Heald, but he declined to do so. To finesse the argument that the book would be over-weighted toward earlier regimes, I noted that in a manuscript covering the Foundation to the end of 1961 the Heald administration would be nearly as long as the Hoffman and Gaither's combined, and longer than each. I also urged that this time around the Foundation waive the right to withhold permission to publish.[49] Matthews declined to transmit the recommendation.

In the meantime, the Foundation still withheld permission to publish the manuscript covering the early Ford philanthropies—seven years after its completion. I urged that it be released, in fairness to Greenleaf and to bolster the possibility that he could be persuaded to carry forward the history of the Foundation.[50]

At one point, the Foundation raised the possibility of transferring rights to the pre-Foundation manuscript to the Ford Motor Company, but company lawyers recommended against it. Greenleaf, by now on the faculty of the University of New Hampshire, then reopened the subject directly with Heald. He observed that if the Foundation continued to refuse permission,

> The subject itself . . . will not remain indefinitely dormant. Since virtually all of the research material . . . is in the public domain, or is accessible to qualified scholars, there will predictably come a time when another writer, working independently, will gather substantially the same data. . . . My

personal opinion is that release of publication rights for my material would be both timely [1963 was the centenary of the birth of Henry Ford], and appropriate.[51]

Greenleaf asked the Foundation to waive its rights. I recommended to Heald that Greenleaf's request be approved and that a decision on the later history be made within a few months.[52] After consulting with Henry Ford II, the Foundation acceded, with the following condition: "That no acknowledgment be made in the book itself or in promotional or advertising material of the fact that the manuscript was written under a consultancy with the Foundation or that the work was commissioned by the Foundation." The Foundation explained its condition "because although the Foundation commissioned the work it is not itself assisting its publication nor has it approved or disapproved details or general findings of the manuscript."[53] The book was published the following year.[54]

In a conversation with me in February 1963, Greenleaf still expressed interest in writing a history of the Foundation, which he said by now had achieved the "administrative stability" necessary to complete the project and approve publication. Still hopeful, he wrote later that year,

> Since the Foundation undertook its expanded program, the scope and complexity of its activities have outstripped any comparable developments in the annals of organized corporate (not corporation!) philanthropy. It would make a magnificent story because it reveals so much that is permanently valuable in our traditions, and, if properly handled, has many of the elements of an exciting tale.[55]

In April 1964, I informed Greenleaf that I was again lobbying for a history, but that by now Greenleaf's work would probably have to be condensed into perhaps one tenth of the total and that, because of Greenleaf's other commitments, someone else would be the author.[56] Ever patient, Greenleaf replied that he was saddened that another author was being contemplated, that he seriously doubted that his manuscript could be so severely condensed, and that he would be available, even on a co-authorship arrangement, to revise the manuscript.[57] That concludes the written record of the sorry affair. Greenleaf died in 1975 at the age of 58.[58]

There is a certain irony in the fact that while the Ford Foundation was waffling on its own history, it launched a major effort to encourage scholars to grapple with the history of philanthropy. In 1957 it made the first of a series of grants that totaled $94,629 to Merle Curti's University of Wisconsin History of Philanthropy Project. Books and articles produced through the project over a decade provided a basic outline of some of the major contributions foundation philanthropy had made, especially in education and welfare, and they began to explore relationships between private foundations and their publics. Curti himself wrote two books, on education and on American philanthropy abroad, in neither of which is the Ford Foundation treated at length.[59]

In the late 1960s and early 1970s, the Foundation took two steps that greatly facilitated the job of scholars. It established an archive and commissioned an oral history project. Although organizing the files into an archive came on the heels of the Tax Reform Act of 1969, there is no evidence of cause and effect. In fact the Act would have been a reason for not undertaking the archival project, on the grounds that public access to the records would open up too many sores. Even after the archive was physically established, it took several years before rules for use by outside researchers were drafted.

Housed in a portion of a basement in the Foundation's headquarters and in a storage warehouse, the archives have 2,000 cubic feet of program records, 14,000 unpublished reports of staff, consultants, and grantees, and 300 linear feet of processed program officer and executive officer files.[60] Also included are general correspondence, records of unsuccessful applications for grants, an index to thousands of books and other publications resulting from grants, and 6,000 rolls of microfilmed grant files.

Although the Ford Archive is sometimes compared unfavorably with the Rockefeller Archive Center, a survey of users conducted for this paper discloses general satisfaction.[61] But in a few cases access to certain files was denied without explanation. "Some of the rules are restrictive," said one scholar, "suggesting that the Foundation is very protective of itself." But the staff is given high marks for its helpfulness. The Archive staff reviews all files given to a researcher. Records are made available "unless otherwise restricted by legal or administrative policy," that is, to protect individual privacy and grantee confidentiality and to prevent disclosure of material that would adversely affect the Foundation.[62] But rarely is anything withheld on these grounds, according to an Archive official. On the other hand, the Ford Archive is more liberal than Rockefeller's in that it gives access to material as recent as ten years ago, and Rockefeller materials are not available for twenty years.

Of course no archive is complete; Foundation officers and staff have walked off with records of their activities without providing copies to the Archives. W. McNeil Lowry's extensive papers, for example, are deposited at the University of Illinois.

Coming two years after the start of the Archive, the oral history was advocated by Julius A. Stratton, president of MIT and chairman of the Ford board of Trustees (1966–1971). Having been a young physicist at MIT's historic Radiation Laboratory in World War II, Stratton saw the need to document "what was new in the world," recalls Charles T. Morrissey, who directed the oral history project. "He was keenly aware of the need to capture the Foundation's history in a deliberate fashion instead of letting the record-keeping process continue as an administrative function which undoubtedly was neglecting some top-level decisions of crucial significance. Ford being then the institutional leader of American philanthropy in terms of size it was important that it look at its own frontier and era."[63]

Oral history itself was a relatively new technique for documenting the past. The Columbia University Oral History Department made a strong bid to do the Ford history. Unlike Carnegie Corporation, however, which had contracted with Columbia to conduct its oral history interviews, Ford invited an oral historian into the Foundation in order to combine the advantages of in-house administration with the independence of an outside professional. When he was chosen to direct the project, Morrissey was president-elect of the Oral History Association, which had been formed only in 1967. Assisting him was Ronald J. Grele, who had worked with him on the John F. Kennedy Library Oral History Project in 1965–1966.

A two-year program, budgeted at $232,800, was approved in June 1971. The scope of the project was drawn cautiously. "[It] was designed to lay an initial foundation for an historical analysis of the organization of the Ford Foundation as a national philanthropy and the evolution of its program, but without the objective of creating currently accessible materials about the Foundation *or preparing for a written history of the institution*" (emphasis added). The Foundation was not looking toward an official published history: "The project does not constitute a full oral history of the Foundation . . . and is not intended to do so. The hundreds of key persons associated with the history of the Ford Foundation as grantees, consultants and otherwise will not be included among the persons interviewed."[64]

Morrissey and Grele interviewed 73 persons, two of whom (trustees John Cowles and Stephen Bechtel) withdrew their transcripts.[65] The result was 230 hours of tape-recorded interviews and 6,730 pages of transcripts, which are open to researchers at intervals specified by the interviewees, stretching to the year 2025. An additional 2,000 pages consist of diary entries of respondents, letters, and other unofficial documents. The oral history includes a name and subject index of 20,000 cards.

"Although we had wide access," Morrissey recalls, "there was a great deal of concern about what would be revealed, what were people talking about, suspiciousness about what we were finding out."[66] "A few interviewees edited (i.e., 'sanitized') some choice portions of their transcripts; others were unduly cautious in stipulating legal restrictions."

Morrissey was impressed as much by how the respondents talked about concepts of foundation behavior as they did about the Foundation itself— "its growth, organization, programs, controversies, leadership, and all the other topics which constitute an integrated, comprehensive history of a prominent social institution with global impact."

"Some of the oral histories are very personal, but most are just solid meat and potatoes," Grele says. "The Archives had no personal correspondence, but we overlaid its rich institutional history, reports, and evaluations with recollections and anecdotes from the interviews to reveal the culture of the Foundation in all its transitions to that time."[67]

Addressing doubts about the historical value of the Foundation oral history and others, Morrissey observes, "Some critics of oral history argue that more vanity than veracity lies in what respondents recall, more forgetfulness than remembrance, more generalities than specifics, more that has been colored by the passage of time and subsequent events than an authentic account of the actual event itself." So why oral history? "Bureaucracies tend to document the minuscule and neglect top-level decisions. . . . Moreover many documents are drafted to obscure the dynamics which underlie a turning point, not to reveal them. Oral history, despite its drawbacks, is often the only adequate way in which the present can document the past for the future. Evaluative judgments are often enhanced by the passage of time instead of being afflicted by the present-mindedness of our times which infers that history is irrelevant."

"People on both sides of funding decisions—grantors as well as grantees—are reluctant to put in writing their candid appraisals of grants which did not produce results in line with expectations. Accordingly, the files of a foundation are likely to contain evaluation reports which historians should view cautiously. Broad claims are made by benefactors as well as by recipients. In oral history, by offering to defer disclosure of forthright opinion until a time when it is unlikely to injure personal feeling, a person can be persuaded to speak frankly."[68]

Expressing concern about the end of the project, Morrissey and Grele said, "It would be unfortunate if the Foundation's history-making activities over the next twenty years or so were to pass without sufficient documentation, and the Foundation be forced to employ another team of oral historians to play a desperate game of 'catch-up' by interviewing, at greatly increased costs, the 'old timers' who survive." They recommended a modest ongoing oral history project. "[It] would focus not necessarily on the long-term leaders who have been with the Foundation for several years but instead focus on the major decisions, issues, turning points, program developments, and personnel action within the past five years. An annual history-keeping project should include the equivalent of a de-briefing session when senior members of the staff approach retirement, or programs are terminated and personnel responsible for them are shifting to new duties. The Foundation would not need to bring in oral historians years later, would not have to deal with fading memories, or voids caused by the sudden demise of key personnel." Among the alternatives, they listed an in-house program through the Archives or the hiring of the Foundation's own historian, to conduct the oral history and perform other duties of a historical nature, such as tracking down private manuscript collections bearing on the history of the Foundation.[69]

Favoring continuation, Willard Hertz, the Foundation liaison person with the project, pointed out that because time and funds had run out, plans for interviewing twenty-two more key figures had been dropped. They included James Armsey, Douglas Ensminger, Paul Hoffman, Mario Fantini, Marshall Robinson, Harold Howe II, and Fred W. Friendly.[70] Alexander Heard, successor to Stratton as chairman of the board, decided "to lower the curtain now. . . . He is concerned lest one exception lead to another and another." Bundy concurred.[71]

Hertz recalls that there was no will at the top to continue the project: "Neither Heard nor other officers besides Lowry took any interest in it. There was a feeling that oral history was not worth much anyway, just a bunch of recollections. Also, this was a time of downsizing in the Foundation. Many people were peeling off, going elsewhere."[72]

In 1976 and 1977, in preparation for Bundy's retirement, the Board of Trustees conducted an extensive study to plan for the future of the Foundation, including "a canvass of the . . . Foundation's experiences, successes, and failures . . . [focussed] on the broad objectives sought, the means pursued to achieve them, and the results." The introductory essay of the study "can help us in measuring the criteria for particular ways and means of making grants—to established institutions, to new ones, to individuals, to groups, for general or for specific purposes, for ideas or for action."[73] I was asked to write the essay, and the staff director of the self-study, Richard S. Sharpe, recommended external publication, "at least in limited edition . . . sanitized to avoid hurting feelings."[74] Bundy agreed, and the essay was published as a book, with the addition of sixteen case studies and a chronology. Of the 2,500 copies printed, the Foundation bought 375, and the publisher sold 1,964. John Simon, a leading scholar and practitioner of foundation philanthropy, called it "informative, balanced, well-written, it subjects the invariably messy history of any institution to as much analytical rigor as possible." Tributes also came from Clark Kerr, John Gardner, Joan Ganz Cooney, Wassily Leontief, and others. Reviews were favorable with the notable exception of William E. Simon, former Secretary of the Treasury and head of the John M. Olin Foundation. Simon faulted the book for paying inadequate tribute to Henry and Edsel Ford and used his long review to criticize several Foundation programs. "The reader is treated," he wrote, "to the spectacle of anti-capitalist intellectuals living in style on grubby capitalist grants, while reordering the traditional institutions and the lives of ordinary citizens."[75]

Reasons for the absence of a formal history of the Foundation vary widely. Merrimon Cuninggim, a former president of the Danforth Foundation whom Bundy invited into the Ford Foundation for a year as a kind of roving critic, noted:

> Those responsible for the foundation's work have seldom paused to consider with meticulous care the primary reasons for the existence of the foundation and the chief ends to which its work should be directed. Action, yes; philosophy, no. Programs, yes, policies, no.[76]

The raw material was in hand, Morrissey and Grele believed:

> We are confident that the oral history transcripts, used in conjunction with the archives and other records of the Foundation . . . would provide ample material for writing a first-rate history of the Foundation since 1948, and for explaining major turning points and characteristics of the Foundation [and] aid in explaining the Foundation's impact on national and international problems. The Foundation has to understand that the independence of the researcher in the long run is the best way to go. There may be some bruises along the way, but better to suffer the bruises than to try to contrive or manipulate the shape of the product."[77]

With the possible exception of Lowry, however, there was no will at the top for a formal history. "There came a point, in 1973 I think," Morrissey recalls, "when Mac Lowry realized his days at Ford were numbered. . . . With his declining stature I don't think there was any champion there to promote the prospect."[78]

The degree of outside interest also comes into play. In connection with a possible observance of the twenty-fifth anniversary of the Foundation as a national institution, Grele reported that several historians he had consulted "dismissed the project as either dull and tedious or impossible to do seriously." One exception was Thomas C. Reeves, author of a history of the Fund for the Republic, who said he would be willing to be considered to write a history of the Foundation.[79] A few nonacademic writers over the years have expressed an interest in undertaking a history but have not followed through.

The fear of appearing to be self-serving may act as a constraint against Foundation financing of a history, says another scholar of philanthropy, Stanley N. Katz, president of the American Council of Learned Societies: "I think many [foundations] feel a big investment in serious history (which is what it would take) would lend itself to the accusation that it was self-serving." He believes, however, that the funds could be assembled apart from Ford funding: "How else to distance the authors from the foundation?"[80]

Accurately evaluating the Foundation poses another challenge. Gordon Harrison, the author of several historical works before coming to Ford, observed:

> The question of trying to ascertain how a foundation program has a societal impact which is measurable is just not addressed, and maybe it can't be. It's a fascinating challenge to try to ask yourself: "Assuming that we have some social consequence, what is it? And how do I go about looking for it?"[81]

Conflicting views among top Foundation policy makers of the Foundation's responsibility to external researchers and the public at large, dating back to the earliest days of the Foundation as a national grant-making entity, also help account for the lack of a history. The assumption of a legitimate and overarching public interest in the Foundation as a key social institution was not universally shared by Trustees, officers, and staff, Hertz observes: "Even at so sophisticated an organization as Ford, there was considerable feeling that the Foundation, as a private organization, had no particular obligation to open its doors to the outside world. It was one thing to announce grants in news releases and to publish an annual report. It was quite another to come clean on the steps that led to these grant decisions."[82]

Past and present presidents of the Foundation have shown scant interest in the prospect of a history. Bundy's early response to one of my prods about commissioning a history was, "I'm not much on semi-official histories. . . . Of course if [Richard] Rovere or some other first-class journalist wanted to do a book—fine."[83] In an interview several months before his death in September 1996, he said, "By its nature it's difficult to do a foundation history because it's known by its grantees. It is too idiosyncratic. The pudding has so many themes." Although he stood by his earlier statement on a history, Bundy declined to speculate on what the Foundation should now do.[84]

During the Thomas presidency, no steps toward a full history of the Foundation were taken. A free-lance writer was commissioned to prepare a brief (sixty-page) historical summary, used solely for orientation of new staff and trustees, and several months before his retirement the director of the Office of Communications was relieved of his regular duties and asked to research and outline the record of the Thomas administration, including a brief account of the earlier history. This material, he says, is to be used to prepare an official history.[85] Also, some retiring staff members were taken on as consultants to write about the Foundation's work in their fields (for example, Louis Winnick on urban affairs, Sutton on the international programs, and Harkavy on population).

Susan Berresford, who became president in April 1996, said the Foundation plans to become more active in informing the public about the role

Ford and other nonprofit organizations play in society: "We all feel that the non-profit sector is less well understood than it should be as a whole—and certainly philanthropy within it. The Foundation now is planning to open a number of public windows into its operations. The options include encouraging members of the program staff to do more public speaking, running public-service advertisements, and distributing information over the Internet."[86] She underscored this intent by creating a vice presidency for communications, to which she appointed a seasoned program officer—Robert Curvin (director of the Foundation's urban poverty program for eight years), who is also a former member of the editorial page of *The New York Times* and dean of urban affairs at The New School.

Will such moves toward greater openness include initiating an independent history of the institution? A foundation-commissioned history is not a priority, Berresford says.[87] "If someone were to take the initiative and come to us with a proposal, asking our financial support, we would evaluate it as we would any proposal, on the merits, and in relation to our other priorities." If the Foundation were ever to finance a history, she adds, it would retain the right to approve or disapprove for publication. A scholar wishing to write a history, coming to the Foundation with his or her own financing, would be given access to the Foundation's archives on the same basis as other scholars, she noted.

Berresford accounts for the absence of a published history of the Foundation on the grounds that "foundations are not of great interest in the public eye." Echoing Bundy's observation, she says, "Their work is understood through the work of their grantees."

"Why [should] the Ford Foundation be an uninviting or perhaps daunting subject," Sutton has wondered. "Institutional history is certainly not one of the more ingratiating literary genres, but even the big banks now seem to find willing chroniclers. . . . Perhaps the Ford Foundation has never again aroused as much public interest as it did in the years Macdonald recounts."[88]

I agree, and although it is now holding record assets of more than $7 billion, the field has expanded so dramatically in the last decade that there are now more than twenty foundations of over $1 billion in assets, including such newcomers as Getty, MacArthur, Annenberg, Packer, California Wellness, and Starr. No longer is Ford "such a towering eminence in the field of philanthropy [that it] tends to establish an attitude toward philanthropy in general," as McKeever said nearly twenty-five years ago. Still, the Ford Foundation is the largest, and its contributions and foibles are significant to American social history. In my view the prospects of the Foundation itself launching an independent, no-strings-attached history are exceedingly dim. But philanthropic studies is a growth guild, if not an industry, and somewhere out there is a scholar who might find the Ford Foundation writ large an attractive challenge. The research resources are richer than they were in Macdonald's and Greenleaf's time. And who knows, outside funding might be available—from the Aspen Fund for Nonprofit Research, from a publisher's advance, or even from the cutting-edge purse of another megafoundation.

Notes

1. The qualifier "national institution" refers to the fact that between 1936 and 1950, when Edsel Ford and Henry Ford, respectively, were its presidents, the Foundation's grants were confined almost entirely to Michigan charities of interest to the Ford family (averaging about $1 million annually); Richard Magat, *The Ford Foundation at Work: Philanthropic Choices, Methods, and Styles* (New York: Plenum, 1979), 7.

2. Waldemar Nielsen, *The Big Foundations* (New York: Columbia University Press, 1972), 1, 294.

3. Report of the Princeton Conference on the History of Philanthropy in the United States (New York: Russell Sage Foundation, 1956), 12.

4. I. Curry, *Brief Sketch of George Peabody and a History of the Peabody Education Fund* (Cambridge: University Press: John Wilson & Son, 1898). A later, necessarily more thorough, history was Hoy Taylor, *An Interpretation of the Early Administration of the Peabody Educational Fund* (Nashville: George Peabody College for Teachers, 1933).

5. Lance E. Jones, *The Jeanes Teacher in the United States* (Chapel Hill: University of North Carolina Press, 1937).

6. John M. Glenn, Lilian Brandt, and F. Emerson Andrews, *Russell Sage Foundation: 1907–1946*, 2 vols. (New York: Russell Sage Foundation, 1947).

7. F. Emerson Andrews, *Foundation Watcher* (Lancaster: Franklin and Marshall College, 1973), 93.

8. Peter Dobkin Hall, "What You See Depends on Where You Stand: Reflections on *The Rockefeller Century* and *The Rockefeller Conscience*," *Philanthropy Monthly* 91 (November 1991): 11–16, 12.

9. Steven C. Wheatley, introduction to *The Story of the Rockefeller Foundation* by Raymond D. Fosdick (1952; reprint, New Brunswick, N.J.: Transaction, 1989), vii.

10. Hall, "What You See Depends on Where You Stand," part II, *Philanthropy Monthly* 92 (January 1992): 7–14.

11. John Ensor Harr and Peter Johnson, *The Rockefeller Century* (New York: Scribners, 1988) and *The Rockefeller Conscience* (New York: Scribners, 1991).

12. John C. Van Dyke, ed., *Autobiography of Andrew Carnegie* (Garden City: Doubleday, Doran, 1933); Joseph Frazier Wall, *Andrew Carnegie* (New York: Oxford University Press, 1970).

13. Ellen Condliffe Lagemann, *Private Power for the Public Good: A History of the Carnegie Foundation for the Advancement of Teaching* (Middletown, Conn.: Wesleyan University Press, 1983); *The Politics of Knowledge: The Carnegie Corporation, Philanthropy, and Public Policy* (Middletown, Conn.: Wesleyan University Press, 1989).

14. Steven C. Wheatley, review of *Private Power for the Public Good* by Ellen Condliffe Lagemann, *Bulletin of the Atomic Scientists* 40 (January 1984): 40.

15. The sensitivity to criticism of homegrown histories was expressed by the authors of a history of the Rosenwald Fund: "This book was written at the request of the Rosenwald family with [their] financial subsidy and with their complete cooperation. [They] have not, however, dictated what would be included and what should be omitted. ... [They] have insisted from the first that they were more interested in a portrait of their father than in a purchased panegyric that would only immerse them in deadly platitude." Edwin R. Embree and Julia Waxman, *Investment in People: The Story of the Julius Rosenwald Fund* (New York: Harper and Brothers, 1949), x–xi.

16. Abraham Flexner, *Henry S. Pritchett: A Biography* (New York: Columbia University Press, 1943).

17. Joseph C. Kiger, *Historiographic Review of Foundation Literature: Motivations and Perceptions* (New York: Foundation Center, 1987).

18. "Even in the year of Henry Ford's death, 1947, John Gunther could write, as if confronted by an enigma, 'Something exists known as the Ford Foundation.'" William Greenleaf, *The Ford Foundation: The Formative Years*, unpublished manuscript, 2 vols. Ford Foundation Archives (hereafter FFA), vol. I, ch. 1, 2.

19. Newsom actually sat in on Foundation board meetings, while Porter McKeever, the Foundation's public relations director, did not (Porter McKeever, Oral History transcript, August 5, 1973, FFA, 4). After leaving the Ford Foundation McKeever went on to an influential career in philanthropy as advisor to John D. Rockefeller 3d.

20. Dwight Macdonald, *The Ford Foundation: The Men and the Millions—An Unauthorized Biography* (1956; reprint, New Brunswick, N.J.: Transaction, 1988).

21. McKeever, Oral History, 14.

22. Fred Rodell, in the *Saturday Review* (June 2, 1956), quoted in an article on Macdonald in *Current Biography* (1969), 279.

23. Paul Woodring, *Investment in Innovation: An Historical Appraisal of the Fund for the Advancement of Education* (Boston: Little, Brown, 1971). Woodring was essentially an insider, having been a consultant to the Fund and editor of the education supplement of the *Saturday Review* when it was subsidized by the Fund.

24. Frank K. Kelly, *Court of Reason: Robert Hutchins and the Fund for the Republic* (New York: Free Press, 1981), and Thomas C. Reeves, *Freedom and the Foundation: The Fund for the Republic in the Era of McCarthyism* (New York: Alfred A. Knopf, 1969).

25. Milton Mayer, *Robert Maynard Hutchins: A Memoir* (Berkeley: University of California Press, 1993).

26. Joan Simpson Burns, *The Awkward Embrace: The Creative Artist and the Institutions in America* (New York: Alfred A. Knopf, 1975).

27. Examples include *The Common Good: Social Welfare and the American Future* (Project on Social Welfare and the American Future, 1989); *South Africa: Time Running Out* (Study Commission on U.S. Policy toward Southern Africa, 1980); and James L. Cochrane, *Industrialism and Industrial Man in Retrospect* (1979), an evaluation of a ten-year, $1,055,000 interuniversity study of labor problems and economic development.

28. Steven Schlossman, Michael Sedlak, and Harold Wechsler, *The New Look: The Ford Foundation and the Revolution in Business Education* (Los Angeles: Graduate Management Admission Council, 1987); Kathleen D. McCarthy, "From Cold War to Cultural Development: The International Culture Activities of the Ford Foundation, 1950–1980," *Daedalus* 116 (Winter 1987): 93–118.

29. Walter Ashely, "Philanthropy and Government: A Study of the Ford Foundation's Overseas Programs" (Ph.D. diss., New York University, 1970).

30. Daniel C. Humphrey, "Teach Them Not to Be Poor: Philanthropy and New Haven School Reform in the 1960s" (Ed.D. diss., Teachers College, Columbia University, 1992).

31. Peter Marris and Martin Rein, *Dilemmas of Social Reform* (New York: Atherton Press, 1967).

32. Peter Seybold, "The Ford Foundation and the Transformation of Political Science," in *The Structure of Power in America: The Corporate Elite as a Ruling Class,* ed. Michael Schwartz (New York: Holmes & Meier, 1987), 185–98.

33. Mary Anna Culleton Colwell, *Philanthropic Foundations and Public Policy: The Political Role of Foundations* (New York: Garland, 1993).

34. Edward H. Berman, *The Influence of Carnegie, Ford, and Rockefeller Foundations on American Foreign Policy: The Ideology of Philanthropy* (Albany: State University of New York Press, 1983); Robert F. Arnove, ed., *Philanthropy and Cultural Imperialism: The Foundations at Home and Abroad* (Bloomington: Indiana University Press, 1982).

35. William H. McIlhany II, *The Tax-Exempt Foundations* (Westport: Arlington House, 1980). The author's earlier books included *The ACLU on Trial* (1976).

36. Rene A. Wormser, *Foundations: Their Power and Influence* (New York: Devin-Adair, 1958).

37. Francis X. Sutton, "The Ford Foundation: The Early Years," *Daedalus* 116 (Winter 1987): 41–92.

38. See also Francis X. Sutton, "International Philanthropy in a Large Foundation," in *Philanthropy in American Society,* ed. Jack Salzman (New York: Center for American Culture Studies, Columbia University, 1987), 139–63.

39. Oscar Harkavy, *Curbing Population Growth: An Insider's Perspective on the Population Movement* (New York: Plenum, 1995).

40. Marshall Robinson, "The Ford Foundation: Sowing the Seeds of a Revolution," *Environment* 35 (April 1993): 10–15, 38; Eugene Staples, *Forty Years: A Learning Curve* (New York: Ford Foundation, 1992).

41. Nielsen, *The Big Foundations,* ix.

42. Waldemar Nielsen, *The Golden Donors: A New Anatomy of the Great Foundations* (New York: Dutton, 1985), 83.

43. Ben Whitaker, *The Philanthropoid: Foundations and Society* (New York: William Morrow, 1974), 7, 92.

44. Allan Nevins, with Frank Ernest Hill, *Ford,* 3 vols. (New York: Scribners, 1954–63). Greenleaf had also written a one-volume condensation of Nevins's two-volume *Study in Power: John D. Rockefeller, Industrialist and Philanthropist* (New York: Scribners, 1953).

45. Memorandum from Porter McKeever to the Program Committee, September 12, 1955, author's files.

46. Greenleaf to Adolph Suehsdorf, January 29, 1957; Suehsdorf to Greenleaf, February 11, 1958. L 57-1209, FFA.

47. Richard Magat, notes on conversation with Greenleaf at the Foundation offices, December 27, 1960, author's files.

48. Greenleaf to Magat, May 25, 1958; Harvey Matthews to Henry Heald, December 2, 1958. L 57-1209, FFA.

49. Magat to Matthews, December 7, 1960, author's files.

50. Magat to Donald Sandberg, January 2, 1963. L 57-1209, FFA.

51. Greenleaf to Heald, February 2, 1963. L 57-1209, FFA.

52. Magat to Heald, February 11, 1963. L 57-1209, FFA.

53. Heald to Greenleaf, February 20, 1963. L 57-1209, FFA.

54. William Greenleaf, *From these Beginnings: The Early Philanthropies of Henry and Edsel Ford, 1911–1936* (Detroit: Wayne State University Press, 1964).

55. Greenleaf to Magat, September 16, 1963. L 57-1209, FFA.

56. Magat to Greenleaf, April 1964. L 57-1209, FFA.

57. Greenleaf to Magat, April 29, 1964. L 57-1209, FFA.

58. His scholarly activity continued, e.g., William Greenleaf, Richard B. Morris, and Robert H. Ferrell, *America: A History of the People* (Chicago: Rand McNally, 1971), and Greenleaf, *American Economic Development since 1960* (Columbia: University of South Carolina Press, 1968).

59. Merle Curti, *American Philanthropy Abroad* (1963; reprint, New Brunswick, N.J.: Transaction, 1988); Curti and Roderick Nash, *Philanthropy in the Shaping of American Higher Education* (New Brunswick, N.J.: Rutgers University Press, 1965).

60. The archives of the Rockefeller Foundation are three times more extensive—6120 cubic feet—but they cover a longer period—77 years compared to 51 for the Ford Foundation. See also David C. Hammack, "Private Organizations, Public Purposes: Non-profits and their Archives," *Journal of American History* 76 (June 1989): 181–91. In a survey of the thousand largest American foundations, the Rockefeller Archive Center found that as of 1993 only 48 had their records in archives or libraries.

61. One dissenting view is that of Ronald Grele, who helped prepare the Foundation's oral history: "The policies of the archives have been self-defeating. People who come back from trying to use the archives at Ford really have horror stories. People at Ford run scared. There are things people can't look at. There's a fearfulness about people finding out what [the Foundation] really did do, when indeed what they really did do was pretty good." Interview with author, March 6, 1996.

62. "Access to Ford Foundation Archives: Outside Researchers." FFA, 1995.

63. Charles T. Morrissey, interview with author, May 13, 1996; "Oral History at the Ford Foundation," A Report by Charles T. Morrissey. 000429 FFA.

64. Lowry to Bundy, June 6, 1971. PA 719-0398 FFA.

65. A third trustee withdrew permission he had granted for immediate release of his interview at the request of a Foundation officer who noticed that it contained intemperate remarks about the wife of another officer. "Heard went to [the trustees] and all agreed to put it under wraps. I thought that decision was stupid. Why not just excise the offending remark? That didn't do the cause any good." Willard Hertz, interview with author, April 4, 1996.

66. Ibid.

67. Ibid.

68. Charles T. Morrissey, "Rhetoric and Role in Philanthropy: Oral History and the Grant-Making Foundations," *Oral History Review* (1978): 5–19, revised and expanded version of a paper, "From Language to Theory in Philanthropy: Some Uses of Oral History at the Ford Foundation," presented at the 12th Annual Oral History Colloquium, Coronado, Calif., October 22, 1977.

69. Morrissey and Grele to Hertz, May 22, 1974; "Interim Evaluation and Recommended Future Direction of the Ford Foundation Oral History Project." FFA.

70. Hertz to Dressner, April 3, 1975.

71. Dressner to Bundy, April 8, 1975. PA 719-0398 FFA.

72. Willard Hertz, interview with author, April 4, 1996. The number of oral histories of foundations is increasing. Several foundations in northern California have participated in an oral history project that they funded with grants to the Regional Oral History Office at the University of California (Berkeley). Columbia University did an oral history of the Pew Charitable Trusts and is currently doing one on the Robert Wood Johnson Foundation. Morrissey is conducting an oral history of the Howard Hughes Medical Institute. A National Film Archive of Philanthropy—videotaped talks with leaders in

philanthropy—was started in 1996 by two former staff members, Nielsen and Siobhan Oppenheimer Nicolau. Franklin A. Thomas was one of the first people interviewed.

73. Memorandum for the Trustees, from Alexander Heard and McGeorge Bundy. September 16, 1975. Richard Sharpe's files on the Trustee Planning Project. Box 6713, FFA.

74. Richard S. Sharpe to McGeorge Bundy, November 24, 1976. Box 6713, FFA.

75. William E. Simon, "Reaping the Whirlwind," *Philanthropy Monthly* 13 (January 1980): 5–8.

76. Merrimon Cuninggim, *Private Money and Public Service: The Role of Foundations in American Society* (New York: McGraw-Hill, 1972), 226.

77. Morrissey and Grele to Hertz, May 22, 1974.

78. Morrisey, interview with author, May 13, 1996.

79. Grele to Magat, December 3, 1973.

80. Katz to Magat, May 2, 1996.

81. Gordon Harrison, Oral History transcript, November 21, 1972. FFA, 9.

82. Hertz to Magat, May 18, 1996.

83. Bundy to Magat, December 19, 1968. Author's files.

84. McGeorge Bundy, interview with author, New York, April 2, 1996. Similarly, Sutton, an astute judge of foundation historiography, has commented, "One reason why general accounts of big foundations are rare is that the abundance and diversity of their programs make them daunting to master and recount." Frank Sutton, book review, *Contemporary Sociology* 19 (1990): 593–94. A notable exception, he says, is Raymond B. Fosdick, *The Story of the Rockefeller Foundation* (New York: Harper & Row, 1952).

85. Lloyd Garrison, interview with author, November 1995.

86. Stephen G. Greene, "Ford Speaks Up for Itself," *Chronicle of Philanthropy,* March 7, 1996, 10.

87. Interview with author, April 5, 1996.

88. Francis X. Sutton, introduction to *The Ford Foundation* by Dwight Macdonald, (1952; reprint, New Brunswick, N.J.: Transaction, 1988), vii.

15 | The History of Philanthropy as Life-History

A Biographer's View of Mrs. Russell Sage

Ruth Crocker

WRITING THE HISTORY of philanthropy involves studying philanthropists and thus leads inescapably to biography. While most major philanthropists have their biographers, scholars have overlooked Margaret Olivia Slocum (Mrs. Russell) Sage (1828–1918). Yet her career, which included five decades of voluntary and reform activity, has significance even apart from the extraordinary philanthropy of her old age. (She disbursed $45 million in her eighties.) Sage's biography offers a case study of philanthropic motivation that will be a point of departure for new scholarship on women donors. Contextualizing her philanthropy within Progressive Era transformations in culture and society yields a more nuanced portrait of the female donor, one informed by new understandings of gender, gifts, and exchange. At its most basic, though, writing this ninety-year life as a continuous narrative means telling a good story.

Aged forty-one in 1869, with no capital but her wit, Syracuse governess and schoolteacher Olivia Slocum escaped from her single state into a spectacular marriage. Her husband was New York multi-millionaire, politician, and financier Russell Sage (1816–1906). Installed on fashionable Fifth Avenue with one of the most eccentric of Gilded Age Wall Street speculators, Mrs. Russell Sage, as she was now called, constructed a separate identity for herself as one of that "New York type of well-to-do committee-working church women."[1] Unable to indulge her longing to give to good causes because of Russell Sage's miserly habits, she became an advocate for moral reform and advancement for women, causes she considered identical. When Russell Sage died in 1906 at the age of ninety, he left her virtually all of his $75 million. Olivia had had to watch every penny during her thirty-seven-year marriage, but now she launched into an astonishing philanthropy, spending about $35 million in her eighties. In addition, she gave $10 million to set up a foundation with the broad goal of "social betterment," naming it the Russell Sage Foundation, and thus erasing her own name as she commemorated the husband who had despised charitable giving in a gesture that we probably should see as ironic.[2]

Olivia Sage's philanthropic gifts to a broad range of benevolent, educational, civic, and religious causes deserve more attention than they have received from scholars, as does her Foundation.[3] Biography, a single life-history, can illuminate philanthropy as economic behavior, cultural practice, or part of elites' self-fashioning, but compared to the historian who can and should explore broad questions spanning centuries or at least decades, the biographer is hemmed in by the life of a single human being whose birth is the starting place and death the terminus. Working through the subject's life forward (as it was lived) from birth to death, the biographer will not normally address questions such as the rise of markets, the ripening of social movements, or the evolution of institutions and state powers, for none of these phenomena is coterminous with the life of an individual. For example, the 1920s may be a vitally important period for the development of American foundations—historians have argued that it is—but Mrs. Russell Sage's biographer has nothing to say about the twenties that carries any weight, since Olivia Sage died in November 1918.[4]

Then why do biography? Certainly, biography is not the most useful genre if we want to know *how* philanthropists spent their money. An early, ambitious article by Merle Curti and associates signaled a brief optimism about the power of quantitative history to tell us all we wanted to know about nineteenth-century philanthropy (or anything else). The authors scoured contemporary newspapers and periodicals for data about American philanthropic gifts and attempted to answer a bank of questions using the then-revolutionary technique of machine data-sorting.[5] Reading their 1963 article today, one is impressed with the data-gathering but struck by the absence of both psychological depth and cultural context. *Why* did wealthy people give, and why *then*, just as national business combinations were transforming Americans' understanding of the relationship of work, wealth, and virtue? How was the defeat of labor protest and agrarian revolt and of visions of alternative America in the 1880s and 1890s linked to the increased giving by captains of industry such as John D. Rockefeller or by their wives and daughters, women like Olivia Sage, Helen Gould, and Nettie McCormick? What were the consequences for women philanthropists of the rise of "scientific giving" and the denigration of sentimental charity? These are questions that biography can help answer, at least in part.

Demolition

Writing a biography of Mrs. Russell Sage has involved three operations: demolition, construction, and revisioning. Demolition, because the only book on the Sages, Paul Sarnoff's *Russell Sage: The Money King* (1965) was little more than caricature. A Wall Street commodities dealer, Sarnoff uncritically adopted the view of the popular press of the time, portraying Russell and Olivia Sage as gendered opposites (she benevolent, he accumulating) and often as no more than a comic duo. Sarnoff's book, useful on Sage's business and financial career, treats Olivia Sage as a problem in Russell Sage's life (she is Camille Claudel to his Rodin), no more than an occasion for light relief in a biography that is strong on topics such as railroads, finance, and politics.[6]

Other treatments of Olivia Sage's philanthropy have been respectful but dismissive, reflecting the contemporary late-Victorian ideology of womanhood as naturally benevolent. Since self-sacrifice was the essence of Christian womanliness, a female philanthropist (even one who set up a $10 million foundation) merely confirmed Victorian gender expectations. My first task in writing about women's philanthropy, therefore, was to problematize female benevolence, to remove it from the realm of the natural and transhistorical and to frame it as an historical problem to be analyzed.[7]

Scholarly neglect of the Russell Sage Foundation occurred for somewhat different reasons. Scholars of American foundations tended to base their conclusions on the more substantial (and better documented) Rockefeller or Carnegie philanthropies.[8] The Russell Sage Foundation, with four women on its first board of trustees, its roots in nineteenth-century missions and moral reform movements, and its associations with social work, seemed anomalous in a foundation history whose practitioners had positioned it as a subfield of, and related to, organizational and business history.[9]

The growth of women's history paradoxically tended to discourage scholarly interest in upper-class women like Olivia Sage for reasons that I discuss elsewhere, notably feminist history's disdain for elite women.[10] When Olivia Sage appeared in women's history narratives, it was as little more than a foil for more activist Progressive Era women. For example, Harriot Stanton Blatch's biographer uses Sage's failure to emerge into public life to emphasize the achievements of Blatch, who did so.[11] Meanwhile, the best biography of Olivia Sage was still the 1971 sketch by Irvin Wyllie in *Notable American Women*.[12]

Construction: Journeys to and with the Subject

The construction of a life history of Mrs. Sage involved me in what has been called a biographer's "journeys to and with the subject."[13] This meant travel to places where she lived, especially Syracuse, Philadelphia, Troy, New York City, and Long Island. I found her modest grave between those of her parents in Oakwood Cemetery, Syracuse, and the graves of Russell Sage and the first Mrs. Sage (Marie Winne Sage) at another Oakwood cemetery, in Troy, New York. At the Emma Willard School (whose splendid buildings were a gift from Mrs. Sage the year after she was widowed), I used the records of the Troy Female Seminary and the Emma Willard Association, and in numerous university archives I read the correspondence of university presidents and fundraisers with Sage and her representatives. I visited Carlisle, Pennsylvania, where in the 1880s Richard Pratt's Indian boarding school inspired the Sages and other evangelical laypeople to pour money into the cause of Protestant "Americanization" of Indian children—an example of the sort of philanthropy that a later age would call into question. On Long Island, I walked by the salt marshes at Lawrence where her summer house once stood, found myself during the season at Sag Harbor and East Hampton, places that she considered sacred because of their connection with two branches of her mother's family, the Piersons and the Jermains.

Then there were journeys *with* the subject. Archival research allowed me to piece together the narrative of various stages in her life: girlhood in Syracuse, education at Troy Female Seminary in 1846–1847, paid work as a teacher and governess from 1851 to 1869, late marriage to financier-politician Russell Sage, and the development of a public role as a benevolent matron between 1869 and 1906. Finally, with her widowhood in 1906, Sage plunged into philanthropy, making it her full-time work during the last twelve years of a ninety-year life, and spending millions on hundreds of different causes. All this satisfying activity of her late years was crowded into her old age: the Foundation was established when she was seventy-eight, and her *eminence grise*, Robert de Forest, tells that at the close of the first trustees' meeting she exclaimed, "I am nearly eighty years old and I feel as if I were 'just beginning to live.'"[14]

New Sources

It is a measure of earlier lack of interest in women philanthropists that the main archival sources for Sage's life, the Russell Sage Foundation Papers at the Rockefeller Archive Center, represent only a remnant, for most of her correspondence and papers (including her large clipping collection) were probably thrown away after her death. None of her papers seem to have been used to write the two-volume official history of the Russell Sage Foundation published in 1949. Whatever remained of Sage's papers seem to have been disposed of long before the Foundation's records were moved from New York City to the Rockefeller Archive Center in 1985.[15] A few years ago, I traveled in great anticipation to read these papers, which had been newly catalogued and opened to researchers. Alas, the five thousand letters turned out to be mainly from the last twelve years of a ninety-year life. Worse still, most of them were begging letters *to* Mrs. Sage, or letters thanking her for gifts and begging for more. Few were written by her. However, the letters often had annotations by Sage or her secretary as to the disposition of the request. I remembered a painting I had seen in the National Gallery in London (a Velasquez, I believe), of a reclining nude, a back view. All you can see of the subject's face is the reflection in the mirror before her. Like the woman in the painting, Olivia Sage controlled what we could know of her. *She* would determine how I could see her.

In fact, the letters told me a great deal. They showed a decisive mind at work, weighing competing claims, rewarding some and rejecting others. How had she formed the criteria by which she gave hundreds of thousands of dollars to one cause and refused to give to another? The letters revealed that her philanthropy operated under a number of unwritten conventions that petitioners broke at their peril.

The letters showed how people framed Sage as a benevolent woman and as "not at all a public woman."[16] But they also revealed that she understood herself rather differently, as an agent of progress for American women, for example, and as the embodiment of duty and longsuffering. "Private greifs [*sic*] must not stand in the way of public duties," she wrote, citing her lifelong model, Emma Willard.[17] They revealed the religious springs of her giving, but they also sounded other, less anticipated themes: education, livelihood, reform, nationality. A female law student at New York University signed a letter to Sage, "Yours with admiration, A fellow-student."[18]

Other sources lay to hand. Sage's essay "The Opportunities and Responsibilities of Leisured Women" (1905) had not been taken seriously as a blueprint for her philanthropy, even though it served this function as surely as Carnegie's essay "Wealth" or John D. Rockefeller's "The Benevolent Trusts" help illuminate those bodies of philanthropy. The essay offers a window into her motivation as she began her philanthropy. Even the title, "Opportunities and Responsibilities," nicely captures the dual aspects of Sage philanthropy as both self-realization and duty.[19]

Revisioning

To a greater extent than I had expected, biographical writing became an exercise in revisioning. The biographer is supposedly more truly "the servant of archival materials" than the historian.[20] But because what I found in the archives did not match Olivia Sage as she had been portrayed by historians, I found myself not only returning to the archives but also attempting an imaginative reconstruction of Sage's life. Disciplines other than history helped me a great deal: from cultural anthropologists I learned that more is involved in gift-giving than altruism. Studies in autobiography and biography taught me to be alert to the subterfuges of self-presentation in historical subjects, to ask not only "What did women give and to what causes?" but also "What were the consequences of women's description of their motives as benevolent?"[21] Autobiographical materials, seemingly the most valuable sources, are also the most mediated, "fraught with questions of self-presentation, emulation, social convention, and self-censorship." I also had to ask of my subject, "When she described her motives as benevolence, was it true?"[22]

Reading the Silences

Dealing with gaps in the evidence and reading the silences is part of any biographer's task. I knew that for twenty-two years, from graduation in 1847 to marriage in 1869, Sage was a wage-earner, a teacher and governess and that she suffered from ill-health. With few primary sources to go on for this stage of her life, I explored the "liminal" position of the governess—the paid employee who is almost (but not quite) a guest in her employer's home. I speculated about the ill-health that rendered Sage (and many other Victorian women) "invalids." And I used studies of domestic fiction to help me understand Sage's taste in novels (George Eliot, Susan and Anna Warner, Jane Austen). These borrowings helped open up useful avenues of speculation and suggested plots and motivation.[23]

By the 1890s Sage was an upper-class matron of formidable respectability but little spending power, crusading for well-paying careers for women and for vocational education, expressing her bitterness about women's lack of professional opportunities and of the right even to speak. Accordingly, when she began to spend, she did not direct her benevolence to the poor but to institutions and to a group I am calling the déclassées—the shabby governesses and retired teachers living on tiny pensions. I read this as a reflection of her experiences as a working woman and her empathy for working women, of her understanding that women's emancipation had an economic dimension.

Finding a Voice

I used the concept "finding a voice" to explain (or more modestly, to explore) Sage's activities in the period before her philanthropy began. In the 1880s and 1890s she was a lady manager for the Women's Hospital of New York, sat on its board of governors, and was a fundraiser and treasurer.

It was enormously important that Sage, stung to anger by the marital infidelities of her husbands, found a voice in the 1890s as the president of the Emma Willard Association.[24] By collecting and publishing the biographies of 3,500 Troy Seminary alumnae in the volume *Emma Willard and Her Pupils*, Sage created a new community of organized women.[25] Shortly afterward, in 1894, she began to support the woman-suffrage amendment in New York State, opening her home parlor to suffrage meetings of hundreds of women.

Now I had a prehistory for my philanthropist: I had a fairly good idea of her mental world (her "imagined communities") and her experiences before she inherited her husband's fortune. I understood her class background and the kinds of exclusions that shaped it. Blacks, for example, came into Olivia Sage's mental world as a romantic absence, connected to the domestic slaves that were part of the fondly imagined past of her mother's Long Island childhood home.

All of this prepared me to deal with Sage's philanthropy from 1906 to 1918. The spectacular philanthropy, with its obsessions and exclusions, could be read in the light of that earlier history of fragmentary activism for suffrage and missions, women's education, and civic commemoration. Except when she was derailed, bamboozled, or pressured into abandoning favorite causes, her philanthropy was essentially an extension of these earlier enthusiasms.[26]

It has been suggested that a single life is, by itself, not a useful analytical tool. In comparison with social science, biography seems "an exceedingly unsystematic way of gleaning patterns or establishing verifiable trends."[27] But my work on Mrs. Russell Sage has not only revealed new information about a neglected and misunderstood figure in early twentieth-century philanthropy, but, by yielding a richer understanding of the role of philanthropy in the activity of Progressive Era elite women, it helps map women's activism across class lines.[28] Perhaps this life story, after all, can suggest ways to reimagine existing paradigms about wealth, gender, and self-representation in the Gilded Age and Progressive Era. It can provide fresh evidence that "Progressivism" was a phenomenon occurring as well in the space between the state and the domestic, outside the arenas of courts and parties. I am encouraged by the recent publication of wonderful biographies that use life stories to present a series of big arguments about American society and reform. I'm thinking of Kathryn Sklar's study of Florence Kelley, Peter Conn's biography of Pearl Buck, of the biographies of anthropologist Elsie Clews Parsons by Desley Deacon, abolitionist Sojourner Truth by Nell Painter, and social worker Miriam Van Waters by Estelle Freedman.[29] All document the agency of individuals, yet they also range widely beyond, illuminating American society and complementing and enriching existing scholarship. They inspire me as I continue to write the history of philanthropy as life history.

Notes

This paper was prepared for the conference "Philanthropy in History" at the Indiana University Center on Philanthropy, Indianapolis, Indiana, September 25–26, 1997. The author gratefully acknowledges the support of the Indiana University Center on Philanthropy, which funded work on this project during 1996. Conference organizers Ellen Lagemann and Susan Kastan provided valuable assistance. Support for research travel on various phases of this study was provided by the National Endowment for the Humanities, by Auburn University's Vice-President for Research, and by research grants from Auburn University's College of Liberal Arts. Paula Backscheider also encouraged me as a biographer.

1. Arthur Huntington Gleason, "Mrs. Russell Sage and Her Interests," *World's Work* 13 (November 1906): 8184.

2. On the establishment of the Foundation, see Robert W. de Forest, "Suggestions for a Possible Sage Foundation. Memorandum Made by R. W. de F. for Mrs. Sage, December 10, 1906"; Margaret Olivia Sage, "Statement of Mrs. Sage for the Press," typed, n.d., Series 1, Box 2, Folder 11, Russell Sage Foundation Papers, Rockefeller Archive Center, Pocantico Hills, North Tarrytown, New York (hereafter cited as RSF). The Foundation received $10 million from Mrs. Sage in 1907 and an additional $5 million in 1918.

3. On Olivia Sage, see Ruth Crocker, "From Widow's Mite to Widow's Might: The Philanthropy of Margaret Olivia Sage," *Journal of Presbyterian History* 74, no. 4 (Winter 1996): 253–64; Irvin Wyllie, "Margaret Olivia Slocum Sage," in Edward T. James et al., eds., *Notable American Women*, vol. 3 (Cambridge, Mass.: Belknap Press of Harvard University Press, 1971), 222–23.

The Foundation has been the subject of several recent studies, especially David C. Hammack and Stanton Wheeler, *Social Science in the Making: Essays on the Russell Sage Foundation, 1907–1972* (New York: Russell Sage Foundation, 1994). See also David C. Hammack, "The Russell Sage Foundation, 1907–1947: An Historical Introduction," in *The Russell Sage Foundation: Social Research and Social Action in America, 1907–1947* (Frederick, Md.: UPA Academic Editions, 1988), and "Russell Sage Foundation," in Howard M. Keele and Joseph C. Kiger, eds., *Foundations: The Greenwood Encyclopedia of American Institutions* (Westport, Conn.: Greenwood, 1984), 373–80. The official foundation history is John M. Glenn, Lilian Brandt, and F. Emerson Andrews, *Russell Sage Foundation, 1907–1946*, 2 vols. (New York: Russell Sage Foundation, 1947). A recent study which includes discussion of the Russell Sage Foundation is Judith Sealander, *Private Wealth and Public Life: Foundation Philanthropy and the Reshaping of American Social Policy from the Progressive Era to the New Deal* (Baltimore: Johns Hopkins University Press, 1997).

4. Guy Alchon, *The Invisible Hand of Planning: Capitalism, Social Science, and the State* (Princeton: Princeton University Press, 1985); James A. Smith, *The Idea Brokers: Think Tanks and the Rise of the New Policy Elite* (New York: Free Press, 1991).

5. Merle Curti, Judith Green, Roderick Nash, "Anatomy of Giving: Millionaires

in the Late Nineteenth Century," *American Quarterly* 15, no. 3 (Fall 1963): 416–35. The authors were inspired by the recently published survey, W. K. Jordan, *Philanthropy in England, 1480–1660* (New York: Russell Sage Foundation, 1959); however, reviewers soon pointed out that the apparent rise in moneys spent on philanthropy actually reflected inflation of the currency.

6. Paul Sarnoff, *Russell Sage: The Money King* (New York: Ivan Obolensky, 1965).

7. Other scholars who have shown the way are Kathleen D. McCarthy, *Women's Culture: American Philanthropy and Art* (Chicago: University of Chicago Press, 1991); *Noblesse Oblige: Cultural Philanthropy in Chicago* (Chicago: University of Chicago Press, 1982); Kathleen McCarthy, ed., *Lady Bountiful Revisited: Women, Philanthropy, and Power* (New Brunswick, N.J.: Rutgers University Press, 1990), and Lori Ginzberg, *Women and the Work of Benevolence: Morality, Politics and Class in the Nineteenth-Century United States* (New Haven: Yale University Press, 1990).

8. Ellen Condliffe Lagemann, *Private Power for the Public Good: A History of the Carnegie Fund for the Advancement of Teaching* (Middletown, Conn.: Wesleyan University Press, 1983); Lagemann, *The Politics of Knowledge: The Carnegie Corporation, Philanthropy and Public Policy* (Middletown, Conn.: Wesleyan University Press, 1989); Barry D. Karl and Stanley N. Katz, "The American Private Philanthropic Foundation and the Public Sphere, 1890–1930," *Minerva* 19 (Summer 1981): 236–70.

9. To Barry Karl and Stanley Katz the Russell Sage Foundation seemed somehow less than authentic. They wrote, "The Russell Sage Foundation, founded in 1907 by Olivia Sage with the inheritance from her despised financier-husband, employed the form and rhetoric of the foundation with a general purpose *but in fact it represented a continuation and modernization of the tradition of social work*" [emphasis added]. Karl and Katz, "The American Private Philanthropic Foundation and the Public Sphere, 1890–1930," 247. Nevertheless, they have provided the essential theorizing on which foundation scholarship rests. See Barry D. Karl and Stanley N. Katz, "Donors, Trustees, Staffs: An Historical View, 1890–1930," in *The Art of Giving: Four Views on American Philanthropy. Proceedings of the Third Rockefeller Archive Center Conference*, October 14, 1977 (Rockefeller Archive Center, 1979), and "Foundations and Ruling Class Elites," *Daedalus* 116 (Winter 1987): 1–40.

Guy Alchon makes an argument similar to mine about the historical literature of foundations. See Guy Alchon, "Mary Van Kleeck and Social-Economic Planning," *Journal of Policy History* 3, no. 1 (1991): 1–23.

10. This reflected the origins of feminist history in social history. Ruth Crocker, "Unrepresentable in Our Narratives: Women's Philanthropy and Women's History," MS in possession of the author; "Mrs. Russell Sage: Power, Difference, Money," paper delivered at the Conference of the Western Association for Women Historians, Asilomar, California, June 1997.

11. Ellen Carol DuBois, "Working Women, Class Relations, and Suffrage Militance: Harriot Stanton Blatch and the New York Woman Suffrage Movement, 1894–1909," *Journal of American History* 74 (June 1987): 34–58. See also Ellen Carol DuBois, *Harriott Stanton Blatch and the Winning of Woman Suffrage* (New Haven: Yale University Press, 1990).

12. Wyllie, "Margaret Olivia Slocum Sage." Wyllie had authored, *The Self-Made Man in America* (New York: Free Press, 1954, 1966), and was familiar with Russell Sage's career.

13. "Journeys to and with the Subject," Introduction to Carol Ascher, Louise de Salva, and Sara Ruddick, eds., *Between Women: Biographers, Novelists, Critics, Teachers,*

and Artists Write about Their Work on Women (Boston: Beacon, 1984). See also Carolyn G. Heilbrun, *Writing a Woman's Life* (New York: Ballantine, 1988); Sara Alpern, Joyce Antler, Elisabeth Israels Perry, and Ingrid Winther Scobie, eds., *The Challenge of Feminist Biography: Writing the Lives of Modern American Women* (Urbana: University of Illinois Press, 1992).

14. Robert W. de Forest, "Margaret Olivia Sage, Philanthropist," *Survey* 41 (1918): 151.

15. Personal communications from Professor Barry Karl to the author, January 8, 1990; February 9, 1998. See also David C. Hammack, Introduction to the Microform Edition, *Russell Sage Foundation: Social Research and Social Action in America, 1907–1947* (Frederick, Md.: UPA Academic Editions, 1988).

16. Gleason, "Mrs. Russell Sage and Her Interests."

17. "'Private greifs [*sic*] must not stand in the way of public duties,' Emma Willard." Handwritten note, [Margaret Olivia Sage], n.d., Emma Willard School.

18. "A fellow-student" to Margaret Olivia Sage, December 19, 1906, RSF Series 10, Box 88, Folder 850.

19. Margaret Olivia Sage, "Opportunities and Responsibilities of Leisured Women," *North American Review* 181 (November 1905): 712–21; Andrew Carnegie, "Wealth," *North American Review* 148 (June 1889): 653–64, and "The Best Fields for Philanthropy," idem, 149 (December 1889): 682–98; John D. Rockefeller, *Random Reminiscences of Men and Events* (New York: Doubleday, Doran, 1933).

20. "Servant of archival materials," Carolyn Steedman, "Biographical Questions, Fictions of the Self," appendix to *Childhood, Culture and Class in Britain: Margaret McMillan, 1860–1931* (New Brunswick, N.J.: Rutgers University Press, 1990), 245.

21. Ginzberg, *Women and the Work of Benevolence.*

22. Nell Irvin Painter, "Review Essay: Writing Biographies of Women," *Journal of Women's History* 9, no. 2 (Summer 1997): 161.

23. Martha Vicinus, *Independent Women: Work and Community for Single Women* (Chicago: University of Chicago Press, 1995); Lee Chambers-Schiller, *Liberty, A Better Husband: Single Women in America, 1780–1840* (New Haven: Yale University Press, 1984); Diane Price Herndl, *Invalid Women: Figuring Feminine Illness in American Fiction and Culture* (Chapel Hill: University of North Carolina Press, 1993).

24. "Russell Sage Made Love: That, at Least, Is the Complaint of Delia Keegan," *The New York Times*, July 19, 1893, 2.

25. Mary Jane Fairbanks, comp., *Emma Willard and Her Pupils, or Fifty Years of the Troy Female Seminary, 1822–1872* (New York: Published by Mrs. Russell Sage, 1898). Historian Anne Scott was the first to recognize the importance of this biographical dictionary. See Anne Firor Scott, "'The Ever-Widening Circle': The Diffusion of Feminist Values from the Troy Female Seminary," *History of Education Quarterly* 19 (Spring 1979): 3–25.

26. In *Splendid Donation: A Life of Mrs. Russell Sage* (Indiana University Press, forthcoming), I discuss at length how Robert W. de Forest, Sage's attorney and advisor, siphoned off Sage's money to his favorite causes.

27. Elliott Gorn and James Grossman, "Materials descriptive of the 1997 NEH seminar, 'Social Historians Write Biography,'" typescript, March 1997. The seminar directors were both social historians embarking on biography.

28. I'm grateful to Nancy Hewitt for this formulation.

29. Kathryn Kish Sklar, *Florence Kelley and the Nation's Work* (New Haven: Yale University Press, 1995); Peter S. Conn, *Pearl Buck: A Cultural Biography* (New York:

Cambridge University Press, 1996); Nell Irvin Painter, *Sojourner Truth: A Life, A Symbol* (New York: W. W. Norton, 1996); Desley Deacon, *Elsie Clews Parsons: Inventing Modern Life* (Chicago: University of Chicago Press, 1997); Estelle Freedman, *Maternal Justice: Miriam Van Waters and the Female Reform Tradition* (Chicago: University of Chicago Press, 1996).

16 Local Philanthropy Matters

Pressing Issues for Research and Practice

William S. McKersie

LOCAL PHILANTHROPY MATTERS. Historians and other scholars have long known this fact. Thousands of donors across American towns and cities have long known this fact. Many more thousands of donees—individuals and institutions working to improve their communities with the help of local private funding—have long known this fact. Some of the broader public, a moderate share of their elected leadership and a handful of their media have long known this fact. The giving of money by private foundations, and the giving of time and expertise by their board or staff members, have been a fact of life in many communities since the mid-1900s, with a few examples of local institutional giving appearing as early as the mid-1800s.

As we approach the year 2000 the matters of local philanthropy are becoming more and more critical. Governance devolution and fiscal austerity have been the dominant public policy trends of the 1980s and 1990s. Basic doubts about largely governmental approaches to a host of public challenges—health care, child care, primary and secondary education, care of the elderly, and welfare—are pervasive. Even the minimal role of governmental agencies in such areas as the arts and humanities has been questioned. These doubts and questions have led to much debate as to how we as a nation address our shared needs and problems. Major changes have begun in several areas (welfare, health care and the arts), with change likely to follow in other areas (child care, education, care of the elderly). Simply put, the press is toward approaches and solutions that are local; small or at least aptly focused; autonomous while being accountable for definite outcomes; flexible and creative; and dependent on initiative and resources from a mix of public and private, if not solely private sources. As a result, local foundations, which have worked to varying degrees on all the issue areas undergoing or facing change, are now in as much flux as the context and targets of their work.

Despite the known fact that local philanthropy matters, and the known fact that it is facing significant change, it remains an area lacking rigorous research and commentary. Considering the nonprofit sector in total, Peter Dobkin Hall in 1995 highlighted the "epistemological problem" hindering knowledge of nonprofits and public policy. Stating that analysts of public and private sector interactions typically study national nonprofit organizations, not state, city or community nonprofits, Hall called for new "conceptual lenses" to understand the more decentralized, long-standing, public-private partnerships.[1] Regarding foundations, research and commentary have targeted individual national foundations or nation-wide foundation activity. While the foundation role in federal (and national) policy has been carefully studied, little scholarly research addresses the consequences of local foundation activism in local public policy, including education reform.[2] A prime example of "decentralized" foundation activity has been public education reform. Recent articles and essays verify that foundations have played an activist role in school reform over the past decade in Boston, Chicago, Cleveland, Los Angeles, New York, Philadelphia, San Diego, and San Francisco. However, these same sources suggest that the ramifications of this activism have not been explored adequately.[3]

This gap in analysis and commentary does not appear to be narrowing much. Most telling is the apparent focus of the various national commissions and panels that have emerged over the last couple of years to examine the future of philanthropy. There were four at last count: the National Commission on Philanthropy and Civic Renewal, supported by the Bradley Foundation, chaired by Lamar Alexander; the Institute for Civil Society's one-year project, "New Century/New Solutions" directed by Pat Shroeder; National Commission on Civic Renewal, chaired by William Bennett and Sam Nunn; and the Future of Philanthropy in a Changing America, sponsored by the American Assembly of Columbia University and Indiana University's Center on Philanthropy. If the first of these is representative, local philanthropy will be a central concern, but will be poorly handled, at least regarding the depictions of past and current behavior of local foundations. The National Commission on Philanthropy and Civic Renewal, despite operating with the premise that local philanthropy is preferred, based its analysis of the entire foundation sector on research and data pertaining to the largest, primarily national foundations.[4] Treating the sector as monolithic, it did not distinguish among foundations with a national, regional or local focus; nor did it distinguish among independent, corporate or community foundations.

The central argument of this essay should be clear by now: Local philanthropy matters and must become the focus of more rigorous research and commentary. I take this stance based on nearly twelve years of professional and academic work in the foundation field. All of it has been at the intersection of philanthropy and urban school reform, with supplementary attention to the funding of higher education, conservation, and the arts. My experiences as a program officer for the Joyce Foundation from 1986 to 1990 (and as a program consultant from 1990 to 1992), working both locally and regionally, suggest that the role and influence of foundations vary according to whether they are on home turf or further afield, especially regarding complex and contentious public policy.

This essay draws most on the data and methods from my recently completed dissertation, which examines the role of three Chicago foundations in the development and initial implementation of the 1988 Chicago School Reform Act (1987 to 1993).[5] The three foundations—the Chicago Community Trust, the Joyce Foundation, and the Woods Fund of Chicago—were selected because of their active role in the school reform process: Between 1987 and 1993, they accounted for $25.7 million of the $52.7 million Chicago foundations contributed to 176 organizations active in the school reform movement. Equally important to a comparative study of local strategic philanthropy, the three foundations also differ in structure, mission, geographic orientation, and size. The Chicago Community Trust is the nation's fourth largest community foundation, both raising and distributing funds to benefit the Chicago metropolitan area, with a board comprised of publicly appointed members. In 1993, out of assets of more than $403 million, it awarded more than $27 million for work on health, social services, arts and humanities, education, and civic affairs. The Joyce Foundation, like the Trust, is one of the 100 largest foundations in the United States. An independent foundation, operating off an endowment with no need to raise funds, Joyce has no ties to its deceased benefactor, other than through the family's former law firm, which has two members on the foundation's board. Joyce focuses its resources on the midwest, targeting conservation, culture, economic development, education, gun violence, and elections and money. In 1993, out of assets of more than $498 million, it awarded nearly $19 million; about one-half went to Chicago initiatives. The Woods Fund of Chicago is far smaller than the other two cases: Its assets in 1993 were approximately $55 million, out of which it awarded $1.8 million to Chicago concerns. Always considered an independent foundation, despite having family members on the board, Woods limited its grants to Lincoln, Nebraska, and Chicago until the end of 1993. Then, with the goal of better serving its distinct cities, two separate foundations were formed: the Woods Charitable Fund in Lincoln and the Woods Fund of Chicago. Woods's Chicago priorities are community organizing, public policies affecting families, community and civic issues, education, and the arts.

The case studies of these foundations were developed with four contrasting methods: participant observation; grant data analysis; archival research; and open-ended interviews with foundation board and staff members and critical actors in the school reform process.

This essay suggests a series of issues that scholarly research should heed if it is to help inform the practice of local philanthropy and extend our understanding of the philanthropic field. Drawn solely from my research on Chicago foundations, these issues could easily be dismissed as site- and situation-specific. Chicago foundations and their work on Chicago school reform may be exceptional, but my hunch is that for local foundations working on major community problems, the Chicago patterns are more typical than many researchers and commentators believe.

Three sets of issues are discussed below: matters of money, context, and local strategic philanthropy. The three sets are part of a comprehensive approach to foundation research and analysis. The first two deal largely with methods and methodology. The last addresses the substance of strategic behavior by local foundations.

Money Matters

A rigorous analysis of the money path is the first step toward understanding the behavior of foundations, locally or nationally. More and more foundation researchers, however, are not starting with this premise. A thorough understanding of the flow of money is the bedrock of foundation analysis, be it for scholarly or practical purposes. While such investigations are often dull, for both researcher and reader, they have to be the starting point. All the other tasks of a grantmaking foundation are rooted in the fundamental process of awarding and declining grants.

Principles of Gathering and Analyzing Grant Data

Several specific problems in data gathering and analysis proved important as I traced the flow of grants for Chicago school reform. Though not complex problems, they require special methods when fine-tuning one's understanding of foundations, especially local institutions working on local issues.

USE DATA FOR THE LEVEL BEING STUDIED

When at all possible, researchers must use data for the level of foundations they are studying. If local foundations are the focus, use data (grant and non-grant) that deal directly with local foundations. It is not wise to analyze the behavior of regional or local foundations using data on national foundations. Until there is solid evidence that foundation behavior is similar regardless of geographic orientation and size, we should not assume so.

This may seem obvious, but it has been ignored in important recent reports and commentaries on philanthropy. David Samuels's prominent 1995 critique in *The New Republic* is one example.[6] A more recent and troubling instance is the National Commission on Philanthropy and Civic Renewal. The commission apparently was stymied by a lack of research and data on local foundations. Its analysis of past and current foundation practice—and thus its recommendations for improvements needed across the foundation sector—were based on macro grant data and observations about the actions of board and staff members from a set of mostly large, national entities.[7] The commission acknowledges that its "dissatisfaction [with the priorities and practices of the foundation sector] . . . stems from misguided giving by the largest foundations."[8] They also admit that "there are . . . magnificent exceptions," but not enough, "particularly among the pacesetter foundations."[9] Unfortunately, the commission assumed that the nation's large foundations, "the organizations most apt to be seen as pacesetters by other donors,"[10] are representative of the entire sector.

My experience and research suggest that local foundations may only weakly model, and often resist, the behavior of national foundations. Indeed, the Chicago foundations I studied took a parochial pride in the role of the city's foundations in the pacesetting nature of Chicago school reform, especially relative to the distant work of the nation's most prominent foundations. While this pride may have been misplaced, and certainly deserves critical inquiry, it counters the idea that local philanthropies mimic their national brethren.

RECOGNIZE THE LIMITS OF FOUNDATION CENTER DATA

In defense of the National Commission on Philanthropy and Civic Renewal, it may have run into the same problem I did in tracking giving by Chicago foundations: The Foundation Center, widely recognized as the primary source of information about foundations, was an imprecise source of data on the work of local foundations. The Center's data did not match the consistency and reliability of the data I had gathered directly from the eleven Chicago foundations most active on Chicago school reform. The Foundation Center underreported the eleven foundations' funding by an average of thirty-five percent, and had no giving records for one-quarter of the years I studied.

This discrepancy is troubling. The Center's data, and our understanding of foundation behavior, become increasingly imprecise as the focus moves from the national to local level. This deficiency is hardly surprising given the monumental data collection and analysis tasks that the Center regularly performs. Small data sets are inherently easier to analyze than giant data sets. Dealing with only eleven Chicago foundations, I was able to scrutinize entire grant reports and accurately assemble totals for primary and secondary education (K–12). In contrast, the Foundation Center's K–12 totals are drawn from its main database, which contains grants from the 100 largest foundations and other private and community foundations that choose to file reports with the Center. Moreover, the Center does not list grants of less than $5,000. Thus, forced to sacrifice precision at the local level, the Center's data is biased toward large foundations and national foundation activity and trends.

USE LONGITUDINAL DATA FOR LONGITUDINAL CONCLUSIONS

A single year of grant data can tell us about foundation behavior only in that year. It should not be used to speak to multi-year patterns. Remarkably, there are recent examples of important research and commentary that draw longitudinal conclusions about foundation behavior from just one or two years of data. For example, Althea K. Nagai, Robert Lerner, and Stanley Rothman—in their book on foundations, public policy and the American political agenda—used Foundation Center grant data from 1986 and 1987 to talk about the public policy work of foundations beyond those two years.[11]

A similar problem occurs in a recent *Harvard Business Review* article by Christine W. Letts, William Ryan, and Allen Grossman, who argue that foundations have much to learn from how venture capitalists guide their portfolio companies through the initial stages of organizational development.[12] Letts et al. only examined grant data from 1995 to support the widely held belief that foundations rarely make multi-year grants, typically end support after two or three years, and avoid covering general operating costs.[13] The authors undermined an otherwise thoughtful article by not using longitudinal data and thus possibly missing the changing reality of foundation giving. A longitudinal analysis might have found what I found in Chicago: that many foundations award a succession of single-year grants to the same agency, that "three-years-and-out" is becoming passé, and that project-based grant recipients often include portions of their general operating needs in the project budget—a practice acknowledged and supported by the foundations.

MEASURE "EFFORT"

It is common practice when comparing foundations to look primarily at dollar totals. This practice short-changes the relative contributions of smaller foundations to particular issues. To avoid this problem, I measured "effort"—the proportion of a foundation's total budget devoted to a particular issue, in this case Chicago school reform. Figure 16.1 shows the important insights provided by this simple measure. Five Chicago foundations

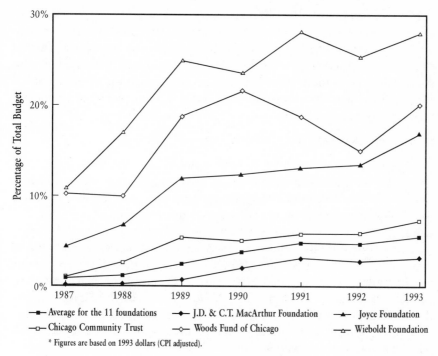

30%

Percentage of Total Budget

20%

10%

0%

1987   1988   1989   1990   1991   1992   1993

—■— Average for the 11 foundations   —◆— J.D. & C.T. MacArthur Foundation   —▲— Joyce Foundation
—□— Chicago Community Trust   —◇— Woods Fund of Chicago   —△— Wieboldt Foundation

* Figures are based on 1993 dollars (CPI adjusted).

Figure 16.1.

are contrasted with each other and with the average for the eleven foundations most active in Chicago school reform. The three largest funders of
school reform from 1987 to 1993 are presented: the John D. and Catherine
T. MacArthur Foundation, the Joyce Foundation and the Chicago Community Trust. Two smaller foundations—the Woods Fund of Chicago and the
Wieboldt Foundation—are also presented.

By this measure, Wieboldt and Woods were found to have exceeded
three much larger foundations in their school reform effort, a conclusion
supported by most observers of Chicago school reform. Thus, by measuring
the effort of these foundations, I achieved a more accurate picture of their
school reform role.

This simple measure also may unveil other differences in foundation
behavior in local public-policy processes. In Chicago, I used it to find variations in "optimal funding levels" and "risk-aversion." Not coincidentally,
the Chicago foundations' rankings for effort were the inverse of their rank
in total annual giving. The large foundations could achieve an optimal
funding level—a level ensuring self-perceived impact—with smaller shares
of total funds than the small foundations. Risk-aversion played out in the

varied proportions the foundations allotted to school reform: The three large foundations gave steady shares, while Wieboldt and Woods had more volatile patterns. The larger foundations, committing a smaller share of funds to school reform, were risking less and felt comfortable holding constant. The smaller foundations, risking larger shares of their funding on reform, felt the need to adjust their commitment annually as good opportunities ebbed and flowed.

COUNT THE NUMBER OF GRANTS

My research underscores that the number of grants awarded (or declined) is a good measure of foundation activity. Most important, it unveils the work of smaller foundations and smaller grants often masked by dollar totals. For instance, an analysis of grant frequency found a more even distribution of foundation involvement in Chicago school reform than was indicated by dollar totals. While the top three foundations accounted for seventy-eight percent of funds awarded for school reform, their share of grants was fifty-three percent. Moreover, the rank order changed when grant number was the measure: most notably, Woods and Wieboldt rose to a strong third and fourth (from fifth and eighth, respectively). As noted in the discussion of "effort," this ranking more accurately measures a foundation's relative involvement in school reform.

An examination of numbers of grants also leads to a finer understanding of the substantive purpose of foundation grantmaking. The Reform Act was centered on the empowerment of parents and community members (primarily through elected local school councils, dominated numerically by parents, with equal numbers of teachers and community members). However, when funding by Chicago foundations for implementation of the Reform Act is analyzed in terms of topic, efforts aimed primarily at parents and community receive just eighteen percent of funds from 1987 to 1993, ranking third in priority. The story changes when grant numbers are counted: parents and community are the top priorities every year, garnering forty-four percent of grants, more than double the twenty percent given the second-ranked topic. The frequency of grants is revealing in Chicago because the vast majority of parent and community grants went to community-based organizations, which typically received relatively small grants from Chicago's foundations (as they do from foundations in most locales). Incidentally, Woods and Wieboldt focused the bulk of their funding and energy on parent and community empowerment, mainly by supporting community-based organizations.

USE ORGANIZATION TYPE CAUTIOUSLY

Many analyses of foundation grantmaking strategies concentrate on the types of funded organizations—such as universities, research and advocacy groups, community-based organizations, or public schools. Analyses based solely on organizational type, especially at the local level, may be faulty, because foundations typically base grantmaking decisions on the substance of potential grantees' work rather than the entity's organizational type. As one grant officer said to me, "Why should I care whether the grantee is a university? I'm looking at what they're doing." There are, of course, exceptions. For instance, the Chicago foundations tended to avoid direct funding of individual public schools, and several gave strong preference to community-based organizations.

Such exceptions make examinations of organizational type useful, but they must be woven together with analysis of the topics funded. Unfortunately, this has not been the approach of several major studies. For instance, Teresa Odendahl, in her provocative book *Charity Begins at Home*, bases her critique of funding patterns largely on the types of organizations supported.[14] The National Commission on Philanthropy and Civic Renewal made the same error when framing its argument by assuming that health agencies and universities, the top recipients of foundation giving, are doing little work related to poverty.[15] Both analyses would have benefitted from a rigorous look at the topics foundations supported, although I suspect they were hindered by a lack of good and manageable topic data for national foundations. Researchers studying local foundations can avoid this major problem because the data sets they build or use are much smaller and more manageable.

Context Matters

> It isn't theme that stamps Chicago writing so much as outlook. It's an outlook from the perspective of the country's third coast, a sweet water inland sea surrounded by prairie, a locus at the center of America where there's not much patience with fads or pretension. It's an outlook in which energy is valued over elegance; instinct over fashionable theories; and street-smarts over the academic; an outlook we used to call "having the scan" in my neighborhood, and that Ernest Hemingway, that kid from Oak Park, called the need for a good crap-detector. It's an outlook that's populist, middle-American, but at the same time too radically anti-establishment to ever be middle of the road; a point of view that takes as given the rigged, crooked nature of power and authority.[16]

Chicago foundations, like Chicago writers, are steeped in the "outlook" of the city, its "point of view." In constructing a behavioral model of foundations in Chicago, or anywhere else, context is just as important as the grants awarded or declined.

Philanthropic research must go beyond accounting. Highly quantitative analyses of foundations can be misleading. According to the late Edward J.

Meade, Jr., education program officer at the Ford Foundation for almost 30 years (1960–1989), studies focused on grant totals and trends do not offer a complete picture of the roles that foundations have played in shaping and improving public schools.[17] Meade stressed the importance of juxtaposing grantmaking statistics with contextual information that reveals the motivations, priorities, limitations, and practices of both foundations and grant seekers.

To put grantmaking in context, researchers need to examine two interrelated dimensions. One is within the foundations being studied, and requires understanding the ideas and approaches, the strategy and tactics, that surround the determination of program direction and grant awards and declines. The other dimension is outside the foundations, and requires understanding the historical and immediate factors shaping foundation behavior.

Mapping the Internal Dimension—The Problem of Access

The internal dimension, though intellectually more manageable than the external one, may be harder to understand. Access to solid data may be the primary reason for the difference. I had uncommon access to the three Chicago foundations' internal documents and members of their staffs and boards for interviews. I was a former program officer at one of the three case study foundations, and for four years I co-chaired a committee of some thirty Chicago foundations concerned with education. I am not certain that other researchers, without the same professional and personal connections, would be given similar access.

Despite this rare access, there is vital internal information that I have been unable to touch or hear: namely, the unwritten and unrecorded discussions and debates that are critical to foundations' strategic and grant decisions. While each foundation worked hard to leave a clear paper trail of its internal deliberations, they left some delicate matters unwritten. Vital but unrecorded "data" include informal interactions among colleagues, comments omitted from board meeting minutes, and matters too delicate to put to paper. Interviews can be used to try to fill these gaps, but there is always the risk that the respondents are imposing order post hoc.

The Chicago Community Trust provides a good example of how some information may be beyond the reach of researchers. I was concerned with understanding each foundation's attention to the racial and ethnic diversity of the institutions most active with Chicago school reform. Unlike those at the two other case study foundations, the Trust's archival documents and grant records revealed little evidence that diversity was a large concern. However, this observation was strongly refuted in each of my interviews with board and staff members. An informant laid it out clearly: "The Trust has not been big on writing down strategic plans, or expansive policy or program statements. Much of the real thinking and discussion about issues, such as racial diversity, occurred during formal and informal discussions, without a paper trail. Given who comprised our staff and executive committee, it would be wrong to conclude we weren't worried about diversity."[18] Subsequently, the informant added that "the Trust had many, many conversations that would not be put on paper, or made public in anyway. Researchers must understand that there is a lot of important information in foundations that is never put to paper, and thus the paper trail does not tell the full story."[19]

Mapping the External Dimension—Sectors and Interdependence

The relations among the various institutions working on a particular issue are important in understanding the external dimension of local foundation behavior. Researchers concerned with mapping this dimension might consider improving on the methodology I used in trying to understand institutional relations regarding Chicago school reform. Two areas need more attention: my consideration of four organizational sectors and my finding of institutional interdependence.

CONSIDERATION OF FOUR ORGANIZATIONAL SECTORS

I examined institutional relations from the standpoint of "organizational fields," defined by Paul J. DiMaggio and Walter Powell as sets of organizations that in the aggregate make up a known area of institutional life, including suppliers, consumers, regulatory agencies, and other organizations producing comparable services or products. DiMaggio and Powell argue that organizational fields entail tangible evidence of "interaction among organizations in the field, the emergence of sharply defined interorganizational structures of domination and patterns of coalition, an increase in the information load with which organizations in a field must contend, and the development of a mutual awareness among participants in a set of organizations that they are involved in a common enterprise."[20]

I defined an organizational field for Chicago school reform as *all the public and private sector organizations responsible for and participating in the formation, development, and implementation of the 1988 Chicago School Reform Act.* This field is comprised of four major sectors:

1. Foundations—independent, community, corporate-sponsored, and operating;
2. Nonprofits—citywide research/advocacy groups, community-based organizations, universities, race-relation agencies, unions, and educational service agencies;

3. Businesses—banks, Chicago-based national and multinational corporations, neighborhood businesses, business associations, business school reform agencies, and business social-policy agencies;
4. Government bodies—schools, central administration, school board, mayor, state department of education, state school board, state legislature, and governor.[21]

Building on the traditional three-sector model of the American social welfare system, first advanced by Theodore Levitt, I create a fourth sector by separating foundations from nonprofits.[22] One of the lessons from my Chicago research is that the nonprofit sector, as legally and popularly construed, is too large and diverse to offer much value as an analytical unit. For example, there are over 1.4 million nonprofit organizations in the United States, including organizational types as diverse as social clubs, business associations, labor unions, political parties, political action agencies, funding intermediaries (e.g., foundations), churches, and service providers.[23] While foundations and other nonprofits fall within the same organizational category for federal tax purposes, they are distinct entities in several ways. Most obviously, other nonprofits must raise or earn funds to do their work, whereas most foundations operate on an endowment of donated funds and do their work when they fund nonprofits. As Hall has argued eloquently, foundations are most subject to the forces of internal and external legitimacy rather than sufficiency of financial resources. Internally, foundation personnel must come to an agreement on mission, objectives, goals, and programs. Externally, they must then seek congruences between those internal arguments and the expectations of outside constituencies—government agencies, legislators, the courts, the press, professional and trade associations, scholars, and donees.[24]

INVESTIGATION OF INTERDEPENDENCY

In keeping with recent scholarship, I considered the four sectors to be highly interdependent. The three-sector model was conceived with the assumption of sectorial independence. Now, the nonprofit sector is thought to be interdependent with the other two sectors.[25] Thus, I entered this study expecting to find far more institutional dependence than independence on the part of foundations. I examined interdependence in Chicago school reform in three ways: 1) the movement of money; 2) the interactions among professionals; and, 3) the flow of ideas.[26] In fact, much of the story regarding institutional relations in Chicago school reform deals with the interdependence of nonprofit agencies and foundations. This finding echoes Lucy Bernholz's research on the relations between private philanthropy and the public schools in San Francisco in the 1960s and 1970s.[27]

Local Strategic Philanthropy Matters

The first two issues—money and context matters—have dealt largely with methods and methodology. The final issue I discuss deals with a purely substantive matter: extending our understanding of strategic philanthropy to the local level and applying it in an era of governance devolution and fiscal constraint.

The phrase strategic philanthropy was coined by the historian Ellen Condliffe Lagemann to describe the national policy work of the Carnegie Corporation between World War II and the early 1980s.[28] Strategic philanthropy's essence is "seeking directly and deliberately to influence public agendas and policies."[29] Within Carnegie, this entailed "finding maximally effective means to achieve agreed-on ends [and] carefully thought-through, articulated, and criticized rationales for action."[30]

Although Lagemann's conception of strategic philanthropy was based on her analysis of a single, national foundation, she was in fact documenting a mode of philanthropy common among a small, yet growing and influential number of national foundations from the 1960s onward.[31] Several recent studies offer evidence that strategic philanthropy remains an influential mode of foundation behavior in the 1990s.[32] These studies concur that the number of foundations pursuing strategic philanthropy, while low, has increased markedly since the 1970s and 1980s, and that these foundations are influencing federal, state, and local governance. Over the last couple of years, *strategic philanthropy* has become prevalent in the philanthropic lexicon. With the recent propagation of commissions and panels examining the future of philanthropy, the phrase even has appeared in the popular press, including the *New York Times*.[33]

Strategic philanthropy has been challenged by a changing public affairs context—whether considered at the national, state, or local level. Simply put, governance devolution and fiscal austerity have combined since the early 1980s to spawn serious reexaminations—and realignment in many cases—of the dispersion of responsibility across the government, business, nonprofit, and foundation sectors for identifying and addressing public needs and problems. In fact, our nation's evolving ideas and approaches for addressing public issues are the main impetus for the recent questions about philanthropy's public roles and responsibilities. Lagemann herself has questioned the wisdom of following the past strategic philanthropy role:

> The quiet partnership that has existed between foundations and federal, state and local governments is unraveling. . . . [T]he government is not going to continue taking foundation programs to scale. Beyond that, as

public authorities retreat from the charitable activities they had assumed, foundations are finding themselves unable to address the social problems that are all around us. . . . And, without government assistance to translate their initiatives into legal regulations or programs or policies, [foundations have] little point in continuing the kind of support for research and program experimentation they have provided in the past.[34]

The challenge may be most pressing for the nation's big foundations, at least those that have been activists on public affairs. Lagemann implies, however, that the legitimacy of the whole foundation sector depends on identifying a new mode of strategic philanthropy: "Foundations will need to find new ways to define themselves and to operate, if they are to continue as viable institutions."[35]

Extending Our Understanding of Strategic Philanthropy

The effort by Chicago foundations to help develop, implement, and evaluate the 1988 Reform Act provides clues about local strategic philanthropy in an increasingly complex and demanding public affairs era. Although site- and scenario-specific, the Chicago story improves our understanding of strategic philanthropy in a local context. First, Chicago school reform was carried out in an environment of governance devolution and fiscal austerity. Second, it entailed extensive activity by local foundations over an extended period. From 1987 to 1993, eleven of Chicago's most active educational foundations provided over $52.7 million to 176 different organizations working on school reform in Chicago, with ninety percent of the funds flowing after the Reform Act's passage. (Of course, the grantmakers were not alone in their efforts. They were the enablers—not the instigators or leaders—of a citywide reform movement.) Finally, case study research, which I have used to capture the Chicago story, allows generalization to theoretical propositions, though not populations or universes. Case studies permit investigators to expand and generalize theories (analytical generalization), but since cases are not technically "samples," they do not allow the enumeration of frequencies (statistical generalization).[36] Therefore, as much as the Chicago case suggests a set of theoretical propositions about local strategic philanthropy, it must be tested and expanded by evidence from other cases of local foundation involvement in local public policy.

A Framework for Local Strategic Philanthropy

My framework articulates the system of ideas and approaches that motivate local foundations to intentionally intervene in local public policy and that influence their strategies and tactics. The framework identifies the key characteristics of the comprehensive mode of local strategic philanthropy exercised by the Chicago Community Trust, the Joyce Foundation, and the Woods Fund of Chicago between 1987 and 1993. I would be overly gener-ous—and creating order post hoc—to conclude that the three foundations pursued this framework in a coherent fashion. Rather, they arrived at the combination of ideas and approaches I describe partly by intent and partly by improvisation. Metaphorically, their strategic work was more like a jazz concert than a symphony performance.

The framework is designed to serve both practitioners and researchers. For practitioners in and around foundations, the framework offers guid-ance for advancing specific public-policy solutions to critical problems in the local arena. For researchers and commentators, it points to aspects of the intersection between foundations and local public affairs that deserve more attention. This framework is far from the final word on local strategic philanthropy. I believe that practice and research are iterative processes: They continually build on, alter, or even reject past work and inquiry. In keeping with this tradition, I hope that subsequent researchers and practi-tioners will probe this framework's validity and reliability.

The framework has three parts: the rationale for pursuing strategic phi-lanthropy, the institutional dimensions of this mode of philanthropy, and its elements. These parts reflect my thinking as a foundation staff member. When I set out to develop and implement a grantmaking program, or at least a set of grants or actions aimed at a particular goal, I consider my plans on three general levels. First, I consider my reasons (the rationale) for undertaking these plans, largely because I need to secure support from fel-low staff members, executive staff, the board, and stakeholders outside the foundation. Second, I contemplate what my efforts will entail both within and outside the foundation (the two main institutional dimensions). Finally, I estimate what I am actually going to do to achieve my goal—what the major elements of my strategic behavior will be.

At the heart of the framework are eight major themes that became ap-parent in my analysis of the case studies, and that now appear essential to the foundations' work on the Reform Act. For each thematic area, I first postulate an ideal mode of strategic philanthropy—"what ought to be"—and then describe how Chicago foundations actually worked with the theme—"what is." In examining "what is," I focus on commonalities in strategic behavior, but also identify places where the foundations differed due to their distinct structures, missions, geographic orientation, and size. I found much merit in the commonalities of their approaches—indeed, they are the basis for most of my arguments about the "ideal" model of local strategic philanthropy. My assertions about the ideal are my interpretations of the ideas and approaches I discovered in Chicago that have wider application.

RATIONALE FOR STRATEGIC PHILANTHROPY

Government Action Is Necessary. These three foundations believed that only government has the resources necessary to meet the largest public challenges. These funders understood that their resources pale compared to the challenge of improving a giant public school system, beset by problems rooted in a mix of organizational, professional, political, economic, and social failings. At the same time, these foundations did not endorse big government or unrestrained public intervention.

Foundation Action Is Necessary. The foundations saw themselves as government's essential partners in addressing the large challenges. While foundations cannot bankroll the development, implementation, and evaluation of major policies or practices intended to reform public education, they can, ideally, bolster the efficiency, creativity, diversity, and flexibility of the public sector's approaches to public problems. Less grandly, the private sector also can help to directly alleviate some of the symptoms of weak schools by supporting remediation or enrichment programs for students and staff.

Nonprofit Action Is Necessary. These foundations recognized that nonprofit organizations are their primary vehicle for influencing public policy. Through research, advocacy, publications, organizing, lobbying (within legal limits), training, and education, nonprofits bring diverse ideas, data, and people into the policy making and political process. In the education arena, they, rather than schools or school systems directly, are the agencies that private dollars typically support to help develop, implement, and evaluate school reform policies and practices.

Foundations Need to Respond to Local Events. Finally, these local foundations felt that they must help with large public processes that generally fit their interests, even if they are not enamored with the specifics. The Chicago Community Trust, whose mission is to respond to community needs and initiatives, could hardly ignore the Reform Act, the community's chosen means for school improvement. The Joyce Foundation, a regional grantmaker, felt a similar obligation to help with the Reform Act because it was "happening in our backyard, our hometown." The Woods Fund of Chicago, with its institutional concern for the intersection of Chicago's communities and citywide policy, naturally felt it had to play an active, ongoing role.

THE DIMENSIONS OF STRATEGIC PHILANTHROPY IN CHICAGO

There are two operational dimensions of strategic philanthropy: *external* and *internal*. Externally, the foundations purposefully involve themselves in selected aspects of the development, implementation, and evaluation of local public agendas and policies. Internally, they establish general action plans, allocate funds, and allot staff time to advance their priorities and those of related public agendas and policies. Strategies are developed and maintained through extensive staff research and staff and board discussion.

ELEMENTS OF STRATEGIC PHILANTHROPY

An Evolving Strategy. The practice of strategic philanthropy regarding particular public issues evolves over time in response to the changing context that surrounds its philanthropic goals and objectives. Complex, quickly changing public issues typically force a foundation to begin with goals and objectives that are not always quantifiable or discretely measurable. Therefore, foundations cannot hope to develop and follow a clean and immutable script of action plans, budget allocations and staff-time allotments to reach their strategic objectives. They need a considerable amount of flexibility to respond to the range of ideas and approaches that are relevant to their goals and that may emerge as events unfold.

The strategies of two of the case study foundations exhibited this evolutionary tendency in different ways. The Trust, after settling on a detailed strategy for a major elementary- and secondary-education initiative in 1988, tended not to make program-wide plans in the subsequent years in order to ensure "maximum flexibility" for responding to unknown, future needs. Joyce, which devoted considerable time every year to developing strategies and tactics for its region-wide education work, valued a certain amount of "muddling around" and "learning by doing." It recognized that an ironclad approach to planning would be foiled by the quicksilver and diverse nature of school reform across its four Midwest cities.

Woods was a counter example—largely due to its small size and clarity of vision. While claiming that its school reform work was "not strategic," Woods made its mark because of strategic focus. For seven years it did not waver from the belief that the first step to improved learning was fostering parent and community participation in school governance and citywide policy formation.

Staff Outreach and Research. Strategic work on a particular issue should begin with an effort to learn what people outside the foundation think about that issue. Staff and board members should extensively debate the findings of the research effort as they are shaped into plans for strategic action. Staff members, in particular, should cultivate and maintain a network of sources for information on the current status of the issue being targeted and on the need for alternative approaches.

Before the Reform Act was developed, program staff for each of the case study foundations conducted separate, formal outreach efforts on school reform, coincidentally during roughly the same period (1985 to 1986). Staff for each foundation interviewed about thirty individuals from Chicago and elsewhere about how public education in Chicago could be reformed. While none of the three conducted formal outreach from 1987 to 1993, most staff and some board members constantly updated their knowledge of emerging reform ideas and approaches through media reports, educational publications, research by reform advocates and academics, and most importantly networks of personal contacts in the field. Staff from Joyce and Woods, which placed a premium on staff action, frequently attended reform meetings and events across the city.

Issue and Institutional Persistence. Foundations must be willing to commit resources to an issue or institution for a five- to ten-year period. Change takes time, especially when the targets are schools and school districts built on complex patterns of organizational and individual behavior. Foundations often find persistence difficult to maintain because it conflicts with several ideal philanthropic operating principles, each rooted in the belief that foundations are uniquely free of market or governmental accountability. Most notable among these principles are

1. *Leverage.* Foundations ideally provide temporary levers for organizations and individuals identifying and solving problems.
2. *Maximum Flexibility.* It is essential to keep funds unencumbered because the power of foundation money lies in flexibility far more than size.
3. *Pluralism.* Funding a mix of ideas, individuals, and institutions is the best way to help a democratic society improve itself.

Each of these principles is threatened by the principle of persistence, which ties foundations' limited funds to a particular set of ideas or institutions.

At the end of 1993, the three foundations were completing at least their seventh consecutive year of supporting the Chicago school-reform effort. School reform garnered a larger share of each foundation's educational budget nearly every year. A core group of grantees, representing about sixty-five percent of the foundations' school reform funding, received five to seven years of continuous support. Considering the "three years and out" stereotype of foundation-grantee relations, seven-plus years of funding is notable. Joyce and Woods knew from experience that changing complex public policies and agencies requires long-haul grantmaking. While the Trust also understood the slow pace of change, its patience was primarily a result of the fact that the Reform Act remained the community's chosen method to improve schools.

Significantly, the foundations' perseverance occurred in the face of doubts about the Reform Act's basic ideas and approaches. The Trust's long-term involvement was secured when the reform movement broadened its agenda from a focus on governance to a concern with teaching and learning issues that more closely fit the Trust's priorities. Joyce overcame its ambivalence because of the board's and staff's fundamental belief that it was more important to get involved than to sit back and criticize the law's deficiencies. Woods, abiding by its faith in community-driven policy change, felt that any concerns it had about the short-term educational effects of the law were outweighed by the long-term value of getting parents and community members involved in schooling.

Gap-Funding. Foundations working on local public-policy issues often have to devote funding and staff time to the implementation of whatever new policies and practices arise from their efforts. This strategy, which governance devolution and fiscal constraint have made necessary, I call "gap-funding." For gap-funding to work, all involved—foundations, nonprofits, and public agencies—must understand that foundations can play this role only temporarily. Regarding such funding as permanent support would undermine (in theory) local foundations' freedom to support creative and diverse solutions to local problems. The obvious tension between the need for persistence and the need for gap-funding to be temporary is manageable. The keys to managing this tension are:

1. Viewing gap-funding as an obligation of at least five years.
2. Expecting the eventual change in funding to occur gradually.
3. Once the initial obligation has been met, shifting to front-end work on the same issue for another five years or so. Parameter-pushing, the next element of local strategic philanthropy, is the prime candidate for any funding taken away from gap-funding.

The Trust, Joyce, and Woods knowingly took on a gap-funding role with Chicago school reform. The Reform Act was major public policy—a state law mandating far-reaching changes in the governance and management of the Chicago public schools. However, the new law came with minimal public funds for implementation (about $1,500 per school). The law did provide individual schools more discretionary money for local initiatives (the typical elementary school and high school annually have about $450,000 and $800,000 to spend, respectively), but most of these funds went to basic local needs, such as more teachers, supplies, or new curriculum materials. As a result, a relatively large share of the three foundations' funding for school reform from 1989 to 1993 went to help implement the law, and often to fill gaps in its design, content, or start-up funding. It was the first- or second-most-funded topic for each foundation and garnered nearly all of Woods's reform funding, about thirty percent of Joyce's, and twenty-five percent of the Trust's.

The Trust's support for implementation of the law's structures and mandates fell annually after 1989 as it shifted attention to other aspects of school reform. Joyce, which undertook gap-funding after much staff deliberation, constantly questioned whether it was an apt role and gradually moved away from supporting basic implementation of the law's particulars. Instead, Joyce concentrated on citywide (or at least multi-site) efforts to broaden the school reform's focus and gauge its effectiveness (in essence, the parameter-pushing described below). Woods, more deeply committed to the Reform Act, maintained support for implementation longer than the other foundations. Its approach was to support implementation until the schools and central office could manage the new governance system. However, this approach left Woods unsettled, fearing that long-term implementation support could distract the Fund's limited dollars from their primary role. "The foundation role," according to Jean Rudd, "is not to provide sustaining support, like the United Way. The role is to help the nonprofit sector look ahead, stimulate studies, demonstrate and advocate new concerns and opportunities to bring about useful change. . . . It is a mathematical reality that foundations cannot support new and upcoming issues, creativity and leaders unless it ceases funding others."[37] Balancing this role with the necessity of temporary gap-funding, Rudd believes, was Woods's greatest challenge: "Our hardest work, our most serious assignment . . . is to make the hard judgement on when to start and stop funding."[38]

All three foundations recognized that gap-funding was not an ideal role, but a necessary one. The Trust, again in a "responsive mode," felt they had to help the community and school system deal with a radically new governance system. Joyce and Woods, to whom public policy was an overarching priority, believed they should offer support at multiple points in the public policy process, including development, implementation, and evaluation. In time, all three came to understand that the implementation process, largely dependent on limited private resources, was not strategic, systematic, or equitable. They and other foundations were mostly funding work in select areas of the city, leaving many schools and neighborhoods unassisted. One lesson from Chicago is that implementation support is a basic necessity and is too important to be left to foundations alone. Over-reliance on private solutions ensures inequity. Simply put, Lester Salamon was correct when he warned that "philanthropic insufficiency" is a pitfall of turning to foundations, and the nonprofit sector generally, to cover gaps in public sector attention to societal problems.[39] The Chicago foundations would likely step to the plate again to help with major policy implementation—as they should. But they would do so with a keener sense—and overt disclaimers—about the limits of their gap-funding role.

Parameter-Pushing. At the same time that foundations are bolstering new policies and practices through gap-funding, they need to expand the range and quality of ideas, approaches, institutions, and individuals working to solve public problems. This may mean critiquing the same policies or practices they are helping to implement. Some grants can accomplish both ends. For example, an ongoing evaluation of a new policy both prompts questions about alternative ways to address the problem and advances effective implementation.

The Trust devoted the bulk of its Chicago school-reform funding to expanding what it considered a "narrow reform agenda." Over seven years, its support for governance reform topics fell, while support for teaching and learning concerns grew. Largely responding to available organizations, the Trust's parameter-pushing increased as the range of groups working on school reform in Chicago broadened. Joyce's funding also went mostly to parameter-pushing. From the birth of the Reform Act, Joyce worked to extend its focus beyond governance, primarily by funding evaluations of the reform process and organizations that would constructively add more "educational" ideas and approaches to the reform process.

Woods, in contrast, did not push hard at the parameters of the Reform Act. One of the more important differences among the three foundations is that what the Trust and Joyce considered narrow and confining about the Reform Act, Woods saw as the means to critical breadth and openness. For Woods, the emphasis on parent and community empowerment ensured a multi-faceted reform movement that encouraged new actors and perspectives. Woods devoted a significant share of its funds to monitoring the progress of the Reform Act. When the school-reform movement broadened its focus in 1993, Woods expanded its grantmaking only slightly.

The three foundations' differing conceptions of school reform and the process required to improve student learning played out in their parameter-pushing. The Trust focused on the needs and abilities of educational professionals, both at the school and central administration levels. Parents and communities were seen as vital supports to effective schooling, but not as important loci of governance. In addition, because the Trust believed that it had to have the flexibility to respond to the community, its conceptions about reform were intentionally general. Joyce's ideas about school reform focused on schools as the unit of change, with reform led collectively by principals, teachers, parents, and community members. But its conception was not school-by-school reform; rather, it viewed public policy, at the state and district levels, as the key means to simultaneously free and enable local-level initiative. Woods approached school reform from outside the traditional education arena, viewing it as a problem of mobilizing the community for more effective public policy. This conception was rooted in Woods's institution-wide faith in community organizing as a way to foster democratic participation in public-policy processes. Like Joyce, Woods was not interested in supporting school-by-school change; it wanted to support city-wide policy efforts that would allow school- and community-level people to improve teaching and learning.

Institutional Interdependence. Foundations and nonprofit organizations are usually interdependent institutions. They are more intensely so in the context of a complex, fast-moving public-policy process. Since foundations find it difficult to create from scratch, they depend on nonprofit institutions able and willing to advance their grantmaking priorities. Generally speaking, a foundation will not advance a grantmaking priority if no organization exists to do the work. While foundations have the power to cultivate institutions to undertake specific lines of work, they do not often do so, either because such multi-year endeavors would miss the window of opportunity presented by the current policy context or because of the risk inherent in creating a new institution. The interdependence of foundations and nonprofits requires both *collaboration*—across and within sectors—and *compromise* as foundations balance their own predilections with the interests and abilities of potential grantees.

The three foundations purposely compromised their ideas and approaches while working on the Reform Act. Only Woods's conception of school reform closely matched the Reform Act's central premise that parent and community empowerment is the first step for improving student learning. For the Trust and Joyce, this concept was too narrow. Nevertheless, all three devoted significant sums and energy to the Reform Act's implementation (the work I have described as gap-funding). Some might criticize the foundations for being co-opted, or yielding too much. I consider their willingness to compromise proof of their wisdom. They correctly understood that ultimately they are part of a community and its public processes, and that their role is to help reform public institutions rather than to sit back and criticize attempts to do so. These foundations understood the reality that little or no progress is made in complex public processes without significant compromise by all involved. The ideas and approaches of the Reform Act were not perfect, but none ever will be and this set had rallied a good part of the city to action. To paraphrase board members at the Trust and

Joyce, it was better to get involved and help improve the reform from within than to sit outside being a naysayer. Moreover, it must be remembered that at least Joyce and the Trust invested more in parameter-pushing than implementing the Reform Act.

Interdependence for the Trust, Joyce, and Woods played out in their relations with two citywide research and advocacy agencies, Designs for Change and the Chicago Panel on School Policy, which were leaders in the development and implementation of the Reform Act. These agencies were the top two recipients of school reform funding among all Chicago foundations, and were also the top two grantees for Joyce (among ninety grantees) and Woods (among forty-eight grantees), and ranked fifth and seventh among the Trust's recipients (among forty-one grantees). Although the three foundations provided the nonprofits with significant funding over a long period, they had mixed feelings about the substantive and tactical moves of Designs and, to a lesser extent, the Chicago Panel. The Trust and Joyce were concerned most by Designs's aggressive, ideological approach to school reform. Although less troubled, Woods paid attention to how much Designs' agenda reflected what a diverse group of Chicagoans wanted. Nevertheless, the foundations recognized that the school reform process depended on the two agencies' talent for developing and analyzing policies and on their ability to complement one another. Finding no other citywide agencies similarly oriented or skilled, and unable to create new institutions, the foundations kept funding Designs and the Chicago Panel.

The problematic nature of interdependence surfaced in the racial and ethnic diversity of the school-reform organizations each foundation supported. The foundations worked to broaden reform's institutional base racially and ethnically, but at least at the Trust and Joyce, as both readily admitted, the track record was mixed. The movement's early days were dominated by citywide organizations that were led largely by whites (i.e., Designs, the Chicago Panel, and business associations). After the reform law's passage, the Trust and Joyce, recognizing the need to diversify the citywide institutions working on school reform, each attempted to fund citywide African-American organizations solely oriented to education. (Chicago's multi-ethnic/national Latino community was represented citywide by two major grantees.) As of 1993, they had not been able to help any African-American organization match the influence or capacity of Designs and the Chicago Panel. In retrospect, the two foundations could have worked harder at searching out organizations that might have been viable grantees after some cultivation. The hard truth remains, however, that the foundations were not turning away strong applicants from Chicago's black community during the 1987 to 1993 period.

Woods once again offers a different scenario. Like the Trust and Joyce,

Woods felt dependent on nonprofits. Board members and staff repeatedly told me that their grant record, although shaped by their interest in linking community organizing with citywide policy work, was the result of who came to them with proposals. However, Woods had few doubts about the reform movement's diversity, primarily because its attention and funding was helping to connect the community level, where the reform process was representative of Chicago, with citywide policy efforts.

Personnel Activism. In order to influence local public issues, the professional staff and board members of local foundations must directly contribute their personal expertise and energies. Grantmaking alone is not a sufficient tool. There are multiple reasons for activism: it amplifies foundations' limited funds, helps foundations stay in touch with particular issue areas, allows foundations to learn first-hand what is or is not working and what needs to be done next, and enables them to clearly communicate grantmaking priorities. Activist roles for professional staff and board members include convening groups and individuals, strategizing, writing opinion pieces, participating on task forces, and giving hands-on assistance in the redesign of particular organizations. All of these roles must be carefully exercised, so that the foundation serves as an enabler, not the leader, of public efforts to solve citywide and community problems. At the same time, personnel activism must be seen as inextricably linked to the foundation's grantmaking. Foundation personnel who take on activist roles must recognize that their credibility—and the reason they have been invited to the table—most likely lies in their financial power and not in any special expertise or knowledge they may possess.

All three foundations espoused activism, especially by staff, as a key aspect of their work on Chicago school reform. The focus and extent of activism in each case was tied to their grantmaking record and priorities. While staff from Woods and Joyce were vigorous during the entire period studied, the Trust's staff were much less active after 1988. Woods led the way, seeing activism by board and staff members as a way to leverage its resources and increase the likelihood of relevant and effective grantmaking. Woods's personnel led several collaborations among Chicago foundations to fund community and school-level reform activity and also convened several citywide meetings of school reform stakeholders. Joyce had a similar rationale for supporting staff activism, which characterized the work of its three successive education officers between 1987 to 1993. Their efforts included participating in Mayor Washington's Educational Summit at a sub-committee level, co-chairing a committee of thirty Chicago foundations concerned with education reform, staffing the first round of the school board nominating process under the Reform Act, and convening professional development meetings among school superintendents from Chicago, Cleveland, Detroit, and Milwaukee (the foundation's four target cities).

The Trust's mixed record on activism illustrates the influence of a foundation's changing local context and its grantmaking priorities. Only the first of the Trust's three successive education officers from 1987 to 1993 played an activist role. Trust personnel were especially active as the ideas and approaches that would comprise the Reform Act were being debated. A board member (as co-chair) and the education program officer played important roles in Mayor Harold Washington's Educational Summit. The education officer also worked with a group of foundations to forge a school-reform plan that went beyond parent and community empowerment. As parent and community empowerment came to dominate the school-reform process in Chicago, the education officer focused her energies on grants that advanced reforms more directly tied to teaching and learning, which were more in line with the Trust's priorities.

After the Reform Act's passage, and the departure of the first education officer for a position in higher education, the two subsequent education officers spent little time on activism. The second of the three officers started out taking an activist role, in part by publicly sharing his criticisms of the Reform Act's limits. When his criticisms were severely rebuked by several reform leaders (some of whom demanded that he be fired), the program officer shifted his energies to funding parameter-pushing efforts. The third education officer, who started in 1991 when the reform process was severely challenged by superintendent turnover and system-wide budget crises, did not take an activist role because the Trust board and staff, though certainly wanting to help with school reform, were apprehensive about the tumultuous politics and were concentrating their activism on initiatives they considered their own.

Evaluation. Foundations must evaluate their policies, grantmaking, and activism. Evaluation informs three constituencies: grantmakers, grantees, and the interested public. Foundations need to go public with their lessons, both good and bad, with the goal of helping to improve current and future work, but in a way that protects grantees. Ideally, evaluation should be based on a series of principles. First, an institutional culture of constructive questioning and criticism is necessary. Institutional patience—recognizing that complex public problems take a long time to rectify—is second. Third, foundations must understand evaluation's value; they need to give as much time to awarding grants as tracking their impact. Fourth, evaluation should not control grantmaking; it should not preclude risk-taking or the funding of efforts with outcomes that are hard to measure. Fifth, evaluation should be based on multiple measures or indicators; qualitative and quantitative measures of process and outcome must be used. Sixth, a mixture of information sources is required, including thoughtful grantees, visits to sites and communities, independent research, media analysis, and other foundation officers. Finally, the types of evaluators should be varied, ranging from the traditional (evaluation specialists and researchers or academics in the particular issue area) to the nontraditional (including practitioners with evaluation experience and freelance journalists).

The Trust, Joyce, and Woods gave attention to evaluation. While their efforts were more monitoring than evaluation, and were not what evaluation experts would necessarily consider best practice, their approaches to assessing results suggest a realistic path for foundations involved in volatile, local public-policy scenarios. To a certain extent, they each acted on the above principles. Constructive questioning and criticism are part of the culture of each of the three foundations, especially at Joyce, where staff were expected to challenge policy and grant proposals across all program areas. As noted in the earlier discussion of "persistence," each foundation was patient with school reform's progress. Proposal review and grant monitoring formed their first line of evaluation. Woods set the pace in this area, with its thorough grant-evaluation process drawing on staff, board members, and consultants. Each foundation used multiple sources of information. *Catalyst* (an independent, foundation-funded publication, devoted to documenting, analyzing, and supporting improvement in Chicago's schools) was the most common source. For more systematic research, all three drew on the Chicago Panel and the foundation-funded work of the Consortium on Chicago School Research, a collective effort by Chicago academics and educational researchers to study longitudinally the multiple effects of school reform. Finally, at least during the 1987 to 1993 period I studied, they each emphasized "soft" indicators, which spotlighted the process of implementation rather than academic outcomes. Nonetheless, the ultimate measure for each foundation was the effect of the Reform Act on student learning.

Conclusion

Local philanthropy matters and must become the focus of more rigorous research and commentary. Comprehensive approaches to understanding the work of local foundations in local public-policy processes are needed. A series of methodological issues, dealing with both matters of money and context, must be attended to carefully. Foundation grant records and the context from which they emerge, taken together, tell us far more than either one in isolation. On the money side, researchers must remember the basics: Use data from the level being studied, do not blur national, regional, and local foundations into a monolithic group (nor should community, independent, and corporate foundations be blurred); know the limits of Foundation Center data for understanding local foundations; draw longitudinal conclusions only from longitudinal data; measure "effort" and count the number of grants, especially if small foundations and small grants are important; and use organization type cautiously, ideally matching it with data on the topics funded. Regarding context, researchers must look at an internal and external dimension. The internal, probably harder to capture due to limited access, is comprised of the strategies and tactics, the ideas and approaches, that guide decisions on programs, grants, and the allocation of staff time. The external dimension is comprised most importantly of the other local institutions working on the same problem or set of problems. The key is to understand the interplay among these institutions and how it shapes, and is shaped by, foundation policy, grants, and activism.

A better handle on methods will help us get a better handle on the role local foundations have been playing, and need to play, in addressing important local public problems. Strategic philanthropy—the intentional intervention of foundations in the public-policy process—faces challenges. Governance devolution and fiscal austerity have combined over the past fifteen years to change the targets and context of strategic philanthropy. Policy trends point toward more devolution, on top of which there is now a growing movement to advocate more local philanthropic activity. How these changes have influenced, and are likely to influence the work of foundations in cities is not well known. The work of three Chicago foundations on Chicago school reform provides one set of clues. They suggest several necessary elements to local strategic philanthropy:

- Foundations should set policies and formulate strategies for grantmaking and activism, but should allow those policies and strategies to evolve, with much learning and responding along the way.
- Staff outreach and research should be formal and ongoing, with the foundation listening to a range of opinions.
- Persistence should prevail over other principles pushing shorter-term support.
- Gap-funding should be provided temporarily and strategically.
- Foundations should push at the limits of the same new policies and practices they are helping to implement. This dual strategy expands the quality of ideas and institutions working on public problems.
- The interdependence of institutions necessitates collaboration and compromise. The tendency to support existing organizations in a fast moving, complex policy process must be leavened with staff outreach to broaden the quality and mix of ideas and institutions.

- Personnel activism is a valuable complement to grantmaking, but must be undertaken with care so that the foundation serves as an enabler, not leader, of public efforts to solve citywide and community problems.
- Foundations working on local issues must evaluate their policies, grantmaking and activism. Evaluation has the basic purpose of informing foundations, grantees, and the interested public. Both good and bad lessons need to be shared, with the goal of improving current and future work.

Notes

1. Peter Dobkin Hall, "Private Initiatives, Public Needs: Privatization and Contracting Human Services in Connecticut, 1980-1994," paper presented at the annual spring research forum of the Independent Sector, Arlington, Va., 22-23 March 1995.

2. For analysis of the foundation role in federal (and national) policy, see Barry Karl, "Philanthropy, Policy Planning and Bureaucratization of the Democratic Ideal," *Daedalus* 105 (1976): 129-50. Jane Mavity and Paul Ylvisaker, "Private Philanthropy and Public Affairs," in *Research Papers Sponsored by the Commission on Private Philanthropy and Public Needs* 2 (Washington, D.C.: U.S. Department of Treasury, 1977), 795-836. Barry Karl and Stanley Katz, "The American Private Foundation and the Public Sphere, 1890-1930," *Minerva* 19 (1981): 236-70. Ellen Condliffe Lagemann, *Private Power for the Public Good: A History of the Carnegie Foundation for the Advancement of Teaching* (Middletown, Conn.: Wesleyan University Press, 1983). Peter Dobkin Hall, "Abandoning the Rhetoric of Independence: Reflections on the Nonprofit Sector in the Post-Liberal Era," in *Shifting the Debate: Public/Private Sector Relations in the Modern Welfare State*, ed. Susan A. Ostrander and Stuart Langton (New Brunswick, N.J.: Transaction Books, 1987), 11-28. Lester Salamon, "Of Market Failure, Voluntary Failure, and Third-Party Government: Toward a Theory of Government-Nonprofit Relations in the Modern Welfare State," in *Shifting the Debate: Public/Private Sector Relations in the Modern Welfare State*, ed. Susan A. Ostrander and Stuart Langton (New Brunswick, N.J.: Transaction Books, 1987), 29-49. Ellen Condliffe Lagemann, *The Politics of Knowledge: The Carnegie Corporation, Philanthropy, and Public Policy* (Chicago: University of Chicago Press, 1989). Peter Dobkin Hall, *Inventing the Nonprofit Sector* (Baltimore: Johns Hopkins University Press, 1992). Mary Anne Colwell, *Private Foundations and Public Policy: The Political Role of Philanthropy* (New York: Garland Publishing, 1993). Althea K. Nagai, Robert Lerner, and Stanley Rothman, *Giving for Social Change: Foundations, Public Policy, and the American Political Agenda* (Westport, Conn.: Praeger, 1994). Sally Covington, *Moving a Public Policy Agenda: The Strategic Philanthropy of Conservative Foundations* (Washington, D.C.: National Committee for Responsive Philanthropy, 1997).

3. Loren Renz, *Foundation Giving, 1991* (New York: Foundation Center, 1991). Jeanne Jehl and Thomas Payzant, "Philanthropy and Public School Reform: A View from San Diego," *Teachers College Record* 93, no. 3 (1992): 472-87. Theodore Lobman, "Public Education Grant Making Styles: More Money, More Vision, More Demands, *Teachers College Record* 93, no. 3 (1992): 382-402. William S. McKersie and Robert Palaich, "Philanthropy and Systemic Reform: Finding a Cross-Sector Blend of Risk-Taking and Political Will," *Education Week*, 4 May 1994, 48. Meg Sommerfeld, "Foundations Seek More Active Role in Replicating Successful Models," *Education Week*, 14

December 1994, 6. Lucy Bernholz, "Private Philanthropy and Public Schools: San Francisco in the 1960s and 1970s" (Ph.D. diss., Stanford University; Ann Arbor: UMI Dissertation Services, 1995).

4. National Commission on Philanthropy and Civic Renewal, *Giving Better Giving Smarter* (Washington, D.C.: National Commission on Philanthropy and Civic Renewal, 1997), 81.

5. William S. McKersie, "Strategic Philanthropy & Local Public Policy: Lessons from Chicago School Reform, 1987-1993" (Ph.D. diss., University of Chicago; Ann Arbor: UMI Dissertation Services, 1998).

6. David Samuels, "Philanthropic Correctness," *New Republic*, 18 and 25 September 1995, 28-36.

7. National Commission on Philanthropy and Civic Renewal, *Giving Better Giving Smarter*, 81.

8. Ibid.

9. Ibid., 87.

10. Ibid., 81.

11. Nagai, Lerner, and Rothman, *Giving for Social Change: Foundations, Public Policy, and the American Political Agenda*, 125-27.

12. Christine W. Letts, William Ryan, and Allen Grossman, "Virtuous Capital: What Foundations Can Learn from Venture Capitalists," *Harvard Business Review*, March-April 1997, 37.

13. Ibid., 39-40.

14. Teresa Odendahl, *Charity Begins at Home: Generosity and Self-Interest among the Philanthropic Elite* (New York: Basic Books, 1990).

15. National Commission on Philanthropy and Civic Renewal, *Giving Better Giving Smarter*, 14, 32-33.

16. Stuart Dybek, "Introduction," in *Chicago Stories*, ed. J. Miller and G. Anderson (San Francisco: Chronicle Books, 1993), xii.

17. Edward J. Meade, Jr., "Foundations and the Public Schools: An Impressionistic Retrospective, 1960-1990," *Phi Delta Kappan* 73, no. 2 (1991): K1-K12.

18. Albert Bennett, Interview with Author, Chicago, Ill., 21 February 1995.

19. Ibid., 17 July 1997.

20. Paul J. DiMaggio and Walter W. Powell, "The Iron Cage Revisited: Institutional Isomorphism and Collective Rationality in Organizational Fields," in *The New Institutionalism in Organizational Analysis*, ed. Walter W. Powell and Paul J. DiMaggio (Chicago: University of Chicago Press, 1991), 64-65.

21. William S. McKersie, "Sectorial Relations and Chicago School Reform: A Preliminary View from the Foundation Sector," paper presented on the panel "School Reform in Chicago: The Role of Business, Foundations and Activist Organizations," Annual Meeting of the American Educational Research Association, New Orleans, 4-8 April 1994.

22. Theodore Levitt, *The Third Sector: New Tactics for a Responsive Society* (New York: Amacom, 1973).

23. Lester M. Salamon, *America's Nonprofit Sector: A Primer* (New York: Foundation Center, 1992).

24. Hall, *Inventing the Nonprofit Sector*, 225.

25. Lester M. Salamon and A. J. Abramson, *The Federal Government and Nonprofit Sector: Implications of the Reagan Budget Proposals* (Washington, D.C.: The Urban Institute, 1981). Hall, "Abandoning the Rhetoric of Independence," 11-28. Salamon, "Of Market Failure, Voluntary Failure and Third Party Government," 29-49.

Odendahl, *Charity Begins at Home*. Jon Van Til, ed., *Critical Issues in American Philanthropy* (San Francisco: Jossey Bass, 1990). Hall, *Inventing the Nonprofit Sector*. McKersie, "Sectorial Relations and Chicago School Reform." Bernholz, *Private Philanthropy and Public Schools*.

26. McKersie, "Sectorial Relations and Chicago School Reform." Hall, *Reinventing the Nonprofit Sector*, 100–104.

27. Bernholz, *Private Philanthropy and Public Schools*.

28. Lagemann, *The Politics of Knowledge*. Ellen Condliffe Lagemann, "Philanthropy, Education, and the Politics of Knowledge," *Teachers College Record* 93, no. 3 (Spring 1992): 361–69.

29. Lagemann, "Philanthropy, Education, and the Politics of Knowledge," 365.

30. Lagemann, *The Politics of Knowledge*, 8.

31. Mavity and Ylvisaker, "Private Philanthropy and Public Affairs." Benjamin Whitaker, *The Foundations: An Anatomy of Philanthropic Societies* (New York: Penguin, 1979). Robert H. Bremner, *American Philanthropy* (Chicago: University of Chicago Press, [1960] 1988).

32. Colwell, *Private Foundations and Public Policy*. Nagai, Lerner, and Rothman, *Giving for Social Change*. Covington, *Moving a Public Policy Agenda*.

33. Peter Goldberger, "In honor of the fund that loves New York," *New York Times*, 9 June 1997, B1–B2.

34. Ellen Condliffe Lagemann, "AERA Comment," Discussant Paper presented at the 1997 Annual Meeting of the American Educational Research Association, Chicago, 26 March 1997, 6–7.

35. Ibid., 7.

36. Robert K. Yin, *Case Study Research: Design and Methods* (Newbury Park, Calif.: SAGE Publications, [1984] 1989), 21.

37. Jean Rudd, "Executive Director's Letter," in *Woods Charitable Fund 1989 Annual Report* (Chicago: Woods Fund of Chicago, 1989), 5.

38. Ibid.

39. Salamon, "Of Market Failure, Voluntary Failure, and Third-Party Government."

17 | The Future of Foundation History
Suggestions for Research and Practice

Lucy Bernholz

Historians are trained to look backward. This paper is an inversion (some might say a perversion) of that training, as I am quite deliberately looking forward. Wearing two different sets of lenses—a practitioner lens and a scholar lens—I have reviewed the historical literature on foundations. I wore the scholarly lenses first, and that review is available at length in my dissertation.[1] More recently I have worn the practitioner lenses, in my current work as a program officer at the Community Foundation of Santa Cruz County. My reviews of the literature through these two lenses reinforce a belief I developed early on in my graduate studies: that academics and practitioners operate in separate worlds and their perceptions of what foundations do rarely intersect. One foundation executive recently said to me, "The scholars who write about foundations don't have a clue about what we do." My sense is that this statement is true in reverse as well, and that both sides contribute to the misunderstandings. This paper offers some suggestions that might begin to bridge that gap.

The following is presented as a "requested historiography." The first section briefly describes the analytic framework used to shape the historiography. The second section presents an overview of three historical approaches to understanding foundations, and lays the groundwork for why new approaches are necessary. Following this brief historiography are ten suggested areas for future research. The tenth such suggestion directly addresses the existing gap between research and practice, and offers an argument for considering a blended approach. Such an approach to the study of philanthropic history would draw on both practical and academic expertise to create a conceptual framework for understanding twentieth-century American foundations and philanthropy that has value to the practice of philanthropy in the future.

A Framework for Looking at Foundation Decisions

Much has been written about the independence and autonomy and "lack of accountability" of foundations. Since Merle Curti's groundbreaking work in 1957, considerable research has been done on how foundations operate, the values that propel their founders, boards, and staff, and their impact on various aspects of society.[2] Political theorists and ideologues from both ends of the spectrum have discussed the nature of foundations' tax-exempt status, the need for reporting, the roles of foundations in a democratic, capitalist society. My interest is not in applying a particular political spin to the philanthropic sector. Rather, my concerns are far more utilitarian. I wish to make explicit the ways foundations operate and the impact, if any, of those operations on society. And I wish to assess these impacts in ways that reflect the place of foundations as one of many influential institutions and forces on any given social issue, and in ways that can guide future practice and research.

This framework does not take it as a given that foundations are influential organizations in modern society. We must do a far better job of parsing the term *influence* before making such an assertion. One of the most misleading results of the cumulative body of knowledge about foundations is this question of influence. While Merle Curti brought the field forth, much of the work on foundations written since his 1957 essay has shined the spotlight directly on the foundations, thereby not asking whether or not they are influential, and, if they are, why and how, but inferring it. If, on the other hand, foundations and philanthropy were included as one source of data, one of many actors in the social-issues arenas in which they provide funding or one point in a study of elites, the questions of influence would move to the forefront. Once a greater body of knowledge exists that looks at foundations and their funding programs in the contexts of the larger histories of the social issues, we will be able to define the true scope, direction, sustainability, and time to maturity of foundation influence.

This framework for understanding foundation decisions draws on organizational theory, social history, and professional practice; it is presented here because it underlies the historiography that follows. Foundations are often portrayed as autonomous and independent organizations. Compared with public-sector funders this is true, as there is no democratic process by which foundation decision makers are chosen. Compared to private industry, foundation shareholders are considerably fewer (although the range is vast considering the differences between community foundations and private family foundations).[3] Much of foundation history to date miscalculates the level of independence. The result of that overemphasis has been a lack of critical understanding of the influences that do guide foundation action. In trying to tackle the autonomy question, historians have placed foundations at the center of their histories and examined the influence that emanates from the organizations. Whether critical or positive, written from inside foundations or outside, from the political right or left, the effect has been to overstate vastly the role of foundations as influences on society and greatly underestimate the degree to which they are responsive organizations.

The influences that drive foundation action can be viewed as a complex web of external and internal factors. The innermost level of this web includes those factors found only in a single organization. For foundations, the number of founding-family members on the board, particular staff expertise, the "age" of currently funded programs, and the staffs' own particular emphasis on "innovation" are all powerful influences on grant decisions. Many organizational theories can be used to analyze these layers of influence. Bill Diaz recently argued that different elements of foundation decision-making can be understood in the "rational actor model," the "organizational process model," or the "bureaucratic politics model." They are all enveloped within the larger "ecology," which contains at least the next two layers of this three-part web.[4]

Outside this innermost level of decision influences is a layer of factors that results from and affects the actions of a community of foundations. For example, an existing set of privately funded programs in a program area often affects decisions about subsequent grants. Informal gatherings of foundation personnel can lead to joint projects or collaborative identification of priorities. Small, local foundations are also subject to the concerns and decisions of wealthier foundations. The larger foundations' actions might sway the local grant makers by virtue of their research reports on a topic, their "market share" in a particular locale, or by the credibility which their support gives to a non-profit organization. It also can be demonstrated that the work of small, local (and especially, community) foundations can influence the work of larger, more distant foundations. The dynamics of this layer, the ways that communities of foundations work, are perhaps the least understood set of dynamics. As foundations multiply in number, staff move from one to another, and professional networks continue to grow, understanding these dynamics should become increasingly important to understanding American philanthropy.

The third and most external layer includes factors located outside of foundations. Examples of external factors include the local, state, and national political climate, contemporary demographics and anticipated population shifts, the fiscal health of local service providers, and the federal tax-code regulations regarding foundation disbursements. The current model of understanding foundations locates their impact in this layer. This "web model," on the other hand, posits that this public environment shapes and influences the foundations. The interaction of foundations and this public environment, which includes public policy, public opinion, and nonprofit agencies funded by philanthropy, is another area ripe for investigation.[5]

Good foundation history must rely, to some extent, on analysis of grantmaking patterns over time. The individual grant decisions that represent much of the relationship between the foundations and the nonprofit or public grantees are dependent on many variables. Each decision, to apply for foundation funding or to make a grant, is affected by the sense of urgency around a particular issue, preferences of staff involved, the novelty of a proposed solution, alternative issues of equal, greater, or lesser urgency, community pressure, public agendas and fiscal strength, national philanthropic priorities, and so on. This is not to say that grant decisions are capricious. Rather, what we see are many levels and sources of contextual constraints which affect every decision by both applicant agencies and foundations. Patterns do emerge over time, and these have their own characteristics. However, it must be remembered that these patterns are the sum of hundreds of individual decisions, each of which is bound by its own particular blend of the myriad external and internal factors identified above.[6]

One final note on this framework. I believe there is almost as much to be learned from what foundations do not do as from what they do. Individual decisions to fund one proposal come at the expense of proposals not chosen. Program areas selected come at the expense of those closed to consideration. If any aspect of foundation work can best capture the degree of their institutional autonomy it is this one (foundations are truly free to choose the scope of their funding programs). Federal law and Internal Revenue Service (IRS) regulations turn foundations away from certain activities (political lobbying, for example) but in no way direct foundations toward any others. Given this, we know distressingly little about their decisions to fund in certain areas or to stay away from certain issues.

The structure for this historiography divides the literature into three categories: 1) operational history, 2) organizational and sector history, and 3) social history (in which political, economic, ethnic, and regional histories are included). These three categories are described below. Following the descriptions and examples, I turn to the question of what is still missing and what type of research is still needed. I hope to move the conversation toward a more practical understanding of philanthropy, one that can be useful to foundation staff and board members who are in fact creating the work of foundations that we study.

Operational History

In this tripartite typology, operational histories are the most common form of foundation history. I include in this category institutional studies, which look at single organizations and are often commissioned works; biographies and autobiographies of philanthropists; and those histories which use particular social or political issues to examine a single foundation.[7] Often, the essential question of these histories is "How did X Foundation make a difference?" In almost all cases these works presuppose that the foundation's work did, in fact, make a difference. This impact is usually seen as either extremely positive or extremely negative, and the foundation is often credited with being on the leading edge or, where critique is the story line, damned for promoting the will of the elite over the masses.

Ironically, the role of nonprofit agencies or charitable groups that use foundation funds to carry out their stated missions is, by and large, absent from these kinds of studies. Foundations, which for the most part do not run programs (operating foundations excepted), actually do not *do* any of the work that matters in a community or society. Whether the mission statement of the organization is "to make Santa Cruz County a better place to live," or "dedicated to an informed California populace," foundations only fund the work of others. Their success in meeting their (often hyperbolic) mission statements is absolutely linked to the work of the organizations that cash their checks.[8] Yet rarely is the dependence of foundations on grantee success noted. Recently, the Ford Foundation started using the advertising tag line "A Resource for Innovative People and Institutions Worldwide." This is as close as any public statement that, in fact, it is foundations that are the support agencies and the grant recipient organizations that get the work done. One would never know this from reading the bulk of foundation histories. These histories most clearly represent the maxim, "History is written by the winners."

Organizational and Sector History

Another type of foundation studies includes those that locate foundations within the larger universe of nonprofit organizations, public charities, and mutual benefit associations. These are often broad-based studies of the so-called independent sector, examinations of dynamics between foundations and program areas, or regional studies of interfoundation relations.[9] These works leave behind much of the rich detail on how foundations operate that is available in studies of individual organizations. However, they may be rich in their understanding of collaborative grantmaking and the political context in which foundations operate, and may present more information on the organizations that were funded by the grantmakers than do the individual studies.[10] These studies often can account for a wider variety of foundation influences and actions, yet invariably the question of foundation as influence is presupposed.

By looking at groups of foundations, either grouped by asset size, location, or priorities, these studies begin to reveal the vast and complex world of external dynamics that shape foundations' work. While these works often pay more attention to the roles of nonprofit grant recipients, these organizations are still rarely presented as initiating actors. What these studies do address is the influence on foundations of the communities in which they operate. However, they generally raise more questions than they answer.

Relations among foundations are, for the most part, not well studied. Yet these relationships abound. From the influence of national funders' large-scale initiatives to the many ways foundations meet and discuss their work, the vertical and horizontal influences that funders have on each other, and potentially on an entire program, need to be better understood. One prime example would be the effects of such recent "challenges" as the Annenberg funding for public schools, which led to the Bay Area School Reform Collaborative in the Bay Area and similar chain reactions of funders interested in school reform in Chicago, Los Angeles, Boston, New York, and rural areas of the country. Another example would be the current challenge by George Soros's Open Society Institute to spur private funding of naturalization and citizenship efforts across the county. In at least one area (Central and Northern California), the response was a regional effort involving twelve counties, eight community foundations, a dozen or so local and state-wide private foundations and dozens of service providers.[11]

These issue-based collaboratives and joint funding opportunities are one type of interaction point for foundations. There are many other forms in which foundations work together. For example, in both the San Francisco Bay Area and metropolitan New York, ongoing, semiformal "think session" groups exist. A dozen or so Bay Area executive directors meet regularly for dinner to discuss the ethics of philanthropy and grantmaking. In New York, the "Presidents' Lunch Club" offers a similar opportunity for its "members." Northern California Grantmakers, one of many regional affiliation groups, sponsors workshops, joint funding projects (such as the citizenship effort mentioned above), and even a reading group for foundation professionals. Much has been made in the literature of foundations regarding interlocking directorates or the *keiretsu* model of decision making. Little has been written about the ways in which staffs meet and work together, formally or informally, and what influence (if any) these idea-exchanges have on the work of "foundations" writ large or the individual foundations whose staff participate. These communities of foundations are increasingly common, and their role in the workings of American philanthropy needs study.

Social History

The third type of history is that which focuses not on the foundations but on the areas of work in which they operate. This would include histories of education, social welfare, health, the arts and humanities, international relations, entrepreneurship, etc. This genre of history also would include city or regional histories, political and economic histories, racial or ethnic histories, and the history of social movements. Examples rich in insight regarding philanthropic roles include James Anderson's work on the history of black education in the south, Ronald Walters' *American Reformers, 1815–1860,* David Farber's work on the 1960s, and Richard DeLeon's studies of San Francisco.[12] Within each of these works one finds an analysis of foundations and private funding. By placing foundations' work in a larger context, the issues of impact and influence become less central to the story. The work of the foundations and the grant-receiving organizations becomes part of the larger fabric of a social movement's, ethnic group's, or city's history.

To my knowledge, only a small amount of research has been done with this focus. At least three research projects or collections contain this type of work. From 1991 to 1994 the University of San Francisco (using a grant from the W. K. Kellogg Foundation) gave support to professors in the humanities and social sciences in California colleges and universities to develop curricula that would include information on philanthropy and nonprofit organizations. The Independent Sector also has a collection of such syllabi. Indiana University's Center on Philanthropy makes available sample syllabi from its humanities and social sciences courses on philanthropy.[13] Increasingly, historians have been examining the political and social contexts in which their histories of leading philanthropic individuals or institutions take place; however, the focus remains on the philanthropic leaders and the rest is often just background. This contextual analysis is important, but in my mind, it still overemphasizes the "influence question."

One final note on influence and independence is necessary. The role of the media on foundation-agency relationships is basically unexamined. Local newspapers, academic journals, foundation annual reports, and the burgeoning infrastructure of philanthropy provided by the Foundation Center, Council on Foundations, regional associations of grantmakers, affinity groups, and professional networks, are all influential in shaping foundation-agency-issue relations. Learning more about how the media works as an influence on agencies and foundations is a research area rich in potential.

Nine Questions Foundation Historians Should Ask and One Suggestion on the Use of History by Foundations

There are ten areas for future research that I would like to present. Many of these share a common bond, the de-emphasis of the concept of the foundation as a central player, and a push for studies of social, political, and economic trends that include philanthropy but don't grandstand. I present these as questions, some of which will require new research and some of which will force us to reexamine the existing literature. They are practical questions, by which I mean that greater understanding of them has strong potential to influence practice. And they are all questions that must draw on the histories of foundations as organizations, of philanthropy as a human value, and of regions, social issues, economics, and politics in order to be answered. The ten research areas follow.

One: How Do Foundations and Nonprofits Influence Each Other?

Philanthropic programs may be set by a board of directors and staff, but nearly all such programs are influenced by the proposals that cross the transom, the public policy agenda, and so forth. In short, there is a mutual dependence (interdependence) between foundations and nonprofit agencies that is vastly misunderstood or overlooked. Setting forth the hypothesis that service providers influence the funding priorities of foundations, and further positing that foundations need the agencies as much as the agencies need the foundations, inverts the current model. Foundations need agencies to succeed if they are to accomplish their own stated goals. Agencies need foundation support to do that work. Greater understanding of the intricacies of this dynamic, this interdependence, would shed light on questions of political elitism, public-policy agenda setting, and the ways in which problems are defined and solutions settled on. It would be most useful to have studies covering various locations and time periods. For example, John Kreidler, in what may be the first history to divide time along foundation-marked axes, posits that Ford Foundation funding in the arts shaped the characteristics of arts funding for years to come. He also asks the key follow-up question, "How then does this arts funding landscape influence subsequent generations of arts funders?" This dynamic of interdependence and mutual influence is the one most frequently missing from foundation histories.[14]

Influence runs in many directions. A diagram of the influences on foundations and agencies would have to show arrows coming from sources as diverse as the national economy, local politics, community activists, unions, and foundation board members. Diagrams of the flow of influences among foundations and agencies would have to show arrows going in both directions. These diagrams also would need to include community groups, the media, research institutes, and other such "intermediary organizations."

Two: What Role Does Innovation Play in Foundation Grant Making?

For all their awareness of limited funds and the enormity of the problems with which they struggle, foundations continue to speak grandly of their own accomplishments and those of their grantees. Lofty mission statements from foundations seem to inspire equally large promises by applicant organizations. The emphasis on innovation put forth by foundations meets with promises of new approaches and projects by applicants. One possible result of such a dynamic is an overabundance of new organizations, each specifically targeted at a certain issue. With regard to public schools in the 1960s, this dynamic played out in the form of funding programs to be added on to the basic core curriculum. This problem-solving-by-accretion was fueled to a great extent by the availability of funds. As the economic picture changed from one of plenty to one of scarcity, redistribution politics came into play. There were not enough resources to continue to fund new programs as well as support those programs already on board. Some foundations responded to these new challenges by questioning their own emphasis on start-up funds and innovative funding. They also reconsidered their aversion to providing operating support; a role once viewed as the sole purview of the public treasury. For example, the Rosenberg Foundation in San Francisco questioned its emphasis on innovation when it chose to establish a program of "longer and larger" grants, funding selected organizations for up to five years. This "experiment" lasted about five years, longer than expected. By the end of 1970s, however, the Foundation had returned to its previous emphasis on short-term grants for innovative projects.[15]

The demand by foundations that programs offer novel solutions and their general preference for one- or two-year grants places applicants in the position of redefining themselves (at least on paper) on an almost annual basis. It also threatens the potential livelihood of programs with a track record for success, the preference being for something new and different. What seems to happen in large bureaucracies dependent on foundation funding for new programs is the marginalization of innovation. Those things which are new and different happen on the edges of the organization, while the core of what institutions do may remain unchanged. A greater understanding of the effects that foundation funding and the resultant "projectitis" have on agencies themselves is needed.

Three: What Are the Trends or Patterns in Foundation Funding?

Are there trends in foundation giving? Are they affected by factors such as public policy, regional funding patterns, staff changes, or asset base? What impact, if any, do these trends have on the program areas in which they take place? Many a grant seeker will tell you that foundations are fickle. They change their priorities frequently and they won't support a program or organization long enough to make a difference. We lack a good historical understanding of these claims, as well as an ability to assess their validity, understand their meaning, or learn about regional or asset-based characteristics of funders. For example, some foundations in the San Francisco Bay area claim that 70 percent of their funding each year is in renewal grants (the Rosenberg Foundation) while others have funded some organizations for eight, nine, or ten years in a row (the Stuart Foundation).[16] These patterns belie the common wisdom, and beg questions regarding how representative they might be, how this funding differs from shorter-term support, how decisions are made for such long-term support, and how the relations between the agencies and funder are similar or different from those with shorter-term grant support.

Four: How Do Foundations Act as Reference Groups for Each Other?

This question slices across the sector of philanthropy, rather than across topic areas. Very little is known about these relations. The only studies that have examined this, at least to the author's knowledge, are those which have examined philanthropy in a particular city or region. In doing so, the best of these studies capture the presence of both locally based philanthropies and out-of-town funders.[17] Although foundations of all sizes contribute to one professional association, the Council of Foundations, there are numerous differences and tensions between local and national grant makers. The importance of regional issues can be seen in the subsequent development of regional associations, such as the Northern California Grantmakers Association and the Southern California Association for Philanthropy. Recently, smaller regions, such as the San Francisco Bay (Bay Bounders) or the Central Coast (three proximal counties in California) have become recognized associational parameters. At the same time, the globalization of the world economy also shapes philanthropy. This can be seen in George Soros's numerous international organizations, off-shore foundations designed to provide founder anonymity, and the recent interest in American community foundations by communities in the emerging democracies of eastern Europe.

The relationships between national funders located outside an area and the local and community foundation of a particular city might very well effect the outcome of programs funded by either or both types of organizations. One would assume that a national funder would prefer to avoid being considered a "carpetbagger," as was the case when a conflict arose between the Russell Sage Foundation of New York and the Rosenberg Foundation in the late 1960s.[18] The San Francisco story revealed both a variability of influence, as in cases where locals valued national support and those where they didn't, and a cycle of influence from local to national to local such as is seen in the stories of Oakland's Marcus Foster Educational Institute and the San Francisco Education Fund. These lessons may or may not apply to other cities, other issues, or other combinations of foundations. We need considerably more work on "communities of foundations," how they work, what they've done, and what they might mean for the future of foundation decision making. The diagrams of influence mentioned earlier need to consider these variations as well. Diagrams of influences between foundations also would show arrows in many directions: from local to national, local to local, national to national, and national to local. These diagrams can only get increasingly complex as they try to capture the many types of influence that must be considered, including money and issues of prestige, inclusion, and reputation.

Five: What Regional Distinctions Shape the Universe of Foundations?

This question has to do with the vastly understudied areas of the country. The majority of the literature still looks at the largest foundations (Kellogg, Ford, Carnegie, Rockefeller). We know relatively little about smaller foundations—foundations located off the beaten path (which is to say most of those not in New York City), and community foundations in general, which one might expect to make their materials more public than private foundations. We can only conclude from examining the full corpus of existing literature that foundations must operate along the same lines regardless of size, location, or founding date. I would like to put forth the alternative hypothesis: that foundations differ greatly and many of those differences may break out according to regional characterizations, date of founding/age of the organization, and asset size. Case histories on southern and western foundations and the regional communities are needed to help test this hypothesis. From the existing body of literature we do not know why the proliferation of foundations has been slowest in the South, why community foundations are the fastest growing form of organized philanthropy today, or why private foundations seem to be turning to community foundations as partners in ever-growing numbers. Nor can we begin to speculate about the longer-term meaning of these trends.

The regional question spins off other related queries, such as how the foundations created by acknowledged civic leaders figure into the history of a city or region. For example, the Haas family and the Levi Strauss Corporation are almost synonymous with the city of San Francisco, yet few histories of the city include information on the family's numerous foundations or their personal charitable giving. What will a history of Silicon Valley be without an understanding of the lives, work, and philanthropy of William Hewlett and David Packard (and their families)?

Similar to the question of regional distinctions are queries regarding ethnic, religious, gender, and other identity-based philanthropic endeavors. While some work exists in this area, it tends to focus on individual giving or the roles of individuals within nonprofits or foundations.[19] Historical understanding of identity-based institutionalized philanthropy, such as gay and lesbian community foundations, women's foundations, or race- and ethnicity-based philanthropic organizations, is considerably less robust.

How these organizations operate, set goals and programs, measure success, and work within or outside more mainstream philanthropic circles are basically unanswered questions. The development of these funders in response to neglect by mainstream philanthropies, and the possibility that their presence then "legitimizes" mainstream philanthropic neglect of these issues, are also inquiries in need of research.

Six: How Do Social Attitudes about Needs, Wealth, and Responsibility Shape the Work of Foundations and Philanthropists?

Here we return to Curti's 1957 work. He called for this same type of study and we have generated volumes of case studies on the question. We still need longitudinal analyses that look at clusters of foundations or focus on the influences on the foundations beyond the founding individuals. Certainly, these attitudes change regularly and cannot easily be aggregated for any one place, time, or people. But the history of media representations of philanthropy, or more likely, the public representation of poverty, government, and individual responsibility, would seem to be important markers against which to assess foundation activity. For example, the popular press is currently full of stories of Silicon Valley millionaires, the need for high-technology executives to share their prodigious wealth, and personal challenges from one executive to another that supposedly lead to multi-million-dollar philanthropic undertakings overnight.[20] Historical analyses of donor motivation that take the media, regional- and identity-based distinctions, and public attitudes into account are still needed.

Seven: What Do We Know about Social or Policy Areas that Foundations Have not Funded?

How does the history of foundations appear when one examines an area such as the gay rights movement? Many of the ethnic- or gender-specific philanthropic affinity groups, such as Asian American/Pacific Islanders in Philanthropy, assert that it was the lack of philanthropic concern for this community's interests that led to their creation. How often does a group mobilize in response to philanthropic disinterest? On a broader scale, histories of well-funded social issues could be compared to histories of unfunded social issues. Such comparisons might shed new light on the ways that foundations make decisions.

Eight: What Can We Learn from Failure?

We know very little about philanthropic initiatives that have not met their goals. Yet, foundations are spending more and more of their funds on evaluation of their individual grants and of their entire portfolios. In the past these reports were rarely made public, and so were not available for external analysis. However, that pattern is changing and evaluations by outside consultants often are available for public review. It is safe to assume that, over time, foundations have funded projects or initiatives that ultimately did not meet the stated goals. Select staff and board members may have learned certain lessons from those grants. Certainly, the element of risk and its potential for reward is a frequent topic of discussion among grant makers. Historical analysis of grant evaluations, portfolio reviews, and even granting collaboratives would no doubt yield important practical information as well as further the larger discussion of philanthropy's role in society.

Nine: How Do Philanthropy and Public Policy Interact at the Local Level?

From the relative prosperity of one decade to economic recession (depression) the next; from conservative public-policy environments to more liberal leadership, how does local institutionalized philanthropic giving reflect or ignore public-spending priorities? Geographically bound private foundations and most community foundations fund in a nonprofit environment that may be quite strongly influenced by the priorities of county or municipal government. Existing research on the questions of public-private intersection or interaction often look at large-scale national funders and initiatives. It is possible that the more close-knit relations that can exist in smaller communities cast into place a different dynamic between public and private funders. Case studies of city- or county-level funding communities that look at both the public and private sector are needed. One hypothesis to be examined is whether or not, in some areas and on some issues, the public sector has not absolved itself of responsibility for certain actions because of private funders' interest (funding the arts in schools, for example).

Suggestion for Foundation Executives on the Use of History or Historical Methods in Their Work

The tenth area of inquiry is more for foundation executives than historians, and focuses on the use of history in foundation work. One encounters the request, "Tell us about the history and mission of your organization" in proposal guidelines from nearly every foundation. What is the purpose of this historical information? What about the foundation's own history of grantmaking to an institution—How does that come into play? Do foundation executives have access to the necessary primary source materials to develop a sense of an organization's history? What about the review of a portfolio of work? How often do foundations examine their own paper trails, their own histories? If they do so, when, why, and how? Do they have access to the necessary primary source materials to develop a sense of an organization, a grants portfolio, a program?

An informal poll of a dozen foundation executives in the San Francisco Bay area shed interesting light on this question of constructing history. With some variation, the following list of information is what these insiders said would be the minimum needed to capture a sense of their organizations: founders' wills; grantee organization records; interviews with board members; foundation oral history series (San Francisco Bay area); grant records; staff memos to the board regarding the construction of guidelines and initiatives; board minutes/agendas; bylaws; correspondence between grant seekers and foundations; individual board members' views on what they were doing; annual reports (only useful for the public presentation of activities); orientation materials for new board members and new staff; proposals not funded (which most organizations don't keep for very long); the internal and unwritten record of why programs and proposals were funded (or not); and media coverage of the geographic area, the social issues, and the times. To a person, there was concern that the scholarly literature was incomplete in its modeling of philanthropic decision making and somewhat irrelevant to practice. Many of these same executives then indicated that their foundations had little or no interest in opening their archives to historians or providing access to the materials identified above. Foundations hold the key to improving scholarly inquiry in the field, and must be persuaded of the potential value of this type of research if they are to open their archives. The research must progress to a point where it is, in fact, of practical value. Once again, the dynamics of interdependence can be seen.

Conclusion—Closing the Gap

This paper's numerous suggestions for future research and writing of philanthropic history can be clustered into three broad categories. First, foundations and philanthropic giving, the interactions between foundations and nonprofits, should become a source of data for historians of larger social issues. This approach would temper the "all or none" positions currently expressed in the literature that exists on foundations as social institutions. In addition, it would serve the needs and interests of both practitioners and scholars. For foundation executives this knowledge would provide a stronger and broader base upon which to consider their work. For scholars, the inclusion of the philanthropic sector would shed new light on the social, political, and economic trends and institutions of interest.

Second, historians and scholars of foundations should look beyond the biggest foundations and into the distant regions of the country (particularly the West and South). By not including studies of small foundations or regional grantmakers, the existing literature contributes to the exaggerated influence credited to (or blamed on) foundations and misses the more compelling stories of communities, regions, and interactions. Foundations can be both reactive and proactive. They vary widely in their characters and approaches, and they should be studied as communities with both common and idiosyncratic features. The stories from the West and the South are valuable in and of themselves, but even more so for what they have to offer to the construction of a larger conceptual model of philanthropic roles, reactions, and influences.

Third, we know only the stories of big foundations and only the history of the work they pursued. Histories of social issues or ethnic groups that do not participate in or benefit from foundation support must be brought to light. Taken out of the context of the full universe of foundations and the vast universe of fundable choices, the presumption of foundation influence that so characterizes existing work becomes all the grander. In the last thirty years historians have done a tremendous job of shining the spotlight directly on foundations. It is now time to reassess that focus, and try to position foundations within the broader histories of place, peoples, and concerns. Studies of foundation communities, professional structures, associations, and regions are critical, given the rapidly changing nature of the philanthropic environment and the demands created for organizational adaptation. A broader, and more nuanced, historical understanding of the field is critical to the present and the future of American philanthropy, as well as to its past.

Notes

The author wishes to thank Ray Bacchetti, Hugh Burroughs, Peter Hero, John Kreidler, Ellen Condliffe Lagemann, Theodore Lobman, Michael O'Neill, Bruce Sievers, David Tyack, Kirke Wilson, and Sylvia Yee for their insights and suggestions in the preparation of this paper. The author takes full responsibility for any mistakes or misrepresentations contained herein.

1. Lucy Bernholz, "Private Philanthropy and Public Schools: San Francisco in the 1960s and 1970s," (Ph.D. diss., Stanford University, 1995).

2. Merle Curti, "The History of American Philanthropy as a Field of Research," *American Historical Review* 62 (1957): 352–63. See also Joseph Kiger, *The Operating Principles of Larger Foundations* (New York: Russell Sage Foundation, 1954).

3. In 1981, Martin Paley, executive director of the San Francisco Foundation, referred to the residents of the five Bay Area counties where the foundation made grants as the "stockholders" of the foundation. This comment was made in the context of one of the foundation world's greatest controversies (the Buck Trust case) and the term was used as a means of reaching out to the angriest constituents, those who felt the Foundation had established a two-tiered system of grantmaking. See Waldemar A Nielsen, *The Golden Donors* (New York: E. P. Dutton, 1985), 261.

4. Bill Diaz, "The 'Black Box' of Foundation Decision Making," *Foundation News and Commentary,* July/August 1997, 38–40.

5. Bernholz, "Private Philanthropy and Public Schools," 58–79.

6. A similar model of decision-making influences can be found in James G. March and P. Olsen, "Garbage Can Models of Decision Making in Organizations," in *Ambiguity and Command,* ed. James G. March and Roger Weissinger-Baylon, (London: Pitman, 1986).

7. Some examples include Raymond Fosdick, *The Story of the Rockefeller Foundation* (New York: Harper and Brothers, 1952); Horace Powell, *The Original Has This Signature—W.K. Kellogg* (Englewood Cliffs, N.J.: Prentice Hall, 1956); William Greenleaf, *From These Beginnings: The Early Philanthropies of Henry and Edsel Ford* (Detroit: Wayne State University Press, 1964). Joseph Kiger's *Historiographic Review of Foundation Literature: Motivations and Perceptions* (New York: Foundation Center, 1987) provides an excellent overview of the field.

8. Mission statements of the Community Foundation of Santa Cruz County and the James F. Irvine Foundation, 1997.

9. Peter Dobkin Hall, *Inventing the Nonprofit Sector and Other Essays on Philanthropy, Voluntarism, and Nonprofit Organizations* (Baltimore, Md.: Johns Hopkins University Press, 1992); Michael O'Neill, *The Third America: The Emergence of the Nonprofit Sector in the United States* (San Francisco: Jossey-Bass, 1989); and *Perspective on Collaborative Funding: A Resource for Grantmakers* (San Francisco: Northern California Grantmakers, 1985).

10. See Waldemar A. Nielsen, *The Big Foundations* (New York: Columbia University Press, 1972); F. Emerson Andrews, *Philanthropic Foundations and Philanthropic Giving* (New York: Russell Sage Foundation, 1950); Robert Bremner, *American Philanthropy* (Chicago: University of Chicago Press, 1960).

11. Council on Foundations, *When Community Foundations and Private and Corporate Funders Collaborate* (Washington, D.C.: Council on Foundations, 1995).

12. James D. Anderson, *The Education of Blacks in the South, 1860–1935* (Chapel Hill: University of North Carolina Press, 1988); Ronald G. Walters, *American Reformers, 1815–1860* (New York: Hill and Wang, 1978); David Farber, *The Age of Great Dreams: America in the 1960s* (New York: Hill and Wang, 1994); and Richard Edward DeLeon, *Left Coast City: Progressive Politics in San Francisco, 1975–1991* (Lawrence: University Press of Kansas, 1992).

13. Indiana University Center on Philanthropy, *Sample Syllabi for Philanthropic Studies, Nonprofit Management, and Civil Society* (Indianapolis: Indiana University Center on Philanthropy, 1997).

14. John Kreidler, "Leverage Lost: The Nonprofit Arts in the Post-Ford Era," *Journal of Arts Management, Law and Society* 26 (1996): 79–100.

15. Author interview, Kirke Wilson, 17 August 1994.

16. Author interviews, Kirke Wilson and Theodore Lobman, 20 June and 9 July 1997.

17. See, for example, Kathleen D. McCarthy, *Noblesse Oblige: Charity and Cultural Philanthropy in Chicago, 1849–1929* (Chicago: University of Chicago Press, 1982), and Diana Tittle, *Rebuilding Cleveland: The Cleveland Foundation and Its Evolving Urban Strategy* (Columbus: Ohio State University Press, 1992).

18. Ruth Close Chance, "Ruth Close Chance: At the Heart of Grants for Youth," interview, 30 May 1974, 36–37, 55–57.

19. See Bradford Smith, S. Shue, J. L. Vest, and Joseph Villarreal, *Ethnic Philanthropy* (San Francisco: Institute for Nonprofit Management, 1994); Teresa Odendahl and Michael O'Neill, *Women and Power in the Nonprofit Sector* (San Francisco: Jossey-Bass, 1994); Herman Gallegos and Michael O'Neill, eds., *Hispanics and the Nonprofit Sector*

(New York: Foundation Center, 1991); and Doug Braley, *Out in Front: A Report of the Lesbian and Gay Philanthropy Project* (San Francisco: Horizons Foundation, 1995).

20. See "The New Rich," *Newsweek*, 4 August 1997, 48–49. Such focus on the wealthy and philanthropy has historical precedents. See Merle Curti, "Anatomy of Giving: Millionaires in the Late 19th Century," *American Quarterly* 15 (1963): 416–35.

BIBLIOGRAPHY
Recent Writings about Foundations in History
Susan Kastan

This is a selected bibliography of historical studies of American philanthropic foundations, with a focus on critical and interpretive work appearing between 1980 and 1997. The emphasis is more on U.S. private, endowed foundations than on community, corporate, or operating funds. These latter types have begun recently to play dynamic and significant roles in American philanthropy, but it is the experience and influence of the endowed funds, a form of philanthropic institution now a century old in the United States, that have increasingly drawn the attention of historians who want more fully to understand changes over time in the nation's cultural, economic, political, and social development.

Included are works that deal centrally with foundations, as well as those that highlight specifically the role and political significance of foundations in broader historical developments. Some of the topics thus emphasized are the arts, African American education, child study, the social sciences and the professions, higher-education history and university research, labor economics and public health. The listings include books and other monographs, dissertations, and journal articles. The bibliography is organized according to the following sections:

I. Archives, Bibliographies, Historiographies, Research Guides, and
   Reference Works
II. Historical Studies of Foundations
III. Historical Studies Highlighting Foundations
IV. Biographies and Autobiographies
V. Oral Histories
VI. Historical Work on Foundation Management, Organization,
   Personnel, and Professionalization

I. Archives, Bibliographies, Historiographies, Research Guides, and Reference Works

This bibliography emphasizes work published in the past seventeen years, yet I have also included in this first section several older works that survey the pertinent earlier literature. F. Emerson Andrews and Merle Curti were pioneers in the field of foundation history, and their work remains important. More recently Robert

Bremner and Robert Payton, for example, have provided good introductions to the general history of philanthropy, including such classic American works as Andrew Carnegie's "The Gospel of Wealth" (1884) and Eduard Lindeman's *Wealth and Culture* (1936). I have excluded government documents, recommending instead Joseph Kiger's essay identifying important and still-influential government reports, such as Jane H. Mavety and Paul N. Ylvisaker's "Private Philanthropy and Public Affairs," in *Research Papers Sponsored by the Commission on Private Philanthropy and Public Needs*, vol. 2, part 1 (Washington, D.C.: Department of the Treasury, 1977). Finally, a number of works listed in other sections include good bibliographies or bibliographic essays, for example those by Donald Critchlow and Ellen Condliffe Lagemann. These are highlighted in the annotations.

Andrews, F. Emerson. *Philanthropic Foundations*. New York: Russell Sage Foundation, 1956. An early history and descriptive taxonomy by the originator of the institution that became the Foundation Center and the compendium that became the *Foundation Directory*.

Bremner, Robert H. *American Philanthropy*. 2nd ed. Chicago: University of Chicago Press, 1988. Concise and erudite overview, originally published in 1960, of the history of American philanthropy in many forms. Includes updates of a helpful chronology and a fine topical bibliographical essay; especially pertinent is the section on foundations, "Benevolent Trusts and Distrusts."

City University of New York (CUNY), The Graduate School and University Center, Center for the Study of Philanthropy. *Making Connections: Information On-Line and In-Print*. New York: CUNY, Fall 1997. Listing of Working Papers of CUNY's Center for the Study of Philanthropy, plus information on bibliographic resources, including guides for curriculum development on the history and practice of elite and multicultural philanthropy, and an on-line World Philanthropy Database (http://www.philanthropy.org/worldbase).

Curti, Merle. "The History of American Philanthropy as a Field of Research." *American Historical Review* 62 (January 1957): 352–63. Seminal essay, important in defining questions, problems and gaps in connecting the study of philanthropic institutions to broader currents in American intellectual and social history.

The Foundation Directory, 19th ed. Edited by Michael N. Tuller. New York: Foundation Center, 1997. First edition was published 1960. Annual listing of foundations with assets over $100,000; data includes year founded, purpose, programs, recent aggregate data on assets and expenditures, contact and leadership information. (The Foundation Center publishes additional directories, indexes, and studies on topics ranging from foundations by state, giving by field, electronic resources, leadership, and the nonprofit sector in general.)

The Foundation Grants Index, 25th ed. Edited by Rebecca MacLean. New York: Foundation Center, 1997. Annual listing of grants of $10,000 or more by large private, corporate, and community foundations with analysis of giving trends.

Hall, Peter Dobkin. "Of Books and the Scholarly Infrastructure." *Nonprofit and Voluntary Sector Quarterly* 22 (Spring 1993): 5–12. Brief essay identifying developments and gaps in the interest of publishers and periodicals in philanthropy and the nonprofit sector.

Hammack, David C. "Private Organizations, Public Purposes: Nonprofits and their Archives." *Journal of American History* 76 (June 1989): 181–91. Essay on sources.

Independent Sector. *Compendium of Resources for Teaching about the Nonprofit Sector, Voluntarism and Philanthropy*, 2nd ed. Edited by Nancy L. Crowder and Virginia Hodgkinson. Washington, D.C.: Independent Sector, November 1991. Useful, general-purpose guide, including listing of periodicals in the field.

Indiana University Center on Philanthropy. *Philanthropic Studies Index: A Reference to Literature on Voluntarism, Nonprofit Organizations, Fund Raising, and Charitable Giving*. Bloomington: Indiana University Press, 1995. Irregular from 1991; the 1995 Cumulative Edition indexes publications from January 1993 to March 1994. Includes occasional historical articles or books; emphasizes topics of current interest across the nonprofit sector. (The Indiana University Center on Philanthropy publishes additional studies, books and working papers, including an August 1997 compilation of *Sample Syllabi for Philanthropic Studies, Nonprofit Management, and Civil Society*.)

Indiana University Center on Philanthropy. *Research in Progress: A National Compilation of Research Projects on Philanthropy, Voluntary Action, and Not-for-Profit Activity*. Indianapolis: Indiana University Center on Philanthropy. Periodic compendium of research reported to the Indiana University Center on Philanthropy; now issued jointly with the Association for Research on Nonprofit Organizations and Voluntary Action (ARNOVA). Includes historical studies underway.

Kiger, Joseph C. *Historiographic Review of Foundation Literature: Motivations and Perceptions*. New York: Foundation Center, 1987. Essay characterizing book-length studies of foundations and government reports from 1898 to 1987; especially useful are his expositions of Congressional committee investigations of foundations, with bibliographic references for important government reports. (Kiger was research director for the Cox Committee in the 1950s.)

Layton, Daphne Niobe. *Philanthropy and Voluntarism: An Annotated Bibliography*. New York: Foundation Center, 1987. Very useful, wide-ranging topical bibliography covering philanthropic concepts, organizational forms, and functions; of special interest are sections on "Historical Setting and Precedents" and on foundations. A joint project of the Association of American Colleges and the Trust for Philanthropy of the American Association of Fund-Raising Counsel (AAFRC).

Otto, Margaret. "A Selected Bibliography in Philanthropy." In *Report of the Princeton Conference on the History of Philanthropy in the United States*. New York: Russell Sage Foundation, 1956. Extensive and heterogeneous compilation of a century of works on American philanthropy, including studies of foundations, to the mid-1950s.

Payton, Robert. "On Discovering Philanthropy: An Informal Guide to the Core Literature." *Change* 20 (November/December 1988): 33–37. Surveys seminal works on the idea and traditions of philanthropy and the voluntary sector in general; lists academic centers for the study of philanthropy and "independent sector" associations.

Rockefeller Archive Center. *Archives and Manuscripts in the Rockefeller Archive*

Center. North Tarrytown, N.Y.: Rockefeller Archive Center, 1982. Guide to holdings.

Rockefeller Archive Center. *Newsletter*. Annual. Lists information on the collections at the Rockefeller Archive Center, reports on conferences, and research grants. Also occasionally compiles recent articles and books by users of the center; thus includes numerous recent references to historical studies, both broad and particular.

Rose, Kenneth W., ed. *The Availability of Foundation Records: A Guide for Researchers*. North Tarrytown, N.Y.: Rockefeller Archive Center, 1990. Archives locations and access policies, based on a national survey of foundations.

Stapleton, Darwin. "Archival Sources and the Study of American Philanthropy." *Nonprofit Management and Leadership* 5 (Winter 1994): 221–24. Essay on sources.

Stapleton, Darwin H., with Kenneth W. Rose, Emily J. Oakhill, and Claire Collier. "Plumbing the Past: Foundation Archives Are Becoming an Invaluable Resource for Those Seeking to Understand Philanthropy's Role in Society." *Foundation News*, November/December 1987, 67–68. Essay on sources.

Yale University, Program on Non-Profit Organizations (PONPO). Publishes long-standing series of working papers and scholarly resources on civil society, foundations and philanthropy, including historical views.

II. Historical Studies of Foundations

Listed here are historical studies, including collections of essays, that take a single American foundation or a group of foundations as their primary focus. Also included are sociological studies that have proved especially useful to historians. Of particular interest are works establishing or epitomizing a specific analytic approach or interpretive paradigm for the historical study of philanthropic foundations. These include, for example, Robert F. Arnove, Edward H. Berman and Donald Fisher as neo-Marxian historians and critics, as well as Peter Dobkin Hall, David C. Hammack, Barry D. Karl, Stanley N. Katz, and Ellen Condliffe Lagemann as liberal historians and interpreters of the social roles of elites and the "politics of knowledge" (as Lagemann has termed it). Waldemar Nielsen has been a friendly yet persistent critic. J. Craig Jenkins and other sociologists have developed theories of the "channeling" influence of foundations on social movements. Merle Curti and Roderick Nash's interpretive history of the role of philanthropy in higher education, though dated, remains useful and important. Curti was also the author of important articles on topics such as philanthropy and national character; see Daphne Niobe Layton's bibliography (listed above) for further citations and descriptions.

A word is needed concerning the geography of foundation activities. From the time of "foreign" missions through today's global development, American foundations have been active and influential internationally. To maintain a manageable scope for this bibliography, however, I have generally excluded articles that focus narrowly on overseas projects or emphasize local cultural effects. There are exceptions. I have included international projects discussed by an author in terms of their wider political impact or their significance in subsequent, important decisions by the foundation or other policy leaders. Further, I used more latitude in including

"American" foundation projects in Canada, Mexico, Central and South America than international projects outside the Americas. Finally, the Rockefeller Foundation's support for medical education in China was so extensive as to demand its inclusion as a special case.

Ahmad, Salma P. "American Foundations and the Development of the Social Sciences between the Wars: Comments on the Debate between Martin Bulmer and Donald Fisher." *Sociology* 25 (August 1991): 511–20. Argues that Bulmer underestimated, and Fisher exaggerated, the influence of elites in philanthropic and research institutions, and the impact of foundations on research. (See also Ahmad, Bulmer, and Fisher, below.)

Ahmad, Salma P. "Institutions and the Growth of Knowledge: The Rockefeller Foundation's Influence on the Social Sciences between the Wars." Ph.D. dissertation, Manchester University, 1987. Sees a strong influence of philanthropic institutions in shaping research agendas.

Arnove, Robert F., ed. *Philanthropy and Cultural Imperialism: The Foundations at Home and Abroad.* Boston: G. K. Hall, 1980. Varied and useful collection of essays with a critical bent, spanning liberal to Marxian viewpoints.

Bennett, Anna Barclay. "The Management of Philanthropic Funding for Institutional Stabilization: A History of the Ford Foundation and New York City Ballet Activities." Ph.D. dissertation, Harvard University, 1989. Retrospective study of Ford support, beginning in 1959, for ballet performance and training. Based on archives and interviews; concerned with illuminating institutional options in climate of competition for grants; emphasizes importance of leadership in both kinds of institutions, problems arising from gaps in communication.

Berliner, Howard S. *A System of Scientific Medicine: Philanthropic Foundations in the Flexner Era.* New York: Tavistock, 1985. Physicians vs. philanthropists, including Carnegie and Rockefeller.

Berman, Edward H. *The Influence of Carnegie, Ford and Rockefeller Foundations on American Foreign Policy: The Ideology of Philanthropy.* Albany: State University of New York Press, 1983. Neo-Marxian interpretation of philanthropy promoting capitalist ideology.

Brown, E. Richard. *Rockefeller Medicine Men: Medicine and Capitalism in America.* Berkeley: University of California Press, 1979. Links corporate interests to the development of modern medicine via the foundation's elite leadership.

Bulmer, Martin. "Philanthropic Foundations and the Development of the Social Sciences in the Early Twentieth Century: A Reply to Donald Fisher." *Sociology* 18 (1984): 572–87. Argues against Donald Fisher's view that philanthropy serves only ruling-class interests, and for a more moderate and multifaceted analysis.

Bulmer, Martin. "Support for Sociology in the 1920s: The Laura Spelman Rockefeller Memorial and the Beginnings of Modern, Large-Scale, Sociological Research in the University." *American Sociologist* 17 (November 1982): 185–92. Argues that though decisions on grants established patterns and emphases (e.g., empiricism, concern for practical application, large-scale projects) in sociological research, these were not mere expressions of the social-class interests of the sponsors but products of subtle and complex relationships between scholars and foundation staff leaders. Bulmer's essay is included in an issue of *American*

Sociologist devoted to the financing of sociological research; see also John H. Stanfield, "The Cracked Back Door," below.

Bulmer, Martin, and Joan Bulmer. "Philanthropy and Social Science in the 1920s: Beardsley Ruml and the Laura Spelman Rockefeller Memorial, 1922–29." *Minerva* 19 (1981): 347–407. Ruml's leadership of the Spelman Memorial before its absorption by the Rockefeller Foundation, and its shaping effect on university economics, political science, and sociology.

Cluff, Leighton. *Helping Shape the Nation's Health Care System: A Report on the Robert Wood Johnson Foundation's Program Activities.* Princeton, N.J.: Robert Wood Johnson Foundation, 1989. Insider account of grantmaking, organizational development, and policy decisions.

Colwell, Mary Anna Culleton. *Private Foundations and Public Policy: The Political Role of Philanthropy.* New York and London: Garland, 1993. Critical account, aligned generally with neo-Marxian interpretations, by a foundation participant-observer. Based on early 1970s sociological study and interviews, and the author's dissertation (University of California–Berkeley, 1980). Includes chapters on conservative funders and policy organizations.

Coon, Horace. *Money to Burn: What the Great American Foundations Do with Their Money.* 1939. Reprint, with an introduction by Patrick D. Reagan, New Brunswick, N.J.: Transaction, 1990. Hearkening back to the 1915 Walsh Commission and the question of whether foundations are a "menace to democracy," Coon saw "no point in moral judgment" but still called for critical attention to foundations' nature, role in economic affairs, and influence in American society.

Crail, Marc L. "The Martha Holden Jennings Foundation: An Institutional History, 1959–1984." Ph.D. dissertation, University of Akron, 1988. Traces "evolutionary growth" of a foundation program to aid Ohio's primary and secondary schools.

Critchlow, Donald T. *The Brookings Institution, 1916–1933: Expertise and the Public Interest in a Democratic Society.* DeKalb: Northern Illinois University Press, 1985. Contextualized institutional study of a philanthropically endowed research institute; good bibliography.

Cueto, Marcos, ed. *Missionaries of Science: The Rockefeller Foundation and Latin America.* Philanthropic Studies Series. Bloomington: Indiana University Press, 1994. Reviews selected Rockefeller programs since 1920, including essays on agriculture, medicine and public health activities, especially in Brazil and Mexico, as well as general surveys of medical, scientific and public-health conditions in Latin America.

Curti, Merle E. *American Philanthropy Abroad: A History.* 1963. Reprint, with a new introduction by the author, New Brunswick, N.J.: Transaction, 1988. Overview of U.S. foundations' international interests, aims, and programs.

Curti, Merle E., and Roderick Nash. *Philanthropy in the Shaping of American Higher Education.* New Brunswick, N.J.: Rutgers University Press, 1965. Dated but still useful and important as an overview of the influence of various forms of philanthropy, including foundations, in the development of higher education.

Fisher, Donald. "Boundary Work: A Model of the Relation between Power and Knowledge." *Knowledge: Creation, Diffusion, Utilization* 10 (December 1988):

156–76. Illustrates "boundary work" (a theoretical, sociological approach to understanding efforts to "change" and "control" knowledge) by analyzing the history of social anthropology between World Wars I and II, including ways that "the control of the ruling class over the production of anthropological knowledge was exercised indirectly through Rockefeller philanthropic foundations."

Fisher, Donald. "The Role of Philanthropic Foundations in the Reproduction and Production of Hegemony." *Sociology* 17 (1983): 206–33. Marxian analysis of Rockefeller funding in the development of social sciences; concludes that philanthropy perpetuates Gramscian hegemony of the ruling class. See also reply by Martin Bulmer along with Fisher, "A Response to Martin Bulmer," *Sociology* 18 (1984): 572–87. See also Ahmad (1991), above.

Fisher, Donald. *Fundamental Development of the Social Sciences: Rockefeller Philanthropy and the United States Social Science Research Council.* Ann Arbor: University of Michigan Press, 1993. Deeply critical, Marxian analysis of the hegemonic effect of social science sponsorship by foundations.

Fitzgerald, Deborah. "Exporting American Agriculture: The Rockefeller Foundation in Mexico, 1945–53." *Social Studies of Science* 16 (1986): 457–83.

Fosdick, Raymond B. *The Story of the Rockefeller Foundation.* 1952. Reprint, with an introduction by Steven C. Wheatley, New Brunswick, N.J.: Transaction, 1989. Illuminating insider account.

Guzzardi, Walter, Jr. *The Henry Luce Foundation: A History, 1936–1986.* Chapel Hill: University of North Carolina Press, 1986. Insider, commissioned account of foundation active in education, East Asia, art, theology, and public affairs.

Hall, Peter Dobkin. "A Historical Overview of the Nonprofit Sector." In *The Nonprofit Sector: A Research Handbook,* edited by Walter W. Powell. New Haven: Yale University Press, 1987. Highlights foundations in characterizing the nonprofit sector; included in a useful, well-edited, wide-ranging volume.

Hall, Peter Dobkin. *Inventing the Nonprofit Sector and Other Essays on Philanthropy, Voluntarism and Nonprofit Organizations.* Baltimore: Johns Hopkins University Press, 1992. Historically grounded general essays; excellent introduction to the field and issues of philanthropy and philanthropic history; specifically discusses foundation history and historiography in several chapters.

Hammack, David C., and Stanton Wheeler. *Social Science in the Making: Essays on the Russell Sage Foundation, 1907–1972.* New York: Russell Sage Foundation, 1994. Four short interpretions: three by historian Hammack on the Foundation's early history through World War II, and one by legal scholar and former foundation officer Wheeler on subsequent history.

Harvey, A. McGehee, and Susan L. Abrams. *"For the Welfare of Mankind": The Commonwealth Fund and American Medicine.* Baltimore: Johns Hopkins University Press, 1986. Useful chronicle.

Humphrey, Daniel Craig. "Teach Them Not to Be Poor: Philanthropy and New Haven School Reform in the 1960s." Ed.D. dissertation, Teachers College, Columbia University, 1993. Historical case study of Ford Foundation's comprehensive "Gray Areas" program with educational, social service and job training components, an example of philanthropic activism during the Kennedy and Johnson administration's War on Poverty. Changes in New Haven public schools were "residual rather than resilient" because of overly optimistic assumptions about educational change, avoidance of issues of race, and emphasis on immediate results and short-term impact on national policy.

Jenkins, J. Craig, and Craig Eckert. "Channeling Black Insurgency: Elite Patronage and Professional Social Movement Organizations in the Development of the Black Movement." *American Sociological Review* 51 (December 1986): 812–89. Articulates sociological theory concerning the role of patrons and resources in directing social movements toward a mainstream politics; see also additional articles elaborating these theories and their historical application.

Jenkins, J. Craig, and Teri Shumate. "Cowboy Capitalists and the Rise of the 'New Right': An Analysis of Contributors to Conservative Policy Formation Organizations." *Social Problems* 33 (December 1985): 130–45.

Jenkins, J. Craig. "Resource Mobilization Theory and the Study of Social Movements." *Annual Review of Sociology* 9 (1983): 527–53.

Jenkins, J. Craig. "Social Protest, Hegemonic Competition, and Social Reform: A Political Struggle Interpretation of the Origins of the American Welfare State." *American Sociological Review* 54 (December 1989): 891–909.

Jiang, Xiao-Yang Sunny. "Cross-Cultural Philanthropy as a Gift Relationship: The Rockefeller Donors and Chinese Recipients, 1913–1921." Ph.D. dissertation, Bowling Green State University, 1994. Failure of donors and recipients to cooperate in administration of a gift and agree on goals, cultural conditions and demands.

Jonas, Gerald. *The Circuit Riders: Rockefeller Money and the Rise of Modern Science*. New York: W. W. Norton, 1989. Written with the support and cooperation of the Rockefeller Foundation. Interestingly chronicles the role of big philanthropy in creating big science.

Karl, Barry D. "Foundations and Public Policy." In *Encyclopedia of the United States in the Twentieth Century*, edited by Stanley I. Kutler, 5 vols. New York: Scribner's, 1996. Overview of stages in the development of the roles assumed by philanthropic foundations in the broadening of public policy making in the United States; highlights research, education, and tax policy.

Karl, Barry D., and Stanley N. Katz. "The American Private Philanthropic Foundation and the Public Sphere, 1890–1930." *Minerva* 19 (1981): 236–70. Definitive essay on foundations and public policy identifies Carnegie and Rockefeller philanthropies as setting early patterns of interpenetrating private and public influences.

Karl, Barry D., and Stanley N. Katz. *The Art of Giving: Four Views in American Philanthropy*. Proceedings of the Third Rockefeller Archive Center Conference, October 14, 1977. North Tarrytown, N.Y.: Rockefeller Archive Center, 1979. Includes early version of Karl and Katz *Minerva* 19 (1981) article; Paul N. Ylvisaker on private philanthropy and government; Alan Pifer on Carnegie Corporation management, 1911–1977; Lloyd N. Morrisett on the history of the John and Mary R. Markle Foundation during the 1920s.

Karl, Barry D., and Stanley N. Katz. "Foundations and Ruling Class Elites." *Daedalus* 116 (Winter 1987): 1–40. Influential general interpretation of the political significance of foundations; this is the introductory essay in an issue collecting several interesting pieces on philanthropy.

Keppel, Frederick. *The Foundation: Its Place in American Life.* 1930. Reprint, with an introduction by Ellen Condliffe Lagemann, New Brunswick, N.J.: Transaction, 1989. Overview of foundation history, purposes, and procedures in the U.S., by the president of the Carnegie Corporation, an early leader in the field.

Kevles, Daniel J. "Foundations, Universities, and Trends in Support for the Physical and Biological Sciences, 1900–1992." *Daedalus* 121 (Fall 1992): 195–235. Analyzes, critically but sympathetically, the role of foundations in supporting innovation in science.

Kohler, Robert E. *Partners in Science: Foundations and National Scientists, 1900–1945.* Chicago: University of Chicago Press, 1991. The interaction of "entrepreneurial science" in universities with the ideas and policies of major foundations and their leaders.

Kohler, Robert E. "Science and Philanthropy: Wickliffe Rose and the International Education Board." *Minerva* 23 (1985): 75–95. Examines foundation leaders' faith in science through the example and ideas of Wickliffe Rose, head of both the International Education Board and the General Education Board from 1923 to 1928.

Kohler, Robert E. "Science, Foundations, and American Universities in the 1920s." *Osiris,* 2nd series, 3 (1987): 135–64. The "partnership" of private philanthropy and American universities, and the investment of foundation dollars, shifted the center of gravity in scientific power from Europe to the United States during the interwar period.

Lagemann, Ellen Condliffe. "Philanthropy, Education, and the Politics of Knowledge." *Teachers College Record* 93 (Spring 1992): 361–69. Introductory essay, outlining an approach for understanding the role of philanthropy in society, in a special issue on the purposes of philanthropy and the nature of education.

Lagemann, Ellen Condliffe. *Private Power for Public Good: A History of the Carnegie Foundation for the Advancement of Teaching.* Middletown, Conn.: Wesleyan University Press, 1983. Richly contextualized study of an institution that shaped medical education and influenced the development of universities through promotion of a pension system for college teachers. Includes review of literature to 1983 on foundations and the historical context for their study.

Lagemann, Ellen Condliffe. *The Politics of Knowledge: The Carnegie Corporation, Philanthropy, and Public Policy.* Chicago: University of Chicago Press, 1989. Study of the Carnegie Corporation shows how philanthropic foundations influence the pursuit and legitimation of knowledge, and thus the framework of political debate and decision making. The bibliographic essay identifies critical histories of foundations published during the 1980s as well as references for deeper historical and political contextualization.

Lagemann, Ellen Condliffe. "The Politics of Knowledge: The Carnegie Corporation and the Formulation of Public Policy." *History of Education Quarterly* 27 (Summer 1987): 205–20. Uses three brief, concrete examples of early Carnegie Corporation grants to illustrate how public-policy options could be informed by a politics of knowledge in which the decisions of philanthropic leaders helped establish the authority of certain kinds of knowledge, specific knowledge-producing organizations, and patterns of access to and communication of knowledge.

Ma, Qiusha. "The Rockefeller Foundation and Modern Medical Education in China, 1915–1951." Ph.D. dissertation, Case Western Reserve University, 1995. Considers Rockefeller's support of Western-style medical education in several contexts: missionary education, medical education reform and professionalization, the Chinese "new intellectuals' reform movements," and Chinese government policies.

Macdonald, Dwight. *The Ford Foundation: The Men and the Millions.* 1956. Reprint, with an introduction by Francis X. Sutton, New Brunswick, N.J.: Transaction, 1988. Not interpretive, but influential and popular; an adaptation of the journalist and critic's witty articles in *The New Yorker.*

Maddox, David C., ed. *The Russell Sage Foundation: Social Research and Social Action in America, 1907–1947.* Frederick, Md.: CIS Academic Editions, 1988. Microform. Selections from Sage Foundation archives at the Rockefeller Archive Center; printed guide includes interpretive essay by David C. Hammack, editorial advisor.

Madison, James H. "John D. Rockefeller's General Education Board and the Rural School Problem in the Midwest, 1900–1930." *History of Education Quarterly* 24 (Summer 1984): 181–200. Identifies mixed legacy, complex relationships, and conflicts arising from the encounter of "cosmopolitan, outside experts" with local communities concerned with schooling in two rural Indiana counties.

Magat, Richard, ed. *An Agile Servant: Community Leadership by Community Foundations.* New York: Foundation Center, 1987. Case studies covering an array of cities, funds, and projects nationwide; among others, includes essays by David C. Hammack on philanthropic purposes; Paul N. Ylvisaker on future roles for community funds; Susan V. Berresford on collaborations and tensions between different foundations.

Magat, Richard. "The Big Chill." *Foundation News* 30 (November/December 1989): 32–40. Historical review of the intent and effect of the Tax Reform Act of 1969.

Magat, Richard. *The Ford Foundation at Work: Philanthropic Choices, Methods and Styles.* New York: Plenum, 1979. Insightful thirty-year retrospective report on foundation objectives and operations, commissioned by the board to aid future planning.

Magat, Richard, ed. *Philanthropic Giving: Studies in Varieties and Goals.* New York: Oxford University Press, 1989. Broad view of the philanthropic sector, with sensitivity to both history and current practice. Along with essays on values, theory, government policy, individual and corporate giving, includes substantive chapters on "Foundations, Donors, Types, and Management." Also includes essays on the control and influence of institutions, including the problems of perpetual trusts, and social movement philanthropy.

McCarthy, Kathleen D. "From Cold War to Cultural Development: The International Cultural Activities of the Ford Foundation, 1950–1980." *Daedalus* 116 (Winter 1987): 93–117. Analyzes shift from Cold War emphasis from cultural programs to create sympathy for the U.S. and democracy, to economic development efforts during the 1960s, and a combination by the 1980s.

McCaughey, Robert A. *International Studies and Academic Enterprise: A Chapter in the Enclosure of American Learning.* New York: Columbia University Press,

1984. A social and institutional history of why and how Americans developed programs of research and education about international cultures; highlights the establishment, termination, and impact of the Ford Foundation's International Training and Research Program (ITR), 1953-1966.

Nielsen, Waldemar A. *The Golden Donors: The New Anatomy of the Great Foundations.* New York: E. P. Dutton, 1985. Successor to Nielsen's 1972 volume *The Big Foundations;* a critical though ultimately sympathetic overview and perceptive characterization of the strengths and weaknesses of foundations.

Ninkovich, Frank. "The Rockefeller Foundation, China, and Cultural Change." *Journal of American History* 70 (March 1984): 799-820. Analyzes Rockefeller Foundation support for Chinese medical education as an "experiment in the management of ideas" and an episode in extragovernmental influence.

Odendahl, Teresa, ed. *America's Wealthy and the Future of Foundations.* New York: Foundation Center, 1987. A volume resulting from a project on "Foundation Formation, Growth, and Termination" sponsored by the Council on Foundations and the Yale University Program on Non-Profit Organizations (PONPO). Essays on Congress and foundations, donors, advisors, large foundations. Appendix on tax law and selected bibliography.

O'Neill, Michael. *The Third America: The Emergence of the Nonprofit Sector in the United States.* San Francisco: Jossey-Bass, 1989. Useful overview of the U.S. nonprofit sector, organized topically but including a chapter on foundations and corporate funders, and an interesting contextual chapter on research and education that touches on the significance of the "information economy."

Ostrander, Susan A. *Money for Change: Social Movement Philanthropy at the Haymarket People's Fund.* Philadelphia: Temple University Press, 1996. Evolution and leadership innovations of a small foundation supporting grassroots organizations.

Payton, Robert. *Philanthropy: Four Views.* New Brunswick, N.J.: Transaction, 1988. Essays by a long-time observer of foundations.

Payton, Robert. *Philanthropy: Voluntary Action for the Public Good.* New York: American Council on Education/Macmillan, 1988. Essays on intellectual traditions and philosophical background of philanthropy as important in a democratic society; bibliography on these topics. Includes Virginia Hodgkinson, "Research on the Independent Sector: A Progress Report."

Radford, Neil A. *The Carnegie Corporation and the Development of American College Libraries, 1928-1941.* Chicago: American Libraries Association, 1984. Useful account of the aims, administration, focus and impact of one foundation's support for selected institutions.

Robinson, Marshall W. "Private Foundations and Social Science Research." *Social Science and Public Policy* 21 (May/June 1984): 76-80. Brief overview, by the then-president of the Russell Sage Foundation, of social-science support by foundations, roughly 1920-1980. Additional brief reports in this issue—by Harvey Brooks, Kenneth Prewitt, and F. Thomas Juster and Roberta Alstad Miller (all from a 1983 symposium at the American Association for the Advancement of Science)—add context on other forms of sponsorship, research on the Third World, and technological change in determining research agenda.

Rose, Kenneth W. "Toward a Universal Heritage: Education and the Development of

Rockefeller Philanthropy, 1884–1913." *Teachers College Record* 93 (Spring 1992): 536–55. The Rockefeller legacy as perpetuated at Spelman College, University of Chicago, Rockefeller University, Rockefeller Foundation.

Samson, Gloria Garrett. *The American Fund for Public Service: Charles Garland and Radical Philanthropy, 1922–1941.* Westport, Conn.: Greenwood, 1996. Studies a "premature" united front of anticapitalists that attempted to revitalize the left through philanthropic investments in the radical press (including *New Masses*), A. Philip Randolph's Brotherhood of Sleeping Car Porters, and workers' education.

Sealander, Judith. *Private Wealth and Public Life: Foundation Philanthropy and the Reshaping of American Social Policy from the Progressive Era to the New Deal.* Baltimore: Johns Hopkins University Press, 1997. Emphasizes comparisons and chronology in analyzing efforts by a small universe of private foundations to shape public policy, 1903–1932; argues that close organizational interrelationships and a style of philanthropy still more "personal" than "corporate" characterized early work. Identifies links, cooperation, and disagreements among several Rockefeller institutions, the Russell Sage Foundation, the Rosenwald and Commonwealth Funds in vocational education, parent education, early social-welfare provision, child-helping and juvenile justice, anti-prostitution campaigns, and public recreation.

Seybold, Peter J. "The Ford Foundation and Social Control." *Science for the People* 14 (May/June 1982): 28–31. Criticizes Ford for narrow, behaviorist focus in research on electoral behavior during the 1950s, perpetuating the dominant order rather than promoting public political engagement. Draws on the author's Ph.D. dissertation (SUNY-Stony Brook, 1978), "The Development of American Political Sociology: A Case Study of the Ford Foundation's Role in the Production of Knowledge."

Silva, Edward T., and Sheila A. Slaughter. *Serving Power: The Making of the Academic Social Science Expert.* Westport, Conn.: Greenwood, 1984. Argues that academic social scientists tend to support vested political and economic interests by "binding knowledge to power," subordinating ideas and research to resource-rich state and capitalist institutions, including philanthropic foundations.

Smith, James A. *The Idea Brokers: Think Tanks and the Rise of the New Policy Elite.* New York: Macmillan/Free Press, 1991. Thoughtful, broad-gauge, and contextualized account of the political impact of "experts" as spawned by such institutions as the Brookings Institution and the Twentieth Century Fund.

Solorzano Ramos, Armando. "The Rockefeller Foundation in Mexico: Nationalism, Public Health and Yellow Fever, 1911–1924." Ph.D. dissertation, University of Wisconsin–Madison, 1990. Symbiosis of foundation's "unofficial diplomacy" 1911–1920 and public health work in the 1920s promotes capitalist interests and softens Mexican attitudes toward U.S. involvement.

Stanfield, John H. "The Cracked Back Door: Foundations and Black Social Scientists between the World Wars." *American Sociologist* 17 (November 1982): 193–204. Argues that while foundations supported and thus to a certain extent advanced the work of a number of emergent, African American social scientists, expectations of "race leader" roles and other presumptions of a racially hierarchical society restricted these scholars' range and control of their research.

Stanfield's essay is included in an issue of *American Sociologist* devoted to the financing of sociological research; see also Martin Bulmer, "Support for Sociology," above.

Sutton, Francis X. "The Ford Foundation: The Early Years." *Daedalus* 116 (Winter 1987): 41–91. Policy formulation and leadership in the 1940s and 1950s; critical essay by an insider.

Van Buren, Martin P. *Reaching Out: America's Volunteer Heritage.* Battle Creek, Mich.: W. K. Kellogg Foundation, 1990. Emphasizes the importance of voluntarism in the U.S. and describes selected Kellogg grants for voluntarism from the 1930s to the present.

Wheatley, Stephen C. *The Politics of Philanthropy: Abraham Flexner and Medical Education.* Madison: University of Wisconsin Press, 1988. Uses a biographical study of Flexner to explore the strategic role of Rockefeller philanthropy in the overall development of American medical education.

Williams, Roger M. "From Inside Right to Out Front." *Foundation News* 32 (May–June 1991): 20–25. The political shift of the Pew Charitable Trusts, from right to left, over their history.

Willie, Charles V. "Philanthropic and Foundation Support for Blacks: A Case Study from the 1960s." *Journal of Negro Education* 50 (Summer 1981): 270–84. Study of motivations, flaws, and changes in support for historically black colleges, and for recruitment of minority students to selective, predominantly white colleges, through the Rockefeller Foundation's "Equal Opportunity Program," begun in 1963.

Wilson, Emily Herring. *For the People of North Carolina: The Z. Smith Reynolds Foundation at Half-Century, 1936–1986.* Chapel Hill: University of North Carolina Press, 1988. Readable, informative chronicle.

Wisely, D. Susan. "A Foundation's Relationship to Its Public: Legacies and Lessons for the Lilly Endowment." Essays on Philanthropy, no. 17. Indianapolis: Indiana University Center on Philanthropy, 1995. In "Series on Foundations and Their Role in American Life."

III. Historical Studies Highlighting Foundations

This section includes studies in which foundation philanthropy is a specific and important part of a wider subject of inquiry. Some of the topics or historical issues covered are broad (capitalism, for example, or the state). Others are specific (one school or cultural institution, for example), and in these cases I have tried to select work that is strongly contextual. The willingness and the ability of historians and other scholars to assess critically the roles of organized philanthropy in wider cultural, economic, political, and social developments is an encouraging historiographical trend. Historical interpretations of foundations and other philanthropic institutions have provided tools for such critical analysis, as well as a growing awareness that the realms of "public" and "private" interests, formerly and popularly considered distinct, are to the contrary intricately interrelated.

Abrams, Sarah E. "Brilliance and Bureaucracy: Nursing and Changes in the Rockefeller Foundation, 1915–1930." *Nursing History Review* 1 (November 1993):

119-37. Puts Rockefeller funding of nursing education in the broad context of a turbulent period in which the professional territories of medicine, public health, nursing, education, and social work were redefined.

Abrams, Sarah E. " 'Dreams and Awakenings': The Rockefeller Foundation and Public Health Nursing Education, 1913-1930." Ph.D. dissertation, University of California, San Francisco, 1992. Contextualized study of support for nursing education.

Addo, Linda D. "A Historical Analysis of the Impact of Selected Teachers on Education for Blacks in Coastal South Carolina, 1862-1970." Ph.D. dissertation, University of North Carolina-Greensboro, 1988. Incorporates discussion of the influence of philanthropic foundations on black southern education, into a study of the careers of eight teachers.

Alchon, Guy. *The Invisible Hand of Planning: Capitalism, Social Science, and the State in the 1920s.* Princeton, N.J.: Princeton University Press, 1985. Discusses, in rich context, the role of foundations in promoting nonstatist planning.

Anderson, James D. *The Education of Blacks in the South, 1860-1935.* Chapel Hill: University of North Carolina Press, 1988. Establishes an interpretive framework for understanding and criticizing the role of northern philanthropy during Reconstruction and beyond.

Benson, Keith R., Jane Maienschein, and Ronald Rainger, eds. *The Expansion of American Biology.* New Brunswick, N.J.: Rutgers University Press, 1991. Analyses of public and foundation funding, leaders and institutional influences are included as part of the deep context in which biology expanded into "big science" between 1920 and 1950. See for example Rainger's introduction (with notes usefully reviewing related literature), Garland E. Allen on the Rockefeller Foundation's role in the transformation of eugenics into population science, and Diane B. Paul on the same foundation and the field of "behavior genetics." This collection is the second of two by these editors on the history of biology; this volume highlights funding issues more fully, but the first also addresses the social and political contexts of scientific development, and touches on philanthropic support (e.g., by the Carnegie Institution of Washington). See also Ronald Rainger, Keith R. Benson and Jane Maienschein, eds., *The American Development of Biology* (Philadelphia: University of Pennsylvania Press, 1988).

Bernholz, Lucy. "Private Philanthropy and Public Schools: San Francisco in the 1960s and 1970s." Ph.D. dissertation, Stanford University, 1995. Mutual dependence of two organizational groups with intersecting missions in efforts to improve schools, including the creation of the San Francisco Education Fund. Contextual factors include political and fiscal influences, Tax Reform Act of 1969, desegregation demands.

Bobinski, George. "The Golden Age of American Librarianship." *Wilson Library Bulletin* 58 (January 1984): 338-44. Library field 1945-1970, including changes in philanthropic and public funding.

Brown, Jerold E., and Patrick D. Reagan, eds. *Voluntarism, Planning, and the State: The American Planning Experience, 1914-1916.* Westport, Conn.: Greenwood, 1988. Includes articles addressing the role of foundations and leaders in state policy formation, e.g., Charles E. Harvey, "John D. Rockefeller, Jr., Herbert Hoover, and President Wilson's Industrial Conferences of 1919-1920," and

Patrick D. Reagan, "Creating the Organizational Nexus for New Deal National Planning."

Bullough, Vern L. "Katharine Bement Davis, Sex Research, and the Rockefeller Foundation." *Bulletin of the History of Medicine* 62 (Spring 1988): 74–89.

Bulmer, Martin. *The Chicago School of Sociology: Institutionalization, Diversity, and the Rise of Sociological Research*. Chicago: University of Chicago Press, 1984. Traces the pervasive influence of the Chicago School on American social science in the intellectual and institutional development of research topics and methodology; includes the role of the Laura Spelman Rockefeller Memorial and Beardsley Ruml in these developments.

Bulmer, Martin, Kevin Bales, and Kathryn Kish Sklar. *The Social Survey in Historical Perspective, 1880–1940*. Cambridge: Cambridge University Press, 1991. Situates the influential role of Russell Sage Foundation in the development of social survey concepts, methods, and applications.

Cahan, Emily D. "Science, Practice, and Gender Roles in Early American Child Psychology." In *Contemporary Constructions of the Child: Essays in Honor of William Kessen*, edited by Frank S. Kessell et al. Hillsdale, N.J.: Lawrence Erlbaum, 1991. Discusses role of Laura Spelman Rockefeller Memorial support in the gendered development of a field.

Carroll, Evelyn Cecelia Jenkins. "Priorities in Philanthropic Support of Private Negro Colleges and Universities, 1930–1973." Ph.D. dissertation, University of Michigan, 1982. A study of grants from twelve major foundations during this period; their support fell short of aiding in the development of a level of excellence comparable to other private institutions, but was adequate for maintenance and gradual development.

Chapman, Bernadine Sharpe. "Northern Philanthropy and African-American Adult Education in the Rural South: Hegemony and Resistance in the Jeanes Movement." Ph.D. dissertation, Northern Illinois University, 1990. Interprets as social control the motives of philanthropists in supporting the Jeanes Industrial Teacher Supervisory Movement, 1907–1968, through which African American teachers, mainly women, trained elementary teachers and engaged adults in community-development activity.

Cravens, Hamilton. *Before Head Start: The Iowa Station and America's Children*. Chapel Hill: University of North Carolina Press, 1993. Comprehensive account of child development research in American universities; includes a chapter on philanthropy and the child welfare movement, especially the Laura Spelman Rockefeller Memorial and Lawrence K. Frank.

Dain, Phyllis. "American Public Libraries and the Third Sector: Historical Reflections and Implications." *Libraries & Culture* 31 (Winter 1996): 56–84. Identifies the importance over time of a "public-private, variegated mix," including individual and foundation philanthropy, in sponsorship of public libraries. This volume of *Libraries & Culture* is a special number on "Libraries and Philanthropy," based on papers from a 1995 seminar, including historical studies by Peter Dobkin Hall on libraries and the origins of U.S. civil society, Mary B. Haskell on Rockefeller philanthropy for libraries, Paula D. Watson on women's roles in Carnegie libraries, and more.

DiMaggio, Paul J., ed. *Nonprofit Enterprise in the Arts: Studies in Mission and Con-*

straint. New York: Oxford University Press, 1986. A collection of studies, historical and contemporary, establishing a framework for understanding the interplay of aesthetic, social, and political concerns in arts institutions; includes essays connecting philanthropy and the organization of culture in the United States.

Fox, Daniel M. *Engines of Culture: Philanthropy and Art Museums*. 1963. Reprint, with a new introduction by the author, New Brunswick, N.J.: Transaction, 1995. Early interpretation of the interpenetration of private and public in the establishment and funding of cultural and philanthropic organizations during the late nineteenth and early twentieth centuries.

Freedman, Estelle B. *Maternal Justice: Miriam Van Waters and the Female Reform Tradition*. Chicago: University of Chicago Press, 1996. Exemplary biography of women's prison reformer Van Waters, including a substantial chapter on a Los Angeles child-guidance clinic she established with support from the Commonwealth Fund.

Freedman, Estelle B. *Their Sisters' Keepers: Women's Prison Reform in America, 1830-1930*. Ann Arbor: University of Michigan Press, 1981. Highlights the anti-prostitution work of the Rockefeller-funded Bureau of Social Hygiene, as well as foundation relationships of reformers such as Frances Kellor and Katharine Bement Davis.

Freedman, Kerry. "The Philanthropic Vision: The Owatonna Art Education Project as an Example of 'Private' Interests in Public Schooling." *Studies in Art Education* 31 (Fall 1989): 15–25. Carnegie philanthropy's role in a Minnesota school art program.

Gagnon, Alain, and Stephen Brooks, eds. *The Political Influence of Ideas: Policy Communities and the Social Sciences*. Westport, Conn.: Greenwood, 1994. Includes William J. Buxton, "From Radio Research to Communications Intelligence: Rockefeller Philanthropy, Communications Specialists, and the American Intelligence Community," 187–209.

Gamble, Vanessa Northington. *Making a Place for Ourselves: The Black Hospital Movement, 1920-1945*. New York: Oxford University Press, 1995. Though American hospitals were generally community-funded and most foundations didn't view them as part of their mission, three national philanthropies—the Julius Rosenwald Fund, the Duke Endowment, and the General Education Board—played crucial roles in assisting and influencing a black-hospitals movement. Gamble views this movement as part of a struggle by black doctors to secure access to hospitals and thereby to careers and professional viability.

Gardner, Deborah. "Practical Philanthropy: The Phelps-Stokes Fund and Housing." *Prospects: An Annual of American Cultural Studies* 15 (1990): 359–411. Low-income housing development in New York City during the early twentieth century is influenced by the Phelps-Stokes Fund (and other philanthropic institutions).

Geiger, Roger. *To Advance Knowledge: The Growth of American Research Universities, 1900-1940*. New York: Oxford University Press, 1986. Includes a chapter discussing the nature and impact of foundation/university interrelationships.

Geiger, Roger. *Research and Relevant Knowledge: American Research Universities since World War II*. New York: Oxford University Press, 1993. Second volume continues Geiger's earlier study; government support is more important in this era, but foundations are still players.

Gillespie, Richard P. "Manufacturing Knowledge: A History of the Hawthorne Experiments." Ph.D. dissertation, University of Pennsylvania, 1985. Western Electric Company as a site of social science research in industrial management, 1924–1933; Gillespie locates his story in the context of changes in work processes, the professionalization of management, and the promotion by philanthropic foundations of new behavioral and social sciences.

Goggin, Jacqueline. *Carter G. Woodson: A Life in Black History*. Baton Rouge: Louisiana State University Press, 1993. Study of the historian, publicist and editor of the *Journal of Negro History*; discusses his interactions with officers of Carnegie and Rockefeller philanthropies, including their denial of support as well as Woodson's resistance to advice.

Grant, Julia. *Raising Baby by the Book: The Education of American Mothers*. New Haven: Yale University Press, 1998. Locates powerful influence of Lawrence K. Frank and the Laura Spelman Rockefeller Memorial in child-study program development. See also Grant, "Modernizing Mothers: Home Economics and the Parent Education Movement," in *Rethinking Home Economics: Women and the History of a Profession*, edited by Sarah Stage and Virginia B. Vincenti (Ithaca, N.Y.: Cornell University Press, 1997).

Grant, Julia. "Caught between Common Sense and Science: The Cornell Child Study Clubs, 1925–45." *History of Education Quarterly* 34 (Winter 1994): 433–52. Grassroots experience of child-study programs as shaped by foundation influence.

Greeley, Dawn M. "From Benevolence to Professionalism: Gender, Class and the Organization of Charity, 1860–1900." Ph.D. dissertation, State University of New York–Stony Brook, 1994. Study of triangular relationships of donors, social workers, and clients in organized charity; touches on the professionalization of social work as influenced by the Russell Sage Foundation's Charity Organization Department.

Haines, Herbert. *Black Radicals and the Civil Rights Mainstream, 1954–1970*. Knoxville: University of Tennessee Press, 1988. Sociological analysis of civil-rights movements; critically considers resource mobilization, highlighting the role of foundations in supporting moderate groups, as contrasted with the "radical flank."

Haug, Ruth Janet Severson. "From the Ground Up: The Institutionalization of Public Health Administration in Mississippi." Ph.D. dissertation, Mississippi State University, 1995. Discusses Rockefeller philanthropy as influential in the development of state public-health programs.

Heffron, John M. "Science, Southernness, and Vocationalism: Rockefeller's 'Comprehensive System' and the Reorganization of Secondary School Science Education, 1900–1920." Ph.D. dissertation, University of Rochester, 1988. General Education Board influence in the creation of "the progressive high school science policy pioneered at the Gary School in Indiana and developed at the Lincoln School in New York."

Hiltzik, Lee R. "The Brooklyn Institute of Arts and Sciences' Biological Laboratory,

1890–1924: A History." Ph.D. dissertation, State University of New York–Stony Brook, 1993. Study of a biological laboratory at Cold Spring Harbor traces transitions in biology and philanthropy, including support from Carnegie and Rockefeller funds.

Hine, Darlene Clark. "Carter G. Woodson, White Philanthropy and Negro Historiography." *History Teacher* 19 (May 1986): 405–25. Philanthropy influences the establishment of the field of African American history.

Hoffschwelle, Mary S. "Organizing Rural Communities for Change: The Commonwealth Fund Child Health Demonstrations in Rutherford County, 1923–27." *Tennessee Historical Quarterly* 53 (Fall 1994): 154–65. Analytic account of a public-health program; sensitive to local politics and social concerns as well as the sponsoring foundation's "demonstration" and policy objectives; narrative enhanced by photographs.

Horn, Margo. *Before It's Too Late: The Child Guidance Movement in the United States, 1922–1945.* Philadelphia: Temple University Press, 1989. Critically contextualized study of the Commonwealth Fund's role in helping to shape the emerging field of child guidance.

Huntzinger, Victoria MacDonald. "The Birth of Southern Public Education: Columbus, Georgia, 1864–1904." Ph.D. dissertation, Harvard University, 1992. Community study differentiates southern public-school development from standard historiography of schooling in the north and west; includes the role of foundation philanthropy as a uniquely southern feature.

Jacobs, Meg. "The Politics of Purchasing Power: Political Economy, Consumption Politics, and American State-Building, 1909–1959." Ph.D. dissertation, University of Virginia, 1998. Study of economic research and policy, highlighting Edward Filene and the Twentieth Century Fund's role in promoting consumer economics.

Jordan, John M. *Machine-Age Ideology: Social Engineering and American Liberalism, 1911–1939.* Chapel Hill: University of North Carolina Press, 1994. Examines the ideas and rhetoric of technocratic reformers (e.g., Edward A. Filene and Beardsley Ruml) and their institutions; sees emphasis on means over ends.

Jordan, John M. " 'To Educate Public Opinion': John D. Rockefeller, Jr. and the Origins of Social Scientific Fact-Finding." *New England Quarterly* 64 (June 1991): 292–97. The text of a 1912 letter from John D. Rockefeller, Jr. to his father's advisor (prior to the establishment of the Rockefeller Foundation), with Jordan's brief analysis of early notions by business and financial leaders to launch campaigns of "public education" and research to undergird corporate interests and values.

Kay, Lily E. *The Molecular Vision of Life: Caltech, the Rockefeller Foundation, and the Rise of the New Biology.* New York: Oxford University Press, 1993. Analyzes the central roles of two institutions and their leaders in the creation and promulgation of new fundamental ideas and approaches in biology between 1930 and 1950; argues that the resulting hegemony of molecular biology was achieved through complex patterns of cooperation and cultural resonance between scientists and patrons.

Kett, Joseph F. *The Pursuit of Knowledge under Difficulties: From Self-Improvement to Adult Education in America, 1750–1990.* Stanford, Calif.: Stanford University Press, 1994. Origins of adult education in universities and community colleges; discusses support of major foundations.

Lazar, Flora E. "From Social Science to Psychosomatic Research: The Failure of an Alliance, 1908–1935." Ph.D. dissertation, Columbia University, 1994. Origins and demise of the Chicago Psychoanalytic Institution as the first attempt to ally psychoanalysis with social science in the United States. Includes contextual analysis of the roles of a broad range of institutions such as the American Sociological Society, Social Science Research Council, the Rockefeller Foundation and the Rosenwald Fund.

Link, William A. *The Paradox of Southern Progressivism, 1880–1930.* Chapel Hill: University of North Carolina Press, 1992. Account of southern progressivism concentrates on the struggle between paternalist reformers and localist communities; touches on the Commonwealth Fund, General Education Board, Rockefeller philanthropies, Julius Rosenwald Fund, and Peabody Education Fund.

Link, William A. "Privies, Progressivism, and Public Schools: Health Reform and Education in the Rural South, 1909–1920." *Journal of Southern History* 54 (November 1988): 623–42. Rockefeller Sanitary Commission involvement in rural public health programs.

Magat, Richard. "Organized Labor and Philanthropic Foundations: Partners or Strangers?" *Nonprofit and Voluntary Sector Quarterly* 23 (Winter 1994): 353–71. Examines the ambivalences, connections, and distance between foundations and labor organizations, the latter often ignored as voluntary associations.

McKersie, William. "Philanthropic Persistence: Chicago Foundations and Public School Reform." In *Advances in Educational Policy*, edited by Kenneth K. Wong. Greenwich, Conn.: JAI Press, 1998.

McKersie, William. "Philanthropy and Systemic Reform: Finding a Cross-Sector Blend of Risk-Taking and Political Will." *Education Week*, May 4, 1994.

McKersie, William. "Philanthropy's Paradox: Chicago School Reform." In *Educational Evaluation and Policy Analysis.* Washington, D.C.: American Educational Research Association, 1993.

McKersie, William. "Strategic Philanthropy and Local Public Policy: Lessons from Chicago School Reform, 1987–1993." Ph.D. dissertation, University of Chicago, 1998. Participant-observer's critical and contextualized account of the role of foundations in promoting a major school-reform initiative during the 1980s in Chicago.

Mitchell, Theodore E., and Robert Lowe. "To Sow Content: Philanthropy, Scientific Agriculture, and the Making of the New South, 1906–1920." *Journal of Social History* 24 (Winter 1990): 317–40. Illuminates little-known educational efforts of Rockefeller philanthropies among white southern farmers and their families.

O'Connor, Alice. "Community Action, Urban Reform and the Fight against Poverty: The Ford Foundation's Gray Areas Program." *Journal of Urban History* 26 (July 1996): 586–625. Highlights the strategies and ideas, accomplishments and limitations of postwar liberal domestic policymaking concerned with cities and poverty; traces the roots, genesis, and internal/external dynamics of the Ford Foundation's urban programs in the 1950s and 1960s.

Porter, Laura Smith. "From Intellectual Sanctuary to Social Responsibility: The

Founding of the Institute for Advanced Study, 1930–1933." Ph.D. dissertation, Princeton University, 1988. Study of an alternative institution, which became a haven for refugee intellectuals, as shaped by foundation executive Abraham Flexner and endowed initially by a Newark merchant.

Proietto, Rosa. "Collaborative Tension in Protest and Patronage: The Women's Studies Movements in Canada and the United States, 1970–1995." Ph.D. dissertation, Duke University, 1995. A sociological study sensitive to history. Explores the differential role of public and philanthropic funding in the development of women's studies programs at universities in two countries; highlights the role of the Ford Foundation in U.S. developments.

Richardson, Theresa M. Rupke. *The Century of the Child: The Mental Hygiene Movement and Social Policy in the United States and Canada.* Albany: State University of New York Press, 1989. Comparative study which includes the influence of large general-purpose foundations such as Rockefeller and Commonwealth on the development of the "medical ideology" of the field in the United States.

Rose, Kenneth W., Benjamin R. Shute, Jr., and Darwin H. Stapleton, eds. "Philanthropy and Institution-Building in the Twentieth Century." *Minerva* 35 (Autumn 1997): 203–205. Introduction to a special issue of *Minerva* collecting research essays that incorporate critical analyses of philanthropic initiatives into wider studies of intercultural or international development, including the building of institutions in a variety of fields and locales. Includes articles on elites, institutions, philanthropic historiography, medical research, hospitals, U.S. and international health policy, and African American higher education— by James D. Anderson, Marcos Cueto, Daniel M. Fox, Vanessa Northington Gamble, Barry D. Karl, Lily E. Kay, Nathan Reingold, and Paul Weindling.

Rossiter, Margaret. *Women Scientists in America: Struggles and Strategies to 1940.* Baltimore: Johns Hopkins University Press, 1982. Overall interpretation of achievements and obstacles faced by women scientists; Rossiter coined the term "coercive" (sometimes "creative") philanthropy to describe the use of funding to leverage institutional change and the accommodation of women; touches on a number of foundations in addition to individual and other funders.

Schlossman, Steven. "Philanthropy and the Gospel of Child Development." *History of Education Quarterly* 21 (Fall 1981): 275–99. Delineates and interprets Laura Spelman Rockefeller Memorial promotion of scientific child-development research and parent education, 1920s.

Sierra, Christine M. "The Political Transformation of a Minority Organization: The Council of La Raza, 1965–1980." Ph.D. dissertation, Stanford University, 1983. The development of a Chicano (Mexican American) community organization between the 1960s and 1980s in the southwest and California. Discusses the impact of Ford Foundation involvement in economic development in minority communities; suggests that La Raza may have lost local legitimacy in cultivating national foundation and government support.

Smuts, Alice Boardman. "Science Discovers the Child, 1893–1935: A History of the Early Scientific Study of Children." Ph.D. dissertation, University of Michigan, 1995. Integrated study of three movements in the institutionalization and professionalization of child study: child development, child guidance, and the Children's Bureau. Discusses science-minded philanthropy in context.

Solovey, Mark. "The Politics of Intellectual Identity and American Social Science, 1945–1970." Ph.D. dissertation, University of Wisconsin–Madison, 1996. Political conditions and a partnership between science and the federal government are keys to understanding the post–World War II development of American social science; touches on philanthropic influence, especially that of the Ford Foundation, in the behavioral sciences and other social sciences.

Sontz, Ann H. L. *Philanthropy and Gerontology: The Role of American Foundations.* Westport, Conn.: Greenwood, 1989. Historical study and contemporary suggestions for research and policy.

Stanfield, John S. II. *Philanthropy and Jim Crow in American Social Science.* Westport, Conn.: Greenwood, 1984. Elite northerners, through institutional philanthropy, concede to southern pressures, stopping short of desegregation in efforts to improve black education.

Stocking, George W., Jr., ed. *Objects and Others: Essays on Museums and Material Culture.* Madison: University of Wisconsin Press, 1985. Includes an essay by George W. Stocking, Jr., "Philanthropies and Vanishing Cultures: Rockefeller Funding and the End of the Museum Era in Anglo-American Anthropology."

Toon, Elizabeth. "Managing the Conduct of the Individual Life: Public Health Education and American Public Health, 1910–1940." Ph.D. dissertation, University of Pennsylvania, 1998.

Urban, Wayne J. "Philanthropy and the Black Scholar: The Case of Horace Mann Bond." *Journal of Negro Education* 58 (Fall 1989): 478–93. The black scholar and educational administrator was supported, yet limited, by Rockefeller's General Education Board and the Julius Rosenwald Fund patronage. See also Urban, *Black Scholar: Horace Mann Bond, 1904–1972* (Athens: University of Georgia Press, 1992).

Van Slyck, Abigail A. "Free to All: Carnegie Libraries and the Transformation of American Culture, 1886–1917." Ph.D. dissertation, University of California–Berkeley, 1989. Addresses how Carnegie influenced philanthropy and redirected library design.

Wenocur, Stanley, and Michael Reisch. *From Charity to Enterprise: The Development of American Social Work in a Market Economy.* Urbana: University of Illinois Press, 1989. Includes an interpretation of the Russell Sage Foundation's role in the professionalization of social work.

Wolch, Jennifer R. *The Shadow State: Government and Voluntary Sector in Transition.* New York: Foundation Center, 1990. Theoretical and practical account comparing the emergence in the U. K. and U.S. of voluntary organizations performing public functions and to some extent subject to state control, though outside traditional realms of democratic accountability. Provides context for the history of U.S. philanthropic foundations in chapters defining the voluntary sector and outlining theories of state-centered and institutional political analysis; discusses foundations directly in a chapter on the history of the U.S. welfare state.

Wollons, Roberta Lyn. "Educating Mothers: Sidonie Matsner Gruenberg and the

Child Study Association of America, 1881–1929." Ph.D. dissertation, University of Chicago, 1983. Includes discussion of role of philanthropy, including funding from Laura Spelman Rockefeller Memorial (LSRM) and the national leadership of LSRM's Lawrence K. Frank in child study and parent education.

IV. Biographies and Autobiographies

The best recent biographical studies incorporate factors such as elite power, gender politics, intellectual history, organizational development, professionalization, and the like in analyses of influential leaders of philanthropic institutions. Some studies of foundations and fields, listed above, also emphasize biography. See for example Martin and Joan Bulmer on Beardsley Ruml and the Laura Spelman Rockefeller Memorial, Robert E. Kohler on Wickliffe Rose and the Rockefeller Foundation, or Steven Wheatley on Abraham Flexner and Rockefeller philanthropy.

Acheson, Roy M. *Wickliffe Rose of the Rockefeller Foundation, 1862–1914: The Formative Years*. Cambridge, UK: Killycarn, 1992. Biographical study.

Alchon, Guy. "Mary Van Kleeck and Social-Economic Planning." *Journal of Policy History* 3 (1991): 1–23. Biographical study of the influence of the Russell Sage Foundation labor economist.

Crocker, Ruth. "From Widow's Mite to Widow's Might: The Philanthropy of Margaret Olivia Sage." *American Presbyterians* 74 (Winter 1996): 253–64. Essay on the founder of the Russell Sage Foundation (1907) by the author of a forthcoming biography (Indiana University Press).

Cross, Stephen J. "Designs for Living: Lawrence K. Frank and the Progressive Legacy in American Social Science." Ph.D. dissertation, Johns Hopkins University, 1994. Career and influence of the head of the Laura Spelman Rockefeller Memorial.

Ernst, Joseph W., ed. *"Dear Father"/"Dear Son": Correspondence of John D. Rockefeller and John D. Rockefeller, Jr.* New York: Fordham University Press, in cooperation with the Rockefeller Archive Center, 1994.

Froh, George Riley. "Edgar B. Davis: Wildcatter Extraordinary." Ph.D. dissertation, Texas A&M University, 1980. Varied business and philanthropic careers of an Eastern industrialist turned oilman, including establishment of the Luling Foundation in Texas and the Pilgrim Foundation in Massachusetts.

Harr, John Ensor, and Peter J. Johnson. *The Rockefeller Century*. New York: Scribner's, 1988. More detailed than critical account of Rockefeller family philanthropy, focusing on John D. Rockefeller 3rd's early years.

Harr, John Ensor, and Peter J. Johnson. *The Rockefeller Conscience: An American Family in Public and Private*. New York: Scribner's, 1991. Sequel account to the authors' previous book (1988); the mature John D. Rockefeller 3rd's philanthropic legacy and activities.

Hijiya, James A. "Four Ways of Looking at a Philanthropist: A Study of Robert Weeks de Forest." *Proceedings of the American Philosophical Society* 124, no. 6 (December 1980): 404–18. Balanced assessment of the multi-faceted railroad attorney and municipal reformer who advised M. Olivia Sage on the establishment of the Russell Sage Foundation and succeeded her as president.

Kert, Bernice. *Abby Aldrich Rockefeller: The Woman in the Family*. New York: Random House, 1993. Light on context and heavy on use of family sources; emphasizes Abby Aldrich Rockefeller's (Mrs. John D., Jr.) role in establishing the Museum of Modern Art.

Lederman, Sarah Henry. "From Poverty to Philanthropy: The Life and Work of Mary E. Richmond." Ph.D. dissertation, Columbia University, 1994. Interpretive biography of the head of the Russell Sage Foundation's Charity Organization Department, influential in shaping social work education and professionalization.

Legacy: The Life of W. K. Kellogg. Kalamazoo, Mich.: Kalamazoo Writing and Video Company, 1990. Videocassette. Biography including Kellogg's business career, company, charitable giving, and foundation.

Madison, James H. *Eli Lilly: A Life, 1885–1977*. Indianapolis: Indiana Historical Society, 1989. Includes chapter "Philanthropy and the Quest for Character."

Marcus, George E., with Peter Dobkin Hall. *Lives in Trust: The Fortunes of Dynastic Families in Late Twentieth-Century America*. Boulder, Colo.: Westview, 1992. Essays, with an anthropological cast, on "dynastic organizations," sensibilities and legacies, including accounts of the Bingham family and the J. Paul Getty Trust. Also includes Peter Dobkin Hall's essay on the Rockefeller legacy, "The Empty Tomb: The Making of Dynastic Identity."

Nielsen, Waldemar A. *Inside American Philanthropy: The Dramas of Donorship*. Norman: University of Oklahoma Press, 1996. Biographical studies of donors, including "three giants of the past" (John D. Rockefeller, Andrew Carnegie, Julius Rosenwald); "three formidable successors" (Mary Lasker, Arnold Backman, Walter Annenberg); and "the new super-rich" (Warren Buffett, Bill Gates, Leslie Wexner, George Soros). Issues discussed include the rising role of women, cautionary cases, the development of family, community and entrepreneurial funds, the "pitfalls of perpetuity," and trusteeship. Sympathetically critical.

Parker, Franklin. "George Peabody: Founder of Modern Philanthropy." *Peabody Journal of Education* 70 (Fall 1994): 17–32. This essay, and others in the same issue, draw on the author's much earlier dissertation on Peabody, an American financier active in London and founder of one of the earliest philanthropic trusts in the United States.

Rockefeller, John D. *Random Reminiscences of Men and Events*. Tarrytown, N.Y.: Sleepy Hollow Press and Rockefeller Archive Center, 1984. Originally published as a series in *World's Work*, 1908–1909.

Schenkel, Albert F. *The Rich Man and the Kingdom: John D. Rockefeller, Jr., and the Protestant Establishment, 1900–1960*. Minneapolis: Fortress, 1994. Rockefeller, central to Protestant establishment, uses institutional philanthropy as a social expression of modernist religion, celebrating science and religion alike.

Scively, Barbara. "Geraldine Rockefeller Dodge." In *Past and Promise: Lives of New Jersey Women*, edited by Joan N. Burstyn. Metuchen, N.J.: Scarecrow, 1990.

Stasz, Clarice. *The Rockefeller Women: Dynasty of Piety, Privacy, and Service*. New York: St. Martin's, 1995. Popular account of the status, roles and influence in family institutions of Rockefeller wives, mothers, and daughters; by the author of a similar account of the Vanderbilt women.

Walton, Andrea M. "With Strength to Reason and the Warmth to Feel: A Portrait of Clementine Miller Tangeman, Philanthropist and Educator." Working Papers Series. New York: New York University, Center for the Study of American Culture and Education, 1998. Biography, incorporating oral history, interpreting local and national philanthropy by Clementine Miller Tangeman (1905–1996), associated with Cummins Engine Co. and the Irwin-Sweeney-Miller Foundation of Indiana.

V. Oral Histories

Some established oral history repositories hold useful historical materials on foundation and program leaders, even when the emphasis is not philanthropy per se. The Oral History Research Collection at Columbia University, for example, includes interviews with James B. Duke, Mary Lasker, John D. Rockefeller, Jr., Warren Weaver, and others. More recent projects have focused on the development of specific philanthropic institutions (e.g., the Spencer Foundation).

Gardner, Joel R. "Oral History and Philanthropy: Private Foundations." *Journal of American History* 79 (September 1992): 601–605. An historian discusses the simultaneously rich and sparse evidence of oral history on philanthropic foundations and urges more extensive (though critical) use. Cites Deborah Brody, "The Past Is Prologue: Oral Histories Are an Effective and Powerful Way to Preserve the Vision of the People Who Shaped a Foundation," *Foundation News* 32 (November/December 1991), in encouraging today's funds to preserve their history. Outlines oral history archives, resources currently available, and projects underway.

Morris, Gabrielle. *Bay Area Foundation History.* 5 vols. History of Bay Area Philanthropy Series. Berkeley: Regional Oral History Office, Bancroft Library, University of California, 1990. Series of oral history interviews with officers and leaders of the San Francisco and Rosenberg Foundations.

Morris, Gabrielle. *Collected Thoughts on Grantmaking and the Hewlett Foundation: An Interview with Roger W. Heyns.* History of Bay Area Philanthropy Series. Berkeley: Regional Oral History Office, Bancroft Library, University of California, 1989. Oral history interviews with a former president of the Hewlett Foundation, plus a talk to the Northern California Grantmakers.

Morris, Gabrielle. *Equity and Diversity: Hispanics in the Nonprofit World: An Interview with Herman E. Gallegos.* History of Bay Area Philanthropy Series. Berkeley: Regional Oral History Office, Bancroft Library, University of California, 1989. Oral history interview with social and civic worker, former president of La Raza, trustee of Rosenberg and Rockefeller Foundations.

Morris, Gabrielle. *Funding Prevention of Nuclear War: An Interview with Sally Lilienthal.* History of Bay Area Philanthropy Series. Berkeley: Regional Oral History Office, Bancroft Library, University of California, 1989. Oral history interview with founder of the antinuclear Ploughshares Fund, a public grantmaking foundation.

Morris, Gabrielle. *Organizational Aspects of Philanthropy, San Francisco Bay Area, 1948–1988: An Interview with Leslie Luttgens.* History of Bay Area Philanthropy Series. Berkeley: Regional Oral History Office, Bancroft Library, University of California, 1990. Oral history interview with trustee of multiple independent-sector organizations, including Council on Foundations and the Rosenberg Foundation; with section on Rosenberg grant-program development.

Morris, Gabrielle. *Specialized Grantmaking with National and International Impact: Interviews with Mary Dee Skaggs and Philip Jelley*. History of Bay Area Philanthropy Series. Berkeley: Regional Oral History Office, Bancroft Library, University of California, 1989. Oral history interviews with a founder of the L. J. and Mary Skaggs Foundation and her attorney, concerning its establishment, administration, staffing, and grantmaking in medical research and the arts.

Morris, Gabrielle. *The Spirit and Morale of Private Philanthropy: Stanford University and the James Irvine Foundation: An Interview with Morris M. Doyle*. History of Bay Area Philanthropy Series. Berkeley: Regional Oral History Office, Bancroft Library, University of California, 1990. Oral history interview with a Stanford trustee who has also served on Irvine Foundation board; wide range of topics, including Irvine grantmaking 1963–1988.

Morris, Gabrielle. *Zellerbach Family Fund Innovations in Support of Human Services and the Arts*. History of Bay Area Philanthropy Series. Berkeley: Regional Oral History Office, Bancroft Library, University of California, 1992.

Spencer Foundation Project: Oral History, 1981–85. In the Oral History Research Collection of Columbia University, New York. Transcripts of interviews with foundation staff; copies are also available at the Regenstein Library, University of Chicago.

VI. Historical Work on Foundation Management, Organization, Personnel, and Professionalization

This highly selective sampling from a burgeoning literature emphasizes work that is strongly historical in focus or interpretation, or that is potentially useful to historians in particular because of the analytic approaches employed or trends identified.

Blumenthal, Andrea K. "Leadership in a Medical Philanthropy: Simon Flexner and the Rockefeller Institute for Medical Research." Ph.D. dissertation, Drew University, 1991. Leadership and management study of the Rockefeller Institute for Medical Research, 1903–1935.

Conley, Darlene J. "Philanthropic Foundations and Organizational Change: The Case of the Southern Education Foundation (SEF) during the Civil Rights Era." Ph.D. dissertation, Northwestern University, 1990. Organizational changes, including a shift from white to black leadership, as the SEF (a philanthropic foundation created by the Peabody, Slater, Jeanes and Virginia Randolph Funds) responded to external changes and developed new strategies to improve black education.

Council on Foundations. *Evaluation for Foundations: Concepts, Cases, Guidelines, and Resources*. San Francisco: Jossey-Bass, 1993. Overview and nine case studies from recent history. Includes annotated bibliography with several references for longer-term perspectives on evaluation.

Frumkin, Peter. "Conflict and the Construction of an Organizational Field: The Tax

Reform Act of 1969 and the Transformation of American Philanthropic Foundations." Ph.D. dissertation, University of Chicago, 1997. Sociological study documenting increasing professionalization in the staffing patterns and norms of foundation work; argues that this trend in part responds to increased regulation, and in many ways stifles the creative and transformative potential of philanthropic organizations.

Frumkin, Peter. "Left and Right in American Philanthropy." *Minerva* 32 (Winter 1994): 469–75. Review essay with historical background on investigations of foundation politics, organization, and personnel; the book reviewed is *Giving for Social Change*, edited by Althea K. Nagai, Robert Lerner, and Stanley Rothman (Westport, Conn.: Praeger, 1994), which finds a liberal bias in contemporary foundation grantmaking concerned with public policy.

Frumkin, Peter. "Strangled Freedom." *American Scholar* 64 (Autumn 1995): 590–97. Professionalization and regulation diminish philanthropic potential.

Hawkins, Beverly Oliver. "The Role of Evaluation in Philanthropic Decision Making." Ph.D. dissertation, University of Minnesota, 1984. Survey of endowed, community, and corporate foundations; emphasizes social psychology.

Joseph, James A. "Building a New Era for Organized Philanthropy." *Fund Raising Management* 21 (April 1989): 42, 44, 46, 48, 112. Joseph, then-president of the Council of Foundations, highlights twenty years of changes in philanthropy that will influence future development: new climate of Congressional debate; new and more sophisticated research used to evaluate programs and understand giving; rise of community foundations filling gaps left by private funds; new rationales for corporate giving; internationalization.

Larson, Deborah A. "An Exploratory Study of Specific Factors That Influence Corporate Foundation Support of Higher Education." Ph.D. dissertation, University of South Dakota, 1987. Survey of corporate foundations in Minnesota, with historical preface on expanding corporate interest in higher education.

McCue, Howard M. III, and Thomas P. Gallanis. "Charitable Foundations: What We Have Learned in Twenty Years." *Trusts and Estates* 131 (August 1992): 12, 14, 16, 18–21. Reviews laws governing private foundations; impact of Tax Reform Act of 1969; statistics on foundation giving since then.

Odendahl, Teresa, and Michael O'Neill, eds. *Women and Power in the Nonprofit Sector*. San Francisco: Jossey-Bass, 1994. Includes chapters and lists of references to additional studies of women's roles on foundation boards; grantmaking for girls' and women's interests, and women's foundations.

Odendahl, Teresa, et al. *Working in Foundations: Career Patterns of Women and Men*. New York: Foundation Center, 1985. Recent history, but case studies and data are revealing on longstanding power dynamics and role assignments in philanthropic foundations.

Roelofs, Joan. "Foundations and the Supreme Court." *Telos* 62 (Winter 1984–85): 59–87. The role of the judiciary as an elite institution, *vis à vis* foundations such as Ford, Rockefeller, Carnegie, Russell Sage, and the Twentieth Century Fund.

Turner, Richard C., ed. *Taking Trusteeship Seriously: Essays on the History, Dynamics, and Practice of Trusteeship*. Indianapolis: Indiana University Center on Philanthropy, 1995. Treats foundation trusteeship in the context of leadership trends and policies in the nonprofit sector overall; historical studies concerning foundations include Fred W. Beuttler, "Morals and Ethics in the Education of a Trustee: Chester I. Barnard at the Rockefeller Foundation"; Jimmy Elaine Wilkinson Meyer, "Intimate Connections: Trusteeship in Historical Perspective—The Maternal Health Association and the Brush Foundation"; and Barry Westin, "The Evolution of Control over Philanthropic Expenditures for Public Education in the South: The Rosenwald Fund in North Carolina."

Van Til, Jon, et al. *Critical Issues in American Philanthropy: Strengthening Theory and Practice*. San Francisco: Jossey-Bass, 1990. Collection includes pieces on historical context of philanthropy (Maurice G. Gurin and Jon Van Til) and philanthropy as a social relation (Susan Ostrander and Paul G. Schervish), among others.

Young, Dennis R., Robert M. Hollister, Virginia A. Hodgkinson, and Associates, eds. *Governing, Leading, and Managing Nonprofit Organizations: New Insights from Research and Practice*. San Francisco: Jossey-Bass, 1993. Essays on boards, values, information systems, evaluation, and human and financial resources in nonprofit organizations. Young's introduction identifies themes, including nonprofits' less-than-wholehearted embrace of sophisticated management and governance techniques, the wide variety of the field, increasing interest in inclusiveness, and the still-guiding influence of values, including religious ones. Hollister's conclusion emphasizes board roles and program evaluation as key issues discussed in the volume, then ventures further to suggest topics for future research, including leadership (transcending mere management), advocacy, and variations in organizational size and type. The collection spans the nonprofit spectrum, but Susan A. Ostrander's chapter, "Diversity and Democracy at Haymarket People's Fund: Doing Philanthropy as Social Change," focuses specifically on a philanthropic foundation, analyzing its deliberate efforts to develop diversity and democratize leadership and management.

CONTRIBUTORS

GUY ALCHON is Associate Professor of History at the University of Delaware and the author of *The Invisible Hand of Planning: Capitalism, Social Science, and the State in the 1920s.*

LUCY BERNHOLZ is President of Blueprint R & D, a consulting company specializing in program development for corporate grantmakers and philanthropic foundations. She completed a Ph.D. at Stanford University in 1995, having written a dissertation entitled "Private Philanthropy and Public Schools: San Francisco in the 1960s and 1970s."

RUTH HUTCHINSON CROCKER is Associate Professor of History at Auburn University and the author of *Social Work and Social Order: The Settlement Movement in Two Industrial Cities, 1889–1930.*

PETER FRUMKIN is Assistant Professor of Public Policy at the John F. Kennedy School of Government, Harvard University. He completed a Ph.D. at the University of Chicago in 1997. His dissertation was entitled "Conflict and Construction of an Organizational Field: The Transformation of American Philanthropic Foundations."

JULIA GRANT is Associate Professor of Social Relations and American Culture at James Madison College, Michigan State University. She is the author of *Raising Baby by the Book: The Education of American Mothers, 1890–1960.*

ABIGAIL L. HALCLI is a member of the Sociology Department of Oxford Brookes University. She is the co-editor of *Theory and Society: Understanding the Present.*

PETER DOBKIN HALL is Director of the Program on Non-Profit Organizations and Senior Research Scholar at the Yale Divinity School. He is the author of numerous books and articles, including *Inventing the Nonprofit Sector and Other Essays on Philanthropy, Voluntarism, and Nonprofit Organizations.*

DAVID C. HAMMACK is Benton Professor of History at Case Western Reserve University. He has written widely on the history of philanthropy and is the author (with Stanton Wheeler) of *Social Science in the Making: Essays on the Russell Sage Foundation* and editor of *Making the Nonprofit Sector in the United States: A Reader*.

MEG JACOBS is Assistant Professor of History at Claremont McKenna College. She completed a Ph.D. at the University of Virginia in 1998, having written a dissertation entitled "The Politics of Purchasing Power: The Rise and Demise of a Consuming Public, 1909–1959."

J. CRAIG JENKINS is Professor of Sociology and Faculty Associate, Mershon Center for International Security, Ohio State University. He is the author of many books and articles, including (with Bert Klandermans) *The Politics of Social Protest: Comparative Perspectives on States and Social Movements*.

BARRY DEAN KARL is Norman and Edna Freehling Professor Emeritus at the University of Chicago and Bloomberg Visiting Professor at the John F. Kennedy School of Government, Harvard University. *The Uneasy State: The United States from 1915 to 1945* is one of his many publications.

SUSAN KASTAN is a doctoral candidate in the History of Education Program at New York University. Her dissertation will be a study of the early years of the Russell Sage Foundation.

ELLEN CONDLIFFE LAGEMANN is Professor of History and Education, Director of the Center for the Study of American Culture and Education, and Chair of the Department of Humanities and the Social Sciences in the School of Education at New York University. She is the author of numerous books and articles, including *The Politics of Knowledge: The Carnegie Corporation, Philanthropy, and Public Policy*.

RICHARD MAGAT is the editor of *An Agile Servant: Community Leadership by Community Foundations*. He was president of the Edward Hazen Foundation and, before that, a longtime staff member at the Ford Foundation.

WILLIAM S. MCKERSIE is Senior Program Officer at the Cleveland Foundation. He completed a doctorate at the University of Chicago in 1998, where he wrote a dissertation entitled "Strategic Philanthropy and Local Public Policy: Lessons from Chicago School Reform, 1987–1993."

ALICE O'CONNOR is Assistant Professor of History at the University of California, Santa Barbara. Her most recent article is "The False Dawn of Poor Law Reform: Nixon, Carter, and the Quest for a Guaranteed Income."

SUSAN OSTRANDER is Associate Professor of Sociology at Tufts University. She has written many books and articles, including *Money for Change: Social Movement Philanthropy at Haymarket People's Fund.*

ROSA PROIETTO is a doctoral candidate in the Sociology Department at Duke University. Her dissertation is entitled "Collaborative Tension in Protest and Patronage: The Women's Studies Movement in Canada and the United States, 1970–1995."

GREGORY K. RAYNOR is a doctoral candidate in the History Department at New York University, where he is completing a dissertation entitled "Engineering the American Century: Henry Ford, the Ford Foundation, and the Rise of the American State, 1908–1969."

ELIZABETH TOON is a doctoral candidate in History and Sociology of Science at the University of Pennsylvania. She is completing a dissertation on the Milbank and Commonwealth Funds.

INDEX

Abalone Alliance, 233

Accountability: and conservative ascendancy, 34–36; and democracy, 258–59; in the era of corporate liberalism, 26–31; and foundation reporting, 75–77; government regulations for, 31–34; grantees' role in, 77–79, 257, 260–64; problem of, 9–17; and the professional code of conduct, 80–84; professionalization and, 84–93; and the public/private debate, 259–60; research into, 359–60; stakeholders' voice in, 17–26; three mechanisms of, 25

Action for Boston Community Development, 176, 179, 181

Activism, philanthropic: by Carnegie, 169; Ford Foundation's turn to, 169, 176–78, 186–89; by Rockefeller, 169

Addams, Jane, 153, 154, 155, 156, 261

Adelphi University, 36

Administrative costs of foundations, 84–85

Advocacy groups, 239–43

Affirmative action, 82, 83

African Americans: child development research on, 145–46; education funds for, 55; health care services for, 56; social movement philanthropy advocacy for, 241–42, 264–66

Agape Foundation, 233, 234

Agendo Fund, 233, 250

Agribusiness Accountability Project, 233

Alchon, Guy, 101

Alexander, Lamar, 330

Alinsky, Saul, 179, 231, 239

Alternative foundations, 234, 236–38, 262

American Assembly, 330

American Association of Small Loan Brokers, 106, 111

American Association of University Women, 139

American Bar Association's Model Nonstock Corporation Statute, 8, 32

American Board of Commissioners for Foreign Missions (ABCFM), 13, 15

American Child Health Association, 134

American Council of Learned Societies, 204

American Council on Education, 204

American Historical Association, 204

American Home Economics Association of America, 139

American Indian Movement, 235

American Medical Association, 127

American Public Health Association, 123

American Social Science Association, 53

American Tract Society (ATS), 13, 15

Amnesty International, 233

Anderson, Florence, 288–89

Anderson, James D., 265, 365

Anderson, Marian, 264

Andrews, F. Emerson, 288, 291, 296

Angell, James, 132

Animal rights campaigns, 236

Annual reports, 75–77

Antin, Mary, 153, 157

Armsey, James, 309

Arnove, Robert F., 300

Ashley, Walter, 300

Ashmore, Harry S., 201–202

Ashmore Report, 201–202, 206

Aspen Institute, xii, 292

Association for Research on Nonprofit Organization and Voluntary Action (ARNOVA), xii, xiii, 259

Association of Black Foundation Executives, 242

Associative state, 101, 170

Astor, Brooke, 216

Astor Foundation, 216